# EVOLUTION OF THE ARCTIC–NORTH ATLANTIC AND THE WESTERN TETHYS

PETER A. ZIEGLER
Shell Internationale Petroleum Maatschappij B.V.

AAPG Memoir 43

Publication of the International Lithosphere Program, no. 0144
for the Inter-Union Commission on the Lithosphere

Published by
The American Association of Petroleum Geologists
Tulsa, Oklahoma, 74101, U.S.A.

Library of Congress Cataloging-In-Publication Data

Ziegler, Peter A.
    Evolution of the Arctic–North Atlantic and the
Western Tethys

    (AAPG memoir, ISSN 0065-731X ; 43)
    "Also published as International Lithosphere Program
publication no. 0144 for the Inter-Union Commission
on the Lithosphere."
    Bibliography: p.          ISBN 0-89181-320-9
    Includes index.
    1.  Paleoceanograph–North Atlantic Ocean.  2.  Pale-
oceanography–Arctic Ocean.  3.  Paleoceanography
–Mediterranean Sea.  I.  Title.  II.  Series.
QE350.22.N65Z53   1988       551.46 '11       88-26275

Association editor: James Helwig
Science director: Ronald L. Hart
Science editor: Victor V. Van Beuren
Project editor: Anne H. Thomas
Special editor: Catherine Skintik, Custom Editorial Productions, Inc.

# CONTENTS

# LIST OF PLATES

Paleogeographic–Paleotectonic maps

Plate 1—Late Caledonian Tectonic Framework.
Plate 2—Middle Devonian, Eifelian–Givetian.
Plate 3—Late Devonian, Frasnian–Famennian.
Plate 4—Early Carboniferous, late Visean.
Plate 5—Middle Carboniferous, late Bashkirian–Moskovian, Westphalian.
Plate 6—Permo-Carboniferous, Kasimovian–Sakmarian, Stephanian–Autunian.
Plate 7—Late Early Permian, Artinskian–Kungurian, "Rotliegend".
Plate 8—Late Permian, Ufimian–Kazanian, "Zechstein".
Plate 9—Middle Triassic, Anisian–Ladinian, "Muschelkalk".
Plate 10—Late Triassic, Carnian–Norian, "Keuper".
Plate 11—Early Jurassic, Sinemurian–Toarcian.
Plate 12—Middle Jurassic, Bajocian–Bathonian.
Plate 13—Late Jurassic, Oxfordian–Tithonian.
Plate 14—Early Cretaceous, Berriasian–Barremian.
Plate 15—Early Cretaceous, Aptian–Albian.
Plate 16—Late Cretaceous, Turonian–Campanian.
Plate 17—Early Tertiary, Paleocene.
Plate 18—Mid-Tertiary, late Oligocene.
Plate 19—Late Tertiary, middle Miocene.
Plate 20—Late Tertiary, Messinian.
Plate 21—Late Tertiary, Pliocene.

Stratigraphic correlation charts

Plate 22—Paleozoic of Arctic–North Atlantic basins.
Plate 23—Paleozoic, northern parts of Variscan foredeep basin.
Plate 24—Paleozoic, southern parts of Variscan foredeep basin and Variscan externides.
Plate 25—Paleozoic, basins located within Variscan fold belt.
Plate 26—Mesozoic and Cenozoic basins, Arctic and Norwegian–Greenland Sea.
Plate 27—Mesozoic and Cenozoic basins, North Atlantic Europe.
Plate 28—Mesozoic and Cenozoic basins, North Atlantic, North Central Atlantic, Labrador Sea.
Plate 29—Mesozoic and Cenozoic basins, Western Europe.
Plate 30—Mesozoic and Cenozoic basins, Northwest and Central Europe.

# PREFACE

This volume is intended to provide earth scientists with a broad, multidisciplinary overview of the late Paleozoic to Recent geological evolution of the continents and shelves bordering the North Atlantic Ocean, the Norwegian–Greenland Sea, the Arctic Ocean, and the Mediterranean Sea.

The evolution of these seas has been the subject of many comprehensive studies and compilations, which discuss the evolution of oceanic basins on the basis of their magnetic sea-floor anomalies. The volume presented here combines this information with geological data from the adjacent shelf and onshore areas. It retraces the evolution of sedimentary basins developed during the rifting phases that preceded the opening of these oceans and highlights the scope of the associated intra-plate phenomena. Moreover, the author presents a reconstruction of the late Paleozoic and early Mesozoic development of Europe, northernmost Africa and northeastern North America–Greenland and discusses the different orogenic cycles that accompanied the stepwise assembly of Pangea and the early rifting phases heralding its break-up.

This volume gives an account of almost continuously changing plate boundaries, of plate kinematics and interactions, and of the dynamics of basin evolution. Its contents are based on published literature and on data gathered by Shell Companies and its affiliates in the course of their exploration activities in the sedimentary basins of Western Europe, North Africa, and Canada.

P.A. Ziegler has undertaken the task of integrating this mass of information in this compilation. In spring 1986, he presented a summary of these studies during his American Association of Petroleum Geologists Distinguished Lecturer tour to 26 universities and petroleum societies in the United States and in Canada. The content of these lectures has been made available to the public through the AAPG slide-tape program under the title "Evolution of the Arctic–North Atlantic Rift System."

The reader will appreciate that the scope and framework of this compilation does not always allow full documentation of the interpretations given in the attached maps and diagrams. Furthermore, some of these data cannot be divulged owing to their proprietary and confidential nature. Yet, despite these constraints, Shell wishes to contribute to the advancement of earth sciences in general and to the further understanding of the geological history of Europe in particular by releasing this book for publication.

P.A. Ziegler is the current chairman of Working Group 3 of the Inter-Union Commission on the Lithosphere; Working Group 3 is charged with the study of intraplate phenomena. This volume is designated publication no. 0144 of the International Lithosphere Programme. As such it represents Shell's and the author's contribution to this international, interdisciplinary research program, which seeks to elucidate the nature, dynamics, origin and evolution of the lithosphere.

The Hague, November 1986
Dr. R.E. Wegmann
Head of Exploration
Shell Internationale Petroleum
Maatschappij B.V.

# Acknowledgments

During the preparation of this compilation, the author had free access to Shell's basin analyses and in-house special studies. These have been prepared by his colleagues in Shell's exploration and research teams both in Europe and overseas. Their indirect contributions to this compilation are herewith acknowledged.

Special thanks are due to the following Shell staff: Drs. E. Haan for his detailed analysis of the Mesozoic and Cenozoic evolution of the Mediterranean area, which formed the basis for the interpretations shown in the attached paleogeographic–paleotectonic maps' Mr. B. K. Balke, M.A., Drs. J. H. Braakman, and Dr. J. de Jager for discussions on the evolution of the Arctic Ocean; Dr. B. van Hoorn, Dr. P. H. Nelson, Dr. C. Bukovics, and Dr. G. Gorin for their contributions on the geology of the UK and Norwegian Shelf areas; Dr. B. M. Reinhardt for comments on Spain, and Dr. O. Friedenreich for discussions on the evolution of the Atlantic shelves of Canada. Specific contributions in the form of cross sections appearing as text figures are acknowledged in the respective captions.

Moreover, the author is indebted to Prof. R. Trümpy, Zürich, and Prof. J. Dercourt, Paris, for stimulating discussions on the Alpine–Mediterranean domain; and to Dr. U. Mayr and Dr. A. F. Embry, Calgary, and Dr. E. Håkonsson, Copenhagen, for their contributions on the evolution of the Sverdrup Basin and northern Greenland. Special thanks are due to my friends and colleagues Prof. A. W. Bally, Houston, and Dr. D. G. Roberts, London, for critically and constructively reviewing this volume.

Thanks are extended to Mrs. Andrea Heijnen and Mrs. Ineke Hilberding for their assistance during the construction of maps and diagrams, to Messrs. E.C.M. Schmidt and W.A. Hoekstra and their teams for their drafting efforts, and to Miss Monique Molenaar for typing the manuscript.

Finally, the author would like to thank his wife for her patience and understanding of his preoccupation with this project, which has taken up so much of his spare time during the last two to three years. This book is dedicated to her as a token of his gratitude.

The author is indebted to Shell Internationale Petroleum Maatschappij B.V. for having given him the opportunity and free hand to carry out this compilation and for releasing it for publication.

# INTRODUCTION

The objective of this volume is to review in broad outlines the Late Silurian to Recent evolution of the Arctic–North Atlantic and Western Tethys domains and their borderlands.

The Arctic–North Atlantic domain is here considered as including part of the oceanic Canada and Eurasian basins, the Norwegian–Greenland Sea, the North Atlantic, the Labrador Sea, and Baffin Bay. The Western Tethys realm embraces the Mediterranean Sea, its Alpine fold belts, and the adjacent cratonic areas. Thus, the area covered by this compilation includes much of northeastern North America and Greenland, all of Europe, and the northern parts of North Africa.

During the past few decades the understanding of the geological framework of the North American and European borderlands of the Arctic–North Atlantic and also of the Tethys domain has greatly advanced as a consequence of research carried out by academic institutions, national geological surveys, and government-sponsored oceanographic institutions. Much has been gained by international cooperation in research projects such as those sponsored by the International Geological Correlation Programme. At the same time, major contributions have been made by the petroleum industry as a result of its exploration activities both in onshore basins and on the continental shelves.

Intensified studies of the classical outcrop areas have led to the development of new stratigraphical and structural concepts, particularly with regard to the evolution of the Caledonian, Hercynian, and Alpine fold belts. This has been paralleled by major efforts in the hitherto little known Arctic frontier areas.

The ever-increasing number of radiometric age determinations has contributed much to the dating of orogenic events and the intraplate igneous activity that accompanied the Paleozoic assembly of Pangea, its Mesozoic and Cenozoic break-up, and the Alpine suturing of Africa and Europe. In addition, faunal analyses and particularly paleomagnetic data have provided new constraints for the paleogeographic reconstruction of the Arctic–North Atlantic and Tethys domains. Regional marine geophysical surveys, supported by deep-sea drilling, have increased our knowledge of the geology and evolution of oceanic basins to the point that the inventory of sea-floor magnetic anomalies has provided a tool for the Mesozoic and Cenozoic palinspastic reconstructions of the Arctic–North Atlantic borderlands. This has greatly enhanced the understanding of the kinematics underlying the Jurassic to Recent evolution of the Mediterranean and Arctic–North Atlantic areas. Moreover, deep reflection surveys and refraction data have contributed substantially to the understanding of processes governing the evolution and destruction of sedimentary basins.

In recent years, the petroleum industry in its quest for new hydrocarbon resources has extended its exploration efforts to the limits of the perennially ice-infested Arctic frontier areas. Apart from establishing substantial new oil and gas reserves, these efforts have yielded a tremendous amount of new stratigraphical and geophysical information from hitherto inaccessible areas, depths and basins that one or two decades ago were hardly known to exist.

This wealth of new data, in combination with the geology of outcrop areas and the oceans, permits us to reconstruct the geological evolution of the Arctic–North Atlantic and Tethys domains in a modern, plate tectonic framework.

During the preparation of this ambitious compilation, the author soon became aware that many questions must be left unanswered and that much remains to be learned from future research and exploration efforts and particularly from the pooling of knowledge. Moreover, the integration of an almost forbiddingly voluminous, multilingual literature demanded such a taxing effort that exhaustive coverage of the areas of interest could never be achieved.

The account of the late Paleozoic to Recent evolution of the Arctic–North Atlantic and Western Tethys domains given in this volume centers on the discussion of 21 paleogeographic–paleotectonic maps (Plates 1–21). These are supported by chronostratigraphic-lithostratigraphic correlation charts (Plates 22–30), numerous cross sections, and detail maps given as text figures.

The individual paleotectonic–paleogeographic maps span large time intervals, and, in view of their scope, they are of an interpretative and in part even a conceptual nature. These maps give for the respective time interval maximum depositional basin outlines, gross lithofacies/depositional environment provinces in color code, and the principal tectonic features. For areas of nondeposition, a distinction was made between cratonic highs, tectonically active orogenic belts, and tectonically inactive fold belts characterized by a considerable topographic relief. Volcanic activity during the respective time interval is indicated by star symbols that distinguish between intraplate volcanism (black stars) and subduction-related volcanism (open stars). In view of the scope of these maps, depositional thickness values or isopachs could not be given; the reader is therefore referred to the literature quoted in the text.

The information given on the paleogeographic–paleotectonic maps was abstracted from more detailed maps that had been compiled for individual basins and provinces on the basis of in-house studies and/or published literature.

The topographic bases of these maps, showing the present-day continental outlines for areas not affected by orogenic activity during the respective time interval, are based on computer-generated palinspastic reconstructions of the Arctic–North Atlantic and the Central Atlantic Oceans as dictated by their sea-floor magnetic anomalies. These reconstructions were carried out at Shell Development Company's Bellaire Research Center in Houston using programs for computer animation of continental drift (Scotese et al., 1980). Devonian to Early Jurassic maps are essentially based on the predrift fit of the continents whereby paleomagnetic constraints were honored (Ziegler et al., 1979; Scotese et al., 1979, 1985; Morel and Irving, 1978). Empirical palinspastic corrections were applied to areas of important intracratonic deformation.

Projections are orthographic with the map center located in the northern part of Scotland. Because in many parts of the Central and North Atlantic, the Norwegian–Greenland and Labrador Sea, and Baffin Bay there is considerable uncertainty about the position of the continent–ocean boundary and the amount of crustal extension that occurred during the rifting phase preceding the opening of the respective ocean basins, the palinspastic reconstruction given in these maps should be regarded as tentative.

Furthermore, palinspastic reconstructions of the Alpine–Mediterranean domain are based on the assumption that during the Late Carboniferous and Permian the area between the African and European cratons was occupied by the Hercynian fold belt and thus, by continental crust. In the eastern Mediterranean–Black Sea area, the Hercynian fold belt probably faced the oceanic Proto- or Paleo-Tethys, which separated it from the northern, passive margin of Gondwana.

The area occupied by continental crust at the end of the Hercynian orogeny in the Western and Central Mediterranean domain was defined on the basis of the late Paleozoic–early Mesozoic trans-Atlantic fit of Laurentia, Africa, and Fennosarmatia. In the eastern Mediterranean–Black Sea area, the limits of the Proto-Tethys Ocean during the latest Carboniferous, and consequently the outlines of the Hercynian fold belt as shown in the Permo-Carboniferous reconstruction given by Plate 6, are conceptual.

As a next step, areas corresponding to the Alpine–Mediterranean domain were subdivided into tectonostratigraphic units such that certain interpretations and assumptions had to be made regarding the correlation and original size of the different units recognized in the Alpine chains. Although the size and shape of the individual tectonostratigraphic units, such as the Italo-Dinarid promontory, had to remain tentative, their distinction and the retention of their dimensions formed the basis for the conceptual Late Permian, Mesozoic, and Cenozoic palinspastic reconstructions given in Plates 7–21. This approach was chosen for the simple reason that reliable palinspastic reconstructions are not yet available for the different segments of the Alpine fold belts in the Mediterranean area. Correspondingly, space allocation to the different tectonostratigraphic units has been arbitrary and is subject to perhaps major changes as new information becomes available. Furthermore, as the inventory of magnetic sea-floor anomalies increases, motions of the major cratonic blocks during the opening phases of the different segments of the Arctic–North Atlantic can be

more closely constrained and a better understanding will be obtained of the width of oceanic basins that opened during the Mesozoic in the Mediterranean domain.

It should therefore be stressed that the paleotectonic-paleogeographic maps presented in Plates 1 to 21 are generalized and that they may have serious shortcomings. Yet they provide a first overview of the post-Caledonian evolution of the entire Arctic–North Atlantic and Western Tethys areas and their borderlands. As such, they are intended to give the reader a broad framework on which to build and against which more local studies can be tested.

The chronostratigraphic–lithostratigraphic correlation charts, given in Plates 22–30, summarize the sedimentary record of selected basins and subbasins that developed through time in the Arctic–North Atlantic borderlands and in Western and Central Europe. Each chart provides the reader with an overview of the geological record of geographically and (generally) also genetically related basins. The lithostratigraphic columns are color coded for depositional environments and distinguish between erosional and nondepositional breaks in sedimentation. The side columns give a summary of the tectonic and igneous activity that accompanied the evolution of the respective basins and, where applicable, also their destruction.

The angularity of unconformities is indicated by symbols and letters that specify whether they are rift or wrench induced or associated with folding.

The text of this volume is organized, from the point of view of plate interaction, into ten chapters in which a chronological account is given of the latest Silurian to Recent evolution of the Arctic–North Atlantic and Western Tethys realms. The tenth chapter contains a discussion of geodynamic processes that governed the subsidence and destruction of sedimentary basins which evolved during the long and complex geological history of the area under consideration.

In this synthesis, a number of new, in part controversial, concepts have been advanced. They should be regarded as working hypotheses. Through their discussion, the reader's attention is focused on areas and subjects of uncertainty, the clarification of which requires further research.

The scope of this review required considerable generalization, and many points raised could not be fully documented within the frame of this volume. However, an effort was made to provide the reader with a comprehensive reference list that is intended to serve as a guide to the pertinent, more specialized literature.

# Chapter 1
# Late Caledonian Tectonic Framework
# (Latest Silurian–Earliest Devonian)

# INTRODUCTION

The late Caledonian megatectonic framework of the Arctic–North Atlantic area and its borderlands is summarized in Plate 1.

The Caledonian orogenic cycle spanned Late Cambrian to earliest Devonian times. It embraced the Late Cambrian to Early Ordovician Grampian/Finnmarkian, the mid- to Late Ordovician Taconic, and the Late Silurian to early Gedinnian Main Scandinavian or late Caledonian orogenies (Gee and Sturt, 1986; Fig. 1).

The late Caledonian evolution of the Arctic–North Atlantic domain involved the convergence of four plates. The Late Ordovician and Silurian sinistral oblique collision of the continental Laurentia–Greenland and Fennosarmatian plates was preceded by the progressive subduction of the oceanic Iapetus plate and culminated in their Late Silurian–Early Devonian suturing along the Arctic–North Atlantic Caledonides. With this the Laurussian Megacontinent, also referred to as the North Continent, was formed (Wilson, 1966; Phillips et al., 1976; Roberts and Gale 1978; Soper and Hutton, 1984).

At the same time, the oceanic Proto-Tethys plate converged northward with the colliding Laurentia–Greenland and Fennosarmatian plates (Fig. 2). Northward subduction of the Proto-Tethys plate at an arc-trench system marking the southeastern margin of Laurentia and the southwestern margin of Fennosarmatia was accompanied by the northward rafting of a number of continental fragments that were rifted off the northern margin of Gondwana during the Cambro-Ordovician and Early Silurian. Some of these micro-continents (allochthonous terranes) became accreted during the Caledonian orogenic cycle to the southern margin of the newly forming North Continent (Laurussia). These continental fragments are enclosed by the North German-Polish, Mid-European, and Ligerian-Moldanubian Caledonian fold belts. In view of the contemporaneous sinistral-oblique convergence of Fennosarmatia and Laurentia–Greenland (Soper and Hutton, 1984), the consolidation of these fold belts involved presumably major sinistral translations (Ziegler 1982a, 1984, 1986; Brochwicz-Lewinski et al., 1984).

In the Arctic domain, the continental Siberian plate converged southward, toward the northern margin of Laurentia–Greenland. This involved the closure of the Proto-Arctic Ocean along a presumably south-dipping subduction system that was associated with the Innuitian fold belt. This fold belt became consolidated, however, only during the latest Devonian to earliest Carboniferous (Chapter 2).

# LATE CALEDONIAN CONTINENT ASSEMBLY (± 410 Ma)

Compared with the classical "Bullard Fit" (Bullard et al., 1965), the continent assembly given in Plate 1 shows a dextral offset of some 1500 km between Laurentia–Greenland and Fennosarmatia–Baltica. Such an offset, which is a minimum value, is suggested by paleomagnetic data (Morris, 1976; van der Voo et al., 1980; Kent, 1982; van der Voo, 1983; Perroud et al., 1984). Although there is considerable uncertainty about the magnitude of this offset, the available paleomagnetic data suggest that a continent assembly comparable to the Bullard Fit was only achieved during the Early Carboniferous as a result of

intra-Devonian and earliest Carboniferous sinistral translations between Laurentia–Greenland and Fennosarmatia–Baltica along a fault system transecting the Arctic–North Atlantic Caledonides (Keppie et al., 1985; Chapter 2).

In Plate 1, the northern Scottish Highlands, the Hebrides, Orkney, and Shetland Isles are shown as being dextrally offset across the Great Glen Fault by some 400 km relative to the Southern Highlands of Scotland (compare with Fig. 12). Such an offset is indicated by paleomagnetic data that support a commensurate intra-Devonian rotation of the northern Highlands along the curvilinear Great Glen Fault (Storedvedt, 1987) but that challenge the 2000 km offset across this fault postulated by van der Voo and Scotese (1981) (Tørsvik et al., 1983, Storedvedt and Tørsvik, 1983). On the other hand, Briden et al. (1984) question even a 400 km offset across the Great Glen Fault and prefer to reduce it to 100–200 km which, according to these authors, is "more in line with the conventional Scottish geological wisdom."

This implies that the bulk of the Late Silurian–Early Devonian offset between Laurentia–Greenland and Fennosarmatia–Baltica had to be taken up by a hypothetical fault system located to the west of the Hebrides Isles.

Plate 1 shows, in accordance with Harland et al. (1984), western Svalbard as forming part of the Greenland Craton, Eastern Svalbard as forming part of Fennosarmatia, and Central Svalbard as taking in an intermediate position. This postulate requires, however, further support by paleomagnetic analyses (see Løvlie et al., 1984).

# CALEDONIAN FOLD BELTS AND ALLOCHTHONOUS TERRANES

The Arctic–North Atlantic Caledonides, corresponding to the Iapetus megasuture, became consolidated during the late Caledonian orogeny (Fig. 1; Gee and Sturt, 1986; Dallmeyer and Gee, 1986). They embrace the Caledonide fold belts of Eastern Greenland, Svalbard, Norway, Sweden, and the northern British Isles. Although the trace of the Caledonian deformation front in the Barents Sea is uncertain, it is questionable whether a branch of the Scandinavian Caledonides extended from northernmost Norway in a northeastern direction, across the Barents Shelf, into the area between Novaya Zemlya and Severnaya Zemlya (North Islands) as suggested by Gortunov et al. (1984) and Khain (1985).

The structural style of the Scandinavian and East Greenland Caledonides is characterized by major basement-involving nappes (Haller, 1971; Roberts and Gales, 1978; Sturt et al., 1978; Hossack, 1985; Hossack et al., 1986). In combination with an extensive high-grade metamorphism and a widespread syn- and late-orogenic plutonism (Gee and Sturt, 1986), this indicates that the evolution of the Arctic–North Atlantic Caledonides was accompanied by major crustal delaminations and the subduction and anatectic remobilization of lower crustal and upper mantle material. The Late Ordovician closure of the Iapetus Ocean and the ensuing Himalaya-type collision of Laurentia–Greenland and Fennosarmatia–Baltica, giving rise to the late Caledonian orogeny, is thought to have been accompanied by important sinistral translations (Mitchell, 1981; Leggett et al., 1983; Soper and Hutton, 1984; Dallmeyer and Gee, 1986).

To the northwest, the Arctic–North Atlantic Caledonides grade into the Innuitian fold belt of northernmost Greenland

and the Canadian Arctic Island and, to the northeast, possibly into the hypothetical Lomonosov fold belt, which is though to have fringed the leading edge of the Siberian Craton. The Innuitian and possibly also the Lomonosov fold belt became finally consolidated during the latest Devonian–Early Carboniferous Ellesmerian orogeny (see Chapter 2). The evolution of the Innuitian fold belt, involving the Mid-Ordovician M'Clintock, the Late Silurian Vølvedal, and the Devonian–earliest Carboniferous Ellesmerian orogenies (Fig. 1), probably reflects the gradual closure of the Proto-Arctic Ocean and the collision of the

Siberian Craton with Laurentia–Greenland (Trettin and Balkwill, 1979; Kerr, 1981a; Trettin, 1987). In such a scenario, the hypothetical Lomonosov fold belt may have been associated, at least during the Ordovician and Silurian, with the essentially transform margin of the Siberian block facing the Ural and Lomonosov oceans.

To the south, in the North Sea area, the Arctic–North Atlantic Caledonides bifurcate into the Scottish–Irish Caledonides, which find their continuation in the Appalachian geosynclinal system and into the North German–Polish Caledonides.

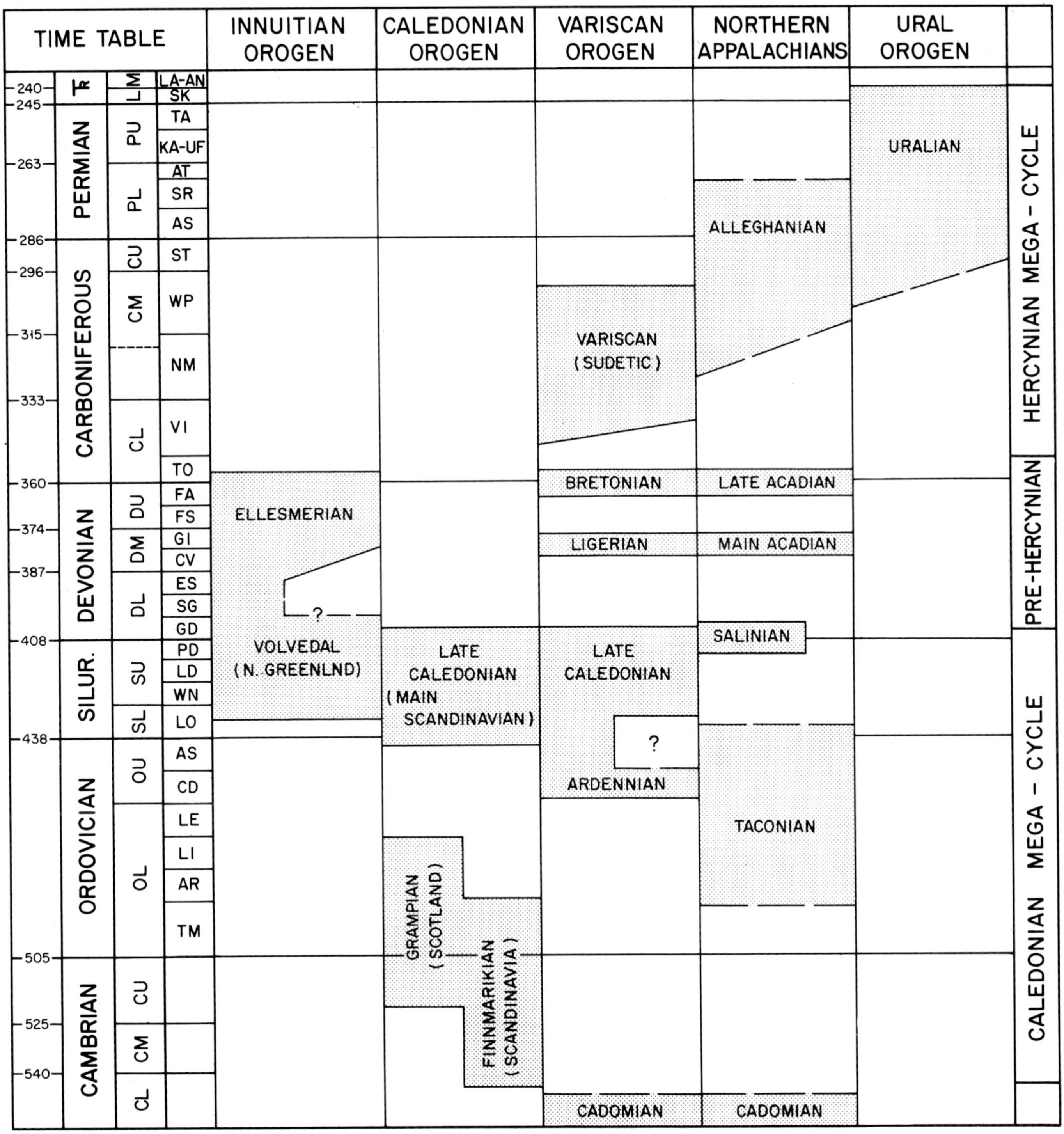

*Figure 1—Correlation of Paleozoic orogenic cycles.*

In the Appalachian domain, the main phase of the Caledonian orogenic cycle corresponds to the Taconian orogeny that terminated during the latest Ordovician–Early Silurian with the accumulation of a thick clastic wedge in the foredeep flanking the rising orogen (Fig. 1; Cook and Bally, 1975). The less pervasive Salinian disturbance, corresponding to the late Caledonian diastrophism, was accompanied by important plutonism in northern Maine and New Brunswick (Poole, 1977; Williams and Hatcher, 1983; Hatcher, 1985; Spariosu and Kent, 1983; Hubacher and Lux, 1987).

The North German–Polish Caledonides, which are deeply buried under the late Paleozoic and younger sediments of the Northwest European Basin, show on the basis of radiometric age determinations evidence for Taconian and late Caledonian deformations (Ziegler, 1982a; Brochwicz-Lewinsky et al., 1984). The Polish Caledonides extend southeastward through the Dobrudgea into the domain of the Caucasus (Sandulescu, 1984; Khain, 1984b).

The Mid-European Caledonides, corresponding to the Ardennes, probably linked the Appalachian area of incomplete Caledonian consolidation with the North German–Polish Caledonian fold belt via the Mid-German High. The Ardennes, which show evidence for Late Ordovician deformation, became consolidated during the latest Silurian–earliest Devonian late Caledonian diastrophism (Waterlot, 1974; André et al., 1986).

On the basis of limited data, it is assumed that the Ligerian–Moldanubian Cordillera developed during the late Caledonian orogeny.

These fold belts enclose the Gondwana-derived cratonic blocks of the Irish Sea Horst, the London–Brabant Massif, the Central Armorican, Saxothuringian, and Barrandian blocks, and the East Silesian Massif. These allochthonous terranes are all characterized by a continental crust that was consolidated to varying degree during the Cadomian (Baikalian, Pan-African) orogenic cycle (Ziegler, 1984, 1986). Paleomagnetic and/or faunal data indicate that these blocks were rifted off the northern margin of Gondwana during the Late Cambrian to Early Silurian and were incorporated during the Late Ordovician and Silurian into the Caledonian orogenic system of Western and Central Europe in conjunction with the northward subduction

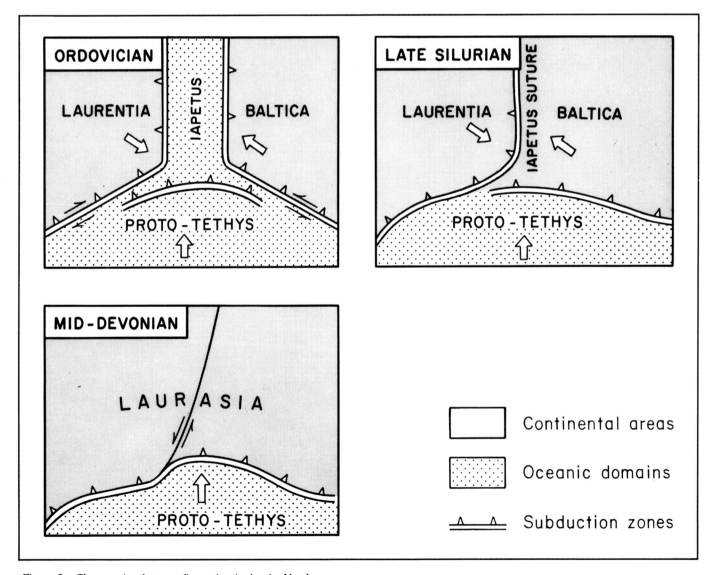

*Figure 2—Changes in plate configuration in Arctic–North Atlantic realm during Ordovician and Early Devonian time.*

of the oceanic Proto-Tethys plate (Perroud and Bonhommet, 1981; Spjeldnaes, 1981; Cocks and Fortney, 1982; Krs, 1982; Séguin, 1983; van der Voo, 1983; Perroud et al., 1984; Bonhommet and Perroud, 1986; McKerrow and Cocks, 1986). Furthermore, preliminary paleomagnetic data also indicate that the Malopolska Massif (Holy Cross Mountains), which forms an important element of the Polish Caledonides, corresponds to a Gondwana-derived terrane (Brochwicz-Lewinski, personal communication, 1986; Lewandowsky, 1987). The occurrence of Ashgillian glaciomarine series in the Armorican Massif (Lardeux et al., 1977; Doré, 1981) and in the Saxothuringian-Barrandian domain (Katzung, 1961; Steiner and Falk, 1981) stress the Late Ordovician Gondwana affinity of these terranes (see also Brenchley and Newall, 1984). Moreover there is widespread evidence for a rift-related Cambro-Ordovician alkaline to peralkaline magmatism in the Central Armorican and Saxothuringian-Barrandian blocks (Weber, 1984; Matte, 1986). This rifting activity presumably preceded their detachment from Gondwana.

Most of these allochthonous terranes were little affected by the Late Caledonian diastrophism; some were, however, intruded by Caledonian granitoids (e.g., Irish Sea Horst, London-Brabant Massif).

In view of the limited control available on the North German-Polish and the Mid-European Caledonides, as well as on the Ligerian-Moldanubian Cordillera, little can be said about their structural style. Moreover, the definitions of these fold belts is hampered in part by their deep burial under younger sediments and in part also by their overprinting during the Acadian-Ligerian, Bretonian, Variscan,* and Alpine orogenic cycles (Fig. 1).

At present, there are insufficient geophysical data on which a palinspastic restoration of the Variscan fold belt could be based. Consequently, areas south of the Variscan deformation front, shown on Plate 1 by a dotted line, are distorted by an unquantifiable amount of post-Caledonian crustal shortening. For want of a palinspastic restoration of these areas, it is difficult to understand the spatial relationship between the various allochthonous terranes and their enclosing Caledonian fold belts. For instance, it is debatable whether the Armorican Craton, underlying the Central Armorican Basin, and the Bohemian Craton, underlying the Saxothuringian and Barrandian basins, formed part of one structural unit, as postulated by Ellenberger and Tamain (1980), or whether they are formed by two or more separate entities as proposed by Behr et al. (1984).

Owing to these constraints and often limited data sets, the stepwise accretion history of the individual continental fragments enclosed by the Caledonian fold belts of Europe is still difficult to resolve.

Furthermore, the controversy is still ongoing whether by the end of the late Caledonian orogeny Europe was occupied by coherent fold belts and intervening successor basins, floored by continental crust, as suggested by Plate 1, or whether a significant oceanic basin (Rheic or Tornquist Sea) was preserved in the area of the Mid-European Caledonides (Rhenohercynian zone).

as postulated by McKerrow and Ziegler (1972), Johnson (1976), Scotese et al.(1979), Lorenz and Nicholls (1984), and Behr et al. (1984).

Paleomagnetic data suggest, however, that during the Early Devonian a major ocean separated Laurasia and Gondwana (Morel and Irving, 1978; van der Voo et al., 1980) with more recent data favoring its location to the south of the Ligerian-Moldanubian Cordillera as indicated on Plate 1 (Briden and Duff, 1981; van der Voo, 1983; Séguin, 1983; Perroud and van der Voo, 1983; Perroud et al., 1984; Bonhommet and Perroud, 1986). The width of oceanic domains separating during the latest Silurian-Early Devonian the Gondwana-derived Avalon-Meguma composite terrane and the Aquitaine-Cantabrian-Intra-Alpine (composite?) microcontinent(s) from the Appalachian and Ligerian-Moldanubian arc-trench systems is, however, uncertain and is therefore only schematically depicted on Plate 1 (see Keppie et al., 1985; Ziegler, 1984, 1986; Johnson and van der Voo, 1985).

## CALEDONIAN FOREDEEP BASINS

Geodynamic considerations suggest that the Caledonian fold belts of the Arctic-North Atlantic domain and those marking the southern margin of Laurasia were associated with extensive foredeep basins. Large parts of these basins were, however, destroyed during post-Caledonian tectonic events or are now obscured by younger sediments.

The foredeep basin of the Caucasus-Dobrugea-Polish Caledonides is only partly preserved (Rizun and Senkovskiy, 1973; Foose and Manheim, 1975; Gluschko et al., 1976; Wjalow and Medwedew, 1977; Pozaryski et al., 1982; Vinsjakov et al., 1984). In southeastern Poland and in the Dobrugea, deposition of the Caledonian Molasse series began during the Siegenian (Plate 24). In the Eastern Baltic, late Early Devonian continental clastics, overlaying conformably marine Silurian strata, may represent a remnant of the distal part of the Caledonian foredeep basin.

The foredeep basin of the North German and the Scandinavian Caledonides has been largely destroyed by post-Caledonian tectonic and erosional events (Ziegler, 1982a). Only in the Oslo Graben is a remnant of this basin preserved owing to latest Carboniferous-Early Permian downfaulting. In it, Upper Silurian marine strata grade upward into Downtonian red molasse series (Holtedahl, 1960; Nilsen, 1973), which became deformed by décollement folding and thrusting during the Gedinnian-Siegenan(?) (Roberts, 1983). On the basis of regional considerations, it can be assumed that much of the Fennoscandian Shield was originally covered by lower Paleozoic open marine platform sediments. These presumably graded upward into lower Silurian to uppermost Devonian continental red beds that accumulated in the foredeep basin paralleling the thrust front of the North German-Scandinavian-Svalbard Caledonides. Whether part of this foredeep is preserved in the Barents Sea is unknown.

The foredeep basin of the Innuitian fold belt is partly preserved in the area of Parry Island fold belt, outcropping along the southern margin of the Sverdrup Basin and, to a lesser extent, in Northern Greenland (Plate 22). In this basin, Late Silurian turbiditic sands were transported along the basin axis in a westward direction, indicating a major clastic source area in northeastern Greenland (Trettin and Balkwill, 1979; Hurst et

---

*The terms, *Hercynian* or *Hercynides*, as used in this paper, refer to the late Paleozoic fold belts of eastern North America, northwest Africa, and Europe. The term *Variscan* is used to refer to the western and central European segments of the Hercynian fold belt and specifically to the late Visean to Westphalian diastrophism that resulted in their consolidation.

al., 1983; Hurst and Surlyk, 1984; Surlyk and Hurst, 1984). This suggests that in the East Greenland foredeep basin, clastics were transported northward along its axis and were deflected at its northern end in northeastern Greenland into the east–west-trending incipient Innuitian foredeep (Franklinian Basin). Ice cover, however, impedes the recognition of a possible foredeep basin paralleling the deformation front of the East Greenland Caledonides. On trend to the south, a remnant of this foredeep basin is preserved in western Newfoundland (Poole et al., 1970). The West Newfoundland Basin was presumably connected with the Appalachian foredeep basin. Scattered outcrops of early Paleozoic and Devonian sediments in Eastern Canada and in Hudson Bay suggest that much of the Laurentia–Greenland Shield was originally covered by Siluro-Ordovician and possibly Early Devonian marine strata (Cook and Bally, 1975).

## CALEDONIAN SUCCESSOR BASINS

In the framework of the Caledonian fold belts of Western and Central Europe, the Central Armorican Basin and the composite Saxothuringian–Barrandian Basin, which are superimposed on the Cadomian consolidated Armorican and Bohemian cratons, can be considered as successor basins (Fig. 3; Ziegler,

1984). These basins are characterized by nearly continuous marine sedimentary sequences that extend from the Cambro-Ordovician into the Devonian and in part even into the Early Carboniferous (Plate 25; Svoboda, 1966; Watznauer et al., 1976; Lardeux et al., 1977; Guillocheau and Rolet, 1982). Eastward, this complex system of successor basins extended into the Sudetic Basin and into the Harz area (Alberti et al., 1977; Walliser and Alberti, 1983). These basins are located to the east and to the north of the Mid-German High. This high represents the easternmost parts of the Mid-European Caledonides (Ziegler, 1982a, 1984; Plate 1).

It is assumed that the Central Armorican–Saxothuringian successor basin was connected to the west with the Proto-Tethys Ocean but was separated from the South Polish–Dobrugea foredeep by the Polish Caledonides. In the area of the London–Brabant and the East Silesian massifs, a major hiatus separates lower and upper Paleozoic sediments (Plates 23, 24).

## EASTERN MARGIN OF FENNOSARMATIA

According to Zonenshain et al. (1984), the eastern margin of Fennosarmatia–Baltica was tectonically inactive during the Late Silurian and Early Devonian and displayed the characteris-

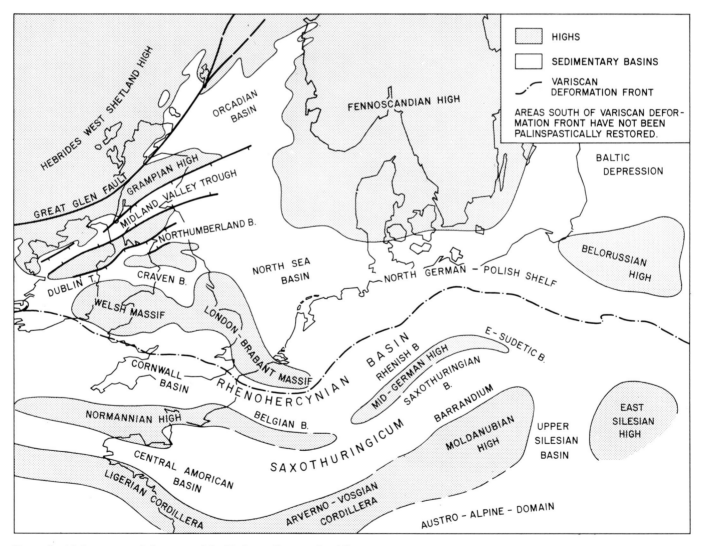

*Figure 3—Main structural elements of the Variscan Geosynclinal System.*

tics of an Atlantic-type passive margin. It faced the Sakmarian Ocean, which was separated from the Ural Ocean by the Sakmarian arc-trench system. This subduction system, which was associated with a west-dipping Benioff zone, came into evidence during the late Early Silurian. Its development is therefore contemporaneous with the onset of the Main–Scandinavian phase of the Caledonian orogeny that involved the continued convergence of the already collided Laurentia–Greenland and Fennosarmatia–Baltica cratons and the emplacement of major, basement-cored nappes (Sturt et al., 1978). This suggests that increasing constraints in the motion of the Fennoscandian–Baltica plate induced the development of the new Sakmarian arc-trench plate boundary within the Ural Ocean. During the Late Silurian, a back-arc compressive system developed within the oceanic Sakmarian Basin. Tectonic activity along the Sakmarian arc-trench system and the Sakmarian back-arc subduction zone apparently abated at the transition from the Silurian to the Devonian but resumed again during the late Early and early Middle Devonian. On the other hand, the subduction system associated with the Arctic–North Atlantic Caledonides became inactive with their final consolidation at the transition from the Silurian to the Devonian.

The existence of a Lomonosov ocean during the Siluro-Ordovician and Early Devonian, separating the northern margin of Fennoscandia–Baltica from the Lomonosov fold belt marking the margin of the cratonic Siberian Block, is hypothetical and is proposed here on geometrical grounds alone. Presumably, this oceanic basin became progressively closed in the course of the Devonian to earliest Carboniferous sinistral northward translation of Fennoscandia–Baltica relative to Laurentia–Greenland (see Plates 2–4 and Chapter 2).

# CHAPTER 2
## DEVONIAN AND EARLY CARBONIFEROUS LAURUSSIA

# INTRODUCTION

With the late Caledonian suturing of Laurentia–Greenland and Fennosarmatia–Baltic along the Arctic–North Atlantic Caledonides, the Laurussian megacontinent was formed. This large cratonic block remained intact for some 350 Ma until its break-up along the Arctic–North Atlantic Caledonian megasuture during the earliest Eocene.

Following the latest Silurian–earliest Devonian consolidation of the Arctic–North Atlantic Caledonides, the Iapetus subduction system became inactive. This entailed a fundamental plate reorganization.

# POST-CALEDONIAN PLATE REORGANIZATION

In the North Atlantic domain, the three-plate convergence system, which governed the evolution of the Caledonian fold belts of Western and Central Europe (Ziegler, 1982a; Soper and Hutton, 1984), gave way at the transition from the Silurian to the Devonian to a two-plate convergence system (Fig. 2). The Devonian and Early Carboniferous evolution of the southern margin of Laurussia was governed by the continued northward subduction of the Proto-Tethys plate at an arc-trench system extending from the Appalachian domain along the southern margin of the Ligerian–Moldanubian Cordillera (Baker and Gayer, 1985) into the area of the Caucasus. For the latter, Adamia et al. (1981) visualize a more southerly located intraoceanic Pontid–Transcaucasus arc that was separated by the Greater Caucasus interarc basins from the Greater Caucasus arc-trench system marking the southern margin of the Sarmatian platform (Plates 2–4).

Devonian subduction of the Proto-Tethys plate was accompanied by the continued northward rafting of the Gondwana-derived Traveler and Avalon–Meguma microcontinents (O'Brian et al., 1983; Williams and Hatcher, 1983; Baker and Gayer, 1985; Keppie et al., 1985) and of the Aquitaine-Cantabrian and the more hypothetical Intra-Alpine continental fragments (Perroud et al., 1984; Ziegler, 1986). These cratonic blocks collided during the Middle Devonian with the Proto-Tethys subduction complex, giving rise to the Acadian-Ligerian orogeny (Fig. 1). It is suspected that the convergence rates between the Proto-Tethys and the Laurasian plates varied though Silurian to Early Carboniferous times. This is evident by the Early Devonian development of an extensive back-arc rift system in Western and Central Europe that remained intermittently active until the Early Carboniferous onset of the Variscan orogeny (Ziegler, 1982a, 1984; Behr et al., 1984). Back-arc extension was, however, temporarily interrupted during the Middle Devonian Acadian-Ligerian orogeny and during the Bretonian orogeny at the transition from the Devonian to the Carboniferous (Plate 2).

During the Devonian and Early Carboniferous, the oceanic Ural plate continued to converge with Laurussia (Zonenshain et al., 1984). However, with the final locking of the Iapetus megasuture and the cessation of related subduction processes in the domain of the Arctic–North Atlantic Caledonides at the transition from the Silurian to the Devonian, the last step in the suture progradation from the Arctic–North Atlantic Caledonides to the Sakmarian arc-trench system, which had already begun during the Middle Silurian, was effected during the Early Devonian. Correspondingly, the Devonian and Carboniferous

evolution of the eastern margin of Laurussia was governed by the Sakmarian (-Magnitogorsk) subduction system (Plates 2–4).

Continued convergence of the Siberian craton with Laurentia–Greenland culminated during the latest Devonian and earliest Carboniferous in the Ellesmerian orogeny, which resulted in the consolidation of the Innuitian fold belt (Trettin, 1973; Trettin and Balkwill, 1979; Fig. 1).

These plate movements were paralleled by a major sinistral translation between the Laurentia-Greenland and the Fennosarmatian subplates along a complex fracture system that transected the axis of the Arctic–North Atlantic Caledonides (see *Arctic–North Atlantic Megashear,* this chapter; Ziegler, 1984; Harland et al., 1984). The development of this megashear can be considered as evolving from the sinistral oblique collision of Laurentia–Greenland and Fennosarmatia during the Caledonian orogeny (Soper and Hutton, 1984). The Devonian and Early Carboniferous northward translation of Fennosarmatia relative to Laurentia–Greenland was presumably accompanied by the progressive closure of the hypothetical Lomonosov ocean and ultimately the collision of the Barents Shelf with the Siberian block and their suturing along the largely hypothetical Lomonosov fold belt (see *Innuitian Fold Belt,* this chapter).

The northern foreland of the Innuitian-Lomonosov fold belt is formed by the East Siberian craton, encompassing Chukotka and the New Siberian Islands. It is uncertain whether this block was separated during the Late Devonian–earliest Carboniferous by an oceanic domain from the West Siberian block or whether these were connected and formed together the larger Siberian Craton, as suggested in Fig. 7 (Scotese et al., 1985). If the latter applies, it may be assumed that during the consolidation of the Innuitian-Lomonosov fold belt a shear zone transected the Siberian Craton in the prolongation of the Sakmarian arc. Such a shear zone could have facilitated the Early Carboniferous separation of the West Siberian block from the East Siberain block and the subsequent convergence of the former with the eastern margin of Fennosarmatia (see *Innuitian Fold Belt,* this chapter, and Ziegler et al., 1979).

The Devonian and Early Carboniferous evolution of Laurussia is summarized by Plates 2–4. On these maps, the palinspastic reconstruction of areas located to the south of the Variscan deformation front is incomplete. Major tectonic units and facies belts shown for areas that later became overprinted by the Variscan and Alpine orogenies are therefore distorted to varying degrees. Moreover, the outline of continental fragments (allochthonous terranes) that converged during the Devonian with the Proto-Tethys subduction zone is only shown schematically on these maps.

# VARISCAN GEOSYNCLINAL SYSTEM

Following the late Caledonian diastrophism, back-arc extension affected the Central Armorican–Saxothuringian–Barrandian successor basins as well as the Mid-European Caledonides. In the area of the latter, the Rhenohercynian Basin (Cornwall–Rhenish–East Sudetic Basin) began to subside during the Early Devonian under a tensional regime (Fig. 3; Ziegler, 1982a). Together, these basins formed important parts of the geosynclinal system out of which the Variscan fold belt of Europe developed during the Late Carboniferous. Their sedimentary record is summarized in Plates 23 and 24. The Rhenohercynian and the Central Armorican–Saxothuringian basins were separated in the west by the Normannian–Mid-German trend of highs but were connected in the east via the East Sudetic Basin. Marine transgressions entered the Rhenohercynian Basin from the east as well as from the west during the Gedinnian, with deeper water conditions being established in its axial parts during the Siegenian and Emsian. A major, in part reef-fringed, carbonate platform occupied the northern margin of the Rhenohercynian Basin during the Middle and Late Devonian and during the Early Carboniferous (Czerminski and Pajchlowa, 1974; Gardiner and MacCarthy, 1981; Ziegler, 1982a; Engel et al., 1983; Langenstrassen, 1983). Clastic influx from the Mid-German High abated during the Siegenian but accelerated again during the Late Devonian and Early Carboniferous (Weber, 1984; Franke and Engel, 1986; Plates 2–4).

In the Central Armorican Basin, Early Devonian shallow marine carbonates and clastics accumulated in depositional continuity with Silurian marine strata (Plate 25). A major influx of deltaic and continental clastics from the Ligerian Cordillera occurred during the Middle Devonian and again during the Early Carboniferous. The latter was preceded by a late Famennian pulse of deeper water flysch deposition. These pulses of clastic influx reflect the orogenic reactivation of the Ligerian Cordillera during the Acadian-Ligerian and the Bretonian diastrophic cycles (Fig. 1; Lardeux et al., 1977; Guillocheau and Rolet, 1982; Rolet, 1983).

In the Saxothuringian Basin, in which marine sedimentation was continuous across the Silurian–Devonian boundary, Devonian and Early Carboniferous series are represented by deeper marine shales and clastics (Plate 25). Shallow marine carbonates developed on local intra-basinal highs during the Middle and Late Devonian and the Early Carboniferous. In the Barrandian Basin, Early and Middle Devonian carbonate deposition was interrupted during the Givetian by the influx of flysch derived from the Moldanubian Cordillera. This is taken as evidence that the Moldanubian Cordillera was also affected by the Acadian–Ligerian diastrophism. The Bretonian orogenic pulse is reflected in the Saxothuringen Basin and in Moravia by the onset of the Early Carboniferous Culm flysch deposition and the reactivation of a south-plunging A-subduction zone (Ziegler, 1982a; Weber, 1984).

The Devonian and Early Carboniferous evolution of the Central Armorican–Saxothuringian and Rhenohercynian back-arc basins was accompanied by a repeated rift-induced, intracontinental alkaline mafic-felsic bimodal volcanism (Floyd, 1982; Ziegler, 1982a, 1984, 1986; Wedepohl et al., 1983; Behr et al., 1984). Facies patterns in these basins were, at least in part, controlled by rift tectonics and by the development of rift-induced volcanic edifices. In the Rhenohercynian Basin, back-arc extension probably progressed during the Early Devonian in some areas to crustal separation and the opening of oceanic basins, as for instance in the Cornwall subbasin (Badham, 1982; Isaac and Barnes, 1985; Rolet et al., 1986) and in the southern parts of the Rhenish subbasin (Engel et al., 1983).

In the Central Armorican and Saxothuringen basins, back-arc extension and volcanism were temporarily interrupted during the Mid-Devonian Acadian–Ligerian and the latest Devonian-earliest Carboniferous Bretonian orogenic pulses. The Early Devonian to earliest Carboniferous evolution of the Rhenohercynian Basin, on the other hand, was governed by persistent back-arc extension as indicated by an almost continuous bimodal alkaline volcanism and a generally low level of clastic influx from the Normannian–Mid-German High (Plate 24).

The eastward continuation of the Variscan geosynclinal system into the Dobrugea–Black Sea area and the Caucasus, schematically shown on Plates 2–4, is essentially based on the paleogeographic maps of Vinogradov (1969). The southeastward prolongation of the Moravian Basin, along the southwestern margin of the East Silesian Massif, is conjectural.

The Donets Graben, which came into evidence during the Middle and Late Devonian, may be considered as forming part of the Devono-Carboniferous back-arc rift system. Its subsidence was accompanied by the updoming of the Ukrainian and Voronesh highs (Vinogradov, 1969).

The Early Devonian development of an extensive back-arc rift system in Western and Central Europe may be interpreted as resulting from a post-Caledonian decrease in the convergence rate between the oceanic Proto-Tethys and the continental Laurussian plates. According to the subduction model of Uyeda (1982), such a decrease of the convergence rate between two colliding plates is associated with a steepening of the Benioff zone and a partial decoupling of the subducting and the overriding plate. With this, compressive stresses exerted on the back-arc areas decrease to the degree that back-arc convection systems can assert themselves and thus can give rise to back-arc extension. This mechanism is apparently reversible if convergence rates accelerate again (Fig. 4).

This model suggests that the Devonian to Early Carboniferous evolution of the Variscan geosynclinal system was governed by the interplay of back-arc extension and back-arc compression, whereby periods of back-arc extension were characterized by an alkaline-bimodal intraplate volcanism and periods of back-arc compression by the shedding of synorogenic clastics from orogenically reactivated highs into the adjacent basins.

The general evolution of the Variscan geosynclinal system shows that it began to subside under a back-arc extensional setting immediately after the late Caledonian orogenic pulse. During the Middle Devonian Acadian–Ligerian orogeny, the southern parts of the Central Armorican, the Saxothuringian, and the Barrandian basins became deformed by back-arc compression while the Rhenohercynian Basin remained in a tensional setting. Back-arc extension resumed in the Central Armorican and Saxothuringian basins during the Late Devonian but was again interrupted during the Bretonian orogeny. At this time, compressive stresses apparently affected also the Mid-German High from which clastics (culm-flysch) were shed into the southern parts of the Rhenohercynian Basin (Weber, 1984). During the Tournaisian and early Visean, back-arc extension again controlled the evolution of the Central Armorican-Saxothuringian and of the Rhenohercynian basins as indicated by renewed rift-induced volcanic activity (Plates 24, 25).

In the following chapters, the geodynamics of the Acadian–Ligerian and Bretonian orogenic cycles are further discussed.

## ACADIAN–LIGERIAN AND BRETONIAN OROGENIES

The Middle Devonian Acadian–Ligerian orogeny and the Bretonian orogeny straddling the Devonian–Carboniferous boundary resulted from the progressive northward subduction of the oceanic Proto-Tethys plate and the ensuing collision and accretion of Gondwana-derived continental fragments (allochthonous terranes) to the southern margin of Laurussia. In view of their association with the Proto-Tethys subduction zone,

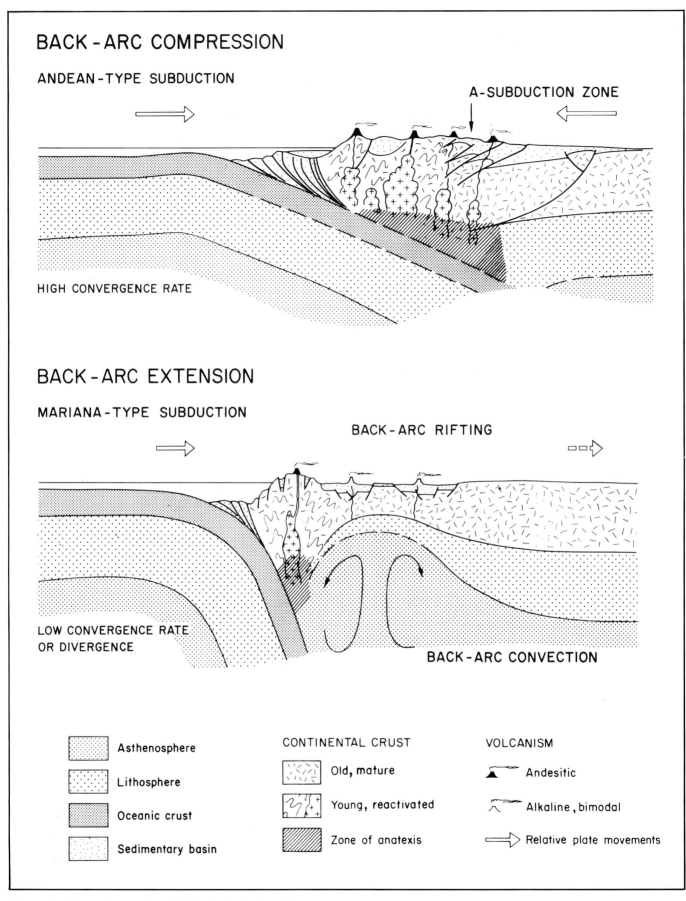

## BACK-ARC COMPRESSION

### ANDEAN-TYPE SUBDUCTION

A-SUBDUCTION ZONE

HIGH CONVERGENCE RATE

## BACK-ARC EXTENSION

### MARIANA-TYPE SUBDUCTION

BACK-ARC RIFTING

LOW CONVERGENCE RATE
OR DIVERGENCE

BACK-ARC CONVECTION

Asthenosphere

Lithosphere

Oceanic crust

Sedimentary basin

CONTINENTAL CRUST

Old, mature

Young, reactivated

Zone of anatexis

VOLCANISM

Andesitic

Alkaline, bimodal

Relative plate movements

*Figure 4—Subduction models. Modified after Bally and Snelson (1980) and Uyeda (1982). (Not to scale.)*

both the Acadian–Ligerian and the Bretonian fold belts can be regarded as "Pacific-type" or "Accretion-type" orogens, as defined by Uyeda (1982). These intermittent orogenic cycles were possibly associated with temporary increases of the convergence rate between the Proto-Tethys and the Laurussian plates and partly correspond to collisional events during which Gondwana-derived continental fragments became accreted to the southern margin of Laurussia. Paleomagnetic data suggest that during the Devonian and the Early Carboniferous the Proto-Tethys narrowed progressively, culminating in the Visean collision of Gondwana and Laurussia and the onset of the "Himalaya-type" Variscan orogeny (Jones et al., 1979; Perroud and Bonhommet, 1981; van der Voo, 1983; Perroud et al., 1984; Ziegler, 1984, 1986).

## Acadian Orogeny

During the Middle Devonian Acadian orogeny, the composite Traveler–Avalon–Meguma terrane collided with the Appalachian subduction system and became accreted to the southern margin of Laurentia (Poole, 1977; Schenk, 1978, 1981; Bradley, 1983; Baker and Gayer, 1985; Keppie, 1985). These terranes apparently became rifted off the northern margin of Gondwana sometime during the Ordovician–Early Silurian. Their Late Ordovician Gondwana affinity is emphasized by the occurrence of glacio-marine deposits in Nova Scotia (Schenk and Lane, 1981).

The megasuture between Laurentia and the Traveler–Avalon–Meguma terrane is characterized by intense deformations, metamorphism, and an extensive Middle to Late Devonian plutonism (Williams and Hatcher, 1983; Chorlton and Dallmeyer, 1986). Consolidation of the Acadian fold belt was accompanied by regional sinistral and local dextral shear movements (Keppie et al., 1985). Because much of the Avalon–Meguma terrane is now buried beneath Mesozoic and Tertiary sediments on the shelves of Nova Scotia and Newfoundland, it is difficult to assess to what extent this cratonic block was deformed during the Acadian orogeny. In Nova Scotia, where the Meguma terrane is exposed, it is characterized by open folds and numerous granitoid intrusions that range in age between 360 and 370 Ma (Reynolds et al., 1981; Keppie, 1982, 1985). These intrusions may be interpreted as being related to the Middle to Late Devonian development of a new B-subduction system along the eastern margin of the Avalon–Meguma block facing the Proto-Tethys. The second, Late Acadian orogenic phase straddles the Devonian–Carboniferous boundary (Keppie, 1985) and is coeval with the Bretonian orogeny of Western and Central Europe. In southwest Newfoundland, time-equivalent metamorphism and granitic intrusions are thought to be related to Bretonian wrench faulting (Chorlton and Dallmeyer, 1986).

In the Canadian Maritime provinces, the accumulation of neo-autochthonous red beds commenced during the late Givetian in the Fundy synclinorium (Magdalen Basin) and possibly also in the Sidney and the St. Anthony basins (Fig. 5). The evolution of these basins was accompanied by repeated wrench deformations and a generally bimodal intraplate volcanism that can be related to the Middle Devonian to earliest Carboniferous Arctic–North Atlantic translation (see Chapter 2). During the Early Carboniferous, marine incursions originating from the Rhenohercynian Basin reached the St. Anthony, Sidney, and Fundy basins where they gave rise to the accumulation of evaporites and carbonates (Plate 22; Howie and Barrs, 1975a, 1975b;

Jansa et al., 1978; Bradley, 1982; Barr et al., 1985; Fyffe and Barr, 1986).

## Ligerian Orogeny

The Ligerian orogeny of Western and Central Europe, which is roughly time equivalent with the Acadian orogeny, was associated with the collision of the Gondwana-derived Aquitaine–Cantabrian and the more hypothetical Intra-Alpine terranes with the Proto-Tethys arc-trench system paralleling the southern margin of the Ligerian–Moldanubian Cordillera. At the same time, the Aquitaine–Cantabrian microcraton collided presumably with the eastern margin of the Avalon–Meguma terrane to which it became sutured along the Central Iberian fold belts (Ziegler, 1986).

It is not certain whether contemporaneous deformations occurred along the southeastern margin of Fennosarmatia. For the Greater Caucasus area, Adamia et al. (1981) indicate the Devonian development of a tensional intra-arc basin in which flysch series accumulated.

The development of the Central Iberian fold belt is related to the closure of a relatively narrow Siluro-Ordovician oceanic basin, the opening of which was preceded by Late Cambrian to Ordovician rifting (Iglesias et al., 1983; Ribeiro et al., 1983) and the intrusion of Ordovician anorogenic granitoids (Priem and den Tex, 1984; Casquero et al., 1985; Lancelot et al., 1985). The occurrence of Ashgillian glacial deposits (Arbey and Tamain, 1971; Carls, 1975; Robardet, 1981) indicates that the Aquitaine–Cantabrian microcontinent became separated from northern Africa presumably during the Early Silurian and began to converge with the South Portuguese Craton with which it ultimately collided during the Middle Devonian. Consolidation of the resulting Central Iberian fold belt was associated with the obduction of a major, east-verging ophiolite nappe in Galicia (Martinez-Garcia, 1972, 1980; Iglesias et al., 1983). In the Ossa Morena zone of Central Iberia, Givetian emplacement of northeast-vergent nappes was followed by sinistral tangential deformations (Chacón et al., 1983). This suggests an oblique collision between the Aquitaine–Cantabrian microcontinent and the South Portuguese Craton; the latter may well form part of the larger continental Avalon–Meguma terrane (Plate 2).

The Middle Devonian consolidation of the Central Iberian range was followed by back-arc extension in the area of southwest Iberia as evident by a Late Devonian–Early Carboniferous bimodal volcanism in the Pyrite Belt and the development of the South Portuguese–Ossa Morena Basin in which Late Devonian and Early Carboniferous shallow marine clastics and flysch series accumulated (Oliveira, 1982; Julivert et al., 1983). This could be taken as an indication that a new subduction complex had developed during the Middle to Late Devonian to the south of Iberia.

In the South Armorican and the Central Massif of France, the Ligerian orogeny gave rise to high-pressure metamorphism, important plutonic activity that persisted into the Late Devonian and the emplacement of major south-vergent basement involving nappes (Bernard-Griffiths et al., 1977, 1985; Autran and Cogné, 1980; Autran and Dercourt, 1980; Matte, 1983, 1986). These important deformations are compatible with the concept that the Ligerian orogeny corresponds to a major continent–continent collisional event (Brun and Burg, 1982; Burg et al., 1987).

The above suggests that by the end of the Acadian–Ligerian orogeny the Aquitaine–Cantabrian terrane was rimmed on three sides by coherent fold belts. Its stratigraphic record shows, however, that in itself this stable cratonic block was little deformed and that its central parts continued to be occupied by carbonate and mixed carbonate-clastic platforms, which were open to the Proto-Tethys ocean to the southeast (Julivert et al., 1983; Kulmann et al., 1982; Plate 25). The deeper water troughs flanking this platform and the Central Iberian and Ligerian ranges were, however, largely destroyed during the Late Carboniferous Variscan orogeny.

Although there is stratigraphic evidence that the Moldanubian Cordillera was also affected by the Ligerian diastrophism, there is only a limited radiometric record of Middle Devonian granitoid plutonism (Bernard and Klominsky, 1975; see Plate 25, Barrandium). It is possible that during this orogenic phase the Barrandian Block became sutured to the Saxothuringian Block (W. Franke, personal communication, 1987).

Areas affected by the Acadian–Ligerian diastrophism possibly extend from the Massif Central, the West Alpine External Massifs, the Vosges, and the Bohemian Massif into the area that is now occupied by the autochthonous basement of the Alps and the basement of the Penninic and Lower and Middle Austro-Alpine nappes (Autran and Cogné, 1980; Lameyre and Autran, 1980; Kornprobst, 1980). The latter contain Siluro-Ordovician and Early and Middle Devonian sedimentary sequences and have yielded limited evidence for a Middle to Late Devonian plutonism (Schönlaub, 1979). Radiometric age determinations indicate, moreover, that the Variscan basement complex of the Central Alps contains Cadomian and older continental crustal elements that were apparently affected by a Caledonian distensional phase (Gebauer and Grüenfelder, 1982). This is compatible with the hypothesis that these areas consist of Gondwana-derived continental fragments and thus represent a truly allochthonous terrane, referred to here as the Intra-Alpine terrane, which was probably accreted to the southern margin of Fennosarmatia during the Ligerian diastrophism. More radiometric datings are, however, required to confirm this

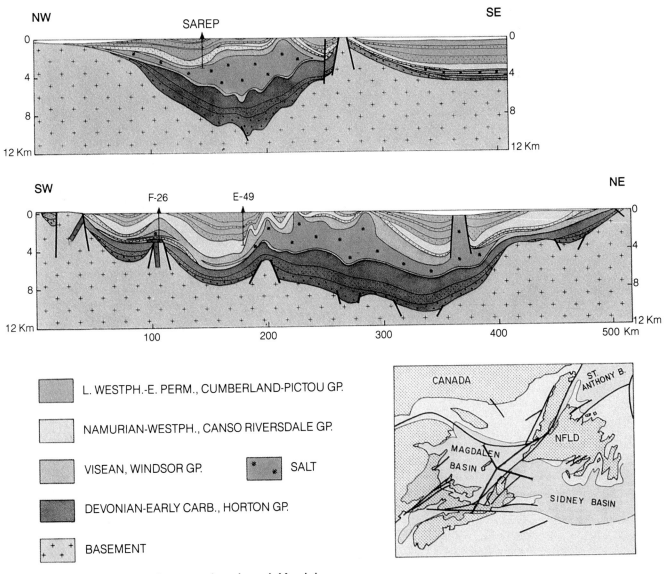

*Figure 5—Regional structural cross sections through Magdalen Basin, Gulf of St. Lawrence. After Howie and Barss (1975b).*

concept (Plate 2).

It is uncertain whether the Aquitaine–Cantabrian and the Intra-Alpine terranes formed part of a single microcraton or whether they represented separate blocks prior to their accretion to the southern margin of Fennosarmatia.

During the Acadian–Ligerian diastrophism, compressive stresses temporarily overcame back-arc extension in the Central Armorican and the Saxothuringian basins. This was apparently accompanied by the first phases of closure of the southwest Cornwall back-arc oceanic basin (Rolet et al., 1986; Holder and Leveridge, 1986). On the other hand, the Middle Devonian evolution of the Rhenohercynian Basin continued to be governed by crustal extension (Ziegler, 1982a). This suggests that during the Acadian–Ligerian orogeny both the subducting Proto-Tethys and the overriding Fennosarmatian plate were partly coupled at the B-subduction zone that paralleled the southern margin of the Ligerian–Moldanubian Cordillera.

Furthermore, it is likely that during the Acadian–Ligerian diastrophism a new B-subduction zone developed along the southern margin of the Intra-Alpine Block. It is, however, uncertain whether this subduction zone linked up to the west with the post-Acadian Proto-Tethys subduction zone along the southeastern margin of the Avalon-Meguma-South Portuguese Terrane (see the beginning of this section, *Acadian–Ligerian and Bretonian orogenies*).

Following the Acadian–Ligerian diastrophism, back-arc extension resumed to control the subsidence of the Central Armorican and the Saxothuringian basins as evident by the resumption of alkaline-bimodal volcanic activity (Sider and Ohnenstetter, 1986). Furthermore, there is evidence that southern Iberia was also affected by back-arc extension causing the subsidence of the South Portuguese Basin and inducing an alkaline-bimodal volcanism (Oliveira, 1982). Whether back-arc extension also affected the Intra-Alpine domain has yet to be resolved.

The resumption of regional back-arc extension during the Late Devonian probably reflects a renewed decrease in the convergence rate (or even a gentle divergence) between the Proto-Tethys plate and the Fennosarmatian subplate, a commensurate steepening of the Proto-Tethys B-subduction zone, and at least a partial decoupling of the subducting and overriding plates. This interpretation is in keeping with the postulated Middle Devonian to Early Carboniferous sinistral translation of Fennosarmatia and Laurentia-Greenland (see *Arctic–North Atlantic Megashear*, this chapter), during which Fennosarmatia may actually have temporarily receded from the Proto-Tethys subduction zone. There is, however, still considerable uncertainty about the width of Proto-Tethys during the Late Devonian, mainly due to insufficient paleomagnetic data from Gondwana in general and specifically from Africa (Kent et al., 1984).

## Bretonian Orogeny

The Bretonian orogenic pulse, straddling the Devonian–Carboniferous boundary, can be related to a second phase of increased convergence between the Fennosarmatia and the Proto-Tethys plates. Renewed shallowing of the Proto-Tethys B-subduction zone and partial coupling of the subducting and the overriding plates resulted, once more, in the exertion of compressive stresses on the back-arc areas. Again, mainly the Ligerian–Moldanubian Cordillera and the southern parts of the Central Armorican (Rolet, 1983; Rolet et al., 1986) and Saxo-thuringian basins (Behr et al., 1982) were affected by compressive stresses, while back-arc extension, giving rise to a commensurate volcanism, persisted in the Rhenohercynian Basin (Plates 3, 24, 25). The Famennian increase in clastic influx into this basin from southern sources indicates, however, that the Mid-German High also became reactivated during the Bretonian orogeny (Engel and Franke, 1983; Behr et al. 1984; Weber, 1984; Franke and Engel, 1986). Furthermore, there is evidence for continued closing of the south Cornwall back-arc oceanic basin (Holder and Leveridge, 1986).

In Iberia, evidence for a Bretonian orogenic phase is largely restricted to Galicia (Martinez-Garcia, 1972; Julivert, 1979, 1983). Contemporaneous granitoids are, however, lacking (Priem and den Tex, 1984). In the South Portuguese–Ossa Morena Basin, back-arc extension apparently persisted across the Devonian–Carboniferous boundary (Oliveira, 1982). In northern Algeria there is, however, evidence for Bretonian orogenic deformations (Bouillin and Perret, 1982), and it is therefore speculated that this area may have formed part of the arc system along which oceanic crust of the Proto-Tethys continued to be subducted.

Limited radiometric age determinations indicate that the Intra-Alpine domain was also affected by the Bretonian orogeny (Schönlaub, 1979; Trümpy, 1980; Oberli et al., 1981; Thélin and Ayrton, 1983). This, however, requires further clarification.

The stratigraphic record of the Gondwana-derived Austro-Alpine Block (Upper Austro-Alpine nappes) lacks evidence of a compressive Bretonian deformation phase. The same applies for the South Alpine–Carnic–Dinarid domain, which is also characterized by a nearly complete Gondwana-type Paleozoic sedimentary sequence.[*] Furthermore, a Devonian separation between the Austro-Alpine and the Carnic–Dinarid blocks is indicated by faunal differences (Schönlaub, 1979; Vai, 1975, 1980; Vai and Cocozza, 1986).

This suggests that the Austro-Alpine block constitutes a separate terrane. Whether the Carnic–Dinarid block was still attached to the northern margin of Gondwana during the Devonian and Early Carboniferous is uncertain. Its tensional evolution, which persisted into the Westphalian, is thought to be related to large-scale dextral strike-slip movements preceding and accompanying the Carboniferous convergence of Gondwana and Laurasia (Vai, 1975, 1980; Vai and Spalletta, 1982; Vai and Cocozza, 1986). Paleomagnetic data may shed further light on the Paleozoic evolution of the Austro-Alpine and the Carnic–Dinarid blocks.

Following the Bretonian orogenic pulse, back-arc extensions resumed and dominated the Tournaisian and early Visean evolution of the Central Armorican, the Saxothuringian, and the Rhenohercynian basins and possibly also of the Intra-Alpine domain.

This may reflect a renewed decrease in the convergence rate of the Proto-Tethys–Gondwana plate and the Fennosarmatia subplate. On the other hand, paleomagnetic data suggest that by early Visean time the collision of Gondwana and Laurasia

---

[*]Gondwana-type Paleozoic sequences are characterized by Ordovician cold-water faunas and the lack of Caledonian compressional deformations. Sedimentation took place in a tensional setting that variably ranged from the Ordovician to the Silurian, Devonian, and Early Carboniferous. The widespread Ordovician magmatism (Caledonian thermal event) is of an essentially anorogenic nature and is probably related to regional tensional tectonics that affected the northern margin of Gondwana; these induced the separation of a number of microcontinents from the northern margin of the Afro-Arabian craton.

was imminent (Jones et al., 1979; Perroud and Bonhommet, 1981; van der Voo and Scotese, 1981; Kent, 1982; van der Voo, 1983). It can, however, not be excluded that already during the Bretonian orogeny cratonic promontories of Gondwana had already collided with the southern margin of Fennosarmatia (see Matte, 1986). This is possibly indicated by the latest Devonian–Early Carboniferous evolution of Northwest Africa where wrench faulting induced the Famennian–Dinantian subsidence of the Sidi Betache Basin in northwest Morocco (Piqué, 1981; Piqué and Kharbouche, 1983) and the concomitant differential subsidence of the Ougarta Trough that extends from the Anti-Atlas in a southeasterly direction into the Sahara Platform (Wendt, 1985; Fig. 8).

From the above it follows that the "Avalon plate," defined by Rast and Skehan (1983) as including, apart from the Avalon–Meguma Terrane, the London–Brabant Massif, the Central Armorican, and the Aquitaine–Cantabrian blocks as well, was not accreted to the southern margin of Laurussia as a single tectonic element but consisted of a mosaic of separate continental fragments that collided stepwise with the Proto-Tethys subduction zone(s). For instance, the London–Brabant, Armorican, and Saxothuringian microcratons were accreted to Laurussia during the Caledonian orogeny whereas the Avalon–Meguma, Aquitaine–Cantabrian, and possibly the Barrandian and Intra-Alpine microcratons were accreted during the Acadian–Ligerian orogeny.

The exact timing of docking and accretion of these different continental fragments to the southern margin of Laurussia is, however, difficult to determine, mainly due to still fragmentary information. Moreover, it should be kept in mind that the definition of the individual suspected allochthonous terranes contained in the European part of the Hercynian fold belt is severely hampered by their intense deformation during the Variscan and partly also the Alpine diastrophism, by limited exposure of the Variscan basement complex, and by incomplete data sets. It is likely that their number is actually greater and their configuration and lateral relationship is more complex than suggested by Plates 2–4. As results of ongoing research become available, the conceptual model developed above will have to be modified and in all likelihood will become considerably more complex.

# ARCTIC–NORTH ATLANTIC MEGASHEAR

As discussed in Chapter 1 and illustrated in Plate 1, Fennoscandia and Laurentia–Greenland were dextrally offset during the latest Silurian by a minimum of 1500 km as compared to the Permo-Triassic Bullard Fit. The bulk of this offset was recovered during the Middle and Late Devonian by sinistral motions along a complex fault system, transecting the axis of the Arctic North Atlantic Caledonides. Relatively minor displacements may still have occurred during the Early Carboniferous (Plates 2–4).

This postulate is supported by modern paleomagnetic data (Irving and Strong, 1984) and is in keeping with the stratigraphic record of the North Atlantic borderlands and those of the Norwegian–Greenland Sea. These data refute the earlier held view (Kent and Opdyke 1978, 1979) that most of these movements had taken place during the Carboniferous (Kent and Opdyke, 1978; Keppie et al., 1985; Kent and Keppie, 1988). Further paleomagnetic support for the Devonian Arctic–North Atlantic translation comes from Scotland where Storedvedt (1987) recognizes a 400–600 km Middle to Late Devonian sinis-

tral displacement along the Great Glen fault.

Definition of the fault systems pertaining to the Arctic–North Atlantic megashear is limited to onshore areas since thick Mesozoic and Cenozoic strata generally mask the Devonian and Carboniferous structural framework of the shelves flanking the North Atlantic and the Norwegian–Greenland Sea. Fault patterns shown on Plates 2–4 are therefore schematic and in offshore areas conceptual.

The stratigraphic record of Devonian and Carboniferous basins associated with the Arctic–North Atlantic megashear is summarized in Plate 22, for which an index is given in Fig. 9.

## Canadian Maritime Provinces

In the Canadian Maritime Provinces, the present juxtaposition of the western and eastern parts of the Acadian fold belt was achieved during the late Visean to Namurian. The bulk of these sinistral displacements was taken up along the Lubec–Belle Isle–Cobequid–Cabot fault system transecting the Fundy Basin (Fundy Synclinorium or Magdalen Basin). The evolution of this complex basin was accompanied by wrench and pull-apart movements and repeated volcanic activity, spanning late Middle Devonian to early Namurian time (Fig. 3; Howie and Barss, 1975a, 1975b; Bradley, 1982; Fyffe and Barr, 1986). Data from Newfoundland indicate that intra-Carboniferous displacements were, however, below the paleomagnetic margin of error (Irving and Strong, 1984). Contemporaneous movements along the Minas (Chedabucto) geofracture, controlling the evolution of the Sidney Basin, are thought to have been dextral (Keppie, 1985). In northeastern Newfoundland, the Cabot fault splits up into the fault systems controlling the subsidence of the St. Anthony Basin (Cutt and Laving, 1977) and those associated with the Devono-Carboniferous basins of the northern British Isles. An important element of this fault system is the Great Glen Fault. In view of the paleomagnetic constraints on the movements along this fault (Storedvedt, 1987), it is likely that the bulk of the Devonian shear movements was taken up along a fault system located to the west of the Hebrides Isles.

The sedimentary record of the Fundy Basin is summarized in Plate 22. In the Post-Acadian basins of the Canadian Maritime Provinces, late Middle Devonian to Tournaisian continental clastics, attaining a thickness of up to 4000 m, are overlain by Visean evaporitic series containing minor carbonates and clastics (Howie and Barss, 1975a, 1975b; Boehner, 1983). Corresponding marine ingressions reached the Sidney and Fundy basins presumably from the West-Iberian segment of the Rhenohercynian Basin and the St. Anthony Basin from the grabens and troughs of southern Ireland (Plates 3, 4).

## Northern British Isles

In the northern British Isles the late Ludlovian to early Emsian lower Old Red continental and lacustrine series accumulated in the largely tensional intramontane Orcadian Basin, the Midland Valley, and the Northumberland–Dublin Trough (Plates 22, 23; Figs. 3, 11). Their development was accompanied by an extensive postorogenic intrusive and extrusive igneous activity. Lower Old Red clastics reach a maximum thickness of 6600 m in the Midland Valley Graben (Leeder, 1976; House et al., 1977; Bluck, 1978, 1984).

During the Middle Devonian, sedimentation in the Northumberland–Dublin Trough and the Midland Valley Graben was interrupted by transpressional deformations giving rise to low relief folds in the Lower Old Red sandstone. In the Orcadian Basin, on the other hand, unconformity-bound Middle Devonian Old Red Series consist of some 5000 m of lacustrine shales and fluviatile sands. Their accumulation was accompanied by syndepositional deformations reflecting the interplay between transtensional and transpressional stresses that can be related to sinistral movements along the Great Glen Fault (House et al., 1977; Anderton et al., 1979; Watson, 1985).

The Middle Devonian Orcadian Basin probably extended across the northern North Sea to the Norwegian coast where great thicknesses of Old Red conglomerates and sand accumulated in the transtensional Hornelen, Solund and two other smaller basins (Nilsen, 1973; Steel, 1976; Steel and Gloppen, 1980; Ziegler, 1982a). The margins of these basins are partly marked by basement-involving overthrusts (Roberts, 1983). These Middle Devonian deformations, which coincide with the Acadian–Ligerian orogeny, can be related to the Arctic–North Atlantic translation. In onshore and offshore areas of northwest Scotland, the subsidence of half-graben-shaped Old Red Sandstone basins involved the tensional reactivation of Caledonian thrust faults. Some of these basins are associated with flat-lying mylonite zones and thus beg a comparison with the Basin and Range Province of the United States Cordillera. This illustrates that the Early to Middle Devonian evolution of the northern North Sea area reflects the interplay between transtensional and transpressional tectonics (Hossack, 1984; Beach, 1985; McClay et al., 1986; Enfield and Coward, 1987).

During the Late Devonian tectonic activity abated in the British Isles and sedimentation resumed in most of its Old Red Sandstone basins. As a result of the progressive overstepping of basin margins, which is partly related to eustatically rising sea levels (House, 1983), these basins became connected with each other and with the Rhenohercynian Basin via southern Ireland and the North Sea. Through these avenues, transgressions advanced from the latter during the early Tournasian. Dinantian and Namurian strata are represented by carbonates, mixed carbonate and clastics and deltaic-paralic series (Plates 3, 4; Ziegler, 1982a).

The Dinantian and early Late Carboniferous evolution of the sedimentary basins of the British Isles (Midland Valley, Northumberland, Solvay, Craven, and Dublin troughs) was governed by crustal extension as documented by the widespread occurrence of an alkaline, bimodal rift volcanism (Francis, 1978; Leeder, 1982; Ziegler, 1982a; Kirton, 1984). During the Early Carboniferous, these basins were connected to the southwest with the basins of the Canadian Maritime Provinces. Together they formed an important part of the Arctic–North Atlantic rift-wrench system (Ziegler, 1984, 1986).

## Norwegian–Greenland Sea Area

Little is known about the Devonian evolution of the West Norwegian coastal and shelf areas. In the Trondheimsfjord, some 1300 m thick Early to Middle Devonian conglomeratic series are preserved in a narrow trough, the southeastern margin of which is overthrust by the Caledonian basement (Siedlicka and Siedlicki, 1972; Nilsen, 1973; Roberts, 1983; Norton, 1986). The age of deformation is unknown but probably Middle Devonian. In the adjacent offshore areas, reflection seismic data indicate the presence of thick pre-Permian sediments, contained in a half-graben, that may include Devonian and Early Carboniferous strata (Figs. 37, 38; Bukovics and Ziegler, 1985).

In Central East Greenland, some 7000 m thick Emsian to early Tournaisian Old Red series, consisting of conglomerates, sandstones, and lacustrine shales, accumulated in the Trail Ø-Hudson Land area (Plates 22; Fig. 9). The evolution of this basin was accompanied by repeated wrench deformations, referred to as the Hudson Land phases, volcanism, and granitic intrusions. The last phase of deformation, involving thrust faulting, is referred to as the Ymerland phase, which cannot be dated closer than intra-Dinantian (Haller, 1971; Friend et al., 1976). From the structural style of this basin it is evident that its development was governed by transtensional and transpressional deformations (Fig. 6). These can be related to the Arctic–North Atlantic megashear. Early Namurian to Early Permian continental clastics, however, were deposited under a tensional setting that persisted through Mesozoic time (Vischer, 1943; Haller, 1971; Pedersen, 1976). The Permo-Carboniferous East Greenland rift system can be followed over a distance of some 1400 km from Scoresby Sound to the Wandel Sea Basin in northeastern Greenland. In the latter, Dinantian coalbearing shales and sands, possibly accumulating in fault-controlled basins, are disconformably overlain by Westphalian–Stephanian marine sands and carbonates (Håkansson et al., 1981b; Håkansson and Stemmerik, 1984; Plate 22).

## Svalbard and Barents Shelf

In the Svalbard archipelago, latest Silurian to earliest Devonian sediments are restricted to the Central Spitsbergen Billefjord Trough where 1500–2000 m thick Downtonian red beds were deposited on a late Caledonian basement complex (Plate 22). These strata were folded and thrusted during the early Gedinnian Haakonian deformation phase. Sedimentation resumed during the late Gedinnian with the accumulation of continental red beds; these grade upward into Middle Devonian marginally marine clastics. These strata, which attain a maximum thickness of 6000 m, were shed from southwestern and southeastern sources. Similar series may be present beneath the Permo-Carboniferous and Mesozoic cover of eastern Svalbard and the Svalbard Bank (Birkenmajer, 1981; Rønnevik and Beskow, 1983). During the Late Devonian, sedimentation was interrupted by the Svalbardian wrench deformations, which probably contributed significantly to the assembly of the western, central, and eastern parts of Svalbard to its present configuration (Harland et al., 1984; Plate 3). The accumulation of a continental coal-bearing series resumed during the latest Devonian under a transtensional setting (Steel and Worsley, 1984).

At the transition from the Visean to the Namurian, wrench movements, referred to as the Adriabukta phase, gave rise locally to important deformations and low-grade metamorphism (Birkenmajer, 1981). In the course of the Namurian, the area of sedimentation gradually increased while subsidence rates of the main grabens slowed down. A last phase of significant wrench deformations, causing partial basin inversion, occurred during the late Namurian (Worsley and Edwards, 1976; Gjelberg and Steel, 1981; Steel and Worsley, 1984).

For Bjørnøya a similar latest Devonian to Carboniferous basin evolution is indicated by Gjelberg and Steel (1983) (Plates 3, 4, 22).

From the above it can be concluded that wrench deformations related to the Arctic–North Atlantic megashear probably terminated during the latest Visean and that post-Visean deformations in the Svalbard area may have been induced by transform movements compensating for crustal extension in the Norwegian–Greenland Sea Rift.

The Devonian and Carboniferous evolutions of the Western Barents Sea has to be derived largely from reflection seismic data that are only partly calibrated by well data. Thus considerable uncertainty exists in the identification of the different Paleozoic seismic reflectors. Yet, these data suggest that Middle(?) to Late Devonian and Early Carboniferous rifting in the southwestern Barents Sea induced the development of a northeast-southwest-trending fault pattern controlling the subsidence of the Nordkapp Basin and possibly also of the Tromsø and Bjørnøya basins (Fig. 10). On the Svalbard Bank, northwest-southeast-striking dextral wrench faults are evident and are interpreted as a conjugate shear to the Arctic–North Atlantic megashear (Rønnevik and Beskow, 1983; Rønnevik and Jacobsen, 1984; Gabrielsen et al., 1984).

During the Devonian and Carboniferous, marine transgressions originating from the eastern Barents Sea advanced westward as illustrated by marginally marine Middle Devonian strata in central Spitsbergen and Bashkirian marine influences in Svalbard and Bjørnoya. The occurrence of suspected Early Carboniferous sandy carbonates in Andøya (West Norway) may be indicative of a major transgression (Sturt et al., 1979). Devonian and Early Carboniferous facies patterns as shown in Plates 2–4 are, however, poorly controlled, and it is uncertain whether evaporites accumulated during the Late Devonian in the Tromsø and Northkapp basins as suggested by Rønnevik and Beskow (1983) and Faleide et al. (1984).

In the coastal area of northernmost Norway, the east–west-trending dextral Trollfjord–Komagelv wrench fault was active during the Devonian and Early Carboniferous (Fig. 10; Johnson et al., 1978). Dyke intrusions associated with this fault are dated as f 355 Ma (Beckinsale et al., 1975).

## Conclusions

In summary, there is ample geological evidence in support of the postulated Devonian to Early Carboniferous Arctic–North Atlantic sinistral megashear. The bulk of these movements occurred apparently during the Middle and Late Devonian with Early Carboniferous displacements being on a relatively minor scale. On the other hand, there is still considerable controversy about the paleomagnetic evidence supporting this concept, as well as about the timing and the magnitude of these movements (e.g., Esang and Piper, 1984; Scotese et al., 1984; Keppie et al., 1985).

## INNUITIAN FOLD BELT

The late Paleozoic stratigraphic record of the Sverdrup Basin, Northern Ellesmere Island and of Northern Greenland, as summarized in Plate 22, reflects the evolution of the Innuitian fold belt.

In northern Greenland, the late Caledonian orogeny resulted in the emplacement of thin-skinned thrust sheets. This was accompanied by the deposition of some 3000 m of synorogenic Silurian flysch series. The youngest sediments involved in these thrust sheets are of Gedinnian age. Although younger Devonian strata are not preserved in the area, last thrust movements occurred probably during the Late Silurian–Early Devonian Vølvedale orogeny (Dawes and Peel, 1981; Håkansson and Pedersen, 1982; Pedersen, 1986).

Time-equivalent deformations are evident in northern Ellesmere Island where Early Devonian shallow marine clastics form part of a neoautochthonous sequence (Mayr, personal communication). In the Innuitian foredeep, the Franklinian Basin, synorogenic flysch series mainly derived from eastern sources continued to accumulate during the Early Devonian.

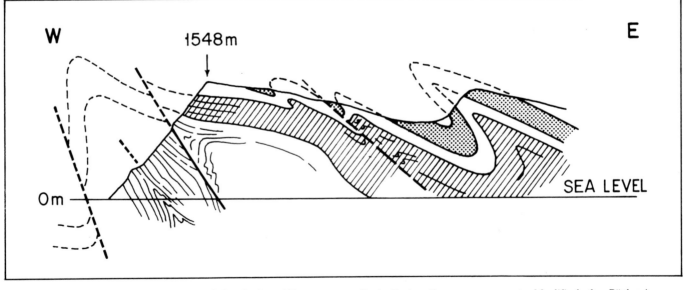

*Figure 6—Structural cross section through Svedenborg Bjerg, Kong Oscar Fjord, Central East Greenland, showing Mid-Devonian Old Red clastics intensely folded and thrusted by* *Early Carboniferous movements. Modified after Bütler, in Haller (1971).*

Carbonate shelves, occupying the distal southern margin of this foredeep basin, persisted into the Emsian and early Eifelian, by which time they became buried beneath deltaic, and later continental, clastics prograding from the northeast and east (Plates 2, 3). These molasse series, which extend into the Frasnian, were deposited during the Ellesmerian orogenic cycle terminating in the Early Carboniferous with the folding of the Franklinian Basin and the consolidation of the thin-skinned Parry Island fold belt that forms the externides of the Innuitian orogen (Plate 4; Fig. 9). Granitic intrusives in the northern part of the Innuitian fold belt are dated as 360 ± 25 Ma and 345 ± 15 Ma (Trettin and Balkwill, 1979; Kerr, 1981a; Balkwill and Fox, 1982; Smith and Stearn, 1982; Fox, 1985).

A palinspastic restoration of the Arctic area, prior to the opening of the Canada Basin, suggests that the direct western exten-

sion of the Innuitian fold belt is formed by the Alaska North Slope and the area of the Brooks Ranges and British Mountains of Ellesmerian deformation from where granitic intrusives ranging in age from 430 to 330 Ma have been reported (Fig. 7; Ziegler, 1969; Bird et al., 1978; Metz et al., 1982; Dutro, 1981; Hubbard et al., 1987). In the northernmost Yukon, the Innuitian deformation front is evident in the northern Richardson Mountains from where it trends in a southwestern direction (Bell, 1973).

The folds and thrusts of the Innuitian orogenic belt are clearly southeast vergent (Kerr, 1981a). South-vergent folds and thrusts of the north Greenland belt, which in part overprint the earlier west-vergent Vølvedal structures, are also attributed to the Ellesmerian orogeny. Because it is impossible to stratigraphically date these deformations more accurately than post-Late

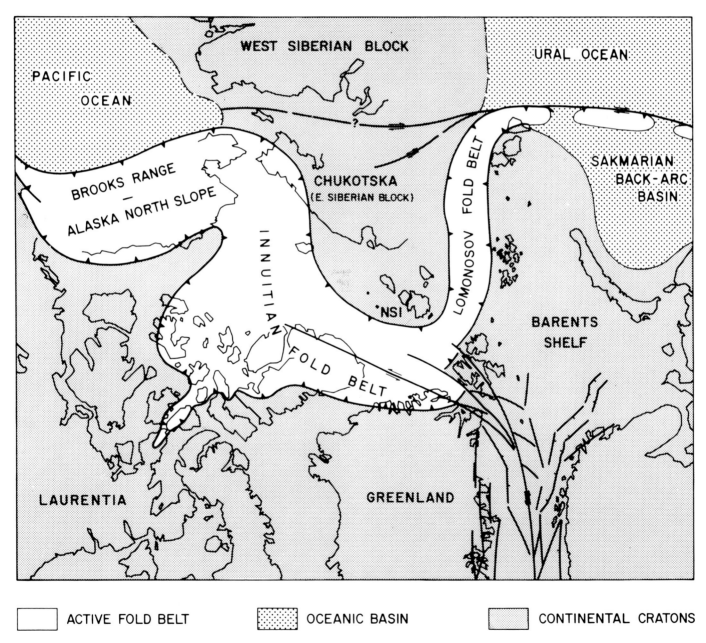

Figure 7—Conceptual Early Carboniferous tectonic framework of the Arctic. NSI = New Siberian Islands.

Silurian, they may actually be of an Early to Middle Devonian age (Dawes and Peel, 1981; Pedersen, 1986). This would be in keeping with the Emsian influx of deltaic clastics into the Innuitian foredeep.

In northern Ellesmere Island, sinistral wrench deformations are thought to have induced the Early to Middle Devonian intrusion of granodiorites and basic plutons and the development of intramontane basins in which thick Late Devonian and also Early Carboniferous continental clastics accumulated (Trettin and Balkwill, 1979; Trettin, 1987; Trettin et al., 1987; Mayr, personal communication). Also in the Brooks Range of Northern Alaska, synorogenic Late Devonian clastics accumulated in intramontane basins (Moore and Nilsen, 1984; Hubbard et al., 1987). In the North Greenland fold belt, wrench deformations probably induced the intrusion of the post-orogenic Middle Devonian Midtkap igneous complex and a low-grade metamorphism straddling the Early to Late Carboniferous boundary (Håkansson and Pedersen, 1982; Pederson and Holm, 1983). The latter is coeval with the the Adriabukta deformation phase in Svalbard that gave rise to local metamorphism (Birkenmajer, 1981). This suggests that the Late Devonian to Early Carboniferous consolidation of the Innuitian fold belt was accompanied by major sinistral wrench deformations related to the Arctic–North Atlantic megashear.

The Innuitian fold belt presumably forms the megasuture between the Siberian Block and Laurentia (Fig. 7; see also Scotese et al., 1979). It is, however, uncertain whether the collision and suturing of these cratons was governed by a south-plunging subduction system located along the northwestern margin of Laurentia–Greenland or by a north-plunging subduction system paralleling the leading edge of the Siberian block (Trettin

and Balkwill, 1979). The rather moderate expression of a Late Devonian to Early Carboniferous calc-alkaline magmatism in northern Alaska and Ellesmere and Axel Heiberg islands, as well as their absence in the North Greenland fold belt, cannot be considered as an argument for or against either of the two hypotheses. Yet, the Late Carboniferous development of the Sverdrup Basin, which may be related to back-arc rifting, would be more easily explained if the first alternative would apply (see Chapter 4).

Assuming that the Innuitian fold belt indeed represents the megasuture between Laurentia–Greenland and the Siberian Craton, and accepting the validity of the Devono-Carboniferous Arctic–North Atlantic megashear, and taking into account the indicated contemporaneous wrench deformations in the internal parts of the Innuitian and North Greenland fold belts, it is likely that the northern margin of the Barents Shelf collided during the Late Devonian to Early Carboniferous with the southeastern margin of the Siberian Craton. Unfortunately, critical areas, including the Lomonosov Ridge, are not accessible to geological investigation. On Franz Josef Land Early(?) Carboniferous paralic clastics overlay late Precambrian (Wendian) metamorphics. On the North-Islands (Severnaya Zemya), Old Red-type Late Devonian sandstones overlay Siluro-Ordovician marine platform series. The latter appear to have been affected by folding that is suggested to be of a "Caledonian" age, and there is apparently evidence for post-Late Devonian folding. Whether these late deformations can be attributed to the Ellesmerian orogeny or to the Permian Uralian orogeny cannot be resolved on the basis of the available literature (Churkin et al., 1981; Karasik et al., 1984). "Caledonian" deformations are furthermore reported from the coastal areas of Taimyr Peninsula

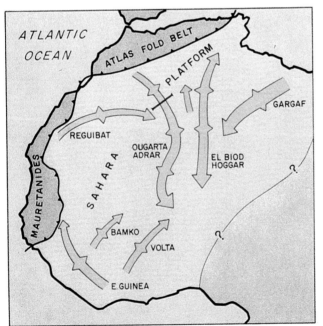

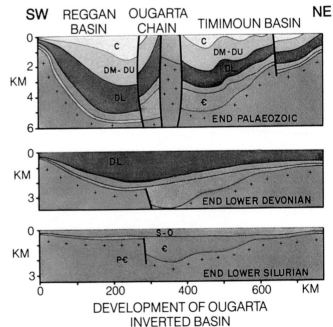

*Figure 8—Carboniferous intraplate deformation of the Sahara Platform and evolutionary diagram of the Ougarta Trough. Arrows indicate axes of major arches.*

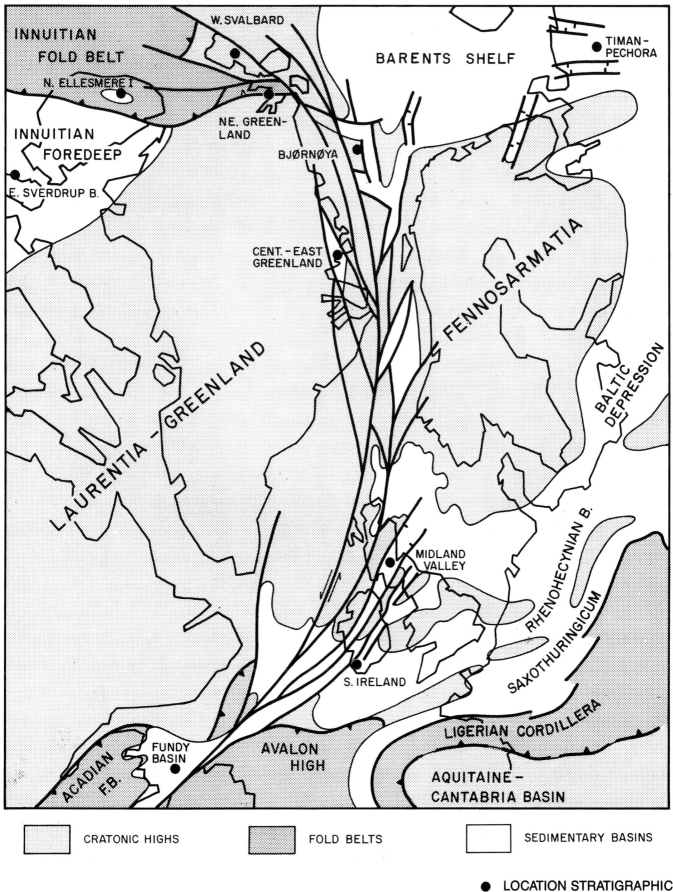

*Figure 9—Arctic–North Atlantic megashear and associated sedimentary basins (location map Plate 22).*

CRATONIC HIGHS     FOLD BELTS     SEDIMENTARY BASINS

● LOCATION STRATIGRAPHIC COLUMNS PLATE 22

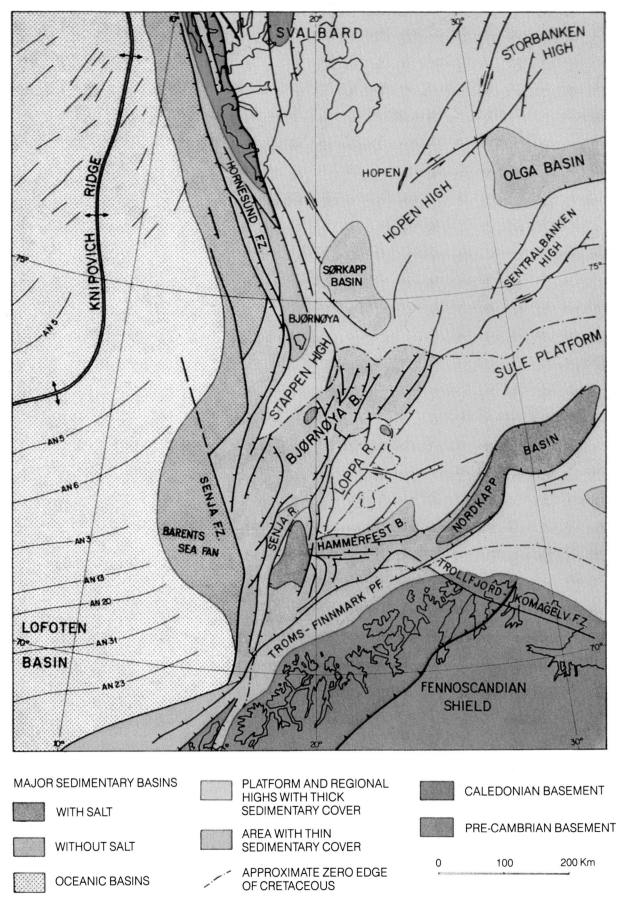

*Figure 10—Tectonic map of the Western Barents Shelf. After Norske Shell.*

MAJOR SEDIMENTARY BASINS

WITH SALT

WITHOUT SALT

OCEANIC BASINS

PLATFORM AND REGIONAL
HIGHS WITH THICK
SEDIMENTARY COVER

AREA WITH THIN
SEDIMENTARY COVER

APPROXIMATE ZERO EDGE
OF CRETACEOUS

CALEDONIAN BASEMENT

PRE-CAMBRIAN BASEMENT

0          100          200 Km

(Hamilton, 1970; Churkin and Trexler, 1981; Pogrebitsky, 1982).

In short, the hypothesis that the Innuitian fold belt finds its eastward extension in the Lomonosov fold belt remains a postulate that begs further analysis.

## EASTERN MARGIN OF FENNOSARMATIA AND THE PRE-URALIAN ARC-TRENCH SYSTEM

Following the earliest Devonian eustatic low stand of sea level, sea levels rose cyclically during the Devonian and Early Carboniferous (Vail et al., 1977; House, 1983; Johnson et al., 1985).

This is reflected on the stable eastern shelves of Fennosarmatia by cyclical late Middle and Late Devonian transgressions inducing the development of vast carbonate, carbonate-evaporite, and mixed carbonate–clastic platforms (Plates 2, 3). These encroached progressively onto the Fennoscandian–Baltic Shield. Similar carbonate platforms characterized the Early Carboniferous setting of the Moscow Platform and probably also of the eastern parts of the Barents Shelf (Vinogradov, 1969).

During the late Eifelian to early Dinantian, the Kola Peninsula, the Timan–Pechora area, and the northern parts of the Moscow Platform became affected by tensional tectonics, giving rise to the differential subsidence of the Kontozero, Pechora, and Kolva grabens and of the Vyatka rift. In the Timan–Pechora area and on the Kola Peninsula, the development of these grabens was accompanied by an alkaline volcanism (Tszyn, 1967; Churkin et al., 1981; Ulmishek, 1982; Gortunov et al., 1984; Plate 22). Whether similar grabens occur in the eastern part of the Barents Shelf is unknown. Moreover, the nature of the geodynamic processes that governed the development of these rifts is not clear. Could they be related to the Arctic–North Atlantic shear via, for instance, the Trollfjord–Kolmagelv fault, or is their development linked with the evolution of the Sakmarian–Magnitogrosk arc-trench and back-arc extension system?

According to Zonenshain et al. (1984), the late Early Devonian to Eifelian reactivation of subduction processes along the Sakmarian–Magnitogorsk arc-trench system was accompanied by the submarine obduction of oceanic crust onto the lower parts of the Fennosarmatian margin (Ruzencev and Samygin, 1979). Emplacement of these nappes was, however, not associated with intense subsidence of the adjacent shelf area (Artyushkov and Baer, 1983). Back-arc compression ceased and gave way to back-arc extension during the late Eifelian, and new oceanic crust was formed during the Givetian, at least in the southern parts of the Sakmarian Basin. The beginning of back-arc extension in the Sakmarian Basin coincided with the onset of rifting in the Timan–Pechora area.

Continued convergence between the Ural oceanic plate and the Sakmarian Magnitogorsk arc-trench system was accompanied by the Famennian collision of the Mugodjarian microcontinent with the latter (Plate 4). Famennian to Tournaisian back-thrusting of the arc induced its uplift and the shedding of clastics into the back-arc basin, where they were deposited as deep sea fans on oceanic crust. These clastics reached the toe of

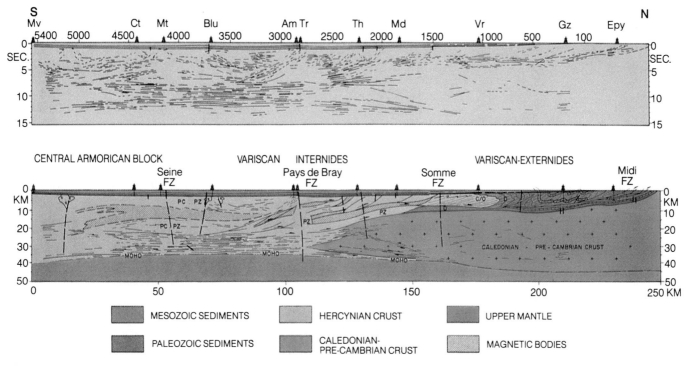

*Figure 11—Crustal structure of the Paris Basin. After Cazes et al. (1985).*

the Fennosarmatian passive margin. During the Tournaisan and early Visean, the Sakmarian–Magnitogorsk arc was characterized by a synorogenic acidic volcanism, which was followed by the middle Visean intrusions of granitic plutons (Plate 4). Subduction processes apparently came to a halt during the middle Visean (Zonenshain et al., 1984).

The evolution of the Pechora and Kolva rifts, on the other hand, suggests that back-arc extension may have persisted into the Tournaisian (Plate 22).

The subsequent evolution of the Uralian orogenic system was governed by a new B-subduction system that developed along the leading edges of the Kazakhstan and the Siberian cratons. The latter apparently became separated from the northern margin of Laurentia (Alaska–Chuckhi block) during the late Visean–early Namurian and began to converge with the now defunct Sakmarian–Magnitogorsk arc and the eastern margin of Fennosarmatia. This marked the onset of the actual Uralian orogenic cycle.

It is unknown how wide the oceanic Sakmarian back-arc basin was at the beginning of the Late Carboniferous. In view of this, the situation shown in Plate 4 should be regarded as conceptual.

# CHAPTER 3
## HERCYNIAN SUTURING OF PANGEA

## INTRODUCTION

The Hercynian orogenic cycle, spanning Visean to Late Permian times, was associated with the collision of Gondwana and of the Kazakhstan and the West Siberian blocks with Laurussia and their suturing along the Appalachian–Mauretanides, the Variscan, and the Ural fold belts (Fig. 1).

Continued dextral oblique convergence between Africa and Fennosarmatia culminated in their intra-Visean collision in the western and central Mediterranean area and the onset of the Himalayan-type Variscan orogeny. Consolidation of the Variscan fold belt of Europe was achieved some 40 Ma later in the latest Westphalian (Plates 4, 5).

The northwestern margin of Africa collided presumably during the Late Carboniferous (Namurian to intra-Westphalian(?); Keppie, 1985) with the subduction system marking the Appalachian margin of the North American Craton. The Appalachian–Mauretanides fold belt became consolidated some 60 to 40 Ma later during the late Early Permian final phases of the Alleghenian diastrophism (Secor et al., 1986; Plate 6). The Stephanian–Autunian phases of the Alleghenian diastrophism were accompanied by a major dextral translation between Africa and Europe giving rise to the development of a complex system of wrench faults transecting the Variscan fold belt and its foreland (Arthaud and Matte, 1977; Lefort and van der Voo, 1981; Ziegler, 1982a).

During the Westphalian the Kazakhstan platform collided with the southeastern margin of Fennosarmatia and at about the same time the West Siberian Craton collided with Kazakhstan. Progressive closure of the Uralian Ocean resulted in the northward propagation of the collision front, which reached the eastern margin of the Barents Shelf during the Stephanian and Early Permian. The Uralian orogeny terminated some 60 Ma later during the Early Triassic (Zonenshain et al., 1984).

In the Arctic–North Atlantic domain, on the other hand, large-scale wrench deformations ceased at the transition from Early to Late Carboniferous and gave way to regional crustal extension and the development of a major rift system in the Norwegian–Greenland Sea. At the same time the Sverdrup Basin subsided rapidly in the area of the Canadian Arctic Islands (Plate 5).

## VARISCAN OROGENY

During the Visean, the megatectonic setting of Western and Central Europe underwent a fundamental change. In the domain of the Variscan geosynclinal system this is expressed by the termination of back-arc extension at the transition from the Early to the Late Visean and the onset of regional compression (Plate 4).

This change in the regional stress regime resulted from a possible renewed acceleration of the convergence rate between the Proto-Tethys–Gondwana and Laurussian plates and the ensuing dextral oblique collision of Africa with the north-dipping B-subduction system located along the southern margin of Fennosarmatia. This marked the onset of the Variscan, Himalaya-type, orogeny, during which the Austro-Alpine, Carnic–Dinarid and possibly additional as yet unidentified microcontinents were incorporated into the Hercynian fold belt of Europe.

Closure of the Proto-Tethys Ocean was probably not synchronous along the trace of the Variscan fold belt. During the final phase of convergence of Gondwana and Laurasia and their ultimate collision in the Western and Central Mediterranean domain, multiple collisions of microcontinents and the commensurate subduction–obduction of intervening oceanic domains presumably took place (Vai, 1980). Correspondingly, the onset of the Variscan orogenic deformation phase varies in time and space in the different Mediterranean parts of the Variscan fold belt. Similarly, the overpowering of the individual Early Carboniferous back-arc extensional basins is not fully synchronous in the different parts of the Variscan geosynclinal system.

For instance, the onset of the Variscan diastrophism, as reflected by the beginning of deep water clastic (Culm-flysch) deposition, is dated in the Asturo–Leonese zone of northwestern Iberia as Early Dinantian, in the Balearic Islands and in Algeria as middle and late Visean, and in the Montagne Noire of southern France as late Visean (Plate 25), whereas the tensional setting of the intra–Alpine Carnic-Dinarid domain came to a close only at the end of the Westphalian-C (Ziegler, 1984; Vai and Cocozza, 1986).

On the other hand, in the eastern Mediterranean and Black Sea domain, the Proto-Tethys remained open during the Carboniferous and Permian. Correspondingly, the eastern parts of the Variscan fold belt continued to be associated with an oceanic subduction complex and thus remained in a Pacific-type setting during its final consolidation phase (Ziegler et al., 1979).

In the Central Armorican and Saxothuringian basins (Fig. 3) back-arc extension and rift-related volcanism ceased at the transition from the early to the late Visean. Uplift of the Ligerian-Arverno–Vosgian–Moldanubian Cordillera, in response to the reactivation-development of south-dipping A-subduction zones along its northern and possibly north-dipping ones along its southern margins, went hand-in-hand with the shedding of the massive synorogenic flysch (Culm series) into the Central Armorican and Saxothuringian basins (Ziegler, 1982a; Behr et al., 1982; Plate 25). Similarly, crustal extension and rift-related volcanism came to a halt in the Rhenohercynian Basin at the beginning of the late Visean. Also in this basin, the accelerated accumulation of synorogenic Culm-flysch, derived from southern sources, probably reflects the reactivation/development of a south-dipping subduction zone presumably along the northern margin of the Normannian–Mid-German High (Engel and Franke, 1983; Franke and Engel, 1986; Plate 24). Closure of a South Rhenish oceanic back-arc basin is reflected by a commensurate calc-alkaline late Visean–Early Naumurian plutonism and volcanism in the Northern Vosges (Holl and Altherr, 1987; Volker and Altherr, 1987). Closure of this basin was followed by tectonic loading of the foreland crust by the advancing nappe systems causing the rapid, asymmetric subsidence of the Rhenohercynian Basin. With this, this long-standing tensional back-arc basin developed into the compression-dominated Variscan foredeep basin. On the other hand, in the Moravian Basin the accumulation of synorogenic Culm-flysch continued from the Late Devonian through the Early into the Late Carboniferous (Dvorak, 1978; Plate 25). This is possibly related to persistent dextral wrench deformations along the eastern margin of the Moldanubian Cordillera. The Central Armorican and Saxothuringian basins became folded and partly destroyed during the latest Visean–earliest Namurian Sudetic, or Variscan main orogenic phase (Pfeiffer, 1971; Schmidt and Franke, 1975; Behr et al., 1984). Subsequently, Namurian and Westphalian continental sequences accumulated in local intramontane basins (Plate 5). These sediments form part of the late Paleozoic neoautochthonous series of the Variscan Internides (Fig. 12; Lützner and Schwab, 1982; Plate 25).

The Variscan foredeep basin, on the other hand, continued to subside during the Namurian and Westphalian under the load of the advancing nappe systems and their clastic aprons. This basin extended over a distance of more than 4000 km from southern Portugal to southern Poland and possibly into the Black Sea area. At the transition from the Visean to the Namurian, the carbonate platforms that occupied the northern, distal parts of this basin (Plate 4) became drowned and covered by Namurian shales and clastics. During the late Namurian and Early Westphalian paralic conditions were established in progressively larger parts of this basin (Plate 5). By mid- to late Westphalian times, coal-measures grading northward into barren red beds were deposited throughout the Variscan foredeep basin (Plates 23, 24). To the north, this basin was in communication with the rifts of the British Isles and to the west with the rift-wrench basins of the Canadian Maritime Provinces (Howie and Barss, 1975a, 1975b; Ziegler, 1982a).

During the Namurian and Westphalian, global sea levels dropped cyclically in response to the progressive glaciation of Gondwana (Caputo and Crowell, 1985). During the Westphalian, temporary glacioeustatic high stands in sea level gave rise to short-lived transgressions that entered the Variscan foredeep presumably from the Appalachian domain via southern Portugal (Bless and Winkler-Prins, 1972). The cyclical nature of these transgressions is reflected by basin-wide correlative marine bands that characterize the Westphalian coal-measures of the Variscan foredeep basin (see correlation charts Plates 23 and 24). The occurrence of late Westphalian Fusulinides of a Tethys affinity in the Oslo Graben suggest that temporary marine transgression presumably advanced westward from the Moscow Platform into this distal part of the Variscan foredeep (Bergström et al., 1985).

During the terminal phase of the Variscan orogeny, the proximal parts of the Variscan foredeep were scooped out by thin-skinned thrust sheets and basement-involving nappes. At the same time, intraplate compressional stresses caused the partial inversion of the graben systems in the British Isles (Plate 5; Fig. 12). These stresses may furthermore have impeded the southward propagation of the Norwegian–Greenland Sea rift system that was initiated during the early Namurian (Vischer, 1943; Steel and Worsley, 1984; Ziegler, 1984). In northwest Africa, Westphalian–Stephanian compressional intraplate stresses induced the deformation of the Sahara Platform and the inversion of the Devono-Carboniferous Ougarta Trough (Fig. 8).

The framework of the Variscan fold belt can only be unraveled in the extra-Alpine areas because reliable palinspastic reconstructions are not yet available for the Alpine and Mediterranean domains (see also Vai and Cocozza, 1986).

The largest intra-Variscan sedimentary basin is the Aquitaine–Cantabrian Basin. In it Westphalian platform carbonates grade laterally into paralic coal-measures fringing the basin margins (Eichmüller and Seibert, 1984; Plate 25). This basin was presumably connected to the marine Sahara Platform occupying the northern parts of the African Craton. Early Westphalian marine strata occur in the intra-Alpine Carnic–Dinaric domain; the outline and tectonic setting of this basin, which became affected by the Variscan diastrophism only during the late Westphalian, is still unknown (Vai, 1975; Castellarin and Vai, 1981; Vai and Cocozza, 1986). Elsewhere within the Variscan fold belt, continental Westphalian coal-measures accumulated in tectonically silled and wrench-induced basins.

These strata form part of late-synorogenic, neoautochthonous sedimentary sequences.

The amount of crustal shortening accomplished during the Variscan paroxysm is difficult to assess. Major nappe structures, in part basement-involving, occur in the Moldanubian area, the southern Massif Central, in Iberia, and also in the Variscan Externides (Thiele, 1977; Julivert et al., 1977; Burg and Matte, 1978; Burg et al., 1984; Meissner et al., 1981; Behr et al., 1982; Matte, 1983, 1986). This is highlighted by the results of the ECORS reflection seismic line, recorded in northern France (Fig. 11). This line demonstrates that the amount of crustal shortening along the Faille du Midi of the Ardennes is at least 50 km, possibly as much as 70 to 80 km or even more (Cazes et al., 1985, 1986; Raoult, 1986).

On the other hand, paleomagnetic data suggest that post-Devonian crustal shortening between the Armorican Massif and the northern Variscan foreland does not exceed the paleomagnetic margin of error and thus cannot be greater than 500 km (Jones et al., 1979).

At present there are, however, still insufficient paleomagnetic data available to permit a detailed comparison of the Carboniferous apparent polar wander paths of Africa, Europe, and North America in order to assess the total amount of crustal shortening that was achieved during the Variscan orogeny (Daly and Irving, 1983). Yet, the widespread occurrence of low-pressure metamorphics and late- to postorogenic calc-alkaline intrusives in the Variscan fold belt can be taken as indirect evidence that significant amounts of crustal shortening, accompanied by crustal delamination, subduction, and anatectic remobilization of lower crustal and upper mantle material had taken place during the Variscan orogeny (Zwart and Dornsiepen, 1978; Matte, 1983, 1986; Ziegler 1984, 1986).

In the western part of the Variscides, the Carboniferous Proto-Tethys suture is to be sought to the south of the Aquitaine–Cantabrian block. In the central and eastern parts of the Variscides, the Proto-Tethys suture is difficult to locate owing to severe Alpine overprinting and limited outcrops of the Variscan basement complex and uncertainties in defining the outlines of potential allochthonous terranes, such as the Austro-Alpine and the Carnic–Dinarid blocks.

Unlike the linear Appalachians and the Uralides, the Variscan fold belt is characterized by a complex arcuate shape (Plate 5). This is partly the result of its being draped around a number of internal microcratons, such as the Aquitaine–Cantabria block, but also because of the irregular geometry of its northern and southern forelands, which were shaped by the pattern of the Devonian and Early Carboniferous back-arc rift systems and by the Ordovician to Carboniferous Gondwana rift systems, respectively (Ziegler, 1982a). In this context, it should be kept in mind that the consolidation of the Variscan fold-belt involved major wrench faulting, the rotation of individual blocks, and considerable rotation of thrust elements (oroclinal bending), particularly in the Ibero-Armorican arc (Perroud and Bonhommet, 1981), the Vosges (Edel et al., 1984), the East Sudetic–Moravian area (Lorenz and Nicholls, 1984), and presumably also in the South Iberian–North African and Intra-Alpine domains.

The paleotectonic map given in Plate 5 shows the eastern Mediterranean area as being occupied by the Variscan deformed "Cimmeria" block, corresponding to the Serbo-Macedonian and Rhodope massifs and the northern parts of Pontides, which is flanked to the south by the Proto-Tethys Ocean. This interpretation is at variance with the interpretation

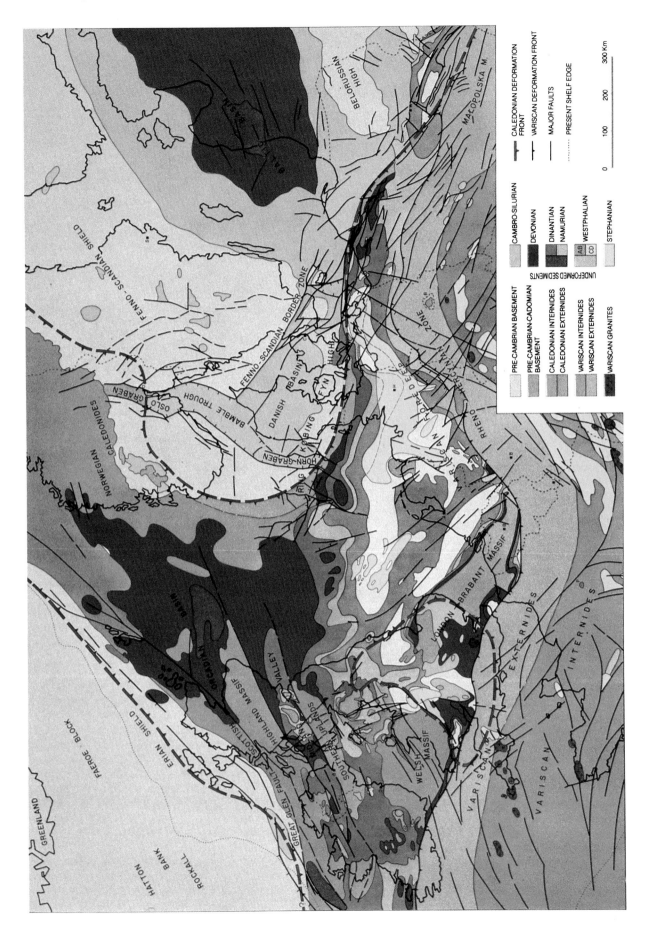

*Figure 12—Pre-Permian subcrop map of Western and Central Europe. Modified after Pozaryski and Dembowski (1984); Teichmüller et al. (1984); and Ziegler (1982a).*

of Brinkmann (1976), Sengör (1977, 1984, 1985), and Vai (1979) who assume that Variscan fold belt splits in the eastern Mediterranean into a northern branch, paralleling the southern margin of Fennosarmatia, and a southern branch extending along the northeastern margin of Gondwana. Such a southern branch of the Variscan fold belt would have to be associated with a south-plunging Proto-Tethys subduction zone.

Based on this assumption, Sengör (1977, 1984, 1985) and Sengör et al. (1984) also suggested that the Balkan and Turkish segments of Cimmeria represent Gondwana-derived allochthonous terranes, which were accreted to the southern margin of Fennosarmatia during the Late Triassic–Early Jurassic Cimmerian orogeny.

The alternate interpretation presented here assumes that the northeastern margin of Gondwana (including the Anatolide and Tauride platforms), facing the Proto-Tethys, remained in a passive margin setting during the Late Carboniferous and Permian and that the Balkan and Turkish parts of Cimmeria, which show clear evidence of Variscan deformation, formed part of the Variscan fold belt paralleling the southern margin of Fennosarmatia (see also Adamia et al., 1981; Zonenshain et al., 1984; Westphal et al., 1986). This interpretation is compatible with the concept that during the Ordovician, Silurian and Devonian several allochthonous terranes were rifted off the northern margin of Gondwana and became accreted during the Acadian–Ligerian and Bretonian orogenies to the southern margin of Fennosarmatia as a consequence of the northward subduction of the Proto-Tethys plate (Ziegler, 1984, 1986). This suggests that only during the late phases of the Variscan orogeny could a south plunging subduction system possibly have developed along the northern margin of Gondwana. This fundamental controversy needs to be resolved in view of its implications for the Permo-Triassic geodynamics of the Eastern Mediterranean domain.

## ALLEGHENIAN OROGENY

The timing of collision of the African craton with the Appalachian subduction system is poorly constrained and has been variably estimated as having occurred at the transition from the Early to the Late Carboniferous (Spariosu et al., 1984; Secor et al., 1986) or during the Westphalian (Fig. 3; Rast, 1984; Keppie, 1985; Ross and Ross, 1985). The latest Namurian to early Westphalian development of the synorogenic, intramontane Narragansett Basin of Rhode Island and Massachusetts speaks in favor of an intra-Namurian onset of the Alleghenian orogenic cycle (Skehan, 1983; Skehan and Rast, 1983; Wintsch and Sutter, 1986). This is in keeping with the geochronological record of the southern Appalachians (Dallmeyer et al., 1986).

The existence of an Early Carboniferous subduction system dipping westward under the margin of "Avalonia" (Traveler–Meguma terranes, east of the Devono-Carboniferous megashear; Rast, 1984) is inferred from the granitic record of the United States Appalachians (360–320 Ma), of New Brunswick (357–327 Ma), and of Nova Scotia (350–300 Ma) (Fyffe et al., 1983; Osberg, 1983; Reynolds et al., 1981).

Collision of the African Craton with this subduction system presumably had repercussions, with only a short delay, on the evolution of the Appalachian fold belt and the Carboniferous basins of the New England states and the Canadian Maritime Provinces. A summary of the scope and timing of the Alleghe-

nian deformations that accompanied the suturing of the African and North American cratons is given by Rast (1984), Osberg (1983), and Hatcher (1985).

The northernmost truly orogenic Alleghenian deformations, involving significant crustal shortening, occur in the New England states and in New Brunswick. Here, polyphase deformations, associated with thrust faulting, were accompanied by metamorphism and the intrusion of granitoids ranging in age from 300 to 260 Ma (Reynolds et al., 1981; Dallmeyer, 1982; Rast, 1983; Skehan, 1983; Mosher and Rast, 1984; Wintsch and Sutter, 1986). These deformations were coupled with important dextral strike-slip movements along the Chedabucto (Minas) geofracture and a paleomagnetically documented 20 rotation of the Meguma terrane (Scotese et al., 1984; Spariosu et al., 1984; Keppie, 1985). Time-equivalent transpressional deformations in the Fundy (Magdalen) Basin and possibly also the St. Anthony Basin are not truly orogenic in nature insofar as they do not involve major crustal shortening and metamorphism. In view of this, they can be regarded as intraplate deformations in the sense of basin inversion (Fig. 5).

In the Fundy (Magdalen) Basin, thermal subsidence and accumulation of early Westphalian red beds and coal-measures (Howie and Barrs; 1975a, 1975b; Bradley, 1982) were interrupted at the end of the Westphalian-B by a first deformation phase attributed to the Alleghenian diastrophism (Keppie, 1982; Keppie et al., 1985). The Westphalian-C to early Autunian Pictu conglomerates and coal-measures, which overlay older strata with an angular unconformity, became in turn deformed during the so-called Maritime Disturbance (Poole, 1977; Plate 22). In the Magdalen Basin, these late Alleghenian deformations, which are largely confined to the basin margins and which involved folding and wrench faulting, partly overprinted preexisting salt-induced structures (Keppie et al., 1975; Mosher and Rast, 1984; Fig. 5).

Also in the St. Anthony Basin the diapirism of Visean halites renders it difficult to determine the importance of Alleghenian deformations, as reported by Lefort and Haworth (1984). If such deformations did occur in this basin, they were probably related to wrench movements along the Cabot–Long Range fault transecting Newfoundland. Whether and to what extent the Sidney Basin was also affected by Alleghenian deformations is unknown.

From the above it is concluded that in the New England states the Alleghenian orogenic cycle started during the Namurian and in the Canadian Maritime Provinces during the late Westphalian, terminated in the late Autunian, and thus spanned a time interval of some 60 to 40 Ma, respectively (Dallmeyer, 1982). Whether a Namurian to Westphalian orogenic belt is hidden beneath the Mesozoic and Cenozoic sedimentary cover of the Nova Scotian Shelf and Georges Bank, as suggested by Plates 5 and 6, is unknown, but could be inferred from the occurrence of granitoids in Nova Scotia that range in age from 320 to 300 Ma (Reynolds et al., 1981) and from the limited control provided by offshore wells that encountered metamorphics yielding an age of ± 300 Ma and a granite dated as ± 329 Ma (Given, 1977). Furthermore, granitic intrusions, dated as 320–290 Ma, have been reported from Eastern Newfoundland (Blenkinsop et al., 1977; Bell et al., 1979). This suggests that the Hercynian–Alleghenian orogeny was associated with a subduction zone dipping under the North American Craton. Moreover, there is evidence that this collisional event was associated with important dextral strike-slip movements spanning the time interval of 324 to 300 Ma (Gates et al., 1986).

In the Mauretanides of northwestern Africa, the occurrence of an Alleghenian deformation phase is difficult to ascertain for want of a late Paleozoic stratigraphic record (Léorché, 1983). A late phase of thrusting is stratigraphically dated as post-Devonian, and geochronological data suggest a late Westphalian age (f 300 Ma) (Léorché and Clauer, 1983; Roussel et al., 1984).

In summary, the Appalachian–Mauretanides fold belt, representing the Hercynian megasuture between the African and North American cratons, became consolidated during the Early Permian. Termination of the Alleghenian diastrophism post-dates by some 30 Ma the last orogenic movements in the Variscan fold belt of Europe (Fig. 3).

During the Late Permian and Early Triassic, progressive erosion and uplift of the Appalachian–Mauretanide fold belt is reflected by retrograde metamorphism. Quantitative analyses in the New England States suggest that this area became uplifted by some 25 km during the Late Permian and Triassic (Wintsch and Sutter, 1986). Whether this uplifting phase was accompanied by extensional tectonics, associated with the decay of the Appalachian–Mauretanide subduction system, is uncertain since the age of the earliest deposits in the Triassic grabens of the Appalachian Piedmont and the adjacent shelf areas is largely unknown. Late Permian to Triassic deformations in the New England states record, however, a gradual rotation of the principal compressional stress direction from northwest to north–northeast (Wintsch and Sutter, 1986).

# URALIAN OROGENY

Following the middle Visean abandonment of the subduction system associated with the Sakmarian–Magnitogorsk arc, a new subduction zone developed, dipping beneath the western and southern margins of the Kazakhstan Craton. This marked the onset of convergence of Kazakhstan with the Fennosarmatian margin and the subduction of the Uralian Ocean. At the same time, the West Siberian Craton became separated from the East Siberian block and started to converge with the Kazakhstan block and Fennosarmatia (Ziegler et al., 1979; Scotese et al., 1979).

During the early Westphalian (Late Bashkirian ± 310 Ma), the Valerianovsk arc-trench system, marking the leading edge of the Kazakhstan block, collided with the Mugodjarian terrane and later with the Fennosarmatian margin. This marked the onset of the Himalayan-type Uralian orogeny and the beginning of the development of the Uralian foredeep basin (Zonenshain et al., 1984; Artyushkov and Baer, 1983). At about the same time, the West Siberian Craton collided with the Kazakhstan block and presumably during the Stephanian with the eastern margin of the Barents Shelf (Ronov et al., 1984; Plates 5, 6).

Convergence of the West Siberian and Kazakhstan cratons with Fennosarmatis persisted during the Permian and into the Early Triassic, by which time the Uralian and Altay–Sayan sutures became consolidated (Hamilton, 1970; Sobolev, 1982; Khain, 1984a; Zonenshain et al., 1984; Plates 7, 8).

The influx of synorogenic flysch into the incipient southern Uralian foredeep is dated as Middle Carboniferous (Bashkirian–Moscovian) (Artyushkov and Baer, 1983). In the northern Urals, earliest flysch series are of Stephanian age (Plate 22). The actual foredeep basin, which is superimposed on the Fennosarmatian Shelf, developed only during the Late Carboniferous in response to tectonic loading of the foreland plate by the advancing nappe systems of the Uralian orogen. This was coupled with a gradual westward migration of the foredeep axis.

In the southern Ural foredeep, Stephanian and Early Permian flysch series, overlain by Kungurian molasse-type clastics, prograded over the earlier carbonate shelf. This clastic prism was separated from the carbonate dominated Moscow platform by a deeper water, sediment-starved trough that became infilled with thick halites during the Kungerian. During the terminal phase of the Uralian orogeny, Late Permian to Early Triassic continental clastics accumulated in this foredeep. The structural style of the external zones of the Urals is characterized by spectacular thin-skinned thrust sheets (Slezinger and Jansin, 1979; Nalivkin, 1982; Artyushkov and Baer, 1983; Dymkin et al., 1984; Kazantseva and Kamaletdinov, 1986).

In the Pechora segment of the Ural foredeep, flysch sedimentation gave way to the accumulation of shallow water marine, molasse-type clastics at the transition from the Asselian to the Sakmarian (Plate 22). These gradually encroached on the Pechora–Southern Barents Sea carbonate platform. At the same time, compressional stresses exerted onto the foreland induced the progressive inversion of the Devonian Pechora and Kolva rifts and the uplift of the Timan anticlinorium. These and other rising anticlinal structures presumably diverted the clastic influx from the rising Urals into a basin-axial, northward direction. During the Kungurian to Tatarian thick continental and coal-bearing paralic clastics accumulated in the Pechora foredeep. These grade northward in the Novaya Zemlya foredeep into flysch-type clastics (Plates 7, 8). Only during the Early Triassic did large continental clastic fans prograde rapidly onto the adjacent Late Permian carbonate platforms of the Barents and Pechora shelves. Deposition of coal-measures ceased, however, at the transition from the Permian to the Triassic. Last folding phases occurred during the Early Triassic. These were followed by further minor folding phases during the Late Triassic and Early Jurassic (Vinogradov, 1969; Churkin and Trexler, 1981; Nalivkin, 1982; Ulmishek, 1982; Matviyevskaya et al., 1986).

Paleomagnetic data suggest that by the end of the Permian Fennosarmatia and the Siberian Craton formed part of a single plate (Gurevich and Slsutsitays, 1985).

From the northern end of Novaya Zemlya, the Hercynian Ural fold belt swings back sharply in an eastern direction into the Taimyr Peninsula. Also in this segment of the fold belt there is evidence for a latest Triassic to Early Jurassic folding phase (Plate 10). Whether the coastal areas of Taimyr Peninsula, which possibly form part of the Caledonian–Ellesmerian Lomonosov fold belt, were also affected by the Uralian diastrophism is uncertain (Hamilton, 1970; Churkin and Trexler, 1981; Pogrebitsky, 1982).

During the Late Permian phases of the Uralian orogeny, the area of the future West Siberian Basin became affected by tensional tectonics that were accompanied by the outpouring of extensive Permo-Triassic flood basalts. This is thought to be the expression of back-arc extension induced by the gradual decay of the east-dipping Uralian subduction zone (Rudkevich, 1976; Aleinikov et al., 1980; Chablinskaia et al., 1982; Ulmishek, 1984).

In summary, the Uralian and Altay–Sayan fold belts form the Hercynian megasutures between the Fennosarmatian, the West Siberian, and the Kazakhstan cratons. Collision of these continental blocks postdates the Visean onset of the Variscan orogeny by 30 to 40 Ma. The consolidation of the Uralian and

Altay–Sayan fold belts during the Late Permian to Early Triassic postdates the late Westphalian consolidation of the Variscan fold belt by some 60 Ma (Fig. 3). The relatively mild Late Triassic–Early Jurassic deformation phase, affecting parts of the late Hercynian Ural and Altay–Sayan orogens, can be related to time-equivalent major orogenic events of Southeast Asia.

## LATE HERCYNIAN FRAGMENTATION OF THE VARISCAN FOLD BELT

Following the latest Westphalian consolidation of the Variscan fold belt and the apparent locking of its subduction system, the convergence direction between Africa and Laurussia changed from a southeast–northwest orientation to one that was essentially east–west directed. During the Stephanian and Autunian, continued crustal shortening in the Appalachian–Mauretanides and in the Uralides was accompanied by a dextral translation between Africa and Fennosarmatia (Plate 6). These motions were taken up by an intracontinental transform fault system linking the southern end of the Uralides with the northern end of the Appalachians (Arthaud and Matte, 1977). This dextral transform fault system transected the newly consolidated Variscan fold belt where it induced the development of a complex set of conjugate shear faults, the subsidence of local transtensional and pull-apart basins, and a widespread volcanism.

The development of this fracture system, which extended also into the foreland of the Variscan fold belt, reflects a diffuse plate boundary between Africa and Fennosarmatia. This fault system remained active until the late Early Permian Alleghenian consolidation of the Appalachians (Ziegler, 1982a).

Whether, and to what degree, back-arc extension, related to the decay of the north-dipping Variscan subduction system, also played a role in the Stephanian and Autunian tectonic evolution of Western and Central Europe is difficult to assess.

In Western and Central Europe, details of the late Hercynian fault systems can only be mapped in the outcropping Variscan massifs and, to a lesser degree, in the subsurface of the major sedimentary basins that are being explored for hydrocarbons (Arthaud and Matte, 1977; Ziegler, 1982a). Fault patterns shown on Plate 6 for the Alpine and Mediterranean areas are conceptual; it should, however, be kept in mind that the available information indicates that these areas had also been affected by the late Hercynian tectonism. Yet, owing to limited control, it is impossible to identify in the Alpine and Mediterranean area even first-order elements of this late Hercynian fault system and to map the outlines of the major Stephanian–Autunian sedimentary basins.

In the Alpine foreland, main elements of the Permo-Carboniferous fault system are the Tornquist–Teisseyre (defining the southeastern limit of the stable East European Platform) and the Bay of Biscay fracture zones. Dextral displacements along the Tornquist–Teisseyre line and its northwestern continuation, the Fennoscandian Borderzone, induced the development of the highly volcanic Oslo Rift during the latest Westphalian and Early Permian (Fig. 12). Similar displacements along the Bay of Biscay fracture zone were accompanied by Stephanian transpressional deformations in Cantabria (Julivert, 1981; Maas and van Ginkel, 1983), the subsidence of the Western Approaches and Porcupine troughs, and possibly crustal extension in the Rockall–Faeroe Rift. For the latter there is,

however, no tangible evidence available.

At the same time, areas located between the Tornquist–Teisseyre and the Bay of Biscay fracture zones became transected by a complex set of conjugate shear faults. Wrench deformation of the Variscan foredeep basin went hand in hand with its regional uplift and the deep truncation of its sedimentary fill, particularly along the Tornquist–Tesseyre line.

In conjunction with these deformations, the Ringkøbing–Fyn High, which played an important role during the Late Permian and Mesozoic evolution of Northwest Europe, became uplifted (Figs. 12 and 16). The regional cross sections through Northern Denmark and Southern Sweden, given in Fig. 44, illustrate that along the Fennoscandian Borderzone up to 5 km thick Cambro-Silurian platform series, which had been deposited in the Caledonian foreland, became dissected by Permo-Carboniferous wrench faults and are now preserved as erosional remnants in half-grabens. Seismic reflection data show that these early Paleozoic series are characterized by parallel bedding and thus indicate that their present structure postdates their deposition. Thick early Paleozoic sediments are also preserved in the Danish Basin and in the Bamble and Horn Graben (Fig. 12).

In Northwestern and Central Europe, Permo-Carboniferous wrench faulting and the associated development of pull-apart features was accompanied by the development of major volcanic centers in Poland, northern Germany, and the North Sea area (Plate 6). This suggests that these deformations were associated with deep crustal fracturing, a major lithospheric thermal surge, and corresponding regional thermal uplift.

It is speculated that tensional stresses developing at the northwestern termination of the Bay of Biscay fracture zone, and of the fault systems crossing the Irish Sea and the British Isles, may have facilitated the southward propagation of the Norwegian–Greenland Sea rift system as suggested in Plate 6 (see Chapter 4).

The Gibraltar and Agadir fracture zones, as indicated on Plate 6, are less well documented. The fault systems shown for Morocco, Algeria, and Tunisia are based on the fault systems that governed the subsidence of Triassic to Early Jurassic rifts in these areas. These were integrated with the fault patterns mapped by Arthaud and Matte (1977) in the area of the Iberian and Morocco Meseta and with those of the Canadian Maritime Provinces (see also Vegas and Banda, 1983).

Deep crustal fracturing, induced by the post-Variscan wrench deformations, triggered in Northwest Europe widespread Stephanian–Autunian extrusive and intrusive activity of a highly variable chemistry (Lorenz and Nicholle, 1984). For instance, extensive Upper Carboniferous tholeiitic dikes and sills are reported from northern Britain (Francis, 1982) whereas the uppermost Carboniferous and Permian igneous rocks of the Oslo Graben display a distinctly mafic-felsic bimodality and are highly alkaline (Oftedahl, 1968; Ramberg, 1976). A similar alkaline bimodality characterized the Lower Permian volcanics in the North Sea, while those in the immediate foreland of the Variscan fold belt are only mildly alkaline with mafic rocks predominating over felsic ones (Eckhardt, 1979; Dixon et al., 1981). In the domain of the Variscan fold belt proper, Lower Permian volcanics consist of rhyolites and andesites and display the typical calc-alkaline composition of a late to postorogenic volcanism (Kramer, 1977; D'Amico, 1979; Dziedzic, 1980).

In Western and Central Europe the latest Carboniferous–Early Permian tectonism induced, in combination with a glacioeustatic low stand in sea level, corresponding to the peak of the Gondwana glaciation, a regional regression and the development of a major erosional unconformity (Martin, 1981; Caputo and Crowell, 1985; Plates 23, 25).

Continental red beds and coal-measures accumulated in wrench-induced half-grabens, pull-apart, and tectonically silled basins (Lützner and Schwab, 1982; Ziegler, 1982a; Lorenz and Nicholls, 1984). Marine sediments were restricted to the margins of the Tethys Ocean (Kamen-Kaye, 1972).

In the framework of the paleotectonic map as given in Plate 7, the occurrence of thick lower Westphalian to uppermost Stephanian marine turbidites in Cantabria (Martinez-Garcia and Wagner, 1982; Maas and van Ginkel, 1983) and Permo-Carboniferous shallow marine series in the Carnic Alps, both containing faunas with Donets-Don area affinity (Flügel, 1974; Schønlaub, 1979; Trümpy, personal communication), is rather difficult to explain and thus highlights the uncertainty of this reconstruction.

In summary, the modification of plate movements during the late Hercynian suturing phases of the Pangean megacontinent induced in Europe a phase of essentially anorogenic faulting, which caused the fragmentation of the Variscan fold belt. The associated magmatic activity was widespread and not so much related to the final phase of consolidation of the Variscan fold belt as to the first phase of its disintegration.

The late Hercynian fault system of Western and Central Europe became reactivated time and again and played a major role during the Mesozoic rifting stage preceding the opening of the Tethys and of the Arctic–North Atlantic Oceans (Ziegler, 1987e).

The dimensions of the proposed Permo-Carboniferous dextral translations between Africa and Fennosarmatia are, however, difficult to quantify. Assuming that the above-developed model applies, these transform motions should equate to the amount of crustal shortening achieved during the late phases of Alleghenian diastrophism in the Appalachian–Mauretanides fold belt.

The COCORP deep reflection seismic data (Cook et al., 1979, 1981; Cook 1983) indicate that Alleghenian crustal shortening in the Appalachians amounts to at least 175 km (Secor et al., 1986). For the entire Appalachian–Mauretanides megasuture, Late Carboniferous–Early Permian crustal shortening of the order of 300 to 400 km or even more can be visualized; however, it appears improbable that latest Carboniferous and Early Permian crustal shortening could be an order of magnitude larger.

In view of this, the Early Permian Pangea A-2 assembly of van der Voo and Peinado (1984) is preferred over the Pangea-B assembly (Morel and Irving, 1978; Daly and Irving, 1983). The latter would require in the latest Carboniferous–earliest Permian time frame of some 30 Ma a counterclockwise rotation of Gondwana relative to Laurussia, involving a 3500 km dextral transform motion between North Africa and Southern Europe. This would correspond to plate movements at the rate of about 11 cm/year. This appears excessive, particularly in a collisional setting. Yet, there is evidence for dextral translations along the axis of the Appalachian orogen during the terminal phase of the Alleghenian orogeny (Secor et al., 1986).

# CHAPTER 4
## LATE CARBONIFEROUS TO PERMIAN EVOLUTION OF ARCTIC BASINS, THE NORWEGIAN–GREENLAND SEA RIFT AND PERMIAN BASINS OF WEST AND CENTRAL EUROPE

# INTRODUCTION

Following the Early Carboniferous consolidation of the Innuitian–Lomonosov(?) fold belt and the termination of the Arctic–North Atlantic sinistral translation, the megatectonic setting of the Arctic areas underwent a fundamental change.

During the Early Carboniferous, the West Siberian Craton apparently became separated from the northern margin of Laurentia (corresponding to the northern margin of the North Alaska–Chukchi–Chukotka [East Siberian Block] and the New Siberian Islands blocks; Fig. 7), started to drift and rotate eastward, and began to converge with the eastern margin of Fennosarmatia and the Kazakhstan block (see Chapter 2, Post-Caledonian Plate Reorganization and Chapter 3, Uralian orogeny; Scotese, 1984). This was accompanied by the postorogenic collapse of the Innuitian fold belt as evident by the development of the Sverdrup Basin (Balkwill, 1978), tensional tectonics in the area of the Alaska North Slope (Hubbard et al., 1987) and rifting in the New Siberian Island (Fujita and Cook, 1986). At the same time, crustal extension governed the subsidence of the Norwegian Greenland Sea Rift through which the Arctic Seas advance southward during the Late Permian and invaded the Permian basins of Northwest and Central Europe (Plates 4–8).

# SVERDRUP BASIN

The Sverdrup Basin is superimposed on the Innuitian fold belt. Its late Paleozoic to Late Cretaceous sedimentary fill attains thicknesses of up to 12 km (Fig. 13). The axis of this basin coincides closely with the trend of the Innuitian fold belt. Its southern margin is formed by the Parry Island fold belt, which represents the externides of the Innuitian orogen (Meneley et al., 1975; Balkwill, 1978; Trettin and Balkwill, 1979; Hea et al., 1980; Kerr, 1981b; Balkwill and Fox, 1982).

Shortly after the Ellesmerian consolidation of the Innuitian fold belt, the Sverdrup Basin began to subside under a tensional regime (Plate 22). Late Visean continental clastics, contained in downfaulted lows, are locally exposed (Emma Fjord formation). Crustal extension apparently accelerated during the early Namurian, leading to regional subsidence and the accumulation of conglomeratic clastics that grade basinward into marine sands (Borup formation). Carbonate deposition set in during the late Namurian, by which time tensional tectonics apparently abated. During the Westphalian and Stephanian, the Sverdrup Basin assumed the geometry of a broad downwarp. The margins of this basin were occupied by extensive reef-fringed carbonate platforms grading shorewards into cyclical mixed carbonate and clastic shelves and coastal sands. In the axial parts of the basin, deeper water conditions were established during the late Namurian. These depressions were infilled by thick halites and sulfates during the early Westphalian. These evaporites are overlain by Lower Westphalian to upper Permian deep water shales reflecting a renewed sediment starvation of basinal areas. During the Early Permian, basin subsidence apparently slowed down and shallow water conditions were gradually established also in the central parts of the Sverdrup Basin while clastic aprons prograded into it from its southern and western margins. Renewed tensional tectonics during the Late Permian, referred to as the Melvillian disturbance, were associated with major normal faulting causing subsidence of the axial parts of the basin in which deeper water conditions

were reestablished. At the same time, the northwestern margin of the basin became uplifted (Balkwill and Fox, 1982). A regional regression and hiatus marks the Permian–Triassic boundary (Plates 5–8).

During the Late Carboniferous and Permian, the Sverdrup Basin was in open marine communication with the Arctic Shelf corresponding to the North Alaska, Chukchi, Chukotka and New Siberian Islands areas. In the northern Brooks Ranges and on the Alaska North Slope, for instance, the late Visean and Westphalian Lisburn carbonate platform is the equivalent of the carbonate shelves fringing the deep water troughs of the Sverdrup Basin (Dutro, 1981; Churkin and Trexler, 1981; Fujita and Cook, 1986). As in the Sverdrup Basin, the Lisburn carbonates are in part underlain by Late Devonian and Early Carboniferous clastics (Kanayut–Hunt Fork Formation and Endicott Group), which accumulated in tensional basins (Fig. 40; Bird and Molenaar, 1983; Hubbard et al., 1987).

Carboniferous and Permian sediments attain a thickness of some 5000 m in the central parts of the Sverdrup Basin. They are overlain by some 7000 m of Mesozoic sands and shales (Fig. 13; Meneley et al., 1975; Trettin and Balkwill, 1979; Balkwill and Fox, 1982). In view of this great overburden it is difficult to assess the scope of the late Visean to Namurian tensional tectonics that governed the initial phase of basin subsidence. Major grabens appear to be northeast- to east-trending and basalt flows are indicative of contemporaneous deep crustal fracturing (Trettin and Balkwill, 1979), possibly related to back-arc extension caused by the decay of the Innuitian subduction system. The Westphalian to Early Permian regional downwarp of the Sverdrup Basin, coupled with a gradual slowing down of subsidence rates, suggest that this second phase of basin evolution was governed by cooling of the thermal anomaly introduced during the earlier rifting phase (Sweeney, 1977). The resumption of tensional tectonics during the Late Permian Melvillian disturbance, which was accompanied locally by igneous activity, is probably related to contemporaneous crustal extension in the Arctic–North Atlantic rift system.

Geophysical data show that the crust of the Sverdrup Basin is drastically thinned, probably due to late Paleozoic and Mesozoic extension (Fig. 14; Sobczak et al., 1986).

# SVALBARD–NORTHEAST GREENLAND OBLIQUE-SLIP ZONE

The stratigraphic record of northern Ellesmere Island, corresponding to the northeastern margin of the Sverdrup Basin, suggests that basin evolution during the Late Carboniferous and Permian was governed by wrench deformations (Plate 22). These induced the intermittent uplift of northeast–southwest-trending outer highs during the Westphalian and Artinskian. From these highs, clastics were shed in a southward direction into the adjacent subsiding troughs (U. Mayr, personal communication, 1985). This wrench system finds its continuation in the fault patterns of Western Svalbard and Northeastern Greenland (Steel and Worsley, 1934; Håkansson and Pedersen, 1982; Hakansson and Stemmerik, 1984).

In Western Svalbard, the Adriabukta wrench deformations at the transition from the Visean to the Namurian were followed by the rapid subsidence of a complex graben system in which alluvial fan-glomerates and sandy, in part coal-bearing, floodplain deposits accumulated. These Namurian series are up to

2000 m thick. Syndepositional oblique-slip movements resulted in local basin inversion at the transition from the Namurian to the Westphalian, while other troughs continued to subside rapidly (Plate 22). Westphalian alluvial fan-glomerates, accumulating at the foot of active fault-scarps, grade laterally into shallow marine and sabkha deposits that give way to open marine carbonates on the Barents Shelf. During the Stephanian and Early Permian, carbonate shelves containing fault-controlled evaporitic basins occupied the area of the Svalbard Archipelago. During the Late Permian, basinal areas were characterized by deeper water cyclical spiculites indicating their sediment starvation while carbonates and shallow marine sands accumulated on the offsetting platforms (Dalland et al., 1982; Plates 5–7). Although syndepositional tectonics continued through Permian time, they were less dramatic than during the Carboniferous and gave rise to local unconformities only. In Svalbard, marine sedimentation was continuous across the Permian–Triassic boundary (Nysaether, 1976; Birkenmajer, 1981; Gjelberg and Steel, 1981; Steel and Worsley, 1984).

The Wandel Sea Basin of northeastern Greenland offsets Svalbard to the southwest, according to the palinspastic reconstruction given in Plates 5–8. In this basin, sedimentation commenced in fault-controlled depressions with the accumulation of Dinantian coal-bearing continental clastics (Plate 22). This series is unconformably overlain by a transgressive cyclical sequence of late Westphalian to Stephanian coastal sands grading laterally into sabkha deposits and carbonates. These give way to Early Permian platform carbonates containing reefal buildups. The increasing tectonic instability of the area is indicated by the Artinskian influx of shallow marine sands and an intra-Ufimian unconformity. Late Permian series are represented by marine conglomerates and sands containing minor carbonates. A regional unconformity marks the Permian–Triassic boundary. These breaks in sedimentation are thought

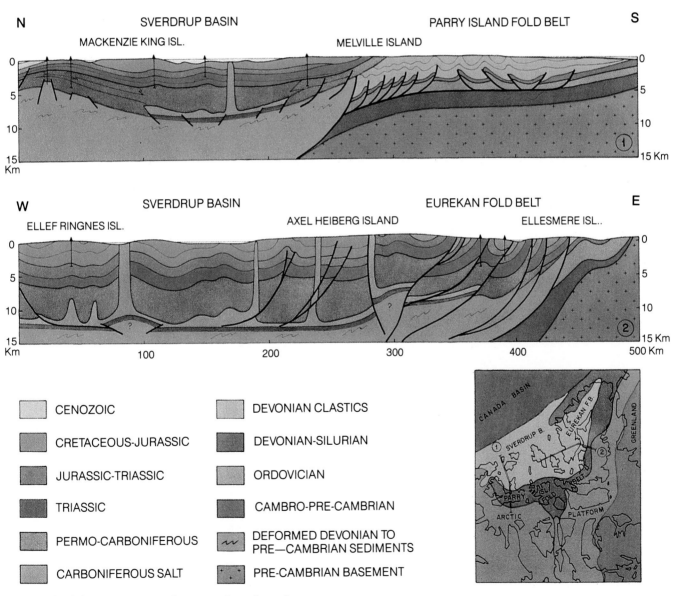

*Figure 13—Schematic structural cross sections through Sverdrup Basin. Modified after Roblesky, Shell Canada (1); Fischer, Shell Canada (2).*

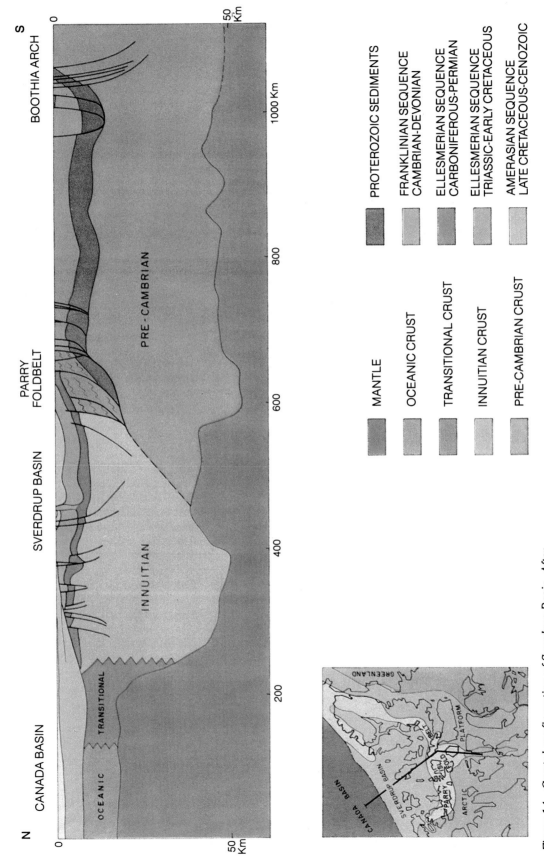

*Figure 14—Crustal configuration of Sverdrup Basin. After Sobczack et al. (1986) and Sweeney et al. (1986).*

to be related to dextral wrench movements along fault zones extending into Northern Ellesmere Island (Håkansson, 1979; Håkansson and Pederson, 1982; Håkansson and Stemmerik, 1984).

The stratigraphic control point located closest to the southern parts of the Wandel Sea Basin is Bear Island (Bjørnøya; Plate 22). Here, a latest Devonian to Namurian continental series accumulated in a half-graben limited to the west by an active fault. Marine transgressions reached this basin during the late Namurian. Sedimentation was interrupted at the transition from the Namurian to the Westphalian. Similar to Svalbard, Westphalian series are represented by thick conglomeratic fan deposits accumulating at the foot of an active fault scarp. These grade eastward into thinner deltaic sand and shallow marine shales that are conformably overlain by late Westphalian carbonates. In turn, these are disconformably overlain by Kazanian–Asselian (Stephanian to early Autunian) marine sands and carbonates. Wrench-induced basin inversion occurred during the Sakmarian. Artinskian clastics and carbonates transgressed over deeply truncated earlier series and the basement complex. Only minor deformations interrupted the Artinskian to Kazanian deposition of platform carbonates. A regional unconformity here also marks the Permian–Triassic boundary (Worsley and Edwards, 1976; Worsley and Gjelberg, 1980; Gjelberg and Steel, 1981, 1983).

From the above it can be concluded that the Late Carboniferous to Late Permian evolution of the Svalbard–Wandel Sea–Bear Island area was governed by extensional and oblique-slip tectonics. The latter probably compensated for contemporaneous crustal extension in the Norwegian–Greenland Sea Rift (Plates 5–8).

## BARENTS SEA AREA

The Late Carboniferous and Permian paleogeographic and structural evolution of the Barents Shelf has to be deducted from reflection seismic data, limited borehole control, and projections from surrounding onshore areas. Regional compilations have been published by Faleide et al. (1984) and Rønnevik and Jacobsen (1984).

Based on regional considerations, it is assumed that much of the eastern Barents Shelf was occupied during the Late Carboniferous and Permian by stable carbonate platforms forming the northern extension of the Moscow Platform (Plates 5–8). On the other hand, the western parts of the Barents Shelf are transected by the Tromsø–Bjørnøya and the Nordkapp grabens (Fig. 10), the subsidence history of which is not yet fully resolved owing to limited well control. These structural features form an integral part of the Norwegian–Greenland Sea Rift and of the fault systems of the Svalbard–Northeast Greenland oblique-slip zone. In this context, the occurrence of massive alkaline intrusions in the Kontozero Rift on Kola Peninsula, dated as ± 300 Ma (Churkin et al., 1981), should be noted. The western Barents Shelf was presumably occupied during the Late Carboniferous by extensive carbonate platforms (Plates 5, 6). In analogy to Svalbard, evaporitic series were probably restricted to the differentially subsiding Tromsö and Nordkapp grabens. These contain thick halites that later gave rise to major diapiric structures (Fig. 39). The age of these halites is tentatively given as Late Carboniferous Bashkirian to earliest Permian. For the Nordkapp Graben, there is reflection seismic evidence for two separate cycles of salt deposition, the earlier being of probably Bashkirian age and the younger of Early Permian age. This suggests that these grabens had subsided differentially during these times.

On the western Barents Shelf, Early Permian strata are thought to be developed in a carbonate and carbonate-evaporitic facies as observed in Western Svalbard and in the Timan–Pechora area. This is supported by limited well data and seismically evident solution features on the eastern flank of the Loppa Ridge (Fig. 15). Late Permian cherty shales and carbonates, similar to those occurring in Svalbard, have been encountered in some of the wells drilled in the southwestern Barents Sea. This suggests an increase in water depth in areas of differential subsidence. On adjacent platforms, carbonate deposition apparently continued during the Late Permian (Plates 7, 8). Seismic and well data indicate that the Loppa Ridge became sharply uplifted at the transition from the Permian to the Triassic while the Bjørnøya Basin was downfaulted (Fig. 15). The uplift of the Loppa Ridge may be interpreted as rift-induced thermal doming. There is reflection seismic evidence that the Nordkapp Graben was also affected by this rifting pulse. In the Tromsø Basin, Cretaceous series exceeding a thickness of 6 km impede seismic resolution at deeper stratigraphic levels; it is therefore uncertain whether this graben also became reactivated at the transition from the Permian to the Triassic (Fig. 39).

Intraplate compressional stresses, related to the Uralian orogeny, apparently did not impede the Permian evolution of rifts in the Western Barents Sea.

## NORWEGIAN–GREENLAND SEA RIFT

Following the last transpressional deformations along the Arctic–North Atlantic megashear, corresponding in East Greenland to the intra-Visean Ymerland phase, crustal extension governed the evolution of the Norwegian–Greenland Sea area.

In Central East Greenland, Namurian to early Stephanian continental conglomerates and sandstones, attaining thicknesses of up to 1500 m, accumulated in a north–south-trending system of half-grabens some 300 km long. After a rift-induced hiatus at the transition from the Carboniferous to the Permian (Scoresby Land unconformity), differential subsidence of these half-grabens continued and 2000–3000 m of Early Permian red conglomerates, fluvial sands and occasional lacustrine black shales were deposited (Plate 22).

An important intra-Kungurian rifting pulse, accompanied by dike intrusions, resulted in a further tilting of major basement-involving rotational fault blocks and an uplift of their leading edges. This rifting phase preceded the transgression of the Late Permian seas. Late Permian strata, some 300 m thick, consist of basal transgressive conglomerates, in part reefal carbonates, evaporites, and organic-rich shales; these are overlain by turbiditic and deltaic sands and coarse conglomerates. A further rifting pulse marks the Permian–Triassic boundary (Vischer, 1943; Haller, 1971; Henriksen and Higgins, 1976; Birkelund and Perch-Nilsen, 1976; Stemmerik and Sørensen, 1980; Surlyk et al., 1984, 1986; Fig. 49).

The overwhelming evidence for Late Carboniferous and Permian rifting available from Central East Greenland cannot, however, be duplicated by the stratigraphic record available for the basins underlying the shelf of Mid-Norway. Seismic data indicate that the Trøndelag Platform, located to the west of the

Mid-Norwegian town Trondheim, is underlain by thick pre-Triassic series contained in a basin that is limited to the east by a major coast parallel fault (Figs. 37, 38; Bukovics and Ziegler, 1985). These strata are not calibrated by well data but are thought to be made up of predominantly upper Paleozoic clastics. The occurrence of Upper Permian carbonates in the West Norway Shelf Basin has, however, been confirmed by well results (Plate 26).

Further south, in the Faeroe–West Shetland Basin, poorly dated Permo-Triassic red beds, which accumulated in rapidly subsiding half-grabens, may extend into the lower Permian and partly into the Stephanian. The occurrence of Upper Permian evaporitic intervals in this red bed series has been established by boreholes. Similarly, Upper Permian carbonates and evaporites have been encountered in wells drilled in the UK part of the northernmost North Sea and also on the northern shelf of Ireland (Plate 27; Fig. 48).

The Carboniferous rifts of the Northern British Isles, which can be considered as forming part of the rift-wrench basins of the Canadian Maritime Provinces, remained active until their partial inversion during the late Westphalian in response to compressional stresses exerted on the foreland during the terminal phase of the Variscan orogeny (Plate 22, 23). These foreland stresses presumably impeded the southward propagation

of the Norwegian–Greenland Sea Rift (Chapter 3). On the other hand, subsequent tensional stresses, developing during the Stephanian and Autunian at the western termination of the Bay of Biscay fracture zone and of subsidiary wrench systems crossing the Irish Sea and the British Isles, may have assisted the southward propagation of this rift system through which the Arctic Seas advanced southward during the Late Permian (see Chapter 3; Ziegler, 1982a).

The Late Carboniferous and Permian Norwegian–Greenland Sea Rift was essentially a-volcanic. The only igneous evidence reported to date are a syenite porphyry dike, dated as 297 ± 8 Ma, and a Lamprophyr dike dated as 278 ± 25 Ma occurring in the coastal area of Mid-Norway near Kristian Sund (Räheim, 1974). On the other hand, extensive Stephanian–Antunian dike systems and sills occur in Scotland (Plate 6).

## PERMIAN BASINS OF WESTERN AND CENTRAL EUROPE

With the final consolidation of the Appalachian-Mauretanides fold belt during the Alleghenian orogenic pulse, the dextral transform system linking this fold belt with the Urals

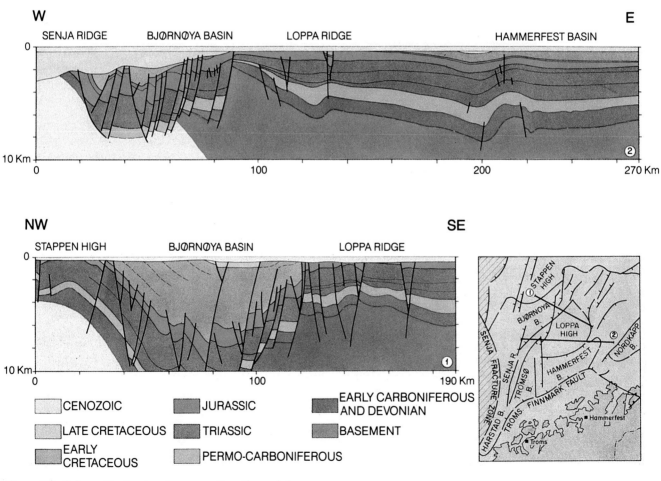

*Figure 15—Schematic structural cross sections through Loppa Ridge and Bjørnøya Basin, southwestern Barents Sea. After Gorin et al., Norske Shell.*

became inactive. Consequently, wrench movements and volcanic activity in Western and Central Europe abated at the transition from the Autunian to the Saxonian. Only in the Oslo Graben did magmatic activity persist into the Late Permian.

The gradual decay of the thermal anomalies, which were induced by the Stephanian–Autunian wrench and pull-apart deformations, is reflected by the progressive subsidence of the Northern and Southern Permian basins of Northwest and Central Europe. In these basins, the thick Rotliegend eolian and intracontinental playa lake deposits accumulated under arid conditions during the late Early Permian (Plate 7; Plein, 1978; Ziegler, 1982a; Glennie, 1984a, 1984b; Sørensen, 1986).

During Rotliegend times, the Northern and Southern Permian basins were separated by the Mid-North Sea–Ringkøbing-Fyn trend of highs; these highs had come into evidence during the Stephanian-Antunian (Fig. 12).

The Southern Permian Basin is essentially superimposed on the Late Carboniferous Variscan foredeep but encroaches in its eastern parts on the Variscan Externides. This basin has the form of a broad, saucer-shaped downwarp. Its depocenter, in which Rotliegend shales and halites reach a thickness of 1500 m, coincides closely with the areas of Permo-Carboniferous volcanism in northern Germany (Ziegler, 1982a; Fig. 16; Plates 6, 7). The Rotliegend sands, which are developed in a broad belt along the southern margin of the Southern Permian Basin, form the reservoir of major gas accumulations in the southern North

Sea and the eastward adjacent Dutch and North German onshore areas (Ziegler, 1980; Glennie, 1986).

Subsidence of the Southern Permian Basin was accompanied by only minor faulting. An exception is the Polish depocenter that was controlled by a northwest–southeast-trending graben (Depowski, 1978). This rift zone extends from Poland into the Black Sea area (Vinogradov, 1969). Its development is contemporaneous with the subsidence of the early Tethys rifts in the Central Mediterranean and with back-arc extension in the eastern Tethys domain. The latter culminated during the latest Permian–Early Triassic in sea-floor spreading in the Black Sea area and the partial separation of the Balkan–Turkish Cimmeria Terrane from the southern margin of Fennosarmatia (Adamia et al., 1981; Khain, 1984a; Chapter 5, Permo-Triassic Tethys Rift Systems).

The outlines and geometry of the Northern Permian Basin(s), located in the Central North Sea, is less well known owing to its deep burial under younger sediments and the intensity of Mesozoic rift tectonics (Fig. 18). Limited well control indicates that Rotliegend clastics in this basin attain thicknesses ranging between 200 and 600 m; there is no evidence for the development of an axial, evaporitic playa lake. The Rotliegend clastics of the Northern Permian basin overlay a variable thickness of Devonian and/or Lower Carboniferous sediments and, particularly in its eastern parts, transgressed directly over the Caledonian basement complex and lower Paleozoic sediments

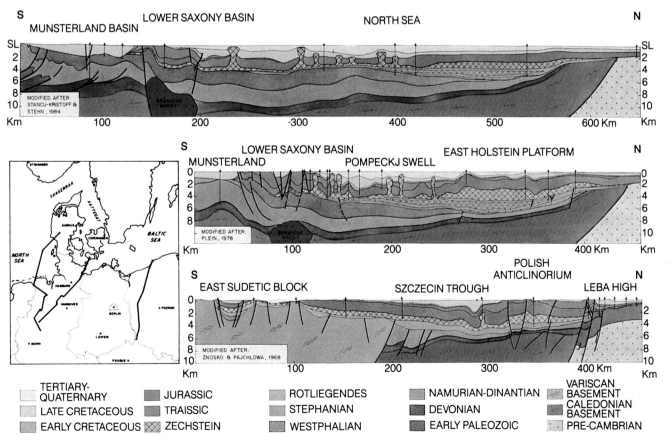

*Figure 16—Regional structural cross sections through North German and Polish Lowlands showing relation of southern Permian Basin to Variscan fold belt and foredeep. Modified after Stancu-Kristoff and Stehn (1984) (top); Plein (1978) (center); and Znosko and Pajchlowa (1968) (bottom).*

preserved in the Caledonian foreland (Fig. 12; Hospers et al., 1986a).

Progressive subsidence of the Norwegian–Greenland Sea Rift, combined with a glacioeustatic rise in sea level related to the deglaciation of Gondwana, resulted in the Late Permian rapid southward transgression of the Arctic Seas (Plate 8). At the transition from the Kungurian to the Ufinian, the barriers separating the Norwegian–Greenland Sea Rift from the Northern and Southern Permian basins of Europe broke down (were overstepped?) and the Arctic Seas invaded the latter, forming the huge Zechstein inland sea, which had a length of some 1700 km and a width of about 600 km. This transgression was apparently catastrophic as indicated by the basin-wide correlative, transgressive Kupferschiefer which corresponds to a sharp time-marker. The depositional water depth of this highly organic shale was clearly below wave-base and could have been in the 200–300 m range in the central parts of these basins. This suggests that the Rotliegend basins had subsided below the global sea level already before the transgression of the Zechstein Sea.

The Zechstein seas entered these intra-continental depressions probably via the incipient Viking Graben of the northern North Sea and via the Faeroe–Rockall Trough, the Irish Sea (Manx–Furness Basin, "Bakevillia Sea"), and across the area of the Pennine High (the Solway–Vale of Eden depression; Fig. 35; Pattinson et al., 1973; Ziegler, 1982a; Glennie, 1984a). Syndepositional faulting is evident in areas bordering the Faeroe–

Rockall Trough, in the Irish Sea, the Moray Firth area, and also in Poland, but otherwise plays only a minor role. On the basis of the available seismic and well data, it is unlikely that the Central North Sea Graben had already started to subside differentially during the Late Permian. In the northern parts of the Viking Graben, presumably thin Zechstein series, if at all present, are confined to its axial parts where they cannot be reached by the drill. Zechstein salts contained in the southern parts of the Viking Graben (Curtin and Ballestad, 1986) and in the Central Graben represent on the basis of seismostratigraphic evidence downfaulted prerift sediments and were not deposited in a differentially subsiding rift. The Horn Graben, on the other hand, forming the southernmost part of the Early Permian Oslo Rift, continued to subside differentially during the Late Permian (Fig. 18).

The depositional cycles recognized in the Zechstein series of the Northern and Southern Permian basins (Fig. 17) are fully correlative and thus illustrated that these basins were in full communication with each other across the Mid-North Sea High (Jenyon et al., 1984). Since Zechstein salts are missing, or only thinly developed, in the central parts of the Danish sector of the North Sea Central Graben, it must also be assumed that this segment of this major Mesozoic rift had not yet started to subside differentially during the Late Permian.

Faunal evidence indicates that during the Ufimian a temporary link was established between the Arctic-dominated Zechstein Seas and the Tethys via the Polish–Dobrugea Rift (Peryt

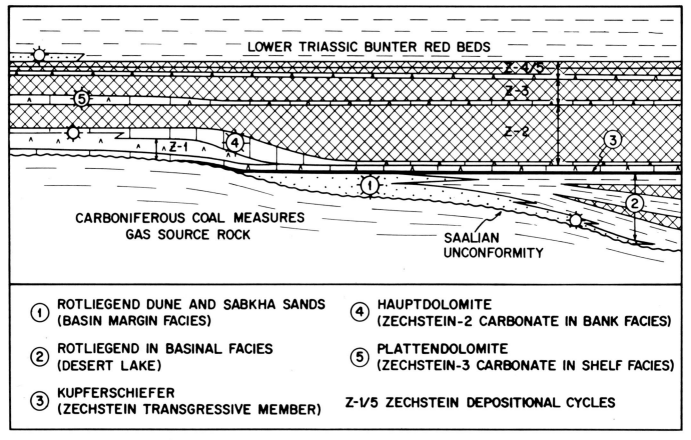

*Figure 17—Permian depositional cycles of the Northern and Southern Permian basins. Star symbol indicates principal gas reservoirs.*

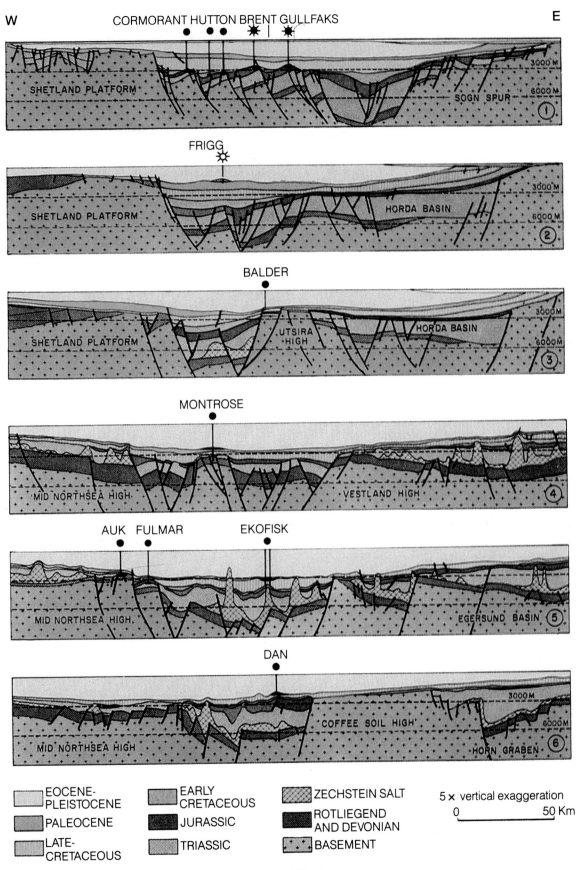

*Figure 18—Structural cross sections of the Central and Northern North Sea. For locations see Figure 19. After Louwerens, SIPM.*

and Peryt, 1977). Following the initial transgression of the Zechstein Seas, repeated glacioeustatic sea level fluctuations resulted in the cyclical restriction of the Northern and Southern Permian basins. This impeded a further faunal exchange between the Arctic and Tethys Seas.

During the deposition of the Zechstein I and II cycles (Fig. 17), water depths increased to some 400–500 m in basinal areas while carbonate and sulfate banks developed along the basin margins. The Dolomites capping these banks and their prograding slopes (Hauptdolomite) contain important gas-condensate accumulations in the Netherlands and Northern Germany (Sannemann et al., 1978; Smith, 1981; Van Adrichem-Boogaert and Burgers, 1983; Taylor, 1984; Clark, 1986; Ziegler, 1980).

Accumulation of the Hauptdolomite was interrupted by a sharp restriction of basinal areas, presumably in response to a sea level drop, causing their infilling by the thick Stassfurth Salts (Z-2 salt). During the subsequent depositional cycles III to V, which were controlled by repeated sea level fluctuations, subsidence and sedimentation rates were more or less in balance and the basinal areas were characterized by relatively shallow water depths (Pakulska and Kuna, 1981). During the latest Permian, the Arctic seas withdrew from Northwest Europe.

The five glacioeustatically induced depositional cycles of the Zechstein Basin correlate with the same number of cycles evident in the spiculite series of Western Svalbard (see Steel and Worsley, 1984).

In the Northern and Southern Permian basins, continued thermal relaxation of the lithosphere, combined with sediment loading and cyclically rising sea levels, resulted during the accumulation of the Zechstein series in a significant overstepping of the basin margins (Ziegler, 1982a).

## CONCLUSIONS

The Late Carboniferous and Permian development of the Norwegian–Greenland Sea Rift opened an avenue through which the Arctic Seas transgressed during the Late Permian into Northwest and Central Europe where they temporarily linked up with the Tethys Seas advancing northwestward through the Polish–Dobrugean Rift. Crustal extension in the Norwegian–Greenland Sea Rift was compensated by transform faults marking the northern margin of the Sverdrup and Wandel Sea basins. The southward propagation of the Norwegian–Greenland Sea Rift was apparently impeded by compressional foreland stresses during the Westphalian phases of the Variscan orogeny. After the relaxation of these stresses, this rift system began to propagate itself southward during the Late Permian into the Faeroe–Rockall Trough and possibly also into the northern North Sea.

In the Tethys domain, back-arc extension in the Black Sea area and rifting in the South Alpine, Dinarid, and Balkan areas heralded the early Mesozoic plate reorganization that culminated in the Mid-Jurassic crustal separation between Laurasia and Africa (Chapter 5).

During the Late Carboniferous and Permian, long-term and short-term eustatic sea level changes played an important role. These can be related to the glaciation of Gondwana that peaked during the latest Carboniferous to earliest Permian and waned rapidly at the beginning of the Late Permian (Hambrey and Harland, 1981; Caputo and Crowell, 1985). Yet, the highly cyclical nature of the Late Permian series is suggestive of continued glacioeustatic sea-level fluctuations. It is, however, uncertain whether during this time span remanent ice sheets still existed, for instance, in Antarctica or whether new ice caps developed in Siberia which, by now, had moved into a circumpolar position (Ustritsky, 1973; Smith and Briden, 1977; Kanasevich et al., 1978; Firstbrook et al., 1979; Scotese et al., 1980).

# CHAPTER 5
# EARLY MESOZOIC PLATE REORGANIZATION

# INTRODUCTION

The initial phase of the post-Hercynian break-up of the Pangea Supercontinent spanned Late Permian to Middle Jurassic times and culminated in the development of a new divergent/transform plate boundary between Gondwana and Laurasia.

In the Arctic–North Atlantic and Tethys domains, this plate reorganization is reflected by the Triassic to Middle Jurassic development of multidirectional rift systems that transected the Variscan fold belt and its European foreland (Plates 9–12). The evolution of these rift systems was governed, on the one hand, by the rapid southward propagation of the Norwegian–Greenland Sea Rift and, on the other hand, by the development and rapid westward propagation of the Tethys Rift system. In the Central and North Atlantic areas, these two megarift systems met and interfered with each other.

As long as crustal separation was not yet achieved in these rift systems wide areas around the future plate margins were subjected to tensional stresses. This is particularly evident in Western and Central Europe where the localization of Mesozoic grabens was to a large extent governed by the reactivation of Permo-Carboniferous fracture systems.

In the Tethys domain, the Late Permian to Early Triassic development of the Neo-Tethys sea floor spreading axis and its gradual westward propagations culminated during the Middle Jurassic in crustal separation between Laurasia and Africa and the opening of new oceanic basins in the Central and Western Mediterranean areas as well as in the Central Atlantic. This fundamental plate reorganization in the Atlantic–Tethys domain, which governed the first break-up phase of Pangea, was paralleled by continued crustal extension across the Norwegian–Greenland Sea Rift and further rifting and wrench deformation in the Svalbard–North Greenland and northern Sverdrup oblique-slip zones.

The Uralian orogeny, on the other hand, abated gradually, and its subduction system apparently became locked during the Early Triassic while back-arc extension, inducing volcanic activity in the incipient West Siberian Basin, reached a peak (Rudkevich, 1976; Nesterov et al., 1984). Subsidence of this basin was temporarily interrupted at the transition from the Triassic to the Jurassic by the early Kimmerian (Indosinian) compressive phase that affected the northern Urals and their continuation into Novaya Zemlya and the Taimyr Peninsula. The subsequent evolution of the West Siberian Basin was governed by the decay of the thermal anomaly induced by Permo-Triassic back-arc rifting.

# TRIASSIC-ARCTIC–NORTH ATLANTIC RIFT SYSTEM

In the Norwegian–Greenland Sea Rift, large rotational fault blocks subsided rapidly during the Triassic in response to accelerated crustal extension. This is evident on seismic data from the Mid-Norway Basin and from surface geology in Central East Greenland (Vischer, 1943; Bukovics and Ziegler, 1985). At the onset of the Triassic, the Norwegian–Greenland Sea Rift propagated southward into the North Sea area where the Viking and Central grabens, as well as the Moray Firth Rift, came into evidence (Figs. 18, 19, 35). Similarly the Horda–Egersund–North Danish system of half-grabens, subparalleling the coast of southern Norway and Sweden, began to subside differentially

during the Early Triassic (Ziegler, 1982a). Whilst the Horn Graben, already evident during the Late Permian, continued to subside, the Oslo Graben apparently did not subside substantially during the Triassic. During the earliest Triassic, the long-standing Mid-North Sea–Ringkøbing–Fyn High, separating the Northern and Southern Permian basins, became transected by the southward-propagating Central North Sea Graben. The North Danish Halfgraben (Fig. 44) linked up to the southeast, via an offset through the western Baltic Rønne Graben, with the Polish–Dobrugea Rift and the Black Sea back-arc sea floor spreading center (Adamia et al., 1981; Ziegler, 1982a; Khain, 1984a).

Regional isopachs of the Triassic series indicate, however, that in Northwest and Central Europe the Northern and Southern Permian basins continued to subside in response to lithospheric cooling and contraction (Ziegler, 1982b; Sørensen, 1985).

Accelerated crustal extension across the Faeroe–Rockall Rift is reflected by the rapid subsidence of major half-grabens on the West Shetland, Hebridean and Northwest Irish shelves (Binns et al., 1975; Jones, 1978; Ridd, 1981, 1983; Naylor and Shannon, 1982; Duindam and van Hoorn, 1987). The subsidence of these basins was controlled by listric normal faults (Fig. 36). Deep reflection seismic lines over the Hebridean Shelf show that some of these faults extend to deeper crustal levels (Brewer and

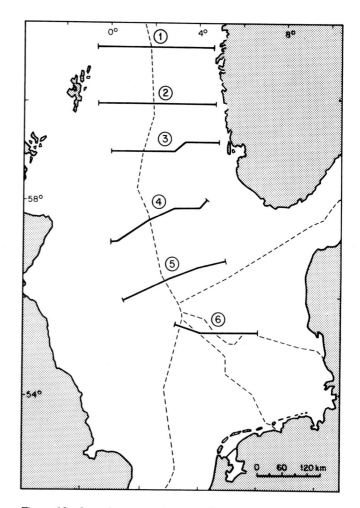

*Figure 19—Location map of structural cross sections given in Figure 18.*

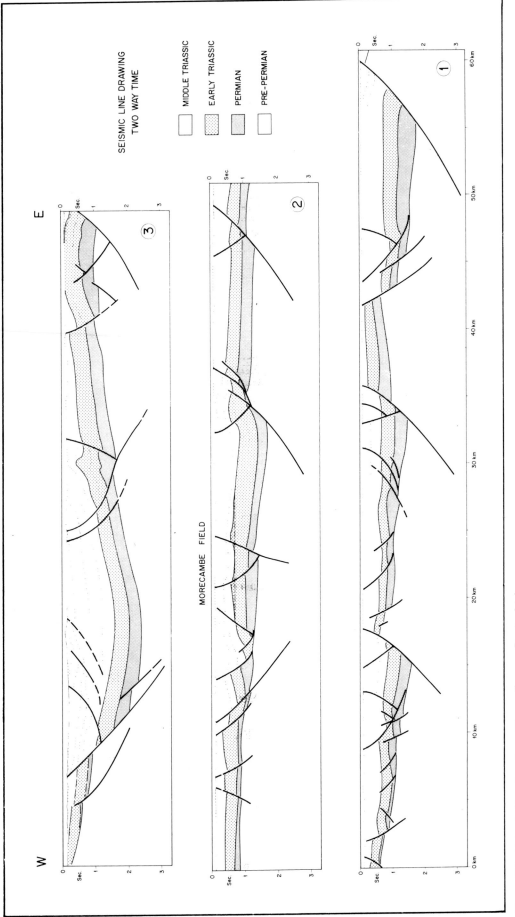

*Figure 20—Seismic line drawings, Manx–Furness Basin, Irish Sea. For location see Figure 21. After Shell UK Expro.*

Smythe, 1984). Similarly, the Donegal, Slyne-Erris, and Porcupine troughs flanking the Rockall Trough (Naylor and Shannon, 1982), as well as the Irish Sea Basin (Figs. 20, 21), and the Celtic Sea, Bristol Channel, and Western Approaches troughs subsided rapidly during the Triassic (Figs. 22, 23; Ziegler, 1982a, 1987e). During the Middle Triassic, the rift systems on the Newfoundland Shelf and between the Grand Banks and Iberia came into evidence. The palinspastic reconstructions given in Plate 9 and 10 suggest that the Porcupine Graben (Fig. 32) finds its

southern extension in the Flemish Pass Rift located between the Orphan Knoll and the Flemish Cap and that the Western Approaches Trough extends into the grabens flanking the Galicia Bank (Masson and Miles, 1986b). The latter open up to the south into the Lusitania–Tagus Abyssal Plain rift system. The complex graben systems of the Flemish Cap–Grand Banks area (Jeanne d'Arc, Flemisch Pass, Carson, Horseshoe, and North and South Whale basins, Fig. 28; Wade, 1981) find their southward extension in the rift basins underlying the shelf of Nova

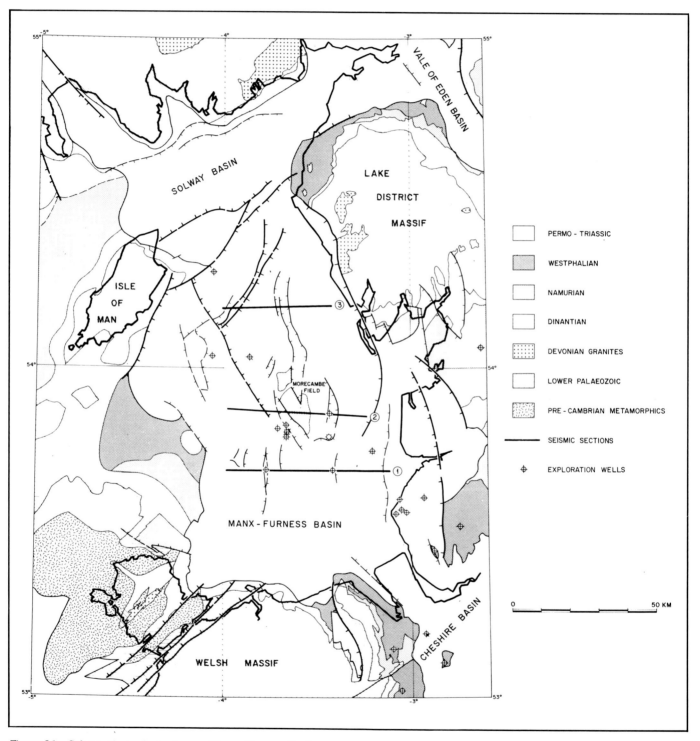

*Figure 21—Schematic geological map, Manx–Furness Basin, Irish Sea. After Shell UK Expro.*

Scotia and in the Fundy Basin. Determination of the inception age of the various rift basins in the North and Central Atlantic domain is, however, hampered by limited control on the age of the basal continental red beds that form the initial synrift deposits (Plates 27, 28). Overall, it appears that rifts on the Nova Scotia Shelf and their counterparts on the Atlantic Shelf of Morocco came into evidence during the Ladinian to Carnian (Wade, 1981; Jansa and Wiedmann, 1982) and that during the Carnian rifting propagated rapidly southward through the Central Atlantic and into the Gulf of Mexico (Wilson, 1981; Manspeizer, 1982, 1985).

The evolution of the Triassic rifts in the North and Central Atlantic area can be related, on the one hand, to the southward propagation of the Norwegian–Greenland Sea Rift and, on the other hand, to the westward propagation of the Tethys rift system (see *Permo-Triassic Tethys Rift Systems,* this chapter). Since the earliest synrift deposits in the Triassic grabens of the Central

Atlantic area are largely not calibrated by wells, they may be as old as Late Permian to earliest Triassic; it is therefore possible that back-arc extension, governed by the decay of the Appalachian–Mauretanide subduction zones, may, at least initially, also have played a role in the development of this megarift system (see Chapter 3).

In the northern parts of the Norwegian–Greenland Sea Rift, the Western Barents Shelf, and the Svalbard area, rifting activity was most intense at the transition from the Permian to the Triassic but abated gradually during the Middle Triassic (Plate 26). This is particularly evident by the evolution of the Byørnøya Graben. Earliest Triassic downfaulting of this rift and contemporaneous uplifting of the Loppa Ridge, forming a classical rift shoulder, was followed by the gradual burial of this high during the Early and Middle Triassic and by regional subsidence of the area during the Late Triassic and Jurassic (Fig. 15). The increase in thickness of the Upper Triassic and Jurassic strata from the

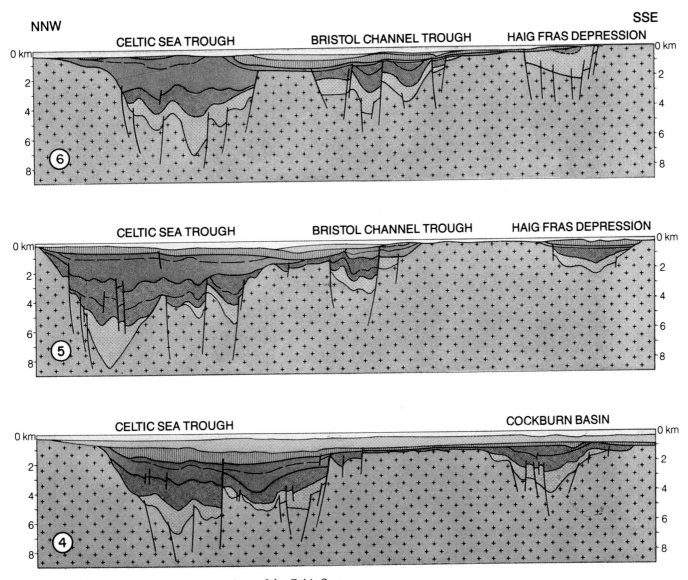

*Figure 22—Schematic structural cross sections of the Celtic Sea and Bristol Channel troughs. For legend and location see Figure 23. After Shell UK Expro and SIPM.*

eastern flank of the Loppa Ridge toward its crest suggests that relaxation of the thermal anomaly, which had caused its Early Triassic uplift, governed its subsequent subsidence (see Faleide et al., 1984).

Also in Western Svalbard there is evidence for Early Triassic differential subsidence of troughs, along preexisting fault zones, while the eastern part of the Svalbard archipelago retained the configuration of a stable platform. Starved basin conditions during the early Middle Triassic were associated with the accumulations of kerogenous oil source rocks in the central and northern parts of the Barents Shelf. During the Late Triassic and earliest Jurassic, deltaic complexes, sourced by the renewed uplift and erosion of the Ural Mountains and also by the uplift of the Lomonosov High and the Fennoscandian Shield prograded

over large parts of the Barents Shelf (Plates 9–11; Mørk et al., 1982; Steel and Worsley, 1984; Jacobsen and van Veen, 1984).

In the Sverdrup Basin, the accumulation of up to 5000 m of Triassic sediments suggests that considerable crustal thinning, presumably induced by crustal extension, must have occurred at least during the late Paleozoic and Early Triassic (Figs. 13, 14). In the axial parts of this basin, deeper water conditions, associated with the development of kerogenous oil source rocks, prevailed during the Early and Middle Triassic (Plates 9, 26). Continued uplift of the northern rim of the Sverdrup Basin during much of the Triassic is suggested by the influx of clastics from northern sources. During the Norian, these source areas apparently subsided and major delta complexes prograded from the southern and southeastern margins of the Sverdrup

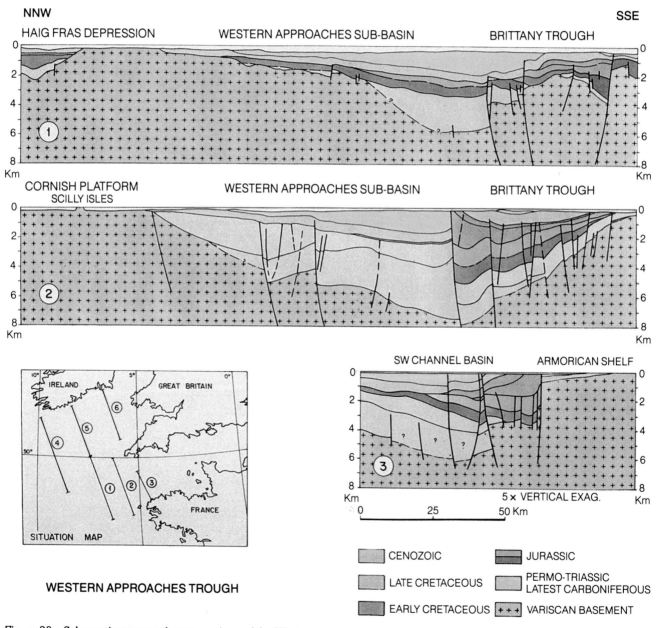

*Figure 23—Schematic structural cross sections of the Western Approaches Trough. After Shell Française.*

Basin into its central parts, causing their shallowing out (Plate 10). The Norian to Pliensbachian continental and deltaic Heiberg Series attain a thickness of some 2500 m in the central parts of the Sverdrup Basin (Meneley et al. 1975; Balkwill, 1978; Kerr, 1981a; Embry, 1982).

The Scythian to Carnian uplift of the northern margin of the Sverdrup Basin was probably caused by transform faulting compensating for crustal extension in the Norwegian–Greenland Sea Rift. Parts of these displacements were presumably taken up by crustal extension in the Makarov Rift (precursor of the future oceanic Makarov Basin, located between the Alpha and the Lomonosov Ridges), which separated the Barents–Lomonosov platform from the Arctic Shelf; the latter encompassed the New Siberian Islands and the Alaska–Chukchi–Chukotka blocks (Fig. 7). An expression of this may be seen in the Late Triassic uplift of the Lomonosov High from which clastics were shed southward into the area of the Svalbard Archipelago and onto the northern parts of the Barents Shelf (Plate 10).

# PERMO-TRIASSIC TETHYS RIFT SYSTEMS

In the eastern Tethys domain, progressive back-arc extension, related to the decay of the Variscan subduction system, culminated during the Late Permian–Early Triassic in sea floor spreading in the Black Sea area and the separation of the Variscan deformed Cimmeria Terrain from the southern margin of Fennosarmatia (Plate 8; Adamia et al., 1981; Khain, 1984a).

Late Permian tensional tectonics affected also the Balkan, Hellenic, Dinarid, and South Alpine domains as indicated, for instance, by the rift-related volcanism of the internal Dinarides (Pamic, 1984) and of the Pindos–Sub-Pelagonian Trough (Roddick et al., 1984).

It is likely that the Permian seas advanced westward along the axes of these rift systems, the outline of which cannot be established on the basis of the sparse data available. In view of this it is difficult to map the distribution and to assess the tectonic setting of the Late Permian basins in the Central and Eastern Mediterranean area; the reconstruction shown in Plate 8, indicating the existence of extensive carbonate platforms on the Tethys shelves, must therefore remain conceptual (see also Kamen-Kay, 1976; Tollmann, 1984). Overall, the later Permian marine basins of the Mediterranean area had the shape of a wide gulf that was open to the east, toward the Tethys Ocean (Argyriadis et al., 1980). During the Late Permian, continental clastics continued to accumulate along the fringes of the marine Mediterranean basin and in intramontane depressions within the Variscan fold belt.

The general absence of Late Permian and Early Triassic sediments in much of Iberia, Northwest Africa, and the Canadian Maritime Provinces suggests that these areas formed a coherent highland during the latest Paleozoic and earliest Mesozoic.

In the eastern Tethys domain, gradual activation of the Tethys sea-floor spreading axis is evident by Late Permian to Early Triassic crustal extension along the northeastern margin of the Afro-Arabian Craton, facing the Paleotethys, resulting in Mid-Triassic crustal separation between the continental Central and East Iranian Terrane and the Arabian Peninsula. This event marked the beginning of the early Mesozoic break-up cycle of Pangea that culminated in the Middle Jurassic development of a divergent plate boundary between Gondwana and Laurasia (see *Mid-Jurassic Crustal Separation between Laurasia and Gondwana,* this chapter).

The Central and East Iranian cratonic block is characterized by a Gondwana-type stratigraphy and was clearly not affected by the Hercynian diastrophism. It formed part of Sengör's (1985) much larger Asian "Cimmerian Continent" (Cimmeria sensu lato), which was accreted to the southern margin of Eurasia during the Late Triassic–Early Jurassic Indosinian orogeny as a consequence of the northward subduction of the Proto-Tethys and opening of the Mesozoic Tethys Ocean. The Late Permian to Early Triassic width of Proto-Tethys in its Arabian segment is, however, difficult to determine in view of the uncertainty about the original dimensions of the Central and East Iranian cratonic blocks (Berberian and King, 1981; Devoudzadeh and Schmidt, 1981, 1982; Sengör, 1985; Kazmin et al., 1986).

During the Triassic, the Tethys sea-floor spreading axis gradually propagated westward into the Mediterranean domain. This was preceded by rift propagation into the Central and Western Mediterranean realm and ultimately into the Central Atlantic (Laubscher and Bernoulli, 1977; Channell et al., 1979). As a consequence of the activation of the northwestward propagating Tethys sea-floor spreading axis, the Balkan–Turkish Cimmeria Terrane (Cimmeria, sensu stricto, Chapters 3 and 4) began to converge with Fennosarmatia during the Mid-Triassic. This entailed the gradual closure of the oceanic Black Sea backarc basin (Sengör et al., 1984). At the same time, a complex rift system developed in the Central and Western Mediterranean area (Plates 9, 10).

Rifting activity, punctuated by an often widespread volcanism, dominated the Triassic evolution of the Hellenides, the Dinarides, the Carnic, Julian, and Southern Alps, the Austroalpine domain, and the Carpathians (Bechstädt, 1978; Bechstädt et al., 1978; Tollmann, 1978, 1984; Argyriadis et al., 1980; Trümpy, 1980; Jacobshagen, 1982; Pe-Piper et al., 1982; Tollmann and Tollmann, 1982; Brandner, 1984; Kovacs, 1984; Pamic, 1984; Garzanti, 1985). Progressive fragmentation of the eastern parts of the Italo-Dinarid Block was paralleled by differential subsidence of the Olenos–Pindos and the Sub-Pelagonian troughs (Aubouin, 1973; Channell et al., 1979; Pe-Piper and Piper, 1984; Mountrakis, 1986). These grabens find their northern continuation in the complex rift systems of the Dinarides (Pamic, 1984) and the Carnic–South Alpine domain. The evolution of these multidirectional rift systems was accompanied by local intra-Triassic transpressional deformations as, for instance, in the area of the Southern and Carnic Alps (Montenegrian tectonic phases; Brandner, 1984).

During the Late Triassic, limited sea-floor spreading occurred in the Sub-Pelagonian Trough, and during the latest Triassic crustal separation was achieved in the domain of the internal Dinarides (Plate 10). This was followed by the gradual opening of the Dinaric–Hellenic Ocean, corresponding to the future Vardar suture zone. By latest Triassic time, rifts flanking this new oceanic basin had become inactive and volcanism ceased in them (Pamic, 1984; Spray et al., 1984). The suggested latest Triassic shift of sea-floor spreading from the Sub-Pelagonian Trough to the Dinaric–Hellenic Basin, resulting in the partial or complete isolation of the Pelagonia–Golija microcraton, could be interpreted as reflecting a ridge jump during the early evolution of the Neo-Tethys sea-floor spreading axis (for an alternate interpretation see Smith and Spray, 1984).

During the Late Triassic, Cimmeria (sensu stricto) became further deformed and the Black Sea back-arc ocean continued to close, whereby a north-dipping subduction zone developed along its northern margin. This was associated with a first phase of mild compressional deformation of the Donets Graben and the uplifting of the Sarmatian platform; from the latter clastics were shed westward into the Northwest European Basin (Sengör et al., 1984).

During the Middle and Late Triassic, the Lagonegro Trough, thought to form the western margin of the Italo-Dinarid block (Apulian platform), also subsided differentially (Channell et al., 1979; d'Argenio and Alvarez, 1980; Argyriadis et al., 1980; Wood, 1981). To the south, this trough opened up into the Ionian Sea Basin, which probably came into evidence at the same time (Escarmed, 1982; Enay et al., 1982). Subsidiary grabens branching off to the west from the Lagonegro–Ionian Sea Basin, such as the Streppanosa Trough of southern Sicily and the Sicani and Imerese basins to its north, also began to subside differentially during the Middle Triassic (Scandone, 1975a). These grabens may find their western extension in the Maghrebian-Gibraltar and the North African rifts (Plates 9, 10).

Tensional reactivation of the Permo-Carboniferous Bay of Biscay fracture zone started during the Late Permian to Early Triassic. For instance, in the Pyrenean–Cantabrian area, and in the region of the Celt–Iberian Ranges, accumulation of continental red beds in a system of pull-apart basins commenced during the Late Permian and Early Triassic. During the Triassic, basin margins became progressively overstepped. Intensified Late Triassic tectonic activity was accompanied by the extrusion of basalts in the Aquitaine Basin, in Cantabria and in the Celt-Iberian Ranges (Plate 27; BRGM et al., 1973; Stévaux and Winnock, 1974; Boury et al., 1977; Vegas and Banda, 1983). Similarly, the Permo-Carboniferous Gibraltar fracture zone apparently became reactivated by tensional tectonics during the latest Early Triassic and developed during the Middle and Late Triassic into a major rift along which the Tethys seas advanced westward (Mákel, 1985).

In Morocco and Algeria, the High, Middle and Sahara Atlas rifts also began to subside during the late Early(?) to Middle Triassic (Plate 28). The evolution of this complex graben system, which was accompanied by sinistral wrench faulting and repeated basaltic volcanism, probably involved the reactivation of Permo-Carboniferous fracture systems (van Houten and Brown, 1977; Mattauer et al., 1977; Manspeizer et al., 1978; Stets and Wurster, 1981; Manspeizer, 1982; Beauchamp and Petit, 1983; Laville and Petit, 1984).

In the North and Central Atlantic domain the westward-propagating Tethys rift system met with the southward-propagating Arctic–North Atlantic rift system (see *Triassic Arctic–North Atlantic Rift System*, this chapter).

## GEODYNAMICS OF TRIASSIC TETHYS–NORTH ATLANTIC RIFTS

In the context of the southward-propagating Arctic–North Atlantic rift system and the westward propagation of the Tethys rifts, Western and Central Europe became progressively subjected to regional extension. This resulted in the development of a complex, multidirectional system of grabens and troughs, many of which are superimposed on Permo-Carboniferous fracture systems (Ziegler, 1982b; compare Plate 6 with Plates 9 and 10).

The subsidence of most of these grabens systems was accompanied by only very minor volcanic activity (Plates 29, 30). In

contrast, the Bay of Biscay, the Gibraltar, and the North African rifts as well as those on the North American shelf are all characterized by significant Late Triassic to Early Jurassic volcanic activity (Plate 28; Vogt, 1973; Manspeizer et al., 1978, Van Houten and Brown, 1977; Stévaux and Winnock, 1974). The Late Triassic subsidence of the Bay of Biscay, the Gibraltar, and the North African rifts was probably accompanied by wrench movements compensating for crustal extension in the Central and North Atlantic realm (Plate 10). Commensurate deep crustal fracturing presumably facilitated the ascent of mantle-derived magmas.

On the other hand, the extremely low level of volcanic activity in the Triassic rifts of Northwest and Central Europe is surprising because their dimensions are comparable to those of the highly volcanic Cenozoic Rhine–Bresse–Rhône graben system or with parts of the East African Rift. From this comparison, it is concluded that the Triassic rift systems of Western and Central Europe subsided in response to regional crustal extension rather than because of the development of a multitude of local hotspots or mantle plumes.

When viewed in the broader framework of the Arctic–North Atlantic and Tethys rift systems, the area affected by tensional stresses, as indicated by the subsidence of multidirectional Triassic grabens and troughs, extended from the Polish Trough to the Atlas grabens over a distance of some 2000 km and from the Grand Banks to the margins of the Tethys Ocean over a distance of about 3500 km.

Such a wide field of crustal extension developed presumably in response to intraplate tensional stresses that may have been induced by frictional forces exerted on the lithosphere of Pangea by gradually developing upwelling asthenospheric convection systems. Such slowly developing new convective systems could be visualized as the driving mechanism for the post-Hercynian plate reorganization that culminated during the Middle Jurassic in crustal separation between Gondwana and Laurussia (see *Mid-Jurassic Crustal Separation between Laurasia and Gondwana,* this chapter).

However, as long as crustal separation was not yet achieved in the Tethys and Arctic–North Atlantic domains, large areas around the future plate boundaries were apparently subjected to tensional stresses.

## TRIASSIC TETHYS TRANSGRESSION AND ARCTIC REGRESSION

The latest Permian (Tatarian) corresponded to a period of global low stand in sea level that is possibly related to a significant deepening of the world oceanic basins in response to decreasing activity along the mid-oceanic ridges and a commensurate cooling and contraction of the oceanic lithosphere (Schopf, 1974; Forney, 1975; Heller and Angevine, 1985). During the Triassic, however, sea levels cyclically rose again to reach a high during the late Early Jurassic (Vail et al., 1977; Hallam, 1978; Biddle, 1984; Brandner, 1984). This rise in sea level is probably an effect of the early Mesozoic plate reorganization and the associated development of new sea-floor spreading axes causing a gradual volume reduction of the oceans (Pitman, 1978). Its cyclical nature is, however, more difficult to explain and could in part be due to the flooding and possibly the desiccation of silled, rift-induced basins (e.g., salt basins of Central and North Atlantic domain) and broad-scale, low-relief lithospheric deformations. On the other hand, it should be kept in mind that northeastern Siberia occupied a near polar position during the Triassic, Jurassic, and Early Cretaceous (Smith and Briden, 1977; Kanasewich et al., 1978; Firstbrook et al., 1979). From these areas, Jurassic and Early Cretaceous glaciomarine deposits have been reposted (Epshteyn, 1978; Kaplan, 1978; Brandt, 1986). Thus, it cannot be precluded that during the Triassic and particularly during the Early and Middle Jurassic and the Early Cretaceous, glacioeustatic sea-level changes also played a role and may be, at least in part, responsible for the cyclical nature of sedimentation during these time spans.

During the Triassic, rising sea levels, combined with the tectonically induced subsidence of the Tethys and Arctic–North Atlantic graben systems, caused a progressive overstepping of the Permian basin margins. This is particularly evident in northwestern Europe where, for instance, the Northern and Southern Permian Basin became fully connected during the Early Triassic, thus forming the much larger Northwest European Basin (Ziegler, 1982a).

In latest Permian times, the Arctic seas withdrew from the Permian basins of Northwest Europe and remained confined throughout Triassic times to the Norwegian–Greenland Sea rift zone and the Barents Shelf (Jacobsen and van Veen, 1984; Plates 8–10, 29, 30). This initial regression may be related to the latest Permian tectonoeustatic low stand in sea level (Schopf, 1974). However, the persistent separation of the Arctic and Tethys seas throughout the Triassic could possibly be explained in terms of upwarping of a rift-induced broad, low-relief dome in the northern North Sea and Faeroe–Shetland area. In this region, a high rate of crustal extension combined with an intensified clastic influx into rapidly subsiding grabens resulted in the accumulation of up to 3000 m of in part coarse red beds ranging in age from the earliest Triassic to late Norian (Ziegler, 1982a).

On the other hand, a moderate clastic influx into the grabens extending from the Tethys shelves into Western and Central Europe and into the North and Central Atlantic realm facilitated the opening of new avenues for the transgression of the Tethys seas.

## Tethys Realm

On the shelves and rift-bounded platforms flanking the Tethys Ocean, extensive carbonate platforms, some of them containing evaporitic basins, were established (reestablished?) during the Early and Middle Triassic, while deeper water carbonates and shales accumulated in the intervening troughs (Auboin, 1973; Biju-Duval et al., 1977; Bechstädt et al., 1978; Channell et al., 1979; Argyriadis et al., 1980; Kovacs, 1984). This is exemplified by the Italo–Dinarid–Austro Alpine block that corresponded through Triassic times to a vast carbonate bank, offset by the probably rift-induced deeper water Olenos–Pindos, Lagonegro, and Ionian Sea troughs (Abbate et al., 1970; Auboin et al., 1970; Papa, 1970; d'Argenio et al., 1975; Pieri, 1975; Scandone, 1975a, 1975b; Pamic, 1984).

The fully marine Alpine–Mediterranean Triassic facies province gives way laterally to the more clastic dominated Germanic facies province that characterized the distal western and northern parts of the Tethys shelves as well as much of the basins in Western and Central Europe (Plates 9, 10). The Germanic facies province closely reflects the interplay between tectonic subsidence, sedimentation rates and sea-level fluctuations. It is char-

acterized by a tripartite subdivision of the Triassic series into the lower, continental Buntsandstein clastics, the middle, marine Muschelkalk carbonates and evaporites, and the upper, tidal flat and playa deposits of the Keuper (Plates 27, 29, 30). The boundaries between these gross lithofacies units are, however, not fully synchronous and as such reflect differences in the subsidence and sedimentation rates in the various basins (Ziegler, 1982a).

During Late Scythian times, the Tethys seas transgressed northward through the Polish–Dobrudgea graben into the eastern parts of the Northwest European Basin, giving rise to the accumulation of early Muschelkalk carbonates in Poland. However, only during the middle Anisian did the deposition of the lower Muschelkalk carbonates become pervasive in the Northwest European Basin (Plate 9). A second link between the Tethys and the Northwest European Basin was opened during the late Ladinian (upper Muschelkalk) between the London–Brabant–Armorican–Massif Central High and the Bohemian Massif via the Western Alps and the graben systems of the Jura Mountains and Central Germany (Burgundy–Hessian Depression). During the Middle and Late Triassic periodic, distal marine transgressions advanced into the south-central North Sea area and across the English Midlands into the rift/wrench basins of the Irish Sea area. During the accumulation of the Carnian and Norian playa and tidal flat Keuper Series, the connection between the Tethys and the Northwest European Basin via the Polish Trough became blocked by a strong clastic influx from the Fennosarmatian hinterland while cyclical transgressions continued to enter the basin via the West Alpine–Burgundy–Hessian route (Plate 10). These transgressive cycles, which gave rise to the accumulation of evaporitic series, were interrupted by regional regressions during which clastic fans prograded from the Fennosarmatian landmass southward across the Northwest European Basin and via the Hessian–Burgundy–West Alpine route onto the Tethys shelves. With the Rhaetian rise in sea level, open marine conditions were established in the Northwest European Basin with the seas encroaching onto the central North Sea area (Plate 30). At the same time, the seaway through the Polish–Dobrudgea Trough reopened (Ziegler, 1982a).

A third avenue of Triassic Tethys transgression followed the Bay of Biscay Rift. In the Aquitaine Basin, lower Anisian halites are overlain by upper Anisian–lower Carnian carbonates, middle Carnian–lower Norian halites, and mid-Norian to lower Rhaetian Keuper playa deposits (Plate 28; BRGM et al., 1973). In Cantabria, Muschelkalk equivalent carbonates and evaporites are of a Late Anisian and Ladinian age. They are overlain by Carnian and Norian halite-bearing Keuper Series. Middle Triassic carbonates occur also in the southwestern parts of the Celtic Sea Trough, the Fastnet Basin. Similarly, temporary marine incursions advanced during Ladinan to Norian time from the Bay of Biscay Rift into the northeastern parts of Celtic Sea Trough, into the Western Approaches Graben, and possibly also into the grabens of the Irish Sea where they gave rise to the accumulation of evaporitic series (Plate 29). This refutes the notion held by Masson and Miles (1986b), who propose that the margin of the Triassic Aquitaine Basin was located to the west of Cantabria and that this basin was therefore not communicating with the Celtic Sea–Western Approaches grabens.

During the Rhaetian, open marine conditions were established in the Bay of Biscay and in the rifts of the Celtic Sea–Western Approaches area and also in the Porcupine Trough. From these areas, seaways extended into the Rockall Trough, possibly as far north as the Minches Basin on the Hebrides Shelf, and via the Irish Sea and the Great Glen fracture zone into the Inner Moray Firth Basin of the northwestern North Sea (Plate 27). Furthermore, marine connections were established between the Paris Basin, the Celtic Sea and Western Approaches troughs and the Northwest European Basin via the English Channel and the English Midlands (Plate 29).

In Norian and Rhaetian times, distal marine transgressions reached from the Bay of Biscay Rift via the East Newfoundland Basin into the Avalon–Jeanne d'Arc graben in which Argo-equivalent halites were deposited (Plate 28). These basins presumably had already started to subside during late Ladinian to early Carnian time (Plates 9, 10). (See also Hubbard et al., 1985; Meneley, 1986; Grant et al., 1986.)

A fourth avenue of Triassic Tethys transgressions corresponds to the Maghrebian–Gibraltar Rift and the Chotte–Sahara Atlas Trough of Tunisia, Algeria, and Morocco. In the Betic and Rift zone (Gibraltar Rift), oldest Muschelkalk carbonates are dated as middle Ladinian (Simon and Kozur, 1977; Wildi, 1983; Mákel, 1985), while the earliest evaporitic series in the Middle and High Atlas troughs are probably of an Anisian age (Plate 28). Carbonate deposition remained largely restricted to the axial parts of the Gibraltar Rift zone through which the Tethys seas advanced westward during the Late Triassic into the Lusitania Basin of West Portugal. In South and West Portugal, mixed carbonate and halite sequences of a Carnian in Hettangian age grade laterally into continental red beds (Antunes et al., 1980). The thick halite sequences in the rift basins of the Atlantic seaboard of Morocco, the New England States, Nova Scotia, and on the Grand Banks (Argo salt) are similarly dated as Carnian-Norian to early Hettangian (Wade, 1981; Jansa and Wiedmann, 1982; see also Emery and Uchupi, 1984). On the other hand, very thick late Middle and Upper Triassic continental clastics and lacustrine shales accumulated in the rifts that are superimposed on the Appalachian internides (e.g., Newark Basin) and in the Fundy Rift of Nova Scotia. The onset of subsidence of these basins, which display the geometry of half-grabens, is difficult to determine because control on the age of their earliest synrift deposits is generally lacking (Manspeizer, 1982).

### Arctic Domain

In the Arctic domain of Svalbard, in the western Barents Sea, and in the Norwegian–Greenland Sea, the accumulation of Triassic strata was governed by syndepositional rift and wrench tectonics. Open marine, in part kerogenous, Lower to Middle Triassic shales occur in Svalbard Archipelago, on Franz Josef Land, and in the central parts of the Barents Sea (Plate 26). These grade toward the basin margins into deltaic complexes, the outbuilding of which was governed by sea level fluctuations, a tectonically controlled clastic influx and by local subsidence patterns (Jacobsen and van Veen, 1984; Mørk and Bjørøy, 1984). During the Late Triassic and earliest Jurassic the renewed uplift of the Ural Mountains and of the Lomonosov High was accompanied by the rapid progradation of coal-bearing deltaic fans over large parts of the Barents Shelf. At the same time, deltaic systems prograded northward from the north coast of Norway onto the Barents Shelf (Plates 9–11).

In the Norwegian–Greenland Sea rift zone, stratigraphic control is limited to the outcrops in East Greenland and to well data from the southern Barents Sea, the Mid-Norway Basin, and the northernmost North Sea. Triassic facies patterns shown in Plates 9 and 10 are therefore highly interpretative. In the South-

ern Barents Sea, Triassic strata are developed in a sandy deltaic to prodelta clay facies. In Eastern Greenland, marine series are restricted to the Lower and Middle Triassic and the Rhaetian (Clemmensen, 1980; Surlyk et al., 1981), while in the Mid-Norway Basin marine and evaporitic series appear to be restricted to the upper Ladinian and lower Norian (Jacobsen and van Veen, 1984). In the northernmost North Sea, there is limited evidence for a Norian incursion of the Arctic Sea (Plate 27). During the Rhaetian and Hettangian, major deltas prograded from all sides into the Norwegian–Greenland Sea Rift and as such reflect an intensified rifting activity. These fluvio-deltaic, partly coal-bearing series form the reservoir for major hydrocarbon accumulations in the northernmost North Sea and in the Mid-Norway Basin (Plates 26, 27).

It is speculated that the subsidence of the Norwegian-Greenland Sea Rift was accompanied by thermal updoming of its flanking areas, particularly during the Late Triassic and earliest Jurassic. The uplift of such marginal highs probably gave rise to the latest Triassic and the earliest Jurassic development of new drainage systems, which governed the massif influx of clastics into the Sverdrup Basin, onto the Barents Shelf, and also into the Northwest European Basin (Plate 10).

Overall, it appears that the accumulation of clastics in the southern parts of the Norwegian–Greenland Sea, the Central and Northern North Sea, and in the Faeroe rifts generally kept balance with subsidence rates and rising sea levels. This apparently impeded the southward transgression of the Arctic Sea and also the northward transgression of the Tethys seas. First tentative connections between the Arctic and the Tethys seas may have been established during the Rhaetian via the Rockall–Faeroe Rift.

### EARLY JURASSIC RIFTING AND LINK-UP OF ARCTIC AND TETHYS SEAS

During the Early Jurassic, both the Arctic–North Atlantic and the Tethys rift systems remained tectonically active while slow northwestward propagation of the Tethys sea-floor spreading axis resulted in the gradual opening of the Dinaric-Hellenic, Transylvanian, and Pienide basins (Plate 11; Smith and Spray, 1984; Sandulescu, 1984). Continued tectonic subsidence of the rift systems of Western Europe, combined with a cyclical rise in sea level (Vail et al., 1977; Hallam, 1978) brought about a link-up of the Arctic and the Tethys seas during the early Liassic. A first permanent seaway connecting these distinct faunal provinces was opened during the Hettangian via the Faeroe-Rockall Rift and the Irish Sea. This permitted the southward migration of Arctic faunas which, for the first time mixed with Tethys faunas during the Hettangian in the area of the English Channel (Ager, 1956; Mégnien, 1980).

During the Rhaetian and Hettangian, the Northwest European Basin and the area of the Channel–Paris Basin and the Franconian Platform were occupied by neritic seas that were connected with the Tethys shelves via relatively narrow, shallow passages through the Rhône Valley and the Western Approaches–Bay of Biscay rift zones. In this enclosed basin, the Belemnitidae evolved during the Hettangian and Sinemurian (Stevens, 1973a). Foundering of the northern North Sea area during the late Sinemurian and early Pliensbachian (Ager,

1956; Ziegler, 1982a), coupled with a progressive overstepping of basin margins in response to rising sea levels, resulted in the derestriction of marine communications between the Norwegian–Greenland Sea area and the basins of Northwest Europe. This facilitated a rapid faunal exchange between the Boreal and Tethys realms and the dispersal of the European Belemnites (Stevens, 1973a; Howarth, 1973; Cariou et al., 1985).

In the Bay of Biscay Rift and in the North and Central Atlantic domains evaporitic conditions gave way to a normal marine environment at the transition from the Hettangian to the Sinemurian and in the Atlas troughs during the Pliensbachian (Plates 27, 28). This was accompanied by the westward and southward migration of bathyal and outer neritic Tethys faunas that reached the Caribbean via the Central Atlantic during the Sinemurian, and the Pacific by the early Pliensbachian time (von Hillebrandt, 1981; Thierry, 1982). Subarctic faunal elements arrived in Iberia and in the Western Mediterranean during the Pliensbachian (Enay and Mangold, 1982; Cariou et al., 1985).

The establishment of normal marine circulation through the Western Mediterranean, the North and Central Atlantic, and Northwestern Europe saw vast carbonate platforms develop in areas dominated by the warm Tethys seas. Elsewhere, shelves dominated by the colder Arctic seas continued to be characterized by clastic sediments. In this context, it should be remembered that Early Jurassic glaciomarine deposits occur in northeastern Siberia (Epshteyn, 1978). In areas where the warm and more saline Tethys seas interfingered with the colder and less saline Arctic seas, repeated stagnant water density stratification developed. This gave rise to the deposition of important kerogenous oil source rocks such as the Hettangian and Toarcian oil shales of the Paris Basin and the southern parts of the Northwest European Basin (Plates 29, 30).

## Tethys–Central Atlantic Rift Systems

In Early Jurassic time, the Neo-Tethys sea-floor spreading axis propagated slowly northwestward resulting in the progressive opening of the Hellenic–Dinaric–Transylvanian–Pienide Ocean while sea-floor spreading in the Sub-Pelagonian Trough is thought to have ceased by the end of Triassic time (Sandulescu, 1984; Smith and Spray, 1984; Mountrakis, 1986; Debelmas and Sandulescu, 1987). This was accompanied by continued deformation of Cimmerian terrane (sensu stricto), the closure of the Black Sea back-arc ocean, and finally the collision of Cimmeria with the southern margin of Fennosarmatia (Plate 11). Resulting compressive stresses induced the deformation of the Moesian Platform (Ganev, 1974; Sandulescu, 1978, 1984; Burchfiel, 1978; Sengör et al., 1984), a second phase of partial inversion of the Donets Trough during the Pliensbachian (Konashov, 1980), and a further uplift of the Sarmatian Platform; from the latter, clastics were shed westward into the eastern parts of the Northwest European Basin (Ziegler, 1982a; Sengör 1977; Sengör et al., 1984; Dercourt et al., 1985, 1986).

During the Early Jurassic, the Central and West Mediterranean areas continued to be affected by rift and wrench tectonics. In the Alpine domain, rifting activity became increasingly important, affecting the South Alpine and Austro-Alpine realms as well as the Penninic, Helvetic, and Dauphinois areas. This led to the gradual individualization of the Briançonnais High separating the North and South Penninic troughs (Baudrimont and Dubois, 1977; Tollmann, 1978; Trümpy, 1980; Bernoulli,

1980; Schwab, 1981; Winterer and Bosselini, 1981; Lemoine, 1985; Lemoine et al., 1986; Lemoine and Trümpy, 1987).

Continued crustal extension and wrench movements along the western and northern margin of the Italio-Dinarid promontory went hand in hand with its further fragmentation. This is expressed by synsedimentary block-faulting and the development of a complex pattern of isolated carbonate platforms and intervening deeper marine basins. For example, the Lagonegro Trough, separating the Lucania–Campania and the Apulia-Karst platforms, continued to subside during the Early Jurassic while the Molise Trough probably came into evidence during this time. The schematic reconstruction, given in Plate 11, shows, according to currently favored interpretations, the Molise Trough as separating the Latium–Abruzzi Platform from the Apulia–Karst Platform and as extending northward into the Umbrian zone (d'Argenio and Alvarez, 1980; Bernoulli et al., 1979; Channell et al., 1979). To the west of the Lagonegro Trough, the Lucania–Campania (or Latium–Lucania) and the Alboran–Kabylia blocks formed an apparently coherent carbonate platform. They were flanked to the south by the differentially subsiding Imerese–Maghrebian–Gibraltar deeper water trough (Scandone, 1975a, 1975b; Channell et al., 1979; Wildi, 1983). In the latter, as well as in the Sahara Atlas, Middle Atlas, and High Atlas troughs, wrench movements induced repeated dike intrusions. These deeper water troughs were offset by carbonate platforms, fringing and partly covering the Morocco and Oran Meseta and the Ain M'Lila High (Plate 28). Similarly, the eastern parts of the Iberian Meseta–Ebro High block were covered by a carbonate platform.

In the axial parts of the Central Atlantic Rift, rapid crustal extension induced the development of deeper water conditions (Thierry, 1982) while reef-fringed carbonate banks were established on its tectonically still active margins (Plate 28; Figs. 20, 21) (Jansa and Wiedmann, 1982; Ruellan and Auzende, 1985). At the same time, the graben systems of the Appalachian Piedmont and on the shelf of the New England States and Nova Scotia (e.g., Newark and Fundy grabens) remained active as indicated by the continued accumulation of continental clastics and lacustrine shales. Differential subsidence of these basins was accompanied by repeated dike and sill intrusions and the extrusion of basaltic flows (Puffer et al., 1981; Manspeizer, 1982; Emery and Uchupi, 1984; Huchison et al., 1986). The occurrence of time-equivalent tholeiitic dike systems on the Sahara Platform indicates that very wide areas around the future plate margins were affected by tensional stresses and that the underlaying lithosphere was thermally destabilized (Bertrand and Westphal, 1977; see also Dooley and Smith, 1982). The megatectonic setting of the Triassic-Early Jurassic Central Atlantic graben system, which is superimposed on the Appalachian–Mauretanid fold belt, could have had some similarities with that of the Basin and Range province of the U.S. Cordillera, which has, however, a much higher frequency of grabens (Allmendinger et al, 1983; Bartley and Wernicke, 1984).

Also in the North Atlantic domain, continued crustal extension induced further differential subsidence of the graben systems on the Grand Banks and in the East Newfoundland Basin (Fig. 28) in which shallow marine carbonates and shales accumulated (Wade, 1981; McWhae, 1981; Meneley, 1986). In these areas, however, there is no evidence for significant Early Jurassic igneous activity. An exception are dikes that intruded along the Trans-Avalon lineament of easternmost Newfoundland (Hodyck and Hayatsu, 1980).

Early Jurassic differential subsidence of the West Portuguese Lusitania Basin (Fig. 27) is evident from well data that indicate a basinward shale-out of the near-shore carbonate banks. It is unknown whether deep water conditions were established already during the late Early Jurassic in the area of the Tagus Abyssal Plain and Flemish Basin (east flank Grand Banks; Fig. 28), corresponding to the axial parts of the North Atlantic Rift. Repeated intrusions along the Messejana dike system, transecting southwestern Iberia, were probably associated with regional tensional stresses affecting the North Atlantic borderlands (Schermerhorn et al., 1978).

## Norwegian–Greenland Sea and Northwest European Rift Systems

The rift systems of Western and Central Europe also remained active during the Early Jurassic. As during the Triassic, there is only very limited evidence for contemporaneous igneous activity. Neritic conditions were pervasive and there is no evidence for discrete rifting pulses. Continued uplifting of the southern parts of the Fennosarmatian Platform is reflected by a strong clastic influx from the east into the Northwest European Basin (Plates 11, 26, 29, 30).

Isopach maps of the Early Jurassic sediments (Ziegler, 1982a) illustrate that the Celtic Sea and Western Approaches grabens (Fig. 22), branching off to the north from the Bay of Biscay Rift, subsided more rapidly than did, for instance, the Viking and Central grabens in the North Sea (Fig. 18). Continued differential subsidence of the Polish Trough was accompanied by the uplift of its southwestern rift shoulder (Czerminski and Pajchlowa, 1975).

Seismic data, calibrated by wells, indicate that the Norwegian–Greenland Sea rift system and the major grabens of the Western Barents Sea remained active during the Early Jurassic (Figs. 10, 11, 35). This is confirmed by outcrop data from Central East Greenland and Svalbard. Deltaic complexes continued to build out from the basin margins into these graben systems in which neritic shales were deposited (Surlyk and Clemmensen, 1983; Rønnevik and Jacobsen, 1984; Steel and Worsley, 1984; Bukovics and Ziegler, 1985).

Regional subsidence of the Sverdrup Basin continued during the Early Jurassic. The massif influx of clastics from southern and southwestern sources slowed down, however, during the Pliensbachian; Toarcian to early Aalenian series are represented by shallow marine shales (Balkwill, 1978; Embry, 1982; Plate 26).

The northern margin of the Sverdrup Basin, and also the area of Alaska North Slope, were apparently tectonically relatively quiescent during the Early Jurassic. In the Wandel Sea Basin of northeastern Greenland, Late Triassic to Mid-Jurassic sediments are absent due to either nondeposition or erosion.

Overall, it appears that the rate of crustal extension across the Norwegian–Greenland Sea Rift slowed down somewhat during the Early Jurassic and that tectonic activity along the North Greenland–Sverdrup oblique-slip zone was at a commensurately lower level than during the Late Triassic. Moreover, gradual subsidence of the uplifted flanks of the Norwegian–Greenland Sea Rift may be reflected by the Early Jurassic decrease in clastic influx from southern sources into the Sverdrup Basin and onto the Barents Shelf as well as from northern sources into the Northwest European Basin.

## MID-JURASSIC CRUSTAL SEPARATION BETWEEN LAURASIA AND GONDWANA

During the Middle Jurassic crustal extension accelerated in the Arctic–North Atlantic and the Tethys–Central Atlantic Rift systems. Rifting culminated during the Bajocian–Bathonian in crustal separation and the onset of sea floor spreading in the Sub-Pannonian Trough, separating the Dacides and the Austro-Alpine domain, in the South Penninic–Piedmont–Ligurian Trough, the Alboran Basin, and in the Central Atlantic (Plate 12) (Tollmann, 1978; Frisch, 1979; Trümpy, 1980; Castellarin, 1980; Vegas and Banda, 1983; Winterer and Hinz, 1984; Emery and Uchupi, 1984; Sandulescu, 1984; Lemoine, 1985; Lemoine et al., 1986; Lemoine and Trümpy, 1987).

### Tethys–Central Atlantic Spreading Ridge-Transform System

During the Mid-Jurassic, rapid sea-floor spreading in the Eastern Mediterranean was coupled with strong compression along the northern margin of the Balkan–Turkish Cimmeria Terrane and its final welding to the southern border of Laurasia. This was accompanied by an extensive calc-alkaline magmatism and the shedding of clastics into northern foredeep basins (Sengör et al., 1984; Khain, 1984a; Dercourt et al., 1985, 1986).

The Middle Jurassic abandonment of the Intra-Carpathian Transylvanian–Pienid sea-floor spreading axis and the initiation of the Sub-Pannonian–Penninic sea-floor spreading axis was preceded by accelerated crustal extension in the Alpine domain. This is reflected by the progressive individualization of the Mid-Penninic–Briançonnais High and the North Penninic-Valais–Dauphinois Trough in which deep water conditions were established while rift margins became uplifted and subjected to erosion. It is uncertain whether crustal thinning in the Valais Trough had already proceeded to crustal failure and limited ses-floor spreading (Tollmann, 1978; Trümpy, 1980; Schwab, 1981; Sandulescu, 1984; Lemoine, 1985; Lemoine et al., 1986; Baudrimont and Dubois, 1977). The Lagonegro and Molise troughs, thought to separate the Latium–Lucania, the Abruzzi–Campania, and the Apulian platforms, presumably continued to subside differentially until crustal separation was achieved in the Piedmont–Ligurian–Alboran Basin (d'Argenio and Alvarez, 1980).

In the Central Atlantic, crustal separation was achieved during the early Bajocian (Emery and Uchupi, 1984). The rapidly westward propagating Neo-Tethys sea-floor spreading axis and the new Central Atlantic sea-floor spreading axis were linked by a sinistral shear zone transecting the Western Mediterranean. This shear zone, which presumably separated the Iberia and Corsica–Sardinia blocks to its north from the Alboran–Kabylia and the Latium–Lucania blocks to its south, extended westward through the Gibraltar Rift and linked up with the Southeast Newfoundland fracture zone marking the northern termination of the nascent Central Atlantic Ocean.

Crustal extension and later sea-floor spreading in the Central Atlantic and in the Piedmont–Ligurian Basin induced a sinistral translation between Laurasia and Africa whereby the Italo-Dinarid and probably also the Alboran–Kabylia and Latium–Campania blocks were still firmly attached to the latter (Laubscher and Bernoulli, 1977; Westphal et al., 1986). Commensurate transtensional movement along the Alboran–Iberian fracture zone presumably caused limited opening of the largely hypothetical Alboran oceanic basin; this postulate is principally based on geometric and paleomagnetic considerations.

For an alternate model, the reader is referred to Dercourt et al. (1985, 1986), who propose that the Alboran–Kabylia block remained attached to Iberia and thus formed part of the Laurasian plate. This model implies that significant sea-floor spreading had occurred in the Lagonegro Trough, the southern termination of which would have to be linked with the northern termination of the Central Atlantic sea-floor spreading axis via the Maghrebian–Gibraltar fracture zone (Ricou et al., 1986).

Following the establishment of this new plate boundary in the Central and Western Mediterranean, the evolution of areas bordering these rapidly opening oceanic basins began to subside according to the pattern of passive margins whereby upward-shoaling Bahamian-type carbonate platforms were interspaced by submarine plateaux, characterized by condensed sequences, and deep water troughs in which radiolarian cherts and shales accumulated (Bernoulli and Jenkyns, 1974; Bernoulli et al., 1979; Argyriadis et al., 1980; Castellarin, 1980; Jenkyns, 1980; Winterer and Bosellini, 1981; Bernoulli, 1984; De Wever and Dercourt, 1985; Lemoine et al., 1986). On the Apulian Platform, the existing topography became consolidated with carbonate platforms remaining stable as a consequence of a balance between sedimentation and subsidence rates and sea-level fluctuations (Abbate et al., 1970; Pieri, 1975; Channell et al., 1979).

Sinistral movements along the Gibraltar fracture zone, across which Iberia and North Africa were not yet fully decoupled, induced wrench deformations along preexisting fault zones. This is reflected by multiple intrusions along the some 500 km long Messejana dolerite dike system of southwestern Iberia (Schermerhorn et al., 1978; Schott et al., 1981) and by volcanic activity in the external Betic Cordillera (Azema et al., 1979). Similarly, extrusions of Mid-Jurassic alkaline volcanics in the Middle and High Atlas troughs are thought to be related to wrench deformations (Plate 28) (Manspeizer et al., 1978; Laville and Harmand, 1982). At the same time, a second shear zone, branching off from the Gibraltar fracture zone, probably developed between the Alboran–Kabylia Block and North Africa in the area of the Maghrebian Trough. While shallow water conditions were established during the Middle Jurassic in the Atlas and Sahara troughs, continued volcanic activity along the Malta Escarpment is taken as an indication for persistent differential subsidence of the Ionian Sea Basin (Stets and Wurster, 1982; Escarmed, 1982; Wildi, 1983; Dercourt et al., 1985, 1986).

In the Central Atlantic, crustal separation was achieved during the early Bajocian (Emery and Uchupi, 1984). This was apparently preceded and accompanied by regional doming of the areas flanking the axial parts of the Central Atlantic rift zone. This concept is supported by the geometry of the Triassic–Early Jurassic rift basins of the Appalachians, the adjacent Piedmont and offshore areas, and also the Fundy Graben of Nova Scotia and New Brunswick. These basins apparently were uplifted during the latest Early and early Middle Jurassic and were subjected to deep truncation.

Reflection seismic data indicate that 2000–3000 m of sediments were removed from these basins during this late Early to Middle Jurassic erosional phase. Contemporaneous wrench deformations are also evident and can be related to a last phase of crustal extension preceding the opening of the Central Atlantic oceanic basin (see, e.g., Hutchison et al., 1986).

Uplift of areas flanking the axial parts of the Central Atlantic rift was probably caused by a thermally induced upward displacement of the asthenosphere–lithosphere boundary immediately prior to and during crustal separation in the Central Atlantic and during the earliest phases of sea-floor spreading. Moreover, convective mantle processes may have been accompanied by the ductile lateral transfer of lower crustal material from the axial rift zone toward the rift flanks (see Moretti and Pinet, 1987). Such a process could explain the lack of postrifting subsidence of the Fundy Graben and the Newark Basin, for example.

Alternatively, it may be assumed that upper crustal extension in marginal grabens was transferred along intracrustal detachment zones to the axial parts of the Central Atlantic rift system where these shear zones dipped to the Moho level. During the rifting stage tectonic unloading of the marginal areas by upper crustal extension and the lack of commensurate lower crustal thinning may explain their isostatic uplift and their limited post rifting subsidence (see Wernicke, 1981, 1985; Wernicke and Burchfiel, 1982; Ussami et al., 1986).

It is likely that both of the processes referred to above may have contributed to the latest Early and Mid-Jurassic development of the graben systems flanking the Central Atlantic rift zone.

Following the early Bajocian crustal separation in the Central Atlantic, basins located on the adjacent North American and African shelves became tectonically inactive and their further evolution was governed by lithospheric cooling and contraction, sedimentary loading, and sea-level fluctuations (Watts and Steckler, 1981; Keen et al., 1981; Hardenbol et al., 1981). Carbonate banks established on the Moroccan Shelf kept balance with subsidence and sea-level fluctuations during the Middle and Late Jurassic (Fig. 24). Similar carbonate shelves on the Nova Scotia Shelf give way northward to the late Bajocian–early Bathonian Mohikan delta. In the same area, deposition of shallow water carbonates and shales resumed, however, during the late Mid-Jurassic and later Jurassic (Plate 28; Fig. 25; Given, 1977; Jansa and Wade, 1975; Jansa, 1981; Jansa and Wiedmann, 1982).

## North Atlantic Area

In the North Atlantic domain, in which crustal separation was only achieved during the late Neocomian and early Aptian (Sullivan, 1983; Masson and Miles, 1984), crustal extension persisted during the Mid-Jurassic as illustrated by the sedimentary record of the Lusitania Basin and the basins of the Newfoundland Shelf.

During the Middle Jurassic, carbonate and shale series accumulated in the differentially subsiding South and North Whale and Horseshoe grabens of the southern Grand Banks area (Fig. 26; Wade, 1981) and in the grabens of the East Newfoundland Basin (Fig. 28), while carbonates prevailed in the Lusitania Basin (Fig. 27; Plate 28). Little can be said about the Middle Jurassic evolution of the axial parts of the North Atlantic Rift, corresponding to the Tagus and Flemish basins, for want of stratigraphic control. These basins are now characterized by a drastically thinned continental crust that is overlain by relatively thick sediments (Masson and Miles, 1984; Olivet et al., 1984). Thus, it is uncertain whether these areas had foundered already during the Middle Jurassic to considerable depth in response to intense crustal attenuation as suggested in Plate 12.

Subsurface data indicate that the Bay of Biscay Rift and the Western Approaches, Celtic Sea, and Porcupine grabens continued to subside differentially during the Middle Jurassic (Plate 27). In these basins, shallow water carbonates and shales, containing minor amounts of sands, accumulated essentially in continuity with Early Jurassic strata. Crustal distension in the Celtic Sea–Western Approaches area was coupled with increased tectonic activity along a system of wrench faults extending into the Paris Basin. Igneous activity in the general area was restricted to a few Bathonian sills in the Fastnet Basin (southeast extension of Celtic Sea Trough) and the Bathonian Fuller's Earth of southwestern England, which cannot be related to a discrete volcanic center (Ziegler, 1982a). Although not supported by hard evidence, it is assumed that the Rockall Rift also subsided differentially during the Middle Jurassic.

## North Sea Rift Dome

The Mid-Jurassic evolution of the Western Shelf area sharply contrasts with that of the North Sea, where accelerated crustal extension was accompanied by the late Aalenian and Bajocian upwarping of a large rift dome (Plate 12). This dome was centered over the Central Graben and embraced much of Scotland and Denmark. During its uplift, an important volcanic complex developed at the triple-junction between the Viking, Central, and Moray Firth rifts with subsidiary volcanic centers occurring in the Viking Graben and in the Horda Basin (Plate 12). Upwarping of this dome was probably associated with the intrusion of asthenospheric material into the upper mantle, at the crust–mantle boundary, and possibly also into the lower crust. Over the crestal parts of this thermally uplifted dome, which had a structural relief of 2000–3000 m, Mesozoic and in part also Permian strata became deeply truncated by subaerial ero-

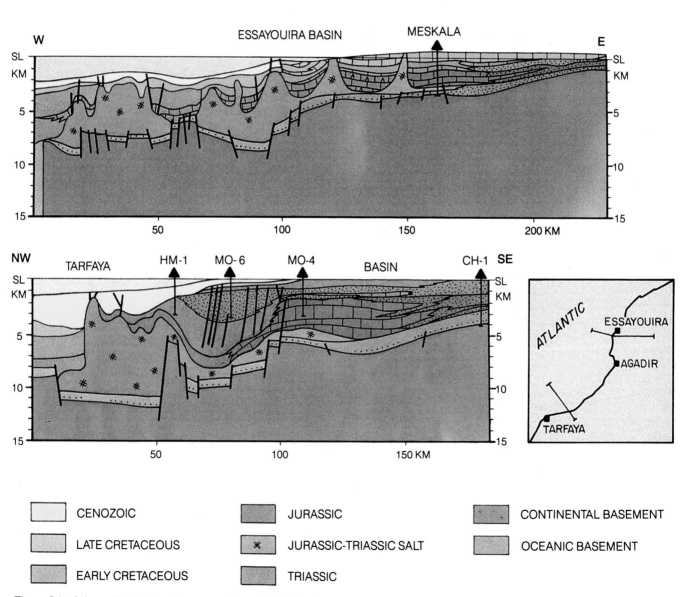

*Figure 24—Schematic structural cross sections of the Atlantic Shelf, Morocco.*

sion (Plate 30; Fig. 18). Erosion products were shed into the adjacent, continuously subsiding basins where they were deposited in major deltaic complexes (Ziegler, 1982a). These sands form the reservoirs of major oil accumulations particularly in the Viking Graben of the northern North Sea (Ziegler, 1980; Brown, 1984; Karlsson, 1986).

In the axial parts of the Central Graben, late Bajocian and Bathonian continental series unconformably overlie locally Early Jurassic, in general deeply truncated Triassic, and in some areas even Late Permian, strata. This indicates that the rate of thermal uplift of the Central North Sea rift dome exceeded the contemporaneous subsidence rate of the Central Graben, induced by continued crustal extension, as evident, for instance, in the northern parts of the Viking Graben (Ziegler, 1982a). An analogous development is seen in the Miocene ther-

mal uplift of the northern Rhine Graben area (see Chapter 9).

The uplift of the North Sea rift dome, in combination with the Aalenian–Bajocian low stand in sea level (Hallam, 1978; Vail and Todd, 1981), caused the interruption of open marine connections between the Arctic and Tethys seas. This is reflected by the late Bajocian and Bathonian break in the faunal exchange between these distinct biogeographical provinces (Stevens, 1973a; Ager, 1975; Callomon, 1979; Mégnien, 1980; Enay and Mangold, 1982; Cariou et al., 1985). During the late Bathonian and Callovian, however, the Central North Sea rift dome began to subside gradually, presumably in response to the combined effects of "subcrustal erosion," cooling of the earlier introduced thermal anomaly, and possibly phase changes at the crust–mantle boundary (see Chapter 10).

Rising sea levels, combined with continued crustal extension

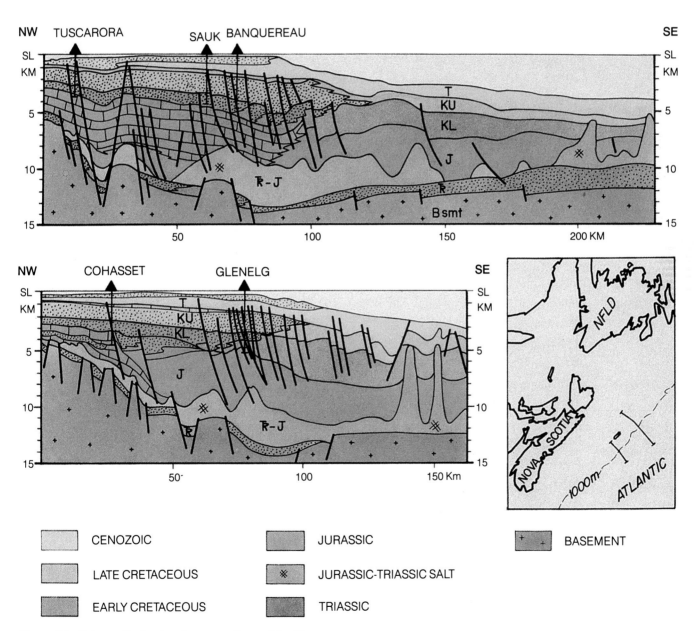

*Figure 25—Schematic structural cross sections of the Nova Scotia Shelf. After Friedenreich (1981), Shell Canada.*

inducing further subsidence of the Northwest European rift systems, led during the Callovian to the reopening of seaways connecting the Tethys and the Arctic seas via the North Sea area and the Faeroe–Rockall Rift. Resumption of the faunal exchange between these biogeographical provinces is reflected by the Callovian appearance of Tethys faunas in Eastern Greenland and of boreal ammonites and belemnites in Iberia and North Africa (Stevens, 1973a; Cariou, 1973; Ager, 1974; Callomon and Birkelund, 1980; Thierry, 1982). At the same time, ammonites of a Pacific affinity appeared for the first time in the Tethys domain and in Western Europe (Cariou et al., 1985), indicating that free water circulation was now established through the gradually opening Central Atlantic Ocean and the Gulf of Mexico.

Unlike the Central North Sea Rift, the Polish Trough and the Norwegian–Greenland Sea Rift continued to subside during the Middle Jurassic without any evidence for thermal doming and volcanism.

## Norwegian–Greenland Sea Rift and Arctic Basins

Throughout the Norwegian–Greenland Sea Rift, on the Barents Shelf, and in the Sverdrup Basin, the indicated early Bajocian low stand in sea level is reflected by the rapid progradation of deltaic complexes. These form the reservoirs of major hydrocarbon accumulations on the Mid-Norway Shelf and also in the southern Barents Sea (Plates 26, 27).

In the Mid-Norway Basin, regressive Middle Jurassic sands were deposited in stratigraphic continuity with Early Jurassic shaly series. Syndepositional faulting is evident and there are indications that the leading edges of some of the major rotational fault blocks became uplifted and were the source of local clastic supply (Bukovics and Ziegler, 1985).

Also in East Greenland, major half-grabens, controlled by listric faults, continued to subside differentially during the Middle Jurassic. After a regional hiatus, corresponding to the Aalenian,

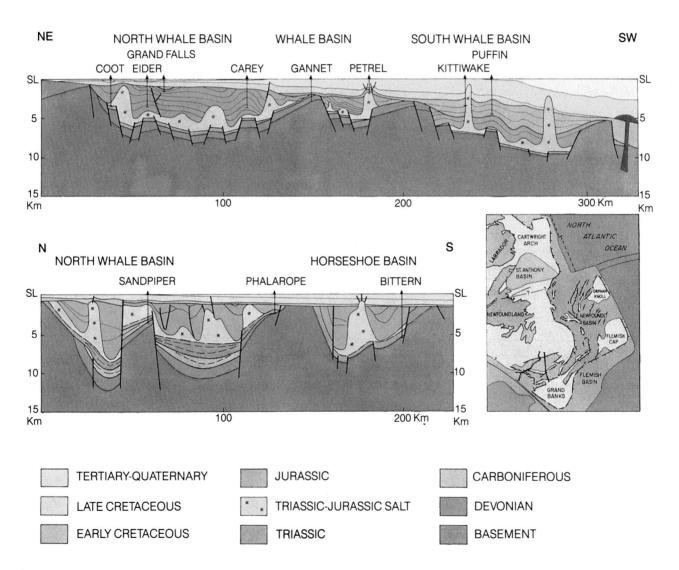

*Figure 26—Schematic structural cross sections of the Southern Grand Banks. After Levesque (1986) Shell Canada; Wade (1981).*

sedimentation resumed whereby the Early Jurassic basin margins were significantly overstepped in a northward direction. This may be taken as evidence for a northward propagation of rifting activity (Surlyk, 1977a, 1977b, 1978; Surlyk and Clemmensen, 1983).

In the northern Barents Sea, tectonic activity was at a moderate level during the Middle Jurassic with thermal subsidence of the Loppa Ridge apparently continuing. Temporary uplift of western Svalbard during the Bajocian and Bathonian can be related to movements along the Svalbard–North Greenland oblique-slip zone. On the other hand, the continued influx of clastics from northeastern sources probably reflects further uplift of the Lomonosov High and tectonic activity in the Makarov Rift (Steel and Worsley, 1984).

In the Sverdrup Basin, the late Aalenian regression was followed by a Bajocian transgression and the deposition of shallow marine shales reflecting slow basin subsidence under a regime of diminished clastic influx (Balkwill, 1978; Embry, 1982). The northern margins of the Sverdrup Basin was apparently tectonically quiescent during the Middle Jurassic while limited extension governed the evolution of the Alaska North Slope (Hubbard et al., 1987). This suggests that the bulk of tensional strain across the Norwegian Greenland Sea Rift was translated by the North Greenland–Svalbard oblique-slip zone into the largely hypothetical Makarov rift zone located between the Lomonosov High and the New Siberian Islands Block.

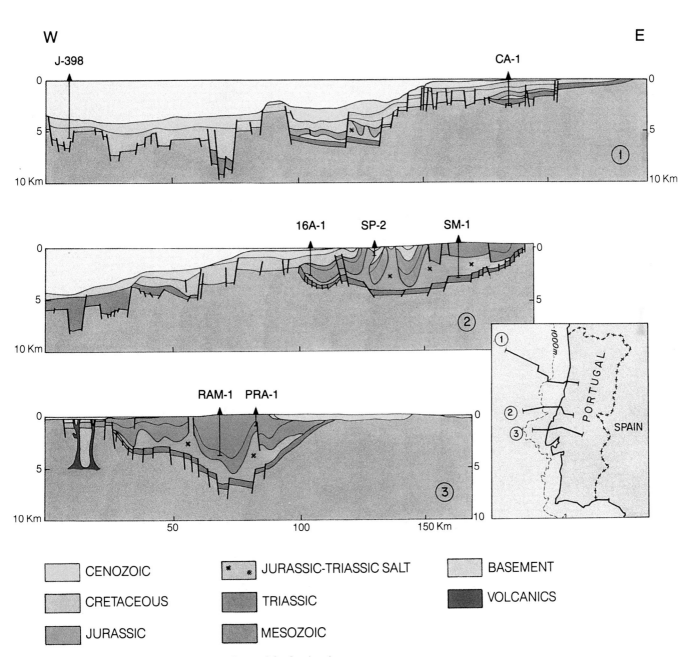

*Figure 27—Schematic structural cross sections of the Lusitania Basin, Portugal.*

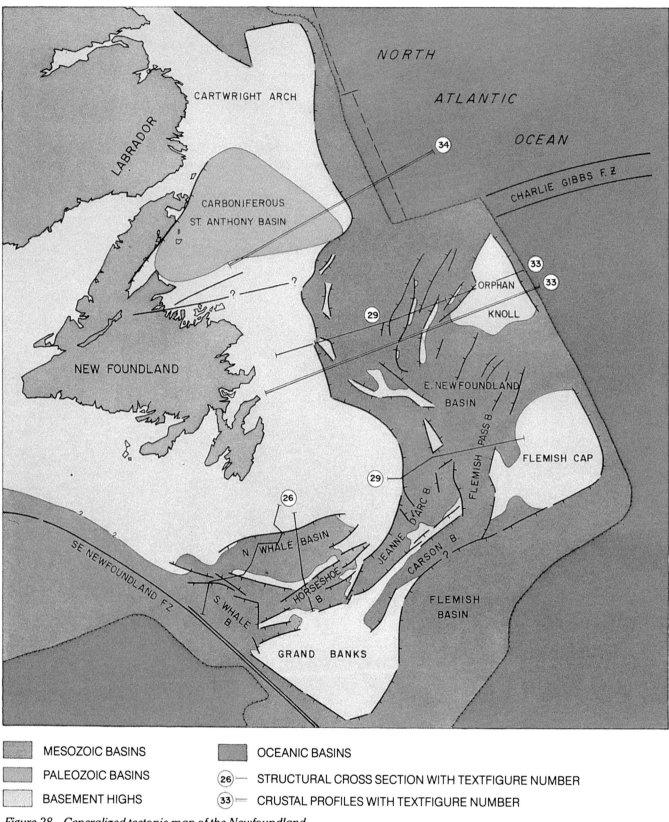

MESOZOIC BASINS

PALEOZOIC BASINS

BASEMENT HIGHS

OCEANIC BASINS

(26)— STRUCTURAL CROSS SECTION WITH TEXTFIGURE NUMBER

(33)═ CRUSTAL PROFILES WITH TEXTFIGURE NUMBER

*Figure 28—Generalized tectonic map of the Newfoundland Shelf. After Shell Canada.*

## Summary

Summing up, the Middle Jurassic was a period of fundamental changes in the megatectonic and paleogeographic setting of the Arctic–Central Atlantic and Tethys domains. With the development of a distinct plate boundary between Africa and Laurasia, a major step was achieved in the disintegration of Pangea. Furthermore, following crustal separation in the Western and Central Mediterranean and the Central Atlantic, stress regimes related to continued crustal extension across the Arctic–North Atlantic rift system now governed exclusively the evolution of its North American and European borderlands.

# CHAPTER 6
## LATE JURASSIC–EARLY CRETACEOUS CENTRAL ATLANTIC SEA-FLOOR SPREADING, CLOSURE OF NEO-TETHYS, AND OPENING OF CANADA BASIN

## INTRODUCTION

The Mid-Jurassic development of a sea-floor spreading axis in the Central Atlantic marked the onset of a new kinematic regime in the Atlantic–Tethys domain, and with this a new chapter commenced in the break-up history of Pangea.

As discussed in Chapter 5, the initial phase of the Pangea break-up, spanning Permian to Mid-Jurassic times, was governed by the southward propagation of the Arctic–North Atlantic and the westward propagation of the Tethys rift systems. It peaked in the development of the Tethys and the Central Atlantic sea-floor spreading axes that linked-up via the Western Mediterranean transform fault system. In contrast, the post-Mid-Jurassic phases of the Atlantic–Tethys plate reorganization were governed by the evolution of the Central Atlantic sea-floor spreading axis and its stepwise northward propagation; this was paralleled by the stepwise opening of the South Atlantic Ocean. The evolution of the Central Atlantic sea-floor spreading axis is suggestive of its association with a major upwelling asthenospheric convective cell that had slowly developed during the Triassic and Early Jurassic.

During the Late Jurassic and Early Cretaceous, the progressive opening of the Central Atlantic caused a major sinistral translation between Africa and Laurasia (Olivet et al., 1984; Livermore and Smith, 1985). This was coupled with the transtensional opening of oceanic basins in the Western Mediterranean domain and a gradual closure of the Dinaric–Hellenic ocean, culminating during the earliest Cretaceous in the collision of the leading edge of the Italo-Dinarid promontory with the southern margin of Fermosarmatia (Plate 13). This collision marked the onset of the Alpine orogeny. During the Early Cretaceous, continued opening of the Central Atlantic and commensurate sinistral translations between Africa and Laurasia went hand in hand with the eastward and westward propagation of the early Alpine collision front, the counterclockwise rotation of the Italo-Dinarid promontory and its partial decoupling from Africa (Plate 14; Chapters 6 and 7).

In the Arctic–North Atlantic rift zone, crustal extension persisted until crustal separation was achieved in its different parts during the Cretaceous and early Cenozoic. In the North Atlantic area, increased tectonic activity, accompanied by rift propagation into the Labrador Sea, preceded the northward propagation of the Central Atlantic sea-floor spreading axis and the intra-Aptian separation of the Iberian microcontinent from Laurasia (see *Opening of the North Atlantic,* this chapter).

Furthermore, the stress system governing the evolution of Northwest Europe changed fundamentally as a consequence of Mid-Jurassic crustal separation in the Western and Central Mediterranean. This is expressed by the abandonment of northeast–southwest-oriented grabens and troughs and the development of new northwest–southeast-trending wrench systems. This late Middle to Late Jurassic "polarization" of the Northwest European rift system indicates that its further evolution was now exclusively governed by stresses related to continued crustal extension across the Arctic–North Atlantic megarift (Ziegler, 1982a; see *Norwegian–Greenland Sea Rift System,* this chapter).

In the Arctic domain, a relatively short rifting phase preceded the Valanginian crustal separation between Laurasia, the Alaska–Chukchi–Chukotka and New Siberian Islands blocks; this was followed by the opening of the oceanic Canada Basin (see *Opening of the Canada Basin,* this chapter).

During the Late Jurassic, the Arctic and Tethys seas were in open communication with each other via the Norwegian–Greenland Sea Rift and the basins of Western and Central Europe (Plate 13). This facilitated a faunal exchange that was only restrained by the vast, shallow carbonate platforms occupying the Tethys shelves (Enay and Mangold, 1982; Enay et al., 1982; Cariou et al., 1985). Although there is paleogeographic evidence for a Neocomian constriction of seaways linking the Canada Basin and the Barents Shelf, the exchange of faunas between the Arctic and Atlantic–Mediterranean provinces continued, mainly via the rift systems of the North Atlantic and the Norwegian–Greenland Sea (Plate 10; Rawson, 1973; Birkelund and Perch-Nielsen, 1976). These tectonically induced constrictions became, however, intensified during the Aptian and Albian, and by late Albian time boreal faunas were completely confined to the Arctic domain (Plate 15; Casey and Rawson, 1973; Owen, 1973; Stevens, 1973b).

The strong tectonoeustatic sea-level fluctuations, which occurred during the Late Jurassic and Early Cretaceous (Vail et al., 1977; Hallam, 1978; Haq et al., 1987), had an important overprinting effect on sedimentation patterns, and it is often difficult to distinguish between their effects and those induced by local tectonics. Glacioeustatic contributions to the observed relative sea-level changes can, however, not be excluded in view of the sedimentary record of the Arctic areas (Epshteyn, 1978; Brandt, 1986; see also Bird, 1986).

## TETHYS SHEAR AND EARLY ALPINE OROGENY

Following crustal separation at about 180 Ma the Central Atlantic Ocean opened during the Late Jurassic at the rapid rate of some 3.4 cm/year. During the Early Cretaceous, spreading rates decreased, however, to some 2.3 cm/year (Emery and Uchupi, 1984; Olivet et al., 1984; see also Savostin et al., 1986).

### Late Jurassic Evolution of the Tethys Domain

The rapid opening of the Central Atlantic was accompanied by a commensurate sinistral translation of Africa relative to Europe whereby during the Late Jurassic the bulk of these movements was taken up by transtensional deformations in the Alboran and Ligurian–Piedmont–South Penninic Ocean (Plate 13). Paleomagnetic data indicate that the Italo-Dinarid promontory, including the Lucania–Campania block and possibly also the Alboran–Kabylia block, moved essentially in unison with Africa (van den Berg, 1979; van den Berg and Zijderveld, 1982; Horner and Freeman, 1983; Westphal et al., 1986). This suggests that during the Late Jurassic only minor movements occurred along the Maghrebian transform zone. Contemporaneous wrench deformations, however, reactivated the fault systems of the Atlas troughs and induced the intrusion of basic plutons (Plate 28; Harmand and Laville, 1983) while alluvial fans prograded from the Sahara Platform onto the carbonate shelves flanking the Tethys (Stets and Wurster, 1982; Wildi, 1983). In the external Betic Cordillera, transtensional deformations associated with minor volcanic activity accompanied the foundering of the southeastern shelves of Iberia (Azema et al., 1979). In the Alpine domain, the Valais–North Penninic–Intra-Carpathian Trough subsided differentially during the Late

Jurassic in response to transtensional movements that paralleled the rapid opening of the Ligurian–Piedmont–South Penninic Ocean. In this basin the formation of oceanic crust is stratigraphically dated as Late Jurassic (Trümpy, 1980; Durand-Delga and Fontboté, 1980; Lemoine, 1985; De Wever and Dercourt, 1985; Weissert and Bernoulli, 1985; Lemoine et al., 1986). At the same time, limited sea-floor spreading took place in the northern part of the Lagonegro Trough (Beccaluva and Piccardo, 1978), suggesting that differential movements occurred between the Lucania–Campania Platform and the composite Latium–Abruzzi–Apulia–Karst Block.

During the Late Jurassic, the northern shelves of the Tethys were occupied by vast, upward-shallowing carbonate platforms. These flanked the deep water troughs of the Dauphinois and the Penninic zone in which pelagic series accumulated, containing mass flow deposits derived from adjacent carbonate platforms such as the Briançonnais High. Also the Lucania–Campania, the Latium–Abruzzi, Apulia, Karst, and Pelagonia–Golija blocks continued to be occupied by stable carbonate platforms while the Trento and Julia blocks became drowned. Submarine plateaux, such as the Austro-Alpine domain, and intervening troughs were generally sediment starved as reflected by the deposition of condensed series, in part containing radiolarites (Abbate et al., 1970; Kälin and Trümpy, 1977; Channell et al., 1979; d'Argenio et al., 1980; Trümpy, 1980; Winterer and Bosellini, 1981; De Wever and Dercourt, 1985; Lemoine et al., 1986).

The Late Jurassic translation of Africa and the Italo-Dinarid promontory induced a gradual narrowing of the Dinaric–Hellenic Ocean in which sea-floor spreading presumably ceased during the Late Jurassic. Compressional deformations are indeed evident along the western and eastern margin of the Pelagonia–Golija microcontinent onto which ophiolites were obducted during the Late Jurassic and at the transition from the Jurassic to the Cretaceous, respectively (Smith and Spray, 1984). Furthermore, there is evidence for the initiation of a subduction zone along the Balkan–Rhodope (Serbo-Macedonian) margin of the Dinaric–Hellenic Ocean (Burchfiel, 1980; Bonneau, 1982; Dercourt et al., 1985; Mountrakis, 1986). At the same time, compressional deformation of Cimmeria (sensu stricto) and its foreland continued with flysch being deposited in the foredeep flanking the Moesian carbonate platform (Foose and Manheim, 1975; Sandulescu, 1978; Sengör, 1984; Sengör et al., 1984; see also Milanovsky et al., 1984). During the later part of the Late Jurassic, alkaline volcanic activity in the Lesser Caucasus area testifies to a phase of back-arc extension that persisted through Early Cretaceous times (Zonnenshain and Le Pichon, 1986).

This suggests that the Late Jurassic rapid opening of the Central Atlantic and the ensuing translation of Laurasia relative to the African plate, including the Italo-Dinarid promontory, induced space constraints in the Central and Eastern Mediterranean domain where they were compensated by the gradual closure of the Dinaric–Hellenic Basin and the subduction/partial obduction of its oceanic crust. This indicates that in the Dinaric–Hellenic Ocean compressional stresses developing as a consequence of sinistral translations between Laurasia and Africa were able to overpower the western parts of the Tethys sea-floor spreading axis, causing its rapid decay. Conversely, it may be speculated that the decay of the western parts of the Tethys sea-floor spreading axis facilitated the rapid opening of the Central Atlantic Ocean. (This is a classical "chicken and egg" question.)

## Early Cretaceous Collision of the Italo-Dinard Promontory with the South European Margin

During the Early Cretaceous, the Pelagonia–Golija Block and the leading edge of the Italo-Dinarid promontory of Africa collided with the Balkan–Rhodope subduction zone (Plate 14). Closure of the Dinaric–Hellenic Ocean along the Vardar suture zone was accompanied by the emplacement of major nappe systems in the internal Dinarides and Hellenides. At the same time, the sub-Pannonian oceanic zone became closed, and deformation of the Dacides Block commenced (Aubouin, 1973; Debelmas et al., 1980; D'Argenio and Alvarez, 1980; Burchfiel, 1980; Mountrakis, 1986; Radulescu and Sandulescu, 1980; Sandulescu, 1984; Dercourt et al., 1986). This collisional event marked the onset of the Himalayan-type Alpine orogeny in this area.

During the Early Cretaceous, the Italo-Dinarid Block, which, due to its collision with Europe, was now no longer able to follow the relative eastward drift of Africa, apparently became partly decoupled from the latter and began to rotate in a counterclockwise direction (van den Berg, 1979; Horner and Freeman, 1983; Westphal et al., 1986). This was accompanied by the gradual closure of Late Jurassic–earliest Cretaceous oceanic basins and the propagation of the Alpine collision front into the area of the Pontides and also into the Carpathians and the Eastern and Central Alps. This is evident by the occurrence of the compressional deformations in the frontal parts of the Austro-Alpine and Penninic nappes and also in the central East Carpathian nappes as well as by the accumulation of extensive synorogenic flysch deposits. In combination with the occurrence of high pressure–low temperature metamorphics in the Central and Eastern Alps and in the Carpathians, this suggests that transtensional opening of the South Penninic Ocean had ceased during the Early Cretaceous. During the Aptian–Albian, development of a south-dipping subduction system accompanied the gradual closure and subduction of the South Penninic Ocean and the development of the first nappe systems (Plate 15; Slazka, 1976; Tollmann, 1978; Frisch, 1979; Faupl et al., 1980; Geyssant, 1980; Homewood et al., 1980; Trümpy, 1980, 1982; Gillet et al., 1986; Debelmas and Sandulescu, 1987).

In the Ligurian–Piedmont Ocean, the production of new oceanic crust under a transtensional tectonic regime decreased at the transition from the Jurassic to the Cretaceous. The extrusion of ophiolitic material continued, however, into the Aptian and Albian (Durand-Delgas and Fontboté, 1980; Trümpy, 1980; Lemoine et al., 1986) and thus illustrates that the Alboran–Piedmont transform system had remained active during this time.

The model given in Plates 14 and 15 for the Early Cretaceous evolution of the Mediterranean area suggests that movements along the Alboran–Piedmont transform zone had drastically decreased during the later parts of the Early Cretaceous and that the rotation of the Italo-Dinarid promontory was accompanied by its partial decoupling from northern Africa along a complex sinistral wrench-fault system extending from Gibraltar eastward through the Ionian Sea into the Eastern Mediterranean area, referred to as the Gibraltar–Maghrebian–South Anatolian fracture zone. For geometric reasons, it is assumed that during its counterclockwise rotation the Italo-Dinarid block became internally deformed by wrench movements, presumably along such preexisting fault systems as those of the Lagonegro and Molise troughs. Such deformations are, however, difficult to establish in view of the severe tectonic overprinting of these areas during the Alpine orogeny (see Chapters 7 and 9).

During the Early Cretaceous, carbonate platforms continued to occupy the stable Lucania–Campania, Latium–Abruzzi, Apulia, Karst, and Anatolia–Taurid platforms with pelagic sedimentation characterizing the intervening submarine plateaux and troughs (Channell et al., 1979; D'Argenio et al., 1980; D'Argenio and Alvarez, 1980).

The Azores fracture zone, delimiting the Central Atlantic Ocean to the north, extended eastward into the Gibraltar–Maghrebian–South Anatolian fracture zone. With the Italo-Dinarid promontory, and probably also the Alboran–Kabylia block, lagging behind the continued relative eastward drift of Africa during the Early Cretaceous, this fracture zone developed into an important transform plate boundary (Plates 14, 15). In the Eastern Mediterranean, this boundary was probably diffuse as reflected by the transtensional opening of limited oceanic basins in the Ionian Sea and along the South Anatolian zone (Michard et al., 1984; Poisson, 1984; Delaloye and Wagner, 1984; Dercourt et al., 1986).

In the Western Mediterranean area, latest Jurassic and Early Cretaceous wrench deformations along the Gibraltar–Maghrebian transform zone were accompanied by the extrusion of pillow lavas in the Maghrebian Trough and alkaline volcanic activity in the Atlas (Plate 28; Durand-Delgas and Fontboté, 1980; Laville and Harmand, 1982; Harmand and Laville, 1983). Wrench-induced reactivation of the Atlas troughs and of the Oran and Morocco Mesetas is reflected by the Neocomian shedding of clastics into the Maghrebian Trough from southern sources. Transpressional deformations may be held responsible for the Aptian–Albian uplift of the Alboran–Kabylia block, the erosion of its sedimentary cover, and the shedding of clastics into the Maghrebian Trough from northern sources (Plate 15; Durand-Delgas and Fontboté, 1980; Stets and Wurster, 1981, 1982; Wildi, 1983).

In summary, the Late Jurassic and Early Cretaceous evolution of the Mediterranean area was governed by the sinistral translation between Africa and Laurasia that was caused by the opening of the Central Atlantic. The resulting earliest Cretaceous oblique, passive collision of the Italo-Dinarid promontory, including the Austro-Alpine domain, with the southern margin of Europe and its ensuing partial decoupling from Africa and subsequent rotation, marked the onset of the Alpine orogenic cycle. This reflects a fundamental change in the plate tectonic setting of the Mediterranean domain.

# OPENING OF THE NORTH ATLANTIC

Following the Mid-Jurassic crustal separation between Africa and North America, sea-floor spreading remained confined to the Central Atlantic for some 50 Ma while rifting activity persisted and accelerated in the North Atlantic domain.

The analysis of sea-floor magnetic anomalies indicates that the Central Atlantic sea-floor spreading axis propagated during the Neocomian into the southern part of the North Atlantic. This involved a first phase of counterclockwise rotation of the Iberian block. With the early Aptian crustal separation between Galicia Bank and Flemish Cap and in the Bay of Biscay, the Iberian microcontinent became isolated from Laurasia (Plate 15). During the middle Aptian to Santonian–early Campanian, sea-floor spreading in the Bay of Biscay and in the North Atlantic induced a second phase of counterclockwise rotation of Iberia

and at the same time its sinistral translation relative to mainland Europe (Plate 16; Masson and Miles, 1984; Olivet et al., 1984).

In middle Albian time, crustal separation was achieved between the Goban Spur and Flemish Cap, the Porcupine Bank and Orphan Knoll, and probably also in the southern parts of the Rockall Trough (Roberts et al., 1981b; Olivet et al., 1984; Masson et al., 1985).

The stratigraphic record of sedimentary basins flanking the North Atlantic, the Bay of Biscay, and the Labrador Sea is summarized in Plates 27 and 28. These diagrams illustrate the correlation of Late Jurassic and Early Cretaceous depositional cycles and tectonic events recognized in these basins.

## North Central Atlantic Shelves

The Late Jurassic and Early Cretaceous evolution of the Moroccan and Nova Scotia shelves, flanking the gradually opening Central Atlantic, essentially followed the pattern of classical passive margins. There is also evidence, however, that these areas were marginally affected by the transform movements along the Azores fracture zone and subsidiary fracture zones in the northern parts of the Central Atlantic.

On the Moroccan Shelf, reef fringed carbonate platforms, established already during the Early Jurassic, kept balance with subsidence rates and eustatically rising sea levels during the Middle and Late Jurassic (Fig. 24). During the late Berriasian–Valanginian to late Albian, a strong influx of clastics from the hinterland dominated sedimentation on these shelves (Jansa and Wiedmann, 1982; Jansa et al., 1984; Winterer and Hinz, 1984). This is probably the combined effect of their thermal downwarping in response to lithospheric cooling of the intra-Berriasian and early Aptian low stands in sea level (Vail et al., 1977) and also of wrench-induced deformation of the Atlas troughs (see above). The reported contemporaneous tensional reactivation of the fault systems of the Mazagan Plateau (northwest Moroccan shelf, Ruellan and Auzende, 1985) may be related to transtensional stresses developing between the Azores and South Atlas fracture zones. In the Essaouira and Tarfaya basins, the Jurassic and Early Cretaceous sedimentary outbuilding of the shelf was accompanied by diapirism of the Late Triassic–earliest Jurassic halites (Fig. 20).

On the Nova Scotia Shelf, the carbonate depositional regime of the Late Jurassic became suppressed during the Berriasian by a massive influx of clastics that persisted until the late Albian (Fig. 25; Jansa and Wade, 1975; Wade, 1981; Jansa and Wiedmann, 1982; Grant et al., 1986). This change in the paleogeographic setting of the Nova Scotia Shelf can only partly be related to its subsidence pattern and the intra-Berriasian and Aptian low stand in sea level. Early Cretaceous basaltic extrusions, ranging in age between 125 and 102 Ma, occur in the Orpheus Graben, which is superimposed on the Chedabukto fault zone. This indicates that this long-standing geofracture became repeatedly reactivated in conjunction with movements along the Azores transform fault zone (Jansa and Pe-Piper, 1985) and intensified rifting activity in the North Atlantic domain. Early Cretaceous alkaline intrusions and dikes occur also in Newfoundland (Helwig et al., 1974; Strong and Harris, 1974), on Anticosti Island (Poole, 1977), in the Monteregian Hills of Quebec (Eby, 1984, 1985; Foland et al., 1986), and in the White Mountains of New England (McHone, 1978). This suggests that during Early Cretaceous opening phases of the north Central Atlantic Ocean large areas of the adjacent Laurentian

Craton became tectonically destabilized whereby intraplate stresses caused the reactivation of the preexisting fracture zones (Bédard, 1985) and triggered a generally short-lived intraplate magmatism. This, combined with a possible thermal doming of the affected areas, could be in part responsible for the strong clastic influx onto the northern Nova Scotia and the southern Newfoundland shelves (Plates 14, 15). Contemporaneous "hotspot" activity has also been recorded from the oceanic domain of the New England seamounts in the western parts of the north Central Atlantic (Swift et al., 1986) and attests to the fact that tectonic instability was not confined to continental cratonic areas only.

The Late Jurassic and Early Cretaceous sedimentary outbuilding of the Nova Scotia Shelf was accompanied by flowage and diapirism of the Late Triassic–Early Jurassic salts and associated growth faulting at shallower stratigraphic levels (Wade, 1981; Friedenreich, 1987; Fig. 21).

## North Atlantic Areas

During the Late Jurassic, sedimentation in the grabens on the Newfoundland shelf, in those of the Celtic Sea–Western Approaches area and in the Bay of Biscay rift zone was dominated by a shallow marine mixed carbonate–clastics depositional regime. Deeper water conditions were essentially confined to the axial parts of the Bay of Biscay Rift and possibly also the Tagus Abyssal Plain area (Plates 13, 27, 28).

A regional rift-induced unconformity, straddling the Callovian–Oxfordian boundary, is evident in the Celtic Sea, Bristol Channel, and Western Approaches troughs, in Cantabria, and in the Lusitania Basin. In the Jeanne d'Arc Basin and in the Porcupine Trough, this tectonic pulse was less intense and is reflected by a regressive–transgressive clastic cycle. In the basins of the Southern Grand Banks (Horseshoe, North and South Whale basins), shallow marine sedimentation was continuous across the Middle to Late Jurassic boundary.

During the Late Jurassic, differential subsidence of the individual grabens and troughs of the North Atlantic rift system resumed/continued. Crustal extension across the Celtic Sea and Western Approaches troughs was compensated by sinistral movements along a system of wrench faults extending from their northeastern termination into the Paris Basin. Similarly, crustal extension between Iberia and Newfoundland was probably accompanied by sinistral wrench movements in the Bay of Biscay Rift. The occurrence of Late Jurassic coast parallel dikes in southwestern Greenland (Watt, 1969) and diatremes on the southeastern coast of Labrador (King and McMillan, 1985) suggests that rifting propagated into the southern parts of the Labrador Sea which, by this time, was presumably occupied by a shallow marine basin (Umpleby, 1979). Although it is likely that the Rockall Trough continued to subside differentially during the Late Jurassic, it is questionable whether the Iceland Sea Rift, delimiting the Rockall–Hatton Bank to the west, was already active during this time, as indicated on Fig. 17. In the Lusitania Basin several intra-Late Jurassic rifting pulses are evident; these were coupled with the influx of clastics from western sources and minor alkaline volcanic activity in onshore areas (Antunes et al., 1980).

At the transition from the Late Jurassic to the Early Cretaceous, a major rifting pulse combined with an important, presumably tectonically induced lowstand in relative sea level (Hallam, 1978; Vail and Todd, 1981) affected the entire North Atlantic rift system. The resulting "Late Kimmerian" uncon-

formity is of regional significance and can be recognized in most basins flanking the North Atlantic and the Bay of Biscay (Plates 31, 32). In the North Atlantic area, this unconformity can be related to a phase of regional thermal doming presumably in response to progressive lithospheric thinning preceding crustal separation and the northward propagation of the Central Atlantic sea-floor spreading axis.

Earliest Cretaceous uplift of the southern Grand Banks area (Fig. 28) induced the deep truncation of Jurassic strata in the Horseshoe and North and South Whale basins in which diapirisms of the Upper Triassic–lowermost Jurassic halites had caused considerable deformation of the Middle and Late Jurassic series (Fig. 26). In the South Whale Basin, which is limited to the south by the Azores fracture zone, erosion cut down into Lower Triassic series indicating that uplift of this area was very strong. Uplift of the southern Grand Banks area was associated with the extrusion of basaltic flows in the South Whale Basin and on the flanks of the Grand Banks High (Gradstein et al., 1977). Following its late Kimmerian uplift, the area became tectonically quiescent and started to subside regionally. Lower Cretaceous shallow marine clastics are relatively thin in the Horseshoe and North Whale Basin but expand rapidly in the South Whale Basin toward the continental margin. The intra-Aptian hiatus coincides with crustal separation between Flemish Cap and Galicia Bank and in the Bay of Biscay (Plates 15, 28; McWhae, 1981; Wade, 1981).

The stratigraphic record of the Jeanne d'Arc–Avalon Basin (Fig. 29, Plate 28), located to the southwest of the Flemish Cap, shows clear evidence for a later Kimmerian, an intra-Aptian and an intra-Albian unconformity. The later Kimmerian rifting pulse induced rapid basin subsidence whereby in the axial parts of the basin deeper water sedimentation was continuous across the Jurassic–Cretaceous boundary. As a result of the progradation of major cyclical deltaic fans the basin shallowed on during the Barremian. The intra-Aptian unconformity and, to a lesser degree, also the intra-Albian unconformity, were associated with tensional tectonics. The subsequent evolution of the basin was governed by salt-induced tectonics and its regional downwarping to the north, toward the East Newfoundland Basin into which the Jeanne d'Arc–Avalon Basin opens up. Cretaceous sands form the principal reservoirs of the hydrocarbon accumulations occurring in the Jeanne d'Arc Basin (Fig. 24; McKenzie, 1981; Arthur et al., 1982; Hubbard et al., 1985; Meneley, 1986).

Also on the Atlantic margin of Iberia, a major unconformity separates Jurassic and Lower Cretaceous strata. During the latest Jurassic and particularly during the late Kimmerian rifting pulse, the outer margin of the Lusitania Basin became progressively uplifted, causing the complete erosion of its former sedimentary cover (Fig. 27). Restored to the late Kimmerian unconformity level, the Lusitania Basin has essentially the geometry of a half-graben, controlled by fault systems forming its landward margin. During the Early Cretaceous, clastics were shed from the uplifted offshore high eastward into the Lusitania Basin (Plate 28). At the same time, major alluvial fans prograded into this basin from its eastern, landward margin. Southward, these deltaic complexes interfinger with shallow marine carbonates (Plate 14). Minor volcanic activity persisted into the Valanginian (Antunes et al., 1980). To the west of the outer basement high, delimiting the Lusitania Basin, reflection seismic data indicate the occurrence of several half-grabens, containing apparently deeply truncated Jurassic–Triassic series. These are buried beneath essentially unfaulted Cretaceous and Cenozoic strata (Fig. 27). This indicates that the Atlantic margin of Iberia, similar to the Grand Banks–Flemish Cap area, became thermally uplifted during the earliest Cretaceous rifting stage preceding crustal separation in the North Atlantic. At the same time, Western Iberia as a whole became uplifted and tilted to the east. This is reflected by the Early Cretaceous shedding of continental clastics onto its eastern shelves facing the Tethys on which shallow marine carbonates and shales had accumulated during the Late Jurassic (Plates 13–15).

To the north of the Lusitania Basin, the area of the complex Galicia Bank horst is characterized by an intensely block-faulted structural relief involving Neocomian and older shallow marine synrift series. These fault blocks are covered by unfaulted Albian and younger pelagic series that represent the postrifting sequence (Mauffret et al., 1978; Group Galice, 1979). Detailed seismostratigraphic analyses indicate that this area also became progressively domed up prior to crustal separation, resulting in subaerial erosion of Jurassic and Neocomian

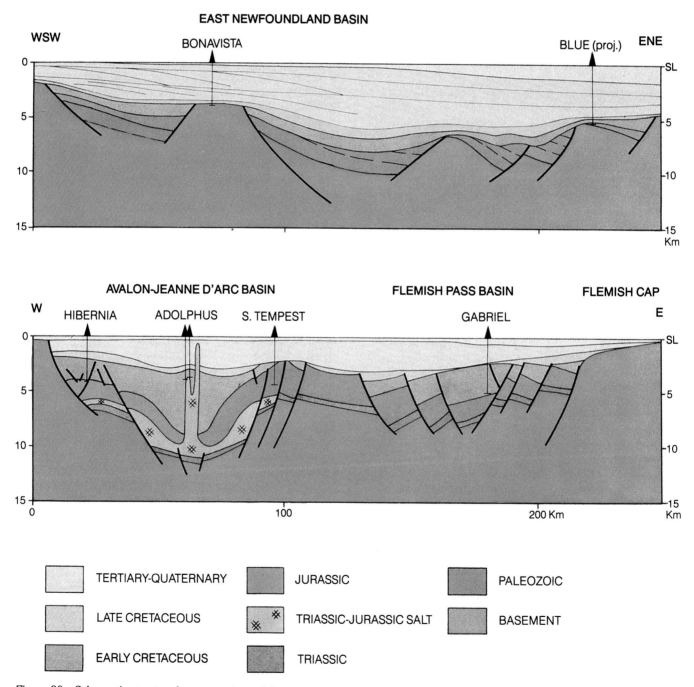

*Figure 29—Schematic structural cross sections of the Jeanne d'Arc and East Newfoundland basins. For location see Figure 20. After Levesque (1985) Shell Canada (top); Faught (1986) Shell Canada (bottom).*

sediments over the crestal parts of rotational fault blocks (Mauffret and Montadert, 1987). Following crustal separation, the North Atlantic margin of Iberia subsided rapidly, largely under sediment-starved condition (Fig. 26).

The continent–ocean transition in the North Atlantic is thought to coincide with the J-anomaly. This suggests that the Flemish Basin and the Tagus Abyssyal Plain are underlain by strongly attenuated continental crust (Boillot et al., 1980; Sullivan, 1983; Masson and Miles, 1984).

## Bay of Biscay

In the stratigraphic record of the sedimentary basins flanking the Bay of Biscay, the late Kimmerian rifting pulse is reflected as a major regression as evident by a regionally correlative unconformity (Plate 27). In the area of the Aquitaine Basin, repeated transtensional deformations caused the rapid subsidence of the Parentis and Adour subbasins in which Lower Cretaceous clastics and carbonates reach a thickness of 4000 and 5000 m, respectively (BRGM et al., 1974; Curnelle et al., 1982). In northern Spain, a counterpart to these wrench-induced basins is the Duero Basin in which 4000 m of continental Lower Cretaceous sediments accumulated (Choukroune and Mattauer, 1978; Salomon, 1983). Contemporaneous wrench deformations are also evident in the Celt-Iberian Ranges transecting the Iberian Craton (Vegas and Banda, 1983). Even after the mid-Aptian crustal separation between Iberia and Southern France, wrench deformations persisted into the Albian and Turonian, by which time they were accompanied by volcanic activity (BRGM et al., 1974; Brunet, 1984).

In Cantabria, several phases of transtensional deformations accompanied the Late Jurassic and Early Cretaceous subsidence of the complex, half-graben-shaped Cantabrian offshore basin that was limited to the north by the Le Danois basement horst. Repeated clastic cycles advanced onto the narrow shelves of this basin, in the axial parts of which deeper water conditions were already established during the Late Jurassic. Following the accumulation of thick halites during the latest Jurassic–earliest Cretaceous deeper water conditions were reestablished. Similar to the Aquitaine Basin, wrench deformations, accompanied by repeated volcanic activity, continued in Cantabria and in the Pyrenean domain, even after crustal separation, into Late Cretaceous times (Boillot et al., 1985; see also Emery and Uchupi, 1984).

## Intersection of the North Atlantic and Bay of Biscay Rifts

The area at the intersection of the North Atlantic–Bay of Biscay, Celtic Sea, Western Approaches, Porcupine and Flemish Pass rifts apparently became thermally domed up during the late Kimmerian rifting pulse.

In the Celtic Sea and the Western Approaches troughs, the deposition of shallow marine, in part evaporitic carbonates and shales, ceased at the transition from the Jurassic to the Early Cretaceous. A regional erosional hiatus, associated with important wrench deformations, corresponds to the late Kimmerian unconformity (Plate 29). This is illustrated by the palinspastic reconstructions of the Western Approaches Trough, given in Figure 70. Contemporaneous wrench and rift deformations are also evident in the Bristol Channel and the Channel basins and also in the basins of the Irish Sea (Plate 29; Fig. 20). Following the late Kimmerian tectonism, the Celtic Sea and Western

Approaches troughs subsided rapidly under a tensional regime (Fig. 22, 23, 75). During the Berriasian to early Aptian, thick continental to lagoonal "Wealden" clastics accumulated in these basins. There is only very limited evidence for syndepositional volcanic activity. During this time, the Celtic Sea Trough was largely isolated from the marine shelves of the Bay of Biscay Rift. On the other hand, the Western Approaches Trough was open to the Bay of Biscay as indicated by the transition of the Wealden clastics into a shallow marine carbonate and shale series near the present-day shelf edge (Ziegler, 1982a, 1987a, 1987b; van Hoorn, 1987a; Robinson et al., 1981; Tucker and Arter, 1987).

During the Early Cretaceous, the Armorican Massif became regionally uplifted and tilted to the northeast. This gave rise to the shedding of the "Wealden" clastics into the Paris Basin (Mégnien, 1980).

Similarly, the area of the Goban Spur, occupying the triangular block at the junction between the Bay of Biscay, Western Approaches, and Porcupine rifts, apparently became uplifted during the earliest Cretaceous. This caused the partial erosion of its Jurassic and Triassic sedimentary cover and a restriction of the marine connection between the Celtic Sea–Fastnet Trough and the Bay of Biscay Rift. At the same time, intense crustal extension along the southern flank of the Goban Spur, locally accompanied by volcanic activity, caused the differential subsidence of a complex array of rotational fault blocks controlled by listric normal faults. Tensional tectonics persisted until crustal separation was achieved between the Goban Spur and the Flemish Cap during the mid-Aptian. Subsequently these fault blocks were covered by relatively thin pelagic series ranging in age from early Aptian to Cenozoic (Fig. 30). Fault block geometries suggest that the crust of the Goban Spur was extended by some 50 km. On the other hand, if it is assumed that during rifting the crust-mantle boundary is not being disturbed, the crustal configuration of the area suggests that the total amount of extension would be as high as 150 km (Fig. 31; Dingle and Scrutton, 1979; Roberts et al., 1981b; Avedik et al., 1982; Masson et al., 1985; Sibuet et al., 1985; de Graciansky et al., 1985; de Graciansky and Poag, 1985; Pinet et al., 1987). This presents a challenge to the pure shear extensional model (McKenzie, 1978) but could be compatible with the simple shear extensional model (Wernicke, 1981; Fig. 74). Alternatively it may be assumed that other processes also contributed to lower crustal attenuation (see Chapter 10).

Mid-Aptian crustal separation in the Bay of Biscay was associated with further wrench deformations and regional uplift of the Celtic Sea and Western Approaches troughs, the Channel area, and probably also the basins of the Irish Sea. With the onset of sea-floor spreading in the Bay of Biscay, these long-standing rifts became tectonically quiescent and their Late Cretaceous evolution followed the pattern of passive margins and aborted rifts (Ziegler, 1982a, 1987a, 1987b; van Hoorn, 1987a; Tucker and Arter, 1987).

The Late Jurassic and Early Cretaceous evolution of the Porcupine Trough differs considerably from that of the rifts of the Celtic Sea–Western Approaches area. In the axial parts of the Porcupine Trough, deeper water conditions were probably established already during the Late Jurassic. The late Kimmerian rifting pulse, inducing further subsidence of this graben along a set of listric normal faults and the progradation of minor clastic fans from its margins, was accompanied by the development of an elongate major volcanic edifice in its south-central parts (Fig. 32). This apparently submarine chain of volcanoes is evident on reflection seismic records and correlates to a major magnetic anomaly (Max et al., 1982). Intra-Aptian, Albian, and Late Cretaceous tensional tectonics were of relatively minor importance and affected mainly the master faults delineating the Porcupine Trough. These rifting pulses accompanied crustal separation between the Porcupine Bank and Orphan Knoll and in the Southern Rockall Trough. Regional southward tilting of the Porcupine Trough during its postrift evolution probably reflects differential crustal thinning in its southern parts. Reflection seismic data refute the earlier held notion that limited sea-floor spreading had occurred in the southern Porcupine Trough (Roberts, 1975; Riddihough and Max, 1976; Naylor and Shannon, 1982; Ziegler, 1982a; Masson and Miles, 1986a).

The structural framework of the East Newfoundland Basin is characterized, at pre-Late Cretaceous levels, by a complex, block-faulted relief involving the basement, Triassic(?), Jurassic, and Early Cretaceous synrift sediments. This relief is overlain by thick Late Cretaceous and Cenozoic postrift sediments,

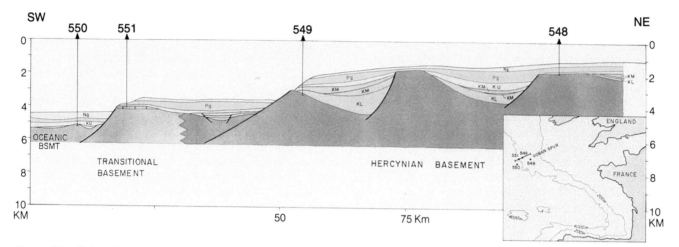

Figure 30—Goban Spur transect, northern Bay of Biscay. After de Graciansky et al. (1985).

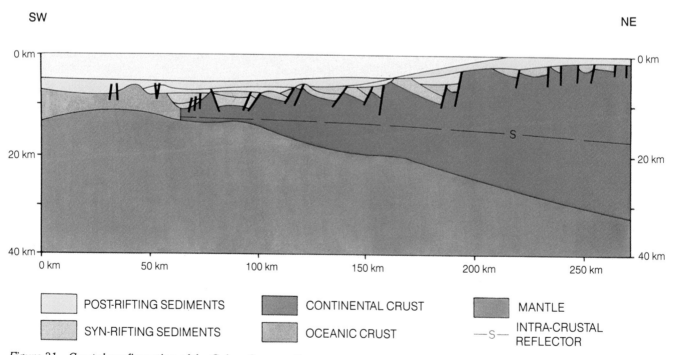

POST-RIFTING SEDIMENTS    CONTINENTAL CRUST    MANTLE

SYN-RIFTING SEDIMENTS    OCEANIC CRUST    —S—  INTRA-CRUSTAL REFLECTOR

Figure 31—Crustal configuration of the Goban Spur continental margin, northern Bay of Biscay. Location similar to Figure 25. After Avedik et al. (1982).

corresponding to the drift sequence (Fig. 33; Grant, 1975; Keen and Hyndman, 1979; Keen and Barret, 1981). The outer margin of the East Newfoundland Basin is marked by the Flemish Cap and Orphan Knoll basement highs (Fig. 28). There is only limited control available on the age and composition of the synrift series. Upper Triassic to Lower Jurassic sediments, if at all present, are devoid of major halites as indicated by the regional absence of diapiric structures. In analogy with the Jeanne d'Arc–Avalon Basin, Jurassic sediments probably consist in the East Newfoundland Basin of shallow marine carbonates, shales, and minor clastics. The JOIDES No. 111 well, drilled on the Orphan Knoll, bottomed in nonmarine Bajocian sands preserved in a synclinal depression (Laughton, 1972; Umpleby, 1979). The late Kimmerian rifting pulse sharply accentuated the structural relief of the East Newfoundland Basin. Differential subsidence and rotation of individual fault blocks was associated with the erosion of their sedimentary cover. It is unknown whether this erosional phase was of a subaerial or a submarine nature. Rifting activity apparently continued into Aptian time under deeper water conditions. A regional hiatus separates Aptian–Albian(?) strata from the Upper Cretaceous and younger drift sequence.

Reflection and refraction seismic data indicate that the East Newfoundland Basin is underlain by strongly attenuated continental crust (Fig. 33). Under the assumption that during rifting the crust is thinned by stretching only (mass conservation), the crustal configuration of the East Newfoundland Basin suggests that its crust has been extended by over 130% or by some 280 km. The available reflection seismic data suggest, however, that the amount of crustal extension at the base of the Mesozoic sedimentary sequence is of the order of only 100 km. Thus, there is a considerable discrepancy between the amount of extension postulated for this basin on the basis of its crustal configuration and on the basis of fault block geometries at top basement level. In this context, it should be noted that an extension of the crust of the East Newfoundland Basin by some 100 km is required if the tight Permo-Triassic fit of the continents in the North Atlantic domain, as shown in Plates 7–10, is to be accepted.

The northern margin of the East Newfoundland Basin coincides with a fracture zone which, on a predrift fit of the continents, can be traced from the northern end of the Porcupine Trough across the Porcupine Bank (Riddihough and Max, 1976) and onto the shelf of Newfoundland (Grant, 1975). This fracture zone could be considered as the precursor of the intraoceanic Charlie Gibbs fracture zone (Fig. 28).

North of this fracture zone, in the area south of the Cartwright Arch and under the Labrador Shelf, the zone of extended continental crust is much narrower than in the East Newfoundland Basin (Keen and Hyndman, 1979; Grant, 1980). From Figure 34 it is evident that in areas north of this fracture zone the continental crust became extended during the rifting phase by a considerably smaller amount than in the East Newfoundland Basin. Moreover, the available stratigraphic and igneous record suggests that rifting started in the Labrador Sea area only during

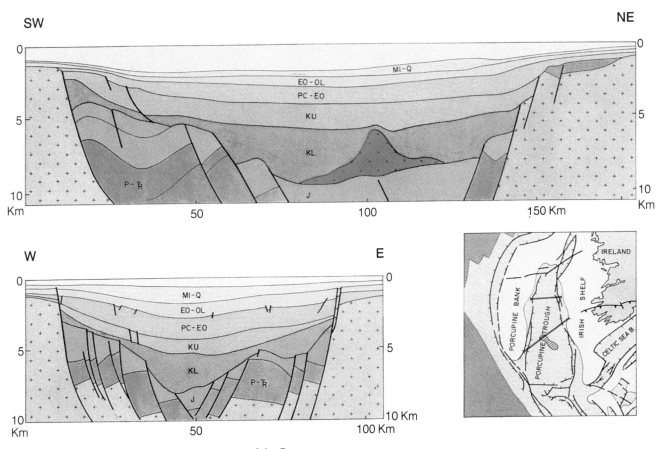

*Figure 32—Schematic structural cross sections of the Porcupine Trough, West Irish Shelf.*

the Late Jurassic whereas in areas of the East Newfoundland Basin and the Grand Banks area, rifting commenced presumably during the Middle to Late Triassic.

## Labrador–Baffin Bay Rift

Wells drilled on the Labrador Shelf indicate that the later Kimmerian rifting pulse strongly affected the Labrador Sea Rift. Differential subsidence of individual graben segments started during the Late Jurassic to Barremian whereby the accumulation of continental clastics was accompanied by intense vol-

canic activity (McMillan, 1979). Contemporaneous dike intrusions are evident in southwestern Greenland and on the coast of Labrador (Watt, 1969; Wanless et al., 1974; Umpleby, 1979; King and McMillan, 1985). By Barremian time, rifting had propagated northward into the area of the Davies Strait and probably also into the southern Baffin Bay (Henderson et al., 1976, 1981; McWhae, 1981; Srivastava et al., 1981; Klose et al., 1982; Plates 13, 14, 28).

Volcanism abated gradually at the beginning of the Aptian, and the area of sedimentation expanded. Aptian and Albian sediments are coal-bearing, and there is evidence for marine

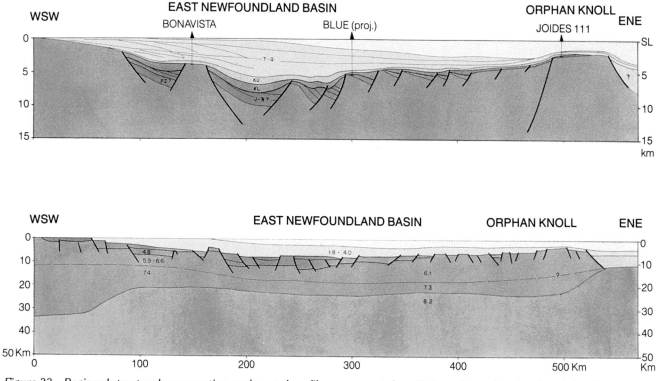

*Figure 33—Regional structural cross section and crustal profile of the East Newfoundland Basin based on multichannel reflection seismic data (after Levesque, 1985, Shell Canada) and* crustal profile based on refraction data (after Keen and Barrett, 1981).

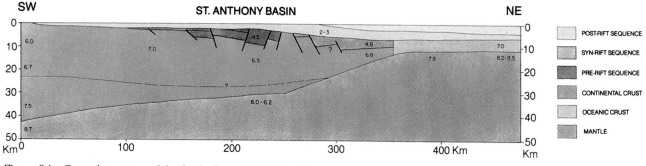

*Figure 34—Crustal structure of the St. Anthony Basin–South Cartwright Arch, Labrador Shelf. After Keen and Hyndman (1979).*

incursions from the North Atlantic area into the southern Labrador Sea Rift. At the same time, rifting propagated into the northern Baffin Bay and via the Lancaster Sound into the Canadian Arctic Archipelago (Plate 15). This is borne out by the onset of differential subsidence of the Eclipse Trough on northern Baffin Island (McWhae, 1981; Kerr, 1981b; Rice and Shade, 1982). Furthermore, there is evidence that in the northward prolongation of the Baffin Bay Rift, Devon Island and the southern parts of Ellesmere Island became affected by crustal extension (Mayr, 1984 and personal communication). Moreover, the purely geophysically defined Melville Bight Graben, located on the northwestern Greenland Shelf may also have started to subside during the Aptian–Albian (Henderson, 1976).

Assuming a constant rate of rift propagation, this suggests that the over-3000-km-long Labrador–Baffin Bay Rift propagated itself during the Late Jurassic and Early Cretaceous from the North Atlantic area into the southern parts of the Canadian Arctic Archipelago at a rate of some 8 cm/year.

## NORWEGIAN–GREENLAND SEA RIFT SYSTEM

During the Late Jurassic and Early Cretaceous, the rate of crustal extension increased in the Norwegian–Greenland Sea

rift system. This was coupled with the rapid subsidence of its axial parts in which deep water conditions were established. At the same time, the tectonic evolution of the Northwest European rift systems became increasingly dominated by the stress systems governing the development of the Norwegian–Greenland Sea Rift. Crustal distension in the latter was compensated by sinistral transform movement along the fracture systems of Northeast Greenland and Western Svalbard. In combination with tectonic activity related to the Early Cretaceous opening of the Canada Basin (see *Opening of the Canada Basin,* this chapter) this resulted in the constriction and ultimately the closure of the seaways linking the Arctic Basin with the Norwegian–Greenland Sea area.

### North Sea Area

In the North Sea, the Viking and Central grabens developed during the late Middle and Late Jurassic into the dominant rift systems while the importance of the Horda–Egesund Halfgraben diminished and the Horn Graben became essentially inactive (Fig. 35). In the Viking and Central grabens, deeper water conditions were established during the Late Jurassic as a result of continued crustal distension and the progressive foundering of the Central North Sea dome. By mid-Kimmeridgian time,

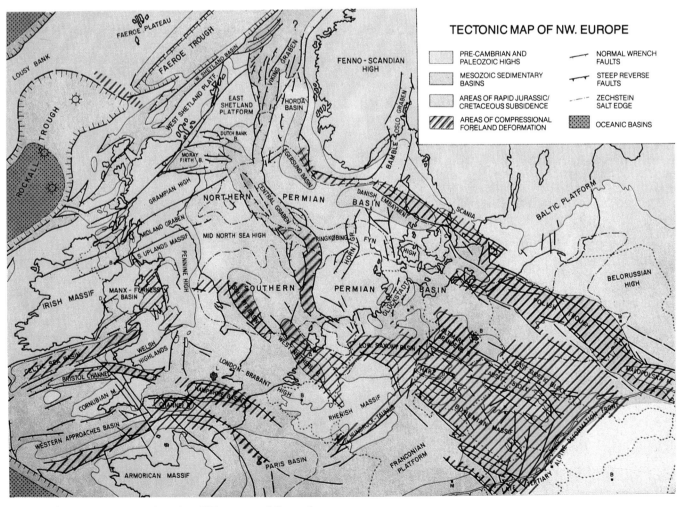

*Figure 35—Mesozoic tectonic units of Western and Central Europe.*

marine connections were established between the Central and Southern North Sea area across the Mid-North Sea High.

In much of the North Sea area, Kimmeridgian and Tithonian sediments are represented by highly organic shales that form the principal source rock for the hydrocarbon accumulations occurring in the Viking and Central grabens. Upper Bajocian and Bathonian continental clastics and Callovian to lower Kimmeridgian transgressive sands, resting unconformably on deeply truncated Triassic red beds (mid-Kimmerian Unconformity), contain a number of important hydrocarbon accumulations in the Central North Sea. Where these clastics are absent by onlap, Triassic sandstones form an important reservoir. These reservoirs rely for their hydrocarbon charge on Kimmeridgian–Tithonian source rocks (Ziegler, 1980, 1982a; Barnard and Cooper, 1981; Cornford, 1984; Baird, 1986).

Crustal extension across the North Sea rift system was taken up at its southern termination in the Dutch offshore by a system of northwest–southeast-striking wrench faults. Dextral displacements along these induced the differential subsidence of the Sole Pit, Broad Fourteens, West and Central Netherlands, Lower Saxony, Sub-Hercynian, and Altmark–Brandenburg basins (Ziegler, 1982a, 1987c). These basins flank the northern margin of the London–Brabant, Rhenish, and Bohemian massifs. The localization of these wrench-induced basins probably involved the reactivation of Permo-Carboniferous fracture systems. Rapid subsidence of these basins, locally accompanied by repeated igneous activity, went hand in hand with the wrench-induced uplift of the London–Brabant, Rhenish, and western Bohemian massifs (Plates 29, 30; Fig. 12). With this, the long-standing seaway, linking the North European Basin with the Tethys shelves via the area of the Rhenish Massif (Hessian Depression), became closed during the early Late Jurassic (Plates 12, 13). On the other hand, the Bohemian Massif became transected during the Callovian by the Saxonian Strait (Malkovsky, 1976, 1987), which provided a new link between the Tethys and the Lower Saxony Basin. The latter started to subside rapidly during the late Oxfordian, while areas offsetting it to the north became uplifted, thus forming the Pompeckj Swell (Fig. 12, 31). At the same time, a number of north-northeast–south-southwest-trending troughs in northern Germany became inactive (Glückstadt, Emsland, Gifhorn troughs; Betz et al., 1987).

Late Middle to Late Jurassic tectonic activity along the Fennoscandian borderzone is evident by the intrusion of basalt necks in southernmost Sweden (Klingspor, 1976) and by the differential subsidence of half-grabens in northern Denmark and southern Sweden (Liboriussen et al., 1987; Norling and Bergström, 1987). The Polish Rift also continued to subside rapidly during the Late Jurassic. During the Kimmeridgian, marine connections were established between the Tethys shelves and the Central North Sea via the Polish–Danish system of grabens.

Overall, a progressive reorganization ("polarization") of the rift systems of Northwest Europe can be observed during the late Middle and Late Jurassic. In the process of this, northeast-southwest-trending grabens and troughs became inactive (e.g., Horn and Glückstadt grabens, Emsland Trough, Weser Depression; Fig. 35) while new northwest–southeast-striking wrench systems came into evidence (e.g. Sole Pit, West-Netherlands, Lower Saxony, and Altmark–Brandenburg Basins, Saxonian Strait; Fig. 35; compare also Plates 11–13). This is thought to reflect changes in the regional stress systems affecting Northwest Europe. These changes were the consequence of mid-Jurassic crustal separation between Europe and the Italo-Dinarid promontory, the resulting relaxation of tensional stresses associated with the Tethys rift system and continued lithospheric stretching in the Arctic–North Atlantic area (see above; Ziegler, 1982a, 1987c).

At the transition from the Jurassic to the Cretaceous, a major rifting phase affected the graben systems of the North Sea. In the Viking Graben, rapid differential subsidence of rotational fault blocks in response to accelerated crustal distension resulted in the development of a submarine relief of some 1000 m. Highs were swept clean by contour currents while pelagic shales accumulated in the intervening lows in which sedimentation was more or less continuous across the Jurassic-Cretaceous boundary. In the Central Graben, contemporaneous rift tectonics are less obvious since much of the tensional deformation at the pre-Permian level was taken up by plastic deformation in the Zechstein salts (Fig. 18).

In the North Sea area, the largely submarine and in many places composite late Kimmerian unconformity is regionally correlative (Rawson and Riley, 1982). Its origin is probably related to drastic changes in the current regime of the area that were caused by the combined effects of rapid subsidence of the Viking and Central grabens and an important drop in relative sea level (Vail et al, 1977; Vail and Todd, 1981). This change in current regime was apparently associated with a stronger oxygenation of the bottom waters. This is reflected by the regional termination of kerogenous shales deposition during the earliest Cretaceous and the subsequent accumulation of shales having a low organic content.

From a geodynamic point of view, it is interesting to note that in the North Sea, the late Kimmerian rifting pulse, which spanned perhaps less than 10 Ma, was not associated with significant volcanic activity nor with a renewed doming of the Central Graben. In this respect, it differed greatly from the mid-Kimmerian rifting pulse at the transition from the Early to the Middle Jurassic, which was coupled with considerable volcanic activity and the uplift of a major rift dome (see Chapter 5). It can only be speculated that the thermally induced ductility of the lower crust and upper mantle had considerably increased as a consequence of the mid-Kimmerian thermal surge. The upper mantle and the lower crust may therefore have been able to yield by ductile deformation during the late Kimmerian phase of rapid crustal extension. This could have impeded a second phase of lithospheric failure and the intrusion of asthenospheric material to the crust–mantle boundary.

Following the late Kimmerian rifting pulse, the rate of crustal extension across the North Sea graben system decreased gradually. Within the Viking and Central grabens, the throw on many faults decreases and fades out upwards in the Lower Cretaceous shales. On the other hand, master-faults delineating these grabens remained active through Early Cretaceous into Late Cretaceous times (Fig. 18; see also Glennie, 1984b, Fig. 2.14). During the Early Cretaceous, continued differential subsidence of this graben system was accompanied by the gradual infilling of its relief with deep water shales and minor pelagic carbonates ranging in age from Berriasian to Albian (Hancock, 1984).

The Fennoscandian Borderzone remained tectonically active through Early Cretaceous times as reflected by repeated volcanic activity in southernmost Sweden (Plate 30; Prinzlau and Larsen, 1972; Klingspor, 1976) and the shedding of clastic from the Fennoscandian Shield into the Danish Basin (Liboriussen et al., 1987; Bergström and Norling, 1987). Similarly, the Polish Trough continued to subside, in such a way that subsidence and sedimentation rates kept balance; correspondingly, marine connections between the Tethys and the North Sea remained intermittently open (Marek and Raczynska, 1972; Raczynska, 1979; Kemper et al., 1981) (Plates 14, 15).

Early Cretaceous high rates of the crustal extension in the North Sea were coupled with the sharp accentuation of the wrench-induced basins along the northern margin of the Rhenish–Bohemian Massif and a further uplift of the latter. During the Neocomian and Barremian, this high linked up to the northwest with the Pennine High of northern England, thus forming a barrier between the North Sea Basin and the Channel–Paris Basin (Plate 14). During this time, only occasional transgressions originating from the North Sea crossed the English Midlands and advanced southward into the Channel area (Allen, 1976, 1981; Rawson et al., 1978). During the late Aptian and Albian, however, permanent marine communications were reestablished between the Channel area and the North Sea via the English Midlands (Plate 15). Uplift of the Rhenish–Bohemian Massif was accompanied by the Early Cretaceous closure of the Saxonian Strait and wrench deformations along its southwestern margin (Malkovsky, 1987; Schröder, 1987; Nachtmann and Wagner, 1987). Clastics shed northwards from the uplifted Rhenish–Bohemian High were deposited in the adjacent continuously subsiding wrench-induced basins. Contemporaneous deep crustal fracturing gave rise to repeated volcanic activity in these basins, and in the Lower Saxony Basin to the Aptian intrusion of felsic and mafic laccoliths (Stadler and Teichmüller, 1971; Deutloff et al., 1980; van Hoorn, 1987b; van Wijhe 1987; Betz et al., 1987). Tectonic activity in the wrench-induced basins flanking the northern and southern margins of the London–Brabant and Rhenish–Bohemian massifs abated gradually during the Albian and Cenomanian.

Early Cretaceous sands contain important oil accumulations in the West Netherlands and Lower Saxony basins (Ziegler, 1980; Boigk, 1981; Bodenhausen and Ott, 1981).

## Rockall and Faeroe–West Shetland Troughs

In the southern and central parts of the Rockall Trough, sea-floor spreading is thought to have commenced during the Albian and to have continued into the Senonian. Subdued magnetic anomalies evident in this area have been related by Roberts et al. (1981a) to anomalies 34 and 33 (see also Bott, 1978). An alternative interpretation, supported by reflection seismic data, has recently been advanced by Megson (1987), who suggests that these anomalies are associated with tilted fault blocks (involving attenuated continental crust?) and interspersed volcanic edifices. The width of oceanic or partly oceanic crust in the southern and central parts of the Rockall Trough could range between 100 and 140 km. Refraction and gravity data indicate for the axial parts of the Rockall Trough a crustal thickness ranging from 5 km in the south to 10 km in the north (Roberts et al., 1983; Scrutton, 1986; Megson, 1987). In the northern parts of the Rockall Trough, seismic definition of its structural configuration at Cretaceous levels is impeded by the presence of extensive uppermost Cretaceous-lower Eocene volcanics that are overlain by up to 3000 km of Cenozoic clastics.

To the north, the Rockall Trough finds its continuation in the Faeroe–West Shetland Trough from which it is now separated by the Wywill–Thomson Ridge, a Paleocene–lowermost Eocene volcanic edifice (Fig. 51; Roberts et al., 1983). Reflection seismic data from the southern parts of the Faeroe Trough, calibrated by wells, indicate that it is floored by highly stretched continental crust (Duindam and van Hoorn, 1987; Fig. 36). This refutes the postulate that crustal extension in this rift had proceeded to crustal separation during the Albian to early Senonian as suggested by Hanisch (1983, 1984a, 1984b) and Price and Rattey (1984; see also Bott, 1984; Bott and Smith, 1984).

In view of the above, it must be assumed that the width of oceanic or para-oceanic crust in the Rockall Trough decreases northward. This implies that limited Cretaceous sea-floor spreading in the southern and central Rockall Trough was accompanied by a counterclockwise rotation of the continental Rockall–Hatton–Faeroe Bank, and that the northern parts of the Rockall Trough are probably floored at least to a large extent by highly attenuated continental crust as suggested by Plates 15–17.

The Faeroe–West Shetland Trough grades northward at its intersection with the Viking Graben, into the Norwegian–Greenland Sea rift system. Seismic and well data from the triple junction between the West Shetland–Faeroe Trough, the Norwegian–Greenland Sea Rift, and the Viking Graben indicate that this area became domed up during the Kimmeridgian. From this high, over which Jurassic and Triassic strata became deeply truncated, clastics were shed southward into the northernmost parts of the Viking Graben where they were deposited as turbiditic sands; these are productive in the Magnus oil field (Plate 27; Fig. 48; De'Ath and Schuyleman, 1981). These sands contain shallow marine faunas which indicate that erosion in their source area was of a subaerial nature. This domed-up area, the dimensions of which are difficult to determine, subsided apparently rapidly during the late Kimmerian rifting pulse.

Similarly, the northwestern margin of the West Shetland Basin, the Sula–Sgeir Platform, and the Faeroe–Shetland Basin became apparently uplifted during the Late Jurassic as erosion cut down into Permo-Triassic red beds and even onto the basement (Fig. 36). Thick Permo-Triassic and Jurassic sediments are only preserved in the relatively narrow half-grabens paralleling the margins of the Shetland Platform and in the Minches Basin (Ridd, 1981; Duindam and van Hoorn, 1987). Uplift of the Faeroe–West Shetland Trough and of the Shetland Platform was accompanied by apparently only minor volcanic activity (Knox, 1977; Ziegler, 1982a) During the Late Jurassic, clastics were shed eastward from the uplifted Shetland Platform into the Morray Firth and southern Viking grabens where they were deposited in submarine fan complexes that form the reservoirs of such oil and gas/condensate fields as Brae, Miller, Tony, and Thelma (Brown, 1984).

The uplifted parts of the Faeroe–West Shetland Trough began to subside during the Kimmeridgian and foundered rapidly during the Early Cretaceous as a consequence of a high rate of crustal distension. Movements along listric normal faults involving the basement continued into the Late Cretaceous (Fig. 36). The marginal half-grabens of this rift system subsided only little during the Early Cretaceous while the Shetland Platform stayed elevated. During the Early Cretaceous, clastics were shed westward from this high into the axial parts of the Faeroe–Shetland Trough where they were deposited as deep water fans along major fault scarps; similarly, clastics were shed eastward into the Morray Firth Graben (Hancock, 1984; Plates 14, 15).

## Norwegian–Greenland Sea Area

During the Late Jurassic, the subsidence of the Norwegian–Greenland Rift was governed by continued crustal extension. In combination with eustatically rising sea levels, this led to the establishment of deep water conditions in its axial parts during the Oxfordian and Kimmeridgian (Plates 13, 26). Similar to the North Sea area, Kimmeridgian to early Berriasian shales are highly kerogenous in large parts of the basins of Eastern Greenland, Mid-Norway, and on the Barents Shelf. These shales form the principal source rocks for the oil and gas accumulations of the Mid-Norway Basin (Heum et al., 1986) and the gas fields of the southwestern Barents Sea (Berglund et al., 1986).

In the Mid-Norway Basin, Late Jurassic extensional and transtensional faulting appears to have been more intense in the western parts of the Trøndelag Platform than in its eastern parts

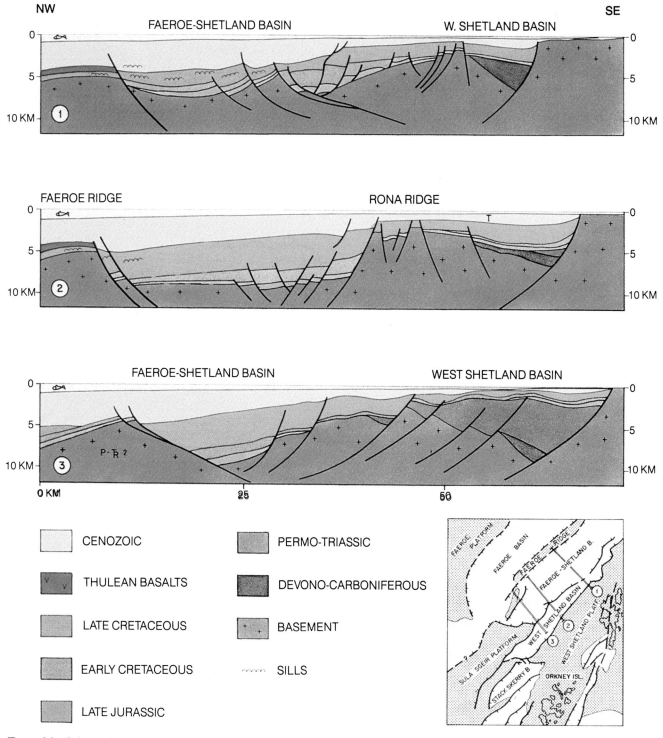

Figure 36—Schematic structural cross sections of the southern Faeroe–West Shetland Trough. After Duindam, Shell UK Expro.

(Figs. 37, 38). During the late Kimmerian rifting pulse the Vøring and Møre basins, forming the axial parts of the Norwegian–Greenland Sea Rift, began to subside rapidly while the Trøndelag Platform was little affected by faulting and subsided only little. At the same time, its western margin became uplifted, presumably in isostatic response to progressive lithospheric thinning. This illustrates that rifting activity was now concentrated in the axial parts of the Norwegian-Greenland Sea Rift (Gowers and Lunde, 1984; Bukovics et al., 1984; Buckovics and Ziegler, 1985). Apart from a thin Kimmeridgian tuff layer observed on Andøya (Dalland and Thusu, 1977; Dalland, 1981), there is no evidence for volcanic activity associated with the Late Jurassic-Early Cretaceous rifting pulses in the Mid-Norway Basin.

In the Møre and Vøring basins, the base of the Cretaceous corresponds to a regional, often angular unconformity and it is unknown whether its origin is related to subaereal or submarine erosion. These basins subsided very rapidly during the Early Cretaceous such that faults offsetting the base of the Cretaceous die out upwards in pelagic Lower Cretaceous shales attaining thicknesses of 3–4 km and more. This sedimentary wedge thins progressively by onlap and condensation toward the zone of future crustal separation along the Faeroe–Shetland and Vøring Plateau escarpments (Fig. 37).

The Late Jurassic and Early Cretaceous evolution of the East Greenland rifted basins is comparable to the development of the Mid-Norway Basin. Continued differential subsidence of major rotational fault blocks led to the establishment of deeper water conditions during the Oxfordian to Kimmeridgian and the accumulation of organic-rich shales. Crustal extension accelerated during the Tithonian to Berriasian with tectonic activity being concentrated on the eastern coast parallel fault zones as indicated by the occurrence of coarse submarine clas-

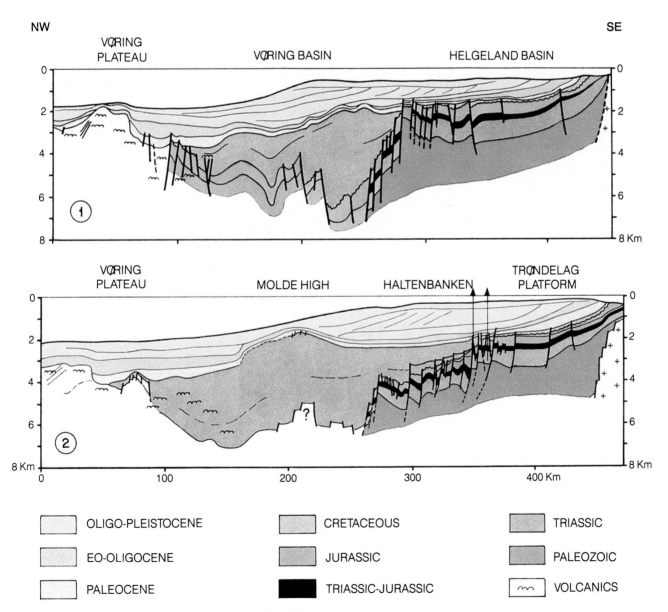

*Figure 37—Schematic structural cross sections of the Mid-Norway Basin. For location see Figure 38. After Bukovicz, Norske Shell.*

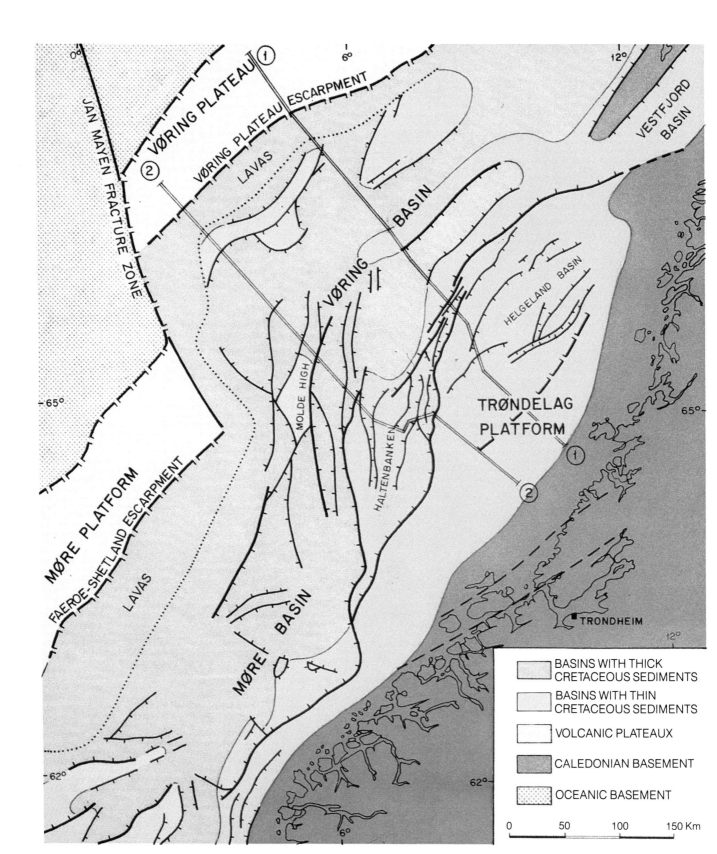

*Figure 38—Generalized tectonic map of the Mid-Norway Basin. (After Norske Shell.)*

tic fans associated with deep water shales. On the other hand, the Jameson Bay Basin, located further to the west, subsided little during the latest Jurassic and earliest Cretaceous. This is reflected by the rapid progradation of deltaic sands over the upper Oxfordian and Kimmeridgian deeper water shales (Surlyk, 1977a, 1977b, 1984; Surlyk et al., 1981; Surlyk and Clemmensen, 1983; Birkelunde et al., 1984). This also suggests that in Central East Greenland rifting activity gradually concentrated toward the zone of future crustal separation. In this context, a similarity can be seen between the Late Jurassic and Early Cretaceous evolution of the Trøndelag Platform of the Mid-Norway Basin and the Jameson Bay Basin of Central East Greenland (Figs. 37, 50).

In Eastern Greenland, there are only limited outcrops of lower Cretaceous series. These consist of deeper water shales containing in part coarse debris-flow deposits along fault scarps (Surlyk et al., 1981). This suggests that the tectonic and depositional regime, which was established during the late Kimmerian rifting pulse, persisted into the Aptian–Albian (Plate 26). It is likely that during this time the large, aeromagnetically defined basins underlaying the northeastern shelf of Greenland subsided differentially (Henderson, 1976). It is uncertain whether the East Greenland rift system that extends southward between Greenland and the Rockall–Hatton Bank, as shown in Plates 14–16, was already active during the Early Cretaceous. Some support for this concept is, however, lent by the occurrence of thin upper Albian to Danian shallow marine shales and clastics in the Kangerdlugssuaq area of south-central East Greenland (Soper et al., 1976; Higgins and Soper, 1981).

## Barents Shelf

On the Barents Shelf, Late Jurassic sediments consist of kerogenous shales as indicated by well results from its southwestern parts and outcrops from the Svalbard Archipelago. Also in the Timan–Pechora area and in the West Siberian Basin, Kimmeridgian to Tithonian (Volgian) sediments are developed in a highly organic, starved basin facies (Rudkevich, 1976; Ulmishek, 1982, 1984; Artyushkov et al., 1986). On Franz Josef Land, Upper Jurassic shales and limestones attain a thickness of some 500 m (Ulmishek, 1982). In the northern parts of the Svalbard Archipelago, Upper Jurassic sediments consist of shallow marine, distal prodelta clays that grade southward into deeper marine, partly kerogenous shales (Smith et al., 1977; Steel and Worsley, 1984; Dypvik, 1984). Overall, it appears that during the Late Jurassic large parts of the Barents Shelf were sediment starved and had subsided well below wave base. These shales form an important hydrocarbon source rock.

In the southwestern Barents Sea, Late Jurassic syndepositional faulting is evident on reflection seismic lines. Rifting activity accelerated sharply at the transition from the Jurassic to the Cretaceous (Rønnevik and Beskowv, 1983; Faleide et al., 1984; Rønnevik and Jacobsen, 1984; Berglund et al., 1986). This is exemplified by the renewed sharp uplift of the Loppa Ridge, which was coupled with downfaulting of the Byørnya Graben (Figs. 3, 15). At the same time, the Hammerfest Graben became accentuated and the Tromsø Basin began to subside rapidly (Fig. 39). The thickness of the Lower Cretaceous sediments contained in these grabens clearly indicates that the Tromsø Graben, which grades southward into the Harstad Basin, paralleling the coast of northwest Norway, subsided considerably faster than the Hammerfest and Byørnøya grabens. This suggests that also on the Barents Shelf, tensional tectonics

gradually concentrated on the axial zones of the Norwegian–Greenland Sea Rift.

In the Svalbard Archipelago, the late Kimmerian pulse of rift and wrench deformation, giving rise to local unconformities, was associated with the intrusion of dolerite dikes and sills (Plate 26). A second phase of volcanic activity is dated as Barremian (Burov et al., 1977). This igneous activity was probably induced by wrench movements along the Svalbard–Northeast Greenland oblique-slip zone. Basaltic flows of a Hauterivian to Albian age cover large parts on Franz Josef Land (Tarakovsky et al., 1983). This volcanic activity was associated with the uplift of the northern margin of the Barents Shelf, the Lomonosov High. The Franz Josef Land hotspot came into evidence during the early phases of sea-floor spreading in the Canada Basin and became extinct with the termination of sea-floor spreading in the latter during the early Late Cretaceous (see *Opening of the Canada Basin,* this chapter). The location of the Franz Josef Land center of igneous activity may coincide with the projection of one of the major sea-floor spreading axes of the Canada Basin into the area of the northern Barents Shelf (see Plates 14, 15). As such, this hotspot could be interpreted as an abortive attempt at splitting the crust of the Lomonosov High at right angles to the strike of the postulated Devonian–Early Carboniferous Lomonosov fold belt. Since the Canada Basin is, however, devoid of clear sea-floor magnetic anomalies, this concept cannot be verified (see *Opening of the Canada Basin,* this chapter).

From the uplifted Lomonosov High, deltaic complexes prograded southward into the area of the Svalbard Archipelago during the Barremian and Aptian. Following a Late Aptian transgression, clastic fans probably built out again over the area and preceded the Late Cretaceous regional uplift of the Lomonosov High and the northern parts of the Svalbard Platform (Birkenmajer, 1981; Steel and Worsley, 1984; Smith et al., 1977; Dypvik, 1984). On much of the Barents Shelf, Early Cretaceous sediments consist of distal prodelta and pelagic clays that have a low organic carbon content.

## Wandel Sea Basin

In the Wandel Sea Basin of Northeast Greenland, sedimentation resumed during the Oxfordian after a hiatus spanning Late Triassic to mid-Jurassic time. Transgressive, shallow marine Oxfordian to Tithonian shales are conformably overlain by shallow marine and continental sandstones and conglomerates ranging in age from Berriasian to early Albian (Plate 26). This is taken as evidence for Early Cretaceous increased tectonic activity in the Hinterland. From northeastern Greenland, clastics apparently prograded during the Barremian into the area of Western Svalbard (Håkansson et al., 198lb; Håkansson and Pedersen, 1982; Birkelund and Hakansson, 1983). On the north coast of Greenland, the peralkaline intrusive and extrusive Kap Washington complex came into evidence during the Aptian–Albian and remained active until early Paleocene time (Dawes and Soper, 1979; Brown and Parson, 1981; Batten, 1982). This igneous activity was probably triggered by wrench movements along the Svalbard–Northeast Greenland oblique-slip zone compensating for continued crustal extension in the Norwegian–Greenland Rift.

## OPENING OF THE CANADA BASIN

During the Late Jurassic to earliest Cretaceous, the Sverdrup Basin subsided relatively slowly. Cyclical deltaic clastics derived from southern sources shale out basinward where pro-delta clays, in part with source rock characteristics, reach a thickness of some 600 m (Plate 26). Late Jurassic and Early Cretaceous basin subsidence was associated with the intrusion of basic dikes indicating renewed tectonic instability (Balkwill, 1978; Trettin and Balkwill, 1979; Balkwill and Fox, 1982). At the same time, increased tectonic activity along the northern margin of the Sverdrup Basin and the Alaska North Slope is reflected by the differential subsidence of fault blocks in the area of the present-day continental shelf and slope and the gradual uplift of the adjacent stable platforms. Reflection seismic data from the northern margin of Alaska indicate its rifted nature and suggest that tensional tectonics were initiated during the Middle Jurassic, intensified during the Late Jurassic, and persisted until Valanginian time (Grantz et al., 1979, 1981; Grantz and May, 1982, 1984; Hohler and Bischoff, 1986; Hubbard et al., 1987). On the Canadian Arctic margin, similar features are less obvious and have been overprinted by Late

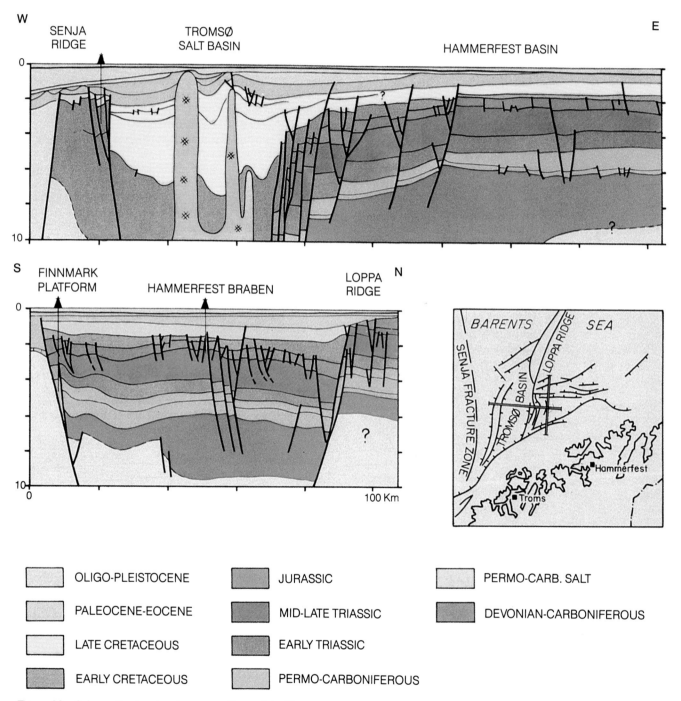

Figure 39—*Schematic structural cross sections of the Tromsø and Hammerfest basins, southwestern Barents Sea. After Norske Shell.*

Cretaceous tensional and wrench tectonics. This is exemplified by the graben system of Banks Island, which subparallels the present-day shelf edge and which started to subside during Middle and Late Jurassic time (Meneley et al., 1975; Miall, 1975; Kerr, 1981a; Norris and Yorath, 1981; Jones, 1982). On the westernmost New Siberian Islands, turbidites of a Middle to Late Jurassic age were probably deposited in a rifted basin (Fujita and Cook, 1986). This basin, referred to as the Makarov Rift, separated the Lomonosov High from the New Siberian Island block.

Overall, it appears that Late Jurassic and earliest Cretaceous rifting along the Canadian and North Alaskan margins progressed rapidly and culminated during the Valanginian in crustal separation between the northern margin of the Sverdrup Basin, the Alaska–Chukchi–Chukotka, and the New Siberian Islands blocks. Doming of areas flanking the incipient Canada Basin gave rise to the development of a pronounced, regional "break-up unconformity" that is clearly evident on the Alaska North Slope (Fig. 40; Bird and Molenaar, 1983; Magoon and Claypool, 1983; Bird, 1986; Hohler and Bischoff, 1986; Hubbard et al., 1987) and also along the northern margin of the Canadian Arctic Archipelago (Balkwill, 1978; Kerr, 1981b; Balkwill and Fox, 1982; Sweeney, 1985; Sobczac et al., 1986;

see also Figs. 13, 14).

Following crustal separation, the Sverdrup Basin continued to subside rapidly with Valanginian to Aptian series attaining a thickness of 1500 m. Tectonic instability continued, however, as indicated by the intrusion of dikes and sills and the extrusion of basaltic flows. During the Valanginian to Aptian, major deltas advanced from the southeast and west into the Sverdrup Basin and to a lesser degree from its northern uplifted margin (Plates 14, 15). During the Aptian and Albian, the northeastern, outer margin of the Sverdrup Basin remained a positive feature. This may be related to persistent transform movements along the Northeast Greenland–Svalbard fracture zone.

In the model proposed here, opening of the Canada Basin involved the counterclockwise rotation of the Alaska–Chukchi block (comprising the Alaska North Slope, the Brooks Range, the Chukchi Sea, and Chukotka) and of the New Siberian Island block, probably representing separate microcratons, away from the Canadian margin (Fig. 7). Sea-floor spreading rates were apparently high with the bulk of the opening of the Canada Basin occurring during the Aptian to Santonian period of single, normal magnetic polarity (see Harland et al., 1982). Furthermore, it is likely that spreading ridge geometries were complex and that several jumps of the sea-floor spreading axes occurred

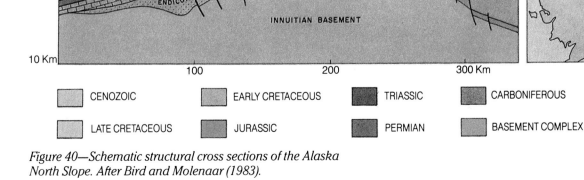

*Figure 40—Schematic structural cross sections of the Alaska North Slope. After Bird and Molenaar (1983).*

during the northwestward drift and rotation of the Alaska–Chuckchi and the New Siberian Islands continental fragments. This could explain the absence of clear magnetic sea-floor anomalies in the Canada Basin (Taylor et al., 1981; Vogt et al., 1982, 1984; Sweeney, 1985). In this model, the Alpha Ridge is interpreted as representing a hotspot track superimposed on a transform fault that can be compared to the Cenozoic Iceland Ridge (Jackson and Johnson, 1984; Forsyth et al., 1986).

During the early phases of opening of the Canada Basin, the northern margin of the Barents–Lomonosov Platform was probably governed by transform faulting. This, in combination with the development of the Franz Josef Land hotspot, may have induced the sharp intra-Valanginian uplift of the Lomonosov High from which deltaic complexes prograded southward onto the Barents Shelf and into the Svalbard Archipelago during the Hauterivian to Albian (Steel and Worsley, 1984).

The Early Cretaceous rotation of the Alaska–Chukchi block cannot be documented paleomagnetically owing to repeated thermal and diagenetic overprinting of the critical strata (Churkin and Trexler, 1981). The proposed predrift reconstruction of the borderlands of the Arctic Ocean (Fig. 7) is, however, supported by the late Paleozoic and early Mesozoic stratigraphic and tectonic framework of the Alaska–Chukchi block, which is fully compatible with that of the Canadian Arctic Islands. In this respect, the trace of the Innuitian deformation front is a major argument in favor of the intra-Cretaceous rotation of the Alaska–Chukchi Block. The Innuitian deformation front leaves the Canadian Arctic Archipelago in the western part of Prince Patrick Island but is recognized again in the northernmost part of the Richardson Mountains (southwest of MacKenzie Delta; Bell, 1973). In northwestern Alaska, the trace of the Innuitian deformation front loops to the south around the eastern Chukchi Sea block and Point Barrow; for this area, seismic data indicate the presence of north-verging thrusts (Grantz et al., 1981). In northeastern Alaska, the Innuitian fold belt underlies the North Slope and is exposed in the British Mountains straddling the Alaska–Canadian border. Detailed structural analyses in the northern Brooks Range suggest, however, that Devonian thrusting was south-vergent (Oldow et al., 1987). This cannot be easily reconciled with the rotational model of Alaska proposed here for the opening of the Canada Basin (for an alternate model for the opening of the Canada Basin, the reader is referred to Hubbard et al., 1987).

According to the model presented here, the Alaska North Slope–Chukchi and the New Siberian Island blocks passed during the opening of the Canada Basin through a polar position and may have been the locus of grounded ice sheets. It is suspected that the Lower Cretaceous Pebble Shale of the Alaska North Slope is a glaciomarine deposit (Bird, 1986). Furthermore, evidence for cold water deposits during the Early Cretaceous comes from the Sverdrup Basin, Western Spitsbergen, and northeastern Siberia (Epshteyn, 1978; Kemper and Hermann, 1981; Brandt, 1986).

# CHAPTER 7
## LATE CRETACEOUS AND PALEOCENE ATLANTIC SEA-FLOOR SPREADING AND ALPINE COLLISION

# INTRODUCTION

In the North Atlantic domain, sea-floor spreading continued during the Cenomanian to early Campanian along axes established during the Aptian and Albian. During the Campanian, crustal separation was achieved between the Labrador Shelf and Greenland and the southern margin of the Rockall–Hutton Bank. With this, the North Atlantic sea-floor spreading axis rapidly propagated northward into the Labrador Sea (Plate 16).

At the same time, the sea-floor spreading axes in the Bay of Biscay and the southern part of the Rockall Trough became extinct (Kristoffersen, 1977; Srivastava, 1978; Olivet et al., 1984). Following this reorganization of sea-floor spreading axes, the North Atlantic–Labrador sea-floor spreading system dominated the late Senonian to Paleocene evolution of the Arctic–North Atlantic rift systems.

Sea-floor spreading in the North Atlantic domain and continued crustal distension in the Baffin Bay and the Norwegian–Greenland Sea rifts (see *Opening of the Labrador Sea* and *Norwegian–Greenland Sea Rift System,* this chapter) was accompanied by the rotation of the Eurasian Craton relative to Greenland and also a rotation of Greenland relative to the North American Craton. This induced transpressional deformations in the northeastern parts of the Sverdrup Basin and possibly also in Svalbard (Kerr, 1981a, 1981b; Price and Shade, 1982; Hanisch, 1983). In the Canada Basin, in which clearly identifiable magnetic sea-floor anomalies are lacking, sea-floor spreading is thought to have terminated during the Late Cretaceous (Sweeney, 1985).

Despite the rotation of Eurasia relative to North America, the sinistral translation between Europe and Africa continued during the Late Cretaceous. This was accompanied by the transtensional opening of oceanic basins along the South Anatolian fracture zone (Whitechurch et al., 1984). Late Cretaceous opening of the South Atlantic–Indian Ocean, on the other hand, induced a change in the drift pattern of Africa, which now began to converge gradually with Laurasia (Olivet et al., 1984; Livermore and Smith, 1985; Savostin et al., 1986; Westphal et al., 1986).

This caused the progressive closure of oceanic basins in the Central and Western Tethys. The Albian to Turonian closure of the south Penninic Ocean and the ensuing collision of the Alpine subduction system with the southern, passive margin of the European Craton was accompanied by the transmission of compressive stresses into the latter. These stresses induced during the Senonian and mid-Paleocene major intraplate compressional and transpressional deformations at distances up to 1300 km to the north of the Alpine collision front (Plate 17; Ziegler, 1987e). Furthermore, there are indications that the rate of crustal extension in the North Sea and Norwegian–Greenland Sea rifts decreased during the Late Cretaceous. Termination of sea-floor spreading in the Bay of Biscay coincides with the onset of convergence of Iberia with the southwestern margin of Europe, their collision, and the early phases of the Pyrenean orogeny (Olivet et al., 1984; Mirouse, 1980).

The coincidence of these phenomena suggests that the northward drift of Africa induced a change in the regional stress patterns affecting the Tethys domain and Western and Central Europe.

The Late Cretaceous is characterized by a major tectonoeustatic rise in sea level, presumably resulting from a global acceleration of sea-floor spreading and a commensurate reduction of the ocean basin volume (Pitman, 1978; Donovan and Jones, 1979). At the end of the Late Cretaceous, sea levels had risen to a maximum high stand of some 110–300 m above the present level, according to some authors (Hays and Pitman, 1973; Vail et al., 1977; Bond, 1978, 1979; Hancock and Kauffmann, 1979). This caused a worldwide overstepping of the Early Cretaceous basin margins and the reopening of seaways linking the colder water Arctic, Barents Shelf and West Siberian Platform seas with the warm water North Atlantic and Tethys oceans. This facilitated a renewed, extensive faunal exchange (Matsumoto, 1973; Tröger, 1978; Wiedmann, 1979). For instance, establishment of a new seaway linking the Arctic Basin and the Norwegian–Greenland Sea is dated as early Cenomanian by the reappearance of boreal faunas in the basins of Northwest and Central Europe from which they were lacking during the late early Aptian and Albian (Stevens, 1973b).

During the Late Cretaceous transgression, extensive carbonate platforms occupied the northern and southern Tethys shelves (Plate 16). In Western, Central, and Eastern Europe much of the Early Cretaceous land areas became inundated. Consequently, the clastic influx into its basins became drastically reduced. This gave rise to the prevalence of clear water conditions and the deposition of the Chalk series (Ziegler, 1982a; Vinogradov, 1969). Detail facies analyses of the chalk of the North Sea area indicate that the depositional water depth of these carbonates ranged from less than 100 m to possibly 1000 m (Hancock and Scholle, 1975; Watts et al., 1980; Hancock, 1984). Upper Cretaceous chalks form an important reservoir for major hydrocarbon accumulations, particularly in the Norwegian and Danish sector of the Central North Sea (Ziegler, 1980; D'Heur, 1986; Sørensen et al., 1986).

In the cold water dominated areas of the Sverdrup Basin, on the Barents Shelf, in the West Siberian Basin, and in the Norwegian–Greenland Sea area, Upper Cretaceous series are represented by open marine shales (Plate 26).

In the Arctic–North Atlantic realm, the mid-Paleocene corresponds to a period of regression (Vail et al., 1977), which was probably induced by regional lithospheric deformations (Cloetingh et al., 1985; Cloetingh, 1986a, 1986b; Plates 17, 26, 27). Particularly in Western and Central Europe, this regression was accompanied by major intra-plate deformations. During the late Paleocene, sea-levels rose again, causing renewed transgressions (Vail et al., 1977).

# EARLY ALPINE OROGENY

The early Alpine orogenic cycle is here defined as spanning Late Cretaceous to mid-Paleocene times (Trümpy, 1980).

During the Late Cretaceous, the Italo-Dinarid promontory continued to rotate counterclockwise relative to Europe as a consequence of the sinistral translation between Africa and Fennosarmatia (Westphal et al., 1986). At the same time, the counterclockwise rotation and northward drift of Africa caused the progressive closure of the South Penninic–Piedmont-Ligurian–Alboran Ocean along a system of south-plunging subduction zones (Tollmann, 1980; Homewood et al., 1980; Trümpy, 1980; Debelmas et al., 1983; Vegas and Banda, 1983). Similarly, gradual closure of the Tethys in the Eastern Mediterranean domain was associated with the eastward propagation of the collision front between the Italo-Dinarid block and the Dinarid–Hellenic–South Pontides subduction system (Michard et al., 1984; Bonneau, 1984; Plate 16).

In the Dinarides and Hellenides, internal nappes became stacked (Aubouin, 1973; Richter, 1978; Channell et al., 1979; Cadet et al., 1980; Bonneau, 1982), and in the southern Pontides Tethyan ophiolites became obducted during the Senonian onto the Anatolid–Tauride Platform (e.g., Bozkir nappes) (Sengör and Yilmaz, 1981; Okay, 1984). In the North Pontides-Transcaucasian arc, the Late Cretaceous corresponds to a major orogenic cycle that was punctuated by widespread calc-alkaline volcanism. This was accompanied by compressional foreland deformations in the Crimean and the Caucasus (Adamia et al., 1981; Borsuk and Sholop, 1983; Khain, 1984a).

In the intra-Carpathian domain, Albian and Late Cretaceous compressional deformation of the internal Dacides was associated with the closure of the oceanic Transylvanian–Pienid basin and the imbrication of the external Dacides. The deformation front of the Dacides looped southward around the stable Moesian platform and linked up to the east with the North Pontide–Transcaucasus thrust front (Burchfiel, 1980; Sandulescu, 1982, 1984). During the Late Cretaceous, extensive synorogenic flysch series were deposited in the Carpatho-Balkan-Pontides foredeep. Laterally, these gave way to carbonate platforms covering the stable foreland (Vinogradov, 1969; Sandulescu, 1984; Borsuk and Sholop, 1983).

In the Alpine domain, progressive closure of the Penninic–Piedmont Ocean culminated during the Albian to Turonian in the collision of the Austro-Alpine subduction systems with the Central Penninic Block and the development of a new subduction zone along its northern margin in the area of the Central and Eastern Alps. Following the imbrication and partial subduction of the North Penninic Basin, which apparently was characterized by a drastically attenuated continental crust, the orogenic front reached probably during the late Turonian to early Senonian the passive Helvetic shelf margin of the Eastern Alps and the Northern Carpathians (Frisch 1979; Geyssant, 1980; Trümpy, 1980; Tollmann, 1980; Debelmas et al., 1983; Winkler and Bernoulli, 1986). This was presumably accompanied by the development of a true A-subduction zone at the Penninic–Helvetic boundary, marking the southern limit of the North European Craton.

As a consequence of the collision of the Alpine orogenic system with the fractured and weakened European foreland, compressional stresses were transmitted into the latter. These stresses induced the intra-Senonian, Sub-Hercynian reactivation of preexisting intraplate discontinuities in the Alpine foreland (see next section of this chapter). In particular, the Mesozoic rifts and wrench-induced basins with their thinned crust, acting like shear-pins in an otherwise rigid craton, started to collapse and became inverted to varying degrees. At the same time, the Permo-Carboniferous and Late Jurassic–Early Cretaceous fracture zones, which transected the Bohemian Massif, became reactivated and governed the gradual uplift of major basement blocks along wrench and steep reverse faults (Malkovsky, 1987; Schröder, 1987). These compressional foreland stresses caused during the Senonian intraplate deformations at distances up to 1200 km to the north and northwest of the Alpine collision front (Fig. 41).

In the west Central and Western Alps, the Late Cretaceous closure of the Penninic–Piedmont Ocean was accompanied by the obduction of oceanic crustal material onto the eastern flanks of the Briançonnais High, the so-called Piedmont domain. Development of an A-subduction zone in the North Penninic Trough did not, however, progress further westward than the Central Alps (Debelmas et al., 1983). Correspondingly compressional

stresses were not yet exerted onto the foreland of the Western Alps where intra-Senonian compressional intraplate deformations are conspicuously absent (Ziegler, 1987c).

In the Ligurian and Alboran oceans, the development of intraoceanic subduction zones was followed by the Senonian obduction of ophiolites onto southern Piedmont and onto the margin of the Corsica–Sardinia block (Debelmas et al., 1983; Harris, 1985). This was accompanied by the compressional deformations of Mesozoic graben systems of the Lower Rhone Valley (Baudrimont and Dubois, 1977). Furthermore, there is evidence that Senonian compressional deformations, giving rise to metamorphism, also affected the margins of the Alboran–Kabylia block corresponding to the internal zones of the Betic Cordillera of southern Iberia and the Maghrebian fold belt of northern Algeria and Tunisia (Wildi, 1983; Vegas and Banda, 1983; Dercourt et al., 1986).

In the Northern Carpathians and in the Alpine domain, the Late Cretaceous evolution of the Austro-Alpine and Penninic nappe systems was accompanied by the accumulation of synorogenic flysch series in the North and South Penninic troughs and in the Piedmont Basin. From the latter, basin axial currents transported clastics into the northern parts of the Lagonegro Trough (Ksiaskiewicz, 1965; Gwinner, 1971; Schwab, 1981; Homewood, 1983; Debelmas et al., 1983). Progressive stacking of the crystalline cored Austro-Alpine and Penninic nappes was associated with high-pressure metamorphism but only a very low level of synorogenic volcanism. In this aspect, the Alps and Northern Carpathian differs from the Southern and Eastern Carpathians in which Late Cretaceous andesitic volcanism played an important role (Burchfiel, 1980; Homewood et al., 1980; Milnes and Pfiffner, 1980; Trümpy, 1980; Tollmann, 1980; Sandulescu, 1982, 1984).

During the late Campanian to Danian, little compressional deformation can be observed in the Alpine foreland and in the Helvetic domain (Trümpy, 1980; Ziegler, 1987c). This may be interpreted as reflecting a decrease or even a pause in the dextral oblique convergence between the Austro-Alpine and Penninic nappe systems and the European foreland. These movements accelerated/resumed again, however, during the mid-Paleocene and gave rise to the second, "Laramide" phase of foreland compression which was even more pervasive than the intra-Senonian, "Sub-Hercynian" one (Fig. 42). Northernmost deformations are recorded from the Central North Sea Egersund Basin, located some 1300 km to the north of the present Alpine deformation front (Pegrum, 1984).

Since the foreland of the Western Alps was also affected by intra-Paleocene compressional deformations, it must be assumed that the collision front between the Penninic nappe system and the Helvetic Shelf had propagated westward. Stratigraphic evidence suggests, however, that the north Penninic Valais Trough of the Western Alps became closed only during the Eocene (Homewood et al., 1980; Laubscher and Bernoulli, 1982; Debelmas et al., 1983). From this it can be inferred that the crust and upper mantle underlying the Valais Trough were sufficiently rigid to facilitate the transmission of tangential stresses into the foreland.

The strong Laramide deformation of the Alpine and North Carpathian foreland indicates that the Central and Eastern Alpine nappe systems were partially mechanically coupled with the foreland at their respective A-subduction zones.

It is likely that during the late Senonian and Paleocene crustal shortening persisted, on a moderate scale, also in the Ligurian–Alboran Sea and along the southern margin of the Alboran-

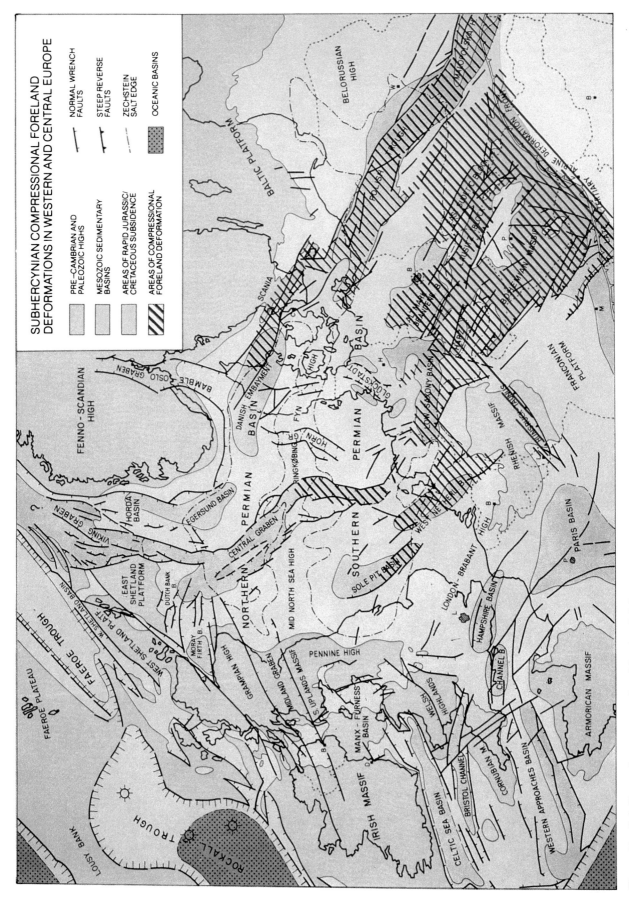

*Figure 41—Sub-Hercynian compressional foreland deformations of Western and Central Europe.*

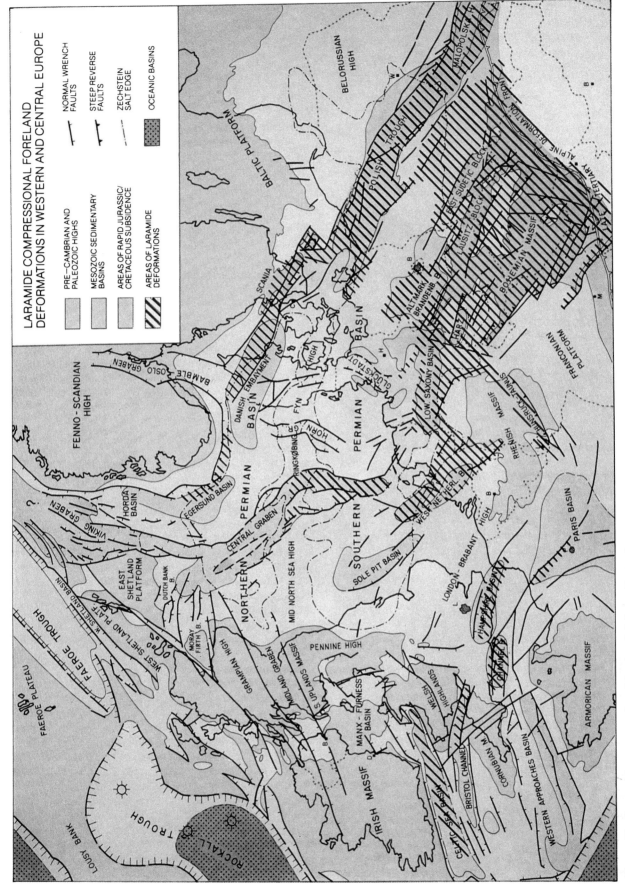

*Figure 42—Laramide compressional foreland deformations of Western and Central Europe.*

Kabylia block (Plate 17). This concept is supported by limited stratigraphic data from the Rif and Tellian nappes of northern Algeria and Tunisia (Wildi, 1983) and the Betic Cordillera of southern Iberia (Diaz de Federico et al., 1980; Durand-Delga and Fontboté, 1980; Vegas and Banda, 1983).

In the Eastern Carpathians, crustal shortening continued during the Paleocene, as evident by the accumulation of flysch in the foredeep basin paralleling the deformation front of the external Dacides (Sandulescu, 1982, 1984). Also in the Hellenides and Dinarides, orogenic movements, paralleled by the deposition of extensive flysch series, gave rise to local metamorphism and the stacking of the most internal isopic zones (Aubouin, 1973; Bonneau, 1982). In Turkey, the Anatolide and Bozkir nappes were emplaced while the Levantine oceanic basins began to close with ophiolites being obducted during the Maastrichtian (Sengör and Yilmaz, 1981; Okay, 1984; Whitechurch et al., 1984; Ricou et al., 1984).

On the other hand, late Senonian to Paleocene back-arc extension induced the opening of two oceanic basins in the Black Sea area (Zonenshain and Le Pichon, 1986).

## COMPRESSIONAL INTRAPLATE DEFORMATIONS IN NORTHWESTERN EUROPE

With the decrease in the rate of crustal extension in the North Sea rift system during the Albian and Late Cretaceous, the wrench-induced basins flanking the northern margins of the London–Brabant and Rhenish–Bohemian massifs became tectonically quiescent (Fig. 35; Plate 30). Similarly, the Polish–Danish Trough ceased to subside differentially and its early Late Cretaceous evolution reflects regional downwarping, possibly in response to progressive lithospheric cooling and contraction.

Following crustal separation in the Bay of Biscay, the rifts of the Celtic Sea–Western Approaches area also became tectonically inactive and the area started to subside regionally (Plate 29). With this, tectonic activity in the wrench-induced basins in the area of the English Channel and also in the Paris Basin abated (Ziegler, 1982a, 1987a).

During the Late Cretaceous, eustatically rising sea levels caused the progressive overstepping of the Early Cretaceous basin margins (Plates 15, 16). By early Senonian time, much of the Irish, Welsh, and Armorican massifs were inundated while the Rhenish–Bohemian Massif remained a positive feature. To the southeast, the Paris Basin was open to the Helvetic Shelf seas. It is, however, uncertain to what extent the area occupied by the Rhine Graben and the South German Franconian Platform were covered by the Late Cretaceous seas since in these areas Mesozoic sediments became deeply truncated during the Cenozoic (Fig. 45). On the other hand, there is clear evidence that the Cretaceous seas encroached onto the Bohemian Massif along the Southwest Bohemian Borderzone. Tectonic activity along this long-standing fracture system had apparently also abated during the early part of the Late Cretaceous (Schröder, 1987).

In the northern foreland of the Carpathians and the Eastern and Central Alps, tectonic activity gradually intensified again during the late Turonian to Campanian as a result of the collision of the Alpine–Carpathian nappe systems with the passive margin of the Helvetic Shelf. This is reflected by the intra-Senonian gradual uplift of major basement blocks along steep reverse and wrench faults in the Bohemian Massif and in southern Sweden and by the inversion of major Mesozoic grabens

and wrench-induced basins in the southern North Sea area, in northern Germany, in Denmark, and in Poland. This phase of intraplate compressional/transpressional deformation is referred to as the Sub-Hercynian tectonism (Plate 30; Fig. 16; Ziegler, 1987c).

Basin inversion is defined as the reversal of the subsidence patterns of a sedimentary basin, which had developed under a tensional or transtensional tectonic regime, in response to compressional or transpressional stresses (Fig. 80). Basin inversion generally involves uplift of the basin floor and deformations of the basin fill, whereby the throw on tensional faults, controlling the original structural relief of the respective graben or trough, becomes partly or totally reversed (Bally, 1984). This implies that during basin inversion a commensurate amount of crustal shortening occurs, which is responsible for the deformation of the basin fill. This is reflected in the buckling-up of major anticlinoria, the crestal parts of which generally become subjected to erosion while in adjacent, secondary basins sedimentation is often continuous. Owing to the greater preinversion sedimentary thickness in basinal areas, the structural relief created by inversion movements is in many inverted basins considerably smaller at depth than at shallower levels (Voigt, 1962; Ziegler, 1982a, 1983b, 1987c; Bally, 1984).

The structural style of inverted basins is very variable and depends on the preinversion configuration of the respective basin, the lithologic composition of its sedimentary fill, the degree of its inversion (amount of strain), and the orientation of the basin axis relative to the greatest principal stress that induced its inversion. In this respect, the presence of major halite and/or shale layers, acting as detachment planes, can play a significant role in the disharmony of the structural style observed at shallow and at deeper levels (e.g., Lower Saxony, Broad Fourteens and Sole Pit basins; van Hoorn, 1987b; van Wijhe, 1987; Betz et al., 1987).

In the northern Alpine and Carpathian foreland intra-Senonian, Sub-Hercynian, compressional/transpressional deformations related to the Alpine collision are restricted to areas between the Polish Trough in the east and the Broad Fourteens–West Netherlands Basin to the west. They are also recognized along the Fennoscandian borderzone in southern Sweden and northern Denmark and in the Danish and Dutch sector of the North Sea Central grabens (Fig. 41; Plates 29, 30).

In the area of the Bohemian Massif, the uplifting of major basement blocks along Permo-Carboniferous and Late Jurassic–Early Cretaceous fracture zones also started during the late Turonian and early Senonian as illustrated by the increased clastic influx into the adjacent basins (Malkovsky, 1987; Nachtmann and Wagner, 1987; Bachmann et al., 1987).

During the Maastrichtian and Danian, compressional foreland deformations abated, at least in the more distal parts of the Alpine foreland, but resumed again during the middle Paleocene, giving rise to the even more pervasive "Laramide" phase of inversion. This is the main inversion phase of the Polish Trough, the Altmark–Brandenburg, the Sub-Hercynian, the Lower Saxony, and the Broad Fourteens–West Netherlands basins as well as of the Dutch and Danish part of the Central North Sea Graben and the Fennoscandian borderzone. Northernmost traces of basin inversion occur in the Egersuud Basin, offshore southern Norway. Mild mid-Paleocene inversion movements have also been recorded in the Celtic Sea Trough, in the Fastnet Basin, the Channel area, and in the Paris Basin. In contrast, the Western Approaches Trough was hardly affected by the Laramide movements (Ziegler, 1987a, 1987b,

1987c), (Fig. 42; Plates 29, 30).

Although not closely bracketed by a corresponding stratigraphic record, the main phase of deformation of the Bohemian Massif and of the areas occupied by the Swiss, German, and Austrian part of the Cenozoic Molasse Basin, is probably also of a mid-Paleocene age. Subsurface data from the Vienna Basin (Wessely, 1987) and the Carpathian foredeep (Kolarova and Roth, 1977; Heller and Moryc, 1984) clearly indicates that the area affected by the Late Cretaceous and mid-Paleocene compressional foreland deformations extends at least some 50 km southward in the autochthonous substratum under the East Alpine and Carpathian nappes (Fig. 45). Similarly, the southern parts of the strongly inverted Polish Trough appear to extend under the Carpathian nappe systems (Pozaryski and Brockwicz-Lewinski, 1978; Pozaryski and Zytko, 1979). In the Central Alps, similar foreland deformations are considered responsible for the latest Cretaceous-Early Tertiary unconformity recognized in the area of the Aare Massif and the sub-Helvetic and Helvetic nappes (Herb, 1965).

The degree to which the different rift- and wrench-induced Mesozoic basins in the northern Alpine and Carpathian foreland became inverted during the Sub-Hercynian and Laramide phases of foreland compression is very variable. In general it can be observed that the intensity of inversion decreases with increasing distance from the Alpine collision front.

This is particularly evident in the case of the Polish–Danish Trough (Fig. 43). The southern parts of the Polish Trough have been inverted to the degree that the graben floor, forming the Malopolska Massif, is now exposed in the Holy Cross Mountains. Its northern parts are characterized by gentle anticlinoria that have been truncated to Jurassic levels and display a structural relief of some 2000 m. Along the Fennoscandian Borderzone, major basement blocks have been tilted up, presumably along steep reverse faults, while in northern Jutland inversion movements induced only gentle undulations at the Late Cretaceous Chalk level (Fig. 44; Norling and Bergström, 1987; Liboriussen et al., 1987).

The scope and effects of the Sub-Hercynian and Laramide phases of compressional deformation in the Alpine foreland can be assessed by a comparison of Fig. 42 with the pre-Tertiary geological map given in Fig. 45 (see also Ziegler, 1982a).

Considering that during the Paleocene the Alpine thrust front was probably located some 75 to 100 km further south than at present, the total area affected by these intra-Paleocene foreland deformations and the structural relief created by them is quite spectacular and can be readily compared with the Lara-

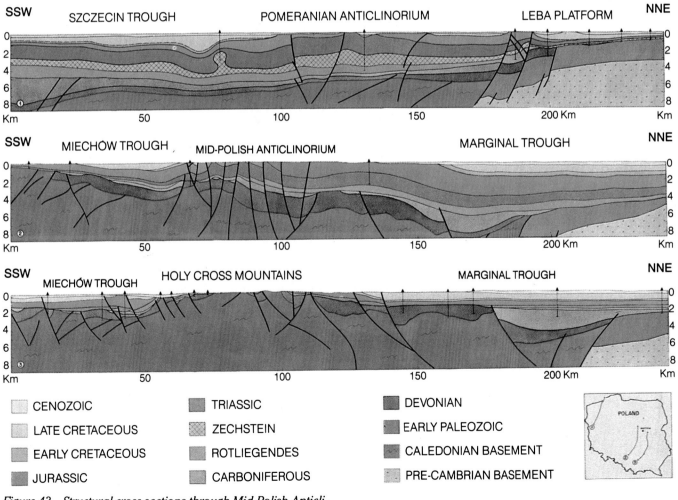

*Figure 43—Structural cross sections through Mid-Polish Anticlinorium. After Znosko and Pajchlowa (1968).*

mide foreland tectonics of the Rocky Mountains (Brewer et al., 1980) and the Permian foreland structures of the Timan–Pechora area (Ulmishek, 1982; Matviyevskaya et al., 1986). While the Rocky Mountains consist essentially of basement blocks carried by reverse faults, to which the Harz Mountains and the Lausitz Block in the Bohemian Massif can be compared, the Timan–Pechora foreland folds, which represent inverted Devonian rifts, are analogs, for example, for the Polish Anticlinorium (Pozaryski and Brochwicz-Lewinski, 1978).

The crustal configuration of the Polish Trough, which is controlled by refraction and deep reflections surveys, indicates that beneath its axial, inverted part the crust–mantle interface is not pulled up but is somewhat depressed and forms the so-called Guterch Graben (Fig. 46; Guterch et al., 1976, 1986). Reconstructions of preinversion profiles across the Polish Graben indicate, however, that in its deepest parts Mesozoic and late Paleozoic sediments attained thicknesses of up to 10 km (Pozaryski and Brochwicz-Lewinski, 1978). In order to accommodate such a thick sedimentary sequence, isostatic considerations require that a significant amount of crustal thinning through mechanical stretching and possible physicochemical processes must have taken place during the Late Permian and Mesozoic rifting stages of the Polish Trough. Its preinversion crustal configuration presumably resembled that of the present-day Central North Sea (Fig. 61).

These features suggest that during the inversion of the Polish Trough, its crust became mechanically thickened again by transpression-induced crustal shortening. As a consequence of its intense inversion, the Polish Trough achieved isostatic and thermal stability during the Early Tertiary.

The amount of crustal shortening associated with the Sub-Hercynian and Laramide inversion of the different basins in the Alpine foreland and the deformation of the Variscan massifs is at present still difficult to estimate but is unlikely to exceed a few tens of kilometers. These displacements require a decoupling within the crust of the foreland and/or between its crust and the underlying upper mantle or even within the upper mantle. On the other hand, as these intraplate deformations are apparently related to collisional events in the Alpine and Carpathian fold belts, a certain amount of mechanical coupling is required between the foreland plate and the nappe system of these orogens at the respective A-subduction zones in order to facilitate the transmission of tangential stresses from collision zones into the foreland. A working model for the transmission of tangential stresses from collision zones into foreland areas has been developed by Neugebauer and Gao (1985).

Crustal shortening induced by these compressional intra-plate deformations requires the subduction of a commensurate

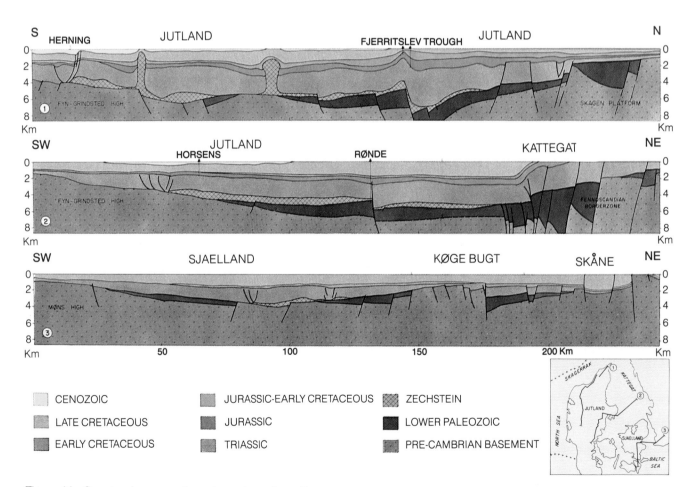

*Figure 44—Structural cross sections through northern Denmark and southern Sweden.*

*Figure 45—Geological map of Western and Central Europe with Cenozoic sediments removed.*

amount of lithosphere, either in the Alpine orogen, if a decoupling occurred within the foreland plate, or locally, if the entire lithosphere is involved in these deformations (see Chapter 10).

## IBERIAN MICROCONTINENT

With the late Aptian onset of sea-floor spreading in the Bay of Biscay, Iberia began to rotate counterclockwise away from the Armorican margin of France (Olivet et al., 1982, 1984). As a consequence of continued sea-floor spreading in the North Atlantic, this motion was accompanied by transtensional shear in the Pyrenean and Cantabrian domain, giving rise to metamorphism, an alkaline magmatism, and the tectonic emplacement ultrabasics during the Albian to early Senonian (Plate 27; Choukroune and Mattauer, 1978; Dubois and Séguin, 1978; Brunet, 1984; Vielzeuf and Kornprobst, 1984; Goldberg et al., 1986; Boess and Hoppe, 1986). The southern limit of the Iberian plate was formed by the Azores and Alboran fracture zones. As such, the Iberian microplate occupied an intermediate position between the Eurasian and the African plates.

During the early Campanian, sea-floor spreading ceased in the Bay of Biscay and Iberia began to converge in a clockwise, oblique sense with the southwestern margin of Europe. In the eastern Pyrenees and in Cantabria, first compressional deformations are evident during the Santonian and Campanian. These probably marked the onset of convergence and the subsequent collision between Iberia and the southern margin of Europe, and with this the beginning of the Pyrenean orogeny during which oceanic crust along the southern margin of the Bay of Biscay became subducted (Bilotte, 1978; Boillot et al., 1979, 1985; Alvarado, 1980; Mirouse, 1980; Olivet et al., 1984; de Luca et al., 1985; Sancho et al., 1987). During the late Senonian and Paleocene, continued convergence of Iberia and Europe resulted in the westward propagation of their mutual collision front. This was accompanied by the accumulation of

late Senonian and Paleogene synorogenic deep water clastics (flysch) in the rapidly narrowing Pyrenean trough. In southern France, contemporaneous intraplate compressional deformations are evident by the uparching of the Durance axis and the Toulouse Peninsula (Baudrimont and Dubois, 1977; Plaziat, 1975, 1981).

In southwestern Portugal there is evidence for late Senonian transpressional deformations along northeast-striking faults. Late Senonian and Paleocene transtensional dislocations along north–northwest-trending fracture systems induced the intrusion of alkaline and ultrabasic magmas in the area of Lisbon and also offshore on Gorringe Bank (Plate 28; Antunes et al., 1980; Mougenot, 1981; Feraud et al., 1982).

During the Cenomanian to Santonian, much of eastern Iberia was occupied by an extensive, shallow marine carbonate platform. The upper Senonian to Paleocene series is developed in a regressive, partly continental facies. Deeper water conditions dominated the southeastern margin of Iberia, which had not yet collided with the Alboran block (Plates 16, 17; Alvarado, 1980; Azema et al., 1974, 1979; Garcia-Hernandez, et al., 1980; Plaziat, 1981).

Transpressional deformations along the margins of the Alboran block were also initiated during the Santonian (Wildi, 1983; Vegas and Banda, 1983).

This was probably a consequence of the northward drift of Africa, which can also be held responsible for the convergence and collision of Iberia and Europe and the reactivation of fracture systems in southwestern Portugal. In this context, it should be noted that the first compressional deformations evident in Cantabria appear to be contemporaneous with the last phases of sea-floor spreading in the Bay of Biscay. The subsequent termination of sea-floor spreading in the Bay of Biscay may be a direct consequence of the build-up of regional compressive stresses in response to the convergence of Africa and Europe. In this respect, it may be surmised that sea-floor spreading in the Bay of Biscay was not directly associated with a deep

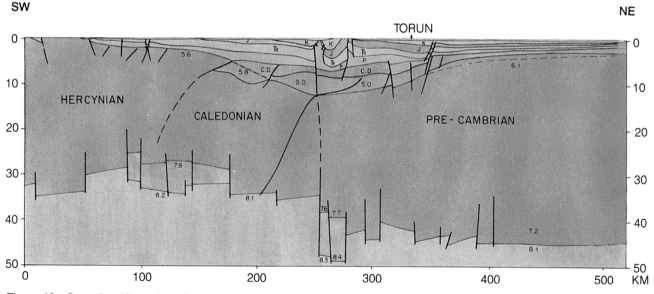

*Figure 46—Crustal configuration of the Polish Trough along DSS profile VII. Interval velocities given in km/sec. After Guterch et al. (1976).*

asthenospheric upwelling convective system, but was rather the result of asthenospheric advection induced by the oblique translation and rotation of Iberia relative to the southern margin of Europe. This motion of Iberia was presumably governed by the North Atlantic sea-floor spreading system, which most likely was associated with deep asthenospheric upwelling convection currents.

## OPENING OF THE LABRADOR SEA

Rifting activity in the Labrador Sea culminated during the Santonian–Campanian in crustal separation and the onset of sea-floor spreading. With this, the Labrador Shelf became tectonically inactive and its further development followed the pattern typical for passive margins (Fig. 47; Umpleby, 1979; Grant, 1980; Gradstein and Srivastava, 1980).

In the southeastern parts of the Labrador Sea, the oldest magnetic sea-floor anomalies recognized are anomalies 34 and 33. In its northwestern parts, where magnetic anomalies are poorly defined, the oldest one identified is anomaly 31 (Srivastava, 1978; Srivastava et al., 1981, 1982; Tucholke and Fry, 1985).

The magnetic sea-floor anomalies of the Labrador Sea show that sea-floor spreading patterns established during the Senonian persisted until late Paleocene time. To the north, the Labrador Sea sea-floor spreading axis terminated in the Davis Strait at the Ungava transform fault zone (McMillan, 1979; Srivastava et al., 1981, 1982; Klose et al., 1982). Seismic and well data indicate that movements along this fault system were of a sinistral transpressional nature and involved the uplifting of high trends (Fig. 52).

In the Baffin Bay, crustal distension continued through Late Cretaceous and Paleocene time. At its northern termination, there is evidence for tensional tectonics in Devon Island and in the southern parts of Ellesmere Island (Mayr, 1984). This suggests that the bulk of crustal stretching taking place in the Baffin Bay was taken up by extension in the Arctic Archipelago and only to a minor degree by strike-slip movements along the Nares Strait transform zone (Plate 16). There is stratigraphic evidence that the Eclipse Trough and probably also the Lancaster

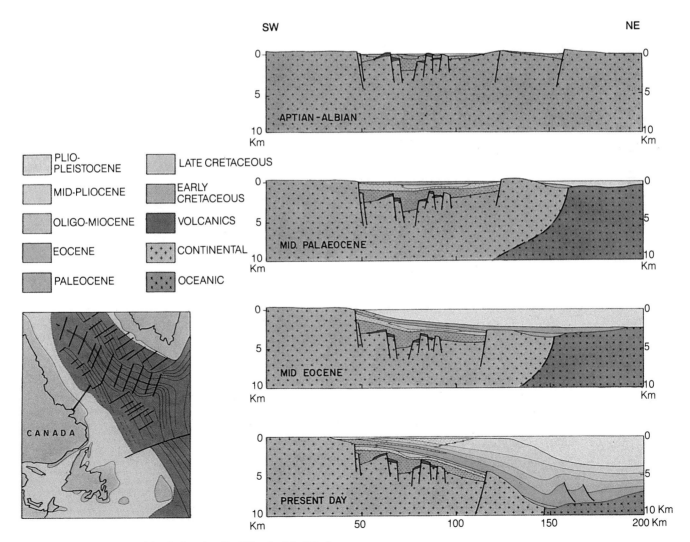

*Figure 47—Evolution of the Labrador Shelf Basin. Modified after Umpleby (1979).*

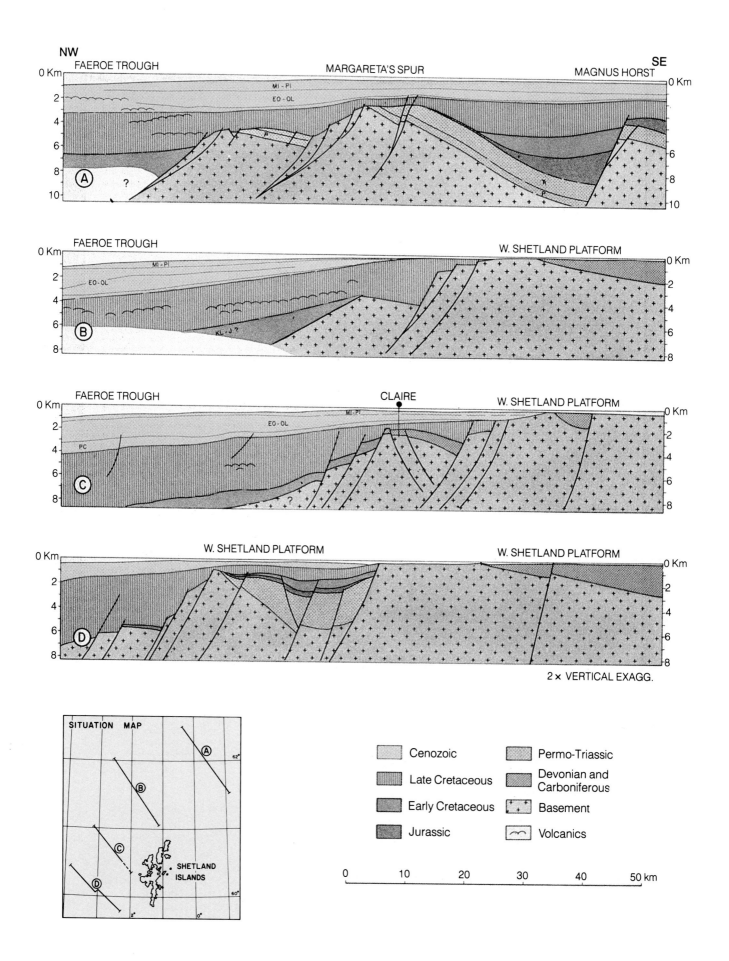

NW
FAEROE TROUGH          MARGARETA'S SPUR          MAGNUS HORST          SE

FAEROE TROUGH          W. SHETLAND PLATFORM

FAEROE TROUGH          CLAIRE          W. SHETLAND PLATFORM

W. SHETLAND PLATFORM          W. SHETLAND PLATFORM

2 × VERTICAL EXAGG.

SITUATION MAP

SHETLAND ISLANDS

| | Cenozoic | | Permo-Triassic |
| | Late Cretaceous | | Devonian and Carboniferous |
| | Early Cretaceous | | Basement |
| | Jurassic | | Volcanics |

0    10    20    30    40    50 km

◄ *Figure 48—Schematic structural cross sections of the northern part of the Faeroe–West Shetland Trough. After Shell UK Expro.*

Sound Rift continued to subside during the Late Cretaceous and Paleocene (Beh, 1975; Miall et al., 1980; McWhae, 1981; Price and Shade, 1982). The Lancaster Sound Graben may extend westward into the Parry Channel fracture zone (Kerr, 1981b). It is also likely that the aeromagnetically defined Melville Bight Graben on the Northwest Greenland Shelf continued to subside differentially during this time (Henderson, 1976). The late Cenomanian to Turonian extrusion of tholeiitic basalts in northern Axel Heiberg Island (Sweeney, 1985), and the occurrence of time equivalent bimodal intrusives and extrusives in northern Ellesmere Island (Trettin and Parrish, 1987) in the onshore prolongation of the Alpha Ridge, may be related to a last phase of transform movements along the latter.

Sea-floor spreading in the Labrador Sea and crustal extension in the Baffin Bay involved a counterclockwise rotation of Greenland relative to the North American Craton (Fig. 55; Beh, 1975; Kerr, 1981b; Price and Shade, 1982). This induced compressional deformations in northeastern Ellesmere Island and with this the onset of the Eurekan orogeny (Balkwill, 1978; Kerr, 1981a, 1981b). In the Sverdrup Basin, this is reflected by the outbuilding of deltaic fans during the Campanian from the gradually uplifted eastern part of Ellesmere Island. During the Maastrichtian and Paleocene, compressional deformations intensified and affected much of Ellesmere Island and also Axel Heiberg Island. At the same time, deltaic clastics spread over much of the northern part of the Canadian Arctic Archipelago (Miall, 1981, 1984a, 1984b). Contemporaneous compressional deformations are also evident on the north coast of Greenland (Håkansson and Pedersen, 1982).

During the Turonian, and possibly even earlier, the Arctic seas ingressed the Baffin Bay Rift as indicated by the occurrence of corresponding marine faunas on Núgssuaq Peninsula (Disko Bay area, central West Greenland; McKenna, 1983). Arctic faunas appeared on the Labrador Shelf for the first time during the Campanian while Atlantic faunas reached the Disko Bay area at the same time. In the latter, Maastrichtian faunas reflect a mixture of Arctic and Atlantic waters (Gradstein and Srivastava, 1980; McKenna, 1983).

This suggests that during the Turonian and early Senonian, the Davis Strait High (Srivastava, 1983) formed an effective barrier between the Arctic-dominated Baffin Bay sea arm and the Atlantic-dominated Labrador Sea (Plate 16). This barrier apparently broke down during the Campanian early phases of sea-floor spreading in the Labrador Sea. This new connection between the Arctic and the Atlantic Seas became constricted, however, and finally interrupted during the Paleocene and Eocene as a consequence of the uplift of the Eurekan fold belt in the eastern Arctic Archipelago (Plates 17, 18).

The occurrence of tuffaceous material in the Late Cretaceous sediments of central West Greenland reflects volcanic activity, possibly associated with the Ungava transform fault system (Plate 28; Henderson et al., 1981; McKenna, 1983; Rolle, 1985).

# NORWEGIAN–GREENLAND SEA RIFT SYSTEM

During the Late Cretaceous, crustal extension across the Norwegian–Greenland Sea Rift was concentrated on its axial parts. Overall it appears, however, that the rate of crustal stretching decreased during the Late Cretaceous and that dike intrusion along the zone of future crustal separation became increasingly important (Bukovics and Ziegler, 1985).

It is also likely that during this time the Iceland Sea Rift, located between the Rockall–Hatton Bank and southeastern Greenland, was active. In view of the limited geophysical data available from this area and its pervasive cover with uppermost Paleocene and lower Eocene volcanics, this hypothesis cannot, however, be supported by concrete evidence (Roberts et al., 1984). On the other hand, the occurrence of Danian shallow marine shales and clastics in the south-central East Greenland Kangerdlugssuaq area lends some support to this concept (Soper et al., 1976; Higgins and Soper, 1981).

## Rockall–Faeroe–West Shetland Trough

Although sea-floor spreading had apparently ceased in the southern Rockall Trough during the Campanian (Roberts et al., 1981a), there is evidence for minor Late Senonian igneous activity on the Rockall Bank (Harrison et al., 1979) and along the north coast of Ireland (Slyne Head, Killala Bay, and southwest Donegal; M.D. Max, personal communication). It is uncertain whether in the northern part of the Rockall Trough, which is probably underlain by a drastically thinned continental crust, the Rosemary Bank, Anton Dohrn Bank, and Hebrides Terrace seamounts had already developed to their full dimensions during the latest Cretaceous or only during the Paleocene–Eocene Thulean volcanic period (see Chapter 8).

During the Late Cretaceous and early Paleogene, the Rockall Trough linked up northward with the Faeroe–West Shetland Trough from which it is now separated by the Wyville–Thomson Ridge. This ridge is formed by predominantly Paleocene–Eocene volcanics (Fig. 51; Roberts et al., 1983).

In the Faeroe–West Shetland Trough, many faults, controlling the base Cretaceous block-faulted relief, die out upwards in Upper Cretaceous shales. Master faults associated with the margins of this rift remained active, however, into Paleocene times. Particularly in the northern parts of the Faeroe–West Shetland Trough, reflection seismic data indicate the occurrence of volcanics and sills within the Upper Cretaceous series (Fig. 48; Plate 27). Some of these have been calibrated by wells and found to consist of dolerites yielding a Campanian to Maastrichtian age. Toward the northwest, the Faeroe–West Shetland Basin is separated from the Faeroe Basin by a geophysically defined major lineament that is partly overlain by Upper Cretaceous shales (Fig. 36). Previously, this lineament was interpreted as an intrusive body, possibly of Campanian–Maastrichtian or Paleocene–Eocene age (Ridd, 1983). Recent seismic evidence suggests, however, that this lineament consists of a heavily intruded basement block (Duindam and van Hoorn, 1987).

Upper Cretaceous shales and marls attain thicknesses of 3–5 km in the Faeroe–West Shetland Trough. The mid-Paleocene low stand in sea level was accompanied by the progradation of deltaic systems over the flanks of this trough and the accumulation of widespread deep water clastic fans in its axial parts (Fig. 48).

Although Late Cretaceous and Paleocene crustal extension in

the Faeroe–West Shetland Trough was accompanied by an increasing level of igneous activity, it is doubtful whether locally crustal separation was achieved in this rift as postulated by Hanisch (1983, 1984b), Price and Rattey (1984), and Bott (1984).

## Central and Northern North Sea

In the Central and Northern North Sea, Upper Cretaceous chalks and marls progressively infilled the sea-floor topography of the Viking and Central grabens and onlapped against intrabasinal highs and the graben flanks (Fig. 18; see also Ziegler et al., 1986). Many of the faults that control the Early Cretaceous graben relief die out within the Upper Cretaceous strata, and only a few master faults show continued displacement growth during the Late Cretaceous. Intra-Senonian block faulting is locally evident, however.

It is inferred that in the Central and Viking Graben, Late Cretaceous sedimentation rates somewhat exceeded subsidence rates. Thus, despite generally rising sea levels, water depths decreased gradually at least until Maastrichtian time. However, true shallower water conditions were never established within the axial parts of the North Sea graben system (Hancock and Scholle, 1975; Watts et al., 1980; Hatton, 1986). This is further supported by the occurrence of Paleocene sandstone turbidites in these grabens, which were deposited in response to the intra-Paleocene low stand in sea level (Morton, 1982). Outside these grabens, Late Cretaceous and Paleocene sedimentation rates apparently remained in step with subsidence rates and cyclically rising sea levels. During the Late Cretaceous, the area of sedimentation expanded substantially and encroached on the Fennoscandian Shield and the Scottish Highlands. Late Cretaceous series attain maximum thicknesses of 1000 to 2000 m in the Central and Viking Graben and also in the Danish Basin (Ziegler, 1982a).

Crustal stretching played only a minor role during the Late Cretaceous and Paleocene evolution of the North Sea Basin. Its regional downwarping can be related to lithospheric cooling whereby water loading in response to rising sea levels and sediment loading of the lithosphere had an overprinting effect (Sclater and Christie, 1980; Wood and Barton, 1983).

## Mid-Norway Basin and Central East Greenland

In the Mid-Norway Basin, tectonic activity abated during the Late Cretaceous. Minor syndepositional faulting, affecting Late Cretaceous strata, is evident on the Trøndelag Platform but is more important along the shoreward margin of the Vøring Plateau (Figs. 37, 38). In the Vøring and Møre basins, Late Cretaceous pelagic shales and marls attain thicknesses on the order of 2–4 km while on the Trøndelage Platform they hardly exceed a thickness of a few hundred meters. The Nordland Ridge forming the outer margin of the Trøndelag Platform remained emergent during the Late Cretaceous. As the Faeroe-Shetland and Vøring escarpment is approached, reflection seismic data indicate the occurrence of volcanics at increasingly shallower levels and also at an increasing frequency. Although not calibrated by well data, these volcanics are likely to be of Late Cretaceous to Paleocene–Eocene age (Plate 26).

Late Cretaceous and Paleocene series onlap and pinch out on the flanks of the Vøring Plateau and thin toward the Faeroe-Shetland escarpment (Fig. 37). These features presumably formed a system of highs that marked the outer margin of the Møre and Vøring basins. In the area of these highs, seismic resolution is, however, impeded by nearly continuous Late Paleocene–Early Eocene basalt flows (Fig. 38; Bøen et al., 1984; Bukovics et al., 1983; Bukovics and Ziegler, 1985).

In Central East Greenland, limited outcrop data suggest that rifting activity continued during the Late Cretaceous as reflected by the accumulation of turbiditic clastics along fault scarps (Surlyk et al., 1981). There is evidence for an Albian-Cenomanian and a Santonian–Campanian transgression (Haller, 1971). Cenomanian faunas are almost exclusively of the European–Atlantic type whereas younger Cretaceous faunas reflect a mixture of Arctic and Atlantic waters (Birkelund and Perch-Nielsen, 1976).

To what extent the coastal areas of East Greenland were inundated by the Late Cretaceous seas is difficult to determine owing to the Paleogene uplift of the area and the corresponding deep truncation of Mesozoic strata.

## Barents Shelf and Wandel Sea Basin

In the Southern Barents Sea area, the Tromsø and Bjørnøya grabens continued to subside rapidly during the Late Cretaceous while the Hammerfest Basin subsided only slowly (Figs. 10, 15, 39). Seismic data indicate that in the Tromsø Basin Upper Cretaceous shales reach a thickness of 2000–3000 m while in the Hammerfest Basin they are generally thinner than 400 m. This suggests that in time, rifting activity concentrated further on grabens subparalleling the zone of future crustal separation.

Late Cretaceous regional subsidence patterns of the Barents Shelf are, however, difficult to determine owing to the Cenozoic truncation of the Upper Cretaceous strata and also owing to their transpressional deformation along the Senja–Svalbard fracture zone (Rønnevik and Jacobsen, 1984; Faleide et al., 1984). Outcrop evidence from Svalbard indicates that a first phase of deformation, involving folding and upthrusting, took place during the Late Cretaceous. This deformation is the expression of space constraints in the motion between Greenland and the Barents Shelf that developed in conjunction with sea-floor spreading in the Labrador Sea and differential crustal extension in Baffin Bay and the southern part of the Norwegian–Greenland Sea Rift (see above). These motions involved the rotation of Eurasia relative to Greenland around a pivot point located in the area of the Senja Ridge (Hanisch, 1984a).

During the Late Cretaceous, the northern parts of the Barents Shelf and probably also the area of the Lomonosov Ridge became uplifted forming together the Lomonosov High (Plate 16). This was accompanied by the intrusion of northwest-southeast-striking dike systems on Franz Joseph Land. Uplift of the Lomonosov High may be related to the inception of the Nansen Rift, which separated the area of the future Lomonosov Ridge from the northern margin of the Barents–Kara Sea Platform.

In the area of the Wandel Sea Basin, dextral strike-slip faulting caused the differential subsidence of a series of pull-apart grabens and their subsequent transpressional deformation. These deformations, which were associated with volcanic activity in northernmost Greenland, can be related to wrench movements along the Senja–De Geer fracture zone (Batten, 1982; Birkelund and Håkansson, 1983; Brown and Parson, 1981; Håkansson and Pederson, 1982).

# CHAPTER 8
# CRUSTAL SEPARATION BETWEEN EURASIA AND NORTH AMERICA–GREENLAND: OPENING OF THE ARCTIC–NORTH ATLANTIC OCEAN

## INTRODUCTION

During the late Paleocene, volcanic activity increased sharply in the area of the Rockall–Faeroe Trough, in the southern parts of the Norwegian–Greenland Sea Rift, between the Rockall–Hatton–Faeroe Bank and Greenland, and in the Davies Strait. Additional volcanic centers developed to the north of Ellesmere Island at the junction between the Nansen Rift and the Senja–De Geer fracture zone (Plate 17).

This regional volcanic surge, during which extensive plateau basalts were extruded, is referred to as the so-called Thulean Volcanism. It is the surface expression of the final rifting phase that preceded crustal separation between Greenland and the Rockall–Hatton–Faeroe Bank and Norway, between the Barents–Kara Sea Shelf and the Lomonosov Ridge, and between Greenland and Baffin Island (Talwani and Eldholm, 1977; Srivastava and Falconer, 1982). Following crustal separation and the beginning of sea-floor spreading in these areas, volcanic activity generally abated quickly but persisted till the present in the Iceland hotspot (Vogt, 1983).

In the Labrador Sea, a major change occurred in the location of its sea-floor spreading axis during the late Paleocene between anomalies 25 and 24 (Tucholke and Fry, 1985). This was paralleled by the development of the Reykjanes sea-floor spreading ridge in the northward prolongation of the North Atlantic spreading axis, and of the Aegir and Mohn's ridges in the Norwegian–Greenland Sea. In the Arctic–North Atlantic, the oldest magnetic sea-floor anomaly recognized is anomaly 24. This suggests that crustal separation between Eurasia and Greenland was achieved around 56 Ma during the earliest Eocene (Talwani and Eldholm, 1977; Vogt et al., 1981; Bott et al., 1983; Olivet et al., 1984). With this, the evolution of the Norwegian-Greenland Sea rift system, which had begun at the transition from the Early to the Late Carboniferous, came to a close after some 275 Ma of intermittent crustal extension.

In the Eurasian Basin, sea-floor spreading probably also began between anomalies 25 and 24 or slightly before (Vogt et al., 1981; Srivastava, 1985).

During the Eocene to earliest Oligocene, simultaneous sea-floor spreading in the Labrador Sea–Baffin Bay, in the northern North Atlantic, in the Norwegian–Greenland Sea, and in the Eurasian Basin caused a northward displacement of Greenland. This induced intensified dextral strike-slip movements between northern Greenland and the Barents Shelf along the Senja–De Geer fracture zone and sinistral movements between Greenland and Ellesmere Island along the Nares fracture zone. Northward movement of Greenland was accompanied by its continued counterclockwise rotation relative to North America in response to northward-decreasing rates of sea-floor spreading in the Labrador Sea and Baffin Bay (Fig. 60). This caused intense deformation of the eastern parts of the Sverdrup Basin, corresponding to the main phases of the Eurekan orogeny, and also the deformation of the western margin of the Barents Shelf where the "Alpine" fold belt of Svalbard came into evidence (Eldholm and Thiede, 1980; Rice and Shade, 1982; Srivastava and Falconer, 1982; Miall, 1984a, 1984b; Srivastava, 1985).

Sea-floor spreading along the Mid-Labrador Sea Ridge ceased during the early Oligocene, prior to anomaly 13 ($\pm$35 Ma) (Tucholke and Fry, 1985) in rough coincidence with the termination of the Eurekan orogeny. From then on, Greenland, which had formed an intermediate plate between North America and Europe during the late Senonian to earliest Oligocene, permanently joined the North American plate (Fig. 78). Correspondingly, the Labrador Sea–Baffin Bay represents now an aborted arm of the Arctic–North Atlantic sea-floor spreading system and as such can be compared to the equally aborted southern Rockall Trough and Bay of Biscay oceanic basins.

In the Norwegian–Greenland Sea, activity along the Aegir Ridge stopped during the late Oligocene around anomaly 7 (27–26 Ma), and a new spreading axis, the Kolbeinsey Ridge, developed some 300 km to its west. This important ridge jump entailed the separation of the Jan Mayen microcontinent from the margin of Greenland (Vogt et al., 1981). The Reykjanes and the Mohn's Ridge, on the other hand, continued to be active and maintained their mid-oceanic position (Plate 18).

The onset of sea-floor spreading between northeastern Greenland and the transpressionally deformed western margin of the Barents Platform coincides also with anomaly 13 (36–35 Ma). It was followed by the late Oligocene development of the Knipovich Ridge (Vogt et al., 1981; Myhre et al., 1982). This coincides with the termination of the sea-floor spreading in the Labrador Sea and the translation of activity from the Aegir to the Kolbeinsey Ridge in the Norwegian–Greenland Sea.

With the early Oligocene change in sea-floor spreading patterns and plate boundaries in the Arctic–North Atlantic domain, the earlier constraints in the movement between Greenland and the northwestern tip of Eurasia were removed and the "Alpine" fold belt of Svalbard, similar to the Eurekan fold belt of the Canadian Arctic Archipelago and northern Greenland, became inactive. Intra-oceanic transform motions in the northernmost parts of the Norwegian–Greenland Sea continued, however, along the Spitsbergen and Molloy fracture zones.

From anomaly 7 onward, sea-floor spreading axes in the Arctic–North Atlantic domain had stabilized to their current median position and lithospheric cooling and contraction governed the progressive deepening of the flanking basins (Thiede, 1979; Vogt et al., 1981).

Only by mid-Miocene time had sea-floor spreading in the Norwegian–Greenland Sea and in the Eurasian Basin progressed to the point where the northeastern point of Greenland finally cleared the northwestern shelf edge of Svalbard (Plates 9–21).

During the late Paleocene to early Eocene Thulean volcanic surge, the connection between the North Atlantic and the Norwegian–Greenland Sea became interrupted by the development of the volcanic Iceland–Faeroe land bridge between Greenland and Scotland (Plate 17). Combined with the tectonically induced barriers in Northwest Europe, caused by intraplate compressional deformations, and a low stand in relative sea level, this resulted in the isolation of the North Sea Basin from the Atlantic and Tethys seas. Although temporary connections were reopened during the Eocene and Oligocene between the North Sea Basin and the North Atlantic, the Tethys, and the Donets basins (Plate 18), these were too restricted to permit a significant faunal exchange (see Chapter 9). Correspondingly, the North Sea Basin was dominated by the colder waters of the Norwegian–Greenland Sea until the mid-Miocene reestablishment of a major crossflow between the North Atlantic and the Norwegian–Greenland Sea across the Greenland–Shetland Ridge (Plate 19).

During the Paleocene, compressional deformation of the Canadian Arctic Archipelago caused the interruption of the marine connection between the Arctic Ocean and the North Atlantic via the Baffin Bay and Labrador Sea (Chapter 7). Moreover, marine connections between the Arctic Basin and the

Norwegian–Greenland Sea apparently also became constrained in the area of the De Geer fracture zone by clastic influx from the rising Eurekan fold belt, the development of the volcanic Morris Jessup Rise and the Yermak Plateau, and possibly also by transpressional deformations. This resulted in the nearly total isolation of the Arctic Basin during the Paleocene (Plate 17). This is reflected in the development of endemic faunas that were only able to migrate southward into the Norwegian–Greenland Sea and the North Sea Basin during the late Paleocene and early Eocene (Marincovich et al., 1985). With the early Oligocene transtensional opening of the Svalbard–Greenland Strait, communications between the Arctic Basin and the Norwegian–Greenland Sea became progressively derestricted and permitted the southward flow of the colder Arctic waters. By late Oligocene–early Miocene times, a deep water connection was finally established between these basins (Eldholm and Thiede, 1980).

During the earliest Eocene, a broad interchange of European and North American terrestrial biotas took place across the Canadian Arctic Archipelago, Greenland, and the Greenland–Shetland Ridge. This land-bridge between North America and Europe was largely formed as a direct result of the Thulean development of the Iceland hotspot. This important migration route became, however, permanently interrupted again during the later part of the early Eocene, possibly because of the opening of a marine channel via the Faeroe–Rockall Trough (McKenna, 1983; Hoch, 1983). Thus, a connection between the North Atlantic and the Norwegian–Greenland Sea was reestablished (Berggren and Schnitker, 1983). Substantial southward flow of waters from the Norwegian–Greenland Sea into the North Atlantic across the Iceland–Faeroe Ridge commenced only at the transition from the Eocene to the Oligocene (Nilsen, 1983). By middle to late Oligocene time, a considerable influx of Atlantic warm waters into the Norwegian–Greenland Sea is evident by the occurrence of calcareous oozes on the Vøring Plateau (Berggren and Schnitker, 1983).

By mid-Miocene time, thermal subsidence of the Iceland–Faeroe Ridge had progressed to the point where a massive crossflow between the cold waters of the Norwegian–Greenland Sea and the warm Atlantic waters occurred (Thiede and Eldholm. 1983). This contributed to the development of the ancestral Gulf Stream as recorded by the early middle Miocene ingression of warm water faunas into the North Sea Basin.

In contrast, the vegetation on Iceland retained a distinctly North American affinity until the late Miocene (Friederich and Simonarson, 1981). This suggests that the Denmark Strait segment of the Greenland–Shetland Ridge became permanently submerged only during the latest Miocene. This is in conflict with calculated subsidence curves which suggest that by late Miocene time a water depth of some 400 m was reached in the Denmark Strait (Thiede and Eldholm, 1983). On the other hand, seismostratigraphic analyses of reflection seismic lines extending from Greenland into the Denmark Strait indicate that water depths in this gradually widening seaway increased during the late Miocene (Larsen, 1984).

## THULEAN VOLCANISM

The Paleocene to early Eocene Thulean volcanism is unique in the geological history of the Arctic–North Atlantic rift systems. Comparable widespread plateau basalt extrusions did not precede the opening of the Canada Basin and North Atlantic Ocean, nor crustal separation in the Western and Central Tethys. The Early Jurassic volcanism preceding the opening of the Central Atlantic was significant and affected wide areas around future plate boundaries but was apparently not of the same dimension as the Thulean volcanic surge.

Thulean volcanic activity, although concentrated on areas flanking the zones of latest Paleocene–earliest Eocene crustal separation, affected wide areas around these incipient plate boundaries. This is particularly evident on the Rockall–Hatton–Faeroe Bank, which is covered by extensive plateau basalts, in the Rockall–Faeroe Trough where several seamounts came into evidence during the Paleocene, and specifically in the British Isles. Scotland and Northern Ireland are the sites of important extrusive and intrusive centers from which dike swarms extend in a southeastward direction to the shores of the North Sea and across the Irish Sea into Wales and the Midlands. The glaciers of Greenland conceal a possible connection between the volcanic fields of Eastern Greenland and those of central West Greenland (Plate 17).

In the coastal areas of East Greenland, Thulean volcanics and intrusives extend over a distance of some 1300 km (Kent-Brooks, 1980) and, if the data from shelf areas and those from the southwestern margin of the Rockall–Hatton Bank are taken into account (Larsen, 1978; Roberts et al., 1984), over a distance of about 2200 km. On the other hand, considering a Paleocene continent assembly, as given in Plate 17, manifestations of Thulean igneous activity extend from coastal Baffin Island to the shores of the central North Sea over a distance of some 2500 km. The Iceland hotspot is located approximately in the center of this area of volcanic activity.

Regional reviews of the Thulean volcanism have been given by Kent-Brooks (1980), Hall (1981), and McKenna (1983). Summaries of the Early Tertiary igneous activity have been presented for Ireland by Preston (1981); for Scotland by Steward (1965), Walker (1975), Vann (1978), Meighan (1979), and Thompson (1982); for Western Greenland by Clarke and Pedersen (1976); and for Eastern Greenland by Haller (1971), Noe-Nygaard (1976), and Deer (1976). Roberts et al. (1983, 1984) discuss the occurrence of Thulean volcanics on the Rockall–Hatton–Faeroe Bank, and Ridd (1983) and Smythe (1983) review those in the Faeroe–West Shetland Trough. The distribution of Paleocene volcanics in the offshore of Mid-Norway is given by Bukovics and Ziegler (1985; Fig. 38).

The Thulean volcanic surge gave rise to the extrusion of extensive flood basalts that attain thicknesses of 2000–3000 m, the injection of regional basaltic dike systems, and the intrusion of gabbros, syenites, granophyres, and granites. The ascent to shallow crustal levels of felsic intrusives, representing late stage differentiates, is generally confined to the last phases of igneous activity. Thulean extrusives are distinctly mafic-felsic bimodal. Tholeiitic and picritic basalts generally predominate. There is evidence for considerable crustal contamination of extrusive and intrusive rocks, particularly in the British Isles and on the Faeroes (Moorbath and Welke, 1968; Bell, 1976; Dickin et al., 1981; Thompson, 1982; Hald and Waagstein, 1983; Watson, 1985). The regional, earliest Eocene ash-marker in the basins flanking the Norwegian–Greenland Sea and also in the North Sea Basin indicates that the late phases of the Thulean magmatism were accompanied by an intensive explosive volcanism (Plates 26, 27, 30; Jacqué and Thouvenin, 1975; Roberts et al.. 1984).

In Western Greenland, volcanic activity commenced during the late Danian and persisted until the early Eocene. The last dikes are dated as ± 30 Ma (Clarke and Pedersen, 1976; McKinna, 1983). In central East Greenland, the extrusion of plateau basalts commenced around 55.5 Ma and probably ceased during the early Eocene; intrusive activity continued, however, into the Oligocene. On the Faeroe Islands, the age range of basaltic extrusion is uncertain with paleontological criteria and radiometric data, suggesting that volcanic activity spanned early Paleocene to early Eocene times (Tarling and Gale, 1968; Lund, 1983). On the British Isles, the age range of Thulean igneous activity is 66–50 Ma (Bell, 1976; Preston, 1981). Volcanic activity in the Faeroe–Shetland Trough commenced during the Late Cretaceous, intensified during the Paleocene, and abated during the early Eocene (Ridd. 1983). Similarly, volcanic activity began in the igneous province of Northwest Scotland at the transition from the Cretaceous to the Tertiary and persisted into the early Eocene (Curry et al., 1978). Along the southwestern flank of the Rockall–Hatton Bank, a 6 km thick pile of basalt was extruded during the late Paleocene and early Eocene (Roberts et al.. 1984).

Overall, the main phases of the Thulean volcanic pulse lasted for some 10 Ma and spanned late early Paleocene to mid-Eocene times (60–50 Ma). Magnetic sea-floor anomaly 24, the earliest recognized in the northern parts of the North Atlantic and in the Norwegian-Greenland Sea, is dated as about 56 Ma and thus indicates that these oceanic basins began to open during the early Eocene. This indicates that the peak of the Thulean volcanism coincides with crustal separation between Greenland and Eurasia.

Following crustal separation in the Arctic–North Atlantic, hotspot activity was concentrated on Iceland where it persisted to the present. Igneous activity in areas flanking the newly developing Reykjanes and Aegir-Mohn's ridges abated rapidly and became extinct during the early Eocene.

The persistence of intrusive activity in north-central East Greenland into the Oligocene (Rex et al., 1978) can be related to the separation of the Jan Mayen microcontinent from Greenland during the late Oligocene. Similarly, intrusive activity in West Greenland lasting into the early Oligocene reflects transform movements along the Ungava fracture zone during the Eocene to earliest Oligocene phases of sea-floor spreading in the Labrador Sea and Baffin Bay.

The occurrence of major igneous centers on the Rockall–Hatton–Faeroe Platform, in the Rockall–Faeroe Trough, and in Scotland and northern Ireland illustrates that during the Thulean thermal surge, profound mantle disturbances were not confined to areas immediately adjacent to the incipient plate boundaries. Development of these intrusive centers was accompanied by regional doming of the respective areas as indicated by the erosion of the formerly extensive Chalk cover of the shelves flanking the Rockall and Faeroe–West Shetland troughs (Vann, 1978; Preston, 1981; Naylor and Shannon, 1982). It should, however, be kept in mind that the regional deep truncation of the Late Cretaceous series in the area of the British Isles can be attributed to Oligocene broad-scale deformations in response to compressional intraplate stresses. This is evident by the relief of the top Cretaceous surface as extrapolated by the distribution of Upper Cretaceous chert nodules representing erosional remnants (George, 1967; D. G. Roberts, personal communication, 1987; see Chapter 9).

Thermal uplift of areas affected by the Thulean volcanism was associated with transtensional deformation of preexisting fracture systems along which basalt dikes were injected over

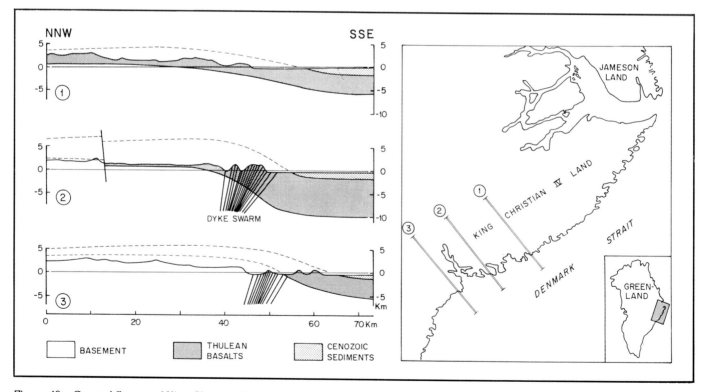

*Figure 49—Coastal flexure of King Christian IV Land, Central East Greenland, showing Eocene radiating dyke systems. After Haller (1971).*

great distances from the respective intrusive centers (Vann, 1978; Ziegler, 1982a). The doming of these areas, in conjunction with the initiation of volcanic activity, is probably the consequence of a heat surge in the mantle causing the diapiric ascent of hot asthenospheric material to the crust–mantle boundary where it spread out laterally while part of the magmas intruded to shallower crustal levels and ultimately reached the surface as alkali olivine basalts. Progressive permeation of the lower and middle crust by mantle-derived magmas, leading to its partial melting, is reflected by the late stage extrusion of contaminated silicic basalts and the intrusion of felsic plutonic differentiates, containing reactivated crustal material (Thompson, 1982). At the same time progressive thermal upward displacement of the asthenosphere–lithosphere boundary induced a second phase of long wavelength doming of the areas affected by the Thulean volcanism (Vann, 1978).

A similar two-phase doming is evident in the coastal areas of central East Greenland, where Thulean flood basalts, partly extruded near sea level, unconformably overlie truncated Cretaceous and older strata and/or the basement (Noe-Nygaard, 1976). The spectacular coastal flexure of the King Christian IV Land area, which involved the intrusion of fan-shaped dike systems and an uplift of the basalt-covered mainland areas by several kilometers, is dated as mid-Eocene to early Oligocene (Fig. 49; Haller, 1971; Kent-Brooks, 1980). This late uplifting phase, which mainly affected areas with a thick continental crust, was probably induced by the thermal upward displacement of the asthenosphere–lithosphere boundary during the early phases of sea-floor spreading, possibly as a consequence of small-scale convection in the upper mantle (Fleitou and Yuen, 1984). Development of such convective systems presumably preceded the Oligocene separation of the continental Jan Mayen Ridge from the margin of Greenland and the spectacular sea-floor spreading axis jump from the Aegir Ridge to the nascent Kolbeinsey Ridge. The location of the East Greenland coastal flexure may coincide with the transition from little to strongly attenuated continental crust. This cannot, however, be ascertained for want of refraction seismic control. Thus, it can only be speculated that the wavelength and amplitude of this coastal flexure is presumably a function of the width of this crustal transition zone, the crustal thickness of the downflexed block, and the thermal state of the crust during its deformation. Yet the lack of substantial postseparation subsidence of King Christian IV Land and of the Mesozoic Jameson Land half-graben (Fig. 50) suggests that these areas are now upheld by a thickened crust, development of which possibly involved lateral ductile transfer of lower crustal material away from the rift zone as proposed by the model of Moretti and Pinet (1987).

In areas underlain by thick continental crust, the bulk of the Thulean sheet flows were extruded under subaerial conditions, close to sea level (Roberts et al., 1984). The accumulation of several-thousand-meters-thick lava piles exerted a load on the lithosphere and induced concomitant subsidence as evident, for instance, from marine sediments capping the flood basalts of Central East Greenland (Deer, 1976). This area became, however, uplifted by several kilometers during the mid-Eocene–early Oligocene in conjunction with the development of the coastal flexure. From plateau areas, flows prograded into adjacent deeper water basins, such as in the Disko Bay area of West Greenland (Henderson et al., 1981) and the Rockall Trough (Roberts et al., 1983), giving rise to foresetting geometries. Within the Rockall Trough, submarine extrusions resulted in the construction of volcanic edifices that built up to sea level and prograded laterally.

This is evident on the seismic line drawings, given in Fig. 51, which crosses the Rosemary Bank Sea Mount. Similar Upper Cretaceous to Lower Tertiary volcanic buildups are the Hebrides Terrace and Anton Dohrn seamounts in the Rockall Trough, the Wyville–Thomson and Ymir Ridge, separating the latter from the Faeroe–West Shetland Trough (Roberts et al., 1983) and the Erland and Brendan igneous complexes in the Faeroe–West Shetland Trough (Ridd, 1983; Smythe, 1983).

In areas immediately adjacent to the developing plate margins, Thulean volcanics were extruded partly under shallow marine to subaerial conditions and partly in a deeper marine environment. In the Mid-Norway Basin, Paleocene sills and dikes are lodged at increasingly shallower stratigraphic levels as the Vøring and Shetland escarpments are approached. The latter are covered by continuous flows (Fig. 37; Bukovics and Ziegler, 1985). On the outer margin of the Vøring Plateau, and also on the southwestern margin of the Rockall–Hatton Plateau, Thulean volcanics are associated with seaward dipping reflection patterns that coincide with magnetic lineations 24a and 24b. These reflection patterns have been interpreted as resulting from the co-magmatic subsidence of seaward-located extrusive centers that built up to sea level (Hinz and Schlüter, 1978; Mutter et al., 1982; Roberts et al., 1984; Roberts and Ginzburg, 1984; Eldholm et al., 1984). During the early phases of volcanism, fissure and explosive eruptions apparently took place over wide areas, as evident in East Greenland (Larsen, 1978), but in time concentrated on the actual zone of crustal separation. During this phase of impending crustal separation, dike injection probably played a greater role than mechanical stretching of the crust (Royden et al., 1980; Dewey, 1982). This was probably coupled with thermal uplifting of the zone of incipient crustal separation, culminating in subaerial volcanism (see *Faeroe–West Shetland Trough and Mid-Norway Basin*, this chapter).

The latest Cretaceous to mid-Paleocene development of the giant Thulean hotspot, centered on Iceland, presumably reflects accelerated diapirism of lower mantle material to the asthenosphere–lithosphere boundary where it reached its density equilibrium and spread out laterally (Artyushkov, 1983). From this reservoir of hot upper mantle, individual plumes ascended to the crust–mantle boundary and later into the crust and to the surface. The location of these secondary plumes was probably predetermined by anomalies at the base of the lithosphere that developed during the preceding rifting phases (Watson, 1985). During the late Paleocene, continued material transfer through the now firmly established asthenospheric heat conduit resulted in rapid thermal attenuation of the lithosphere, the injection of mantle-derived magmas into the crust, and finally in crustal separation.

The onset of sea-floor spreading in the northern North Atlantic and the Norwegian–Greenland Sea coincides roughly with the relaxation of compressional stresses related to the Laramide phase of foreland deformation in Northwest Europe (Chapter 7). This raises the question of whether compressional stresses, originating from the Alpine collision zone, impeded the tensional separation of North America–Greenland and Eurasia and their drifting apart during the Paleocene. In such a model, the restriction in the movement of these megacratons may at least in part be indirectly responsible for the build-up of the Thulean hotspot. Under unrestricted conditions, crustal separation presumably would have been effected considerably earlier with the thermally upwelling asthenospheric material being accreted at the new plate boundary as oceanic crust.

## LABRADOR SEA AND BAFFIN BAY

In the southern parts of the Labrador Sea, sea-floor magnetic anomalies are well defined and readily permit the reconstruction of its spreading history, which terminated around anomaly 13 in the early Oligocene. In the northern parts of the Labrador Sea, and particularly as the Davis Strait is approached, sea-floor magnetic lineations are poorly defined. This is largely due to complex wrench deformations along the Ungava transform zone (Srivastava, 1978; Srivastava et al., 1981, 1982; Tucholke and Fry, 1985).

The western margin of the Labrador Sea is characterized by a Late Cretaceous to recent passive margin prism that prograded onto oceanic basement (Fig. 47). This clastic wedge attains maximum thicknesses of some 10 km under the present shelf edge and partly obscures the oldest sea-floor magnetic anomalies

(Umpleby, 1979; McMillan, 1979; Grant, 1980, 1982; McWhae, 1981). In contrast, the Greenland margin of the Labrador Sea is sediment starved. However, a major deltaic complex prograded from Greenland further northward into the Davis Strait during the Eocene to Pliocene. Cenozoic clastics reach a maximum thickness of some 4000 m near the present shelf edge at latitude 67 °N (Henderson et al., 1981; Rolle, 1985).

In the Davis Strait, wrench deformations, compensating for sea-floor spreading in the Labrador Sea, led to the development of a complex system of block-faulted and transpressional anticlinal and synclinal structures (Fig. 52). These features involve oceanic and continental basement. Seismic data, calibrated by wells, indicate that the main phase of deformation occurred during the Eocene and that tectonic activity abated during the early Oligocene (Klose et al., 1982; MacLean et al., 1982). Late dike intrusions in coastal West Greenland are dated as 30.6–

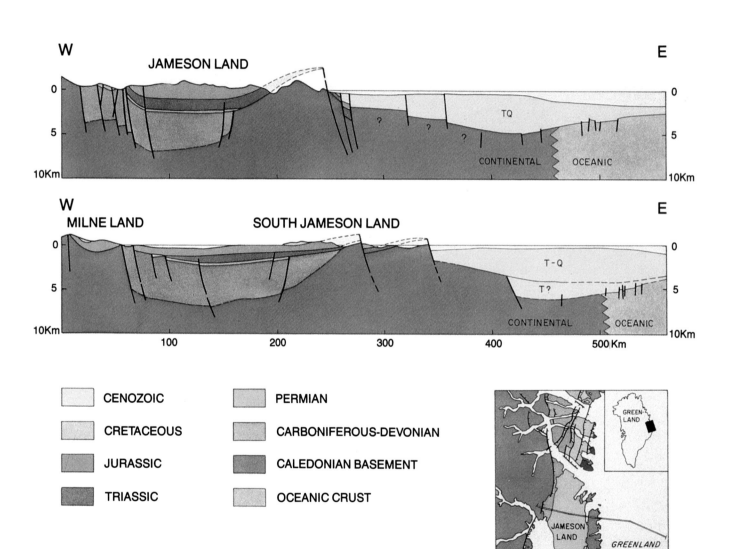

*Figure 50—Schematic structural cross section through Jameson Land Halfgraben and Central East Greenland shelf. After Cleintuar (1985), SIPM.*

30.2 Ma (McKenna, 1983). Termination of tectonic activity along the Ungava fracture zone is thus in keeping with the termination of sea-floor spreading in the Labrador Sea, as derived from its sea-floor magnetic anomalies.

It is uncertain to what extent the Baffin Bay is underlain by oceanic crust. Gravity and refraction data show that under its axial parts the crust–mantle boundary is pulled up to about 10 km, that the crust is thinned to 3–5 km and that it is overlain by a substantial thickness of sediments. Magnetic data indicate the presence of small-amplitude anomalies that are difficult to correlate from line to line; however, a case can be made for their linearity, subparalleling the basin axis. These anomalies cannot be calibrated in terms of the magnetostratigraphic time scale. The subdued nature of these anomalies is probably the result of the blanketing effect of the Cenozoic sediments. These attain thicknesses of 3000–4000 m in its axial zone of the Baffin Bay (Keen et al., 1974; Jackson et al., 1977, 1979; Srivastava et al., 1981; Rice and Shade, 1982; Menzies, 1982).

The regional cross section through the Baffin Bay, given in Fig. 53, is based on published refraction and gravity data (Srivastava et al., 1981; Menzies, 1982) and information derived from a multichannel reflection line. It illustrates that a young clastic sequence up to 3.5 km thick, deposited under a tectonically quiescent regime, overlies a regional unconformity characterized by a considerable relief.

In the west-central parts of the basin, this relief is upheld by a system of volcanic build-ups. These were presumably extruded under submarine conditions since they neither are associated with foresetting geometries nor display seaward-dipping reflec-

tion patterns. The area underlain by volcanic edifices has a minimum width of 160 km but could possibly be as wide as 210 km. The relief of the volcanic edifices between shotpoints C-3 and 37/38 displays a rough symmetry.

In the remainder of the profile, the young clastic sequence overlies a block-faulted relief upheld by older sediments. Near shotpoint C-9 a small volcanic mound is evident on the dipslope of one of these fault blocks. There is some uncertainty whether volcanics are involved in the block-faulted structures between shotpoints 37/38 and C-8. Refraction data indicate, however, that this segment of the profile is underlain by 2–3 km thick sediments having an average velocity of 3.7 km/sec. Under the shelf and slope of Baffin Island, possible sub-unconformity sediments have a velocity of 5.1–5.4 km/sec.

The age of the pre- and post-unconformity sediments and of the volcanics can only be inferred from regional correlations.

Seismic and well data from central West Greenland show that tensional faulting affected Cretaceous to Eocene series, that the area became tectonically quiescent during the early Oligocene, and that mid-Oligocene and younger sediments accumulated under a passive margin setting (Henderson et al., 1981; Rolle, 1985). Volcanic activity started during the late Danian and persisted into the early Eocene. Last volcanic manifestations are early Oligocene dikes on Nugssuaq Peninsula (McKenna, 1983).

Seismic data from the shelf of Baffin Island indicate that tensional faulting affected mainly Late Cretaceous sediments, persisted into the Early Tertiary, and that Mid-Tertiary to recent series were deposited under a passive margin regime. Further-

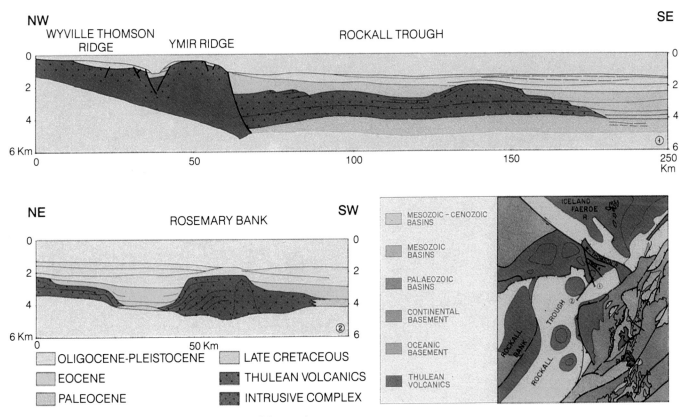

*Figure 51—Schematic structural cross sections of the northern Rockall Trough. After Shell UK Expro.*

more, there is evidence for Early Tertiary crustal extension at the northern end of the Baffin Bay in the Lancaster Sound and in the Eclipse Trough. Contemporaneous rifting may also have affected the Parry Channel fracture zone (McWhae, 1981; Kerr, 1981a, 1981b; Rice and Shade, 1982; see next section of this chapter).

In conjunction with the late Paleocene reorganization of the sea-floor spreading axis in the Labrador Sea (Tucholke and Fry, 1985), this suggests that crustal separation was achieved in the Baffin Bay during the late Paleocene, that the regional unconformity evident on Fig. 53 has a corresponding age, and that sea-floor spreading persisted into the early Oligocene. The width of the oceanic crust generated during this period is, however, difficult to define on the basis of the available data because the boundary between oceanic and continental crust generally is ill defined.

In view of the magnitude of the latest Cretaceous and Paleogene motion of Greenland relative to the North American Craton, as indicated by the sea-floor magnetic anomalies in the Labrador Sea and by the transect through the Baffin Bay given in Fig. 52, it is unlikely that the Baffin Bay is entirely underlain

by highly stretched continental crust, as suggested by Kerr (1967) and van der Linden (1975). On the other hand, the area occupied by oceanic crust in the Baffin Bay is probably not as wide as assumed by Srivastava (1978; see also Keen et al., 1974).

Yet, palinspastic reconstructions, taking into account the sea-floor magnetic anomalies of the Labrador Sea (Fig. 55), indicate that during the opening of the Labrador Sea the distance between Cape Dyer on Baffin Island and Disko Island in central West Greenland increased by some 350 km; of this, 150 km were presumably achieved by crustal extension and sinistral translation during the Cretaceous and Paleocene and some 200 km by sea-floor spreading during the latest Paleocene to early Oligocene.

Although the width of oceanic crust underlaying the Baffin Bay probably decreases northward, as suggested by the rotational movements of Greenland (Menzies, 1982; Rice and Shade, 1982), the above-postulated values for crustal extension and sea-floor spreading are difficult to reconcile with the transect given in Fig. 53. In this context, it should be noted that the available data do not permit estimations of the amount of

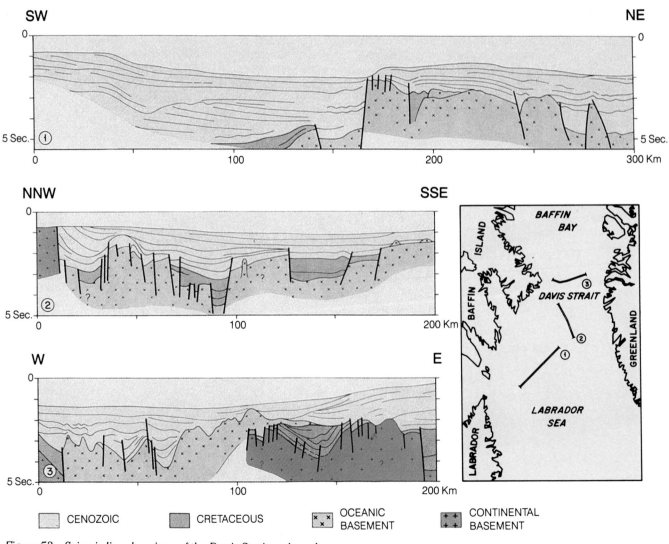

CENOZOIC    CRETACEOUS    OCEANIC BASEMENT    CONTINENTAL BASEMENT

*Figure 52—Seismic line drawings of the Davis Strait and northern Labrador Sea.*

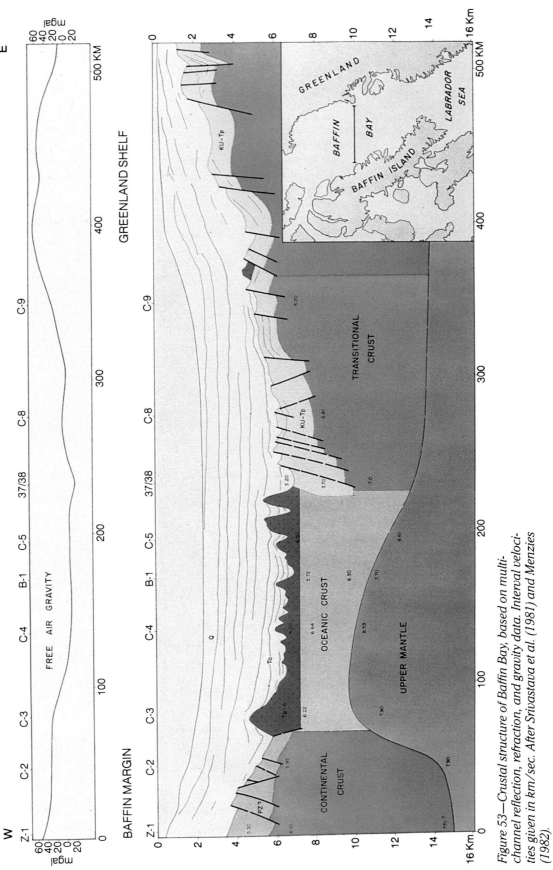

Figure 53—Crustal structure of Baffin Bay, based on multi-channel reflection, refraction, and gravity data. Interval velocities given in km/sec. After Srivastava et al. (1981) and Menzies (1982).

crustal extension that took place in the shelf and slope areas of Western Greenland and Baffin Island.

Clearly, additional combined reflection and refraction seismic traverses are needed to constrain the rifting and sea-floor spreading history of the Baffin Bay and of the drift patterns of Greenland.

# GREENLAND–ARCTIC ARCHIPELAGO DIFFUSE PLATE BOUNDARY

Cenozoic displacements between Greenland and the North American Craton, caused by sea-floor spreading in the Labrador Sea and in the Baffin Bay, were taken up by crustal extension in southern parts of the Canadian Arctic Archipelago, by sinistral strike-slip movements along the Nares Strait fracture zone, and mainly by compressional deformations in the eastern Sverdrup Basin; the latter resulted in the consolidation of the Eurekan fold belt (Trettin and Balkwill, 1979; Kerr, 1981a, 1981b; Miall, 1981; Srivastava and Falconer, 1982; Srivastava, 1985).

The main element of the Late Cretaceous and Paleogene rift system transecting the southeastern parts of the Canadian Arc-

tic Islands is the Parry Channel fracture zone, which is linked via the Lancaster Sound Graben with the Baffin Bay (Kerr, 1981a). From the Lancaster Graben, the Eclipse Trough branches off to the south, and additional grabens may underlay the westward adjacent Admiralty and the Prince Regent inlets (Plate 17). Moreover, there is evidence that Devon Island and the southeastern part of Ellesmere Island were also affected by tensional tectonics and that the Jones Sound, separating them, is underlain by a latest Cretaceous to Cenozoic graben (Kerr, 1981a; Mayr, 1984). Apart from the Eclipse Trough, the age of the sedimentary fill of these grabens is, however, unknown (Miall et al., 1980; Kerr, 1981b; McWhae, 1981). Yet, the occurrence of a mid-Eocene alkaline bimodal volcanic suite on southeastern Bathurst Island (central parts of Canadian Arctic Archipelago; Mitchell and Platt, 1984) indicates that this rift system was active during the tensional evolution of the Baffin Bay. The amount of crustal extension, which was achieved within this Arctic rift system, is unknown, and, correspondingly, it is uncertain to what extent it compensated for crustal dilation and sea-floor spreading in the Baffin Bay.

In the northernmost parts of the Baffin Bay (North Water Bay, at the transition from the Baffin Bay to the Nares Strait), marine geophysical data indicate the presence of a Cretaceous–Tertiary

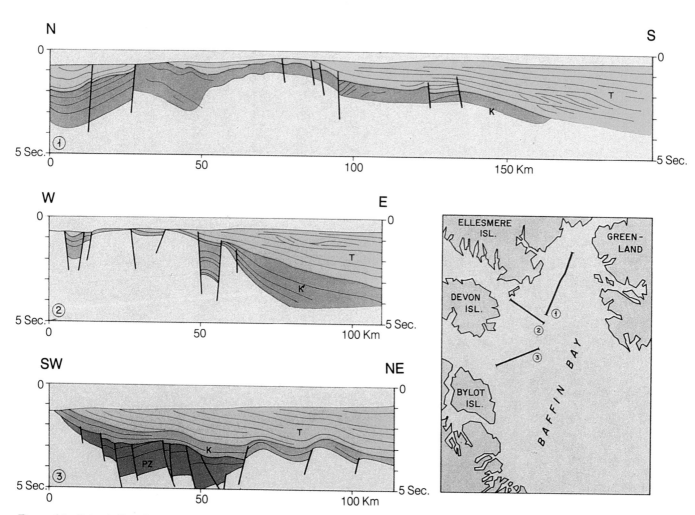

*Figure 54—Seismic line drawings of North Water Bay, northern Baffin Bay.*

sedimentary sequence, which is involved in synclinal and complex anticlinal structures (Fig. 54; Newman, 1982). The development of these features was probably caused by transpressional movements along the intracontinental Nares Strait fracture zone. The magnitude of these indicated sinistral movements is, however, still being debated with estimates ranging from a low of 25 km or less (Dawes and Kerr, 1982) to some 125 km (Miall, 1983; Srivastava, 1985).

The third mechanism compensating for movements between Greenland and the North American Craton was crustal shortening in the Eurekan fold belt. This intracratonic orogen developed during Maastrichtian to early Oligocene time (Miall, 1981, 1984a, 1984b). Compressional and transpressional Eurekan deformations are evident along the northern margin of Greenland (Håkansson and Pedersen, 1982), in northwestern Ellesmere Island and along its coast facing the northern part of the Nares Strait (Mayr and de Vries, 1982), and on Axel Heiberg Island. To the west, Eurekan deformations fade out on Amund Ringnes and Corwall Island. It is possible that the north–south-trending Boothia Arch also became reactivated during the Eurekan diastrophism (Trettin and Balkwill, 1979; Balkwill and Bustin, 1980; Kerr, 1981a; Hugon, 1983).

On Ellesmere and Axel Heiberg Island the Eurekan fold belt

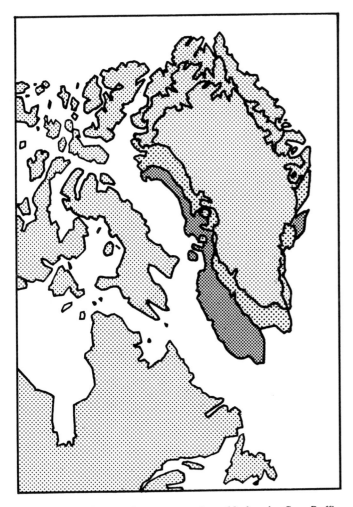

*Figure 55—Palinspastic reconstruction of Labrador Sea–Baffin Bay area illustrating relative motions between Greenland and North America. Dark shading: anomaly 31 (68 Ma); medium shading: anomaly 24 (56 Ma); light shading: present position.*

is characterized by folds, evaporite-cored diapiric structures, steep reverse and thrust faults involving Ellesmerian deformed sequences, and the late Paleozoic to Mesozoic series of the Sverdrup Basin (Osadetz, 1982; van der Berkel et al., 1983). Northwest- and southeast-verging thrust faults are evident with southeastward thrusting and overturning prevailing (Fig. 13). The amount of crustal shortening achieved during the consolidation of the Eurekan fold belt is difficult to determine for want of reflection seismic control and due to extensive ice cover. On individual thrust faults, horizontal displacements of the order of 10 km have been estimated by Osadetz (1982), while other structures are interpreted as steep reverse faults or up-thrusts (Higgins and Soper, 1983). Overall deformation patterns are suggestive of left-lateral ductile shear (Hugon, 1983).

The timing of the Eurekan diastrophism is constrained by the accumulation of the Eureka Sound synorogenic molasse sequence that ranges in age from Maastrichtian to early Oligocene (Miall, 1981, 1984a, 1984b, 1986). This series is unconformably overlain by the mid- to upper Miocene Beaufort clastics that were deposited after a major erosional hiatus, corresponding to a phase of postorogenic uplifting (Reidiger et al., 1984; Miall, 1984b).

The stratigraphically dated termination of the Eurekan diastrophism coincides with the cessation of sea-floor spreading in the Labrador Sea (Miall, 1984a, 1984b). A genetic link between these two megatectonic processes is therefore plausible (Kerr, 1981a, 1981b; Pierce, 1982; Srivastava, 1985).

Palinspastic reconstructions, based on the closure of the Labrador Seas as dictated by its magnetic sea-floor anomalies, suggest that a major gap should have existed between Ellesmere Island and Greenland prior to the Eurekan orogeny, if the present shape of Canadian Arctic Islands is retained (Fig. 55). Such a gap, which would have to be occupied by oceanic crust, obviously never existed as is evident from the late Paleozoic and Mesozoic paleogeography of the Sverdrup Basin and the Svalbard area. In order to close this gap, the Eurekan fold belt has to be restored palinspastically to the end that the southeastern coast of Ellesmere Island was always located adjacent to Greenland. This entails a significant enlargement of the northeastern parts of the Sverdrup Basin. On the paleogeographic–paleotectonic maps given in Plates 4–16, this was taken care of in a simplistic way by spreading out the eastern part of the Arctic Islands over the available space.

Detailed analyses of the generally accepted drift patterns of Greenland relative to Baffin Island and the Arctic Archipelago indicated that the late Senonian and Paleocene rotation of Greenland induced a first phase of compression of the eastern parts of the Sverdrup Basin. During the late Paleocene to early Oligocene phase of sea-floor spreading in the Labrador Sea and in the Baffin Bay, Greenland underwent a second phase of rotation and at the same time a sinistral translation relative to Ellesmere Island. This gave rise to the second phase of the Eurekan orogeny. The total amount of crustal shortening achieved in northern Ellesmere Island should therefore be of the order of 300–350 km (Srivastava, 1985). In this context, it should be kept in mind that the Eurekan deformation front passes through southeastern Ellesmere Island and only touches the northwestern promontory of Devon Island. These undeformed areas thus formed part of the North American Craton, although they were affected by crustal distension during the evolution of the Baffin Bay and the consolidation of the Eurekan fold belt.

Paleomagnetic data suggest that during the Eurekan diastrophism, northern Ellesmere Island had undergone a ±36°

counterclockwise rotation but no detectable latitudinal translation (Wynne et al., 1983). As the late Senonian to early Oligocene counterclockwise rotation of Greenland amounts to only 10°, it must be assumed that the bulk of the paleomagnetically detectable rotation in northern Ellesmere Island is of a local nature, probably involving large-scale structural rotations (oroclinal bending).

The dimensions and timing of sinistral translation along the Nares Strait fracture zone (Senonian–Paleocene or Eocene–early Oligocene) depends essentially on the amount and timing of crustal extension and sea-floor spreading in the Baffin Bay. The latter is difficult to quantify on the basis of the available data, and information from the Eurekan fold belt is too imprecise to provide further constraints (see above).

The Nares Strait fracture zone, combined with the Eurekan fold belt, represent a diffuse plate boundary between Greenland and the North American Craton (Hugon, 1983; Miall, 1983, 1984b). The Eurekan fold belt can be considered as an inverted basin and its evolution is probably the effect of intraplate compressional stresses. Under the impact of the northwestward-rotating stable Greenland Craton, inversion of the eastern parts of the Sverdrup Basin was presumably predetermined by its basement configuration and composition. In this respect, it should be kept in mind that the "basement" of the Sverdrup Basin is largely formed by the externides of the Ellesmerian fold belt and that it was subjected to considerable extension during the late Paleozoic and Mesozoic subsidence of the Sverdrup Basin (see Fig. 14 and Chapter 4). This immature, tensionally attenuated basement complex was prone to deform under the influence of tangential stresses. It is, however, uncertain whether the total amount of crustal shortening implied by the drift of Greenland was taken up in the presently exposed Eurekan fold belt or whether imbrication of the continental margin prism facing the Arctic Ocean and possibly even subduction of oceanic crust also played an important role (e.g., comparable to the Cantabrian margin of Iberia, Chapter 9).

In view of the substantial amount of crustal shortening that was achieved during the consolidation of the Eurekan fold belt, a commensurate amount of crustal thickening and subduction of upper mantle material must have occurred. With the termination of sea-floor spreading in the Labrador Sea, compressional stresses relaxed in the Eurekan fold belt and the thickened lithosphere of the eastern part of the Canadian Arctic Archipelago became isostatically uplifted. This uplifting phase is probably responsible for the late Cenozoic reactivation of the Arctic graben system and, in particular, of the Parry Channel fracture zone (Kerr, 1981a, 1981b; Miall, 1984b).

In conclusion, it appears that opening of the Labrador Sea and Baffin Bay entailing a 10° counterclockwise rotation of Greenland away from the Canadian Shield (Fig. 55) caused rifting in the southeastern Canadian Arctic Archipelago (Lancaster and Jones Sound, Parry Channel rifts), important sinistral translations between Greenland and Ellesmere Island, and major crustal shortening in the Eurekan fold belt.

## OPENING OF THE EURASIAN BASIN

Sea-floor magnetic anomalies indicate that crustal separation between the Barents–Kara Sea Shelf and the Lomonosov Ridge was achieved at the transition from the Paleocene to the Eocene between anomalies 25 and 24, or slightly earlier (Plate 17). With the onset of sea-floor spreading in the Eurasian Basin along the mid-oceanic Nansen–Gakkle Ridge, the Lomonosov Ridge became part of the North American plate (Vogt et al., 1981; Sweeney, 1985; Srivastava, 1985).

The Lomonosov Ridge has a flat-topped sea-floor relief of some 3000 m. It is about 1800 km long, and its width ranges between 20 and 100 km. On geophysical evidence, this ridge represents a clearly block-faulted, partly sediment-covered continental fragment that is offset by the oceanic Makarov and Fram basins (Blasco et al., 1979; Mair and Forsyth, 1982; Sweeney et al., 1982; Weber and Sweeney, 1985). Separation of such a long narrow piece of continental crust from the northern margin of Eurasia was presumably preconditioned by the structural grain of its basement. Such a basement fabric was probably provided by the hypothetical latest Devonian–earliest Carboniferous Lomonosov fold belt, forming the eastern continuation of the Innuitian fold belt (see Chapter 2, Innuitian Fold Belt).

Little is known about the rifting stage preceding the onset of sea-floor spreading in the Eurasian Basin. Repeated uplift of a land mass (Lomonosov High) in the area of the future Eurasian Basin is reflected by the influx of clastics into Franz Josef Land and Svalbard during the Late Triassic to Middle Jurassic (Plates 9–12) and again during the late Early Cretaceous (Plate 15). This may be related to tectonic activity, including possible shearing, along the ancestral Makarov and Nansen rifts. During the Late Cretaceous the northern parts of the Barents Platform became uplifted and remained emergent during the Cenozoic opening of the Eurasian Basin (Plates 16–21).

In northern Svalbard, volcanic activity resumed during the Paleocene and persisted into the early Miocene (Burov and Zagrusina, 1976; Prestvik, 1977). Similarly, there is evidence for Paleocene volcanic activity in northeastern Greenland (Dawes, 1976; Larsen, 1982). This volcanism can be related to Paleocene hotspot activity at the junction of the Nansen Rift and the Senja–De Geer fracture zone, which led to the development of the submarine volcanic Morris Jessup Rise and the Yermak Plateau (Plate 18; Crane et al., 1982; McKenna, 1983).

Volcanic activity in the area of the Yermak Plateau and the Morris Jessup Rise apparently persisted during the early phases of sea-floor spreading along the Nansen–Gakkle Ridge. Progressive opening of the Eurasian Basin ultimately resulted in the separation of the Yermak Plateau and the Morris Jessup Rise and their drifting apart. Because of their young, volcanic nature and their location at the continent–ocean transition, the Yermak Plateau and the Morris Jessup Rise can be suppressed in predrift assemblies of the Barents–Kara Shelf and the Lomonosov Ridge (Crane et al., 1982).

## NORTHERN NORTH ATLANTIC AND NORWEGIAN–GREENLAND SEA

Following crustal separation between Greenland and the Rockall–Hatton–Faeroe Bank and Norway, the northern North Atlantic and the Norwegian–Greenland Sea oceanic basins opened during the early Eocene at sea-floor spreading rates on the order of 1.3–1.5 cm/year. After anomaly 20, spreading rates decreased gradually to about 0.7 cm/year during the Oligocene but subsequently accelerated again to an average rate of 0.9 cm/year.

Throughout the opening history of the northern North Atlantic and the Norwegian–Greenland Sea, the Reykjanes and Mohn's ridges maintained their mid-oceanic position. Along the Aegir Ridge, normal sea-floor spreading occurred during anomaly 24B to 20 time. Between anomalies 20 to 7, sea-floor spreading rates decreased more rapidly in the southern parts of the Aegir Ridge than in its northern parts. This resulted in the development of a northward-divergent magnetic anomaly pattern (Plate 18). At the same time, the Jan Mayen microcontinent became gradually separated from Greenland as a consequence of northward-decreasing, slow sea-floor spreading along the nascent Kolbeinsey Ridge. With anomaly 13, sea-floor spreading began in the southern parts of the Greenland Sea, and with anomaly 7, normal sea-floor spreading began in the prolongation of the Mohn's Ridge along the Knipovich Ridge, while the Aegir Ridge became extinct (Plates 19, 20; Eldholm and Thiede, 1980; Vogt et al., 1981; Myhre et al., 1982; Nunns, 1983; Nunns et al., 1983; Eldholm et al., 1984; Skogseid and Eldholm, 1987).

The segment of the Norwegian–Greenland Sea, which formed by sea-floor spreading along the Aegir Ridge and later along the Kolbeinsey Ridge, is limited to the north by the Jan Mayen fracture zone and to the south by the Iceland Ridge transform zone. These fracture zones apparently projected beneath the European Craton where important wrench deformations occurred during the Oligocene period of sea-floor spreading ridge reorganization in the Norwegian Basin. The onset of this reorganization coincides with the termination of sea-floor spreading in the Labrador Sea and its completion coincides with the beginning of sea-floor spreading between the Barents Shelf margin and northeastern Greenland along the Knipovich Ridge.

The latest Cretaceous to mid-Oligocene evolution of the Western Barents Shelf margin reflects a complex sequence of transpressional and transtensional deformations that accompanied the early sea-floor spreading phases in the Norwegian–Greenland Sea (Faleide et al., 1984; Spencer et al., 1984).

### East Greenland Margin

The structural and stratigraphic framework of the sedimentary basins underlaying the vast continental shelves of East Greenland is known in rough outlines only because sea-ice and icebergs impede seismic surveys and even more so the drilling of exploratory wells.

Aeromagnetic and limited reflection seismic surveys indicate that major sedimentary basins occupy the northeastern and the south-central shelves of Greenland. These contain up to 10 km of sediments. Little is known, however, about the age of these sediments and the structural configuration of the respective basins (Henderson, 1976; Featherstone et al., 1977; Larsen, 1980, 1984).

Reflection seismic data from Central East Greenland show that its shelf and continental rise are underlain by a 3–5-km thick, seaward prograding clastic wedge that was deposited under a passive margin setting (Fig. 50). These clastics overlie a partly block-faulted acoustic basement (Hinz and Schlüter, 1978, 1980; Larsen, 1984).

Because this is the area from which the Jan Mayen Ridge was separated during the mid-Oligocene, it is likely that this passive margin prism overlies partly downfaulted and downflexed continental crust and older sediments covered by Paleocene–Eocene volcanics, and partly Oligocene and younger oceanic crust (Fig. 50). The age of this passive margin wedge probably ranges from late Oligocene to Recent and its dimensions suggest that after crustal separation between the Jan Mayen microcontinent and Greenland was achieved, a major eastward-directed drainage system had developed in the latter.

In Central East Greenland, development of the coastal flexure during the mid-Eocene to early Oligocene was accompanied by syenitic and alkali-granitic intrusions. These range in age between 40 and 28 Ma (Haller, 1971; Brown et al., 1977; Rex et al., 1978). This magmatic activity coincides with the gradual development of the Kolbeinsey Ridge during the mid-Eocene to mid-Oligocene and the separation of the Jan Mayen Ridge from Greenland. Moreover, mid-Eocene basalt flows have been encountered at DSPD site 350 on the Jan Mayen Ridge. Reflection seismic lines crossing this continental fragment indicate the presence of a mid-Oligocene separation unconformity that truncates Eocene and early Oligocene clastics that were presumably derived from Greenland (Talwani and Udintsev, 1976; Hinz and Schluter, 1978a; Nunns, 1982).

Aeromagnetic data over the Northeast Greenland Shelf suggest the presence of a system of grabens containing 8 to 10 km of late Paleozoic and Mesozoic sediments that are covered by a 2–4 km thick Cenozoic passive margin wedge (Larsen, 1984).

Along the East Greenland margin, the continent–ocean transition is only loosely defined in view of the widespread occurrence of Thulean volcanics and the progradation of a thick post-separation clastic wedge over oceanic basement. Furthermore, the amount of crustal extension that occurred during its late Paleozoic to early Cenozoic rifting stage is essentially unknown. Correspondingly, palinspastic reconstructions have to contend with considerable uncertainties.

### Rockall–Hatton–Faeroe Bank, Rockall and Porcupine Troughs

The continental Rockall–Hatton–Faeroe Bank subsided only slowly during the opening phase of the northern North Atlantic. Water depth over this large, sediment-starved submarine plateau vary from less than 500 m to 1500 m.

Deep-Sea drilling results show that pelagic sediments consisting of shales, spiculites, and chalks attain thicknesses of up to 1000 m in the Rockall–Hatton Basin (Roberts, 1975; Roberts et al., 1984; Bott, 1983).

The post-Thulean subsidence of the Rockall Trough is difficult to quantify. For instance, the present water depth over the crests of the Anton Dohrn and Rosemarie Bank seamounts is 500 and 600 m, respectively. These volcanic edifices had built up to sea level during their Paleocene–early Eocene development. It is uncertain whether the present water depth over the crestal parts of these structures reflects the total post–Thulean subsidence of the Rockall Trough, since it is unknown whether these seamounts were originally capped by subaerial volcanic cones that were later beveled off by wave action. On the other hand, the relief and internal configuration of the Rosemarie Bank and the morphology of the stepwise retreating constructional lava scarps along the flanks of Ymir Ridge (Fig. 51) indicate that during Paleocene–early Eocene time, water depths in the northern parts of the Rockall Trough increased from some 1000 m to 3000 m. At present, water depths in the Rockall Trough range from 1500 m in the north to 3000 m in its southern parts. On the other hand, the thickness of Cenozoic deep water clastics contained in the Rockall Trough decreases from some 2500 m in its northern parts to about 1000 m in its southern parts. This suggests that lithospheric cooling and sedimentary loading played an important role in the late Eocene to Recent subsidence of the Rockall Trough. The clastics that accumulated in the Rockall Trough and that only partially bury the Rosemary Bank, Hebrides and Anton Dohrn seamounts were derived from the Hebrides and northwest Irish Shelves. These shelves and their steep, fault-controlled slopes are characterized by considerably less intense Mesozoic crustal extension than, for instance, the West Shetland Shelf. Following their Paleocene uplift, these shelves subsided only little and were largely bypassed by clastic. With the progressive inundation of these shelves during the Neogene, the Rockall Trough became sediment starved (Roberts, 1975; Bott, 1978; Scrutton, 1986).

In the Porcupine Trough, Cenozoic sediments attain a thickness of some 3500 m and consist predominantly of deep water clastics (Fig. 32). On the Porcupine Bank and the Irish Shelf, only thin Cenozoic sediments accumulated (Max, 1978; Roberts et al., 1981b; Naylor and Shannon. 1982). Following the Thulean volcanic outburst, subsidence of the Porcupine Trough was probably governed by continued lithospheric cooling and sediment loading of its thinned crust. Particularly during the late Cenozoic, clastic supply to the Porcupine Trough lagged behind its subsidence; consequently, present water depths over much of the basin are in excess of 1000 m. Some of the border faults of the Porcupine Trough remained active, however, through much of Cenozoic time; this may be only partly an effect of differential crustal loading (see Beaumont and Sweeney, 1978). On the other hand, the occurrence of late Oligocene doleriitic tholeiitic sills in the northern parts of the Porcupine Trough (Seemann, 1984) and of similar aged dikes on Dingle Peninsula (Western Ireland, Horne and MacIntyre, 1975) is probably related to small-scale wrench deformations in the onshore prolongation of the Charlie Gibbs fracture zone.

Time-equivalent wrench deformations are also evident at the northern termination of the Rockall Trough. Here the northwest–southeast-trending Ymir and Wyville Thomson ridges, which are upheld by Thulean volcanics, are bounded by faults offsetting Eocene and lower Oligocene sediments (Fig. 51; Roberts et al., 1983). These deformations may be the expression of transform movements along the Iceland–Faeroe fracture zone during the Oligocene reorganization of sea-floor spreading axes in the Norwegian Basin.

It is also possible that the Oligocene sinistral wrench deformations in the Irish Sea, the Cardigan Bay, and the Bristol Channel area, which were associated with the subsidence of local transtensional basins (Lake and Karner, 1987), are genetically related to transform movements along the Greenland–Scotland Ridge (see Chapter 9, *Intraplate Deformations in Northwest Europe*).

## Faeroe–West Shetland Trough and Mid-Norway Basin

The Cenozoic subsidence patterns of the Faeroe–West Shetland Trough are difficult to assess, since much of its sedimentary fill from the Late Cretaceous and the Cenozoic consists of deep water clastics. Regional downwarping of the area is indicated, however, by the geometry of deltaic lobes prograding northwestward from the West Shetland Shelf. These foresetting units provided the source for extensive deep water clastic fans accumulating in the axial parts of the Faeroe–West Shetland Trough where Paleocene series attain a thickness of some 2000 m and Eocene to Oligocene sediments range between 2000 and 3000 m. With the progressive inundation of the Shetland Platform, clastic supply diminished and basinal areas became sediment starved; Mio-Pliocene series are generally only a few hundred meters thick (Fig. 48). There is only minor evidence for Cenozoic syndepositional faulting, much of which is related

to gravitational instability of depositional slopes. From the Faeroe Platform, which is upheld by Thulean volcanics, only minor amounts of sediments were shed into the Faeroe–West Shetland Trough.

It is uncertain whether Paleocene igneous activity along the axial zone of the Faeroe–West Shetland Trough was of a subaerial or submarine nature. This trend of intrusive centers and basalt flows, of which the Faeroe Ridge forms part (Fig. 36), may be associated with an incipient, albeit abortive Paleocene sea-floor spreading axis (Ridd, 1983; Duindam and van Hoorn, 1987).

In the Mid-Norway Basin, the Cenozoic series forms a prograding wedge that attains a thickness of 3 km beneath the present shelf edge offshore Kristianssund in the Møre subbasin and further north, in the Vøring subbasin, some 2 km (Figs. 37, 38; Bøen et al., 1983). The toe of this wedge onlaps against and partly oversteps the volcanic Møre and Outer Vøring plateaux, the crests of which have subsided to a present depth ranging between 1.5 and 3 km. DSDP drilling results from the Vøring Plateau indicate that it became submerged during the early Eocene (Caston, 1976). This is in keeping with the assumption that the seaward-dipping reflection patterns associated with the outer margins of these plateaux are related to an initial phase of subaerial sea-floor spreading (Mutter et al., 1982; Skogseid and Eldholm, 1987). The present depth of the crests of these plateaux is, however, considerably smaller than would be expected from subsidence curves of normal oceanic crust but is roughly compatible with the subsidence curve of a-seismic oceanic ridges and also of attenuated continental crust (Detrick et al., 1977; Sawyer et al., 1983).

The sedimentary cover of the Møre Platform and the Vøring Plateau is generally less than 1 km. This suggests that they are upheld either by anomalously thick oceanic crust or by thinned continental crust that was covered and permeated by mantle-derived material immediately prior to and during the crustal separation stage (Skogseid and Eldholm, 1987). In general, the latter interpretation is favored, and it is therefore assumed that the continent–ocean transition lies to the west of the Møre Platform and in the western part of the Outer Vøring Plateau (Fig. 38; Bukovics and Ziegler, 1985). This concept is supported by the chemical composition of volcanics drilled during Leg 104 on the Vøring Plateau, which show evidence of crustal contamination (Taylor et al., 1986).

The lack of a regional separation unconformity in the Mid-Norway Basin indicates that crustal separation between Greenland and Norway was not associated with a major tensional event and regional thermal doming, but was rather accompanied by a phase of intense dike intrusion along the axis of impending crustal separation.

Following crustal separation, deep water clastics, ponded behind the gradually subsiding Faeroe-Shetland and Vøring Plateau highs, accumulated in the Møre and Vøring subbasins during the Eocene and Oligocene. In these basins, Paleogene sediments reach maximum thicknesses of 1 km.

During the Oligocene, a system of anticlinal structures became upwarped in the Vøring Basin (Figs. 37, 38). Development of these compressional features, which are superimposed on deep Cretaceous sedimentary troughs, is probably related to transform movements along the Jan Mayen fracture zone during the Oligocene rearrangement of sea-floor spreading axes in the Norwegian Basin. The largest of these structures, referred to as the Molde High, has at base Tertiary level a structural relief of 1200 m (Bukovics and Ziegler, 1985).

Miocene and Pliocene sediments onlap the flanks of these inversion structures and ultimately overstep them. During the Pliocene, an increase in clastic influx resulted in a rapid outward building of the shelf margin. Neogene sediments attain maximum thicknesses of the order of 2–2.5 km.

During the Plio-Pleistocene, the shoreward margin of the Mid-Norway Basin became uplifted and truncated as erosion cut down into the Triassic series as evident by the erosional truncation of Mesozoic series (Bukovicz and Ziegler, 1985; Bukovicz et al., 1984; Bugge et al., 1984). The mechanism governing this uplift is uncertain but may be related to isostatic adjustments of the crust to glaciation and deglaciation of the Fennoscandian Shield.

The crustal configuration of the Mid-Norway continental margin is given in Fig. 56. This profile, which crosses the shelf 80 km to the south of Andøya, is based on refraction and gravity data and illustrates that the continental crust thins from some 43 km beneath the eastern Caledonides to some 16 km beneath the Vøring Plateau. Significantly, westward thinning of the lower crust sets in some 100 km to the east of the shoreward margin of the Mid-Norway sedimentary basin. Within the Mid-Norway Basin, available reflection seismic data do not permit quantification of the amount of crustal extension at the base of the synrift sediments. A wider zone of lower crustal attenuation than at shallow crustal levels is compatible with the "depth dependent extension" model of Beaumont et al. (1982a, 1982b) and Hellinger and Sclater (1983; in their paper referred to as "non-uniform stretching model"). This model was introduced to approximate the inhomogenous response of the lithosphere to stresses, thought to be caused by depth-related changes of the rheological properties of the crust and lithosphere (see Chapter 10).

Although in the case of the Mid-Norway margin attenuation factors at shallow and deeper crustal levels cannot be established, it is suspected that similar to the North Biscay margin (Fig. 31) and the East Newfoundland Basin (Fig. 33), subcrustal erosion contributed substantially to the observed lower crustal thinning, particularly under the Western Caledonides and possibly also in the area of the Mid-Norway Basin.

## Western Barents Shelf and Spitsbergen Orogen

The stratigraphic record and the structural framework of the western margin of the Barents Shelf and of Svalbard provide an account of tectonic processes that accompanied the early phase of sea-floor spreading in the Norwegian Greenland Sea and of the dextral oblique separation between northeastern Greenland and the northwestern tip of the Eurasian Craton (Plate 26).

The main structural elements of the southwestern Barents Sea are summarized in Fig. 10.

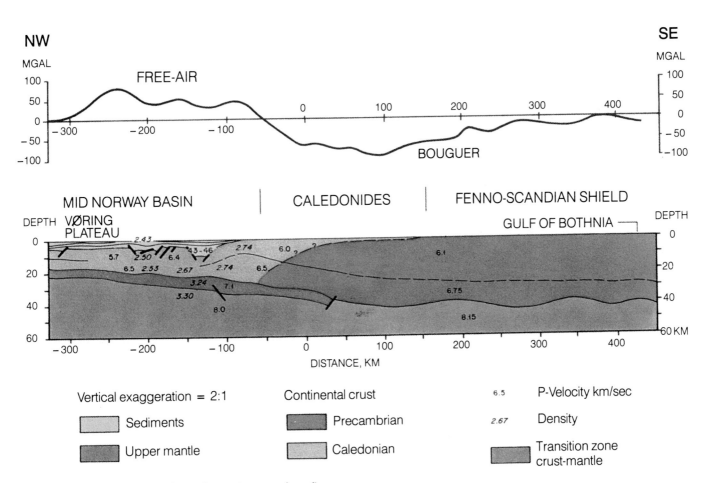

*Figure 56—Mid-Norway continental margin, crustal configuration, based on "Blue Norma" refraction profile. After Meissner, personal communication.*

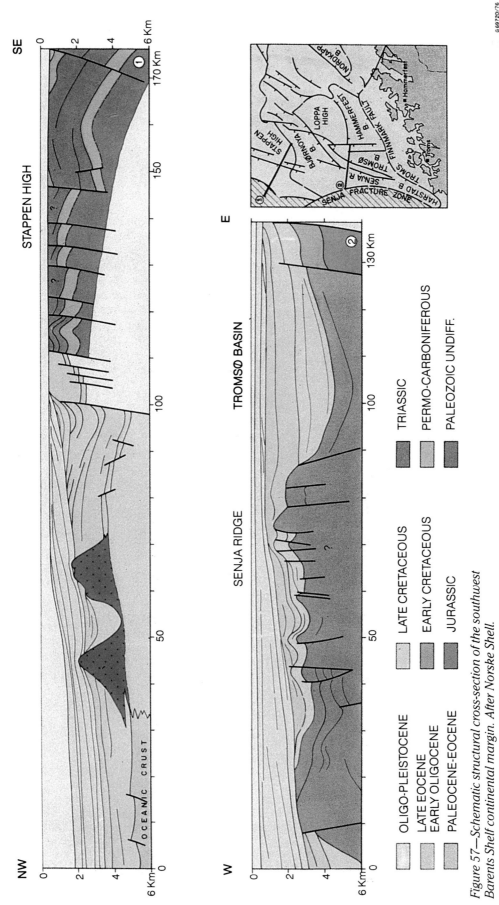

Figure 57—Schematic structural cross-section of the southwest
Barents Shelf continental margin. After Norske Shell.

Latest Cretaceous to Paleocene transpressional deformation of the Senja Ridge, and probably also of the Stappen High (Fig. 15), coincides with the termination of differential subsidence of the Tromsø and Bjørnøya basins (Fig. 39). Latest Cretaceous to Paleocene compressional deformations have been reported from Western Svalbard (Hanisch, 1984a). Late Cretaceous uplift of the Svalbard Platform may be related partly to these transpressional deformations and partly to tectonic activity along the Nansen Rift.

In the area of the Senja Ridge, a major unconformity separates deformed and deeply truncated Cretaceous strata from the late Paleocene and younger series (Spencer et al., 1984; Fig. 57). This early Paleocene erosional event was followed by late Paleocene regional subsidence of the area. In the Tromsø Basin, on the other hand, sedimentation was continuous across the Cretaceous–Cenozoic boundary (see also Fig. 39). However, compressional structures appear to have continued to grow in the western parts of the Senja Ridge as suggested by onlap patterns of the Paleocene to Eocene series. Tectonic activity intensified during the late Eocene to early Oligocene. This was accompanied by the upthrusting of the western margin of the Senja Ridge where a major, regional unconformity marks the base of the Oligocene and younger series. These were deposited under a passive margin regime and formed the Barents Sea submarine clastic fan that prograded over the newly generated oceanic crust of the Norway Basin (Lofoten Basin). This clastic wedge is up to 4 km thick (Hinz and Schluter, 1978b; Faleide et al., 1984; Eldholm et al., 1984).

The Stappen High represents a major inverted Mesozoic basin that probably formed part of the Bjørnøya Basin (Fig. 57). Uplift of this large positive feature, which culminates in Bjørnøya, probably occurred during the late Eocene to early Oligocene with possible precursor phases during the latest Cretaceous and early Paleocene (Faleide et al., 1984). During the development of the Stappen High, the northern parts of the Bjørnøya Basin also became uplifted and deeply truncated (Fig. 15). In its southern parts, where a more complete stratigraphic record is preserved, the main phase of deformation can be dated as late Eocene to early Oligocene. Moreover, seismic data indicate that the Loppa Ridge also became transpressionally reactivated and uplifted during this time.

Structural features associated with the Stappen High show that it developed in response to transpressional stresses. The western margin of the Stappen High is marked by a major normal fault zone to the west of which a thick Paleogene sedimentary sequence is preserved near the continent–ocean transition (Fig. 57). Furthermore, there is evidence for the occurrence of two major Paleocene(?) submarine volcanic buildups in this half-graben. An important erosional unconformity marks the base of the Oligocene and younger series that were deposited under a passive margin tectonic regime (Spencer et al., 1984).

During the late Oligocene and Mio-Pliocene, much of the Barents Shelf and probably also the North Kara Sea area was emergent, thus forming the clastic source area for the Barents Sea fan.

In the Svalbard area, major Cenozoic basins are the Central Tertiary Basin, located to the east of the Spitsbergen "Alpine" fold belt, the Forlandsundet Graben paralleling the west coast of Spitsbergen, and the continental margin prism (Steel et al., 1985).

The Central Tertiary Basin contains up to 2.5 km of Danian to early Eocene, brackish marine and deltaic sediments (Plate 26). Carbonization analyses indicated that an additional 1–1.7 km of

sediments has been eroded from the present basin surface (Manum and Throndsen, 1978). This suggests that sedimentation had continued into the middle to late Eocene.

During the early Paleocene, the basin subsided presumably under a transtensional regime with clastics being derived from the north and east. Subsidence exceeded sedimentation rates, and deeper water conditions developed along its western, sheared margin. From the latter, conglomerates were shed during the late Paleocene, suggesting transpressional uplift of a marginal high. During the early Eocene, clastic influx into the basin increased, particularly from the west, and resulted in its shallowing out. The early Eocene series consists of 1000 m of sandy, coastal plain deposits (Kellogg, 1975; Steel et al., 1981, 1985; Steel and Worsley, 1984). Differential subsidence of the basin probably continued into the late Eocene, by which time dextral, transpressional stresses induced the uplift of the West Spitsbergen "Alpine" fold belt. This fold belt, which is up to 40 km wide, is characterized by east-verging, basement-involving, en echelon thrust faults and upthrusts and folds (Birkenmajer, 1972; Lowell, 1972; Kellogg, 1975; Lepvrier and Geyssant, 1984; Steel et al.. 1985; Maher et al., 1986).

The Forlandsundet Graben on the west coast of Spitsbergen contains a 3–5 km thick succession of clastics; this basin probably developed during Eocene and Oligocene as a transtensional feature. Subsidence of this graben is at least partly contemporaneous with the deformation of the Spitsbergen fold belt (Steel and Worsley, 1984; Steel et al., 1985).

The continental margin prism of Svalbard consists of a 6–7-km-thick sequence of presumably Oligocene and Neogene clastics that prograde over oceanic crust. This clastic wedge was dammed up by the Knipovich sea-floor spreading ridge. There is little evidence for syndepositional deformation. The continent–ocean transition is rather sharp and coincides with the Hornesund fault zone (Schlüter and Hinz, 1978; Myhre et al., 1982; Eldholm et al., 1984). This fault probably evolved out of a Late Cretaceous to Eocene shear zone into an early Oligocene rifted margin at the time sea-floor spreading commenced between the Barents Platform and northeastern Greenland. During this phase of crustal separation, the Hovgaard continental fragment, now located in the northern parts of the Greenland basin, became isolated (Myhre et al., 1982).

In the Wandel Sea Basin of northeastern Greenland, there is evidence for post–Paleocene graben formation associated with a substantial heat flow increase (Håkansson and Pedersen, 1982). These deformations could be interpreted as being equivalent to the Paleocene to early Oligocene wrench and rift activity along the margin of Svalbard. Whether a counterpart of the Spitsbergen "Alpine" fold belt occurs along the submerged northeastern shelf margin of Greenland is unknown, but probable.

Overall, the latest Cretaceous and Paleogene evolution of the western margin of the Barents Sea–Svalbard platform reflects a sequence of transpressional deformations that can be considered as equivalents to the far more dramatic Eurekan orogeny of the Eastern Sverdrup Basin (see above).

## CENOZOIC NORTH SEA BASIN

The North Sea Basin forms part of the large Cenozoic Northwest European Basin, which extends from the Atlantic shelves of Norway and the Shetland Isles to the Carpathians and the Ukraine. Within this megabasin, the North Sea area stands out

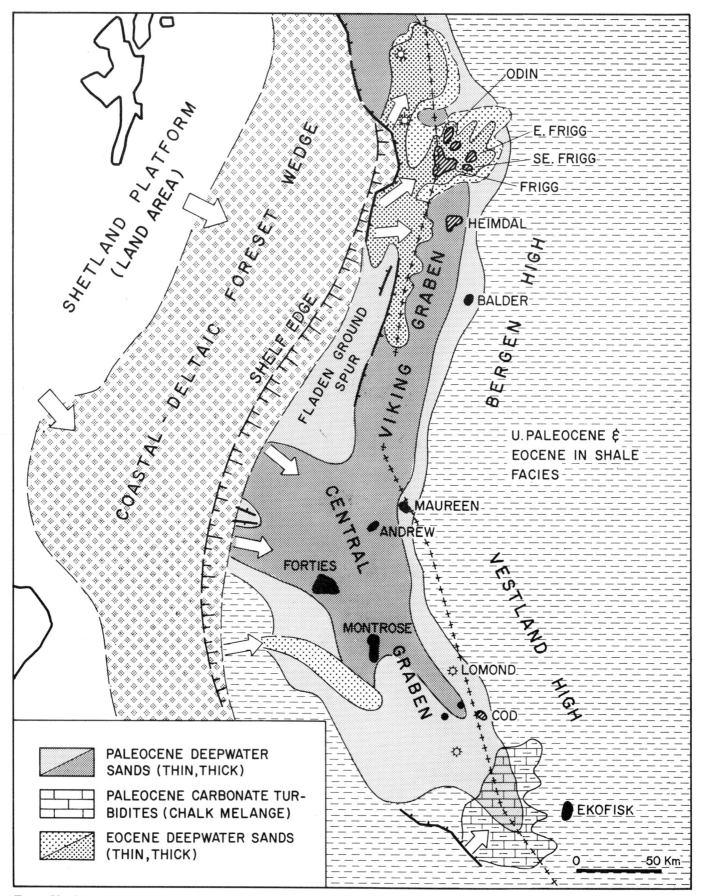

*Figure 58—Schematic facies map of late Paleocene and early Eocene series, central and northern North Sea. Ziegler and Louwerens (1978).*

because of its great thickness of Tertiary and Quaternary sediments (Ziegler, 1982a).

## Paleogene Deep Water Stage

In the North Sea, chalk deposition gave way to a clastic regime in the Viking Graben during the Danian and in the Central and Southern North Sea at the onset of the late Paleocene. This shows that denudation of the Shetland Platform, in response to thermal uplift and falling sea levels, began earlier than the erosion of the Chalk series on the shelves flanking the central and southern parts of the North Sea Basin.

The late Paleocene–earliest Eocene crustal separation stage in the Norwegian–Greenland Sea corresponds in the North Sea to a last, albeit mild, rifting phase. This is reflected by the reactivation of the eastern border faults of the Shetland Platform, the Great Glen Fault, and parts of the Moray Firth fault system. Furthermore, some of the faults marking the northeastern margin of the Mid-North Sea High also became reactivated; this triggered mass-flow of Chalk debris from the Mid-North Sea High into the Central Graben (Fig. 58).

Paleocene uplift and eastward tilting of the Shetland Platform gave rise to the development of an eastward-directed drainage system and the outbuilding of deltaic complexes along the margins of the Viking and Central grabens; in the latter, water depths were of the order of 500–900 m (Parker, 1975). At the intersection of these deltaic and barrier-bar complexes with the tectonically still active graben margins, recurrent slope instability triggered density currents, which transported sands into these troughs where they accumulated as extensive deep water fans (Rochow, 1981; Knox et al., 1981; Morton, 1982; Enjolras et al., 1986). The geometry of these fans illustrates that the Viking and Central grabens formed an elongate deep-water trough during the late Paleocene and early Eocene, while somewhat shallower seas occupied the remainder of the North Sea Basin (Fig. 58). Progressive subsidence of the North Sea Basin, combined with rising sea levels, induced a regional transgression during the latest Paleocene and early Eocene. This is reflected by a gradual reduction of the sand influx into the Central Graben and somewhat later, also into the Viking Graben. In much of the North Sea area, late Paleocene and Eocene strata are developed in a pelagic shale facies, and there is only limited evidence for clastics being derived from the Fennoscandian Shield. Paleogene shorelines were probably located much further inland than today's coastlines of Norway and Sweden (Ziegler and Louwerens, 1979). Upper Paleocene and lower Eocene deeper water sands contain major oil and gas accumulations in the Central and Northern North Sea (Ziegler, 1980).

Over large parts of the North Sea, Oligocene strata consist of pelagic, partly deeper water clays containing minor carbonate intercalations. These contain Arctic cold-water faunas that do not permit a reliable determination of depositional water depths. In the Central North Sea, Oligocene clays reach a thickness of 800 m and represent, on the basis of seismostratigraphic criteria, a basinal facies. During the early Oligocene, sedimentation and subsidence rates probably were more or less in balance so that no appreciable shallowing of the basin took place. The Shetland Platform continued to act as a major source of sand as evidenced by a fringe of delta complexes. During the mid-Oligocene low stand in sea level, a major foreset unit prograded into the Viking Graben. This coal-bearing, sandy sequence reaches a thickness of 500 m and is laterally offset by 200 m of pelagic, deep water clays. Clastic influx from eastern sources remained also during the Oligocene at a very low level. On the other hand, thin, deltaic sheet sands prograded during the Oligocene from the southern margin of the North Sea Basin (Ziegler, 1982a).

## Neogene Shallowing of the Basin

During the Miocene and Pliocene, repeated sea-level fluctuations strongly influenced sedimentation patterns in the North Sea, especially in its shallower parts where regionally correlative disconformities are evident, for instance, at the base and top of the Miocene.

The Neogene uplift of the Rhenish Shield was coupled with the development of deltaic conditions in the Southern North Sea and in Northern Germany during the Miocene and Pliocene. Similarly, deltas began to prograde from the Fennoscandian Borderzone through Denmark. This was accompanied by an increase in clastic influx into the Central North Sea where Neogene and Quaternary open-marine clays are some 2000 m thick (Fig. 59). From mid-Miocene time onwards, warm water microfaunas indicate a progressive shallowing of the central parts of the North Sea Basin. This shows that during the Miocene and Plio-Pleistocene, sedimentation rates outpaced subsidence rates. Also in the northern North Sea, Neogene strata reflect a progressive shallowing of the basin whereby progradation of deltaic complexes from the Shetland Platform into the Viking Graben continued to play an important role.

Throughout the Neogene, clastic influx from the Norwegian coast remained, however, at a rather low level. This is suggested by continued open marine connections between the Central North Sea and the Norwegian–Greenland Sea.

In the glacially scoured Norwegian and Skagerrak trenches, and also in Northern Denmark, Mio-Pliocene and older strata, forming a gently dipping monocline, are deeply truncated. This illustrates that during the Pleistocene the eastern margin of the North Sea Basin became uplifted and subjected to erosion in conjunction with the isostatic adjustment of the Fennoscandian Shield to cyclical Pleistocene glaciation and deglaciation (Figs. 18, 59).

## Subsidence Patterns and Mechanisms

The regional structure map of the top Chalk series, given in Fig. 60, describes the geometry of the Cenozoic North Sea Basin and indicates that it developed by broad downwarping (Ziegler and Louwerens, 1979).

Cenozoic series reach a thickness of 3.5 km in the central parts of this saucer-shaped basin. The axis of this basin is aligned with the trace of the Viking and the Central grabens.

Most faults affecting the base of the Tertiary strata die out rapidly in Paleogene sediments. There is no evidence for a Neogene reactivation of the Mesozoic North Sea Graben system, and the Tertiary Ruhr Graben, forming the northwestern branch of the Rhine Rift, dies out in the Dutch onshore areas near the coast of the southern North Sea.

Diapirism of Permian salts caused local subsidence anomalies and faulting that interrupt the otherwise smooth Cenozoic isopachs. In the southern North Sea, additional anomalies are related to the Paleogene inversion of the West and Central Netherlands Basin, of the Sole Pit Basin, and of the southern parts of the Central Graben (see in Chapter 9, *Compressional Deformation of the Alpine Foreland*).

In general, Paleogene to Quaternary strata increase in thickness from the margins of the North Sea Basin toward its center. Notable exceptions are, however, the Oligocene deltaic complexes that prograded from the Shetland Platform into the deeper waters of the Viking Graben and also the Paleocene and Eocene series, in which both sandy shelf and turbiditic basinal facies stand out by their thickness (Fig. 59).

Refraction and deep reflection data indicate that the Moho Discontinuity is located in the coastal area of Norway at a depth of 33–34 km, under the Viking and the Central grabens at a depth of 22–24 km and 20 km, respectively, and under the Shetland Platform and the British Isles at a depth of 30 km and 32 km, respectively (Fig. 61; Solli, 1976; Christie and Sclater, 1980; Wood and Barton, 1983; Barton and Wood, 1984). Under the axial parts of the Central and Viking Graben, in which sediments reach a thickness of 8–10 km, the continental crust is 60–70% thinner than beneath adjacent Britain, the Shetland Platform, and the Fennoscandian Shield. Throughout these refraction profiles, the upper mantle displays a normal velocity of 8.1–8.2 km/sec. Deep reflection profiles show that the lower crust is highly reflective and diffractive under the Viking Graben and that its reflectivity decreases toward the Norwegian Coast and the Shetland Platform where a fairly discrete Moho reflection is evident (Beach, 1985; Fig. 62).

If it is assumed that the crust of the Viking and the Central grabens was thinned by mechanical stretching only (McKenzie, 1978), then the amount of extension across the Viking Graben would be on the order of 80–100 km and for the Central Graben

about 110 km (Wood and Barton, 1983; Barton and Wood, 1984; Sclater et al., 1986).

Multichannel reflection seismic data acquired by the petroleum industry show, however, that in the northern North Sea extension of the synrift sediments by faulting is, at the Jurassic level, on the order of only 10–15 km. In the Viking Graben, Triassic series transgressed over Caledonian basement and Devonian clastics. The base of the Lower Triassic sediments, representing the earliest synrift deposits, can be mapped only locally. Thus, the extension at the base of the synrift sediments cannot be readily determined from reflection seismic data. Yet, to judge from the geometry of the individual fault blocks and the lack of significant divergence of Triassic reflectors, it seems unlikely that the total amount of Mesozoic crustal extension across the Viking Graben exceeds 20–30 km.

In the Central North Sea, where the Zechstein Salt forms part of the prerift sequence, its base corresponds to a regionally correlative stratigraphical and seismic marker. Thus, the extension mapped at this level gives a reasonable constraint to the amount of extension that can have occurred during the Mesozoic rifting stage. Amounts of extension by faulting at the base Zechstein Salt level are in the range of 25–30 km. It is very unlikely that a multitude of additional, small faults, undetectable on multichannel seismic reflection data, could account for a doubling or even a quadrupling of this amount as suggested by the stretching model (McKenzie, 1978; Wood and Barton, 1983; Barton and Wood, 1984; Ziegler, 1983a; Sclater et al., 1986).

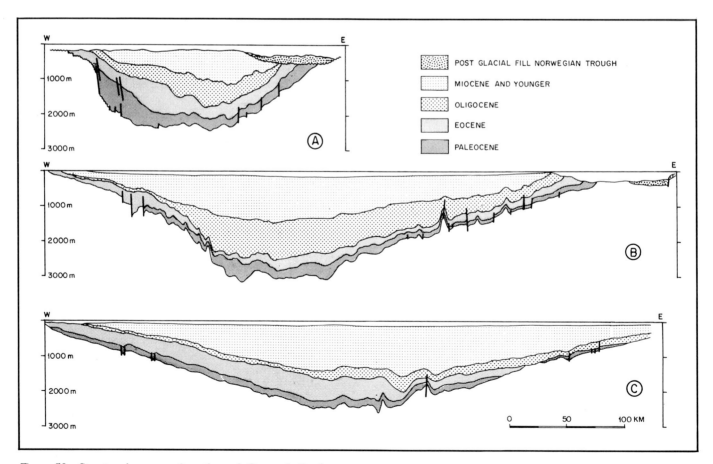

*Figure 59—Structural cross sections through Cenozoic North Sea Basin. For location see Figure 60.*

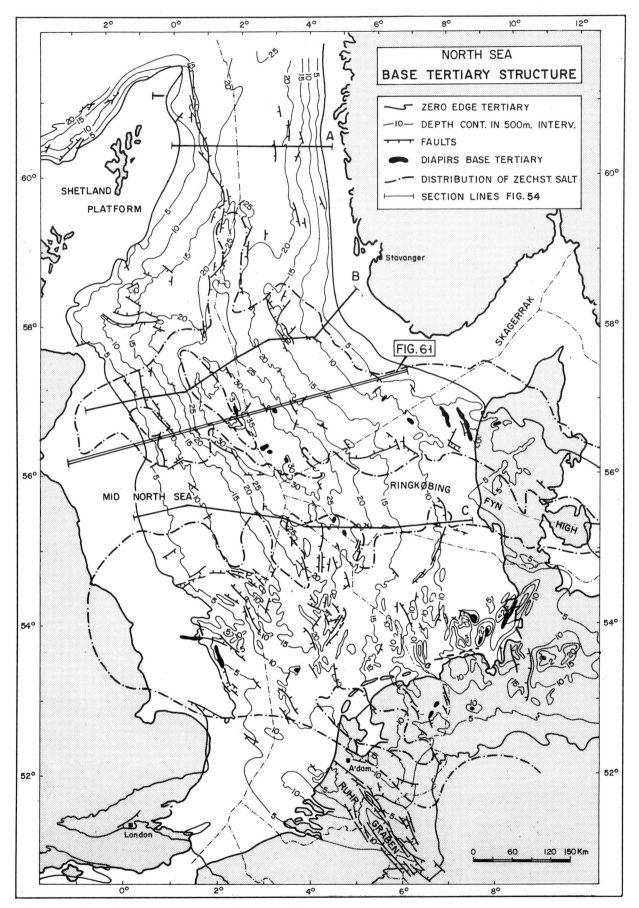

*Figure 60—North Sea, structural map base Tertiary clastics.*
*Ziegler and Louwerens (1978).*

Similarly, the amount of crustal extension postulated by the stretching model for the Witchground and Buchan grabens in the outer Moray Firth area of the northwestern North Sea (Christie and Sclater, 1980) is at variance with the amount of extension observed on reflection lines (Smythe et al., 1980).

For the Danish part of the Central Graben and for the Permo-Triassic Horn Graben, reflection seismic data indicate that at the base Zechstein Salt level, the combined amount of crustal extension ranges from about 10 km to a maximum of 15 km. This is less than the values determined for the Central Graben. Therefore, it must be assumed that part of the crustal dilation that occurred in the Central North Sea was taken up in the North Danish Basin (Fig. 44; Sorensen, 1985).

Gravity data show the presence of a mass excess beneath the low-density sediments of the Viking and Central grabens. The deepest parts of the Cenozoic North Sea Basin coincide with the largest gravity anomaly in the area of the Central Graben (Donato and Tully, 1981; Hospers et al., 1986b).

The Cenozoic subsidence patterns of the North Sea Basin can be explained by the decay of the thermal anomaly that had developed during its Mesozoic rifting stage, spanning some 175 Ma. Although not yet quantifiable, the rate of crustal extension appears to have accelerated during the Triassic to reach a peak at the transition from the Jurassic to the Cretaceous. A major subcrustal thermal anomaly was probably introduced during the Mid-Jurassic doming of the Central North Sea area (Chapter 5). During the Cretaceous, the rate of crustal extension decreased rapidly. The last tensional events occurred during the late Paleocene and earliest Eocene. In this context, it should be kept in mind that the maximum thermal disturbance of the lithosphere of the North Sea area probably did not coincide with termination of rifting activity during the early Eocene but with the Mid-Jurassic and earliest Cretaceous tensional events. Thus, cooling and contraction of the lithosphere started already during the earliest Cretaceous; the subsequent minor rifting events, as well as the Thulean volcanic surge, interfered with or even temporarily reversed this cooling process. Only after the late Paleocene Laramide rifting pulse was the evolution of the

North Sea Basin exclusively governed by progressive lithospheric cooling and contraction and its isostatic adjustment to sedimentary loading and sea-level fluctuations (Watts and Steckler, 1979; Royden et al., 1980; Watts et al., 1982; Watts and Thorne, 1984).

For the Central North Sea, Wood and Barton (1983) postulated, on the basis of quantitative subsidence analyses, a $\beta$-value of 1.5 for its stretched crust, while reflection data indicate a $\beta$-value of 1.1–1.2. On a basin-wide scale, this translates into an extension by 50–80 km, as derived from thermal subsidence analyses versus 110 km as derived from crustal configuration and 20–30 km as derived from reflection data (Ziegler, 1982a, 1983a; Beach, 1985; Sclater et al., 1986). Similar discrepancies between stretching factors derived from subsidence analyses, crustal configuration, and reflection data are also observed in the eastern Moray Firth Rift (Witch Ground–Buchan grabens; Fig. 35; Christie and Sclater, 1980; Smythe et al., 1980) and also in the Viking Graben (Sclater and Christie, 1980; Ziegler, 1982a).

This has led to the development of the "linked tectonics" concept that stresses oblique extension across the Viking and Central grabens to the end that the amount of extension measured in cross sections normal to these rifts may not give a true value of the actual amount of crustal extension achieved in them. This concept requires major sinistral displacements along the Viking Graben and the Fennoscandian Borderzone (Fig. 35; Beach, 1985), the magnitude of which is difficult to reconcile with the available data. Although there is evidence for minor lateral displacements along the fault systems of the Viking and Central grabens, these are unlikely to account for the major discrepancies between extension factors derived from subsidence analyses and reflection and refraction data.

The available data point toward an important discrepancy between upper and lower crustal "stretching" factors and the possibility that the mass of the lower crust is not being conserved during rifting. This leads to the assumption that crustal attenuation of the Central and Northern North Sea, as defined by gravity, refraction, and reflection data was achieved not only

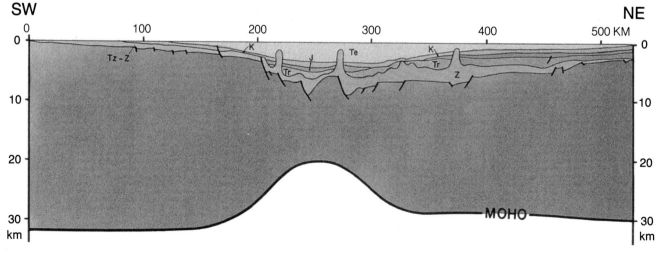

*Figure 61—Crustal configuration of Central North Sea. After Barton and Wood, 1983. For location see Figure 60.*

by mechanical stretching of the crust but also by thermally induced physicochemical processes that affected the lower crust and caused an upward displacement of the crust–mantle boundary. These processes, which are still poorly understood and which are apparently irreversible, are here referred to in generalized terms as "subcrustal erosion." It is speculated that the high reflectivity of the attenuated lower crust, as evident in the Viking Graben (Fig. 62), may be in some way related to these processes. It is, however, realized that intracrustal shear zones can also give rise to deep, intracrustal reflections (Brewer and Smythe, 1984; Gibbs, 1984; Beach, 1985; see in Chapter 10: *Rifting Processes*).

Lower crustal attenuation processes appear to have been more effective in the area of the Mid-Jurassic Central North Sea dome (see in Chapter 5: *North Sea Rift Dome*) than in the Northern Viking Graben where sedimentation was continuous throughout the Jurassic. This suggests that the Cenozoic Central North Sea subsidence maximum is probably related to an area of maximum crustal attenuation and the decay of a maximum thermal anomaly, resulting from the Mid-Jurassic intrusion of asthenospheric material to the crust–mantle boundary and further crustal extension during the late Kimmerian rifting pulse.

It is obvious that additional refraction and deep reflection data are required to evaluate the validity of these concepts.

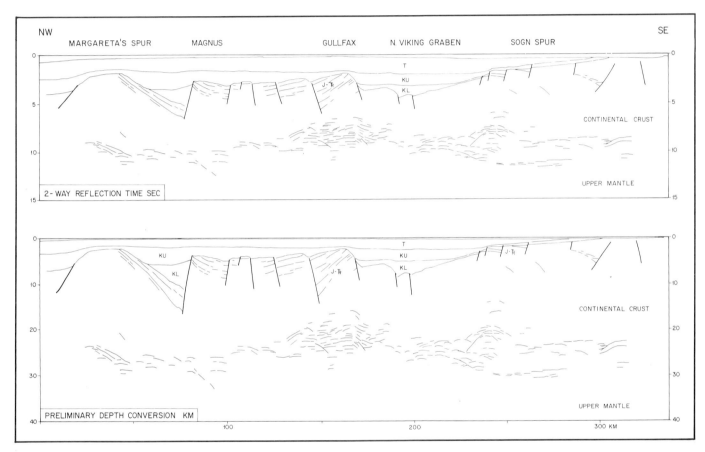

*Figure 62—Seismic line drawing of a deep sounding line crossing northernmost Viking Graben, showing patterns of lower crustal reflectivity. See also Beach (1985).*

# CHAPTER 9
## CENOZOIC SUTURING OF EURASIA AND AFRICA–ARABIA

# INTRODUCTION

Crustal separation between Europe and North America–Greenland during the earliest Eocene, followed by the progressive opening of the Arctic–North Atlantic Ocean, was paralleled by collision of Africa–Arabia and Eurasia leading to their welding together along the Alpine megasuture.

This involved continued northward drift and also the counterclockwise rotation of Africa–Arabia relative to Eurasia in response to the progressive opening of the Central and South Atlantic and the Indian oceans (Hsü, 1982; Livermore and Smith, 1985; Savostin et al., 1986; Dercourt et al., 1986).

Sinistral differential movements between Africa–Arabia and Europe, which had decreased substantially during the latest Cretaceous and early Paleocene, ceased altogether during the latest Paleocene–earliest Eocene as a consequence of the onset of sea-floor spreading in the northern North Atlantic, the Norwegian–Greenland Sea, and the Eurasian Basin (Plate 17).

Africa–Arabia and Europe converged during the Eocene in an approximately north–south direction; during the Oligocene and early Miocene, their convergence direction changed, however, to a northwesterly dextral oblique one (Plate 18). This was the effect of differences in the rates of sea-floor spreading in the Central Atlantic and in the Arctic–North Atlantic. Magnetic sea-floor anomalies indicate that sea-floor spreading slowed down in the Central Atlantic after anomaly 13 ($\pm$ 37 Ma, Rupelian) whereas no corresponding change in spreading rates is evident in the North Atlantic until after anomaly 6 ($\pm$ 20 Ma, Burdigalian) (Savostin et al., 1986). This would explain the dextral translation between Europe and Africa–Arabia that was superposed on their continued northward convergence. These plate motions governed the Main–Alpine orogenic phases during which the collision front between Africa, its Italo-Dinarid promontory, and Europe propagated rapidly into the Western Mediterranean domain.

After anomaly 6, sea-floor spreading rates in the Arctic–North Atlantic were more or less in balance with the spreading rates of the Central Atlantic (Dercourt et al., 1986). Deformation patterns of the Alpine fold belts suggest, however, that dextral oblique motions between Africa–Arabia and Europe continued to play an important role during the mid-Miocene and Pliocene late Alpine orogenic phases and even persist to the present (Plates 19–21).

The assessment of the underlaying plate motions requires a further detailed analysis of the magnetic sea-floor anomalies 7 to 1. Earthquake focal mechanisms indicate that the Alpine Mediterranean domain is at present affected by dextral compressive stresses (Udias, 1982, 1985).

# EOCENE TO EARLY MIOCENE MAIN–ALPINE OROGENIC PHASES

The Eocene and Oligocene convergence of Africa–Arabia and Europe induced major crustal shortening in the Taurides, Hellenides, Dinarides, Carpathians, and Alps (Aubouin, 1973; Burchfiel, 1980; Sengör and Yilmaz, 1981; Bonneau, 1982; Debelmas et al., 1983; Dercourt et al., 1986). This was accompanied by the closure of the Ligurian–Alboran Ocean and the collision of the Alboran–Kabylia–Calabria block with the southeastern margin of Iberia and the Corsica–Sardinia block, presumably during the late Eocene (Rondeel and Simon, 1974; Harris, 1985; Diaz de Federico et al., 1980).

With the closure of the last of the Middle Jurassic to Early Cretaceous oceanic basins in the Mediterranean domain, the collision front between the Italo-Dinarid promontory and Europe propagated rapidly into the Western Mediterranean area (Plate 18).

## Western Mediterranean Area

Along the southern margin of the Alboran–Kabylia block, crustal shortening intensified during the late Eocene as indicated by the deformation of the internal Kabylian and ultra-Tellian nappes of northern Algeria and Tunisia. At the same time, compressional intraplate stresses induced the inversion of the early Mesozoic Atlas troughs (Guiraud, 1975; Michard, 1976; see *Inversion of the Atlas Troughs,* this chapter). During the Oligocene, tectonic activity abated in this area and the deeper water Numidian clastics accumulated in narrow elongate basins paralleling the incipient Rif and Kabylian-Tellian fold belts (Plate 18). These clastics were derived from the uplifted Alboran and Kabylia blocks as well as from the African Craton. During the early Miocene, crustal shortening accelerated sharply and caused the emplacement of the Rif and Tellian flysch nappes (Caire, 1974; Michard, 1976; Wildi, 1983).

Progressive Senonian–Paleocene closure of the Ligurian–Alboran Ocean and obduction of ophiolites on the southern margin of the Corsica–Sardinia block was governed by a south-dipping subduction zone marking the northern margin of the Alboran–Calabrian block. Following the early Eocene collision of the Calabria and Corsica–Sardinia blocks, this subduction system became locked (Cocozza and Jacobacci, 1975; Harris, 1985). During the Eocene, southeastward-directed back-thrusting heralded the development of a new, northwest-dipping subduction zone, activity along which resulted in the Oligocene and early Miocene compressional deformation of the Calabria block and the Lucania–Campania Platform, the development of the Apennine foredeep basin, and calc-alkaline volcanic activity in Sardinia (Sestini, 1974; Pieri, 1975; Cohen, 1980; Boccaletti et al., 1984; Rehault et al., 1985). This change in the subduction polarity was, at least partly, the consequence of the onsetting dextral-oblique convergence of Africa and Europe.

The Eocene closure of the Alboran Ocean and the ensuing collision of the Alboran–Kabylia block with Iberia was followed by their Oligocene to early Miocene continued dextral oblique convergence, and the emplacement of the internal Betic nappes that contain ophiolitic complexes in their western parts at the boundary between the external and internal Betic zones (Rondeel and Simon, 1974; Durand-Delga and Fontboté, 1980; Diaz de Federico et al., 1980; Vegas and Banda, 1983). These orogenic events coincide with the main orogenic phases of the Pyrenees (Mattauer and Henry, 1974; Mirouse, 1980), the compressional deformation of the Iberian Craton as a whole (see *Accretion of the Iberian Microcontinent,* this chapter), its northwestward displacement (escape), and the subduction of oceanic crust along its leading edge in the southern Bay of Biscay (Grimaud et al., 1982).

At the same time, convergence between Africa and the Alboran–Kabylia block accelerated. This is reflected by the main phase of obduction of the Kabylian nappes onto the Tellian margin of Africa, which is dated as early Miocene (Caire, 1974; Michard, 1976; Wildi, 1983).

During the Oligocene, the Gulf of Lion–Valencia rift system, forming the southern extension of the Rhine-Bresse-Rhône

Graben system, transecting Western Europe, came into evidence (Plate 18). From the Gulf of Lion a complex system of grabens extended along the northwestern margin of the Corsica–Sardinia block into the area of the present-day Ligurian Sea (Lemoine, 1978; Cohen, 1980; Thomas and Gennesseaux, 1986). The evolution of this rift system culminated during the mid-Aquitanian in crustal separation between the Corsica–Sardinia block and France and between the Alboran and Kabylia blocks. During the late Aquitanian to early Burdigalian (21–18 Ma), rapid sea-floor spreading along the Liguro-Provençal, Sardo-Balearic, and North Algerian spreading axes induced the counterclockwise rotation of the Corsica–Sardinia block and the clockwise rotation of the Kabylia block and further compressional deformation in the Apennine and Maghrebian fold belts, respectively (Plate 19; Pieri, 1975; Carmignani et al., 1978; Cohen, 1980; Horner and Lowrie, 1981; Burrus, 1984; Rehault et al., 1984a, 1984b, 1985; Morelli, 1985; Westphal et al., 1986).

The evolution of the Algero-Provençal oceanic basin may have been governed by a combination of geodynamic processes such as back-arc extension behind the Apennine–Maghrebian arc, intracontinental rifting related to the Rhine–Rhône–Valencia graben system, and transtensional deformations induced by the dextral translation between Africa and Europe (Laubscher, 1974; Tapponier, 1977; Burrus, 1984; Ricou et al., 1986). Whatever the principal mechanism was, the opening of the Algero-Provençal oceanic basin was contemporaneous with the main orogenic phases of the Maghrebian–Tellian and Apennine fold belts (Durand-Delga, 1978). Shortly after the rotation of the Corsica–Sardina block, back-arc extension shifted from the Algero-Provençal Basin to the Tyrrhenian Basin (Malinverno and Ryan, 1986) while the former apparently became inactive and started to subside in response to lithospheric cooling and sediment loading. The present thermal regime of the Algero-Provençal Basin does not, however, conform to the standard age/heat flow relation established for oceanic and attenuated continental lithosphere, probably due to the Plio-Pleistocene reactivation of the Valencia Rift and phenomena that may be related to continued subduction along the Calabrian Arc (Burrus and Foucher, 1986; see *Western Mediterranean Area,* this chapter).

## Alpine–Carpathian Fold Belt

In the Alpine domain, the basement-cored Austro-Alpine and Penninic nappes became emplaced on the Helvetic Shelf of northern Europe during the Main–Alpine orogenic phases (Tollmann, 1978, 1980; Trümpy, 1980; Milnes and Pfiffner, 1980; Homewood et al., 1980; Faupl et al., 1980; Debelmas et al., 1983). The emplacement of these nappes involved crustal delamination and the subduction of lower crustal and upper mantle material (Müller, 1982). At the same time, the sedimentary sequence of the Helvetic Shelf became imbricated. Compressional deformation of the Briançonnais Platform went hand in hand with the late Eocene closure of the Valais Trough. In the Western and Central Alps, the gradual uplift of the Mont Blanc and Gotthard massifs is indicative for A-subduction progradation into the basement of the Helvetic Shelf. By the early Miocene, the Alpine and North Carpathian nappes were emplaced near their present location (Birkenmajer, 1974; Faupl et al., 1980; Tollmann, 1980; Debelmas et al., 1983; Ricou and Siddans, 1986).

The Eocene–early Miocene obduction of the Austro-Alpine and Penninic nappes onto the margin of the North European Craton was accompanied by the development of the Alpine foredeep, the Molasse Basin (Fig. 63). Through time, the axis of this basin migrated craton-ward in response to the tectonic load exerted onto the foreland crust by the advancing nappe systems. Flexural downbending of the foreland crust was accompanied by the development of a complex set of often basin-parallel tensional faults, as evident, for instance, in the Molasse Basin of Germany and Austria (Bachmann et al., 1987; Nachtmann and Wagner, 1987).

During the Eocene, an extensive synorogenic flysch series was deposited in the southern, proximal parts of this basin. On the other hand, along its northern, distal margin shallow marine clastics and carbonates transgressed over the deeply truncated Mesozoic series that had been deformed during the Sub-Hercynian and Laramide pulses of foreland compression (see Chapter 7, *Compressional Intraplate Deformation in NW Europe*). During the Oligocene, shallow marine and deltaic conditions prevailed in the western and central parts of the Alpine foredeep whereas deeper water conditions persisted in the foredeep of the Eastern Alps and the northern Carpathian (Plates 18, 30; Mahel and Buday, 1968; Gwinner, 1971; Büchi and Schlanke, 1977; Elias, 1977; Kollmann, 1977; Lemke, 1977; Kerckhove et al., 1980; Trümpy, 1980; Ziegler, 1982a; Homewood, 1983).

In the Alpine domain, the Main–Alpine orogeny was associated with minor synorogenic volcanic activity, extensive high-pressure/low-temperature metamorphism, and the late Eocene to Oligocene intrusion of granites in the Southern Alps (Oxburgh, 1974; Trümpy, 1980; Faupl et al., 1980).

## Eastern Mediterranean Area

The Dinarid–Hellenic fold belt was also strongly affected by the Main–Alpine orogeny. During the Eocene, the Karst and the southward adjacent Gavrovo–Tripolitza platforms became incorporated into the flysch troughs paralleling the advancing nappe systems and ultimately themselves became folded and imbricated during the Oligocene and early Miocene (Plate 18; Richter, 1978; Burchfiel, 1980; Bonneau, 1982). The Oligocene to early Miocene emplacement of major nappe systems in the Dinarides and Hellenides was associated with an extensive high-pressure/low-temperature metamorphism and the subduction of substantial volumes of crustal and upper mantle material as reflected by a well-developed calc-alkaline synorogenic magmatism in Greece and Yugoslavia (Aubouin, 1973; Burchfiel, 1980; Celet et al., 1980; D'Argenio et al., 1980; Bonneau, 1982).

During the Eocene and Oligocene, the Taurid Platform (Plate 16) also subsided rapidly in front of the southward-advancing Anatolide nappes and became the site of extensive flysch deposits. Simultaneously, the Taurid thrust sheets became activated (Brinkmann, 1976; Sengör and Yilmaz, 1981; Bonneau, 1982).

In the Eastern Carpathians and the Balkan Ranges, crustal shortening during the Main–Alpine orogenic cycle was of relatively minor dimensions compared to the Alpine and Dinarid–Hellenic fold belts (Radulescu and Sandulescu, 1980; Burchfiel, 1980; Sandulescu, 1984). On the other hand, crustal shortening continued in the northern Pontides during the Oligocene. This was accompanied by the accumulation of synorogenic flysch in the Black Sea Basin (Letouzey et al., 1977; Zonnenshain and Le Pichon, 1986).

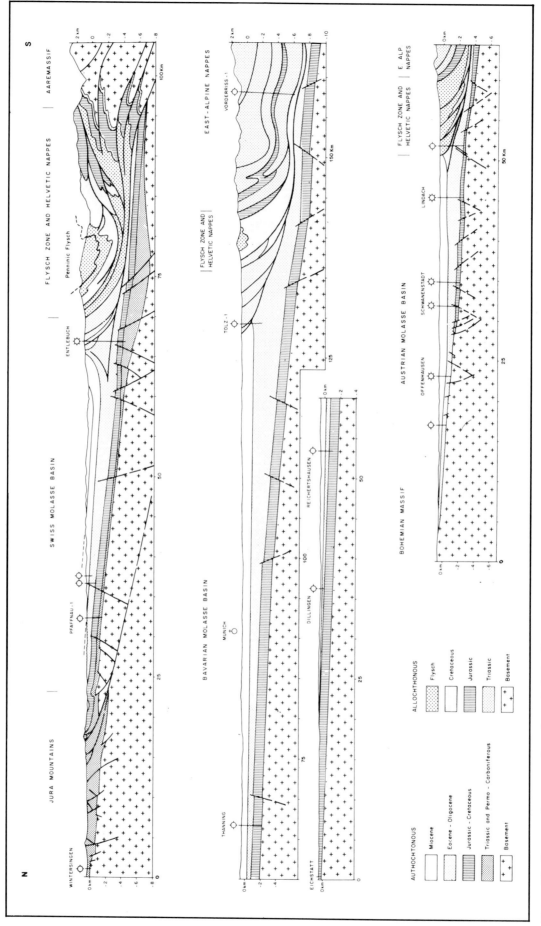

*Figure 63—Structural cross sections through Swiss, Bavarian, and Austrian Molasse Basin.*

General east–west compression of the Italo-Dinarid promontory during the Main–Alpine orogenic cycle is evident by the rapid progradation of the Apennine and Dinarid–Hellenic deformation fronts. By late Oligocene–early Miocene time, the latter had reached the area now occupied by the Adriatic Sea (Pieri, 1975; Boccaletti et al., 1984). With this, the Adriatic Basin began to assume its present-day shape.

The Ionian and Levantine Sea basins are characterized by a thin crust, the much disputed nature of which plays an important role in the different models that have been advanced for the evolution of the Eastern Mediterranean (Makris, 1981; Bonneau, 1982; Finetti, 1985; Dercourt et al., 1986; Ricou et al., 1986). Geophysical evidence suggests that the Ionian Sea is either underlain by drastically thinned continental or truly oceanic crust and that the Levantine Basin may be largely underlain by thinned continental crust (Finetti, 1985; Morelli, 1985; Neev et al., 1985).

During the Eocene to early Miocene, the Pelagian Shelf, the Cyrenaica Plateau, as well as the Latium–Abruzzi and the western parts of the Apulian platforms were occupied by stable carbonate shelves (Plate 18).

# MIO-PLIOCENE LATE ALPINE OROGENIC PHASES

During the late Alpine orogenic phases, spanning essentially Burdigalian to Recent times, Africa–Arabia and Eurasia continued to converge whereby convergence rates, as derived from magnetic sea-floor anomalies, were lower in the Western Mediterranean than in its eastern parts (Dercourt et al., 1986; Savostin et al., 1986). The pattern of tectonic activity along the individual fold belts of the Alpine–Mediterranean orogenic system, as well as the development of a new set of transcurrent fault systems and back-arc basins, indicate that the dextral translation between Eurasia and Africa-Arabia persisted and, in time, possibly gained in importance (Plates 19–21). This concept is further born out by the determination of paleostress patterns as derived from macro- and micro-tectonics in the northern and southern Alpine foreland (Letouzey, 1986) and by focal mechanisms of earthquakes (Udias, 1982, 1985).

During the late Alpine evolution of the Mediterranean area, the latest Miocene Messinian salinity crises correspond to a major incision in sedimentation patterns (Plate 20). Partial and possibly temporary total isolation of the Mediterranean basins from the world oceans by tectonic restriction of seaways through the foredeeps of the Betic Cordillera, the Rif–Tellian (Maghrebian), and the South Anatolian fold belts resulted from the continued convergence of Africa–Arabia and Europe. Contemporaneous glacioeustatic sea-level fluctuations probably had an overprinting effect. Temporary seaways may have been open during the Messinian between the Aegean and the Black Sea (Para-Tethys Basin) via the Bosporus and possibly between the Eastern Mediterranean and the Indian Ocean via the Red Sea and the Gulf of Suez (Hsü 1972, 1978; Hsü et al., 1973; Rögel and Steininger, 1983; Steininger and Rögel, 1984; Sonnenfeld and Finetti, 1985).

Sharp restriction of the water influx into the Mediterranean basins, combined with a high evaporation rate, caused a rapid salinity increase and the accumulation of carbonates and sulfates on shallow platform areas and the deposition of up to 2000 m thick halites in basinal areas, possibly under deeper water

conditions. This was associated with a cyclical lowering of the Mediterranean sea level by several hundred meters and erosion, under arid conditions, of the new land areas surrounding the highly saline basins. Moreover, isostatic uplift of the Mediterranean area, in response to its evaporation-induced water-unloading, may have significantly contributed to the relief of the Messinian unconformities. In view of this, the magnitude of the Messinian drop in sea level in the different basins of the Mediterranean area is not easy to estimate, particularly because at least part of the relief of the erosional unconformities evident along the margins of these evaporitic basins may be of a submarine origin (Fig. 64). The apparent lack of highly soluble salts in the Messinian evaporites speaks in favor of the "continuous (or better, intermittent) inflow and outflow model" (Sonnenfeld and Finetti, 1985), which precludes a persistent kilometer scale drop of the Mediterranean sea level below that of the world oceans and, even more so, its total drying out. This model operates on an evaporation-induced deficiency in the Mediterranean water budget, caused by a restriction of the water inflow from the Atlantic and Indian oceans, but permits a periodic reflux of brines during temporary high stands in sea level. The principal Messinian salt basins are the Provençal–Algerian Basin, the Ionian Sea, and the Levantine Basin (Hsü et al., 1973, 1978; Mulder et al., 1975; Debenetti, 1982; Cita, 1982; Sonnenfeld, 1985).

During the earliest Pliocene, marine connections between the Atlantic and the Mediterranean Basin were reopened and normal water salinities were reestablished in the latter owing to breaching of the Gibraltar orocline (Plate 21).

## Western Mediterranean Area

In the Betic–Balearic Cordillera and in the Maghrebian (Rif–Tellian) fold belt, crustal shortening culminated in the intra-Tortonian phase of folding and nappe emplacement (Rondeel and Simon, 1974; Azema et al., 1974; Michard, 1976; Durand-Delga and Fontboté, 1980; Wildi, 1983). During this last major orogenic pulse, the Gibraltar orocline became sharply accentuated whereby massif olistostromes derived from the rising fold belt blocked the marine connections between the Atlantic and the Mediterranean via the foredeeps of the Maghrebian (Rif-Tellian) fold belt and the Betic Cordillera (Guadalquivir Basin; Plates 19, 20; Fig. 62). This resulted in the sharp restriction of the Mediterranean Basin that culminated in the Messinian salinity crises (Mulder, 1973; Mulder et al., 1975; Hsü et al., 1978; Debenetti, 1982; Sonnenfeld, 1985). Following this intra-Tortonian orogenic event, the Alboran Sea Basin, occupying the internal parts of the Gibraltar orocline, began to subside rapidly under a back-arc tensional setting; with this, the Gibraltar Strait reopened during the earliest Pliocene (Plate 21; Mulder and Parry, 1977; Durand-Delga, 1978; Diaz-de-Federico, et al., 1980; Wildi, 1983). The Alboran Sea Basin is floored by thinned continental crust, and its tensional subsidence was accompanied by a widespread calc-alkaline volcanism and further compressional deformations in the Rif fold belt and the Betic Cordillera (Michard, 1976; Dillon et al., 1980; Horváth and Berkhemer, 1982; Vegas and Banda, 1983; Morelli, 1985).

Late Pliocene and Quaternary compressional deformations of considerable importance are also evident in the Tellian–Sahara Atlas and northeast Tunisian domain (Guiraud, 1975; Cohen et al., 1980; Wildi, 1983; Philip et al., 1986).

During the latest Miocene and Plio-Pleistocene, a chain of alkaline volcanic centers, extending from northeastern Spain across the Rif fold belt to the Cape Verdes Islands, came into evidence (Michard, 1976; Schminke, 1982; Horváth and Berkhemer, 1982; Hernandez et al., 1987). The axis of this rift-related volcanic chain is located on trend with the Rhine–Bresse–Rhône–Valencia Graben. Sea-floor spreading in the Algero-Provençal Basin had, however, ceased around 19 Ma during the Burdigalian.

There is limited evidence for a Plio-Pleistocene tensional reactivation of the Valencia Graben system offshore northeastern Spain (Fig. 64). In Morocco a first phase of alkaline volcanism is dated as mid-Miocene and the second phase as Pleistocene (Harmand and Moukadiri, 1986).

In the Apennine fold belt, crustal shortening continued through Miocene and Pliocene times to the present (Pieri, 1975; Cadet et al., 1980; Reutter, 1981). Progressive stacking of major nappes, cored by Mesozoic carbonates, went hand in hand with the eastward migration of the axis of the Apennine foredeep in which a thick flysch series accumulated. During the Pliocene, the Apennine deformation front reached well beyond the present-day Adriatic shore (Fig. 65). On the other hand, the Dinarid deformation front had already become largely inactive during the middle Miocene. The present Adriatic Basin is clearly polarized toward the still-active Apennine fold belt and contains near the Italian coast up to 7 km of post-Messinian flysch-type clastics (Ricci-Lucchi, 1975, 1978; Pieri and Mattavelli, 1986; Mostardini and Merlini, 1986).

During the Miocene and Pliocene, the nappe systems of the Calabrian Arc, linking the Apennines with the Maghrebian fold belt of Tunisia and Algeria, became emplaced on the margins of the Apulian Platform and the Pelagian Shelf (Plates 19–21; Ogniben and Vezzani, 1975; Roeder, 1978; Cohen et al., 1980). Rapid foundering of the Tyrrhenian Sea during the middle to late Miocene and Pliocene was caused by back-arc extension, inducing a widespread alkaline and tholeiitic basaltic volcanism that is superimposed on the subduction-related calc-alkaline and shoshonitic magmatism of the Calabrian–Apennine Arc. However, only limited truly oceanic crust was probably formed in the Tyrrhenian Basin (Wezel, 1982, 1985; Horváth and Berkhemer, 1982; Locardi, 1985; Malinverno and Ryan, 1986).

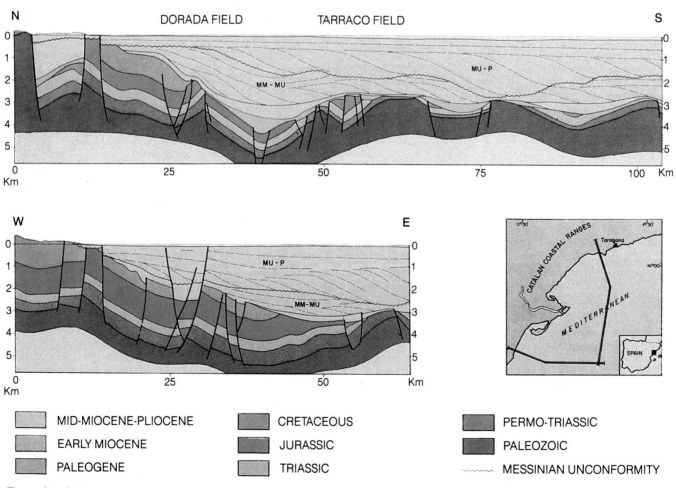

*Figure 64—Schematic structural cross section of the Ebro Delta, Spain, Mediterranean Shelf. After Shell España.*

Similar to the Apennines, crustal shortening persisted in the Calabrian Arc to the present as evident on seismic lines from the western parts of the Ionian Sea (Finetti, 1985) and by surface geology in northeastern Tunisia (Cohen et al., 1980). The dextral, volcanic Pantelleria–Malta rift-wrench zone, transecting the Plagian Platform in a northwesterly direction, came into evidence during the latest Miocene and is presently also still active (Illies, 1981; Winnock, 1981; Finetti, 1985; Jongsma et al., 1987). Mio-Pliocene grabens paralleling the trend of the Pantelleria–Malta Rift occur also in northeastern Tunisia (Cohen et al., 1980; Burollet and Ellouz, 1986; Letouzey, 1986).

## Alpine–Carpathian Fold Belt

Following the Oligocene–early Miocene emplacement of the Penninic and Austro-Alpine nappe systems, the convergence direction between the Alpine orogen and its foreland changed from an essentially southeast–northwest orientation to a more east–west one.

East of Munich, the Alpine deformation front remained essentially inactive during mid-Miocene to Pliocene times (Fig. 63; Kollmann and Malzer, 1980). In the Central and Western Alps, crustal shortening continued, however, as indicated by the further imbrication of the Helvetic nappes and the uplift of the external massifs of the Swiss and French Alps (e.g., Aare, Aiguilles Rouges, Pelvoux, Belledonne, Argentera massifs); these basement uplifts, which represent imbrications of the European foreland crust, evolved partly by compressional reactivation of Mesozoic tensional fault systems (Trümpy, 1980; Homewood et al., 1980; Milnes and Pfiffner, 1980; Debelmas et al., 1983; Lemoine et al., 1986). Their development clearly indicates that during the late Alpine orogenic phases, the foreland

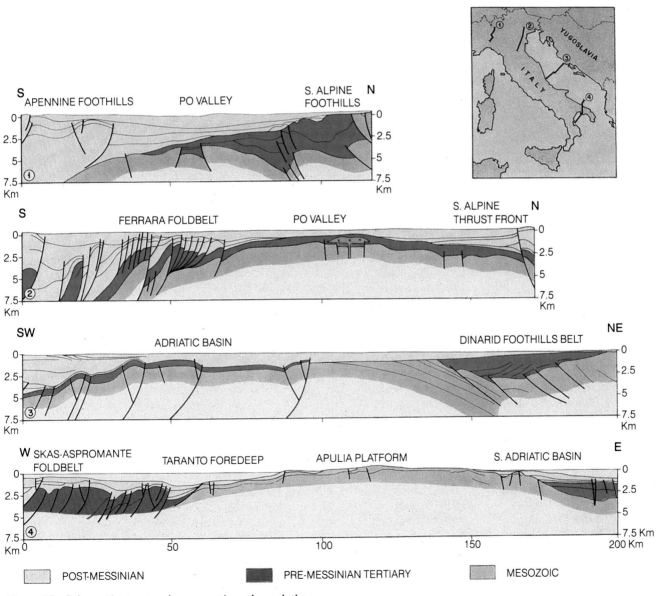

*Figure 65—Schematic structural cross-sections through the Apennine foredeep basin. Sections 1 and 2 after Pieri and Groppi (1981).*

and the orogen were strongly coupled at the respective A-subduction zones and that these prograded stepwise into the foreland.

During the late Miocene and Pliocene, compressional stresses were apparently intermittently exerted onto the north-western foreland of the Alps as evident from the folding of the Jura Mountains and of the external chains of the Western Alps, the Dauphine Zone (Kerckhove et al., 1980; Laubscher, 1980; Debelmas et al., 1983) as well as by the continued inversion movements in the Mesozoic troughs of the Celtic Sea–Western Approaches and Channel areas and wrench deformations in the Armorican Massif and the Paris Basin (see *Compressional Deformation of the Alpine Foreland*, this chapter).

Seismic and well data from the Po Valley (Northern Italy), forming the northernmost part of the Adria Basin, show that along the southern margin of the Alps south-verging thrusts were active during the Miocene and Pliocene (Fig. 65). The essentially pre-Messinian south-verging South Alpine thrusts oppose the north-verging thrusts of the northern Apennines, which were active during the Plio-Pleistocene (Pieri and Groppi, 1981; Pieri, 1983; Cassano et al., 1986).

The late Alpine orogenic phases were accompanied by the development of a complex wrench-fault system that transected the Central and Eastern Alps in an east–west direction (Guillaume, 1978). The pattern of these wrench faults, which are clearly evident on satellite images (e.g., BRGM-BEICIP landsat mosaic "La chaîne des Alpes," 1:1,000,000, 1978), is indicative of dextral shear movements. This fault system extends east-wards into the Pannonian Basin and appears to be genetically linked with the development of this late Alpine back-arc basin (Plates 19–21; Ziegler, 1982a).

Following the Oligocene–early Miocene main diastrophism of the Northern Carpathians and the Dinarides, the area of the Pannonian Basin was uplifted and became the site of extensive calc-alkaline volcanism. This was accompanied during the Carpathian to Sarmatian (17.5–10.5 Ma, late Burdigalian to early Tortonian) by a major extensional phase that induced the rapid subsidence of a system of fault-bounded basins, such as the Pannonian, Danube, Zala–Drava, and Vienna basins. The latter is superimposed on the external parts of the Western Carpathians (Horváth et al., 1981, 1986; Horváth and Berkhemer, 1982; Royden et al., 1982; Burchfiel and Royden, 1982; Poka, 1982; Royden, 1985). In these basins, shallow marine and, in part, deeper water clastics accumulated during the middle and late Miocene. With increasing clastic influx and decreasing subsidence rates, these basins shallowed out during the Pliocene and Quaternary. Following the late early to early late Miocene initial rifting pulse, tectonic and volcanic activity gradually abated and the area began to subside regionally. Tensional and wrench tectonics, periodically interrupted by minor compressional deformations, persisted, however, during late Miocene to Recent times. Pliocene and Quaternary volcanics consists of alkaline basalts (Stegena and Horváth, 1982; Horváth and Berkhemer, 1982).

Neogene and Quaternary sediments exceed a thickness of 4000 m in the deeper parts of the Pannonian Basin and reach 7000 m locally in the deepest grabens. In this intramontane, back–arc basin, marine and brackish sedimentation gave way, at the onset of the Pliocene, to a lacustrine and continental depositional regime (Trunko, 1969; Senes and Marinescu, 1974). At present, the Pannonian Basin is still seismically active and continues to subside (Sclater et al., 1980; Royden et al., 1982; Horváth et al., 1986).

Thrusting in the outer Carpathians was contemporaneous with the subsidence of the Pannonian Basin. Movement along thrust faults of the Northern Carpathian Externides ceased during the late Miocene, along with those of the Eastern Carpathian Externides during the Pliocene, and movement still persists in the seismically active Southern Carpathian Externides (Buday and Cicha, 1968; Sandulescu, 1975, 1984; Brix et al., 1977; Burchfiel, 1980; Royden et al., 1982).

The amount of Neogene crustal shortening in the Eastern Carpathians is substantial and has been estimated by Burchfiel and Bleahu (1976) to be of the order of 100 km. The amount of contemporaneous crustal extension in the Pannonian Basin seems to be considerably smaller as indicated by the geometry of the base-Neogene fault tectonics evident on reflection seismic data (Stegena and Horváth, 1982; Horváth and Berkhemer, 1982; Horváth and Rumpler, 1984; Horváth et al., 1986). The depth to the Moho Discontinuity ranges in the Pannonian Basin between 25 and 30 km and increases under the Carpathian and Dinarid fold belts to 45–60 km.

Subsidence of the individual subbasins of the Pannonian Basin is partly related to late early Miocene and younger crustal extension and in part to late Miocene and Plio-Pleistocene lower crustal attenuation. The latter probably involved ponding of partly mantle-derived magmas at the crust–mantle boundary, inducing a gradual upward displacement of the Moho Discontinuity, presumably by physicochemical processes (Stegena and Horváth, 1982). Both processes caused a significant thinning of the crust and thus induced the linear, rather fast subsidence of the Central Pannonian Basin, which is even now characterized by an elevated heat flow (Sclater et al., 1980; Horváth et al., 1981, 1986).

It is likely that wrench-related crustal extension, triggering the initial calc-alkaline volcanism, also induced the subcrustal heat surge that is responsible for the second, more regional phase of basin subsidence.

The geometric relationship between the fault systems of the Pannonian Basin and those transecting the Alps indicates that both developed during the Neogene. There is probably a genetic relationship between the late Alpine compressional deformations of the Western and Central Alps and of the Carpathians and the inception of this complex wrench and pull-apart system which finds its continuation in the southeast-trending wrench faults transecting the Internides of the Dinarides (peri-Adriatic–Vardar fault system).

The amount of crustal extension achieved in the Pannonian Basin during its Neogene evolution cannot be quantified on the basis of the published data. It is, however, unlikely to correspond to the total amount of crustal shortening achieved during the late Alpine orogenic phases in the Western Alps and in the Carpathians. Neogene dextral oblique convergence between Africa and Europe was apparently taken up by dextral shear along the peri-Adriatic–Vandar and intra-Alpine fault systems and by compression in the Western and Central Alps, in the Apennines, and in the Carpathians. Splays of the peri-Adriatic–Alpine wrench system extended into the intra-Carpathian area where a complex fault pattern developed; it governed the subsidence of transtensional basins trending essentially in a north-easterly direction and facilitated the ascent of anatectic calc-alkaline magmas. During the Badenian (middle Miocene), the intra-Carpathian block apparently became pressed (and escaped) in a northeastward and later in an eastward direction as indicated by the timing of imbrication of the Northern and Eastern Carpathian foredeep sequences. The Plio-Pleistocene decay of the west-dipping Carpathian subduction system was accompanied by limited back-arc extension and alkaline volcanism (Burchfiel and Royden, 1982; Horváth and Royden, 1981; Royden et al., 1982; Stegena and Horváth, 1982).

As such, the bulk of the subsidence of the Pannonian Basin cannot be related to back-arc extension in the classical sense of Uyeda (1982). It is highly unlikely that the late Alpine deformation of the Carpathian fold belt was caused by upwelling mantle currents in the intra-Carpathian area as postulated by Burchfiel and Royden (1982) and Royden et al. (1982). It is more likely that these deformations are the result of the transpressional, wrench-related expulsion of the Intra-Carpathian block (Tapponier, 1977), which triggered in the area of the Pannonian Basin the ascent of partly mantle-derived magmas to the crust–mantle boundary.

## Eastern Mediterranean Area

The late Alpine evolution of the Eastern Mediterranean area reflects the continued convergence of Africa–Arabia and Eurasia whereby the progressive indentation of the stable Arabian block into the Taurid–Anatolid fold belt played an important kinematic role. This effect was intensified by Miocene crustal extension and later by Plio-Pleistocene sea-floor spreading in the Red Sea and the activation of the left-lateral Dead Sea transform fault system, along which Arabia was translated northward relative to the East Mediterranean domain. Miocene sinistral movements along the Dead Sea transform fault were accompanied by the deformation of the Negev and Syrian fold belts. With the Pliocene onset of sea-floor spreading in the Red Sea, these fold belts became inactive while differential movements between the Arabian and Levantine blocks were taken up along the Dead Sea transform fault system (Plates 19–21; Juteau et al., 1983; Chenet and Letouzey, 1983; Quennell, 1984; Chorowicz et al., 1987; note shift of map frame between Plates 19 and 20).

In the eastern Black Sea–Caucasus area, compressional deformations, initiated during the Oligocene, accompanied the gradual uplift of the axial parts of the Caucasus and the development of the Caucasian foredeep basin (Borsuk and Sholop, 1983). During the latest Miocene, uplift and folding of the Caucasus was intensified in conjunction with the development of a north-dipping subduction system paralleling the northeastern margin of the Black Sea (Plate 21). Activity along this subduction zone probably triggered the extrusion of Plio-Pleistocene calc-alkaline volcanics in the Greater Caucasus. Further to the east, in the area of the Lesser Caucasus, the polarity of this subduction zone changed to a south-dipping one as indicated by the Plio-Pleistocene calc-alkaline volcanism in the Armenian Highlands. This change in subduction polarity occurs in the projection of the sinistral East Anatolian fault system, the conjugate of which is the dextral Talish transform system, paralleling the southwestern margin of the Caspian Sea (Zonnenshain and Le Pichon, 1986; Dewey et al., 1986). Contemporaneous crustal shortening is evident in the South Taurid (South Anatolian) fold belt, which was thrust over the Arabian Craton (Ilhan, 1974; Horstink, 1980; Sengör and Yilmaz, 1981). The triangular zone delimited by the East Anatolian and the Talish transform zones describes the indenter cone of the Arabian Craton.

During late Miocene and Plio-Pleistocene times, progressive indentation of Eurasia by the Arabian block and development of the right-lateral Zagros shear zone was accompanied by the partial decoupling of Anatolia from the northern Pontides along the dextral North Anatolian fault system and its lateral expulsion into the domain of the Hellenides (Tapponier, 1977; Sengör and Yilmaz, 1981; Sengör and Canitez, 1982; Dercourt et al., 1986; Dewey et al., 1986). The North Anatolian fault system came into evidence during the middle to late Miocene and is presently still active. Dextral displacements along its eastern parts are estimated to be on the order of 90 km. To the west, the North Anatolian fault splits up into a number of splays that transect the Balkan ranges in an east–west direction and the northern Aegean area in a southwesterly direction. These fault systems are associated with important pull-apart structures in which part of the displacements along the North Anatolian fault was presumably taken up by crustal extensions (Sengör and Canitez, 1982; Lybéris, 1984). To the northwest, this system of wrench faults and pull-apart basins links up with the dextral peri-Adriatic–Vardar fault system (Burchfiel, 1980).

Development of the northeastern Mediterranean dextral transform system, and late Miocene to Plio-Pleistocene movements along it, went hand in hand with the late Alpine orogenic evolution of the Hellenic and Cyprus Arcs, the subsidence of the Aegean back-arc basin, and sinistral movements along the Levantine–East Anatolian system of shear faults (Le Pichon and Angelier, 1979; Angelier et al., 1982; Bonneau, 1982; Horváth and Berkhemer, 1982; Neev et al., 1985).

During the late middle to late Miocene, subduction prograded from the Hellenides southward (i.e., to the southern margin of the Gavrovo–Tripolitza block; Plates 19, 20); with this, the modern Hellenic (Cretan) arc-trench system came into evidence (Richter, 1978; Bonneau, 1982). Late Miocene and Pliocene deformations play a major role in the South Dinarid–Hellenic Externides, but to the north of Albania are apparently of minor importance only (Plate 21; Burchfiel, 1980). Marine geophysical data show that subduction is still active in the Ionian Sea segment of the Hellenic Arc where "fore-arc scraping" affects even the lower slope of the Cyrenaica Platform (Finetti, 1985). Similarly, the Cretan segment of the Hellenic Arc is apparently still active as evidenced by its seismicity (Udias, 1985) and sea bottom deformation on the outer Hellenic Ridge (Mascle et al., 1981; Le Pichon et al., 1982; Kenyon et al., 1982). Paleomagnetic data show that the Plio-Pleistocene evolution of the Hellenic Arc involved considerable clockwise rotation (oroclinal bending) of its northwestern parts (Kissel et al., 1984) and counterclockwise bending of its southeastern parts (Laj et al., 1978). In the Cyprus (Tauric) Arc, crustal shortening persisted at least until late Miocene to early Pliocene time (Letouzey and Trémolières, 1980). Earthquake focal mechanisms suggest that the Eastern Mediterranean foreland continues to converge in a northeast–southwest direction with the Hellenic Arc (Angelier and Le Pichon, 1980; Udias, 1982, 1985).

Late Miocene to Plio-Pleistocene crustal shortening in the Hellenic–Cyprus Arc was paralleled by the development of the Aegean–West Anatolian back-arc extension system and wrench-faulting in Central Anatolia (Dewey and Sengör, 1979; Sengör and Kidd, 1979; Angelier and Le Pichon, 1980; Le Pichon et al., 1984; Lybéris, 1984). This was accompanied by an extensive back-arc volcanism that is predominantly andesitic in the South Aegean volcanic belt and alkaline in the North Aegean and West Anatolian area (Jacobshagen et al., 1978; Fytikas et al., 1984). The calc-alkaline South Aegean volcanism (basalts to rhyolites) is related to the late Miocene to Plio-Pleistocene subduction of the thinned continental to oceanic crust of the Eastern Mediterranean foreland. The alkaline North

Aegean and West Anatolian volcanism, possibly involving crustal contamination of mantle-derived magmas, is thought to be related to crustal extension along fault systems that developed in response to back-arc extension, presumably induced by the gradual slowing down of the subduction rate along the Hellenic–Cyprus arcs and a commensurate steepening of the respective Benioff zones (Jacobshagen et al., 1978; Angelier and Le Pichon, 1980; Fytikas et al., 1984).

In the North Aegean area, splays of the North Anatolian wrench fault and associated pull-apart basins form an integral part of this back-arc rift system. A major element of this graben system is the Saros Trough, which began to subside during the late Miocene and which contains up to 5000 m of Neogene sediments (Angelier and Le Pichon, 1980; Lybéris, 1984; Le Pichon, 1984).

Overall, the Aegean area, similar to the Pannonian Basin, is characterized by a high heat flow. In contrast to the latter, the Aegean area is presently being uplifted and actively extended. The combination of the westward escape of Anatolia along the North Anatolian fault, in response to the impact of the Arabian indenter, and back-arc upwelling mantle currents are the likely causes for the late Miocene to Recent tensional evolution of the Aegean area and continued subduction along the Hellenic arc-trench system (Udias, 1982, 1985; Horváth and Berkhemer, 1982; Makris, 1985). These processes apparently induced the southward bulging of the Hellenic arc which, during the Oligocene and early to middle Miocene, was more linear (Plates 18, 19). In its Cretan segment, this involved a southward suture-progradation (Plates 20, 21), and in its Ionian and Rhodes segments paleomagnetically documented oroclinal bending (Le Pichon and Angelier, 1979; Bonneau, 1982). The late Miocene to Plio-Pleistocene crustal shortening evident in the Hellenic arc probably equates to the bulk of the combined amount of convergence between Africa and Europe, crustal extension in the Aegean back-arc basins, and the dextral displacements along the North Anatolian transform fault system (Horváth and Berkhemer, 1982). However, part of the displacement along the latter were probably taken up by dextral movements along the peri-Adriatic–Vardar fault system leading into the Pannonian Basin, by the expulsion of the Intra-Carpathian Block and by crustal shortening in the Carpathians (see above).

## ACCRETION OF THE IBERIAN MICROCONTINENT

Collision of the Iberian microcontinent with the southern margin of France, which had commenced already during the Santonian and Campanian, culminated during the Oligocene to early Miocene in the consolidation of the Pyrenean fold belt (Pugdefubregas and Souquet, 1986). Suturing of Iberia and Europe was accompanied by dextral translations and a possible minor clockwise rotation of Iberia. The Pyrenean orogeny was paralleled by important intraplate deformations in cratonic Iberia and by the emplacement of the Betic nappe systems on its southern margin (Vegas and Banda, 1983).

Following the late Senonian initial collision of the northeastern margin of Iberia with southern France (see Chapter 7, *Iberian Microcontinent*) and a relatively tectonically quiescent period during the Paleocene, tectonic activity accelerated sharply at the transition from the Paleocene to the Eocene. This is reflected by the shedding of conglomeratic and deltaic series from the rapidly rising Pyrenees into the incipient Ebro and Aquitaine foredeeps and the mid- to late-Eocene compressional deformation of the Languedoc area of southeastern France (Durand-Delga and Lemoine, 1978; Plaziat, 1981; Vaillard, 1985a). During the Eocene and Oligocene, continued dextral convergence between Iberia and Europe, giving rise to transpressional deformation along their mutual collision zone, resulted in the rapid westward propagation of the Pyrenean deformation front into Cantabria and Asturia and the progressive emergence of the Pyrenean fold belt (Plate 18).

This involved the upthrusting of major basement blocks, now forming the crystalline core zone of the Pyrenees, and the possible partly gravitational emplacement of sedimentary nappes in the Ebro basins (Fig. 66; see also Farrell et al., 1987). This was accompanied by a retreat of the sea from the marine embayment which, hitherto, extended from the Bay of Biscay into the Ebro Basin. This basin became, to a large extent, scooped out by thin-skinned thrust sheets during the Oligocene and early Miocene (Plate 19). Essentially thin-skinned thrusts characterize the northwestern Pyrenean foothills while their northeastern parts are typified by basement imbrications that developed out of tensional fault blocks (Jaffrezo and Obert, 1978; Alvarado, 1980; Mirouse, 1980; Choukroune et al., 1980). Mild Pyrenean deformations are also evident in the more distal parts of the Aquitaine Basin and along the southern margin of the Massif Central (Fig. 67; Vaillard, 1985a; Mathieu, 1986). Crustal shortening achieved during the consolidation of the Pyrenees is estimated to amount to a minimum of 80 km in their eastern and to 50 km in their western parts (Seguret and Daignières, 1985).

Along the northern continental margin of Iberia, Pyrenean deformations were associated with a south-dipping subduction zone along which oceanic crust of the Bay of Biscay was consumed. This subduction zone extends westward beyond Galicia Bank into the North Atlantic where it terminates in the tensional Kings Trough and Palmer Ridge (Plate 18; Grimaud et al., 1982). Contemporaneous transpressional deformations are evident along the Torre–Madera and Azores–Biscay ridges. These deformation patterns are interpreted by Olivet et al. (1984) to reflect the dextral translation of Iberia along the Pyrenean collision zone and its finite counterclockwise rotation around a pole located initially to the west of Gibraltar and later to the northwest of Madeira.

The continental slope of northern Iberia is formed by an accretion prism consisting of imbricated Mesozoic and Cenozoic sediments (Boillot et al., 1979, 1985). The shelf of Cantabria is underlain by the inverted Cantabrian Mesozoic Basin (Peñas Trough), which is seaward delimited by the stable Le Danois Bank block and landward by the Asturias Massif (Fig. 67). In the Peñas Trough, compressional deformations commenced after the late Senonian and Paleocene precursor phases, during the Eocene, and culminated during the earliest Miocene in its main inversion phase. Tectonic activity ceased essentially at the end of the Aquitanian; minor deformations continued, however, into the late Miocene (Plate 27).

During the early phases of the Pyrenean orogeny, tangential stresses were transmitted through the oceanic lithosphere of the Bay of Biscay and induced during the Eocene minor compressional and wrench deformations along the lower slope of the Armorican margin (Olivet et al., 1984; Sibuet et al., 1985; Boillot et al., 1985). The lack of younger compressional deformation along the northern margin of the Bay of Biscay suggests that during the Oligocene and earliest Miocene phases of the Pyrenean orogeny the bulk of stresses was absorbed at the

North Iberian subduction zone. This subduction zone apparently developed in response to regional compressional stresses that were induced by the progressive convergence of Africa and Europe. Crustal shortening in the Pyrenees of the order of 50–80 km resulted in penetrative deformation, crustal thickening and the subduction of a commensurate amount of upper mantle material. There is, however, no evidence for a syn- or post-orogenic magmatism.

During the Pyrenean diastrophism, cratonic Iberia became deformed by compressional stresses, reactivating a system of Permo-Carboniferous and Mesozoic fractures. Main features of this deformation pattern are the northeast-striking basement uplift of the Guadarrama Mountains, the northwest-trending Celt–Iberian fold belt, and the northeast-striking Catalonian Coast Range (Fig. 67).

The Celt–Iberian intracratonic fold belt developed through inversion of a northwest–southeast-trending Permo-Triassic sedimentary trough that had continued to subside differentially during the Jurassic (Alvarado, 1980; Vegas and Banda, 1983). Only its northwestern element, the Sierra de la Demanda, developed by inversion of the tensional Early Cretaceous Duero Wealden Basin (Julivert, 1978). The structural style of the Celt–Iberian ranges is characterized at the level of Cretaceous and Jurassic carbonates by open, often steep-flanked, thrusted folds and at deeper levels by upthrusted basement blocks. Deformation patterns are indicative of their transpressional origin involving right-lateral displacements between the stable Madrid Basin and Ebro Basin blocks. The basement-involving Catalonian coast ranges (Anadón et al., 1985), delimiting the Paleogene Ebro foredeep basin to the southeast, grade southwestward into the fold systems of the Celt–Iberian ranges and probably also represent an inverted Mesozoic basin.

The Neogene passive margin prism of the Iberian Mediterranean coast overlies deformed and deeply truncated Mesozoic series that contain important oil accumulations in block-faulted, buried-hill structures (Fig. 59; Sineriz et al., 1980; Watson, 1982). This offshore area of Paleogene deformations forms an integral part of the intraplate deformation of cratonic Iberia. The zone affected by these deformations extends southward into the Prebetic fold belt and into the area of the Baleares where it became overprinted by late Miocene northeast-southwest-trending fold systems and thrusts (Fig. 67).

Transpressional deformation of the Celt–Iberian chains probably started during the earliest Tertiary, as evident in the area of their junction with the Prebetic fold belt (Azema et al., 1974) and terminated during the late Oligocene to early Miocene.

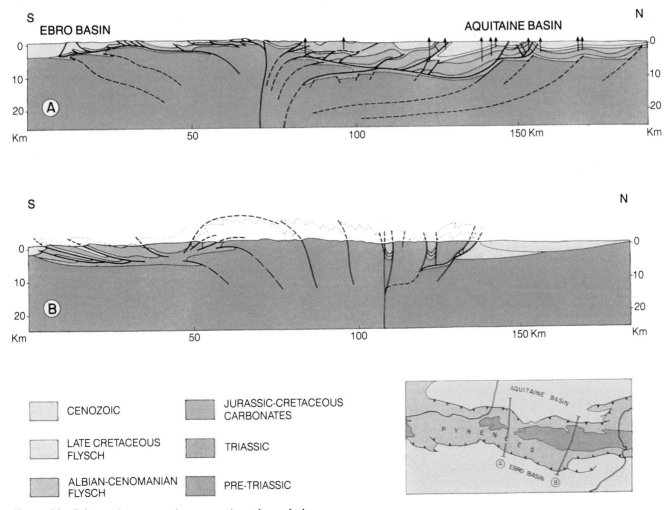

CENOZOIC

LATE CRETACEOUS FLYSCH

ALBIAN-CENOMANIAN FLYSCH

JURASSIC-CRETACEOUS CARBONATES

TRIASSIC

PRE-TRIASSIC

*Figure 66—Schematic structural cross sections through the Pyrenean fold belt. After Seguret and Daignières (1985).*

Main deformation occurred during the Oligocene (Plate 18; Julivert, 1978; Vaillard, 1985b).

This is borne out by the evolution of the Madrid Basin in which middle to late Eocene to mid-Miocene lacustrine and continental sabkha deposits attain a maximum thickness of 3500 m. Development of this basin went hand in hand with the upthrusting of the Guadarrama basement block (Fig. 67). Seismic data calibrated by wells indicate that embryonic movements along the Guadarrama borderfault, delimiting the Madrid Basin to the northwest, occurred during the Late Cretaceous and Eocene; however, the main deformation, involving sinistral transpressional movements, can be dated as mid-Oligocene to early Miocene.

The main phases of the Pyrenean orogeny and of the compressional deformation of cratonic Iberia coincide with the collision of the Alboran Block with Iberia and the early orogenic phases of the Betic Cordillera (Plate 18).

As a result of space constraints induced by the convergence of Africa and Europe, Iberia became increasingly affected by compressional stresses and escaped in a northwesterly direction. These stresses were absorbed partly in the Pyrenean collision zone and by intraoceanic deformation in the North Atlantic and the Bay of Biscay and partly by the compressional deformation of cratonic Iberia. Whether these displacements involved a commensurate counterclockwise rotation of Iberia, as postulated by Olivet et al. (1984), or its clockwise rotation, as suggested by the Senonian to Paleogene westward progression of the Pyrenean deformation front, is unclear. In this respect, it should be noted that the amount of crustal shortening achieved along the Cantabrian–Galician Pyrenean subduction zone cannot be quantified but was of insufficient magnitude to induce anatectic remobilization of subducted crustal and upper mantle material. In view of this, estimates of the Pyrenean displacement of Iberia relative to southern France, which involved not only the shortening of continental crust but probably also the subduction of oceanic crust, are unlikely to be accurate enough to provide constraints for either the clockwise or the counterclockwise rotation model (see Seguret and Daignières, 1985). However, the important shortening evident in the offshore areas of Cantabria add further weight to the clockwise rotation model. These rotations were probably below the paleomagnetic margin of error (van den Berg and Zijderveld, 1982).

During the middle and late Miocene emplacement of the Betic nappes and the folding and imbrication of the Prebetic–Balearic zone, no further compressional deformations occurred in cratonic Iberia and in the Pyrenees. This suggests that by this time the Betic orogen was decoupled from its foreland at the respective A-subduction zone (Plates 19–21).

The amount of crustal shortening that was achieved during the Eocene and Oligocene folding of the Celt–Iberian and coastal Catalonian ranges was probably substantial; however, no systematic analyses and quantitative estimates are available, mainly because strike-slip movements along preexisting fracture zones accompanied the development of these intracratonic

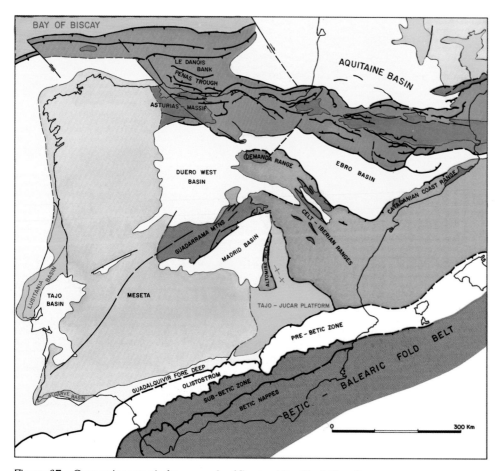

*Figure 67—Cenozoic tectonic framework of Iberia. After Shell España.*

fold belts.

The last phases of compressional deformation of cratonic Iberia were paralleled by the late Oligocene–early Miocene development of the Rhône–Gulf of Lion–Valencia rift system (see above). With the Aquitanian–Burdigalian opening of the Algero-Provençal Basin, the Gulf of Lion–Valencia grabens became inactive and buried beneath a Neogene passive margin sedimentary prism (Watson, 1982; Rehault et al., 1985; Fig. 59). During the latest Miocene and Plio-Pleistocene, alkaline basaltic extrusions in Catalonia, offshore Valencia (Columbretes Islands), and in Central Spain and of calc-alkaline volcanics along its southeastern coast accompanied the regional uplift of Iberia, under a new tensional regime (Plates 20, 21; Alvarado, 1980; Vegas and Banda, 1983; Hernandez et al., 1987).

## INVERSION OF THE ATLAS TROUGHS

In the foreland of the Maghrebian (Rif–Tellian) fold belt, the High and Middle Atlas, and Sahara Atlas ranges correspond to major, inverted Mesozoic rift basins that originally formed during the Triassic and Early Jurassic. A further inverted graben feature is the Saoura–Ougarta chain that developed out of a Late Devonian–Early Carboniferous basin extending in a southeastern direction into the Sahara Platform (Fig. 8).

In the Atlas troughs, first mild inversion movements occurred during the Senonian (Plate 28; Guiraud, 1975; Stets and Wurster, 1981, 1982). This deformation coincides with the early Alpine onset of compressional deformation along the southern margin of the Alboran–Kabylia block (Wildi, 1983; Dercourt et al., 1986).

The main phase of inversion of the Atlas troughs is dated as late middle to late Eocene (Guiraud, 1975; Michard, 1976; Robillard, 1979; Durand-Delga and Fontboté, 1980). This important deformation phase coincides with early movements of the internal Kabylian and Ultra-Tellian nappes (Caire, 1974; Wildi, 1983), the collision of the Alboran block with the southern margin of Iberia, and with the onset of the main orogenic phase of the Pyrenees (see above).

During the Oligocene and Miocene development of the Maghrebian foredeep and the late Miocene emplacement of the Rif and Tellian nappe systems, the Middle and High Atlas and the Sahara Atlas were apparently little deformed. These foreland chains became, however, reactivated and further uplifted during the late Pliocene and Pleistocene (Guiraud, 1975; Michard, 1976; Robillard, 1979).

Contemporaneous compressional deformation is evident in northeastern Tunisia where the Sahara Atlas grades into the external fold systems of the Calabrian arc (Cohen et al., 1980).

Inversion of the Atlas troughs involved the compressional/transpressional reactivation of tensional/transtensional fault systems delimiting these basins and the buckling up of their sedimentary fill, which is partly thrusted over the original basin margins. The structural style of these intracratonic fold belts is strongly influenced by the Triassic–Early Jurassic salts, which act as a detachment horizon (Guiraud, 1975; Michard, 1976; Stets and Wurster, 1981, 1982; Jenny, 1983). The amount of north–south crustal shortening achieved during the inversion of the Middle and High Atlas is estimated to amount to 10–30 km (Mattauer et al., 1977) and for the Sahara Atlas 15–30 km (Guiraud, 1975).

In view of the geometric association of the Atlas Ranges with the Calabrian arc, it is likely that their Plio-Pleistocene reactivation involved dextral translations along the South Atlas fracture zone. This is compatible with focal mechanisms of earthquakes which indicate that the Atlas Ranges are presently being deformed by right-lateral transpression (Udias, 1983). These deformations are contemporaneous with the Quaternary resumption of alkaline volcanic activity along a southwest-trending sinistral fracture system transecting the Rif fold belt and the Middle and High Atlas (Harmand and Moukadiri, 1986).

The Saoura–Ougarta anticlinorium, which extends for a distance of some 500 km from the basement uplift of the Anti-Atlas in a southeastern direction into the Sahara Platform, represents a major intraplate compressional feature (Fig. 8). Its initial phase of uplift occurred during the Late Carboniferous and can be related to compressional foreland stresses exerted on the Sahara Platform during the Hercynian orogeny. This inversion feature became reactivated, presumably during the late Eocene, as evident by the deformation of Mesozoic continental clastics that in the vicinity of the town of Adrar show dips of as much as 70°.

## INTRAPLATE DEFORMATIONS IN NORTHWEST EUROPE

Following the mid-Paleocene Laramide phase of compressional foreland deformation (see Chapter 7), tectonic activity in the northern and northwestern foreland of the Carpathians and Alps was at a low level.

By mid-Eocene time, rising sea levels, in conjunction with the progressive degradation of the tectonic relief induced by the Laramide phase of foreland compression (Plate 17), caused a regional transgression and the reopening of a seaway linking the cold-water-dominated Northwest European Basin and the North Atlantic via the Channel and Western Approaches basins (Kaasschieter, 1961; Murray and Wright, 1974; Ziegler, 1982a). By late Eocene time, marine connections with the Tethys were also reestablished via southwestern Poland and with the Donets Basin via eastern Poland (Pozaryska, 1977, 1978). These seaways, which were presumably too restricted to permit a full exchange between the respective faunal provinces, again became interrupted during the early Oligocene by the upwarping of anticlinal features in the Channel area, the permanent silting up of the North Polish Strait, and the thermal uplift of the eastern parts of the Bohemian Massif. At the same time, a new, albeit narrow sea arm opened, connecting the Alpine foredeep basin and the North-West European Basin through the Bresse–Rhine Graben. Yet, by late Oligocene time, this seaway also became constricted and finally closed off all together by the rift-induced upwarping of the Rhenish Shield (Plate 18).

The mid-Oligocene regression, which caused a renewed complete separation of the cold-water-dominated North-West European Basin from the warm-water-dominated Tethys and Atlantic seas, may have been induced by the combined effects of the onset of the first major glaciation of Antarctica (Donovan and Jones, 1979) and lithospheric deformations in the Alpine foreland (Lambeck et al., 1987). Neogene sea-level fluctuations in the different basins of Northwest Europe therefore reflect the interplay between glacioeustasy and broad-scale tectonic deformations. The latter involved the late Eocene resumption of compressional deformation and inversion of the Mesozoic basins in the northwestern Alpine foreland and the development of the Rhône–Bresse–Rhine and Eger grabens rift system (Ziegler, 1982a).

## Compressional Deformation of the Alpine Foreland

By late Eocene to early Oligocene time, compressional deformation of the northwestern Alpine foreland resumed again as evident from inversion movements in the West Netherlands–Broad Fourteens and Sole Pit basins, the Channel area, and also the Celtic Sea–Western Approaches area (Fig. 68; Plate 29; Ziegler, 1987c). The main phase of inversion of the Sole Pit Basin is dated as straddling the Eocene–Oligocene boundary (van Hoorn, 1987b). In conjunction with the gradual inversion of the Channel and the Hampshire basins, the Artois Axis, crossing the English Channel, became upwarped and blocked the marine connection between the North Atlantic and the North-West European Basin (Plate 19; Ziegler, 1982a).

Late Eocene and Oligocene compressional foreland deformations are of minor importance only in the Lower Saxony Basin (Betz et al., 1987) and are lacking in the area of the Bohemian Massif, in the Polish Trough, and along the Fennoscandian Borderzone. Last inversion movements are dated in the West Netherlands–Broad Fourteens Basin as mid-Oligocene and in the Sole Pit Basin as late Oligocene (Plate 30).

On the other hand, the main inversion of the Channel area, the Bristol Channel and Western Approaches troughs, occurred during the Oligocene and Miocene (Figs. 22, 69, 70) with tectonic activity intermittently continuing possibly into the Pliocene and the Pleistocene (Plate 29; Lake and Karner, 1987; van Hoorn, 1987a; Tucker and Arter, 1987; Gibbs, 1987; Ziegler, 1987b). Contemporaneous wrench deformations are also evident in the Armorican Massif and the Paris Basin. In the Paris Basin, dextral reactivation of preexisting fracture systems resulted in the upwarping of, for instance, the Pays-de-Bray anticline (Pommerole, 1978; Mégnien, 1980; Ziegler, 1982a). On the other hand, Oligocene and younger inversion movements play a very subordinate role in the Celtic Sea Trough and in the Fastnet Basin (Robinson et al., 1981; Tucker and Arter, 1987).

Oligocene wrench deformation in the area of the Irish Sea, Cardigan Bay, and Bristol Channel can be inferred from the rapid subsidence of local transtensional basins such as the Lough Neagh Basin of Northern Ireland (Plates 18, 29). The subsidence of these basins is related by Lake and Karner (1987) to a short-lived phase of sinistral motion along preexisting wrench faults, activity along which was sinistral during the Mesozoic subsidence of the Celtic Sea, Bristol Channel, and Western Approaches troughs, and dextral during their Cenozoic inversion. This short-lived Oligocene phase of renewed sinistral motion along this fault system may be the effect of temporary changes in the sea-floor spreading rates in the different segments of the northern North Atlantic–Norwegian–Greenland Sea (Chapter 8).

Crustal shortening accompanying the late Paleogene to Neogene inversion of the Mesozoic troughs in the Channel–Western Approaches area was compensated by dextral wrench deformations along preexisting fracture systems in the Armorican Massif, the Paris Basin, Channel area, and southwestern England. These entailed a northwestward displacement of the Armorican–Massif Central block as a whole relative to the London–Brabant and Irish massifs. The magnitude of this displacement can, however, not be quantified but is unlikely to exceed 10 km. At the same time, the British Isles as a whole became uplifted as evident by the structural relief of the reconstructed top Cretaceous erosional surface (George, 1967; Vann, 1978; D.G. Roberts, personal communication, 1987).

A comparison of the distribution of the Sub-Hercynian, Laramide, Eo-Oligocene, and late Oligocene to Mio-Pliocene compressional deformations in the Alpine foreland illustrates a gradual westward shift of tectonic activity (Figs. 41, 42, 68, 69). The lack of Eocene and younger compressional deformations in the foreland of the Eastern Alps and the Carpathians indicates that during this important phase of the Alpine orogeny, stresses transmitted into the foreland were no longer large enough to cause significant strain. Based on this observation, it must be assumed that in the East Alpine and Carpathian domain the rising orogen and its foreland were essentially decoupled during the emplacement of the basement-cored Austro-Alpine and Penninic nappes. On the other hand, increasing coupling between the West and Central Alpine orogen and its foreland is evident by the Eocene and younger inversion of the Mesozoic basins in the Channel and Celtic Sea, Western Approaches area (see above; Ziegler, 1987c). This sequence of events is the expression of the continued convergence of Africa and Europe and of the gradual rotation of the principal compressive stress exerted on the Alpine foreland from a northwesterly direction to a westerly one (Letouzey, 1986).

## Cenozoic Rift Systems

The late Eocene to Mio-Pliocene compressional deformation of the northwestern Alpine foreland was broadly contemporaneous with the evolution of the Rhine–Bresse–Rhône Graben system and the Eger Graben; the latter transects the Bohemian Massif in a northeasterly direction (Malkovsky, 1987).

Differential subsidence of the Bresse and Rhine Graben started during the late Eocene (Sittler, 1969a, 1969b; Rat, 1974; Doebl and Teichmüller, 1979). Already by latest Eocene-earliest Oligocene time, a sea arm extended from the Alpine foredeep through the Bresse Graben via the Burgundy area into the southwestern parts of the Rhine Graben. A first peak of volcanic activity occurred in the Rhine Graben during the late Eocene (Lippolt, 1983). In the Massif Central, volcanism began during the late Paleocene–early Eocene (Brousse and Bellon, 1983) and in the Eger Graben during late Oligocene time (Malkovsky, 1987). There was only minor volcanic activity in the Rhône Graben (Brousse and Bellon, 1983).

By mid-Oligocene time, a marine connection was established between the Alpine foredeep and the North Sea Basin via the actively subsiding Rhine Graben; this connection remained open intermittently throughout late Oligocene time (Plate 18). Temporary marine connections may also have existed between the Bresse–Limagne Graben and the Paris Basin. By early Miocene time, these marine connections were severed by the thermal upwarping of the Massif Central and the Rhenish Massif. In the latter, volcanic activity was concentrated in the area of the Rhine–Leine–Ruhr Graben triple junction where extensive trap basalts were extruded during the middle and late Miocene (Plates 19, 20; Lippolt, 1983). Uplift of the southern Rhine Graben Vosges–Black Forest rift dome apparently started somewhat earlier (Illies, 1978). Crustal stretching in the Rhine and Bresse grabens induced the development of the complex transform fault system transecting the Burgundy area (Plate 19; Bergerat, 1977; Rat, 1978).

The different parts of the Bresse–Rhine–Ruhr–Leine Graben subsided only intermittently during the Neogene and Quaternary. This is thought to reflect changes in the regional stress pattern (Villemin and Bergerat, 1987).

During the Miocene, the Bresse Graben and the southern

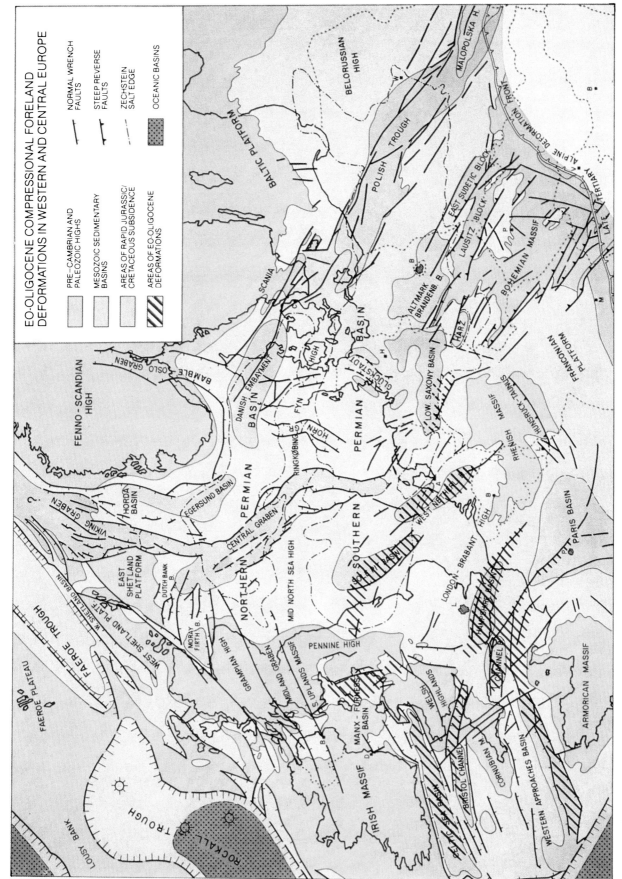

*Figure 68—Eo-Oligocene compressional foreland deformations in Western and Central Europe.*

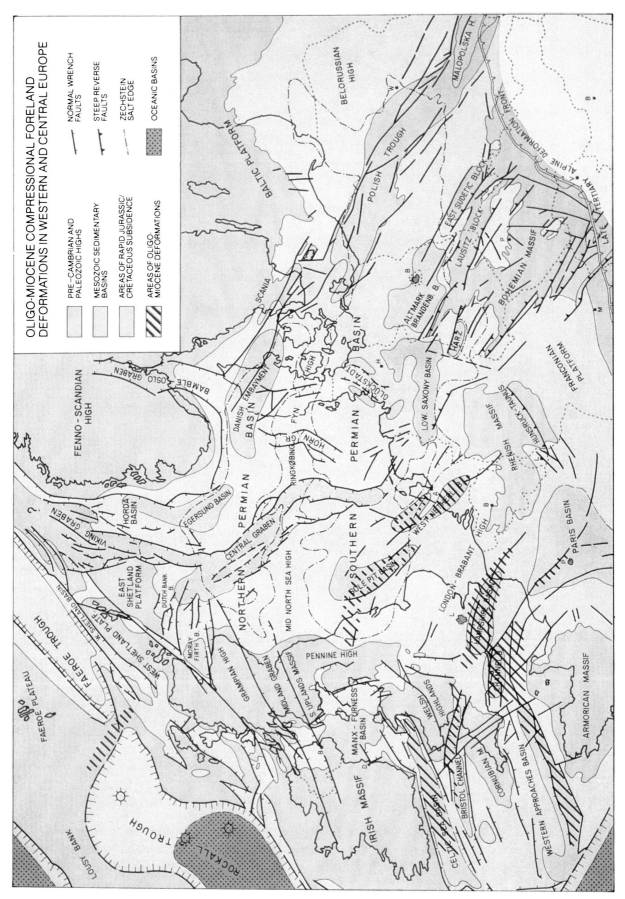

*Figure 69—Oligo-Miocene compressional foreland deformations in Western and Central Europe.*

parts of the Rhine Graben ceased to subside differentially (Rat, 1978; Illies, 1978). This coincides with the main inversion phase of the Mesozoic troughs in the Western Approaches and Channel area (Fig. 69). During the Pliocene, the Bresse Graben once more began to subside while the evolution of the Rhine Graben was controlled by sinistral shear motions (Plate 21). At the same time, the southern margins of the Rhine Graben and the eastern rim of the Bresse Graben were overridden by the frontal thrusts of the Jura Mountains (Ziegler, 1982a).

The present stress field indicates that the Rhine Graben is being deformed by sinistral strike-slip movements and that it is in an incipient stage of inversion. In contrast, the Ruhr Graben,

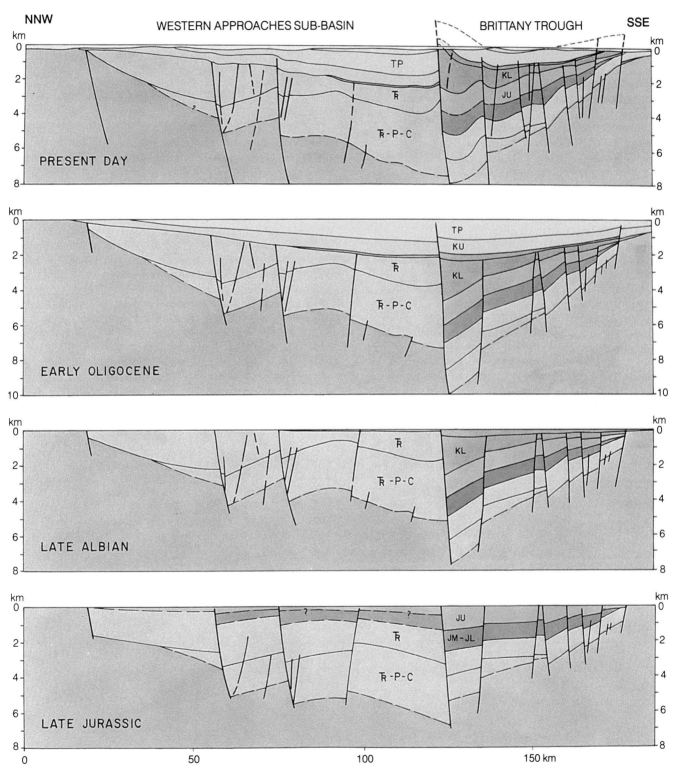

*Figure 70—Evolution of the Western Approaches Trough. For location see Figure 23.*

forming the northwestern branch of the Rhine Rift, is currently subsiding actively in response to tensional stresses (Illies and Greiner, 1978; Ahorner et al., 1983). This graben feathers out to the northwest and loses its identity before reaching the shores of the North Sea. Similarly, the currently inactive Leine Graben, forming the northeastern branch of the Rhine Rift, dies out northward at the edge of the North German Lowland.

The Bresse and Limagne grabens and the grabens in the Massif Central are currently being uplifted. The grabens of the Rhône Valley and the Gulf of Lion ceased to subside differentially after the early Miocene (Rehault et al., 1985). Neotectonics indicate that France is presently being affected by northwest-directed compressional stresses (Bousquet and Philip, 1981).

Cenozoic strata attain maximum thicknesses of some 3000 m in the Rhine Graben and 2000 m in the Bresse Graben.

The Eger Graben, transecting the Bohemian Massif in a northeasterly direction, came into evidence during the Oligocene and remained intermittently active until the present. It is characterized by an intense volcanic activity but contains only limited thicknesses of sediments (Malkovsky, 1987).

During the Plio-Pleistocene, the Rhenish Massif, the Vosges–Black Forest, the Massif Central, and the Bohemian Massif became thermally domed up further. This was accompanied by a resumption of volcanic activity in the Rhenish and Bohemian massifs and in the Massif Central (Plate 21).

Geophysical data show that these rift domes are associated with an elevated Moho Discontinuity that is underlain by an anomalous low-density, low-velocity upper mantle (Fig. 71; Perrier and Ruegg, 1973; Fuchs et al., 1981; Mechie et al., 1983). Such upper mantle anomalies, which probably reflect the intrusion of asthenospheric material to the crust–mantle interface, are typical of active volcanic rifts. Deep reflection seismic data, moreover, show that under the Black Forest the lower crust is highly reflective and that this laminated lower crustal zone thins with increasing distance from the culmination of the

southern Rhine Graben rift dome. Figure 72 shows that in the Black Forest area the top of the highly reflective lower crust coincides with the base of a high conductivity zone that in itself is characterized by low reflectivity (Fuchs et al., 1987).

The chemistry of the volcanics associated with the Cenozoic rifts in the Alpine foreland is typically alkaline and bimodal mafic-felsic. The rift-induced doming of the northern and southern parts of the Rhine Graben and of the Massif Central, combined with the wrench-related upwarping of the Burgundy area and the Armorican Massif, caused the regional truncation of their Mesozoic and Cenozoic sedimentary cover, and hence the erosional partial isolation of the Paris Basin (Mégnien, 1980) and of the South German Franconian Platform (Ziegler, 1982a).

## GEODYNAMIC CONSIDERATIONS

The Cenozoic convergence of Africa–Arabia and Europe, involving a counterclockwise rotation of the former, was governed by sea-floor spreading in the Atlantic and Indian oceans rather than by active subduction processes in the Mediterranean. In view of this, the gradual consolidation of the different parts of the Mediterranean Alpine fold belts, forming the suture between Africa–Arabia and Europe, is the result of their "passive" collision. Large-scale body wave tomographic analysis of the mantle suggests that this collision zone is associated in the western and eastern Mediterranean area with a north-plunging subduction zone reaching to depths between 250 and 600 km (Spakman, 1986).

Although a gradual decrease in the convergence rates between Africa–Arabia and Europe is evident from the analysis of the magnetic sea-floor anomalies of the Atlantic and Indian oceans (Savostin et al., 1986), the distribution of earthquakes in the Mediterranean area and their focal mechanisms, and the nature of neotectonic deformations, indicate that crustal short-

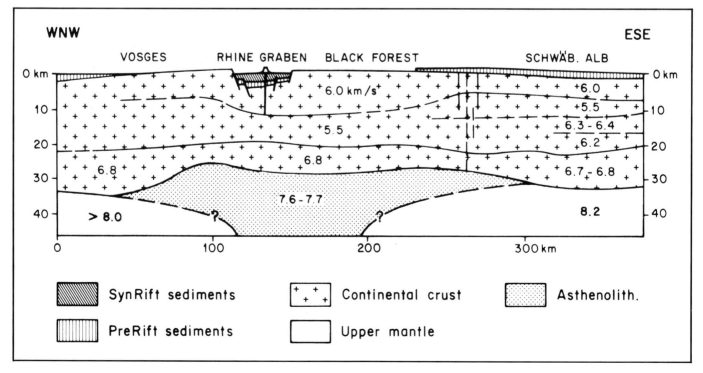

*Figure 71—Crustal configuration of the Southern Rhine Graben.*

ening still persists in the Western Alps, in the Apennine–Calabrian and Hellenic–Cyprus arcs, and in the southern Carpathians (Plate 21; Udias, 1982, 1985). These still-active fold belts are relayed by a system of transform faults that transect the now-inactive Pontides, Dinarides, Eastern, Central, and Ligurian Alps, and the Maghrebides–Atlas fold belt. The subduction systems associated with these already consolidated fold belts, including the Northern and Eastern Carpathians, became locked variably during the late Miocene and Pliocene. On the other hand, the Red Sea–Lybian–Pelagian rift system appears to propagate northwestward into the Tyrrhenian and Algerian Sea, while the Rhine–Bresse–Limagne–Valencia–Rif–Atlas–Cape Verdes tensional system transects the Alpine fold belts of the Western Mediterranean.

Among the different Mediterranean–Alpine fold belts, only the Pontides of Turkey and the southern Balkans were associated with long-standing subduction zones along which oceanic crust of the Permo-Triassic Black Sea back-arc ocean and later oceanic crust of the Tethys were consumed. In the Dinarides and Hellenides, subduction of the Jurassic Vardar (Hellenic-Dinarid) Ocean commenced during the latest Jurassic and earliest Cretaceous. In the Central Alpine and the Western Mediterranean domain, subduction of Mid–Jurassic to Early Cretaceous oceanic crust began during the Late Cretaceous. The late Senonian–early Miocene Pyrenean diastrophism was associated with limited consumption of Late Cretaceous oceanic crust of the Bay of Biscay.

The initiation of subduction of young oceanic crust in the Western and Central Mediterranean domain during the Alpine orogeny cannot be easily explained in terms of gravitational sinking of oceanic lithosphere into the asthenosphere and the development of an arc-trench system driven by the pull of the downgoing lithospheric slab. Long-standing island-arc systems, characterized by an andesitic magmatism, are clearly lacking in the Western Mediterranean. In this area, the onset of subduction processes was probably induced by space constraints, caused by the northward drift of Africa–Arabia and its convergence with Europe. In the Western and Central Mediterranean, the resultant build-up of compressional stresses led ultimately to the development of lithospheric imbrication zones, either within oceanic domains or at continent–ocean transitions. It appears that subduction systems of this type, depending on the amount of lithosphere consumed along them, can be associated with or without an anatectic remobilization of the subducted crustal and upper mantle material and a corresponding calc-alkaline magmatism (e.g., Southern Alps versus Pyrenees). In this respect, it is noteworthy that Alpine granitoid plutons play a far smaller role in the Western and Central Mediterranean domain than in the Rhodope–Pontides segment of the Alpine chains (Ricou et al., 1986).

On the other hand, the inception of syn-, late-, and post-orogenic tensional and wrench fault systems in back-arc areas,

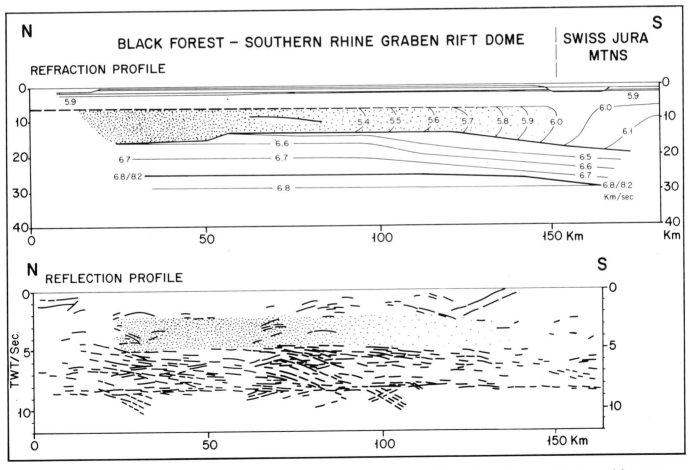

*Figure 72—Crustal structure and reflection seismic signature of Black Forest, forming the eastern flank of the southern Rhine Graben rift dome. After Fuchs et al. (1987). Stippled area corresponds to high conductivity zone at the base of the upper crust. This zone coincides with the top of the highly reflective lower crust.*

such as those of the Alboran and Tyrrhenian Sea, the Pannonian Basin, and Aegean Sea, is apparently coupled with, and probably governed by, the rapid ascent of anatectically remobilized crustal and upper mantle material and later also of mantle-derived alkaline magmas.

The Cenozoic evolution of the Alpine–Mediterranean fold belts was accompanied by major compressional intraplate deformations in their forelands at often considerable distances from the respective collision zones. This is evident in Northwest Europe, in Iberia, and in Northwest Africa. The folding and uplifting of the Pyrenees and of the Caucasus can also be regarded as a particularly dramatic expression of compressional foreland deformation. The spatial relationship between areas affected by intraplate compressional deformations and the respective collisional plate boundaries indicates that during the collision of major cratonic blocks compressional stresses, inducing readily discernible strain, can be transmitted through continental crust and lithosphere over distances of at least some 1300 km. The occurrence of compressional deformations within and along the northern margin of the Bay of Biscay and also within the North Atlantic demonstrates that compressional stresses can also be transmitted through oceanic lithosphere (see Cloetingh and Wortel, 1985).

The Eo-Oligocene and Neogene evolution of the Alpine–Mediterranean area reflects the interplay between compressional stress systems, related to the convergence of Africa–Arabia and Europe, and tensional stress systems associated with the development of new intracontinental rift systems such as those of the Red Sea, Northwest Libya, the Pelagian Shelf, the Eger–Rhine–Bresse–Rhône–Valencia grabens, and the Plio-Pleistocene Spanish–Rif–Cape Verdes volcanic chain.

Particularly the Eocene and younger intraplate deformations in the northwestern Alpine foreland reflect the interplay between collision-related compressional stresses, inducing basin inversion, and the development of an active rift system. The main phases of basin inversion in the Celtic Sea–Western Approaches area appear to alternate with the main phases of differential subsidence of the Limagne–Bresse–Rhine Graben system and thus suggests that compressional intraplate stresses can interfere with the evolution of an active rift system and impede its development (Figs. 68, 69; Plates 18–20).

The interplay between Cenozoic tensional and compressional stresses in the northwestern Alpine foreland is, from a geodynamic point of view, puzzling and cannot be explained alone in terms of hotspot activity or the collision of Africa and Europe and their dextral translation during the Main and late Alpine orogenic phases (Tapponier, 1977; Ziegler, 1982a).

The evolution of the Limagne–Bresse–Rhine Rift indicates that crustal extension preceded the development of discrete hotspots. For example, crustal extension in the Rhine Graben is estimated to amount to some 5 km (Laubscher, 1970; see also Sittler, 1969a; Doebl and Teichmüller, 1979), which is considerably more than could result solely from the uparching of a rift dome in response to the development of a mantle plume.

Rifting activity persisted in the Limagne–Bresse–Rhine graben systems even during and after the Aquitanian–Burdigalian phase of sea-floor spreading in the Algero-Provençal Basin that evolved out of the southwestern extension of this rift system.

Following the late Miocene–early Pliocene consolidation of the Betic Cordillera, the Valencia Graben became reactivated as illustrated by alkaline and basaltic volcanism along the Spanish Mediterranean coast. At the same time, crustal extension governed the subsidence of the Alboran Sea and the development of the alkaline volcanic chain transecting the Rif fold belt and the inverted basins of the Middle and High Atlas (see above). This, together with intensified volcanism in the Limagne–Bresse–Rhine grabens, testifies to continued tectonic activity along this megarift system that transects the Western Mediterranean Alpine fold belts and the compressionally deformed areas in their foreland. This rift system dies out to the north in the Dutch onshore area, and there is no evidence for a Neogene reactivation of the Mesozoic North Sea Rift system. Oligocene and Neogene crustal extension across the Valencia–Rhône–Rhine rift probably involved a small-scale counterclockwise rotation of areas located to its west relative to the remainder of Europe; this may have contributed to the Oligocene and younger wrench-induced uplift of the Ardennes–Artois axis and the broad upwarping of England. Although the evolution of Limagne–Bresse–Rhine graben system was broadly contemporaneous with the inversion of Mesozoic grabens and troughs in the northwestern Alpine foreland, it is doubtful whether crustal extension across this rift provided the driving forces responsible for the inversion of these basins, as postulated by Gillchrist et al. (1987). In this context, it should be noted that the albeit mild Laramide deformation evident in the Channel and Celtic Sea–Western Approaches area predates the subsidence of the Limagne–Bresse–Rhine Rift.

A similar interference of extensional and compressional deformations can be observed in the late Miocene to Recent evolution of the northeast Tunisian–Pelagian rift systems that find their extension in the volcanic fields of northwest Libya.

Among the different back-arc basins of the Mediterranean Alpine system, it could be envisaged that the development of the Gulf of Lion–Valencia Rift and the subsequent opening of the oceanic Algero-Provençal Basin was related to the evolution of the intracratonic Rhine–Bresse–Rhône Rift in the Alpine foreland. Similarly, it can be speculated that development of the Neogene and Quaternary grabens, which are superimposed on the internal nappe systems of the Apennines and transect the Calabrian arc, and which are associated with an active alkaline volcanism (Ghisetti, 1984; Locardi, 1985; Mostardini and Merlini, 1986), may partly be related to the Tyrrhenian back-arc extension system and partly to a northward-propagating branch of the Libyan–Pelagian rift system. The latter appears to be relayed to the northern end of the Gulf of Suez Graben by a dextral transform fault paralleling the shelf margin of North Africa (Ben-Avraham et al., 1987)

The tensional Pannonian and North Aegean back-arc basins are closely associated with the Alpine–peri-Adriatic–Vardar–North Anatolian dextral transform system. Tensional systems in the South Aegean and West Anatolian area may have developed as a consequence of decreasing activity along the Hellenic subduction zone and its gradual steepening (Le Pichon and Angelier, 1979; Spakman, 1986). To what degree back-arc extension, related to the decay of the Dinarid and Carpathian subduction systems, played a role in the Plio-Pleistocene evolution of the Pannonian Basin is not clear.

Overall, the Neogene and Quaternary evolution of the Mediterranean–Alpine fold belts and their foreland can be interpreted as reflecting the interaction between the last phases of the Alpine orogeny and the gradual assertion of a new tensional kinematic regime that ultimately may cause the break-up of the present continental assembly. This incipient plate reorganization is heralded by the Neogene and Quaternary development of the Red Sea–Libyan–Pelagian and of the Rhine–West Mediterranean–Cape Verdes rift systems.

# CHAPTER 10
## THOUGHTS AND SPECULATIONS ON GEODYNAMIC PROCESSES

## INTRODUCTION

The structural and stratigraphic record of the Arctic–North Atlantic borderlands and the Tethys domain reflects their complex geological evolution during which orogenic events, associated with the accretion of continental fragments and the collision of major continents, alternated with periods of wrench faulting and crustal extension. The latter resulted in the destruction of preexisting fold belts and culminated ultimately in the break-up of the newly formed continent assemblies, to a large extent along their Paleozoic megasuture zones. Yet, it should be noted that some of the Pangea break-up axes are quite discordant with the Paleozoic megasutures (e.g., North Atlantic) and cut even across the Precambrian basement grain (e.g., Labrador Sea–Baffin Bay).

The geological evolution of the different parts of the Arctic–North Atlantic and Tethys domains reflects, through time, repeated changes in their megatectonic setting and, correspondingly, changes in the geodynamic processes that governed the subsidence and/or destruction of sedimentary basins. Thus, in time and space, basins of different geotectonic origin developed. Some of these were stacked on top of one another while others were partly destroyed during subsequent tectonic events.

These changes can be related to an almost unbroken sequence of tectonic processes that preceded and accompanied the reorganization of plate boundaries during the late Paleozoic to Recent evolution of the Arctic–North Atlantic and Tethys realms. The main steps of these reorganizations are recapitulated in this chapter.

## MAIN PHASES OF PLATE REORGANIZATION IN ARCTIC–NORTH ATLANTIC AND TETHYS

The late Paleozoic progressive suturing of Pangea and its Mesozoic and Cenozoic disintegration, which was partly interrupted and even reversed by the Alpine collision of Africa with Europe, was accompanied by repeated changes in plate boundaries and changes in plate motions relative to each other. During the suturing phases of Pangea and also during the Alpine orogenic cycle, major oceanic basins became closed and important fold belts developed. The Mesozoic and Cenozoic break-up of Pangea, on the other hand, was associated with the opening of new oceanic basins, some of which are today no longer characterized by active spreading ridges.

The main phases of plate boundary reorganization that accompanied the late Paleozoic assembly of Pangea and its subsequent disintegration are summarized below.

### Caledonian and Pre-Hercynian Cycles (Ordovician–Devonian)

The Caledonian orogenic cycle, spanning Late Cambrian to Silurian time, involved the collision of Laurentia–Greenland and Fennosarmatia and their suturing along the Arctic–North Atlantic Caledonides (Fig. 1). This was accompanied by the northward subduction of the Proto-Tethys Ocean along an arc-trench system paralleling the southern margin of the newly forming Laurussian megacontinent to which a number of Gondwana-derived continental terranes became accreted.

These terranes were rifted off the northern margin of Gondwana during the Ordovician and Early Silurian. Moreover, during the Caledonian orogenic cycle, the Arctic Craton converged and collided with the northern margin of Laurentia–Greenland (Chapter 1).

The Late Silurian–Early Devonian, late- to post-Caledonian plate reorganization is reflected by the abandonment of the Arctic–North Atlantic Caledonide subduction system, the inception of the intraoceanic Sakmarian arc-trench system to the east of Fennosarmatia–Baltica, and the development of a sinistral megashear system transecting the Arctic–North Atlantic Caledonides along their axis. During the Devonian and earliest Carboniferous, continued northward subduction of the Proto-Tethys plate, possibly at variable rates, was associated with intermittent back-arc extension in the domain of the Variscan geosynclinal system and the accretion of additional Gondwana-derived microcontinents (terranes) to the southern margin of Laurussia during the Middle Devonian Acado-Ligerian diastrophism. The latest Devonian–earliest Carboniferous suturing of Laurussia and the Arctic Craton along the Innuitian–Lomonosov fold belt was accompanied by major sinistral translations between Laurentia–Greenland and Fennosarmatia–Baltica. In the domain of the oceanic Sakmarian back-arc basin, a phase of back-arc compression, at the transition from the Early to the Middle Devonian, was followed by back-arc extension during the Givetian and the resumption of back-arc compression during the earliest Carboniferous (Chapter 2).

### Hercynian Megacycle (Carboniferous–Early Permian)

The Early Carboniferous collision of Gondwana with Laurussia marked the onset of the Hercynian orogenic cycle and the ensuing reorganization of plate boundaries. In Western and Central Europe, this is expressed by the compressional overpowering of the longstanding Variscan geosynclinal back-arc extension systems and the late Westphalian consolidation of the Variscan fold belt. The Early Permian consolidation of the Appalachian–Mauretanide fold belt during the Alleghenian diastrophism was associated with a change in the convergence direction between Gondwana and Laurussia. This gave rise to latest Carboniferous–Early Permian development of a dextral shear system transecting the newly consolidated Variscan fold belt; this shear system represented a diffuse plate boundary between Africa and Fennosarmatia (Chapter 3).

In the Arctic domain, the Hercynian plate reorganization is expressed by back-arc rifting in the area of the Innuitian fold belt, inducing the Carboniferous subsidence of the Sverdrup Basin, possibly by the separation of the West Siberian Craton from Laurussia, and by the development of the Norwegian–Greenland Sea rift system (Chapter 4).

During the Carboniferous, the West Siberian Craton rotated away from the northern margin of Laurussia and began to converge with the Kazakhstan Craton and the eastern margin of Fennosarmatia. This marked the onset of the Uralian orogenic cycle that culminated during the Late Permian–Early Triassic in the consolidation of the Ural–Novaya Zemlya–Taimir and the Altay–Sayan fold belts. Back-arc extension, causing subsidence of the West Siberian Basin, commenced during the Late Permian and persisted into Late Triassic–Early Jurassic times (Chapter 3).

## Post-Hercynian Plate Reorganization
## (Late Permian–Mid-Jurassic)

The Uralian diastrophism was paralleled by the first phases of the post-Hercynian plate reorganization in the Tethys and Arctic–North Atlantic domains. This is evident from the Late Permian and Triassic southward propagation of the Norwegian–Greenland Sea rift system into the North and Central Atlantic area and the gradual westward propagation of the Tethys rift system. Particularly during the Triassic and Early Jurassic, large areas around future plate boundaries in the Tethys and Central and North Atlantic area were affected by tensional stresses (Chapter 5).

Furthermore, Late Permian–Early Triassic back-arc extension, related to the decay of the Variscan subduction system, is thought to underlie the separation of the Cimmerian terrane sensu stricto (Balkan–northern Turkey) from the southern margin of Fennosarmatia and the opening of the oceanic Black Sea Basin. Mid-Triassic separation of the continental Central and East Iranian terrane from Arabia, on the other hand, was accompanied by the development of the Tethys sea-floor spreading axis. With this, the northward subductions of the remnant Paleo-Tethys Ocean, at an arc-trench system paralleling its northern margin, was initiated. This gave rise to the Cimmerian orogenic cycle spanning Mid-Triassic to Mid-Jurassic times during which the Central and East Iranian and the Cimmerian terranes were accreted to the southern margin of Eurasia.

Triassic and Early Jurassic gradual westward propagation of the Tethys sea-floor spreading axis and accelerated crustal distension in the Central Atlantic culminated during the Middle Jurassic in crustal separation between Gondwana and Laurussia along the axis of their Hercynian sutures.

## Late Mesozoic Break-up Phase
## (Mid-Jurassic–Early Cretaceous)

Mid-Jurassic development of a discrete plate boundary between Africa–South America and Laurussia marked the onset of the late Mesozoic plate reorganization of the Atlantic–Tethys domain during which the new Central Atlantic sea-floor spreading system played a preeminent role (Chapter 6). Late Jurassic–Early Cretaceous rapid opening of the Central Atlantic induced a sinistral translation between Fennosarmatia and Africa–Arabia whereby the western parts of the Tethys sea-floor spreading system became overpowered and decayed. Ensuing transtensional opening of oceanic basins in the Western and Central Mediterranean domains were followed by the earliest Cretaceous collision of the Italo-Dinarid promontory with the southern margin of Fennosarmatia. This gave rise to the early Alpine orogenic phases. Continued sinistral translation between Africa and Fennosarmatia was accompanied by the partial decoupling of the Italo-Dinarid Block from Africa, its counterclockwise rotation, and the westward and eastward propagation of the early Alpine collision front.

Following crustal separation in the Tethys area, evolution of the Northwest European graben systems was exclusively governed by tensional stress systems related to the Arctic–North Atlantic megarift. During the Early Cretaceous, the Central Atlantic sea-floor spreading axis propagated into the North Atlantic domain and during the Late Cretaceous into the Labrador Sea. This was associated with northward rift propagation into the Baffin Bay and the southeastern parts of the Canadian Arctic Archipelago.

Late Jurassic rifting along the northern margin of the latter culminated during the Valanginian in crustal separation, the counterclockwise rotation of the Alaska–Chukotka–Chukchi and New Siberian Island blocks away from Laurussia, and the opening of the oceanic Canada Basin. This fundamental plate reorganization in the Arctic eventually paved the way for crustal separation between Laurentia–Greenland and Fennosarmatia. Sea-floor spreading in the Canada Basin terminated at about the same time that sea-floor spreading was initiated in the Labrador Sea.

Aptian crustal separation between Africa and South America and linking up of the Central Atlantic and the southern South Atlantic sea-floor spreading axes was followed during the Late Cretaceous by sea-floor spreading in the South Atlantic–Indian Ocean. The resulting counterclockwise rotation and northward drift of Africa–Arabia underlies the Alpine plate reorganization of the Tethys domain during which collisional plate boundaries propagated rapidly into the Western and Eastern Mediterranean areas (Chapter 7).

## Alpine Megacycle (Late Cretaceous–Cenozoic)

During the early Alpine orogenic cycle, spanning Late Cretaceous and Paleogene times, progressive closure of young oceanic domains in the Western and Central Mediterranean area was followed by the collision of Africa and Europe. This was accompanied by important intraplate compressional deformations in Europe and in North Africa.

The Main Alpine orogeny paralleled the second Arctic plate boundary reorganization (Chapter 8). During the latest Paleocene–earliest Eocene, the North Atlantic sea-floor spreading axis propagated northward into the Baffin Bay, the Norwegian–Greenland Sea, and the Eurasian Basin. During the early phase of sea-floor spreading north of the Charlie Gibbs fracture zone, rotation of North America, Greenland, and Eurasia relative to each other induced the compressional deformation of the Eastern Sverdrup Basin and of the western margin of the Barents Shelf. The resulting Eurekan and Spitsbergen orogens are of a passive collisional nature and are not associated with long-standing subduction zones.

Following the early Oligocene abandonment of the Labrador–Baffin Bay sea-floor spreading axis, and the late Oligocene stabilization of spreading axes in the Norwegian–Greenland Sea, crustal separation was achieved between Northeast Greenland and the Barents Shelf. With this, present-day plate boundaries were established in the Arctic–North Atlantic.

The late Paleogene and Neogene Main and late Alpine plate reorganization of the Tethys domain can be related to dextral translations between Europe and Africa in response to differentials in sea-floor spreading rates in the Central Atlantic and the Arctic–North Atlantic (Chapter 9). This plate reorganization was accompanied by the Miocene and Pliocene development of important intramontane wrench systems, the subsidence of the Aegean and Pannonian basins, the opening of the oceanic Algero-Provençal Basin, and later the subsidence of the Tyrrhenian back-arc basin. This was accompanied by the gradual concentration of crustal shortening to the Western Alps, the Apenninen–Calabrian Arc, the southern Carpathian, and the Hellenic–Taurid Arc.

During the Oligocene and Neogene, the Indian Ocean seafloor spreading axis propagated under the Afro-Arabian Craton, causing the opening of the Red Sea Rift and possibly the subsidence of the North Lybian–Pelagian Shelf rifts. This was paralleled by the evolution of the Rhine–Rhône graben system that extends southwestwards through the western Mediterranean and crosses the Rif fold belt. Development of these rift systems can be construed as heralding a post-Alpine plate reorganization that may ultimately lead to the disintegration of the present continent assembly.

This summary illustrates that the Late Silurian to Recent evolution of the Arctic–North Atlantic and Tethys domains was governed by a sequence of plate reorganizations during which a broad spectrum of geodynamic processes was responsible for the development and subsequent partial to total destruction of sedimentary basins.

During the last decade, a number of geophysical models have been advanced in an attempt to explain the development of sedimentary basins under different geodynamic settings. Moreover, the dynamics and evolution of asthenospheric convective systems have been the focus of important research.

In the following chapters, implications drawn from the evolution of sedimentary basins in the Arctic–North Atlantic and Tethys domains are compared with currently favored models of basin evolution, and some speculations are advanced as food for thought.

# RIFTING PROCESSES

Rifts and rift-related passive margin basins play a preeminent role among the sedimentary basins that have developed through time in the Arctic–North Atlantic and Tethys domains. During the late Paleozoic to Cenozoic time span, several cycles of rifting are recognized whereby the subsidence of graben-shaped basins took place under different megatectonic settings.

In this respect, a distinction is made between rifting that led to the break-up of cratonic areas and the opening of major Atlantic-type oceans and back-arc rifting that is related either to decreased convergence rates of a continental and an oceanic plate (Uyeda, 1982) or to the decay of a subduction system following the consolidation of an intracontinental suture (e.g. West Siberian Basin, Chapter 3).

The development of pull-apart features associated with major wrench faulting (e.g., Oslo Graben, Chapter 3) represents a special category of often rapidly subsiding grabens. Development of such pull-apart basins can be associated with Atlantic-type and also back-arc rifting (e.g., late Paleozoic and Mesozoic basins of Svalbard and northern Ellesmere Island, Chapters 4 and 5, and Neogene Aegean and Pannonian basins, Chapter 9).

## Intracratonic Rifts

Numerous models have been proposed for the development of intracratonic rifts and passive margins. These models can be subdivided into two groups. The first group deals principally with the mechanical behavior and deformation patterns at upper and lower crustal and subcrustal lithospheric levels, whereby the emphasis is on mechanical stretching of the lithosphere. The second group addresses the thermally induced upward displacement of the asthenosphere–lithosphere boundary in response to upwelling asthenospheric currents.

One of the earliest rifting models is the uniform stretching or pure shear model (McKenzie, 1978), which assumes that the crust and subcrustal lithosphere are attenuated by an equal amount of stretching whereby deformations are confined to the actual rift zone (Figs. 73, 74). This model has later been modified to the so-called nonuniform or discontinuous depth-dependent stretching model (Royden and Keen, 1980; Beaumont et al., 1982a, 1872b; Hellinger and Sclater, 1983) in which the amount of stretching at crustal and subcrustal lithospheric levels is not the same. This model, which requires an intralithospheric discontinuity (base of the crust), entails space problems at subcrustal lithospheric levels and is therefore not satisfactory. A further modification to the discontinuous nonuniform stretching model has recently been proposed by Rowley and Sahagian (1986) whose continuous (uniform), depth-dependent stretching concept assumes an equal amount of extension at upper and lower lithospheric levels whereby extensional strain is diffused at deeper levels over a wider area than at shallower levels. Both depth-dependent stretching models attempt to account for the broad symmetrical shoulder uplift that is often associated with active rifts (Salveson, 1981; Maréschal, 1983; Turcotte and Emerman, 1983).

On the other hand, the simple shear model (Wernicke, 1981, 1985; Davis et al., 1986; Ussami et al., 1986) invokes, during periods of lithospheric extension, the development of an intracrustal shear zone along which upper crustal distension by faulting is taken up along a discrete shear zone that dips laterally into lower crustal and possibly through upper mantle levels (Fig. 74). In this model, zones of upper and lower crustal and subcrustal lithospheric attenuation do not necessarily coincide as in the pure shear model. The simple shear model satisfies many of the geometric relationships evident on reflection seismic data at upper and middle crustal levels and may explain the absence of post-rifting subsidence of marginal grabens, which are apparently underlain by nonattenuated lower crust (see, e.g., Ussami et al., 1986). Yet the transfer of tensional strain at subcrustal lithospheric levels to one side of the respective rift system would entail an asymmetric uplift of rift shoulders (Wernicke, 1981, 1985; Wernicke and Burchfiel, 1982; Coward, 1986). In extreme cases of the simple shear model, the zone of lower crustal and subcrustal lithospheric attenuation could lie entirely outside the zone of upper crustal stretching. During the rifting stage, this area of nonattenuated upper crust would become progressively uplifted and, during the postrifting stage, develop into a thermal sag basin. This concept has led to the development of the "linked tectonics" model (Beach, 1985).

This concept is, however, difficult to reconcile with the geological record and the heat flow patterns of many rifts (e.g., Rhine Graben, Red Sea).

Barbier et al. (1986) have modified the simple shear model by assuming that the intracrustal shear zone, into which faulting at upper crustal levels soles out, coincides with the transition zone of brittle and ductile deformation. This model suggests, similar to the continuous depth-dependent stretching concept, that tensional strain is dissipated at lower crustal and subcrustal lithospheric levels by ductile flow over a wide zone extending beyond both margins of the upper crustal rift. This would account for a more or less symmetrical doming of rift flanks. Permutations to this combined simple and pure shear model are discussed by Kusznir et al. (1987).

The validity of the different rift models needs to be tested against examples of rift zones for which full geophysical data sets are available, including gravity, shallow and deep reflection, and refraction seismic surveys. These data ought to be of sufficient quality and extent to determine the depth converted crustal configuration of the respective rift zone, the attenuation (stretching) factors at upper and lower crustal levels, the reflectivity of the upper and lower crust as well as the definition of potential intracrustal detachment and/or shear zones. Moreover, such "case history" analyses must also take into consideration heat flow data and the distribution and chemical composition of rift-related igneous activity.

Partial data sets, available for a number of rift zones (e.g., North Sea, Fig. 56; Rhine Graben, Fig. 66) and also for passive margins (e.g., Bay of Biscay, Fig. 27; East Newfoundland Basin, Fig. 29), indicate that the stretching factor determined for lower

crustal attenuation by refraction data exceeds the $\beta$-factor at upper crust at levels as derived from reflection seismic data. The observed discrepancy is generally in the order of 3:1. Although the reliability of stretching factors derived from reflection seismic data for shallow crustal levels has been repeatedly challenged (Wood and Barton, 1983; Barton and Wood, 1984; see also Sclater et al., 1986) the magnitude of these observed discrepancies is too large to be simply attributable to "margins of error" or "linked tectonics" (Beach, 1985) as advocated by the original simple shear model.

This suggests that during rifting phases, attenuation of the lower crust may be achieved not only by its mechanical stretching but also by other mechanisms; moreover, the question is

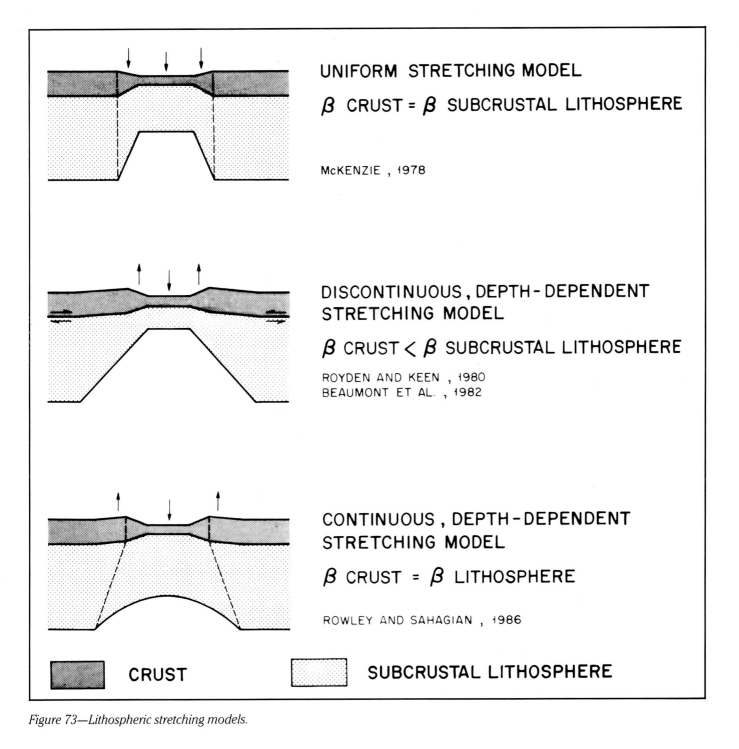

UNIFORM STRETCHING MODEL

$\beta$ CRUST = $\beta$ SUBCRUSTAL LITHOSPHERE

McKENZIE , 1978

DISCONTINUOUS , DEPTH - DEPENDENT STRETCHING MODEL

$\beta$ CRUST < $\beta$ SUBCRUSTAL LITHOSPHERE

ROYDEN AND KEEN , 1980
BEAUMONT ET AL. , 1982

CONTINUOUS , DEPTH - DEPENDENT STRETCHING MODEL

$\beta$ CRUST = $\beta$ LITHOSPHERE

ROWLEY AND SAHAGIAN , 1986

CRUST          SUBCRUSTAL LITHOSPHERE

*Figure 73—Lithospheric stretching models.*

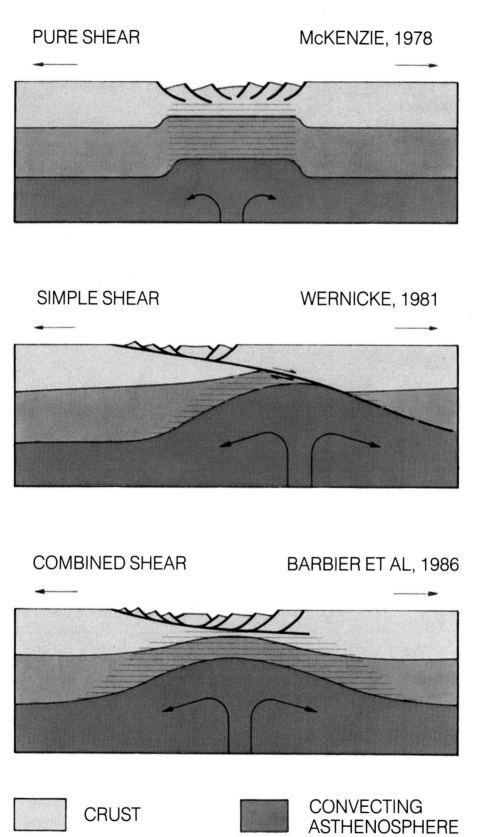

*Figure 74—Lithospheric shear models. After McKenzie (1978) (top); Wernicke (1981) (center); and Barbier et al. (1986) (bottom).*

raised whether during advanced rifting stages lower crustal material conservation and stability of the Moho Discontinuity are still valid concepts (see below; Meissner, 1986).

The driving mechanism of lithospheric extension has been variably attributed to plate boundary forces acting at trenches, particularly when subduction takes place at opposite sides of large continental masses, to mantle plume activity and to the projection and/or gradual development of upwelling asthenospheric convective systems under continents (Bott, 1982; Turcotte, 1981; Turcotte and Emerman, 1983; Neugebauer, 1983).

The Mesozoic and Cenozoic break-up of Pangea, as evident by the evolution of the Arctic–Central Atlantic and Tethys rift systems, suggests that the latter processes are probably the dominant driving force of large-scale lithospheric extension. As discussed in Chapter 5, the Triassic–Early Jurassic rift systems of the North Atlantic and Tethys domains and of West-Central Europe cover an area of 2000 km by 3500 km. Most of these grabens were a-volcanic and crustal doming played only a subordinate role. This speaks against the development of these rifts in response to the emplacement of a multitude of hotspots. Furthermore, it is questionable whether subduction processes along the distant margins of Pangea played a major role in the development of the Triassic Gondwana rifts and those of the Arctic–North Atlantic and Tethys domains.

On the other hand, the Mid-Triassic separation of the Central and East Iranian terrane from Arabia testifies to the evolution of the Tethys sea-floor spreading axis. Jurassic westward propagation of this axis, in conjunction with the development of the West Mediterranean–Central Atlantic–Gulf of Mexico ridge-transform system, resulted in crustal separation between Gondwana and Laurasia (Chapter 5).

This sequence of events suggests that the multidirectional graben systems of the North and Central Atlantic, Tethys, and West-Central European areas developed probably in response to frictional forces exerted on the lithosphere by gradually developing upwelling convective systems beneath the central parts of Pangea. These systems asserted themselves during the Mid-Jurassic by the development of the Tethys–Central Atlantic sea-floor spreading systems (Chapter 5) and during the Cretaceous and Paleogene by the development of the North Atlantic and Norwegian–Greenland sea-floor spreading axes (Chapter 8).

Upwelling asthenospheric currents are thought to cause thinning of the lithosphere by inducing a thermal upward displacement of its lower boundary whereby they probably exert tensional stresses on it. In time, this can lead to lithospheric failure, crustal separation, and the opening of new oceanic basins (Richter and McKenzie, 1978; Chase, 1979; McKenzie et al., 1980). The regional lithospheric extension that precedes continental splitting can affect wide areas around the future plate boundaries. This is exemplified by the Triassic Tethys, Central, and North Atlantic rift systems. With the progression of crustal extension, rifting activity frequently concentrates to the axial rift zones whereby peripheral grabens and fault systems become inactive (e.g., rift systems of Western Europe and Barents Sea relative to Norwegian–Greenland Sea Rift).

In such a tectonic setting, the duration of the rifting stage of "abortive" rifts, in which crustal separation is not achieved, and of "successful" rifts, culminating in crustal separation, is highly variable. This is illustrated by the diagrams given in Figures 75 and 76. For instance, opening of the Central Atlantic Ocean was preceded by a rifting stage spanning some 50 Ma while intermittent rifting lasted in the Norwegian–Greenland Sea for some 275 Ma.

The observed variations in the duration of the rifting stage of successful rifts is probably a function of the time required for the evolution of upwelling asthenospheric convective systems to a point where they are able to drive apart major continents. Prior to crustal separation, these convective systems are probably partially decoupled from the overlying lithosphere, with full coupling being established during or immediately after crustal separation. This concept cannot, however, be generalized as suggested by the abandonment of early sea-floor spreading axes in favor of new ones. This is exemplified by the Oligocene abandonment of the Labrador–Baffin Bay and the Aegir spreading axes in favor of the Reykjanes–Kolbeinsey–Mohn's spreading axis (Chapter 8). Furthermore, minor oceanic basins, such as those of the southern Rockall Trough and the Bay of Biscay, are characterized by only a short period of sea-floor spreading after which they cease to open further (Fig. 77). Such basins are probably not directly associated with major asthenospheric upwelling systems, and their oceanic crust may have formed by passive asthenospheric advection into a lead opening in response to regional stress patterns (Chapter 7). Similar mechanisms may have played a role during the opening of the Labrador Sea–Baffin Bay and northern North Atlantic–Norwegian-Greenland Sea. The early phases of sea-floor spreading in the Labrador Sea were paralleled by continued crustal extension in the northern North Atlantic and the Norwegian–Greenland Sea (Fig. 78). Ultimate abandonment of the Labrador Sea–Baffin Bay spreading axis, and late Oligocene stabilization of spreading axes in the Norwegian–Greenland Sea to the Kolbeinsey Ridge, also suggests that the Labrador Sea spreading system and the Aegir Ridge were not superimposed on a permanent, deep asthenospheric upwelling cell. In turn, this indicates that opening of the Labrador Sea was induced by the rotation of North America, driven by the Central and North Atlantic spreading system, and not so much by the active northward propagation of the latter.

The apparent nearly simultaneous abandonment and inception of distant sea-floor spreading systems may give an indication of the magnitude of the asthenospheric convection cells and their evolution, a subject that is not further analyzed here (Fig. 77).

If tensional forces exerted on the lithosphere by gradually developing asthenospheric upwelling systems are indeed the main driving mechanism of lithospheric extension, it should be kept in mind that lithospheric attenuation can be achieved not only by its stretching but also, at the same time, by a thermal upward displacement of the asthenosphere–lithosphere boundary (Morgan and Baker, 1983; Fleitou et al., 1986). These processes are apparently associated with the decompression of the asthenosphere inducing partial melting at the base of the lithosphere and, on the other hand, with the advection of hot asthenospheric material to the base of the lithosphere (Spohn and Schubert, 1983; Neugebauer, 1983). Both processes can apparently trigger the diapiric ascent of alkaline, mafic-felsic bimodal magmas to shallower lithospheric levels, to the crust–mantle boundary and ultimately to the surface, whereby their composition reflects through time the gradual upward displacement of the asthenosphere–lithosphere boundary (see Wendlandt, 1981; Wendlandt and Morgan, 1982; Fuchs et al., 1983).

Thermal upward displacement of the asthenosphere–lithosphere boundary, probably involving small-scale convective processes even during the precrustal separation stage (Bott, 1976, 1981; Spohn and Schubert, 1983), combined with mechanical stretching of the lithosphere, can result in greater subcrustal lithospheric attenuation ($\beta$m) than at crustal levels ($\beta$c), to the end that $\beta$m is greater than $\beta$c (see nonuniform or depth-dependent stretching model, Royden and Keen, 1980; Beaumont et al., 1982b; Hellinger and Sclater, 1983; Steckler, 1985). Progressive, thermally induced, upward displacement of the asthenosphere–lithosphere boundary causes the gradual upwarp of broad rift domes that reach their maximum dimensions prior to or at the moment of crustal separation (mantle plume model, Fig. 79; e.g., Red Sea, East African Rift, Early Jurassic Central Atlantic).

During the crustal separation stage, dike intrusions in the axial rift zones and convective lateral subcrustal lithospheric thinning (Fleitou and Yuen, 1984), accompanied by lower crustal flowage (Moretti and Pinet, 1987), are thought to play an important role. A further possible mechanism for lower crustal thinning may involve the injection of asthenospheric material into the lower crust leading to its gradual basification (sub-crustal erosion). These processes are irreversible and may have contributed in many passive margin basins to substantially greater lower crustal attenuation than the upper crustal thinning by tensional faulting as evident on reflection seismic data (e.g., northern margin of Bay of Biscay, Fig. 31; East Newfoundland Basin, Fig. 33; West Norway basins, Fig. 51; and also on the northwestern margin of the Provençal Basin (Le Douaran et al., 1984; Bessis and Burrus, 1986; Moretti and Pinet, 1987). This raises the question of whether during rifting the mass of the lower crust is actually being conserved or whether the geophysically defined Moho Discontinuity can be displaced upward by physicochemical processes (Olsen, 1983; Pinet et al., 1987).

Furthermore, at high rates of extension, even at an early stage of rifting, temporary, local failure of the lithosphere may trigger the diapiric rise of asthenospheric material to upper mantle levels and/or to the crust–mantle boundary, where it reaches a density equilibrium and spreads out laterally to form a so-called asthenolith, referred to also as a "rift pillow" (tensional failure model, Fig. 79; Turcotte, 1981; Turcotte and Emerman, 1983). The emplacement of such low-density, low-velocity

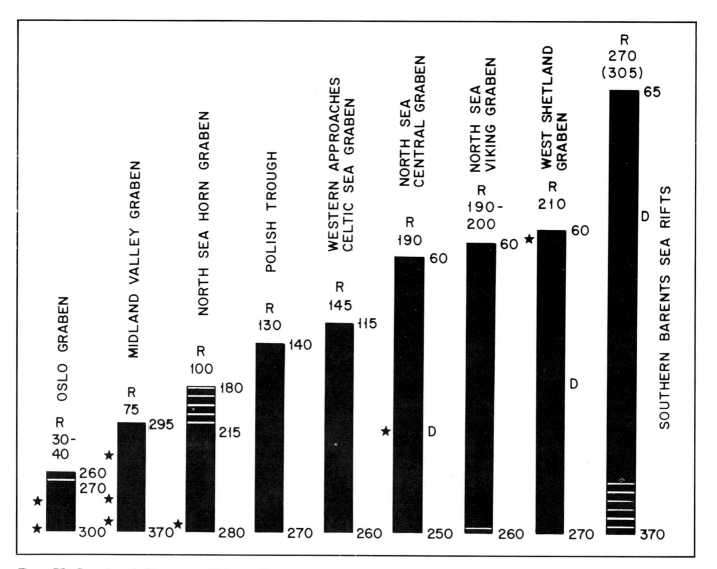

*Figure 75—Duration of rifting stage of "abortive" rifts (paleorifts, failed arms). Vertical scale in Ma. Figures on side of vertical columns indicate onset and termination of rifting stage in Ma. Figures under R on top of each column give duration of rifting stage in Ma. Stars: periods of main volcanic activity; D: doming stage.*

upper mantle anomalies as observed, for instance, beneath the southern Rhine Graben (Fig. 71) and the Massif Central (Perrier and Ruegg, 1973; Fuchs et al., 1981; Mechie et al., 1983) can cause the temporary uplift of a graben and with this a reversal of its subsidence pattern. This is exemplified by the Mid-Jurassic doming of the Central North Sea Graben area and the early Miocene upwarping of the Rhenish Shield. In both cases, earlier accumulated synrift deposits became deeply truncated during the doming stage, even in the axial rift zone.

Asthenoliths are thermally unstable upper mantle anomalies and are apparently resorbed into the upper mantle upon cooling, once the supply of hot asthenospheric material has ceased. This probably involves phase changes that may cause rapid subsidence of the overlying rift zone (Artyushkov, 1983) as evident, for instance, by the late Middle and Late Jurassic collapse of the Central North Sea rift dome (Chapter 5). The evolution of the Loppa Ridge, flanking the Byørnøya Graben of the Western Barents Sea, which underwent a first phase of uplifting at the transition from the Permian to the Triassic and a second one at the Jurassic–Cretaceous boundary (Fig. 15), suggests that such intermittent doming can be recurrent.

During the development of an asthenolith, emplacement of hot asthenospheric material at the crust–mantle boundary probably induces, even in the face of limited crustal extension, additional lower crustal attenuation by subcrustal erosional processes, possibly involving the injection of mantle-derived material into the lower crust. These processes may be associated with the development of the reflection seismically defined lower crustal laminations. These high amplitude, intra-lower crustal reflections, as evident, for instance, in the southern Rhine Graben (Fig. 72; Meissner, 1986; Meissner and Kusznir, 1986), in the northern North Sea (Fig. 62), in the area of the Celtic Sea and Western Approaches troughs (Pinet et al., 1987), and in the rift-wrench-induced Paris Basin (Fig. 11), indicate the presence of high density-velocity contrasts within the lower crust. Such lower crustal impedance contrasts may be associated with high density, mantle derived sills, metamorphic layering, or shear zones (Wever and Meissner, 1986; Moretti and Pinet, 1987). In general, these lower crustal laminations disappear away from the actual rift zones and are absent in areas of flanking, stable cratonic blocks; thus they appear to be, in a way, related to rifting processes. If these lower crustal laminations can, indeed, be related to the injection of mantle-derived material into the lower crust (Meissner, 1986; Bois et al., 1987), it would seem plausible that this process may ultimately lead to the basification of the lower crust and to an upward displacement of the geophysically defined crust–mantle boundary (subcrustal erosion), a process akin to the ones discussed by

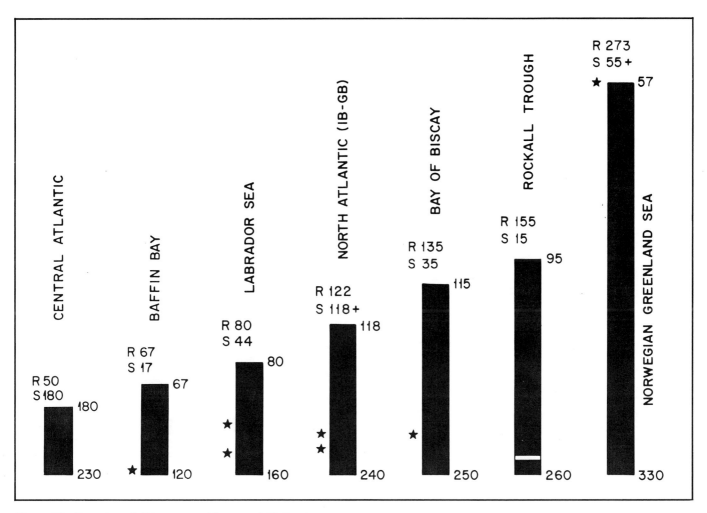

*Figure 76—Duration of rifting stage of "successful" rifts. Legend same as Figure 75. Figures beside letter S indicate duration of sea floor spreading stage.*

Beloussov (1960, 1962, 1975).

At the same time, heating up of the lower crust probably increases its ductility and induces a gradual upward displacement of the brittle/ductile deformation transition zone (Pinet et al., 1987). Correspondingly, simple shear deformations may play a dominant role during early rifting phases, and pure shear deformations may be the prevailing mechanism during advanced stages of crustal extension particularly when the asthenosphere has ascended to the base of the crust (see Barbier et al., 1986).

Many rifts are totally devoid of volcanic activity or show only a very low level of volcanism (e.g., Triassic rifts of Western and Central Europe). Such rifts are generally not associated with progressive, wide-radius doming. Other rifts, however, display a high level of volcanic activity right from the onset of crustal extension, such as the Rhine Graben, or become temporarily volcanic after an initial stage of nonvolcanic subsidence (e.g., North Sea Central Graben during the Middle Jurassic). Such volcanic activity is often associated with symmetrical doming of the rift zone.

Major variations in intensity and timing of volcanic activity are also evident during the rifting stage of passive margins. For instance, the early rifting stages of the Labrador Sea were accompanied by a high level of volcanic activity while the Mid-Norway Basin remained apparently nonvolcanic during its long rifting history until the latest Cretaceous–early Eocene Thulean

*Figure 79—Rift models.*▶

volcanic surge preceded and accompanied crustal separation in the Norwegian–Greenland Sea (Figs. 75, 76).

Volcanism associated with intracratonic rifts is typically alkaline and felsic-bimodal (Martin and Piwinsky, 1972; Burke and Dewey, 1973; Lameyre et al., 1984). Initial volcanic activity is frequently alkaline felsic but changes with increasing lithospheric thinning to a tholeiitic basalt (Wendlandt, 1981; Wendlandt and Morgan, 1982). In wrench-related troughs initial magmatism is, however, often basaltic (e.g., Aquitaine Basin).

Triple junctions, where crustal and subcrustal lithospheric attenuation is most intense, are the likely places for an early manifestation of rift volcanism (e.g., northern Rhine Graben and North Sea Rift). However, while volcanic activity is not necessarily restricted to zones of upper crustal extension, the occurrence of lateral volcanic centers appears to be limited to the area of the corresponding rift dome and by implication to

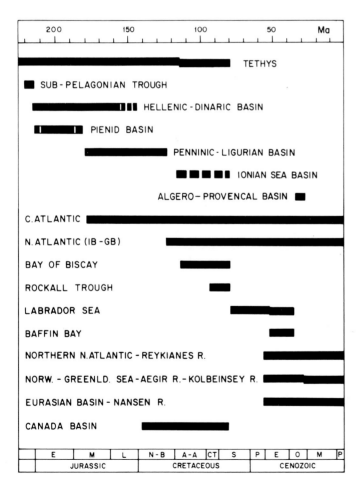

Figure 77—Timetable of sea floor spreading in the Tethys and Arctic–North Atlantic domains.

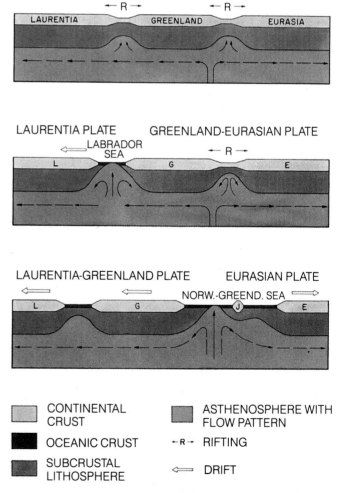

Figure 78—Evolution and dynamics of Mesozoic and Cenozoic plate boundaries in the Arctic–North Atlantic. J = Jan Mayen Ridge.

# MANTLE PLUME MODEL

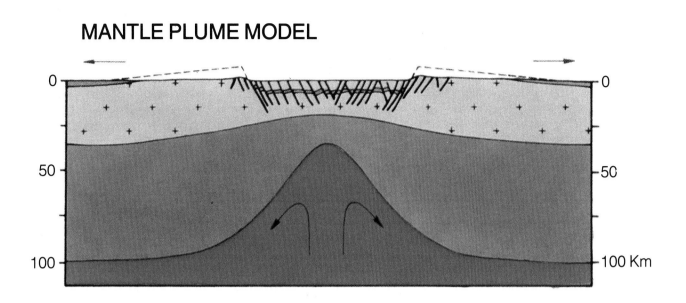

# TENSIONAL FAILURE MODEL

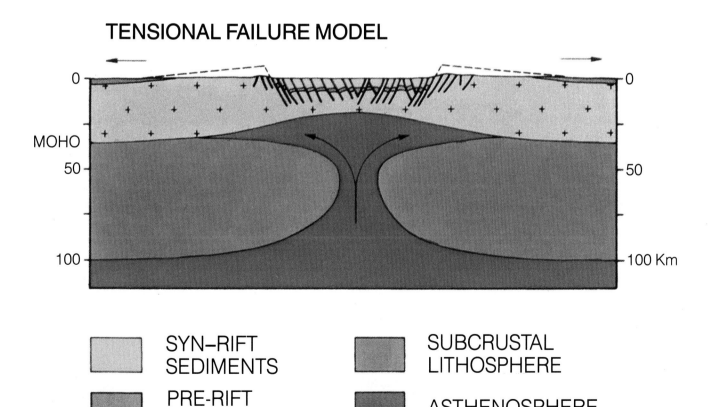

SYN–RIFT
SEDIMENTS

PRE-RIFT
SEDIMENTS

CRUST

SUBCRUSTAL
LITHOSPHERE

ASTHENOSPHERE

FLOW PATTERN

the zone of the thermally upward-displaced asthenosphere–lithosphere boundary. In the case of the Rhine Graben, lateral volcanic centers are confined to the outlines of the subcrustal asthenolith (Fig. 71). Chemical differences between volcanics extruded within the actual rift zone and those extruded in peripheral areas are related to the differences in depth of magma generation (Wendlandt, 1981; Lameyre et al., 1984).

The extrusion of major volumes of plateau basalts, immediately preceding and accompanying crustal separation, is not characteristic for all passive margins. For instance, crustal separation between Iberia, the Grand Banks, and the southwestern margin of Europe and also between the Canadian Arctic Archipelago and the Chukotka–Chukchi block of Alaska were not accompanied by a volcanic surge of the dimensions of, for instance, the Thulean volcanism of the northern North Atlantic and the Norwegian–Greenland Sea. In this respect, it is suspected that, if the motion of incipient diverging plates is unrestrained, crustal separation can be effected relatively easily and thermally upwelling asthenospheric material will be accreted to the new plate boundaries as oceanic lithosphere. Conversely, if the divergence of continental blocks is impeded, the advecting mantle material will be injected into the crust and ultimately be extruded as flood basalts. Restraints in the separation of continents can be caused, on the one hand, by their partial coherence on trend of the respective rift zone (e.g., Jurassic–Early Cretaceous opening of the South Atlantic and Karoo basalts of South Africa and Sierra Geral basalts of Brazil), and, on the other hand, by collision-related tangential compressional stresses (e.g., Thulean volcanism of northern North Atlantic, Plate 17, Chapter 8). Once these constraints in plate motion are removed, sea-floor spreading will commence and intracratonic volcanism will cease in the adjacent borderlands at the expense of accretion of new oceanic crust at the new spreading ridge.

Igneous activity in many highly volcanic rifts can culminate in the intrusion of felsic plutonic differentiates which, on trace element analyses, contain substantial amounts of reactivated crustal material.

This is exemplified by the Ordovician magmatism accompanying the separation of microcontinents from the northern margin of Gondwana (Priem and den Tex, 1984; Weber, 1984; Matte, 1986), the magmatic history of the Permian Oslo Rift (Neumann, 1985), and of the Permo-Triassic Dinarid rift system (Pamic, 1984). A further example is provided by the Early Tertiary Thulean volcanism (Thompson, 1982; Chapter 8). This suggests that crustal contamination of rising mantle-derived magmas involving anatectic remobilization of the lower crust can play an important role during the evolution of a rift. This supports the concept that the crust–mantle boundary can become seriously destabilized during rifting processes and, by implication, casts doubt on the assumption that lower crustal attenuation can be translated, without reservations, into a stretching factor.

Clearly, the evolution of intracratonic rifts shows many variations, which cannot be explained by a few simplistic models. Much has yet to be learned from a multidisciplinary approach and the careful integration of geological and geophysical data. It is important that such studies are based on full data sets, including stratigraphic information from wells, results of shallow and deep reflection seismic surveys calibrated by refraction data, and gravity surveys. Moreover, it should be taken into account that the igneous record of a rift can provide important information on the depth of magma generation through time and space, on the gradual ascent of the asthenosphere–lithosphere boundary, and on the location of the asthenosphere–lithosphere boundary anomaly relative to the zone of upper crustal extension.

## Back-Arc Extension

Several forms of back-arc extension are recognized, all of which differ to varying degrees in their megatectonic setting and possibly also their driving mechanisms.

The classical form of back-arc extension is the Pacific type, described by Uyeda (1982), which is associated with intraoceanic island arcs and also arc-trench systems marking the collision zone between an oceanic and a continental plate. In such a setting, back-arc extension is thought to be related to the development and assertion of secondary upwelling convection currents in the mantle wedge immediately above the subducting lithospheric slab (Fig. 4). Tensional stresses exerted by such convective systems on the overriding plate are apparently capable of inducing back-arc rifting and sea-floor spreading only if the convergence rate between the subducting and the overriding plates is relatively low or if the plates diverge. This is presumably accompanied by partial decoupling of the two colliding plates at the Benioff zone which, under these conditions, is likely to display a relatively steep dip (Mariana-type). On the other hand, if convergence rates are relatively high, stronger coupling at the Benioff zone results in compressive deformation of the back-arc areas and the overpowering of back-arc convective systems. Under these conditions, the Benioff zone is likely to dip relatively gently under the overriding plate (Andean type) (Uyeda, 1981, 1982; Hsui and Toksöz, 1981; Zonenshain and Savostin, 1981). Moreover, the dip of a Benioff zone and the associated stress regime in back-arc areas appear to be related to the age of the subducting oceanic lithosphere whereby Benioff zones involving the subduction of old oceanic lithosphere generally display a steeper dip than those involving the subduction of young oceanic lithosphere (Jarrard, 1986). Nevertheless, as convergence rates and directions between plates are not constant and appear to change through time, periods of back-arc extension and back-arc compression can alternate with each other. Correspondingly, back-arc rifts and back-arc oceanic basins are prone to destruction, particularly under the impact of continent-to-continent collision.

The Devonian to Early Carboniferous Variscan geosynclinal system of back-arc basins can be considered as reflecting the evolution of an intracontinental Pacific-type back-arc system. Its destruction during the Variscan orogeny is related to the collision of Gondwana with Laurussia (Chapters 2 and 3).

The Late Silurian to Early Carboniferous Sakmarian arc-trench and back-arc basin reflects the evolution of an intraoceanic, Pacific-type back-arc system in which periods of back-arc compression alternated with back-arc extension. This system was destroyed during the Uralian orogeny when the Kazakhstan and Siberian cratons converged and collided with the eastern margin of Fennosarmatia (Chapters 2 and 3).

The Permo-Triassic phase of sea-floor spreading in the Black Sea was probably induced by back-arc extension, and as such is likely to reflect the decay of the Variscan subduction system (Chapter 4). Late Triassic and Early Jurassic closure of this basin was induced by the convergence of Cimmeria with the southern margin of Fennosarmatia in response to increasing activity along the Tethys sea-floor spreading axis (Chapter 5). The late Senonian to Paleocene second phase of back-arc sea-floor spreading in the Black Sea is probably related to the early

Alpine reduced activity along, and the decay of, the Pontides subduction system since by that time the bulk of crustal shortening was taken up along the Hellenic–Anatolid subduction zone (Chapter 6).

A second type of back-arc extension is associated with the late-to-postorogenic collapse of fold belts forming the megasutures between major cratons. This is exemplified by the Permo-Triassic evolution of the West Siberian Basin (Chapter 3), the Permo-Carboniferous evolution of the Sverdrup Basin (Chapter 4), and the Neogene development of the Pannonian Basin (Chapter 7).

The subsidence of this type of back-arc basin may be induced by the decay of a long-standing subduction zone along which oceanic lithosphere and later continental lower crustal and upper mantle material were consumed whereby the Benioff zone dipped gently under the areas that subsequently were affected by extension. Gradual steepening of such a Benioff zone as a consequence of decreasing convergence rates of the colliding cratons and ultimately its locking may permit the development of secondary upwelling convection systems in the mantle wedge above the subducting lithosphere slab. Rapid extension of the overlying, immature, and thickened crust, which is partly permeated by synorogenic calc-alkaline plutons, is often associated with the extrusion of widespread basaltic to rhyolitic flows (e.g., West Siberian Basin, Plates 8–10).

The duration of such a phase of active back-arc extension is poorly constrained but apparently lasted in the case of the West Siberian and Sverdrup basins some 50 to 60 Ma. However, the time required for the decay of a fully locked subduction system, associated with a Himalayan-type orogen, may be shorter. In this context, it should be kept in mind that in the case of the West Siberian Basin, the early phases of back-arc extension coincided with the last phases of crustal shortening in the external Uralides.

In back-arc basins, the extension-induced thermal surge and initial phase of basin subsidence is followed by a period of lithospheric cooling and contraction causing regional basin subsidence. This is particularly well illustrated by the evolution of the West Siberian Basin (Artyushkov and Baer, 1986).

The Neogene Pannonian and Aegean back-arc basins, which developed during the late Alpine orogenic cycle, represent a modified form of this type of back-arc extension (Chapter 9). Tensional subsidence of these basins was associated with major wrench deformations and important crustal shortening in the related arc-systems. These deformations are, to a large extent, the expression of changes in the convergence direction between the colliding continents and also of indenter effects and ensuing "escape tectonics" (Chapter 9).

In such basins, wrench-induced deep crustal fracturing, accompanying the development of pull-apart structures, can apparently trigger an intense, predominantly calc-alkaline initial volcanism. Alkaline bimodal suites play only a subordinate role, but in time may gain in importance. The thermal surge, associated at least with the early subsidence phases of such back-arc basins, may be coupled with an upward displacement of the crust mantle boundary by physicochemical processes (subcrustal erosion) as evident in the Pannonian Basin (Chapter 9).

The latest Carboniferous–Early Permian evolution of the Variscan fold belt probably reflects a phase of wrench-dominated back-arc extension that was governed, on the one hand, by the decay of the Variscan subduction system, and on the other hand, by the dextral translation of Gondwana relative

to Laurussia during the Alleghenian orogenic cycle (Lorenz and Nicholls, 1984; Jowett and Jarvis, 1984, Chapter 3).

A further form of synorogenic back-arc extension is represented by the Neogene opening of the oceanic Algero-Provençal Basin and the subsidence of the only partly oceanic Tyrrhenian Basin. It is suspected that the evolution of these basins was at least in part governed by the development of new intracratonic rifts, such as the Rhine–Rhône and Lybian–Pelagian Shelf graben systems. These rifts propagated into and possibly across still-active fold belts and as such many have assisted or even triggered back-arc extension. Significantly, the volcanism of the Tyrrhenian Basin has a mixed calc-alkaline-shoshonitic and alkaline composition; furthermore, alkaline, presently subactive volcanoes are superimposed on the still-active externides of the Apennine–Calabrian Arc (Plate 21). In addition, it is likely that changes in the convergence direction between Africa and Europe have played an important role in the evolution of these West-Mediterranean back-arc basins (Chapter 9).

The structural style of back-arc tensional basins is in many respects similar to that of intracratonic rifts. In back-arc basins, however, tensional reactivation of listric thrust faults can play a locally important role (Bally, 1982). Principal differences in mechanisms of crustal attenuation between intracratonic and back-arc rift systems may arise from the fact that the latter are generally superimposed on young orogenic belts (e.g., Basin and Range Province of U.S. Cordillera, West Siberian, and Pannonian basins) which are characterized by a 60–70 km thick immature continental crust and a thermally destabilized subcrustal lithosphere. Intracratonic rifts, on the other hand, develop in areas of thermally stabilized lithosphere and mature crust having a thickness of 35–45 km. These differences probably play an important role during the early rifting phases by determining the depth at which the brittle/ductile crustal deformation transition zone occurs.

Back-arc extensional basins are generally superimposed on preexisting calc-alkaline magmatic arcs (e.g., Aegean, Pannonian, West Siberian basins, Basin and Range Province). The early subsidence phases of such basins is generally accompanied by an intense calc-alkaline initial volcanism that only in time becomes alkaline bimodal as a consequence of progressive lithospheric thinning (e.g., Pannonian Basin, Chapter 9). The generally high level of magmatic activity in back-arc basins is probably associated with magma ponding at the crust–mantle boundary and a progressive upward displacement of the Moho Discontinuity in response to "subcrustal erosion" processes, as indicated for the Pannonian Basin (Stegena and Horváth, 1982) and the Basin and Range Province (Klemperer et al., 1986).

## PASSIVE MARGINS AND INACTIVE RIFTS

Following crustal separation, the subsidence of the newly formed "passive continental margins" is controlled by lithospheric thermal contraction and sediment loading of the crust. Similar mechanisms govern the subsidence of rifts that have become inactive (Beck and Lehner, 1973; Sleep, 1973, 1976; McKenzie, 1978; Sclater and Tapscott, 1979; Jarvis and McKenzie, 1980; Royden et al., 1980; Le Pichon and Sibuet, 1981; Beaumont et al., 1982a, 1982b; Steckler and Watts, 1982; Watts et al., 1982; Watts and Thorne, 1984). In the following discussion, the basic principles of thermal subsidence, which are well documented in the literature, will not be reiterated and only some points of uncertainty and concern with established models will be highlighted.

The amount of postrifting, tectonic subsidence of passive margins and inactive grabens, which is caused by cooling and contraction of the lithosphere and its return to thermal equilibrium, is controlled by the magnitude of the thermal anomaly that was induced during crustal separation or the crustal attenuation stage. Maximum thermal anomalies presumably developed during continental separation when hot, asthenospheric material welled up to the sea-floor or even to the surface. Thermal anomalies induced by rifting that did not progress to crustal separation are relatively smaller; their magnitude depends on the degree to which the asthenosphere–lithosphere boundary became displaced upward during the rifting stage and/or whether asthenospheric material had risen diapirically to upper mantle levels or to the crust–mantle boundary.

It follows that the postseparation evolution of passive continental margins probably reflects the decay of maximum thermal anomalies, while the subsidence of inactive rifts is governed by the decay of smaller thermal anomalies. On the other hand, the postrifting development of volcanic rifts is likely to be governed by the decay of larger thermal anomalies than that of nonvolcanic rifts. In this context, it should be kept in mind that deep-seated thermal anomalies associated with major pull-ups of the asthenosphere–lithosphere boundary (mantle plume model) decay more slowly than the thermal anomalies induced by the emplacement of an asthenolith at the crust–mantle boundary (tensional failure model, see Fig. 80).

The thickness of the sedimentary column that can accumulate in passive margin basins and in basins developing on top of inactive rifts is not only a function of the magnitude of the thermal anomaly associated with these basins at the end of their rifting stage but also a function of the amount of crustal attenuation achieved in them during the rifting stage by stretching, subcrustal and supracrustal erosion, the water depth at the end of the rifting stage and the density of the infilling postrifting sediments (carbonates, clastics).

Quantitative analyses of the postrifting subsidence of a rift permit the determination of the amount of thermal contraction of the lithosphere and, conversely, the magnitude of the thermal anomaly that was induced during its rifting stage. However, for reasons discussed in Chapter 10, the magnitude of such a thermal anomaly can, however, not be directly related to the amount of crustal attenuation by stretching and other mechanisms. In this context, it ought to be borne in mind that crustal thinning by extension and concomitant subcrustal erosion (basification and/or lateral ductile mass transfer) can take place intermittently over very long periods of time. In long-lived rifts, thermal anomalies that were induced by, and were associated with, early phases of crustal attenuation start to decay during subsequent periods of decreased rate of extension. Thus, the thermal anomaly associated with a rift may not be at its maximum when crustal stretching terminates and the rift becomes inactive. Similarly, late rifting pulses and/or regional magmatic events (e.g., Thulean volcanism) may interrupt and can even reverse the lithospheric cooling processes (e.g., two-stage doming of the Loppa Ridge, Fig. 15). Therefore, analyses of the subsidence patterns of rifts, which evolved in response to repeated rifting phases or a long period of more or less continued rifting, must take into account their entire rifting history.

This is illustrated by the result of several early analyses of the subsidence patterns of the North Sea. These analyses, depending on their approach, came to widely divergent conclusions on the amount of crustal stretching that occurred during the rifting stage (Sclater and Christie, 1980; Barton and Wood, 1984; Chapter 8). More recent time-dependent stretching analyses achieved, however, a better fit with the available data (Sclater et al., 1986). Yet stretching factors determined from subsidence analyses appear to be substantially greater than the amount of extension derived from reflection seismic data and fall short of the amount of extension derived from the present-day crustal configuration of the North Sea (Fig. 61). In none of these analyses was the introduction of a subcrustal thermal anomaly associated with the Bajocian doming of the Central North Sea taken into account. An additional source of error in these analyses is the neglect of lateral heat transfer in relatively narrow rifts (Cochran, 1983; Alvarez et al., 1984).

A special problem is presented by the lack of postrifting or postseparation subsidence or even the uplift of grabens that are located marginal to main rift systems. Examples in case are the Triassic–Early Jurassic grabens of the Appalachian Piedmont, the late Paleozoic–Mesozoic Jameson Land Basin of Central East Greenland, and the deeply truncated Triassic half-grabens on the Hebrides shelf. This phenomenon could be explained, either in terms of the simple shear model by crustal unloading as a consequence of upper crustal extension and the lack of commensurate lower crustal attenuation (Ussami et al., 1986) or by the ductile transfer of lower crustal material away from the axial rift zone to peripheral areas where lower crustal thickening caused isostatic uplift (Moretti and Pinet, 1987). Since these two processes are not mutually exclusive, their combined effects could possibly explain the observed phenomenon.

The above throws further doubt on the concept that stretching factors can indeed be derived from the thermal subsidence analysis of rifted basins. However, such analyses, in combination with other data, may contribute substantially to the understanding of rifting processes, particularly by quantifying the thermal anomalies that were introduced during their rifting stage. This applies not only for passive margins and intracratonic rifts but also to back-arc extensional basins (e.g., Pannonian Basin, Sclater et al., 1980).

# WRENCH FAULTING

Wrench-induced deformations played an important role during the late Paleozoic to Recent evolution of the Arctic–North Atlantic and Western Tethys domain.

In continental areas, basically four different geotectonic habitats of wrench deformation can be recognized. These are associated either with regional crustal distension, collisional tectonics, the translation of major cratonic blocks as a consequence of postorogenic plate reorganizations, or movements along oceanic transform zones projecting beneath the adjacent continental lithosphere.

Under all four megatectonic settings, wrench deformations, depending on fault geometries at fault offsets, can cause folding (transpression) or the subsidence of pull-apart grabens and/or of relatively narrow tension gash basins (transtension). Intracratonic transtensional deformations can be associated with an intense, often basaltic volcanism (e.g., Triassic–Early Jurassic basalts of Aquitaine Basin and rifts of Northwest Africa, Chapter 5) and/or the intrusion of deep-seated plutons (e.g., Aptian, Lower Saxony Basin, Chapter 6). Particularly, pull-apart structures at the termination of major intracratonic wrench faults, such as the Oslo Graben, can be highly volcanic with magmatic activity persisting for some time even after wrench deformations have ceased (Chapter 3; Plate 6). This indicates that major wrench-fault systems probably transect the entire crust and possibly also the subcrustal lithosphere. Alternatively, at least one of the moving blocks may be decoupled from the underlying mantle.

In complex wrench zones associated with large-scale lateral displacements, transpressional and transtensional deformations can apparently alternate (e.g., Arctic–North Atlantic

NAPPE EMPLACEMENT

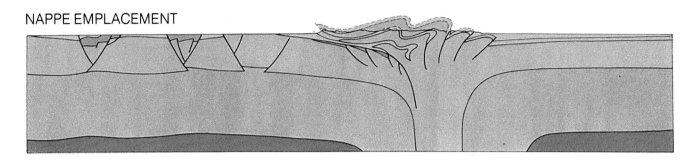

COLLISION

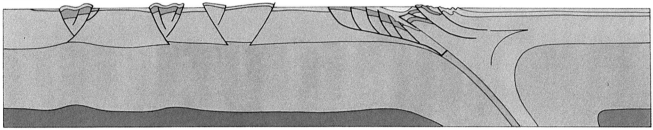

CONVERGENCE

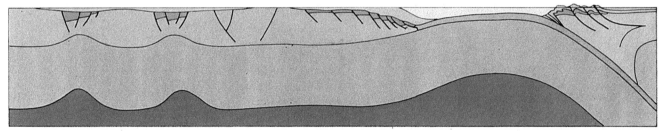

CRUSTAL EXTENSION

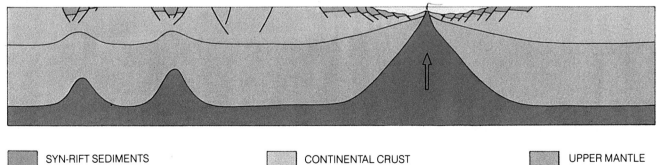

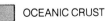

| | SYN-RIFT SEDIMENTS | | CONTINENTAL CRUST | | UPPER MANTLE |
| | POST-RIFT AND SYNOROGENIC SEDIMENTS | | OCEANIC CRUST | | ASTHENOSPHERE |

*Figure 80—Tectonic model illustrating the development of tensional intraplate discontinuities and their reactivation during a collisional event. Not to scale.*

megashear, Chapter 2). This is probably a function of changing local stress patterns with increasing strain.

## Rift-Related Wrench Deformations

Wrench deformations associated with rifting and the opening of oceanic basins can range from local deformations within a rift to regional deformations affecting large areas outside the actual rift zone. In general, the scope of such deformations is directly related to the amount of strain achieved within the respective rift system.

Local wrench deformations within a rift can be associated with transform zones (transfer zones) across which the polarity of asymmetric graben segments changes (Bally, 1982; Angelier and Bergerat, 1983). Similarly oblique extension across a major rift system can be accompanied by the development of negative and positive wrench-induced "flower structures" (Beach, 1985).

In multidirectional rift systems, progressive crustal extension is intimately coupled with wrench movements that locally can lead to transpressional deformations. This is evident, for instance, in the structural style of the Jurassic series in the Mid-Norway Basin (Bukovics et al., 1984). In large multidirectional rift systems, such as the Triassic Tethys rift system, synrift transpressional deformations can assume rather important proportions as illustrated by the Montenegrian folding phase of the Carnic–South Alpine domain (Chapter 5).

Furthermore, important transtensional and transpressional deformations can be associated with wrench faults that offset rift segments or against which major rifts terminate. Examples in case are the complex transform system linking the southern end of the Cenozoic Rhine Graben with the northern end of the Bresse Graben (Bergerat, 1977; Rat, 1978), the late Paleozoic and Mesozoic Svalbard–Northeast Greenland oblique-slip zone compensating for crustal extension in the Norwegian–Greenland Sea (Chapter 4), and the fault systems of southern England and the Paris Basin along which Mesozoic crustal distension in the graben systems of the Western Approaches–Celtic Sea area was taken up by sinistral wrench movements (Fig. 31; Ziegler, 1982a). The classical example of major rift-related wrench faulting is the Dead Sea transform zone that came into evidence in conjunction with the evolution of the Red Sea Rift (Plates 20, 21). Development of this major geofracture was accompanied by compressional deformation of the Sinai and Palmyra fold belts, the tensional subsidence of the Dead Sea Rift, and the extrusion of major flood basalt sheets in Syria and Jordan (Garfunkel, 1981; Quennell, 1984; Chorowicz et al., 1987).

Following crustal separation in a rift and the onset of sea-floor spreading, wrench deformations associated with transform faults delimiting the newly forming oceanic basin can be greatly amplified. This is illustrated for example by the Eurekan and Spitsbergen transpressional deformations along the northern margin of the Greenland Craton that accompanied sea-floor spreading in the Labrador Sea–Baffin Bay and the opening of the northern North Atlantic–Norwegian–Greenland Sea (Chapter 8). Similarly, the Late Jurassic-Early Cretaceous transtensional opening of oceanic basins in the Western Mediterranean can be related to sinistral movements along the Western Tethys transform shear zone compensating for sea-floor spreading in the Central Atlantic (Chapter 8).

Furthermore, in Northwest Europe, the Late Jurassic-Early Cretaceous wrench-induced inversion of rift basins, which was accompanied by the subsidence of new transtensional basins (Chapter 6; Ziegler 1982a), reflects a change in the regional stress pattern. This change in the regional stress field was probably the direct consequence of crustal separation in the Tethys and continued crustal extension in the Arctic–North Atlantic rift system. The resultant "polarization" of the Northwest European rift system reflects its adaptation to the new regional stress regime.

## Collision-Related Wrench Tectonics

Consolidation of the Himalayan-type Variscan fold belt, in response to the dextral oblique collision of Gondwana and Laurussia, was accompanied by important wrench deformations, oroclinal bending, and the rotation of individual blocks. In this context, indenter effects of, for instance, the stable Aquitaine–Cantabrian block, played an important role (Matte, 1986; Chapter 3; Plate 5).

Similarly, major wrench-fault systems, transecting the Alpine fold belts of the Mediterranean area, developed during the Neogene, Late Alpine orogenic cycle (Plates 19–21). Evolution of these fault systems can be related, on the one hand, to a reorientation of the collision direction of Africa and Europe and, on the other hand, to the progressive indentation of the Arabian Craton into the East Mediterranean fold belt and also to the draping of fold belts around the stable Apulian block. This was accompanied by "escape tectonics" that apparently underlie the Neogene evolution of the Carpathians and the Hellenic arc and the partly wrench-induced subsidence of the Aegean and Pannonian back-arc basins (Chapter 9).

An even more dramatic phase of wrench faulting affected the Variscan fold belt immediately after its consolidation during the latest Carboniferous–Early Permian Alleghenian diastrophism of the Appalachians (Chapter 3). These late Hercynian wrench deformations are thought to reflect a reorientation of the convergence direction between Gondwana and Laurussia. They resulted in the disintegration of the Variscan fold belt, which ceased during the Early Permian to play the role of a coherent morphotectonic unit. The late Hercynian system of wrench faults transecting the Variscan fold belt and its foreland is interpreted as representing a diffuse, dextral transform plate boundary between Africa and Europe.

Wrench-fault systems transecting young or still active fold belts can trigger an intense late- to post-orogenic volcanism that is of a calc-alkaline to basaltic composition. Deep crustal fracturing presumably facilitates the initial ascent of subduction-related anatectically remobilized crustal and upper mantle material and, in time also of asthenosphere-derived melts. This is exemplified by the Permo-Carboniferous volcanic surge of Western and Central Europe and the intense Neogene volcanism of Turkey, the Aegean, and also the Pannonian Basin.

## Arctic–North Atlantic Megashear

The Devonian Arctic–North Atlantic megashear evolved during the post-Caledonian plate reorganization out of the Silurian sinistral oblique collision of Laurentia–Greenland and Fennosarmatia (Chapter 2). During the Devonian to earliest Carboniferous, lateral displacements along this complex transform fault system, transecting the axis of the Arctic–North Atlantic Caleonides, were of the order of 1500–2000 km; they were accompanied by transtensional and transpressional deformations. This intracratonic transform plate boundary linked the Acado-Ligerian and Bretonian orogenic systems of the southern margin of Laurussia with the Innuitian (–Lomonosov?) orogen on its northern margin. The driving force of this megashear system, which had remained active from 70 Ma, may be seen in the continued northward subduction of the Proto-Tethys. Significantly, activity along the Arctic–North Atlantic megashear abated with the Early Carboniferous consolidation of the Innuitian (–Lomonosov?) fold belt, and ceased altogether with the Visean onset of the Variscan collision of Gondwana and Laurussia.

In view of its association with the late Caledonian plate reorganization and its geodynamic setting, the Arctic–North Atlantic megashear system can be considered as a special type of postorogenic, intracratonic transform faulting. The magnitude of the postulated translations along this shear system suggest that either the asthenospheric flow regime underlying Laurentia–Greenland differed from that underlying Fennosarmatia or that Fennosarmatia as a whole was fully decoupled from its asthenosphere.

## Wrench Deformations in Prolongation of Oceanic Transform Zones

Particularly during early phases of sea-floor spreading, newly formed passive margins may be repeatedly affected by wrench deformations in the prolongation of oceanic transform faults. Such deformations may or may not trigger igneous activity.

For instance, during the Oligocene reorganization of sea-floor spreading axes in the Norwegian–Greenland Sea, wrench deformations in the prolongation of the Jan Mayen fracture zone induced the transpressional upwarping of anticlinal features in the Mid-Norway Basin (Chapter 8; Fig. 37). Contemporaneous transpressional deformations are evident in the volcanic Yimir and Wyville Thomson ridges at the northern termination of the Rockall Trough (Fig. 51), and sinistral transtensional faulting induced the subsidence of local pull-apart basins in the Irish Sea–Bristol Channel area (Chapter 9). These deformations are probably related to transform movements along the Iceland–Faeroe Ridge. A similar mechanism may have to be invoked for the mild late Eocene wrench deformations in the northern North Sea, described by Pegrum and Ljones (1984). Furthermore, Oligocene dike intrusions in the Porcupine Trough and in northwestern Ireland are possibly related to small-scale wrench deformations in the prolongation of the Charlie Gibbs fracture zone (Chapters 8 and 9).

Early Cretaceous igneous activity in areas bordering the northern parts of the Central Atlantic was probably also induced by tectonic activity along oceanic transform faults and particularly along the Azores fracture zone, which, at that time, delimited the Central Atlantic Ocean to the north (Chapter 6).

This suggests that stresses exerted on the continental lithosphere in response to differential rates of sea-floor spreading across an oceanic transform zone can be large enough to cause substantial strain. At the same time, this can be taken as evidence for coupling between the oceanic and continental crust and the subcrustal lithosphere and possibly the asthenosphere.

Circumstantial evidence indicates that such passive margin deformations occur only during periods of impeded movement of the diverging continental cratons. However, this concept needs to be tested against a wider set of examples.

## COLLISION ZONES, FOREDEEPS, AND INTRAPLATE COMPRESSIONAL DEFORMATIONS

Orogenic belts that developed during the late Paleozoic to Recent evolution of the Arctic–North Atlantic and Tethys domains can be grouped, in the sense of Uyeda (1982), into Accretion- or Pacific-type and Himalayan-type orogens.

Pacific-type orogens involve the collision of an oceanic and a continental plate whereby allochthonous terranes, forming part of the oceanic plate, are being pulled into the arc-trench system as a consequence of progressive subduction of oceanic lithosphere and become accreted to the continental plate. This model can be applied, for instance, to the Caledonian, Acado-Ligerian, and Bretonian orogens that evolved during the Silurian and Devonian along the southern margin of Laurussia as a consequence of the northward subduction of Proto-Tethys. The Mesozoic Cimmerian orogen of the Eastern Mediterranean area, which developed in response to the activation of the Mesozoic Tethys sea-floor spreading axis, also conforms essentially to this model.

Himalayan-type orogens involve the collision of two continental cratons and generally develop out of a Pacific-type setting by subduction of major oceanic basins. Examples are the Arctic–North Atlantic Caledonides, possibly the Innuitian fold belt, the Hercynian Appalachian, Variscan, and Uralian orogens, and also the Alpine orogen of the Eastern Mediterranean area.

All of these fold belts were associated with long-standing B-subduction zones along which old oceanic lithosphere was consumed. The consolidation of these fold belts was accompanied by an often intense synorogenic calc-alkaline magmatism, indicative of anatectic remobilization of substantial amounts of subducted lower crustal and upper mantle material.

Exceptions are the Alpine fold belts of the Western and Central Mediterranean in which subduction-related magmatism plays a very subordinate role (Chapter 9). These fold belts are not associated with long-standing arc-trench systems and the closure of old oceanic basins.

In the Western and Central Mediterranean, lithospheric imbrications, involving relatively young oceanic crust, developed during the Late Cretaceous in response to the build-up of regional compressional stresses. These were induced by the northward drift of Africa–Arabia as a consequence of sea-floor spreading in the South Atlantic–Indian Ocean. Initiation of these subduction zones cannot be related to the gravitational sinking of old oceanic crust and subcrustal lithosphere into the asthenosphere, but rather to "ridge push." In this context, it should be kept in mind that on a finite globe, the generation of new oceanic crust must be compensated by plate consumption elsewhere (Forsyth and Uyeda, 1975; McKenzie, 1977; Bott, 1982; Cloetingh and Wortel, 1985; Chapter 9).

Similarly, distant "ridge push" is held responsible for limited lithospheric subduction accompanying the consolidation of the Pyrenean orogen (Chapter 9) and also of the Eurekan fold belt of Northwest Greenland and the Canadian Arctic Islands (Chapter 8).

Once regional stresses governing such "passive" collisions relax, e.g., due to decay of the respective spreading systems, the corresponding orogens become inactive and subduction processes cease abruptly. This is illustrated by the Eurekan fold belt that became inactive with the termination of sea-floor spreading in the Labrador Sea–Baffin Bay (Chapter 8). Depending on the amount of lithospheric shortening achieved in such "passive" orogens, they can be associated with or without a limited subduction-related anatectic magmatism (e.g., Southern Alps, Chapter 9; versus Pyrenees, Chapter 9).

Overall, the evolution of the Arctic–North Atlantic and Tethys domains highlights the coincidence of the opening of new oceanic basins, the onset of convergence between cratonic blocks, and the ensuing initiation or acceleration of subduction processes. Examples of this phenomenon are the Triassic development of the Tethys sea-floor spreading axis and the onset of the Cimmerian orogenic cycle (Chapter 5), the Jurassic–Cretaceous opening of the Central Atlantic inducing the collision of the Italo-Dinarid promontory with the southern margin of Europe (Chapter 6), and the Late Cretaceous-Cenozoic opening of the South Atlantic–Indian Ocean causing convergence between Africa and Eurasia and their collision during the Alpine orogenic cycle (Chapters 7 and 9).

This suggests that the primary driving force of plate movements is directly related to the generation of new lithosphere at sea-floor spreading axes ("ridge push") and that tensional forces associated with the gravitational subduction and sinking of old oceanic lithosphere into the asthenosphere (slab pull) probably play a secondary role only. Moreover, circumstantial evidence, as well as present-day stress analyses, indicate that compressional stresses can be transmitted over great distances through continental and oceanic lithosphere (Letouzey and Trémoliére, 1980; Cloetingh and Wortel, 1985). In these processes, drag forces exerted on the lithosphere by asthenospheric flow may play an important role (Forsyth and Uyeda, 1975; McKenzie, 1977; Richter and McKenzie, 1978; Christensen, 1983; Gough, 1984; Wortel, 1986).

## Foredeeps

During the convergence of a continental and an oceanic plate, and particularly during the collision of two continents, A-subduction zones can develop along which continental lithosphere is being consumed (Fig. 2; Bally and Snelson, 1980). Development and progradation of A-subduction zones is generally associated with the obduction of ophiolites, the emplacement of nappes, and large-scale thrusting and décollement folding of the sedimentary cover of the foreland plate; these deformations can also involve the crust of the foreland (e.g., Western and Central Alps; Fig. 58).

The advancing thrust sheets and nappes have a tectonic loading effect on the foreland plate that is amplified when they involve upper crustal material. Through their weight, these allochthonous masses induce the isostatic, viscoelastic downbending of the thick, cold crust and subcrustal lithosphere of the foreland and, by this means, cause the development of foredeep basins (Beaumont, 1978, 1981). Downflexing of the foreland crust can be associated with tensional faulting of its upper parts whereby fault patterns generally parallel the basin axis. Throws on individual faults may be of the order of a few hundred meters with synthetic faults somewhat predominating over antithetic faults (e.g., German and Austrian Molasse Basin, Fig. 63; Chapter 9). However, because in such a setting the lower crust and subcrustal lithosphere are in compression, this type of extension faulting and graben formation is not associated with volcanic activity.

The evolution of many foredeep basins is not, however, associated with the development of flexure-induced normal fault systems. For instance, subsidence of the Apennine foredeep,

which contains up to 7 km of late Miocene to Pleistocene clastics, was accompanied by the imbrication of the thick carbonate series that underlay these clastics (Fig. 65). Similarly, the sedimentary prism of the foreland of the Western Alps became compressionally deformed during the late Alpine orogenic cycle whereby the preexisting incipient early Alpine foredeep basin was destroyed.

During the subsidence of the German and Austrian Alpine Molasse Basin, the advancing nappe systems appear to have been mechanically decoupled from the foreland at the A-subduction zone marking their common boundary (Chapter 9). In this case, continued underthrusting of the foreland, combined with the advance of the nappe systems, caused the migration of the foredeep basin axis toward the foreland. At the same time, tensional fault systems affected progressively more distal* parts of the foredeep. This was coupled with the partial destruction of the deeper, proximal* parts of the foredeep basin that were scooped out by thin-skinned thrust sheets (Fig. 63).

In the case of the Western and Central Alps, emplacement of nappes onto the foreland was accompanied by a stepwise progradation of the A-subduction zone and the imbrication of the foreland crust and its sedimentary cover. This suggests that strong mechanical coupling between the rising orogen and the foreland can induce intense compressional deformation of the foreland whereby preexisting tensional fault systems may be reactivated. This can impede the development of pronounced foredeep basins and/or the destruction of such basins that had developed during earlier orogenic phases (see Rif–Tellian fold belt and Atlas ranges of Morocco and northern Algeria, Chapter 9).

The Cenozoic development of the Alpine–Carpathian foreland does not provide evidence for the development of a pronounced peripheral bulge in response to downflexing of the adjacent foredeep areas (Roeder, 1980; Beaumont, 1981; Quinlan and Beaumont, 1984). This concept, therefore, requires rigorous testing against well-documented examples of foredeep development.

Following the termination of underthrusting/subduction, the thickened lithosphere of a fold belt, which penetrates deep into the asthenosphere, rebounds isostatically in response to heating and its unloading by subaerial erosion. At the same time, the elastically downbent foreland crust is also unloaded and rebounds correspondingly. This mechanism controls the post-orogenic uplift and erosion of foredeep basins (Dickinson, 1976; Bally and Snelson, 1980; Bally, 1981; Beaumont, 1981; Quinlan and Beaumont, 1984).

## Collision-Related Intraplate Compressional Deformations

Intraplate compressional and transpressional deformations related to plate collisions can result at distances of up to 1300 km from the collision front in the uplift of major basement blocks and the inversion of rift- and wrench-induced sedimentary troughs. These deformations involve the reactivation of preexisting intraplate discontinuities. This is exemplified by the Late Carboniferous intraplate deformations in the northern and southern forelands of the Variscan fold belt (Chapter 1; Ziegler 1982a), the Permian inversion of grabens in the Timan-

---

*proximal: near thrust front; distal: near foreland edge of foredeep.

Pechora area forming the foreland of the northern Uralides (Chapter 3), and the latest Cretaceous and Cenozoic deformations in the northern and southern forelands of the Alpine orogen (Chapters 7, 9; Ziegler 1987c).

Furthermore, circumstantial evidence points to the likelihood that compressional stresses can be transmitted through continental and oceanic lithosphere over even greater distances than the most distal observed megascopic deformations. For instance, tangential compressional stresses impeded the Senonian northward propagation of the Rockall sea-floor spreading axis and the Paleocene opening of the northern North Atlantic and the Norwegian–Greenland Sea (Chapter 8).

Among different intraplate discontinuities, rifts with a strongly thinned crust appear to be prone to early inversion in response to collision-related intraplate tangential compressional stresses. Major wrench faults, which penetrate much of the crust and possibly extend into the upper mantle, are also prone to compressional reactivation. On the other hand, thrust faults and ancient A-subduction zones appear less prone to compressional reactivation; this contrasts with their frequently observed tensional reactivation.

Depending on the pattern of preexisting intraplate discontinuities, the boundary between an orogen and compressional intraplate deformations can become diffuse, as for instance in the Western Alps.

The structural style of inverted basins and associated basement uplifts indicate that these deformations were accompanied by a commensurate amount of crustal shortening. Correspondingly, collision-related compressional intraplate deformations require, on the one hand, a certain amount of coupling, facilitating stress transmission, between the foreland plate and the associated orogen at the A-subduction zone marking their common boundary (Fig. 80). On the other hand, within the foreland plate, a decoupling is required at intracrustal levels (low-velocity channel?), at the crust–mantle boundary or possibly within the upper mantle or even at the base of the lithosphere to accommodate crustal shortening associated with the inversion of basins and the uptilting of basement blocks along steep reverse faults. Major inversion features such as the Pyrenees are probably associated with the development of lithospheric subduction zones rooting locally in the asthenosphere.

The example of the Polish Trough suggests that during inversion, the thinned crust of a rift can be mechanically thickened as a result of crustal shortening (Chapter 7). Depending on the degree of inversion, an abandoned rift with a thermally still destabilized upper mantle may, by a commensurate thickening of the lithosphere, attain isostatic and thermal stability.

The evolution of the Rhône–Bresse–Rhine graben system and of the North Atlantic–Norwegian–Greenland Sea rift system illustrate that compressional, intraplate stresses can apparently interfere with the evolution of an active rift system and impede its development (Chapter 9).

The timing of inversion of the different Mesozoic grabens in the Alpine foreland of Europe indicates that rifts with strongly attenuated crust, forming the "weakest" link in a chain of inversion-prone basins, will deform first. This can lead to either a "retrogradation" (backward, orogen-ward stepping) or a "progradation" (forward, foreland-ward stepping) of inversion movements (Ziegler, 1987c).

It is uncertain whether the yield strength of a rift zone, which is subjected to tangential compressional stresses, is purely controlled by its crustal thickness (degree of crustal attenuation) or whether its thermal regime and lithospheric configuration also play an important role.

Empirically, it appears plausible that, under the assumption of similar crustal attenuation, the thermally destabilized crust and subcrustal lithosphere of an active rift (e.g., Rhine Graben) has a lower yield strength than that of a thermally stabilized paleorift. On the other hand, the example of the Paleozoic Ougarta Rift (Fig. 8), which was inverted during Late Carboniferous and again during the Cenozoic, shows that stabilized paleorifts can also be deformed under conditions of intense foreland compression.

The stratigraphic record of collision-related intraplate compressional deformations can provide valuable information on the dating of major orogenic events affecting the collisional margin of the respective plate and thus can complement the stratigraphic record preserved in the corresponding orogen. In this context, it should be kept in mind that within orogenic systems the stratigraphic record of earlier orogenic events is often cannibalized during subsequent deformation phases. Moreover, the emplacement of major nappes can mask the stratigraphic record preserved in their substratum.

Although compressional intraplate deformations appear to be most commonly associated with Himalayan-type orogens (e.g., Variscan, Uralian, and Alpine foreland deformations), they can also be associated with Pacific- or Accretion-type orogens that formed in response to the high convergence rate between a continental and an oceanic plate (e.g., Argentinian Andean foreland, Rocky Mountains).

The lack of compressional intraplate deformations in the foreland of an orogen can be related either to the absence of major intraplate discontinuities in the respective foreland and/or to the lack of mechanical coupling between it and the orogen during the evolution of the latter.

The mechanisms that govern the coupling, or the lack thereof, between a foreland plate and its associated orogen at an A-subduction zone are not yet understood but could possibly be a function of the crustal configuration of the collisionally involved passive margin (abrupt crustal thinning versus gentle basement ramp covered by a thick passive margin sedimentary prism), the rate of convergence, and whether or not crustal delamination of the overriding plate facilitates the obduction of major basement-cored nappes.

For example, the main phases of compressional deformations in the foreland of the Eastern Alps and Northern Carpathians appear to correlate with the initial phases of collision of the Austro-Alpine and Penninic nappe complexes with the North European foreland (Chapter 7). During the subsequent phase of emplacement of these basement-cored nappes, the orogen and the foreland were apparently largely decoupled (Chapter 9; Figs. 63, 80).

On the other hand, in the Western and Central Alps, in which corresponding basement-cored nappes play a far smaller role (Debelmas et al., 1983), coupling between the orogen and the foreland seems to have gradually increased during the Oligocene and Miocene as illustrated by the uplift of the external Alpine massifs and the inversion of Mesozoic basins in the Celtic Sea–Western Approaches area (Figs. 68, 69).

Finally, it should be noted that compressional/transpressional intraplate deformations, resulting in the inversion of sedimentary basins, can also occur under nonorogenic settings. For example, the Early Tertiary inversion of the Central African Benue, Bongor, and Doseo troughs (Ngaoundere rift) reflects a fundamental change in the overall stress pattern affecting

Africa, which can be related to the opening of the South Atlantic-Indian Ocean and the ensuing modification of the drift direction of Africa (Olade, 1975; Browne and Fairhead, 1983). Similarly, the Late Jurassic–Early Cretaceous polarization of the Northwest European rift systems was associated with wrench-induced partial inversion of, for instance, the West-Netherlands and Broad Fourteen basins (see Chapter 9, *Rift-Related Wrench Deformations*).

Overall, circumstantial evidence suggests, however, that the most important intraplate compressional/transpressional deformations, such as those in the Alpine, Uralian, North American Cordilleran, and Andean foreland can be related to orogenic events affecting the respective foldbelts.

# RELATIVE AND EUSTATIC SEA-LEVEL CHANGES

Changes in sea level have an overprinting effect on the tectonic subsidence of basins by altering, apart from the water load on the crust, the erosional base level or, in other words, the level to which sediments can accumulate (Sleep, 1976; Bond, 1978).

Curves describing changes in sea level through time have been presented by Vail et al. (1977), Hallam (1978, 1984), and others (Watts and Thorne, 1984; Heller and Angevine, 1985; Haq et al., 1987). Since these publications, mechanisms underlying changes in sea level have been debated and their significance in terms of global eustasy and/or only regional validity as "relative sea-level changes" has been the source of much controversy.

Truly eustatic, global sea-level changes are thought to result, for example, from changes in the water mass stored in polar ice-caps or from changes in volume of the oceanic basins.

Glacioeustatic sea-level changes can only be invoked for periods during which continents occupied high latitudinal positions, thus providing for the development of major grounded ice-sheets. The sedimentary record of Gondwana gives evidence for its partial glaciation during the Late Ordovician to Middle Silurian and during the Late Devonian to early Late Permian (Hambrey and Harland, 1981; Caputo and Crowell, 1985). Although not documented by a corresponding stratigraphic record, it cannot be precluded that minor continental ice-caps existed in Gondwana during the Late Silurian to Middle Devonian. Similarly, the cyclicity of Upper Permian series suggests that either remanent ice-sheets existed in Gondwana or that new ones developed in northeastern Siberia which, by this time, had moved into a polar position (Ustritsky, 1973; Smith and Briden, 1977; Kanasewich et al., 1978; Firstbrook et al., 1979; Scotese et al., 1980). Northeast Siberia remained in a polar position until Early Cretaceous times; this is supported by the occurrence of glaciomarine deposits ranging in age from Early Jurassic to Barremian (Epshteyn, 1978; Kaplan, 1978; Brandt, 1986). In Antarctica, major inland ice-caps developed again during the Eocene, and ice cover became pervasive during the Middle Oligocene. In Arctic areas, mountain glaciation commenced during the Miocene and regional ice-sheets developed during the Pleistocene (Hambrey and Harland, 1981).

This indicates that from Late Ordovician time onward, the globe was probably truly ice-free for relatively short periods only whereby the mass of water stored on the continents was subject to major short-term and long-term fluctuations, giving rise to important glacioeustatic sea-level changes.

Changes in the ocean volume may have been induced by changes in the ocean ridge geometry due to acceleration or deceleration of the spreading rates, by uplift and subsidence of intraoceanic plateaux, or by the desiccation and flooding of restricted basins (Pitman, 1978; Donovan and Jones, 1979; Pitman and Golovchenko, 1983; Hallam, 1984; Kominz, 1984). In this context, periods of major plate reorganizations, following the assembly of a supercontinent, such as Pangea at the end of the Hercynian orogenic cycles, which involve rifting and later the opening of new oceanic basins, and consequently changes in the global average age of oceanic crust and ocean depth, are apparently associated with significant long-term eustatic sea-level changes (Schwan, 1980; Bally, 1982). The model of Heller and Angevine (1985) predicts that a rifting-induced increase of the percentage of the globe occupied by continental crust, followed by the opening of Atlantic-type oceans (rimmed by passive margins), is associated with a gradual eustatic rise in sea level. On the other hand, the initiation of major orogenic cycles, involving the conversion of Atlantic-type oceans into Pacific-type oceans (rimmed by subduction zones) and collisional reduction of the percentage of the earth's surface occupied by continents, is associated with a eustatic fall in sea level. This model appears to be successful insofar as it provides a rationale for the first-order sea-level high stands during the Ordovician and Late Cretaceous, the Permian–Triassic low stand in sea level, and the Cenozoic fall in sea level.

Possible other, though not readily verifiable, mechanisms for eustatic changes in sea level could be limited changes in the radius of the globe (McElhinny et al., 1978; Stewart, 1978) combined with changes in the volume of the hydrosphere due to its continued dewatering.

Furthermore, the magnitude of eustatic sea-level changes has been the subject of considerably divergent views (see Hallam, 1984). Heller and Angevine (1985) suggest for post-Paleozoic sea-level changes an amplitude of less than 200 m and assume that larger deviations were probably caused by local or regional deformation of the lithosphere.

The sedimentary record of most basins reflects repeated changes in erosional base level. Often it is, however, difficult to distinguish between regressions and transgressions that were caused by tectonic phenomena directly affecting the area under consideration and those that were induced by events lying beyond the frame of the area under study. In view of these uncertainties it has become customary to refer to such sea-level changes as "relative changes of sea level" (Vail et al., 1977).

The relative changes of sea-level curves of Vail et al. (1977) and Haq et al. (1987), which were derived from the cumulative seismostratigraphic record of a considerable number of sedimentary basins, are heavily weighted by data from basins flanking the Gulf of Mexico and the Central and North Atlantic. The sedimentary and tectonic record of the basins of Northwest Europe reflects a close correlation between tectonic events and short-term relative sea-level fluctuations as given by the Vail (1977) curve (Ziegler, 1982a). This, in combination with the acceptance of the concept that tectonic stresses of a tensional as well as a compressional nature can induce wide radius lithospheric deformations in continental cratons, has led to the hypothesis that short-term regional relative changes in sea level may, among others, result from changes in paleo-stress conditions (Cloetingh, 1986a, 1986b; Lambeck et al., 1987). Based on this concept, it appears plausible that during periods of major plate reorganization, intraplate stresses affecting large areas can cause lithospheric deformations giving rise to short-term changes of the erosional base level that interfere with long-term and short-term eustatic sea-level changes. Furthermore, deflection of the lithosphere caused by sediment, ice, or tectonic loading can also induce regionally important changes in relative sea level (Cloetingh et al., 1985).

Regional stress patterns affecting the subsidence of sedimentary basins and in part also causing their destruction are related to plate boundary forces and to deep intra-asthenospheric processes. The latter are thought to govern the present-day shape of the geoid that has a relief of about 180 m. The geological record of the globe gives evidence for nearly continuously changing lithospheric plate configurations. These probably reflect changes in the asthenospheric flow patterns, which, in turn, were presumably associated with changes of the geoid shape. On a global scale, changes of the geoid shape are in all likelihood compensatory in the sense that certain areas become uplifted while others subside. Resultant changes in relative sea level are therefore neither global nor uniformly positive or negative and are thus not of a eustatic nature (Chase, 1979; Mörner, 1977, 1981; Bowin, 1983, 1985; McKenzie et al., 1980).

Relative sea-level changes induced by changes of the geoid shape and by lithospheric stresses interfere with such truly eustatic sea-level changes as induced, for instance, by continental glaciations (Peltier, 1980). This illustrates that relative change in sea level can be the product of a multitude of different mechanisms. This emphasizes the need for establishing sea-level fluctuation curves for individual basins and casts doubt on the reliability of correlations based on short-term superregional depositional sequence boundaries, particularly if these do not coincide with periods or epochs of major continental glaciations.

# POSTSCRIPT

*Si non è vero,*
*è ben trovato*
(Italian Proverb)

This volume presents the author's attempt at a stepwise reconstruction of the mid-Paleozoic to Recent evolution of the Arctic–North Atlantic and Western Tethys domain.

During the integration of the mass of geological and geophysical data available to the author, he has drawn widely on the experience of his colleagues, and their contributions are here fully acknowledged. The product of this compilation is, however, the author's sole responsibility, and he bears the blame for misinterpretations and the omission of important facts. Moreover, the author recognizes that, having dared to extend some of his interpretations to the limit, he may have arrived at some hypotheses that are difficult to defend on the basis of the available data. An effort has been made to make the reader aware of such potentially controversial points.

During the preparation of the maps and text making up this volume, the writer was well aware of the limitations placed on him by data availability for certain areas and by his capacity to integrate and synthesize the pertinent multilingual literature. Much could have been gained by involving a much broader international group of earth scientists in this project, perhaps at the expense of never getting it completed.

Nevertheless, the writer believes that this compilation, despite its shortcomings, was well worthwhile if it can be used as a frame upon which others can build.

# REFERENCES

Abbate E., Bortolotti V., Passerini P., and Sangri M., 1980, Introduction to the geology of the Northern Apennines: Sed. Geol., 4:207–249.

Adamia S. A., Chkhotua T., Kelelia M., Lordkipanidze M., and Shavishvili I., 1981, Tectonics of the Caucasus and adjoining regions: Implications for the evolution of the Tethys Ocean: J. Struct. Geol. 3(4):437–447.

Adrichem-Boogaert H.A. van and Burgers W.F.J., 1983, The development of the Zechstein in the Netherlands, in J.P.H. Kaasschieter and T.J.A. Reijers (eds.), Petroleum geology of the southeastern North Sea and adjacent onshore areas: Spec. Ed. Geol. Mijnbouw 62:83–92.

Ager D.V., 1956, The geographical distribution of brachiopods in the British middle Lias: Q. J. Geol. Soc. London 112:157–182.

Ager D.V., 1974, The Western High Atlas of Morocco and their significance in the history of the North Atlantic: Proc. Geol. Assoc. 85:23–41.

Ager D.V., 1975, The Jurassic world ocean (with special reference to the North Atlantic), in K.G. Finstad and R.C. Selley (eds.), Jurassic North Sea Symposium 1975: Norw. Petrol. Soc. JNNSS/2 p. 1–24.

Ahorner L., Baier B. and Bonjer K.P., 1983, General patterns of seismotectonic dislocation and earthquake-generating stressfield in Central Europe between the Alps and the North Sea, in K. Fuchs, K. von Gehlen, H. Malzer, H. Murawski, and A. Semmel (eds.), Plateau uplift, the Rhenish Shield, a case history. Berlin Heidelberg New York Tokyo; Springer-Verlag, p. 187–197.

Alberti H., Schüffler S., Solonwar R., Stoppel D., Wachendorf H. and Walliser O., 1977, Palaegraphische und tektonische Entwicklung des Westharzes: Exkursionsführer Geo-Tagung 77, Univ. Göttingen Publ. p. 171–221.

Aleinikov A.L., Bellavin O.V., Bulashevich Y.P., Tarvin I.F., Maksimov E.M., Rudkevich M.Y., Nalivkin V.D., Shablinskaya N.V. and Sutkov V.S., 1980, Dynamics of the Russian and West Siberian Platforms, in A.W. Bally, P.L. Bender, T.R. McGretchin and R.I. Walcott (eds.), Dynamics of plate interiors. Am. Geophys. Union, Geol. Soc. Am., Geodynam. Ser. 1: 53–72.

Allen P., 1976, Wealden of the Weald: A new model: Proc. Geol. Assoc. 86:389–437.

Allen P., 1981, Pursuit of Wealde models: J. Geol. Soc. London 138:375–405.

Allmendinger R.W., Sharp J.W., Tish D. von, Serpa L., Brown L., Kaufmann S. and Oliver J., 1983, Cenozic and Mesozoic structure of the eastern Basin and Range province of Utah, from COCORP seismic reflection data: Geology 11: 532–536.

Alvarado M., 1980, Introducción a la Geología de Espana: Bol. Geol. Min. XCI-I:1–65.

Alvarez F., Virieux J. and Le Pichon X., 1984, Thermal consequences of lithospheric extension over continental margins: The initial stretching phase: Geophys. J.R. Astr. Soc. London 78: 389–411.

Anadón P., Cabrera L., Guimerà J. and Santanch P., 1985, Paleogene strike-slip deformation and sedimentation along the southeastern margin of the Ebro Basin, in K.T. Biddle and N. Christie-Blick (eds.), Strike-slip deformation, basin formation and sedimentation: Soc. Econ. Paleont. Mineral. Spec. Publ. 37:302–318.

Anderton R., Bridges P.H., Leeder M.R. and Sellwood B.W., 1979, A dynamic stratigraphy of the British Isles: A study in crustal evolution: London, George Allen & Unwin, 301 p.

André L., Hertogen J. and Deutsch S., 1986, Ordovician-Silurian magmatic provinces in Belgium and the Caledonian orogeny in middle Europe: Geology 14:879–882.

Angelier J. and Bergerat F., 1983, Systèmes de contrainte et extension intracontinentale: Bull. Cent. Rech.-Expl. Elf-Aquitaine 7(1):137–147.

Angelier J. and Le Pichon X., 1980, Néotectonique horizontale et verticale de l'Egée: Subduction et expansion, in J. Aubouin, J. Debelmas and M. Latreille (eds.), Géologie de chaines alpines issues de la Tethys: Mem. B.R.G.M. 115: 249–260.

Angelier J., Lybéris N., Le Pichon X., Barrier E., and Huchon P., 1982, The tectonic development of the Hellenic Arc and the Sea of Crete: A synthesis: Tectonophysics 86:159–196.

Antunes M.T., Ferreira M.P., Rocha R.B., Soares A.F. and Zbyszewski G., 1980, Essai de réconstruction paleogéographique par cycle orogénique—le cycle Alpine, in Portugal, introduction à la géologie générale: 26th Internat. Geol. Congr., guide book; Excursion 016A-045A, p. 45–89.

Arbey F. and Tamain G., 1971, Existence d'une glaciation Siluro-Ordovicienne en Sierra Morena (Espagne): C.R. Acad. Sci. Paris 272 (Ser. D):1721–1723.

Argyriadis I., de Graciansky P.C., Marcoux J. and Ricou L.E., 1980, The opening of the Mesozoic Tethys between Eurasia and Arabia-Africa, in Géologie des chaînes alpines issues de la Tethys: 26th Internat. Geol. Congr. Paris, Coll. 05; Mem. B.R.G.M. 115:198–214.

Arthaud F. and Matte P., 1977, Late Palaeozoic strike-slip faulting in southern Europe and North Africa: Results of a right-lateral shear zone between the Appalachians and the Urals: Geol. Soc. Am. Bull. 88:1305–1320.

Arthur K.R., Cole D.R., Henderson G.G.L. and Kushnir D.W., 1982, Geology of the Hibernia discovery, in M.T. Halbouty (ed.), The deliberate search for the subtle trap: Am. Assoc. Petrol. Geol. Mem. 32:181–195.

Artyushkov E.V., 1983, Geodynamics: Development in Geotectonics 18, Amsterdam/Oxford/New York/Tokyo, Elsevier, 312 p.

Artyushkov E.V. and Baer M.A., 1983, Mechanism of continental crust subsidence in fold belts: The Urals, Appalachians and Scandinavian Caledonides: Tectonophysics 100:5–42.

Artyushkov E.V., Baer M.A., and Mikhail A., 1986, Mechanism of formation of hydrocarbon basins: The West Siberian, Volga-Ural, Timan-Pechora and the Permian Basin of Texas: Tectonophysics 122: 3–4.

Aubouin J., 1973, Des tectoniques superposées et de leur signification par rapport aux modèles géophysiques: l'exemple des Dinarides: Paléotectonique, Tectonique, Tarditectonique, Néo-Tectonique: Bull. Soc. Géol. France (7)XV(5-6):426–460.

Aubouin J., Blanchet R., Cadet J.P., Celet P., Charvet J., Chorowicz J., Cousin M. and Rampnoux J.P., 1970, Essai sur la géologie des Dinarides: Bull. Soc. Géol. France (7)XII(69):1060–1095.

Autran A. and Cogné J., 1980, La zone interne de l'orogène Varisque dans l'ouest de la France et sa place dans le développment de la chaîne Hercynienne: Mem. B.R.G.M. 108:90–111.

Autran A. and Dercourt J. (eds.), 1980, Evolution géologique de la France: Mem. B.R.G.M. 107:335 p.

Avedik F., Camus A.L., Ginzburg A., Montadert L., Roberts D.G. and Whitemarsh R.B., 1982, A seismic refraction and reflection study of the continent-ocean transition beneath the North Biscay Margin: Phil.-Trans. R. Soc. London 305 Ser. A:5–25.

Azema J., Bourrouilh R., Champetier Y., Fourcade E. and Rangheard Y., 1974, Rapports stratigraphiques, paléogéographiques et structuraux entre la Chaîne Ibérique, les Cordillières bétiques et les Baléares: Bull. Soc. Géol. France (7)XVI(2):140–159.

Azema J. et al., 1979, Las Microfacies del Jurassico y Cretacico de las zonas externas de las Cordilleras Beticas: University of Granada Publ., 83 p.

Bachmann G.H., Müller M. and Weggen K., 1987, Late Paleozoic to Early Tertiary evolution of the Molasse Basin (Germany, Switzerland): Tectonophysics 137:77–92.

Badham G.P.N., 1982, Strike-slip orogens—an extrapolation for the Hercynides: J. Geol. Soc. Lond. 13A: 493–504.

Baird R.A., 1986, Maturation and source rock evaluation of Kimmeridge Clay, Norwegian North Sea: Bull. Am. Assoc. Petrol. 70(1):1–11.

Baker A.J. and Gayer, R.A., 1985, Caledonide-Appalachian tectonic analysis and evolution of related oceans, *in* R.A. Gayer (ed.), The tectonic evolution of the Caledonide-Appalachian Orogen: Braunschweig/Wiesbaden, Fried. Vieweg & Son, p. 126–165.

Balkwill H.R., 1978, Evolution of Sverdrup Basin, Arctic Canada: Bull. Am. Assoc. Petrol. Geol. 62:1004–1028.

Balkwill H.R. and Bustin R.M., 1980, Late Phanerozoic structures, Canadian Arctic Archipelago: Palaeogeogr., Palaeoclim., Palaeoecol. 30:219–227.

Balkwill H.R. and Fox F.G., 1982, Incipient rift zone, Western Sverdrup Basin, Arctic Canada, *in* A.F. Embry and H.R. Balkwill (eds.), Arctic geology and geophysics: Can. Soc. Petrol. Geol. Mem. 8:171–186.

Bally A.W., 1981, Thoughts on the tectonics of folded belts, *in* K.R. McClay and N.J. Price (eds.), Thrust and nappe tectonics: Geol. Soc. London Spec. Publ. 9:13–32.

Bally A.W., 1982; Musing over sedimentary basin evolution, *in* Sir Peter Kent, M.H.P. Bott, D.P. McKenzie and C.A. Williams (eds.), The evolution of sedimentary basins: Phil. Trans. R. Soc. London 305A:325–338.

Bally A.W., 1984, Tectogenèse et sismique réflexion: Bull. Soc. Géol. France (7)XIV(2):279–285.

Bally A.W. and Snelson S., 1980, Realms of subsidence, *in* A.D. Miall (ed.), Facts and principles of world petroleum occurrence: Can. Soc. Petrol. Geol. Mem. 6:9–94.

Barbier F., Duvergé J. and Le Pichon X., 1986, Structure profonde de la marge Nord-Gascogne. Implications sur le méchanisme de rifting et de formation de la marge continentale: Bull. Cent. Rech. Expl.-Prod. Elf- Aquitaine 10(1):105–121.

Barnard P.C. and Cooper B.S., 1981, Oils and source rocks of the North Sea area, *in* L.V. Illing and G.D. Hobson (eds.), Petroleum geology of the continental shelf of north-west Europe: London, Heyden and Son, p. 169–175.

Barr S.M., Brisebois D. and MacDonald A.S., 1985, Carboniferous volcanic rocks of the Magdalen Islands, Gulf of St. Lawrence: Can. J. Earth Sci. 22:1679–1688.

Bartley J.M. and Wernicke B.P., 1984, The Snake Range décollement interpreted as a major extensional shear zone: Tectonics 3:647–683.

Barton P. and Wood R., 1984, Tectonic evolution of the North Sea Basin-crustal stretching and subsidence: Geophys. J.R. Astr. Soc. 79:987–1022.

Batten D.J., 1982, Palynology of shales associated with the Kap Washington Group volcanics, Central North Greenland: Grønlands Geol. Unders. Rapp. 108:15–23.

Baudrimont A.P. and Dubois P., 1977, Un bassin Mésogéen du domaine péri-Alpin: Le sud-est de la France: Bull. Cent. Rech. Explor.-Prod. Elf-Aquitaine 1(1):261–308.

Beach A., 1985, Some comments on sedimentary basin development in the northern North Sea: Scott. J. Geol. 21(4):493–512.

Beauchamp J. and Petit J.P., 1983, Sédimentation et taphrogenèse Triassique du Maroc: L'exemple du Haute Atlas de Marrakech: Bull. Cent. Rech. Expl.-Prod. Elf-Aquitaine 7(1):389–397.

Beaumont C., 1978, The evolution of sedimentary basins on a viscoelastic lithosphere: Theory and examples: Geophys. J. R. Astr. Soc. 55:471–497.

Beaumont C., 1981, Foreland basins: Geophys. J.R. Astr. Soc. 65:291–329.

Beaumont C. and Sweeney J.F., 1978, Graben generation of major sedimentary basins: Tectonophysics 50:T19–T23.

Beaumont C., Keen C.E. and Boutillier R., 1982a, Comparison of foreland and Atlantic type basins, *in* Sir Peter Kent, M.H.P. Bott, D.P. McKenzie and C.A. Williams (eds.), The evolution of sedimentary basins: Phil. Trans. R. Soc., London, 305A:295–317.

Beaumont C., Keen C.E. and Boutillier R., 1982b, On the evolution of rifted continental margins: Comparison of models and observation for the Nova Scotian margin: R. Astr. Soc. Geophys. J. 70:667–715.

Beccaluva L. and Piccardo G.B., 1978, Petrology of the northern Apennine ophiolites and their significance in the western Mediterranean area, *in* H. Closs, D. Roeder and K. Schmidt (eds.), Alps, Apennines, Hellenides: Inter-Union Commission on Geodynamics, Sci. Rept. No. 38, Stuttgart, E. Schweizerbart'sche Verlagsbuchhandlung, p. 243–253.

Bechstädt T., 1978, Faziesanalyse permischer und triadischer Sedimente des Drauzuges als Hinweis auf eine grossräumige Lateralverschiebung innerhald des Ostalpins: Jb. Geol. A-B (Wien) 121 (1):1–121.

Bechstädt T., Brandner R., Mostler H. and Schmidt K., 1978, Aborted rifting in the Triassic of the eastern and southern Alps: N. Jb. Geol. Palaeont. Abh. 156(2):157–178.

Beck R.A. and Lehner P., 1973, Oceans, new frontier in exploration: Bull. Am. Assoc. Petrol. Geol. 58:376–395.

Beckinsale R.D., Reading H.G. and Rex D.C., 1975, Potassium-argon ages from basic dykes from eastern Finnmark: Stratigraphic and structural implications: Scott. J. Geol. 12:51–65.

Bédard J.H., 1985, The opening of the Atlantic, the Mesozoic New England igneous province, and mechanisms of continental breakup: Tectonophysics 113:209–232.

Beh R.L., 1975, Evolution and geology of western Baffin Bay and Davis Strait, Canada, *in* C.J. Yorath, E.R. Parker and D.J. Glass (eds.), Canada's continental margins and offshore petroleum exploration: Can. Soc. Petrol. Geol. Mem. 4:453–476.

Behr H.-J., Engel W. and Franke W., 1982, Variscan wildflysch and nappe tectonics in the Saxothuringian zone (northeast Bavaria, West Germany). Am. J. Sci. 282:1438–1470.

Behr H.-J., Engel W., Franke W., Giese P. and Weber K., 1984, The Variscan Belt in Central Europe: Main structure and geodynamic implications: Open questions: Tectonophysics 109:15–40.

Bell J.D., 1976, The Tertiary intrusive complex on the Isle of

Sky: Proc. Geol. Assoc. 87(3):247–271.

Bell J.S, 1973, Late Paleozoic orogeny in the Northern Yukon, *in* J.D. Aitken and D.J. Glass (eds.), Proceedings of th Symposium on the Geology of the Canadian Arctic, Saskatoon, May 1973, Geol. Assoc. Can. and Can. Soc. Petrol. Geol., p. 25–38.

Bell K., Blenkinsop J., Berger A.R. and Jayasinghe N.R., 1979, The Newport granite: Its age, geological setting, and implications for the geology of northeastern Newfoundland: Can. J. Earth Sci. 16:264–269.

Beloussov V.V., 1960, Development of the earth and tectogenesis: J. Geophys. Res. 65:4127–4146.

Beloussov V.V., 1962, Basic problems in geotectonics: New York, McGraw-Hill, 809 p.

Beloussov V.V., 1975, Foundations of geotectonics (in Russian): Moscow, Nyedra, 260 p.

Ben-Avraham Z., Nur A. and Cello G., 1987, Active transcurrent fault system along the North African passive margin: Tectonophysics 141: 249–260.

Berberian M. and King G.C.P., 1981, Towards a paleogeorgraphy and tectonic evolution of Iran: Can. J. Earth Sci. 18:210–265.

Berg J. van den, 1979, Palaeomagnetism and the changing configuration of the western Mediterranean area in the Mesozoic and early Cenozoic eras: Geologica Ultraiectina, Medd. Geol. Inst., Rijksuniversiteit Utrecht No. 20, 179 p.

Berg J. van den, and Zijderveld D.A., 1982, Paleomagnetism in the Mediterranean area, *in* H. Berckhemer and K. Hsü (eds.), Alpine- Mediterranean geodynamics: Am. Geophys. Union, Geol. Soc. Am., Geodynam. Ser. 7: 83–112.

Bergerat F., 1977, La fracturation de l'avant-pays Jurassien entre les fossés de la Saône et du Rhin, analyse et essai d'interprétation dynamique: Rev. Geogr. Phys. Géol. Dyn. (2)XIX(4):325–338.

Berggren W.A. and Schnitker D., 1983, Cenozic marine environments in the North Atlantic and Norwegian-Greenland Sea, *in* M.H.P. Bott, S. Saxoy, M. Talwani and J. Thiede (eds.), Structure and development of the Greenland-Scotland Ridge-New Methods and Concepts: (New York/London, Plenum Press, p. 495–548.

Berglund L.T., Augustson J., Faerseth R., Gielberg J. and Ramberg-Moe H., 1986, The evolution of the Hammerfest Basin, *in* A.M. Spencer et al. (eds.), Habitat of hydrocarbons on the Norwegian continental shelf: London, Graham and Trotman, p. 319–338.

Bergström J., Bless M.J.M. and Paproth E., 1985, The marine Knabberud Limestone in the Oslo Graben: Possible implications for the model of Silesian palaeogeography: Z. Dt. Geol. Ges. 136:181–194.

Berkel J.T. van der, Hugon H., Schwerdtner W.M. and Bouchez J.L., 1983, Study of anticlines, faults and diapirs in the Central Eurekan Sound Fold Belt, Canadian Arctic Islands: Preliminary results: Bull. Can. Soc. Petrol. Geol. 32(2):109–116.

Bernard J.H. and Klominsky J.K., 1975, Geochronology of the Variscan plutonism and mineralisation in the Bohemian Massif: Vest.ústřed.ûst.Geol. 50:71–81.

Bernard-Griffiths J., Cantagrel J.M. and Duthon J.C., 1977, Radiometric evidence for an Acadian tectonometamorphic event in the Western Massif Central Francais: Contr. Miner. Petrol. 61:199–212.

Bernard-Griffiths, J., Gebauer D., Grünenfelder M. and Pibouk M., 1985, The Tonalite belt of Limousin (French Central Massif): U-Pb zircon ages and geotectonic implications: Bull. Soc.

Géol. France (8)I(4):523–529.

Bernoulli D., 1980, Southern Alps of Ticino, *in* R. Trümpy, Geology of Switzerland—a guidebook: Basel/New York, Wepf. & Co. Publ., p. 80–82.

Bernoulli D., 1984, The early history of the Atlantic-Tethyan system: Ann. Geophys. 2(2):133–136.

Bernoulli D. and Jenkyns H.C., 1974, Alpine, Mediterranean and Central Atlantic Mesozoic facies in relation to the early evolution of the Tethys, *in* R.H. Dott and R.H. Shaver (ed.), Modern and ancient geosynclinal sedimentation: Soc. Econ. Paleont. Mineral. Spec. Publ. 19:129–160.

Bernoulli D., Kälin O. and Patacca E., 1979, A sunken continental margin of the Mesozoic Tethys: The northern and central Apennines: Symp. "Sédimentation jurassic W. Européene," A.S.F. Publ. Spec. 1: 197–210.

Bertrand H. and Westphal M., 1977, Comparisons géologiques et palaeomagnétiques des tholeiites du Maroc et de la Côte orientale de l'Amérique du Nord: implictions pour l'ouverture de l'Atlantique: Bull. Soc. Géol. France (7)XIX(3):513–520.

Bessis F. and Burrus J., 1986, Etude de la subsidence de la marge du Golfe de Lion: Bull. Cent. Rech. Exp.-Prod. Elf-Aquitaine 10(1):123–141.

Betz D., Führer F., Greiner G. and Plein E., 1987, Evolution of the Lower Saxony Basin: Tectonophysics 137: in press.

Biddle K.T., 1984, Triassic sea level changes and the Ladinian-Carnian boundary: Nature, London 308:631–633.

Biju-Duval B., Dercourt J. and Le Pichon X., 1977, From the Tethys Ocean to the Mediterranean Seas: A plate tectonic model of the evolution of the Western Alpine Sytem, *in* B. Biju-Duval (ed.), Structural history of the Mediterranean Basins: Paris, Edition Technip., p. 143–164.

Bilotte M., 1978, Evolution sédimentaire et tectonique du bassin sous-pyrénéen à la fin du Crétacé, à l'est de la Garonne: Bull. Soc. Géol. France (7)XX(5):649–655.

Binns P.E., McQuillin R., Fannin N.G.T., Kenolty N. and Ardus D.A., 1975, Structure and stratigraphy of sedimentary basins in the Sea of the Hebrides and the Minches, *in* A.W. Woodland (ed.), Petroleum and the continental shelf of NW Europe. Vol. 1. Geology: Applied Science Publ., Barking, England, p. 93–104.

Bird K.J., 1986, The framework geology of the North Slope of Alaska as related to oil-source rock correlations, *in* L.B. Magoon and G.E. Claypool (eds.), Alaska North Slope oil-rock correlation study, analysis of North Slope crude: Am. Assoc. Petrol. Geol. Stud. Geol. 20: 3–29.

Bird K.J. and Molenaar C.M., 1983, The framework geology of the North Slope of Alaska as related to oil-source rock correlations, *in* L. Magoon and G. Claypool (eds.), Alaska North Slope oil-source rock correlation study: Am. Assoc. Petrol. Geol. short course.

Bird K.J., Connor C.L., Tailleur I.L., Silberman M.L. and Christie J.L., 1978, Granite on the Barrow Arch, northeast NPR-A, *in* K.M. Johnson (ed.), The U.S. Geological Survey in Alaska: Accomplishments during 1977: U.S. Geol. Surv. Circ. 772B: B24–B25.

Birkelund T. and Håkansson E., 1983, The Cretaceous of North Greenland-a stratigraphic and biogeographical analysis: Zitteliana 10:7–25.

Birkelund T. and Perch-Nilsen K., 1976, Late Palaeozoic-Mesozoic evolution of central East Greenland, *in* A. Escher and W.S. Watt (eds.), Geology of Greenland: Grønlands Geol. Unders., p. 305–339.

Birkelund T., Callomon J.H. and Fürsich F.T., 1984, The stratigraphy of the Upper Jurassic and Lower Cretaceous sediments of Milnes Land, central East Greenland: Grønlands Geol. Unders. 147: 56 p.

Birkenmajer K., 1972, Alpine fold belt of Spitsbergen: 24th Internat. Geol. Congr. Montreal, 1972, Sec. 3, p. 282–292.

Birkenmajer K., 1974, Carpathian Mountains, in A.M. Spencer (ed.), Mesozoic-Cenozoic orogenic belts, data for orogenic studies: Geol. Soc. London Spec. Publ. 4: 127–157.

Birkenmajer K., 1981, The geology of Svalbard, the western part of the Barents Sea, and the continental margin of Scandinavia, in A.E.M. Nairn, M. Churkin Jr. and F.G. Stehli (eds.), The ocean basins and margins. Vol. 5. The Arctic Ocean: New York, Plenum Press, p. 265–329.

Blasco S.M., Bornhold B.D. and Lewis C.F.M., 1979, Preliminary results of surficial geology and geomorpholoyg studies of the Lomonosov Ridge, central Arctic Basin: Geol. Surv. Can. Paper 79:78–83.

Blenkinsop J., Cucman P.F. and Bell K., 1977, Geochronological evidence of Hercynian activity in Newfoundland: Nature, London 265:616–618.

Bless M.J.M. and Winkler-Prins C.F., 1972, Paleoecology and paleogeography of the Aegir Marine Band and its equivalents in north-western Europe: 72 Congr. Internat. Stratigr. Géol. Carbonif. Krehfeld 1971, C.R. 1:231–239.

Bluck B.J., 1978, Sedimentation in a late orogenic basin: The Old Red Sandstone of the Midland Valley, in D.R. Bowes and B.E. Leake (eds.), Crustal evolution in NW Britain and adjacent regions: Geol. J. Spec. Iss. 10:249–278.

Bluck B.J., 1984, Pre-Carboniferous history of the Middle Valley of Scotland: Trans. R. Soc. Edinburgh Earth Sci. 75:275–295.

Boccaletti M., Nicolich R. and Tortorici L., 1984, The Calabrian Arc and the Ionian Sea in the dynamic evolution of the Mediterranean: Mar. Geol. 55:219– 245.

Bodenhausen J.W.A. and Ott W.F., 1981, Habitat of the Rijswijk oil province, onshore The Netherlands, in L.V. Illings and G.D. Hobson (eds.), Petroleum geology of the continental shelf of north-west Europe: London, Heyden and Sons, p. 301–304.

Boehner R., 1983, Windsor Group salt and potash in Nova Scotia, Canada: Sixth Internat. Symp. on Salt, Salt Institute 1:99–113.

Bøen F., Eggen S. and Vollset J., 1983, Structure and basins of the margin from 62 °N to 69 °N and their development, in A.M. Spencer et al. (eds.), Petroleum geology of the north European margin: London, Graham and Trotman, p. 253–270.

Boess J. and Hoppe A., 1986, Mesozoischer Vulkanismus in Nordspanien: Rifting in Keuper and Kreide-Vulkanismus auf Transform—Störungen: Geol. Rundsch. 75(2):353–369.

Boigk H., 1981, Erdöl und Erdölgas in der Bundesrepublik Deutschland. Erdölprovinzen, Felder, Förderung, Vorräte, Lagerstättentechnik: Stuttgart, Ferdinand Enke Verlag, 330 p.

Boillot G., Dupeuble P.A. and Malod J., 1979, Subduction and tectonics on the continental margin of northern Spain: Mar. Geol. 32:53–70.

Boillot G., Grimand S., Mauffret A., Mougenot D., Kornprobst J., Mergoil- Daniel J. and Torrent G., 1980, Ocean-continent boundary of the Iberian Margin: A serpentinite diapir west of Galicia Bank: Earth Planet. Sci. Lett. 48:23–34.

Boillot G., Temime D., Malod J.A., et al., 1985, Exploration par submersible de la marge continetnale au nord-ouest de l'Espagne: Bull. Soc. Géol. France (8)I(1):89–102.

Bois C., Cazes M., Hirn A., Mascle A., Matte P., Montadert L. and Pinet B., 1987, Crustal laminations in deep seismic profiles in France and neighbouring areas, in D.H. Matthews and BIRPS Group (eds.), Deep seismic reflection profiling of the continental lithosphere: Geophys. J.R. Astr. Soc. 89(1): 297–304.

Bond G.C., 1978, Speculations on real sea level changes and vertical motions of continents at selected times in the Cretaceous and Tertiary periods: Geology 6:247–250.

Bond G.C., 1979, Evidence for some uplifts of large magnitude in continental platforms, in T.R. McGetchin and R.B. Merill (eds.), Plateau uplift: Model and mechanism: Tectonophysics 61:285–305.

Bonhommet N. and Perroud H., 1986, Apport du paléomagnétisme à la compréhension de l'orogenèse hercynienne en Europe occidentale: Bull. Soc. Géol. France (8)II(1):35–42.

Bonneau M., 1982, Evolution géodynamique de l'arc Egéen depuis le Jurassique supérieur jusqu'au Miocène: Bull. Soc. Géol. France (7)XIV(2):229–242.

Bonneau M., 1984, Correlation of the Hellenides nappes in the southeastern Aegean and their tectonic reconstruction, in J.E. Dixon and A.A.F. Robertson (eds.), The geological evolution of the Mediterranean: Geol. Soc. London Spec. Publ. 4: 517–527.

Borsuk A.M. and Sholop V.N., 1983, Correlation of endogenous processes in the Alpine cycle of the Caucasus, in N. Rast and F.M. Delany (eds.), Profiles of orogenic belts: Am. Geophys. Union, Geol. Soc. Am., Geodynam. Ser. 10:97–143.

Bott M.H.P., 1976, Mechanisms of basin subsidence-an introductory review: Tectonophysics 36:1–4.

Bott M.H.P., 1978, The origin and development of the continental margins between the British Isles and south-eastern Greenland, in D.R. Bowes and B.E. Leake (eds), Crustal evolution in NW Britain and adjacent regions: Geol. J. Spec. Iss. 10:377–392.

Bott M.H.P., 1981, Crustal doming and mechanisms of continental rifting: Tectonophysics 73:1–8.

Bott M.H.P., 1982, Origin of the lithospheric tension causing basin formation, in Sir Peter Kent, M.H.P. Bott, D.P. McKenzie and C.A. Williams (eds.), The evolution of sedimentary basins: Phil. Trans. R. Soc. London 305A:319–324.

Bott M.H.P., 1983, The crust beneath the Iceland-Faeroe Ridge, in M.H.P. Bott, S. Saxov, M. Talwani and J. Thiede (eds), Structure and development of the Greenland-Scotland Ridge-new methods and concepts: New York/London Plenum Press, p. 63–75.

Bott M.H.P., 1984, Deep structure and origin of the Faeroe-Shetland Channel, in A.M. Spencer et al. (eds.), Petroleum geology of the north European Margin: London, Graham and Trotman,p. 341–347.

Bott M.H.P. and Smith P.J., 1984, Crustal structure of the Faeroe-Shetland Channel: Geophys. J.R. Astr. Soc. 76:383–398.

Bott M.H.P., Saxov S., Talwani M. and Thiede J. (eds.), 1983, Structure and development of the Greenland-Scotland Ridge—new methods and concepts: New York/London, Plenum Press, 685 p.

Bouillin J.P. and Perret M.-F., 1982, Datation par conodonts du Carbonifère inférieur et mise en évidence d'une phase tectonique bretonne en Petit Kabylie (Algérie): C.R. Acad. Sci. Paris Ser. II 295:47–50.

Boury J., Stévaux J. and Winnock E., 1977, Le Trias d'Afrique et ses relations avec le Trias des Pyrénées et du bassin de l'Ebre: Bull. B.R.G.M. IV:215–244.

Bousquet J.C. and Philip H., 1981, Les characteristiques de la néotectonique en Mediterranée occidentale, in F.-C. Wezel (ed.), Sedimentary basins of Mediterranean margins: C.N.R. Italian Project of Oceanography Bologna, Tecnoprint, p. 389–405.

Bowin C., 1983, Depth of principal mass anomalies contributing to the Earth's geoidal undulations and gravity anomalies: Mar. Geod. 7(1-4):61–100.

Bowin C., 1985, Global gravity maps and the structure of the Earth, in W.J. Hinze (ed.), The utility of regional gravity and magnetic anomaly maps: Soc. Expl. Geophys., 88–101.

Bradley D.C., 1982, Subsidence in late Paleozoic basins in the northern Appalachians: Tectonics 1(1):107–123.

Bradley D.C., 1983, Tectonics of the Acadian orogeny in New England and adjacent Canada: J. Geol. 91:381–400.

Brandner R., 1984, Meeresspiegelschwankungen und Tektonik in der Trias der NW- Tethys: Jb. Geol. A-B (Wien) 126(4):435–475.

Brandt K., 1986, Glacioeustatic cycles in the Early Jurassic: N.Jb. Geol. Paläont. Mh. 17:257–274.

Brenchley P.J. and Newall G., 1984, Late Ordovician environmental changes and their effect on faunas, in D.L. Bruton (ed.), Aspects of the Ordovician System: Palaeontological contributions from the University of Oslo, No. 295, p. 65–79.

Brewer J.A. and Smythe D.K., 1984, MOIST and the continuity of crustal reflector geometry along the Caledonian-Appalachian Orogen: J. Geol. Soc. London 141(1):105–120.

Brewer J.A., Smithson S.B., Oiver J.E., Kaufman S. and Brown L.D., 1980, The Laramide orogeny: Evidence from COCORP deep crustal seismic profiles in the Windriver Mountains, Wyoming: Tectonophysics 63:165–189.

BRGM, Soc. Elf-Aquitaine, Esso-REP and SNPA, 1973, Géologie du Bassin d'Aquitaine: Paris, Ed. BRGM.

Briden J.C. and Duff B.A., 1981, Pre-Carboniferous palaeomagnetism of Europe north of the Alpine orogenic belt, in M.W. McElhinny and D.A. Valencio (eds.), Palaeoreconstructions of the continents: Am. Geophys. Union, Geol. Soc. Am., Geodynam. Ser. 2: 137–150.

Briden J.C., Turnell H.B. and Watts D.R, 1984, British palaeomagnetism, Iapetus Ocean, and the Great Glen fault: Geology 12:428–431.

Brinkmann R., 1976, Geology of Turkey: Amsterdam, Elsevier Sci. Publ. Co., 158 p.

Brix F., Kröll A. and Wessely G., 1977, Die Molassezone und deren Untergrund in Niederösterreich: Erdöl-Erdgas-Z. Spec. Iss. 93:12–35.

Brochwicz-Lewinski W., Pozaryski W. and Tomczyk H., 1984, Sinistral strike-slip movements in Central Europe in the Palaeozoic: Publ. Inst. Geophys. Pol. Acad. Sci. A-13(160):3–13.

Brousse R. and Bellon H., 1983, Réflexions chronologiques et pétrologiques sur le volcanism associé du development des rifts de France: Bull. Cent. Rech. Expl.-Prod. Elf-Aquitaine 7(1):409–424.

Brown P.E. and Parson I., 1981, The Kap Washington Group Volcanics: Grønlands Geol. Unders. Rapp. 106:65–68.

Brown P.E., Breemen O. van, Nobel R.H. and MacIntyre R.M., 1977, Mid-Tertiary igneous activity in East Greenland-the Kialineq complex: Crontrib. Mineral. Petrol. 64(1):109–122.

Brown S., 1984, Jurassic, in K.W. Glennie (ed.), Introduction to the petroleum geology of the North Sea: Oxford, Blackwell Sci. Publ., p. 103–131.

Browne S.E. and Fairhead J.D., 1983, Gravity study of the Central African rift system: A model of continental disruption. Tectonophysics 94:187–203.

Brun J.-P. and Burg J.-P., 1982, Combined thrusting and wrenching at the Ibero- Armorican arc: A corner effect during continental collision: Earth Planet. Sci. Lett. 61:319–332.

Brunet, M.F., 1984, Subsidence history of the Aquitaine basin determined from subsidence curves: Geol. Mag. 121(5):421–428.

Büchi U.P. and Schlanke S., 1977, Zur Paläogeographie der Schweizerischen Molasse: Erdöl-Erdgas-Z. Spec. Iss. 93:57–69.

Buday T. and Cicha I., 1968, Fore-Carpathian Basin in Moravia (the Foredeep), in M. Mahel and T. Buday (eds.), Regional geology of Czechoslovakia. Part II. The West Carpathians: Stuttgart, Schweizerbart, p. 562–570.

Bugge T., Knarud R. and Mørk A., 1984, Bedrock geology on the Mid- Norwegian Shelf, in A.M. Spencer et al. (eds.), Petroleum geology of the North European Margin: Norw. Petrol. Soc., London, Graham and Trotman Ltd., p. 271–283.

Bukovics C. and Ziegler P.A., 1985, Tectonic development of the Mid-Norway continental margin: Mar. Petrol. Geol. 2(1):2–22.

Bukovics C., Cartier E.G., Shaw N.D. and Ziegler P.A., 1984, Structure and development of the Mid-Norway continental margin, in A.M. Spencer et al. (eds.), Petroleum geology of the North European margin: Norw. Petrol. Soc., London, Graham and Trotman, p. 407–423.

Bullard E.C., Everett J.E. and Smtih A.G., 1965, The fit of the continents around the Atlantic, in A symposium on Continental Drift: Phil. Trans. R. Soc. London, 258 (Ser. A):41–51.

Burchfiel B.C., and Bleahu M., 1976, Geology of Romania: Geol. Soc. Am. Spec. Paper 158: 82 p.

Burchfiel B.C., 1980, East European Alpine System and the Carpathian orocline as an example of collision tectonics: Tectonophysics 63:31–61.

Burchfiel B.C. and Royden L., 1982, Carpathian foreland fold and thrust belt and its relation to Pannonian and other basins: Am. Assoc. Petrol. Geol. Bull. 66(9):1179–1195.

Burg J.P. and Matte J.P., 1978, A cross-section through the French Massif Central and the scope of its Variscan geodynamic evolution: Z.Dt.Geol. Ges. 129:429–460.

Burg J.P., Leyreloup A., Marchand J. and Matte P. 1984, Inverted metamorphic zonation and large-scale thrusting in the Variscan Belt: An example in the French Massif Central, in D.H.W. Hutton and D.J. Sanderson (eds.), Variscan tectonics of the North Atlantic region: Geol. Soc. London, Spec. Publ. 14:47–61.

Burg J.P., Bale P., Brun J.P., and Girardeau J., 1987, Stretching lineation and transport direction in the Ibero-Armorican arc during Siluro-Devonian collision: Geodynamica Acta 1(1):71–87.

Burke K. and Dewey J.F., 1973, Plume-generated triple junctions: Key indicators in applying plate tectonics to older rocks: J. Geol. 81:406–433.

Burollet P.F. and Ellouz N., 1986, L'évolution des bassins sédimentaires de la Tunisie centrale et orientale: Bull. Cent. Rech. Expl.-Prod. Elf-Aquitaine 10(1):49–68.

Burov Y.P. and Zagruzina I.A., 1976, Results of determination of absolute ages of Cenozoic basalt rocks in the northern part of the Island of Spitsbergen, in Geology of Svalbard, NISGA,

Leningrad, p. 139–140, 146 (in Russian).

Burov Y.P., Krasilshchikov A.A., Firsov L.V. and Klubov B.A., 1977, The age of Spitsbergen dolerites: Norsk Polarinst. Årbok. 1977:101–108.

Burrus J., 1984, Contribution to a geodynamic synthesis of the Provençal Basin (north-western Mediterranean): Mar. Geol. 55:247–269.

Burrus J. and Foucher J.P., 1986, Contribution to the structural regime of the Provençal Basin based on flumed heat flow surveys and previous investigatins: Tectonophysics 128:303–334.

Cadet J.-P., Bonneau M., Charvet J., Dürr S., Elter P., Ferrière J., Scandone P. and Thiébault F., 1980, Les chaînes de la Méditerranée moyenne et orientale, in J. Aubouin, J. Debelmas and M. Latreille (eds.), Geology of the Alpine chains born of the Tethys: Mém. B.R.G.M. 115:98–118.

Caire A., 1974, Eastern Atlas, in A.M. Spencer (ed.), Mesozoic-Cenozoic orogenic belts, data for orogenic studies: Geol. Soc. London Spec. Publ. 4: 47–59.

Callomon J.H., 1979, Marine boreal Bathonian fossils from the northern North Sea and their palaeogeographical significance: Proc. Geol. Assoc. 90:163–169.

Callomon J.H. and Birkelund T., 1980, The Jurassic transgression and the mid-Late Jurassic succession in Milnes Land, central East Greenland: Geol. Mag. 177:211–310.

Caputo M.V. and Crowell J.C., 1985, Migration of glacial centers across Gondwana during Paleozoic Era: Geol. Soc. Am. Bull. 96:1020–1036.

Cariou E., 1973, Ammonites of the Callovian and Oxfordian, in A. Hallam (ed.), Atlas of palaeobiogeography: Amsterdam, Elsevier Sci. Publ. Co., p. 287–295.

Cariou E., Contini D., Dommergues J.L., Enay R., Geyssant J.R., Mangold C. and Thierry J., 1985, Biogéographie des ammonites et évolution structurale de la Tethys du cours de Jurassique: Bull. Soc. Géol. France (8)I(5):679–697.

Carls P., 1975, The Ordovician of the Eastern Iberian Chains near Fombuena and Lusema (Prov. Zaragoza, Spain): N. Jb. Geol. Paläont. Abh. 152(2):127–146.

Carmignani L., Giglia G. and Klingfield R., 1978, Structural evolution of the Apuane Alps: An example of continental margin deformation in the northern Apennines: J. Geol. 86:487–504.

Casey R. and Rawson P.F., 1973, A review of the Boreal Lower Cretaceous, in R. Casey and P.F. Rawson (eds.), The Boreal Lower Cretaceous: Geol. J. Spec. Iss. 5:415–430.

Casquero J.L.G., Boetrijk N.A.I.M., Chacón J. and Priem H.N.A., 1985, Rb–Sr evidence for the presence of Ordovician granites in the deformed basement of the Badajoz–Cordoba belt, SW Spain: Geol. Rundsch. 74(2):379–384.

Cassano E., Anelli L., Fichera R. and Cappelli V., 1986, Pianura Padana, interpretazione integrata di data geofisici e geologici: 73° Congresso Societa' Geologica Italiana, Roma, 1986, AGIP publication, 27 p.

Castellarin A., 1980, Jurassique et Crétacé: Italie, introduction à la géologie génerale: 26th Internat. Geol. Congr.-G13, Excursion 122A, guide book, p. 65–75.

Castellarin A. and Vai G.B., 1981, Importance of Hercynian tectonics within the framework of the southern Alps: J. Struct. Geol. 3(4):477–486.

Caston V.N.D., 1976, Tertiary sediments of the Vøring Plateau, Norwegian Sea, recovered by Leg 38 of the Deep Sea Drilling Project: Initial Reports of Deep Sea Drilling Project, 38, Washington, DC: US Govt. Printing Office, p. 761–782.

Cazes M., Torreilles G., Bois G., Damotte B., Galdeano A., Hirn A., Mascle A., Matte P., van Ngoc P. and Raoult J.F., 1985, Structure de la coûte hercynienne du Nord de la France: Premiers résultats du profil ECORS: Bull. Soc. Géol. France (8)I(6):925–941.

Cazes M., Mascle A., Torreilles X., Bois C., Damotte X., Matte P., Raoult X., Pham V.N., Hirn A., and Galdeano X., 1986, Large Variscan overthrusts beneath the Paris Basin: Nature, London 323:144–142.

Celet P., Clement B., Ferrière J. and Thiébault F., 1980, Tableau des principaux évènements tectoniques, métamorphiques et magmatiques dans les Hellenides au cours du cycle alpin, in Géologie des chaînes alpines issues de la Tethys: 26th Internat. Geol. Congr., Paris, Coll. 05, Mem. B.R.G.H. 115:306–308.

Chablinskaia N.V., Koulikov P.K., Nalivkin V.D., Pogrebitsk Y.E., Polkin I.I, Rostovtsev N.N., Rudkevich M.I. and Smirnov V.G., 1982, La plateforme de la Siberie occidentale, in Tectonics of Europe and adjacent areas, Variscides, Epi-Paleozoic platforms, Alpides. Explanatory note to the International Tectonic Map of Europe and Adjacent Areas, scale 1:2.500.000: Moscow, "Nauk" Publ. House, p. 265–276.

Chacón J., Oliveira V., Ribeiro A. and Oliveira J.T., 1983, La estrutura de la zona de Ossa Morena, in Libro Jubilar J.M. Ramos, Geologia de Espana, Tomo I, Inst. Geol. Minero Espana Publ., p. 490–504.

Cannell J.E.T., D'Argenio B. and Horváth E., 1979, Aria, the African Promontory, in Mesozoic Mediterranean palaeogeography: Earth Sci. Rev. 15:213–292.

Chase C.G., 1979, Subduction, the geoïd, and lower mantle convection: Nature, London, 282:464–468.

Chenet P.Y. and Letouzey J., 1983, Tectonique de la zone comprise entre Abu Durba et Gebel Mezzazat (Sinaï, Egypte) dans le contexte de l'evolution du rift Suez: Bull. Cent. Rech. Expl.-Prod. Elf-Aquitaine 7(1):201–215.

Chorlton C.B. and Dallmeyer R.D., 1986, Geochronology of early to middle Paleozoic tectonic development in the southwest Newfoundland Gander zone: J. Geol. 94:67–89.

Chorowicz J., Henry C. and Lybéris N., 1987, Tectoniques superposées synsédimentaires des secteurs des golfes de Suez et d'Aquaba: Bull. Soc. Géol. France (8)III(2):223–234.

Choukroune P. and Mattauer M., 1978, Tectonique des plaques et Pyrénées: Sur le fonctionnement de la faille transformante nord-pyrénéenue: comparaison avec des modèles actuels: Bull. Soc. Géol. France (7)XX(5):689–700.

Choukroune P., Mattauer M., and Rios L.M., 1890, Estrùctura de los Pireneos: Bol. Geol. Minero XCI-I:213–248.

Christensen U., 1983, A numerical model of coupled subcontinental and oceanic convection: Tectonophysics 95:1–23.

Christie P.A. and Sclater J.G., 1980, An extensional origin of the Buchan and Witchground Graben in the North Sea: Nature, London, 283:729–732.

Churkin M. Jr. and Trexler J.H. Jr., 1981, Continental plates and accreted oceanic terranes in the Arctic, in A.E.M. Nairn, M. Churkin Jr., and E.G. Stelhli (eds.), The ocean basins and margins. Vol. 5, The Arctic Ocean: New York/London, Plenum Press, p. 1–20.

Churkin M. Jr., Soleimani G., Carter G. and Robinson R., 1981, Geology of the Soviet Arctic: Kola Peninsula to Lena River, in A.E.M. Nairn, M. Churkin Jr. and F.G. Stehlin (eds.), The ocean basins and margins. Vol. 5. The Arctic Ocean: New York/London, Plenum Press, p 331–375.

Cita M.B., 1982, The Messinian salinity crisis in the Mediterranean area: A review, *in* H. Berkhemer and K. Hsü (eds.), Alpine–Mediterranean geodynamics: Am. Geophys. Union, Geol. Soc. Am., Geodynam. Ser. 7: 113–140.

Clark D.N., 1986, The distribution of porosity in Zechstein carbonates, *in* J. Brooks, J.C. Goff and B. van Hoorn (eds.), Habitat of Palaeozoic gas in N.W. Europe: Geol. Soc. Spec. Publ. 23:212–149.

Clarke D.B. and Pedersen A.K., 1976, Tertiary volcanic province of West Greenland, *in* A. Escher and W.S. Watt (eds.), Geology of Greenland: Geol. Surv. Greenland, p. 365–385.

Clemmensen L.B., 1980, Triassic rift sedimentatin and palaeogeography of central East Greenland: Grønlands. Geol. Unders. 136:1–72.

Cloetingh S., 1986a, Intraplate stresses: A new tectonic mechanism for relative sealevel fluctuations: Geology 14:617–620.

Cloetingh S., 1986b, Tectonics of passive margins: Implications for the stratigraphic record: Geol. Mijnbouw 65:103–117.

Cloetingh S. and Wortel R., 1985, Regional stress field of the Indian Plate: Geophys. Res. Lett. 12(2):77–80.

Cloetingh S. and Wortel R., 1986, Stress in the Indo-Australian plate, *in* B. Johnson and A.W. Bally (eds.), Proceedings 1985 Geodynamics Conference on Intraplate Tectonics, Texas A & M University: Tectonophysics, 132:49–67.

Cloetingh S., McQueen H. and Lambeck K., 1985, On a tectonic mechanism for regional sea level variations: Earth Planet. Sci. Lett. 75:157–166.

Coccozza T. and Jacobacci A., 1975, Geological outlines of Sardinia, *in* C.H. Squires (ed.), Geology of Italy: Tripoli, The Earth Sciences Society of Libyan Arab Republic, p. 49–81.

Cochran J.R., 1983, Effect of rifting times on the development of sedimentary basins: Earth Planet. Sci. Lett. 66:289–302.

Cocks L.R.M. and Fortney R.A., 1982, Faunal evidence for oceanic separation in the Palaeozoic of Britain: J. Geol. Soc. London 139:465–478.

Cohen C.R., 1980, Plate tectonic model for the Oligo-Miocene evolution of the western Mediterranean area: Tectonophysics 68:283–311.

Cohen C.R., Schamel S. and Body-Kaygi P., 1980, Neogene deformation in northern Tunisia: Origin of the eastern Atlas by microplate continental margin collision: Geol. Soc. Am. Bull. 91:255–237.

Cook F.A., 1983, Some consequences of palinspastic reconstruction in the southern Appalachians: Geology 11:86–89.

Cook F.A., Albaugh D.S., Brown L.D., Kaufman S., Oliver J.E. and Hatcher R.D. Jr., 1979, Thin-skinned tectonics in the crystalline southern Appalachians: COCORP seismic-reflection profiling of the Blue Ridge and Piedmont: Geology 7:563–567.

Cook F.A., Brown L.D., Kaufman S., Oliver J.E. and Petersen T.A., 1981, COCORP seismic profiling of the Appalachian orogen beneath the coastal plain of Georgia, Part I: Geol. Soc. Am. Bull. 92:738–748.

Cook T.D. and Bally A.W., 1975, Strtigraphic Atlas, North and Central America: Shell Oil Co., Exploration Department, Houston, Texas.

Cornford C., 1984, Source rocks and hydrocarbons of the North Sea, *in* K.W. Glennie (ed.), Introduction to the petroleum geology of the North Sea: Oxford, Blackwell Sci. Publ., p. 171–204.

Coward M.P., 1986, Heterogenous stretching, simple shear and basin development: Earth Planet. Sci. Lett. 80:325–336.

Crane K., Eldholm O., Myhre A.M. and Sundvor E., 1982, Thermal implications for the evolution of the Spitsbergen Trans-

form fault: Tectonophysics 89:1–32.

Curnelle R., Dubois P. and Seguin J.C., 1982, The Mesozoic-Tertiary evolution of the Aquitaine Basin, *in* Sir Peter Kent, M.H.P. Bott, D.P. McKenzie and C.A. Williams (ed.), The evolution of sedimentary basins: Phil. Trans. R. Soc. London, 305A:63–84.

Curry D., Adams C.G., Boulter M.C., Dilley F.C., Eames F.E., Funnell B.M. and Wells M.K., 1978, A correlation of Tertiary rocks in the British Isles: Geol. Soc. London Spec. Rep. 12:72 p.

Curtin D.P. and Ballestad S., 1986, South Viking Graben: Habitat of Mesozoic hydrocarbons, *in* A.M. Spencer et al. (eds.), Habitat of hydrocarbons on the Norwegian Shelf: London, Graham and Trotman, p. 153–157.

Cutt B.J. and Laving J.G., 1977, Tectonic elements and geologic history of the South Labrador and Newfoundland continental shelf, eastern Canada: Can. Petrol. Geol. Bull. 25:1037–1058.

Czerminski J. and Pajchlowa M., 1974, Atlas lithologiczno-paleogeograficzny obszarow platformowych Polski Czesc I—Proterozoik i Paleozoik: Warszawa: Wydawnictwa Geologiczne, 1974.

Czerminski J. and Pajchlowa M., 1975, Atlas lithologiczno-paleogeograficzny obszarow platformòwych Polski Czese II—Mezozoik (Bez Kredy gornej): Warszawa: Wydawnictwa Geologiczne.

Dalland A., 1981, Mesozoic sedimentary succession at Andøya, northern Norway, and relation to structural development of the North Atlantic area, *in* J.W. Kerr and A.J. Fergusson (eds.), Geology of the North Atlantic borderlands: Can. Soc. Petrol. Geol. Mem. 7:563–584.

Dalland A. and Thusu B., 1977, Kimmeridgian volcanic ash in Andøya, north Norway, *in* Mesozoic northern North Sea Symposium, Norwegian Petroleum Society, Oslo, MNSS 9:1–14.

Dalland A., Gjelberg J., Nysaether E. and Nøttvedt A., 1982, The geology of Spitsbergen, a summary prepared for field excursions: Universiyt of Bergen publ., 97 p.

Dallmeyer R.D., 1982, $^{40}AR/^{39}Ar$ ages from the Narragansett Basin and southern Rhode Island basement terrane: Their bearing on the extent and timing of Alleghenian tectonothermal events in New England: Geol. Soc. Am. Bull. 93:1118–1130.

Dallmeyer R.D. and Gee D.G., 1986, $^{40}Ar/^{39}Ar$ mineral dates from retrogressed eclogites within the Baltoscandian Miogeocline: Implications for a polyphase Caledonian orogenic evolution: Geol. Soc. Am. Bull. 97:26–34.

Dallmeyer R.D., Wright J.E., Secor D.T. and Snoke A.W., 1986, Character of the Alleghenian orogeny in the southern Appalachians. Part II. Geochronological constraints on the tectonothermal evolution of the eastern Piedmont in South Carolina: Geol. Soc. Am. Bull. 97:1329–1344.

Daly L. and Irving E., 1983, Paléomagnetism des roches Carbonifères du Sahara Central; analyse et aimanations juxtaposées; configurations de la Pangée: Ann. Geophys. 1(3):207–216.

D'Amico C., 1979, General picture of Hercynian magmatism in the Alps, Calabria-Peloritani and Corsica-Sardinia: IGCP Project No. 5, Correlation of pre-Variscan and Variscan events of the Alpine-Mediterranean Mountain Belt, Newsletter 1:33–68.

D'Argenio B. and Alvarez W., 1980, Stratigraphic evidence for crustal thickness changes on the southern Tethys Margin during the Alpine cycle: Geol. Soc. Am. Bull. 91:681–689.

D'Argenio B., Pescatore T. and Scandone P., 1975, Structural pattern of the Campania–Lucania Apennines, in L. Ogniben et al. (eds.), Structural model of Italy: C.N.R., p. 313–329.

D'Argenio B., Horváth F. and Channell J.E.T., 1980, Palaeotectonic evolution of Adria, the African promontory, in Géologie des Chaînes Alpines issues de la Tethys: 26th Internat. Geol. Congr., Paris, Coll. C-5, Mem. B.R.G.M. Mem. 115:331–351.

Davis G.A., Lister G.S. and Reynolds S.J., 1986, Structural evolution of the Whipple and South mountains shear zones, southwestern United States: Geology 14:7–10.

Dawes P.R., 1976, Precambrian to Tertiary in northern Greenland, in A. Escher and W.S. Watt (eds.), Geology of Greenland: Geol. Surv. Greenland, p. 248–303.

Dawes P.R. and Kerr J.W., 1982, The case against major displacement along Nares Strait, in P.R. Dawes and J.W. Kerr (eds.), Nares Strait and the drift of Greenland: A conflict in plate tectonics: Meddel. Grønland, Geoscience 8:369–386.

Dawes P.R. and Peel J.S., 1981, The northern margin of Greenland from Baffin Bay to the Greenland Sea, in A.E.M. Nairn, M. Churkin Jr., and F.G. Stehli (eds.), The ocean basins and margins. Vol. 5. The Arctic Ocean: New York, Plenum Press, p. 201–264.

Dawes P.R. and Soper N.J., 1979, Structural and stratigraphic framework of the North Greenland fold belt in Johannes V. Jens Land., Peary Land: Grønlands Geol. Unders. Rapp. 93–1–40.

De'Ath N.G. and Schuyleman S.F., 1981, The geology of the Magnus Field, in L.V. Illings and G.D. Hobson (eds.), Petroleum geology of the continental shelf of north-west Europe. Vol. 1 Geology: London, Heyden and Son, p. 342–351.

Debelmas J. and Sandulescu M., 1987, Transformante nord-penninique et problèmes de correlation palinspastique entre les Alpes et les Carpathes: Bull. Soc. Géol. France (8)III(2):403–408.

Debelmas J., Oberhauser R., Sandulescu M. and Trümpy R., 1980, L'arc alpino-carpathique, in Géologie des chaînes alpines issues de la Tethys: 26th Internat. Geol. Congr., Paris, Coll. 05, Mem. B.R.G.M. 115:86–96.

Debelmas J., Escher A. and Trümpy R., 1983, Profiles through the Western Alps, in N. Rast and F.M. Delany (eds.), Profiles of orogenic belts: Am. Geophys. Union, Geol. Soc. Am., Geodynam. Ser. 10:83–96.

Debenetti A., 1982, The problem of the origin of the salt deposits in the Mediterranean and of their relations to other salt occurrences in the Neogene formations of the contiguous regions: Mar. Geol. 49:91–114.

Deer W.A., 1976, Tertiary igneous rocks between Scoresby Sund and Kap Gustav Holm, East Greenland, in A. Escher and W.S. Watt (eds.), Geology of Greenland: Geol. Surv. Greenland, p. 405–429.

Delaloye M. and Wagner J.J., 1984, Ophiolites and volcanic activity near the western edge of the Arabian plate, in J.E. Dixon and A.H.F. Robertson (eds.), The geological evolution of the eastern Mediterranean: Geol. Soc. Spec. Publ. 17:225–233.

Depowski S., 1978, Lithofacies-palaeogeographical atlas of the Permian of platform areas of Poland: Warszawa, Institut Geologiczny.

Dercourt J., Zonenshain L.P., Ricou L.E., Kazmin V.G., Le Pichon X., Knipper A.L., Grandjacquet C., Sborshchikov I.M., Boulin J., Sorokhtin O., Geyssant J., Lepvrier C., Biju-Duval B., Sibuet J.C., Savostin L.A., Westphal M. and Laner

J.P., 1985, Présentation de 9 cartes paléogeographiques au 1/20.000.000 s'étendant de l'Atlantique du Pamir pour la periode du Lias à l'actuel: Bull. Soc. Géol. France (8)I(5):637–652.

Dercourt J. et al., 1986, Geological evolution of the Tethys belt from Atlantic to Pamir since Liassic: Tectonophysics 123(1–4):241–315.

Detrick R.S., Sclater J.G. and Thiede J., 1977, The subsidence of aseismic ridges: Earth Planet. Sci. Lett. 34:185–196.

Deutloff O., Teichmüller M., Teichmüller R. and Wolf M., 1980, Inkohlungsuntersuchungen im Mesozoikum des Massivs von Vlotho (Niedersächsisches Tektogen): N. Jb. Geol. Paläont. Mh. 6:321–341.

Devoudzadeh M. and Schmidt K., 1981, Contribution to the paleogeography of the Upper Triassic to Middle Jurassic of Iran: N. Jb. Geol. Pal. Abh. 162(2):137–163.

Devoudzadeh M. and Schmidt K., 1982, Zur Trias des Iran: Geol. Rundsch. 71(3):1021–1039.

De Wever P. and Dercourt J., 1985, Les Radiolarites triasico-jurassiques marqueurs stratigraphiques et paléogéographiques dans les chaînes alpines périméditerranéennes: Une revue: Bull. Soc. Géol. France (8)I(5):653–662.

Dewey J.F., 1982, Plate tectonics and the evolution of the British Isles: J. Geol. Soc. London 139:371–412.

Dewey J.F. and Sengör A.M.C., 1979, Aegean and surrounding regions: Complex multiplate and continuum tectonics in a convergent zone: Geol. Soc. Am. Bull. 90(I):84–92.

Dewey J.F., Hempton M.R., Kidd W.S.F., Saroglu F. and Sengör A.M.C., 1986, Shortening of continental lithosphere: The neotectonics of eastern Anatolia-a young collision zone, in M.P. Coward and A.C. Ries (eds.), Collision tectonics: Geol. Soc. London, Spec. Publ. 19: 3–36.

D'Heur M., 1986, The Norwegian chalk fields, in A.M. Spencer et al. (eds.), Habitat of hydrocarbons on the Norwegian continental shelf: London, Graham and Trotman, p. 77–89.

Diaz de Federico A., Puga E., Torres Roldan R. and Vera J.A., 1980, Correlation of the phases of deformation, metamorphism and magmatism in the Betic ranges, in J. Aubouin, J. Debelmas and M. Latreille (eds.), Geology of the Alpine chains born of the Tethys: Mem. B.R.G.M. 115:291–293.

Dicken A.P., Moorbath S. and Welke H.J., 1981, Isotope, trace element and major element geochemistry of Tertiary igneous rocks, Isle of Aram, Scotland: Trans. R. Soc. Edinburgh Earth Sci. 72:159–170.

Dickinson W.R., 1976, Sedimentary basins developed during evolution of Mesozoic-Cenozoic arc-trench systems in western North America: Can. J. Earth Sci. 13:1268–1287.

Dillon W.P., Robb J.M., Green H.G. and Lucena J.L., 1980, Evolution of the continental margin of southern Spain and Alboran Sea: Mar. Geol. 36:205–226.

Dingle R.V. and Scrutton R.A., 1979, Sedimentary succession and tectonic history of a marginal plateau (Goban Spur, southwest Ireland): Mar. Geol. 33:45–69.

Dixon J.E., Fitton J.G., and Frost R.T.C., Tectonic significance of post-Carboniferous igneous activity in the North Sea Basin, in L. V. Illing and G. D. Hobson (eds.), Petroleum geology of the continental shelf of N.W. Europe: London, Institute of Petroleum, p. 121–137.

Doebl F. and Teichmüller R., 1979, Zur Geologie und heutigen Geothermik in mittleren Oberrhein Graben: Fortschr. Geol. Rheinld. u. Westf. 27:1–17.

Donato J.A. and Tully M.C., 1981, A regional interpretation of North Sea gravity data, in L.V. Illing and G.D. Hobson (eds.),

Petroleum geology of the continental shelf of N.W. Europe: London, Institute of Petroleum, p. 65–75.

Donovan D.T. and Jones E.J.W., 1979, Causes for world-wide changes in sea level: J. Geol. Soc. London 136:187–192.

Dooley R.E. and Smith W.A., 1982, Age and magnetism of diabase dykes and tilting of the Piedmont: Tectonophysics 90:283–307.

Doré F., 1981, The Late Ordovician tillites in Normany (Armorican Massif), in M.J. Hambrey and W.B. Harland (eds.), Earth's pre-Pleistocene glacial record: Cambridge, Cambridge University Press, p. 582–584.

Dubois P. and Séquin J.C., 1978, Les Flyschs crétacé et éocene de la zone commingeoise et leur environment: Bull. Soc. Géol. France (7)XX(5):657–671.

Duindam P. and Hoorn B. van, 1987, Structural evolution of the West Shetland continental margin, in J. Brooks and K. Glennie (eds.), Petroleum geology of northwest Europe: London, Graham and Trotman, in press.

Durand-Delga M., 1978, Alpine chains of the western Mediterranean (Betic Cordillera and Maghrebides), in M. Lemoine (ed.), Geological atlas of Alpine Europe and adjoining areas: Amsterdam/Oxford/New York, Elsevier Sci. Publ. Co. p. 103–170.

Durand-Delga M. and Fontboté J.M., 1980, Le cadre structurale de la Méditerranée occidentale, in Géologie des chaînes alpines issues de la Tethys: 26th Internat. Geol. Congr., Paris, Coll. 05, Mem. B.R.G.M. 115:67–85.

Durand-Delga M. and Lemoine M., 1978, The Pyrenees and the Lower Provence, in M. Lemoine (ed.), Geological atlas of Alpine Europe and adjoining areas: Amsterdam/Oxford/New York, Elsevier Sci. Publ. Co., p. 113–162.

Dutro J.T. Jr., 1981, Geology of Alaska bordering the Arctic Ocean, in A.E.M. Nairn, M. Churkin Jr. and F.G. Stehli (eds.), The ocean basins and margins. Vol. 5. The Arctic Ocean: New York, Plenum Press, p. 21–36.

Dvorak J., 1978, Proterozoischer Untergrund der Variszischen Geosynklinale in Mähren (CSSR) und ihre Entwicklung: Z.dt. Geol. Ges. 129:383–390.

Dymkin A.M.D., Ivanov S.N., Kamaletdinov M.A., Popov B.A., Puchkow V.N., Zoloev K.K. and Fishman M.V.F., 1984, Geology of the Urals, in Geology of the USSR: Proc. 27th Internat. Geol. Congr., Col. 01, Vol. 1, p. 61–71.

Dypvik H., 1984, Jurassic and Cretaceous black shales of the Janusfjellet Formation, Svalbard, Norway: Sed. Geol. 41:235–284.

Dziedzic K., 1980, Subvolcanic intrusions of Permian volcanic rocks in the Central Sudetes: Z. Geol. Wiss. Berlin 8:1181–1200.

Eby G.N., 1984, Geochronology of the Monteregian Hills, alkaline igneous province, Quebec: Geology 12:468–470.

Eby G.N., 1985, Age relations, chemistry, and petrogenesis of mafic alkaline dykes from the Monteregian Hills and younger White Mountains igneous provinces: Can. J. Earth Sci. 22:1103–1111.

Eckhardt F.J., 1979, Der permische Vulkanismus Mitteleuropas Geol. Jb. Reihe D, 35: 84 p.

Edel J.B., Coulon M. and Hernot M.P., 1984, Mise en évidence par le paléomagnetisme d'une importance rotation antihoraire des Vosges méridionales entre le Viséen terminal et le Westphalien supérieur: Tectonophysics 106:239–257.

Eichmüller K. and Seibert P., 1984, Faziesentwicklung zwischen Tournai und Westphal D im Kantabrischem Gebirge: Z. Dt. Geol. Ges. 135:163–191.

Eldholm O. and Thiede J., 1980, Cenozoic continental separation between Europe and Greenland: Palaeogeogr., Palaeoclim., Palaeoecol. 30:243–259.

Eldholm O., Sundvor E., Myhre A.M. and Faleide J.I., 1984, Cenozoic evolution of the continental margin of Norway and West Svalbard, in A.M. Spencer et al. (eds.), Petroleum geology of the North European Margin: Norw. Petrol. Soc., London, Graham and Trotman, p. 3–18.

Elias M., 1977, Paläogeographische und paläotektonische Entwicklung des Mesozoikums und des Tertiärs am Rande der Karpaten und des Böhmischen Massivs: Erdöl-Erdgas Z. Spec. Iss. 93:5–11.

Ellenberger F. and Tamain A.C.G., 1980, Hercynian Europe: Episodes 1:22–27.

Embry A.F., 1982, The Upper Triassic-Lower Jurassic Heiberg Deltaic complex of the Sverdrup Basin, in A.F. Embry and H.R. Balkwill (eds.), Arctic geology and geophysics: Can. Soc. Petrol. Geol. Mem. 8:189–217.

Emery K.O. and Uchupi E., 1984, The geology of the Atlantic Ocean: New York/Berlin/Heidelberg/Tokyo, Springer-Verlag, 1050 p.

Enay R. and Mangold Ch., 1982, Dynamique biogéographique et évolution des faunes d'Ammonites au Jurassique: Bull. Soc. Géol. France (7)XXIV(5–6):1025–1046.

Enay R., Bizon J.J., Mascle G., Morel Y., Perrier R., Biju-Duval B., 1982, Faunes du Jurassique supérieur dans les series pélagiques de l'escarpement de Malte (Mer Ionienne), implications paléogéographiques: Rev. Inst. Fra. Petro. 37(6):733–757.

Enfield M.A. and Coward M.P., 1987, The structure of the West Orkney Basin, northern Scotland: J. Geo. Soc. London, 144(6): 871–884.

Engel W. and Franke W., 1983, Flysch sedimentation: Its relations to tectonism in the European Variscides, in H. Martin and F.W. Eder (eds.), Intracontinental fold belts: Berlin/Heidelberg, Springer-Verlag, p. 289–321.

Engel W. Franke W. and Langenstrassen F., 1983, Palaeozoic sedimenttion in the northern branch of the mid-European Variscides—essay of an interpretation, in H. Martin and F.W. Eder (eds.), Intracontinental fold belts: Berlin/Heidelberg, Springer-Verlag, p. 9–42.

Enjolras J.M., Gouadain J., Mutti E. and Pizon J., 1986, New turbiditic model for the Lower Tertiary sands in the South Viking Graben, in A.M. Spencer et al. (eds.), Habitat of hydrocarbons on the Norwegian continental shelf: London, Graham and Trotman, p. 171–178.

Epshteyn O.G., 1978, Mesozoic-Cenozoic climates of Northern Asia and glacial-marine deposits: Internat. Geol. Rev. 20(1):49–58.

Esang, C.B. and Piper J.D.A., 1984, Palaeomagnetism and Caledonian intrusive suites in the northern Highlands of Scotland: Constraints to tectonic movements within the Caledonian orogenic belt: Tectonophysics 104:1–34.

Escarmed, 1982, Donnés nouvelles sur les marges du Bassin ionien profond (Méditerranée orientale), resultats des campagnes Escarmed Rev. Inst. Fr. Pétr. 37:713–731.

Faleide J.I., Gudlaugsson S.T. and Jacquart G., 1984, Evolution of the Western Barents Sea: Mar. Petrol. Geol. 1(2):123–150.

Farrell S.G., Williams G.D., and Atkinson C.D., 1987, Constraints on the age of the Montsech and Cotrella thrusts, south Central Pyrenees: J. Geol. Soc. London, 144: 907–914.

Faupl P., Frank W. and Frisch W., 1980, Phases of the evolution of the Eastern Alps, in Géologie des chaînes alpines issues de la Tethys: 26th Internat. Geol. Congr., Paris, Mem. B.R.G.M. 115:297–300.

Featherstone P.S., Bott M.H.P. and Peacock J.H., 1977, Structure of the continental margin of south-eastern Greenland: Geophys. J.R. Astr. Soc. 48:15–27.

Féraud G., Gastaud J., Auzende J.M., Olivet J.L. and Cornen G., 1982, 40Ar/39/Ar ages for alkaline volcanism on the basement of Gorringe Bank, North Atlantic: Earth Planet. Sci. Lett. 57:211–226.

Finetti I., 1985, Structure and evolution of the Central Mediterranean (Pelagian and Ionian Seas), in D.J. Stanley and F.-C. Wezel (eds.), Geological evolution of the Mediterranean Basin: New York/Berlin/Heidelberg/ Tokyo, Springer-Verlag, p. 215–230.

Firstbrook P.L., Funnel B.M., Hurley A.M. and Smith A.G., 1979, Paleoceanic reconstructions 160-0 Ma.: Deep Sea Drilling Project A-031, Scripps Inst. Oceanography, La Jolla, California, 41 p.

Fleitou L. and Yuen D., 1984, Steady state, secondary convection beneath lithospheric plates with temperature and pressure dependent viscosity: J. Geophys. Res. 89:9227–9244.

Fleitou L., Froidevaux C. and Yuen D., 1986, Active lithospheric thinning: Tectonophysics 132:271–278.

Floyd P.A., 1982, Chemical variation in Hercynian basalts relative to plate tectonics: J. Geol. Soc. London 139:505–520.

Flügel E., 1974, Fazies-Interpretation der unterpermischen Sedimente in den Karnischen Alpen: Carinthia, II, 164/84:43–62.

Foland K.A., Gilbert L.A., Sebring C.A. and Jiang-Feng C., 1986, 40Ar/39Ar ages for plutons of the Monteregian Hills, Quebec: Evidence for a single episode of Cretaceous magmatism: Geol. Soc. Am. Bull. 97:966–974.

Foose R.M. and Manheim F., 1975, Geology of Bulgaria: Bull. Am. Assoc. Petrol. Geol. 59(2):303–335.

Forney G.G., 1975, Permo-Triassic sea level change: J. Geol. 83:773–779.

Forsyth D. and Uyeda S., 1975, On the relative importance of the driving forces of plate motion: Geophys. J.R. Astr. Soc. 43:163–200.

Forsyth D.A., Asued I., Green A.G. and Jackson H.R., 1986, Crustal structure of the northern Alpha Ridge beneath the Arctic Ocean: Nature, London 322:349–352.

Fox F.G., 1985, Structural geology of the Parry Islands fold belt: Bull. Can. Petrol. Geol. 33(3):306–340.

Francis E.H., 1978, Igneous activity in a fractured craton: Carboniferous volcanism in northern Britain, in D.R. Bowes and B.E. Leake (eds.), Crustal evolution in NW Britain and adjacent regions: Geol. J. Spec. Iss. 10:279–296.

Francis E.H., 1982, Magma and sediments. I. Emplacement of Late Carboniferous tholeïte sills in northern Britain: J. Geol. Soc. London 139:1–20.

Franke W. and Engel W., 1986, Synorogenic sedimentation in the Variscan Belt of Europe: Bull. Soc. Géol. France (8)II(1):25–33.

Friedenreich O., 1987, Regional seismic reflection profile in the Scotian Basin, offshore Nova Scotia, in C. Beaumont and T. Tankard (eds.), Sedimentary basins and basin-forming mechanisms: Can. Soc. Petrol. Geol. Mem. 12, Atl. Geosci. Spec. Publ. 5: 71–73.

Friederich W.L. and Simonarson L.A., 1981, Die fossile Flora Islands: Zeugin der Thule-Landbrücke: Spek. Wiss. 10:22–31.

Friend P.F., Alexander-Marrack P.E., Nicholson J. and Yeats A.K., 1976, Devonian sediments of East Greenland. I. Introduction, classification of sequences, petrographic notes: Medd. Grønland 206(1):56 p.

Frisch W., 1979, Tectonic progradation and plate tectonic evolution of the Alps: Tectonophysics 60:121–139.

Fuchs K., Bonjer K.P. and Prodhel C., 1981, The continental rift system of the Rhine Graben structure, physical properties and dynamical processes: Tectonophysics 73:79–90.

Fuchs K., Gehlen K. von, Mälzer H., Murawski H. and Semmel A., 1983, Epilogue: Mode and mechanism of Rhenish Plateau uplift, in K. Fuchs, K. von Gehlen, H. Mälzer, H. Murawski and S. Semmel (eds.), Plateau uplift, the Rhenish Shield—a case history: Berlin Heidelberg New York Tokyo, Springer-Verlag, p. 405–411.

Fuchs K., Bonjer K.-P., Gajewski D., Lüschen E., Prodehl C., Sandmeier K.-J., Wenzel F. and Willhelm H., 1987, Crustal evolution of the Rhinegraben area. I. Exploring the lower crust in the Rhinegraben Rift by unified geophysical experiments: Tectonophysics, 141: 261–275.

Fujita K. and Cook D.B., 1986, Northeastern Siberia, in The Arctic region, The decade of North American geology. Vol. 1. The Arctic Ocean region, Chapter G., continental margin. In press.

Fyffe L.R. and Barr S.M., 1986, Petrochemistry and tectonic significance of Carboniferous volcanic rocks in New Brunswick: Can. J. Earth Sci. 23:1243–1256.

Fyffe L.R., Rankin D., Size W.G. and Wones D.R., 1983, Volcanism and plutonism in the Appalachian Orogen, in P.E. Schenk (ed.), Regional trends in the geology of the Appalachian-Caledonian-Hercynian-Mauretanid Orogen: Dordrecht, D. Reidel Publ. Co., p. 173–185.

Fytikas M., Innocenti F., Manetti P., Mazzuoli R., Peccerillo A. and Villari L., 1984, Tertiary to Quaternary evolution of volcanism in the Aegean region, in J.E. Dixon and A.H.F. Robertson (eds.), The geological evolution of the eastern Mediterranean: Geol. Soc. London Spec. Publ. 17: 689–699.

Gabrielsen R.H., Foerseth R., Hamar G. and Rønnevik H., 1984, Nomenclature of the main structural features ont eh Norwegian continental shelf north of 62nd parallel, in A.M. Spencer et al. (eds.), Petroleum geology of the north European margin: Norw. Petrol. Soc., London, Graham and Trotman, p. 41–60.

Ganev M., 1974, Stand der Kenntnisse über die Stratigraphie der Trias Bulgariens, in H. Zapfe (ed.), Die Stratigraphie der Alpin-Mediterranen Trias: Berlin, Springer-Verlag, p. 93–99.

Garcia-Hernandez M., Lopez-Garrido A.C., Rivas P., Sanze de Galiano S. and Vera J.A., 1980, Mesozoic palaeogeographic evolution of the external zones of the Betic Cordillera: Geol. Mijnbouw 59(2):155–168.

Gardiner P.R.R. and MacCarthy I.A.J., 1981, The late Palaezoic evolution of southern Ireland in the context of tectonic basins and their transatlantic significance: Can. Soc. Petrol. Geol. Mem. 7: 683–725.

Garfunkel Z., 1981, Internal structure of the Dead Sea leaky transform (rift) in relation to plate kinematics: Tectonophysics 80:81–108.

Garzanti E., 1985, The sandstone memory of the evolution of a Triassic volcanic arc in the southern Alps, Italy: Sedimentology 32:423–433.

Gates A.E., Simpson C. and Glover L. III, 1986, Appalachian Carboniferous dextral strike-slip faults: An example from Brookneal, Virginia: Tectonics 5(1):119–133.

Gebauer D. and Grünenfelder M., 1982, Geological development of the Hercynian Belt of Europe based on age and origing of high-grade and high-pressure mafic and ultra mafic rocks: Proc. 5 Internat. Conf. on geochronology, Cosmochronology, Isotope Geology, Nikko National Park, Japan, Geochem. Soc. Japan Publ. p. 111–112.

Gee D.G. and Sturt B.A. (eds.), 1986, The Caledonide Orogen-Scandinavia and related areas, part 1 and 2, 1266 p.: New York, John Wiley and Sons.

George T.N., 1967, Landform and structure of Ulster: Scot. J. Geol. 3:400–440.

Geyssant J., 1980, Corrélations péri-adriatiques le long des Alpes orientales: Rapport entre domaines austro-alpin et sud-alpin et tectogénèse Crétacé: Bull. Soc. Géol. France (7)XCII(1):31–42.

Ghisetti F., 1984, Recent deformations and the seismogenic source in the Messinian Strait (southern Italy): Tectonophysics 109:191–208.

Gibbs A.D., 1984, Structural evolution of extensional basin margins: J. Geol. Soc. London 141:609–620.

Gibbs A.D., 1987, Basin development, examples from the United Kingdom and comments on hydrocarbon prospectivity: Tectonophysics 133:189–198.

Gillchrist R., Coward M. and Mugnier J.-L., 1987, Structural inversion and its controls: Examples from the Alpine foreland and the French Alps: Geodin. Acta 1(1):5–34.

Gillet P., Choukroune P., Ballèvre M. and Davy P., 1986, Thickening history of the Western Alps: Earth Planet. Sci. Lett. 78:44–52.

Given M.M., 1977, Mesozoic and early Cenozoic geology of offshore Nova Scotia: Bull. Can. Petrol. Geol. 25(1):63–91.

Gjelberg J.G. and Steel R.J., 1981, An outline of Lower–Middle Carboniferous sedimentation on Svalbard: Effects of tectonic, climatic and sea level changes in rift basin sequences: Can. Soc. Petrol. Geol. Mem. 7:543–561.

Gjelberg J. and Steel R., 1983, Middle Carboniferous marine transgression, Bjørnøya, Svalbard: Facies sequences from an interplay of sea level changes and tectonics: Geol. J. 18:1–19.

Glennie K.W., 1984a, Early Permian-Rotliegend, in K.W. Glennie (ed.), Introduction to the petroleum geology of the North Sea: Oxford, Blackwell Scient. Publ. p. 41–60.

Glennie K.W., 1984b, The structural framework and Pre-Permian history of the North Sea area, in K.W. Glennie (ed.), Introduction to the petroleum geology of the North Sea: Oxford, Blackwell Scient. Publ., p. 17–39.

Glennie K.W., 1986, Development of N.W. Europe's southern Permian gas basin, in J. Brooks, J.C. Goff and B. van Hoorn (eds.), Habitat of Palaeozoic gas in N.W. Europe: Geol. Soc. Spec. Publ. 23:3–22.

Gluschko W.W., Skorduli W.D. and Tarchanow M.I., 1976, Über den geologischen Bau der Lwower paläozoischen Senke: Zeitschr. Angew. Geol. 22(1):166–176.

Goldberg J.M., Maluski H. and Leyreloup A.F., 1986, Age de 95 Ma (méthode $^{39}$Ar-$^{40}$Ar) du schonkinite des Corbières de la brèche magmatique du col d'Agnes, et du métamorphisme statique dans la zone nord-pyrénéenne: Bull. Soc. Géol. France (8)II(4):623–628.

Gortunov G.I., Zagorodny V.G., Makievsky S.I. and Suetnor V.V., 1984, The structure and history of the formation of the Barents Sea South Frame, in Arctic geology: Proc. 27th Internat. Geol. Congr., Coll. 04, Vol. 4, pp. 84–93.

Gough D.I., 1984, Mantle upflow under North America and plate dynamics: Nature, London 311:428–432.

Gowers M.B. and Lunde G., 1984, The geological history of Traenabanken, in A.M. Spencer et al. (eds.), Petroleum geology of the north European margin: Norw. Petrol. Soc., London, Graham and Trotman, p. 231–251.

Graciansky P.C. de and Poag C.W. et al., 1985, Geological history of Goban Spur, northwest Europe continental margin, in P.C. de Graciansky, C.W. Poag et al., Initial Reports of Deep Sea Drilling Project, 80, Washington, DC, US Govt Printing Office, p. 1187–1216.

Graciansky P.C. de et al., 1985, The Goban Spur transsect: Geologic evolution of a sediment-starved passive continental margin: Geol. Soc. Am. Bull. 96:58–76.

Gradstein F.M. and Srivastava S.P., 1980, Aspects of Cenozoic stratigraphy and paleoceanography of the Labrador Sea and Baffin Bay: Palaeogeogr., Palaeoclim., Palaeoecol. 30:261–295.

Gradstein F.M., Grant A.C. and Jansa L.F., 1977, Grand Banks and Janomaly Ridge: Geological comparison: Science 197:1074–1076.

Grant A.C., 1975, Structural modes of the western margin of the Labrador Sea, in W.J.M. van der Linden and J.A. Wade (eds.), Offshore geology of eastern Canada: Geol. Surv. Can. Paper 74–30:217–231.

Grant A.C., 1980, Problems with plate tectonics: The Labrador Sea: Bull. Can. Petrol. Geol. 28(2):252–278.

Grant A.C., 1982, Problems with plate tectonic models for Baffin Bay—Nares Strait: Evidence from the Labrador Sea, in P.R. Dawes and J.W. Kerr (eds.), Nares Strait and the drift of Greenland: A conflict in plate tectonics: Meddel. Grønland, Geoscience 8:313–326.

Grant A.C., McAlpine K.D. and Wade J.A., 1986, The continental margin of eastern Canada: Geological framework and petroleum potential, in M.T. Halbouty (ed.), Future petroleum provinces of the world: Am. Assoc. Petrol. Geol. Mem. 40:177–205.

Grantz A. and May S.D., 1982, Rifting history and structural development of the continental margin of Alaska, in J.S. Watkins and C.L. Drake (eds.), Studies in continental margin geology: Am. Assoc. Petrol. Geol. Mem. 34:77–100.

Grantz A. and May S.D., 1984, Sedimentary basins and geologic structure of the continental margin north of Alaska: 27th Internat. Geol. Congr. Moscow, Publ. Office "Nauka," Moscow, Arctic Geology, Coll. 04, Reports Vol. 4, p. 125–142.

Grantz A., Eittreim S. and Dinter D.A., 1979, Geology and tectonic development of the continental margin north of Alaska: Tectonophysics 59:263–291.

Grantz A., Eittreim S. and Whitney O.T., 1981, Geology and physiography of the continental margin of Alaska and implications for the origin of the Canada Basin, in A.E.M. Nairn, M. Churkin Jr. and F.G. Stehli (eds.), The ocean basins and margins. Vol. 5. The Arctic Ocean: New York London, Plenum Press, p. 439–492.

Grimaud S., Boillot G., Collette B.J., Manffret A., Miles P.R. and Roberts D.G., 1982, Western extension of the Iberian-European plate boundary during the early Cenozic (Pyrenean) convergence, a new model: Mar. Geol. 45:63–77.

Groupe Galice, 1979, The continental margin of Galicia and Portugal: Accoustical stratigraphy, dredge stratigraphy and structural evolution, in J.C. Sibuet, W.B.F. Ryan et al., Initial Reports of Deep Sea Drilling Project, 47, Part 2, Washington, D.C. US Govt. Printing Office, p 633–662.

Guillaume A., 1978, La ligne du Tonale (Alpes centrales et orientales); sens de décrochements et prolongements: Tectonophysics 48:T7–T14.

Guillocheau F. and Rolet J., 1982, La sédimentation paléozoique Ouest-Armoricaine: Bull. Soc. Géol. Mineral. Bretagne (C)14(2):45–62.

Guiraud R., 1975, L'évolution post-Triassique de l'avant-pays de la chaîne Alpine en Algérie d'après l'étude du Bassin de Hodna et des régions voisines: Rev. Geogr. Phys. Geol. Dyn. (2)17(4):427–446.

Gurevich Y.L. and Slautsitays I.P., 1985, A paleomagnetic section in the Upper Permian and Triassic deposits of Novaya Zemlya: Int. Geol. Rev. 27:168–177.

Guterch A., Kowalski T., Materzok R. and Toporkiewica S., 1976, Seismic refraction study of the Earth's crust in the Teisseyre-Tornquist line zone in Poland along the regional profile LT-2: Publs. Inst. Geophys. Pol. Ac. Sci. A- 2(101):15–23.

Guterch A., Grad M., Materzok R. and Perchuc E., 1986, Deep structure of the Earth's crust in the contact zone of the Palaeozoic and Precambrian platforms of Poland (Tornquist–Teisseyre zone): Tectonophysics 128:251–279.

Gwinner M.P., 1971, Geologie der Alpen: Stratigraphie, Paläogeographie, Tektonik: Stuttgart, E. Schweizerbart'sche Verlagsbuchhandlung (Nägele und Obermiller), 477 p.

Håkansson E., 1979, Carboniferous to Tertiary development of the Wandel Sea Basin, eastern North Greenland: Grønlands Geol. Unders. Rapp. 88:73– 83.

Håkansson E. and Pedersen S.A.S., 1982, Late Palaeozoic to Tertiary tectonic evolution of the continental margin in North Greenland, in A.F. Embry and H.R. Balkwill (eds.), Arctic geology and geophysics: Can. Soc. Petrol. Geol. Mem. 8:331–348.

Håkansson E. and Stemmerik L., 1984, Wandel Sea Basin, the North Greenland equivalent to Svalbard and the Barents Shelf, in A.M. Spencer et al. (eds.), Petroleum geology of the north European margin: Norw. Petrol. Soc., London, Graham and Trotman, p. 97–107.

Håkansson E., Birkelund T., Piaseki S. and Zakarov V., 1981a, Jurassic-Cretaceous boundary strata of the extreme Arctic (Peary Land, North Greenland): Bull. Geol. Soc. Denmark 30:11–42.

Håkansson E., Heinberg C. and Stemmerik L., 1981b, The Wandel Sea Basin from Holm Land to Lookwood Ø, east North Greenland: Grønlands Geol. Unders. Rapp. 106:47–63.

Hald N. and Waagstein R., 1983. Silicic basalts from the Faeroe Islands: Evidence of crustal contamination, in M.H.P. Bott, S. Saxov, M. Talwani and J. Thiede (eds.), Structure and development of the Greenland–Scotland Ridge—new methods and concepts: New York/London, Plenum Press, p. 343–349.

Hall J.M., 1981, The Thulean volcanic line, in J.W. Kerr, A.J. Fergusson and L.C. Machan (eds.), Geology of the North Atlantic borderlands: Can. Soc. Petrol. Geol. Mem. 7:231–244.

Hallam A., 1978, Eustatic cycles in the Jurassic: Palaeogeogr., Palaeoclim., Palaeoecol. 23:1–32.

Hallam A., 1984, Pre-Quaternary sea-level changes: Ann. Rev. Earth Planet. Sci. 12:205–243.

Haller J., 1971, Geology of the East Greenland Caledonides, in L.V. de Sitter (ed.), Regional geology series: London, Interscience Publ., 413 p.

Hambrey M.J. and Harland W.B. (eds.), 1981, Earth's pre-Pleistocene glacial record: Cambridge, Cambridge University Press, 1044 p.

Hamilton W., 1970, The Uralides and the motion of the Russian-Siberian platforms: Geol. Soc. Am. Bull. 81:2553–2576.

Hancock J.M., 1984, Cretaceous, in K.W. Glennie (ed.), Introduction to the petroleum geology of the North Sea: Oxford, Blackwell Scient. Publ., p. 133–150.

Hancock J.M. and Kauffman E.G., 1979, The great transgressions of the Late Cretaceous: J. Geol. Soc. London, 136:175–186.

Hancock J.M. and Scholle P.A., 1975, Chalk of the North Sea, in A.W. Woodland (ed.), Petroleum and the continental shelf of NW Europe. Vol. I. Geology, Barking, England, p. 413–427.

Hanisch J., 1983, The structural evolution of the NE Atlantic region: Geol. Jb., B, 52: 37 p.

Hanisch J., 1984a, West Spitsbergen Fold Belt and Cretaceous opening of the northeast Atlantic, in A.M. Spencer et al. (eds.), Petroleum geology of the north European margin: Norw. Petrol. Soc., London, Graham and Trotman, p. 187–198.

Hanisch J., 1984b, The Cretaceous opening of the northeast Atlantic: Tectonophysics 101:1–23.

Haq B.U., Hardenbol J. and Vail P.R., 1987, Chronology of fluctuating sea levels since the Triassic (250 million years ago to present): Science, 235(4793): 1156–1167.

Hardenbol J., Vail P.R. and Ferrer J., 1981, Interpreting palaeoenvironments, subsidence history and sea level changes of passive margins from seismic and biostratigraphy: Proc. 26th Internat. Geol. Congr. Geology of Continental Margins Symp., Oceanologica Acta Supp. 4:33–44.

Harland W.B., Cox A.V., Llewellyn P.G., Pickton C.A.G., Smith A.G. and Walters R., 1982, A geological timescale: Cambridge Earth Sci. Ser., Cambridge University Press, 131 p.

Harland W.B., Gaskell B.A., Heafford A.P., Lind E.K. and Perkins P.J., 1984, Outline of Arctic post-Silurian continental displacements, in A.M. Spencer et al. (eds.), Petroleum geology of the north European margin: Norw. Petorl Soc., London, Graham and Trotman, p. 137–148.

Harmand C. and Laville E., 1983, Magmatisme alcalin Mésozoique et phénomènes thermiques associés dans le Haute-Atlas Saharien (Maroc): Bull. Cent. Rech. Explor.-Prod., Elf-Aquitaine 7(1):367–376.

Harmand C. and Moukadiri A., 1986, Synchronisme entre tectonique compressive et volcanisme alcalin: Exemple de la province quaternaire du Moyen Atlas: Bull. Soc. Géol. France (8)II(4):595–603.

Harris A.L. and Fettes D.J. (eds.). The Caledonian–Appalachian orogen: Geol. Soc. London Spec. Publication (in press).

Harris L.B., 1985, Direction changes in thrusting of the Schistes Lustrés in Alpine Corsica: Tectonophysics 120:37–56.

Harrison R.K., Jeans C.V. and Merriman R.J., 1979, Mesozoic igneous rocks, hydrothermal mineralisation and volcanic sediments in Britain and adjacent regions: Bull. Geol. Surv. Gt. Br. 70:57–65.

Hatcher R.D. Jr., 1985, The North American Appalachian Orogen, in R.A. Gayer (ed.), The tectonic evolution of the Caledonide-Appalachian Orogen: Braunsschweig/ Wiesbaden, F. Vieweg & Son, p. 48–56.

Hatton I.R., 1986, Geometry of allochthonous chalk group members, Central Trough, North Sea: Mar. Petrol. Geol. 3:79–98.

Hays J.D. and Pitmann W.C. III, 1973, Lithsopheric plate motion, sea level changes and climatic and ecological consequences: Nature, London, 246:18–22.

Hea J.P., Arcuri J., Campbell G.R., Fraser I., Fuglem M.O.,

O'Bertos J.J., Smith D.R. and Zayat M., 1980, Post-Ellesmerian basins of Arctic Canada: Their depocentres, rates of sedimentation and petroleum potential, *in* A.D. Miall (ed.), Facts and principles of world petroleum occurrence: Can. Soc. Petrol. Geol. Mem. 6:447–488.

Heller I. and Moryc W., 1984, Stratigraphy of the Upper Cretaceous deposits in the Carpathian foreland: Biul. Inst. Geol., Warszawa 346(XXIV):63–116.

Heller P.L. and Angevine C.L., 1985, Sea-level cycles during the growth of Atlantic-type oceans: Earth Planet. Sci. Lett. 75:417–426.

Hellinger J.S. and Sclater J.G., 1983, Some comments on two-layer extension models for the evolution of sedimentary basins: J. Geophys. Res. B. 88(10):8251–8269.

Helwig J., Aronson J. and Day D.S., 1974, A Late Jurassic mafic pluton in Newfoundland: Can. J. Earth Sci. 11(9):1314–1319.

Henderson G., 1976, Petroleum geology, *in* A. Escher and W.S. Watt (eds.), Geology of Greenland: Greenland Geol. Surv., p. 489–505.

Henderson G., Rosenkrantz A. and Schiener E.J., 1976, Cretaceous-Tertiary sedimentary rocks of West Greenland, *in* A. Escher and W.S. Watt (eds.), Geology of Greenland: Greenland Geol. Surv., p. 341–362.

Henderson G., Schiener E.J., Risum J.B., Croxton C.A. and Andersen B.B., 1981, The West Greenland Basin, *in* J.W. Kerr, A.J. Fergusson and L.C. Machan (eds.), Geology of the North Atlantic borderlands: Can. Soc. Petrol. Geol. Mem. 7:399–428.

Henriksen N. and Higgins A.K., 1976, East Greenland Caledonian fold belt, *in* A. Escher and W.S. Watt (eds.), Geology of Greenland: Greenland Geol. Surv., p. 183–246.

Herb R., 1965, Das Tertiär der helvetischen Decken der Ostschweiz: Bull. Verh. Schweiz. Petrol. Geol. u. Ing. 31(81):135–151.

Hernandez J., Larouziere F.D. de, Bolze J. and Bordet P., 1987, Le magmatisme néogène bético-rifain et le couloir de décrochement trans-Alboran: Bull. Soc. Géol. France (8)III(2):257–267.

Heum O.R., Dalland A. and Meisingset K.K., 1986, Habitat of hydrocarbons at Haltenbanken (PVT-modelling as a predictive tool in hydrocarbon exploration), *in* A.M. Spencer et al. (eds.), Habitat of hydrocarbons on the Norwegian continental shelf: London, Graham and Trotman, p. 259–274.

Higgins A.K. and Soper N.J., 1981, Cretaceous-Paleogene sub-basaltic and intra-basaltic sediments of the Kangerdlugssuaq area-Central-East Greenland: Geol. Mag. 118(4):337–353.

Higgins A.K. and Soper N.J., 1983, The Lake Hazen fault zone, Ellesmere Island: Transpressional upthrust, *in* Current research, Part B: Geol. Surv. Can. Paper 83–1B: 215–221.

Hillebrandt A. von, 1981, Kontinentalverschiebung und die paläozoographischen Beziehungen des Südamerikanischen Lias: Geol. Rundsch. 70(2):570–582.

Hinz K. and Schlüter H.-U., 1978a, Der Nordatlantik—Ergebnisse geophysikalischer Untersuchungen der Bundesanstalt für Geowissenschaften und Rohstoffe an nordatlantischen Kontinentalrändern: Erdöl-Erdgas Zeitschr. 94:271–280.

Hinz K. and Schlüter H.-U., 1978b, The geological structure of the western Barents Sea: Mar. Geol. 26:199–230.

Hinz K. and Schüter H.-U., 1980, Continental margin of East Greenland: Proc. 10th World Petrol. Congr., Bucharest, Vol. 2, Exploration Supply and Demand, London, Heyden and Son, Ltd., p. 405–418.

Hoch E., 1983, Fossil evidence of Early Tertiary North Atlantic events viewed in European context, *in* M.H.P. Bott, S. Saxov, M. Talwani and J. Thiede (eds.), Structure and development of the Greenland-Scotland Ridge-new methods and concepts: New York London, Plenum Press, p. 401–415.

Hodyck J.P. and Hayatsu A., 1980, K-Ar isochron age and palaeomagnetism of diabase along the trans-Avalon aeromagnetic lineament—evidence of Late Jurassic rifting in Newfoundland: Can. J. Earth Sci. 17:491–499.

Hohler J.J. and Bischoff W.E., 1986, Alaska: Potential for giant fields, *in* M.T. Halbouty (ed.), Future petroleum provinces of the world: Am. Assoc. Petrol. Geol. Mem. 40:131–142.

Holder M.T. and Leveridge B.E., 1986, A model for the tectonic evolution of South Cornwall: J. Geol. Soc. London, 143:125–134.

Holl A. and Altherr R., 1987, Hercynian I-type granitoids of northern Vosges: Documents of increasing arc maturity: Terr. Cog. 7(2–3):74 (abstract).

Holtedahl O., 1960, Geology of Norway: Norges Geol. Undersø kelse 208:540 p.

Homewood p., 1983, Palaeogeography of Alpine Flysch: Palaeogeogr., Palaeoclim., Palaeoecol. 44(3–4):169–184.

Homewood P., Gosso G., Escher A., Milnes A., 1980, Cretaceous and Tertiary evolution along the Besançon-Bielta traverse (western Alps): Ecl. Geol. Helv. 73(2):635–649.

Hoorn B. van, 1987a, Evolution of the Bristol Channel basin: Tectonophysics 137:309–334.

Hoorn B. van, 1987b, Structural evolution, timing and tectonic style of the Sole Pit inversion: Tectonophysics 137:239–284.

Horne R.R. and MacIntyre R.M., 1975, Apparent age and significance of Tertiary dykes in the Dingle Peninsula, SW Ireland: Scient. Proc. R. Dublin Soc. 5A:293–299.

Horner F. and Freeman R., 1983, Palaeomagnetic evidence form pelagic limestones for clockwise rotation of the Ionian zone, western Greece: Tectonophysics 98:11–27.

Horner F. and Lowrie W., 1981, Palaeomagnetic evidence from Mesozoic carbonate rocks for rotation of Sardinia: J. Geophys. 49:11–19.

Horstink J., 1980, Oil exploration in southeastern Turkey: Bull. Am. Assoc. Petrol. Geol. 64(5):724 (abstract).

Horváth F. and Berkhemer H., 1982, Mediterranean back-arc basins, *in* A. Berkhemer and K. Hsü (eds.), Alpine-Mediterranean geodynamics: Am. Geophys. Union, Geol. Soc. Am., Geodynam. Ser. 7:141–173.

Horváth F. and Royden L., 1981, Mechanism for the formation of the Intra-Carpathian basins: A review: Earth Evol. Sci. 3–4:307–316.

Horváth F. and Rumpler J., 1984, The Pannonian Basement: Extension and subsidence of an Alpine Orogen: Acta Geol. Hungar. 27(3–4):229–235.

Horváth F., Dövényi P. and Liebe P., 1981, Geothermics of the Pannonian Basin: Earth Evol. Sci. 3– 4:285–291.

Horváth F., Szalay A., Dövényi P. and Rumpler J., 1986, Structural and thermal evolution of the Pannonian Basin: An overview, *in* J. Burrus (ed.), Thermal modelling in sedimentary basins: Paris, Editions Technip, Collection Colloques et Seminaries 44:339–358.

Hospers J., Rathore J.S., Jianhua F. and Finnstrøm E.G., 1986a, Thickness of pre-Zechstein salt Palaeozoic sediments in the southern part of the Norwegian sector of the North Sea: Norsk Geol. Tidsk. 66:295–304.

Hospers J., Finnstrøm E.G. and Rathore J.S., 1986b, A regional gravity study of the northern North Sea (56°-62°N):

Geophys. Prosp. 33:543–566.

Hossack J.R., 1984, The geometry of listric growth faults in the Devonian basins of Sunnfjord, W. Norway: J. Geol. Soc. London 141:629–638.

Hossack J.R., 1985, The role of thrusting in the Scandinavian Caledonides, in R.A. Gayer (ed.), The tectonic evolution of the Caledonide-Appalachian orogen: Braunschweig/Wiesbaden, F. Vieweg & Sohn, p. 97–116.

Hossack J.R., Garton M.R. and Nickelsen R.P., 1986, The geological section from the foreland up to the Jotun thrust street in the Valderes area, south Norway, in D.G. Gee and A.B. Sturt (eds.), The Caledonide Orogen-Scandinavia and related areas: New York, John Wiley and Sons Ltd., p. 443–456.

House M.R., 1983, Devonian eustatic events: Proc. Uscher Soc. 5:396–405.

House M.R., Richardson J.B., Chaloner W.G., Alten J.R.L., Holland C.H. and Westoll T.S., 1977, A correlation of Devonian rocks of the British Isles: Geol. Soc. London Spec. Rep. 8:110 p.

Houten F.B. van and Brown R.H., 1977, Latest Palaeozoic-early Mesozoic palaeogeography, northwestern Africa: J. Geol. 85:143–156.

Howarth M.K., 1973, Lower Jurassic (Pliensbachian and Toarcian) ammonites, in A. Hallam (ed.), Atlas of palaeobiogeography: Amsterdam, Elsevier Sci. Publ. Co., p. 274–285.

Howie R.D. and Barss M.S., 1975a, Palaeogeography and sedimentation in the upper Palaeozoic, eastern Canada, in C.J. Yorath, E.R. Parker and D.J. Glass (eds.), Canada's continental margins and offshore petroleum exploration: Can. Soc. Petrol. Geol. Mem. 4:45–57.

Howie R.D. and Barss M.S., 1975b, Upper Paleozoic rocks of the Atlantic provinces, Gulf of St. Lawrence, and adjacent continental shelf: Geol. Surv. Can. Pap. 74-30, 2:35–50.

Hsü K.J., 1972, Origin of saline giants: A critical review after the discovery of the Mediterranean evaporite: Earth Sci. Rev. 8:371–396.

Hsü K.J., 1978, When the Black Sea was drained: Sci. Am. 238:53–63.

Hsü K.J., 1982, Editors introduction: Alpine-Mediterranean geodynamics: past, present, and future, in H. Berkhemer and K. Hsü (eds.), Alpine-Mediterranean geodynamics: Am. Geophys. Union, Geol. Soc. Am., Geodynam. Ser. 7:7–14.

Hsü K.J., Ryan W.B.F. and Cita M.B., 1973, Late Miocene dessication in the Mediterranean: Nature, London 242:240–244.

Hsü K.J., Montadert L., Bernoulli D., Cita M.B., Erickson A., Garrison A.T., Kidd A.B., Mélières F., Müller C. and Wright R., 1978, History of the Mediterranean salinity crisis, in K.J. Hsü et al. (eds.), Initial Reports of Deep Sea Drilling Project, 42, Washington, DC, U.S. Govt. Printing Office, p. 1053–1078.

Hsui A. and Toksöz N., 1981, Back-arc spreading: Trench migration, continental pull or induced convection: Tectonophysics 74:89–98.

Hubacher F.A. and Lux D.R., 1987, Timing of Acadian deformation in northeastern Maine: Geology 15:80–83.

Hubbard R.J., Pape J. and Roberts D.G., 1985, Depositional sequence mapping to illustrate the evolution of passive continental margins: Am. Assoc. Petrol. Geol. Mem. 39:93–115.

Hubbard R.J., Edrich S.P. and Rattey R.P., 1987, Geologic evolution and hydrocarbon habitat of the "Arctic Alaska Microplate": Mar. Petrol. Geol. 4(1):2–34.

Hugon H., 1983, Ellesmere-Greenland fold belt: Structural evidence for left-lateral shearing: Tectonophysics 100:215–225.

Hurst J.M. and Surlyk F., 1984, Tectonic control of Silurian carbonate shelf margin morphology and facies, North Greenland: Bull. Am. Assoc. Petrol. Geol. 68(1):1–17.

Hurst J.M., McKerrow W.S., Soper N.J. and Surlyk F., 1983, The relationship between Caledonian nappe tectonics and Silurian turbidite deposits in northern Greenland: J. Geol. Soc. London 140:123–131.

Hutchison D.R., Klitgord K.D. and Detrick R.S., 1986, Rift basins of the Long Island Platform: Geol. Soc. Am. Bull. 97:688–702.

Iglesias M., Ribeiro M.L. and Ribeiro A., 1983, La interpretacion alloctonista de la estrutura del noroeste peninsular, in Libro Jubilar J.M. Ramos, Geologia de Espana, Tomo I., Inst. Geol., Minero Espana Publ., p. 459–467.

Ilhan E., 1974, Eastern Turkey, in A.M. Spencer (ed.), Mesozoic-Cenozoic orogenic belts, data for orogenic studies: Geol. Soc. London Spec. Publ. 4:187–197.

Illies J.H., 1978, Two stage Rhinegraben rifting, in I.B. Ramberg and E.-R. Neumann (eds.), Tectonics and geophysics of continental rifts: vol. N.A.T.O. Advanced Study Institute Series C, Math. Phys. Sci., Dordrecht, D. Reidel 37:63–71.

Illies J.H., 1981, Graben formation—the Maltese Islands, a case history: Tectonophysics 73:151–168.

Illies J.H. and Greiner G., 1978, Rhinegraben and the Alpine system: Geol. Soc. Am. Bull. 89:770–782.

Irving E. and Strong D.H., 1984, Evidence against large-scale Carboniferous strike-slip faulting in the Appalachian-Caledonian orogen: Nature, London, 310:762–764.

Isaac K.P. and Barnes R.P., 1985, Discussion of papers on the Hercynian back-arc marginal basin of SW England: J. Geol. Soc. London, 142(5):927–929.

Jackson H.R. and Johnson G.L., 1984, Structure and history of the Amerasian Basin, in Arctic geology: 27th Internat. Geol. Congr., Moscow, Coll. 04, p. 143–151.

Jackson H.R., Keen C.E. and Barrett D.C., 1977, Geophysical studies on the eastern continental margin of Baffin Bay and in Lancaster Sound: Can. J. Earth Sci. 14:1991–2001.

Jackson H.R., Keen C.E., Falconer R.K.H. and Appleton K.P., 1979, New geophysical evidence for sea-floor spreading in the Central Baffin Bay: Can. J. Earth Sci. 16:2122–2135.

Jacobsen V.W. and Van Veen P., 1984, The Triassic offshore Norway north of 62 °N, in A.M. Spencer et al. (eds.), Petroleum geology of the north European margin: Norw. Petrol. Soc., London, Graham and Trotman, p. 317–327.

Jacobshagen V.W., 1982, Mediterrane Trias—Grundzüge und Probleme: Geol. Rundsch. 71(3):973–985.

Jacobshagen V., Dürr St., Kockel F., Kopp K.-O., Kowalczyk G., Berkheimer H. and Büttner D., 1978, Structure and geodynamic evolution of the Aegean region, in H. Closs, D. Roeder and K. Schmidt (eds.), Alps, Apennines, Hellenides: Inter-Union Commission on Geodynamics, Sci. Rept. 38, Stuttgart, Schweizerbart'sche Verlagsbuchhandlung, p. 537–564.

Jacqué M. and Thouvenin J., 1975, Lower Tertiary tuffs and volcanic activity in the North Sea, in A.W. Woodland (ed.), Petroleum and the continental shelf of NW Europe. Vol. 1. Geology: Barking, England, Applied Science Publishers, p. 455–465.

Jaffrezo M. and Obert D., 1978, Les Pyrénées: Bull. Soc. Géol. France (7)XX(5):587–629.

Jansa L.F., 1981, Mesozoic carbonate platforms and banks of the eastern North American margin: Mar. Geol. 44:97–117.

Jansa L.F. and Pe-Piper G., 1985, Early Cretaceous volcanism on the north-eastern Atlantic margin and implications for plate tectonic: Geol. Soc. Am. Bull. 96:83–91.

Jansa L.F. and Wade J.A., 1975, Palaeogeography and sedimentation in the Mesozoic and Cenozoic, southeastern Canada: in C.J. Yorath, E.R. Parker and D.J. Glass (eds.), Canada's continental margins and offshore petroleum exploration: Can. Soc. Petrol. Geol. Mem. 4:79–102.

Jansa L.F. and Wiedmann J., 1982, Mesozoic and Cenozoic development of the eastern North American and northwest African continental margin, in U. von Rad, K. Hinz and E. Seibold (eds.), Geology of the northwest African continental margin: Berlin/Heidelberg, Springer-Verlag, p. 215–269.

Jansa L.F., Mamet B. and Roux A., 1978, Visean limestones from the Newfoundland Shelf: Can. J. Earth Sci. 15(9):1422–1436.

Jansa L.F., Steiger T.H. and Bradshaw M., 1984, Mesozoic carbonate deposition on the outer continental margin of Morocco, in K. Hinz, E.L. Winterer et al., Initial Reports of Deep Sea Drilling Project, 79, Washington, DC, U.S. Govt. Printing Office, p. 857–891.

Jarrard R.D., 1986, Causes of compression and extension behind trenches: Tectonophysics 132:89–102.

Jarvis G.T. and McKenzie D.P., 1980, Sedimentary basin formation with finite extention rates: Earth Planet. Sci. Lett. 48:42–52.

Jenkyns H.C., 1980, Tethys: Past and present: Proc. Geol. Assoc., 91(1 & 2):107–118.

Jenny J., 1983, Les décrochements de l'Atlas de Demnat (Haut Atlas central, Maroc): prolongation orientale de la zone de décrochement du Tizi-n-Test et clef de la compréhension de la tectonique atlasique: Ecl. Geol. Helv. 76:243–251.

Jenyon M.K., Cresswell P.M. and Taylor J.C.M., 1984, Nature of the connection between the northern and southern Zechstein basins across the mid North Sea High: Mar. Petrol. Geol. 1:355–363.

Johnson G.A.L., 1976, Palaeozoic accretion of western Europe: Ann. Soc. Geol. Nord. 96:347–352.

Johnson H.D., Levell B.K. and Siedlicki S., 1978, Late Precambrian sedimentary rocks in East Finnmark, north Norway, and their relationship to the Trollfjord-Komagelv fault: J. Geol. Soc. London 135:517–533.

Johnson J.G., Klapper G. and Sandberg C.A., 1985, Devonian eustatic fluctuations in Euramerica: Geol. Soc. Am. Bull. 96:567–587.

Johnson R.J.E. and van der Voo R., 1985, Middle Cambrian palaeomagnetism of the Avalon Terrane in Cape Breton Island, Nova Scotia: Tectonics 4(7):629–651.

Jones E.J.W., 1978, Seismic evidence for sedimentary troughs of Mesozoic age on the Hebridean continental margin: Nature, London 272:789–792.

Jones M., Voo R. van der and Bonhommet N., 1979, Late Devonian to Early Carboniferous palaeomagnetic poles from the Armorican Massif, France: Geophys. J.R. Astr. Soc. 58:287–308.

Jones P.B., 1982, Mesozoic rifting in the western Arctic Ocean Basin and its relationship to Pacific seafloor spreading, in A.F. Embry and H.R. Balkwill (eds.), Arctic geology and geophysics: Can. Soc. Petrol. Geol. Mem. 8:83–99.

Jongsma D., Woodwise J.M., King G.C.P. and van Hinte J.E., 1987, The Medina Wrench: A key to the kinematics of the central and eastern Mediterranean over the past 5 Ma: Earth Planet. Sci. Lett. 82:87–106.

Jowett E.C. and Jaruis G.T., 1984, Formation of foreland rifts, in L.F. Jansa, P.F. Burrollet and A.C. Grant (eds.), Basin

analysis: principles and application: Sedim. Geology 40:51–72.

Julivert M., 1978, The areas of Alpine folded cover in the Iberian Meseta (Iberian chain, Catalanides, etc.), in M. Lemoine (eds.), Geological atlas of Alpine Europe and adjoining areas: Amsterdam/Oxford/New York, Elsevier Sci. Publ. Co., p. 93–112.

Julivert M., 1979, A cross-section through the northern part of the Iberian Massif, its position within the Hercynian fold belt: Krystallinikum 14:51–57.

Julivert M., 1981, A cross-section through the northern part of the Iberian Massif: Geol. Mijnbouw 60:107–126.

Julivert M., 1983, La evolucion sedimentaria durante el Paleozoico y el registro de la deformacion en la columna estratigraphica paleozoica, in Libro Jubilar J.M. Ramos, Geologia de Espana, Tomo I., Inst. Geol. Minero Espana Publ., p. 593–600.

Julivert M., Marcos A. and Perez-Estaun A., 1977, La structure de la chaîne Hercynienne dans le secteur Ibérique et l'arc Ibéro-Armoricain, in La chaîne varisque d'Europe moyenne et occidentale: Colloque Int. C.N.R.S., Rennes 243:429–440.

Julivert M., Truyols J. and Vergés J., 1983, El Devonico en el Macizo Iberico, in Libro Jubilar J.M. Ramos, Geologia de Espana, Tomo I, Inst. Geol. Minero Espana Publ., p. 265–310.

Juteau T., Eissen J.P., Monin A.S., Zonenshain L.P., Sorokhtin O.G., Matveenkov V.V. and Almukhamedov A.I., 1983, Structure et pétrologie du rift axial de la Mer Rouge vers 18° Nord: Bull. Cent. Rech. Expl.-Prod. Elf-Aquitaine 7(1):217–229.

Kaaschieter J.P.H., 1961, Foraminifera of the Eocene of Belgium: Mem. Inst. R. Sci. Nat. Belg. 147:271 p.

Kälin O. and Trümpy D.M., 1977, Sedimentation und Paläotektonik in den westlichen Südalpen: Zur triasisch-jurassischen Geschichte des Monte Nudo Beckens: Ecl. Geol. Helv. 70:295–350.

Kamen-Kaye M., 1972, Permian Tethys and Indian Ocean: Bull. Am. Assoc. Petrol. Geol. 56:1984–1999.

Kamen-Kaye M., 1976, Mediterranean Permian Tethys: Bull. Am. Assoc. Petrol. Geol. 60:623–626.

Kanasewich E.R., Havskov J. and Evans M.E., 1978, Plate tectonics in the Phanerozoic: Can. J. Earth Sci. 15(6):919–955.

Kaplan M.E., 1978, Calcite pseudomorphoses in Jurassic and Lower Cretaceous deposits of the northern area of eastern Siberia: Geolog. Geofis. 19(2):62–70.

Karasik A.M., Ustritsky V.I. and Khramov A.N., 1984, History of the formation of the Arctic Ocean: Proc. 27th Internat. Geol. Congr., Moscow, Coll. 04, Arctic Geology, Rep. 4:179–189.

Karlsson W., 1986, The Snorre, Statfjord and Gullfaks oilfields and the habitat of hydrocarbons on the Tampen Spur, offshore Norway, in A.M. Spencer et al. (eds.), Habitat of hydrocarbons on the Norwegian continental shelf: London, Graham and Trotman, p. 181–197.

Katzung G., 1961, Die Geröllführung des Lederschiefers (Ordovicium) an der S.E. Flanke des Schwarzenburger Sattels (Thüringen): Geologie 10(7):778–802.

Kazantseva T.T. and Kamaletditov M.A., 1986, The geosynclinal development of the Urals: Tectonophysics 127:371–381.

Kazmin V.G., Sbortshikov I.M., Ricou L.E., Zonnenshain L.P., Boulin J. and Knipper A.L., 1986, Volcanic belts as markers of the Mesozoic-Cenozoic active margin of Eurasia: Tectonophysics 123:123–152.

Keen C.E. and Barrett D.C., 1981, Thinned and subsided continental crust on the rifted margin of eastern Canada: Crustal structure, thermal evolution and subsidence history: Geophys. J.R. Astrol. Soc. 65:443–465.

Keen C.E. and Hyndman R.D., 1979, Geophysical review of the continental margins of eastern and western Canada: Can. J. Earth Sci., 16:712–747.

Keen C.E., Beaumont C. and Boutilier R., 1981, Preliminary results from a thermo-mechanical model for the evolution of Atlantic type continental margins: Proc. 26th Internat. Geol. Congr. Geology of Continental Margins Symp. Oceanologia Acta Suppl. 4:123–128.

Keen C.E., Keen M.J., Ross D.I. and Lack M., 1974, Baffin Bay: Small ocean basin formed by sea floor spreading: Bull. Am. Assoc. Petrol. Geol., 58:1089–1108.

Kellogg H.E., 1975, Tertiary stratigraphy and tectonism in Svalbard and continental drift: Bull. Am. Assoc. Petrol. Geol. 59(3):465–485.

Kemper E. and Hermann H., 1981, Glendonite-Indikatoren des polarmarinen Ablagerungsmilieus: Geol. Rundsch. 70(2):759–773.

Kemper E., Rawson P.F. and Thieuloy J.P., 1981, Ammonites of tethyan ancestry in the early Lower Cretaceous of north-west Europe: Palaeontology 24(2):251–311.

Kent D.V., 1982, Palaeomagnetic evidence for Post-Devonian displacement of the Avalon platform (Newfoundland): J. Geoph. Res. 87:8709–8716.

Kent D.V. and Keppie J.D., 1988, Silurian-Permian paleocontinental reconstruction and tectonics: In press.

Kent D.V. and Opdyke N.D., 1978, Palaeomagnetism of the Devonian Catskill red beds: Evidence of motion of the coastal New England-Canadian Maritime region relative to cratonic North America: J. Geophys. Res. 83:4441–4450.

Kent D.V. and Opdyke N.D., 1979, The Early Carboniferous palaeomagnetic field of North America and its bearing on tectonics of the northern Appalachians: Earth Planet. Sci. Lett. 44:365–372.

Kent D.V., Dia O. and Sougy J.M.A., 1984, Paleomagnetism of Lower-Middle Devonian and upper Proterozoic-Cambrian(?) rocks form Mejeria (Mauretania, West Africa), in R. van der Voo, C.R. Scotese and N. Bonhommet (eds.), Plate reconstruction from Paleozoic paleomagnetism: Am. Geophy. Union., Geol. Soc. Am. Geodynam. Ser. 12: 99–115.

Kent-Brooks C., 1980, Episodic volcanism, epirogenesis and the formation of the North Atlantic ocean: Palaeogeogr., Palaeoclim., Palaeoecol. 30:229–242.

Kenyon N.H., Belderson R.H. and Stride A.H., 1982, Detailed tectonic trends on the central part of the Hellenic outer ridge and in the Hellenic trench system, in J.K. Legget (ed.), Trench-forearc geology: Sedimentation and tectonics on modern and ancient active plate margins: Geol. Soc. London Spec. Publ. 10:335–343.

Keppie J.D., 1982, Tectonic map of the Province of Nova Scotia, 1:500.000: Dept. of Mines and Energy, Nova Scotia.

Keppie J.D., 1985, Geology and tectonics of Nova Scotia, in Appalachian geotraverse (Canadian mainland)—field excursions, Vol. I: Geol. Assoc. Can., Mineral. Assoc. Can., University of New Brunswick, p. 23–108.

Keppie J.D., Currie K.L., Murphy J.B., Pickerill R.K., Fyffe L.R. and St. Julien P., 1985, Appalachian geotraverse (Canadian mainland)—field excursions, Vol. I: Geol. Assoc. Can., Mineral. Assoc. Can., University of New Brunswick, p. 181.

Kerckhove C., Caron C., Charollais J. and Pairis J.L., 1980, Panorama des series synorogéniques des Alpes occidentales, in A. Autran and J. Dercourt (eds.), Evolution géologique de la France: Mem. B.R.G.M. 107:234–255.

Kerr J.W., 1967, A submerged continental remnant beneath the Labrador Sea: Earth Planet. Sci. Lett. 2:283–289.

Kerr J.W., 1981a, Evolution of the Canadian Arctic Islands: A transition between the Atlantic and Arctic Ocean, in A.E.M. Nairn, M. Churkin Jr. and F.G. Stehli (eds.), The ocean basins and margins. Vol. 5. The Arctic Ocean: New York, Plenum Press, p. 105–199.

Kerr J.W., 1981b, Stretching of the North American plate by a now dormant Atlantic spreading centre, in J.W. Kerr, A.J. Fergusson and L.C. Machan (eds.), Geology of the North Atlantic borderlands: Can. Soc. Petrol. Geol. Mem. 7:245–278.

Khain V., 1984a, The Alpine-Mediterranean fold belt of the USSR: Episodes 7(3):20–29.

Khain V.E., 1984b, General structural features of continents and oceans, in Short explanatory note to the international tectonic map of the world: 27th Internat. Geol. Congr., Moscow, "Nauka," Publ. Office p. 21–38.

Khain V.E., 1985, Geology of the USSR, first part: Old cratons and Paleozoic fold belts: Beiträge zur Regionalen Geologie der Erde—Band 17, Berlin Stuttgart, Gebrüder Bornträger, 272 p.

King A.F. and McMillan N.J., 1985, A mid-Mesozoic breccia from the Coast of Labrador: Can. J. Earth Sci. 12:44–51.

Kirton S.R., 1984, Carboniferous volcanicity in England with special reference to the Westphalian of the E. and W. Midlands: J. Geol. Soc. London 141(1):161–170.

Kissel C., Jamet M. and Laj C., 1984, Palaeomagnetic evidence of Miocene and Pliocene rotational deformation of the Aegean area, in J.E. Dixon and A.H.F. Robertson (eds.), The geological evolution of the eastern Mediterranean: Geol. Soc. Lond. Spec. Publ. 17:669–679.

Klemperer S.L., Hauge T.A., Hauser E.C., Oliver J.E. and Potter C.J., 1986, The Moho in the northern Basin and Range province, Nevada along COCORP 40 °N seismic-reflection transect: Geol. Soc. Am. Bull. 97:603–618.

Klingspor I., 1976, Radiometric age determinations on basalts and dolerites and related syenites in Skäne, South Sweden: Geol. For. Stockh. Förh. 98:195–215.

Klose G.W., Malterre E., McMillan N.J. and Zinkan C.g., 1982, Petroleum exploration offshore southern Baffin Island, Northern Labrador Sea, in A.F. Embry and H.R. Balkwill (eds.), Arctic geology and geophysics: Can. Soc. Petrol. Geol. Mem. 8:233–244.

Knox R.W.O'B, 1977, Upper Jurassic pyroclastic rocks in Skye, West Scotland: Nature London 265:323–324.

Knox R.W.O'B, Morton A.C. and Harland R., 1981, Stratigraphic relationships of Palaeocene sands in the U.K. sector of the Central North Sea, in L.V. Illings and G.D. Hobson (eds.), Petroleum geology of the continental shelf of N.W. Europe: London, Institute of Petroleum, p. 267–281.

Kolarova M. and Roth Z., 1977, Geology of the platform entering below the Carpathian Foredeep and its Carpathian nappes in S.E. Moravia: Bull. Geol. Surv. Prag. 52(5):257–265.

Kollmann K., 1977, Die Öl- und Gasexploration der Molassezone Oberösterreichs und Salzburgs aus regionalgeologischer Sicht: Erdöl-Erdgas Z., Spec. Iss. 93:36–49.

Kollmann K. and Malzer O., 1980, Die Molassezone Oberösterreichs und Salzburgs, in F. Brix and O. Schultz (eds.), Erdöl und Erdgas in Osterreich: Wien, Nat. Hist. Museum, p. 179–201.

Kominz M.A., 1984, Ocean ridge volumes and sea-level changes—an error analysis, in J.S. Schlee (ed.), Interregional unconformities and hydrocarbon accumulations: Am. Assoc. Petro. Geol. Mem. 36:109–127.

Konashov V.C, 1980, Expression of early Kimmerian folding phase in the Donets basin: Geotectonics 14(4):268–272.

Kornprobst J., 1980, Le métamorphisme en France, in A. Autran and J. Dercourt (eds.), Evolution géologique de la France: Mem. B.R.G.M. 107:161–189.

Kovacs S., 1984, North Hungarian Triassic facies types: A review: Acta geol. Hung. 27(2–4):251–264.

Kramer W., 1977, Vergleichende geochemische Untersuchungen an permosilesischen basischen Magmatiten der Norddeutschen-Polnischen Senke und ihre geotektonische Bedeutung: Z. Geol. Wiss. Berlin 5:7–20.

Kristoffersen Y., 1977, Late Cretaceous seafloor spreading and the early opening of the North Atlantic: N.P.F. Mesozoic Northern North Sea Symp. Oslo 17-18 October 1977, Norw. Petrol. Soc. Publ. MNNSS/5, p. 1–25.

Krs M., 1982, Implications of statistical evaluations of Phanerozoic palaemagnetic data (Europe, Africa): Rozpravy Czechoslovense, Akademic Ved.-Rada, Mathematickych, A Priordnich. Ved-Rocnik 93, Sesil 3, 86 p.

Ksiazkiewicz M., 1965, Les Cordillières dans les mers crétacées et paléogènes dans les Carpathes du Nord: Bull. Soc. Géol. France (7)7:443–455.

Kullmann J., Schönenberg R. and Wiedmann J. (eds.), 1982, Subsidenz-Entwicklung im Kantabrischen Variszikum und an passiven Kontinentalrändern der Kreide, Teil 1, Variszikum: N. Jb. Geol. Paläont. 163(2):137–300.

Kusznir N.J., Karner G.D. and Egan S., 1987, Geometric, thermal and isostatic consequences of detachment in continental lithosphere extension and basin formation, in C. Beaumont and T. Tankard (eds.), Sedimentary basins and basin-forming mechanisms: Can. Soc. Petrol. Geol. Mem. 12. Atl. Geosci. Soc. Spec. Publ. 5.

Laj C., Gauthier A.J. and Kerandren B., 1978, Mise en evidence d'une rotation plio-quaternaire de l'îsle de Rhodes, Rhodes: Réunion Ann. Soc. de la Terre, Orsay 6:224.

Lake S.D. and Karner G.D., 1987, The structure and evolution of the Wessex Basin, Southern England, an example of inversion tectonics: Tectonophysics 137:347–378.

Lambeck K., Cloetingh S. and McQueen H., 1987, Intraplate stresses and apparent changes in sea level: The basins of north-west Europeern, in C. Beaumont and T. Tankard (eds.), Sedimentary basins and basin-forming mechanisms: Can. Soc. Petrol. Geol. Mem. 12. Atl. Geosci. Soc. Spec. Publ. 5: 259–268.

Lameyre I. and Autran A., 1980, Les granitoides de France, in A. Autran and J. Dercourt (eds.), Evolution géologique de la France: Mem. B.R.G.M. 107:51–97.

Lameyre I., Black R., Bonin B. and Giret A., 1984, Les provinces magmatiques de l'Est américain, de l'Ouest africain et des Kerguelen, indications d'un contrôle tectonique et d'une initiation superficelle du magmatisme intraplaque et des processus associés: Ann. Soc. Géol. Nord CIII:101–114.

Lancelot J.R., Alleget A. and Poncedeleon M.I., 1985, Outline of upper Precambrian and lower Palaeozoic evolution of the Iberian Peninsula according to U-Pb dating of zircons: Earth Planet. Sci. Lett. 74:325–337.

Langenstrassen F., 1983, Neritic sedimentation of the Lower and Middle Devonian in the Rhenisches Schiefergebirge East of the Rhine, in H. Martin and F.W. Eder (eds.), Intracontinental fold belts: Berlin Heidelberg, Springer-Verlag, p. 43–76.

Lardeux H., Chauvel J.J., Hery J.L., Morzadec P., Paris F., Racheboeuf P. and Robardet M., 1977, Evolution géologique du Massif Armoricain au cours des temps Ordoviciens, Siluriens et Devoniens, in La chaîne varisque d'Europe moyenne et occidentale: Coll. Intern. CNRS, Rennes 243:181–192.

Larsen H.C., 1978, Offshore continuation of East Greenland dyke swarm and North Atlantic Ocean formation: Nature, London 274:220–223.

Larsen H.C., 1980, Geological perspectives of the East Greenland continental margin: Bull. Geol. Soc. Denmark 29:77–101.

Larsen H.C., 1984, Geology of the East Greenland Shelf, in A.M. Spencer et al. (eds.), Petroleum geology of the north European margin: Norw. Petrol. Soc., London, Graham and Trotman, p. 329–339.

Larsen O., 1982, The age of the Kap Washington Group volcanics, North Greenland: Bull. Geol. Soc. Denmark 31:49–55.

Laubscher H.P., 1970, Grundsätzliches zur Tektonik des Rheingrabens, in J.H. Illies and S. Müller (eds.), Graben problems: Int. Upper Mantle Project Sci. Report 27:79–87.

Laubscher H.P., 1974, Evoluzione e struttura delli Alpi: Le Scienze 72:48–59.

Laubscher P., 1980, Die Entwicklung des Faltenjuras-Daten und Vorstellungen: Jb. Geol. Paläont. Abh. 160:289–320.

Laubscher H. and Bernoulli D., 1977, Mediterranean and Tethys, in A.E.M. Nairn, W.H. Kanes and F.G. Stehli (eds.), The ocean basins and margins. Vol. 4A. The Western Mediterranean: New York, Plenum Press, p. 1–28.

Laubscher H. and Bernoulli D., 1982, History of deformation of the Alps, in K.J. Hsü (ed.), Mountain building processes: London New York, Academic Press, p. 109–180.

Laughton A.S., 1972, The South Labrador Sea—a key to the Mesozoic and Early Tertiary evolution of the North Atlantic: Initial Reports of Deep Sea Drilling Project, 12, Washington, DC, U.S. Govt. Printing Office, p. 1155–1179.

Laville E. and Harmand C., 1982, Evolution magmatique et tectonique du bassin intracontinental mésozoïque du Haute Atlas (Maroc): Un modèle de mise en place synsédimentaire des massifs "Anorogéniques" lies à des décrochements: Bull. Soc. Géol. France (1)XXIV(2):213–227.

Laville E. and Petit J.P., 1984, Role of synsedimentary strike-slip faults in the formation of Moroccan Triassic basins: Geology 12:424–427.

Lécorché J.P., 1983, Structure of the Mauretanides, in P.E. Schenk (ed.), Regional trends in the geology of the Appalachian-Caledonian-Hercynian-Mauretanide Orogen: Dordrecht, D. Reidel Publ. Co., p. 347–353.

Lécorché J.P. and Clauer N., 1983, First radiometric data (K/Ar) on the front of Mauretanides in the Akjouit region (Mauretania), in The Caledonide orogen: IGCP project 27, Symposium, Morocco and Paleozoic Orogenesis, Rabat, p. 23.

Le Douaran S., Burrus J. and Avedick F., 1984, Deep structure of the north-west Mediterranean basin: Results of two-ship seismic survey: Mar. Geol. 55:325–345.

Leeder M.R., 1976, Sedimentary facies and the origin of basin subsidence along the northern margin of the supposed Hercynian Ocean: Tectonophysics 36:167–179.

Leeder M.R., 1982, Upper Palaeozoic basins in the British Isle—Caledonian inheritance versus Hercynian plate margin processes: J. Geol. Soc. London, 139:479–491.

Lefort J.-P. and Haworth R.T., 1984, Geophysical evidence for the extension of the Variscan front onto the Canadian continental margin: Geodynamic and palaeogeographic consequences, *in* D.H. Hutton and D.J. Sanderson (eds.), Variscan tectonics of the north Atlantic region: Geol. Soc. Lond. Spec. Publ. 14: 219–231.

Lefort J.-P. and Voo R. van der, 1981, A kinematic model for the collision and complete suturing between Gondwanaland and Laurussia in the Carboniferous: J. Geol. 89(5):537–550.

Leggett J.K., McKerrow W.S. and Soper N.J., 1983, A model for the crustal evolution of southern Scotland: Tectonics 2(2):187–210.

Lemke K., 1977, Erdölgeologisch-wichtige Vorgänge in der Geschichte des süd-deutschen Alpenvorlandes: Erdöl-Erdgas Spec. Iss. 93:50–56.

Lemoine M., 1978, The peri-Tyrrhenian System: Corso-Sardinian Block, Apennines and Padan Basin, Calabro-Sicilian Arc, *in* M. Lemoine (ed.), Geological atlas of Alpine Europe and adjoining areas: Amsterdam/Oxford/New York, Elsevier Sci. Publ. Co., p. 227–311.

Lemoine M., 1985, Structuration jurassique des Alpes occidentales et palinspastique de la Tethys ligure: Bull. Soc. Géol. France (8)I(1):126–137.

Lemoine M. and Trümpy R., 1987, Pre-oceanic rifting in the Alps: Tectonophysics 133:305–320.

Lemoine M., Bas T., Arnaud-Vanneau A., Arnaud H., Gidon M., Bourbon M., De Graciansky P.-C., Rudkiewicz J.-L., Megard-Galli J. and Tricart P., 1986, The continental margin of the Mesozoic Tethys in the western Alps: Mar. Petrol. Geol. 3(3):179–199.

Le Pichon X. and Angelier I., 1979, The Hellenic arc and trench system: A key to the Neotectonic evolution of the eastern Mediterranean: Tectonophysics 60:1–42.

Le Pichon X. and Sibuet J.C., 1981, Passive margins: A model of formation: J. Geophys. Res. 86:3708–3720.

Le Pichon X., Huchon P., Angelier C., Lybéris N., Boulin J., Bureau D., Cadet J.P., Dercourt J., Glaçon G., Got H., Karig D., Mascle J., Ricou L.E. and Thiebault F., 1982, Subduction in the Hellenic Trench: Probable role of a thick evaporitic layer based on Sea Beam and submersible studies, *in* J.K. Legget (ed.), Trench-forearc geology: Sedimentation and tectonics on modern and ancient active plate margins: Geol. Soc. Lond. Spec. Publ. 10: 319–333.

Le Pichon X., Lybéris N. and Alvarez F., 1984, Subsidence history of the North Aegean Trough, *in* J.E. Dixon and A.H.F. Robertson (eds.), The geological evolution of the eastern Mediterranean: Spec. Publ. Geol. Soc. London Spec. Publ. 17:727–741.

Lepvrier C. and Geyssant J., 1984, Tectonique cassante et champs de contrainte tertiaires le long de la marge en coulissement du Spitsberg: Corrélations avec les mécanismes d'ouverture de la mer du Norvège-Groënland: Ann. Soc. Géol. Nord. CIII:333–344.

Letouzey J., 1986, Cenozoic paleo-stress pattern in the Alpine Foreland and structural interpretation in a platform basin: Tectonophysics 132:215–231.

Letouzey J. and Trémolière P., 1980, Paleo-stress fields around the Mediterranean since the Mesozoic derived from micro-tectonics: Comparison with plate tectonic data, *in* J. Aubouin, J. Debelmas and M. Latraille (eds.), Geology of the Alpine chains born of the Tethys: Mem. B.R.G.M. 115:261–273.

Letouzey J., Biju-Duval B., Dorkel D., Gonnard R., Kritschev K., Montadert L. and Sungurulu O., 1977, The Black Sea: A marginal basin, geophysical and geological data, *in* B. Bijou-Duval and L. Montadert (eds.), International sysposium on the structural history of the Mediterranean Basins: Split (Yugoslavia), Edition Technip, p 363–376.

Lewandowski M., 1987, Results of preliminary paleomagnetic investigations of some lower Paleozoic rocks from the Holy Cross Mountains (Poland): Kwartalnik Geologiczny, in press.

Liboriussen J., Ashton P. and Tygesen T., 1987, The tectonic evolution of the Fennoscandian border zone in Denmark: Tectonophysics 137: 21–30.

Linden W.J.M. van der, 1975, Crustal attenuation and sea floor spreading in the Labrador Sea: Earth Planet. Sci. Lett. 27:409–423.

Lippolt H.J., 1983, Distribution of volcanic activity in space and time, *in* K. Fuchs, K. von Gehlen, H. Mälzer, H. Murawski and A. Semmel (eds.), Plateau uplift, the Rhenish Shield—a case hsitory: Berlin/Heidelberg/New York/Tokyo, Springer-Verlag, p. 112–120.

Livermore R.A. and Smith A.G., 1985, Some boundary conditions for the evolution of the Mediterranean region, *in* D.J. Stanley and F.-C. Wezel (eds.), Geological evolution of the Mediterranean Basin-Raimond Selli commemorative voluem. Berlin/Heidelberg/New York/Tokyo, Springer-Verlag, p. 83–100.

Locardi E., 1985, Neogene and Quaternary Mediterranean volcanism; the Tyrrhenian example, *in* D.J. Stanley and F.-C. Wezel (eds.), Geological evolution of the Mediterranean Basin: Raimondo Selli commemorative volume. New York/Berlin/Heidelberg/Tokyo, Springer-Verlag, p. 273–291.

Lorenz V. and Nicholls J.A., 1984, Plate and intraplate processes of Hercynian Europe during the late Palaeozoic: Tectonophysics 107:25–56.

Løvlie R., Torsvik T., Jelenska M. and Levandowski M., 1984, Evidence for detrited remanent magnetisation carried by hematite in Devonian red beds from Spitsbergen; palaeomagnetic implications: Geophys. J.R. Astr. Soc. 79:573–588.

Lowell J.D., 1972, Spitsbergen Tertiary Orogenic Belt and the Spitsbergen Fracture Zone: Geol. Soc. Am. Bull. 83:3091–3102.

Luca P. de, Duée G. and Hervouet Y., 1985, Evolution et deformations du bassin flysch du Crétacé supérieur de la haute chaîne (Pyrénée Basco-béarnaises-region du Pic d'Orhy): Bull. Soc. Géol. France (8)I(2):249–262.

Lund J., 1983, Biostratigraphy of interbasaltic coals from the Faeroe Islands, *in* M.H.P. Bott, S. Saxov, M. Talwani and J. Thiede (eds.), Structure and development of the Greenland-Scotland ridge—new methods and concepts: New York/London, Plenum Press, p. 417–423.

Lützner H. and Schwab G., 1982, Tectonic regime of Molasse Epochs: Akad. Wiss D.D.R. Veröff. Zent. Inst. Physik der Erde 66:395 p. and enclosures.

Lybéris N., 1984, Tectonic evolution of the North Aegean Trough, *in* J.E. Dixon and A.H.F. Robertson (eds.), The geological evolution of the eastern Mediterranean: Geol. Soc. London Spec. Publ. 17: 709–725.

Maas K. and Ginkel A.C. van, 1983, Variscan olistostrome deposition and synsedimentary nappe emplacement, Valdeon Area, Cantabrian Mountains, Spain: Leidse Geol. Meded. 52(2):341–381.

Maclean B., Srivastava S.P. and Haworth R.T., 1982, Bedrock

structures off Cumberland Sound, Baffin Island Shelf: Core sample and geophysical data, in A.F. Embry and H.R. Balkwill (eds.), Arctic geology and geophysics: Can. Soc. Petrol. Geol. Mem. 8:279–295.

Magoon L.B. and Claypool G.E., 1983, Petroleum geochemistry of the North Slope of Alaska: Time and degree of thermal maturity, in Advances in organic geochemistry: New York, John Wiley and Sons Ltd., p. 28–38.

Mahel M. and Buday T., 1968, Regional geology of Czechoslovakia. Part II. The western Carpathians: Stuttgart, Schweizerbarth, 723 p.

Maher H.D. Jr., Craddock C. and Maher K., 1976, Kinematics of Tertiary structures in upper Paleozoic and Mesozoic strata on Midterhuken, West Spitsbergen: Geol. Soc. Am. Bull. 97:1411–1421.

Mair J.A. and Forsyth D.A., 1982, Crustal structure of the Canada Basin near Alaska, the Lomonosov Ridge and adjoining basins near the North Pole: Tectonophysics 89:239–253.

Mäkel G.H., 1985, The geology of the Malaguide complex and its bearing on the Geodynamic evolution of the Betic-Rif Orogen (southern Spain and northern Morocco): Geological University Amsterdam, Papers of Geology Ser. 1, No. 22, 263 p.

Makris J., 1981, Deep structure of the eastern Mediterranean deduced from refraction seismic data, in F.-C. Wezel (ed.), Sedimentary basins of Mediterranean margins: Bologna, Tecnoprint, p. 63–84.

Makris, J. 1985, Geophysics and geodynamic implications for the evolution of the Hellenides, in D.J. Stanley and F.-C. Wezel (eds.), Geological evolution of the Mediterranean Basin: New York/Berlin/Heidelberg/Tokyo, Springer-Verlag, p. 231–248.

Malinverno A. and Ryan W.B., 1986, Extension in the Tyrrhenian Sea and shortening in the Apennines as a result of arc migration driven by sinking of the lithosphere: Tectonics 5(2):227–245.

Malkovsky M., 1976, Saxonische Tektonik der Böhmischen Masse: Geol. Rundsch. 65:127–143.

Malkovsky M., 1987, The Mesozoic and Tertiary basins of the Bohemian Massif and their evolution: Tectonophysics 137:31–42.

Manspeizer W., 1982, Triassic-Liassic basins and climate of the Atlantic passive margins: Geol. Rundsch. 77(3):897–917.

Manspeizer W., 1985, Early Mesozoic history of the Atlantic passive margin, in C.W. Poag (ed.), Geologic evolution of the United States Atlantic margin: New York, Van Nostrand Reinhold Co. Ltd., 1–23.

Manspeizer W., Puffer J.H. and Cousminier H.L., 1978, Separation of Morocco and eastern North America: A Triassic-Liassic stratigraphic record: Geol. Soc. Am. Bull., 89:901–920.

Manum S.B. and Throndsen T., 1978, Rank of coal and dispersed organic matter and its geological bearing in the Spitsbergen Tertiary: Norsk Polarinst. Arbok 1977:159–177.

Marek S. and Raczynska, A., 1972, The stratigraphy and palaeogeography of the Lower Cretaceous deposits of the Polish Lowland Area, in R. Casey and P.F. Rawson (eds.), The Boreal Cretaceous: Geol. J. Spec. Iss. 5:369–386.

Maréschal J.-C., 1983, Mechanisms of uplift preceding rifting: Tectonophysics 94:51–66.

Marincovich L. Jr., Browers E.M. and Carter L.D., 1985, Early Tertiary marine fossils from northern Alaska: Implictions for Arctic Ocean paleogeography and faunal evolution: Geology 13:770–773.

Martin H., 1981, The late Palaeozic Gondwana glaciation: Geol. Rundsch. 70(2):480–496.

Martin R.F. and Piwinsky A.J., 1987, Magmatism and tectonic settings: J. Geophys. Res. 77:4966–4975.

Martinez-Garcia E., 1972, El Silurico de San Vitero (Zamora), comparacion con series vecinas e importancia orogenica: Acta Geol. Hispanica VII(4):104–108.

Martinez-Garcia E., 1980, El Macizo Herciniano del dominio Iberico Central: Bol. Geol. Minero. XCI-I:67–90.

Martinez-Garcia E. and Wagner R.H., 1982, Una cuenca marina del Estephaniense superior an el Noroeste de España: Trabajos de Geologica, Univ. de Oviedo 12:119–124.

Mascle J., Lequellec P. and Leite O., 1981, Cadre tectonique de la marge active hellenique de Zakynthos à Karpathos, in F.-C. Wezel (ed.), Sedimentary basins of Mediterranean margins: Bologna, Tecnoprint, p. 147–159.

Masson D.G. and Miles P.R., 1984, Mesozoic sea floor spreading between Iberia and North America: Mar. Geol. 56:229–287.

Masson D.G. and Miles P.R., 1986a, Structure and development of the Porcupine Seabight sedimentary basin, offshore, southwest Ireland: Bull. Am. Assoc. Petrol. Geol. 70(5):536–548.

Masson D.G. and Miles P.R., 1986b, Development and hydrocarbon potential of Mesozoic basins around margins of North Atlantic: Bull. Am. Assoc. Petrol. Geol. 70(6):721–729.

Masson D.G., Montadert L. and Scrutton R.A., 1985, Regional geology of the Goban Spur continental margin, in P.C. de Gracianski, C.W. Poag, et al., Initial Reports of Deep Sea Drilling Project, 80, Washington, DC, U.S. Govt. Printing office, p. 1115–1139.

Mathieu C., 1986, Histoire géologique du sous-bassin de Parentis: Bull. Cent. Rech. Expl.-Prod. Elf-Aquitaine 10(1):33–47.

Matsumoto T., 1973, Late Cretaceous Ammonoidea, in A. Hallam (ed.), Atlas of palaeobiogeography: Amsterdam, Elsevier Sci. Publ. Co., p. 421–429.

Mattauer M. and Henry J., 1974, Pyrenees, in A.M. Spencer (ed.), Mesozoic-Cenozoic orogenic belts, data for orogenic studies: Geol. Soc. Lond. Spec. Publ. 4: 3–21.

Mattauer M., Tapponier P. and Proust F., 1977, Sur les mécanismes de formation des chaînes intracontinentales, l'exemple des chaînes atlasiques du Maroc: Bull. Soc. Géol. France (1)14(3):521–526.

Matte P., 1983, Two geotraverses across the Ibero-Armorican Variscan arc of Western Europe, in Profiles of orogenic belts: Am. Geophys. Union, Geol. Soc. Am., Geodynam. Ser. 20: 53–81.

Matte P., 1986, La chaîne varisque parmi les chaînes paléozoiques peri-atlantiques, modèle d'évolution et position des grandes blocs continenteaux au Permo-Carbonifère: Bull. Soc. Géol. France (8)II(1):9–24.

Matviyevskaya N.O., Bogatsky V.I., Vasserman B.Y., Gobanov L.A. and Shafran Y.B., 1986, Geological history of oil-gas potential of the Pechora-Kolvin aulacogen: Petrol. Geol. 21(7):301–305.

Mauffret A. and Montadert L., 1987, Rift tectonics on the passive continental margin of Galicia (Spain): Mar. Petrol. Geol. 4:49–70.

Mauffret A., Boillot G., Auxiète J.-L. and Dunand, J.-P., 1978, Evolution structurale de la marge continentale en nord-ouest de la péninsule ibérique: Bull. Soc. Géol. France (7)XX(4):375–388.

Max M.D., 1978, Tectonic control of offshore sedimentary basins to the north and west of Ireland: J. Petrol. Geol.

1:103–110.

Max M.D., Inamdar D.D. and McIntyre T., 1982, Compilation magnetic map: The Irish continental shelf and adjacent areas. Geol. Survey Ireland, Rep. Ser. RS82/2 (Geophysics), 7 p.

Mayr U., 1984, Craig Harbor, Cardigan Strait geological map: Open File Dossier, Public. No. 1036, Can. Geol. Survey.

Mayr U. and De Vries D.S., 1982, Reconnaissance of Tertiary structures along Nares Strait, Ellesmere Island, Canadian Arctic Archipelago, *in* P.R. Dawes and J.W. Kerr (eds.), Nares Strait and the drift of Greenland: Conflict in plate tectonics: Meddel. Grønland, Geoscience 8: 167–175.

McClay K.R., Norton M.G., Coney P. and Davis G.H., 1986, Collapse of the Caledonian orogen and the Old Red Sandstone: Nature, London 323:147–149.

McElhinny M.W., Taylor S.R. and Stevenson D.J., 1978, Limits to the expansion of Earth, Moon, Mars and Mercury and to changes in the gravitational constant: Nature, London 271:316–320.

McHone J.G., 1978, Distribution, orientation and ages of mafic dykes in Central New England: Geol. Soc. Am. Bull. 89:1645–1655.

McKenna M.C., 1983, Cenozic palaeogeography of North Atlantic land bridges, *in* H.P. Bott, S. Saxov, M. Talwani and J. Thiede (eds.), Structure and development of the Greenland-Scotland ridge-new methods and concepts: New York/London, Plenum Press, p. 351–383.

McKenzie D.P., 1977, Initiation of trenches: A finite amplitude instability, *in* Island arcs, deep sea trenches and back-arc basins: Maurice Ewing Series, Vol. 1, Am. Geophys. Union, p. 57–61.

McKenzie D.P., 1978, Some remarks on the development of sedimentary basins: Earth Planet. Sci. Lett. 40:25–32.

McKenzie D., Watts A., Parson B. and Roufosse M., 1980, Planform of mantle convection beneath the Pacific: Nature, London 288:442–446.

McKenzie R.M., 1981, The Hibernia...a classic structure: Oil and Gas J. 79 (38):240–246.

McKerrow W.S. and Cocks L.R.M., 1986, Oceans, island arcs and olistostromes: The use of fossils in distinguishing sutures, terranes and environments around the Iapetus Ocean: J. Geol. Soc. London 143:185–191.

McKerrow W.S. and Ziegler A.M., 1972, Palaeozoic oceans: Nature, London, Phys. Sci. 240:92–94.

McMillan N.J., 1979, Geology of the Labrador Sea and its petroleum potential: Proc. 10th World Petroleum Congr., Bucharest, Vol. 2, Exploration, Supply and Demand, London/Philadelphia/Rheine, Heyden, p. 165–175.

McWhae, J.R.H., 1981, Structure and spreading history of the northwestern Atlantic region from the Scotian Shelf to Baffin Bay, *in* J.W. Kerr, A.J. Fergusson and L.C. Machan (eds.), Geology of the North Atlantic borderlands: Can. Soc. Petrol. Geol. Mem. 7:299–332.

Mechie J., Prodhel C. and Fuchs K., 1983, The long-range seismic refraction experiment in the Rhenish Massif, *in* K. Fuchs, K. von Gehlen, H. Mälzer, H. Murawski and A. Semmel (eds.), Plateau uplift, the Rhenish Shield—a case history: Berlin/Heidelberg/New York/Tokyo, p. 260–275.

Mégnien C. (ed.), 1980, Synthèse géologique du Bassin de Paris, Vol. I, II and III: Mem. B.R.G.M. 102.

Megson J.B., 1987, The evolution of the Rockall Trough, *in* J. Brooks and K. Glennie (eds.), Petroleum geology of northwest Europe: London, Graham and Trotman, 653–665.

Meighan I.G., 1979, The acid igneous rocks of the British Tertiary Province: Bull. Geol. Surv. Gt. Brit. 70:10–22.

Meissner R., 1986, The continental crust, a geophysical approach, *in* W.L. Donn (ed.), International geophysical series, Vol. 34: Academic Press, 426 p.

Meissner R. and Kusznir N.J., 1986, Continental crustal rheology and the reflectivity of the lower Crust: Ter. Cogn. 6(3):347 (abstract).

Meissner R., Bartelsen H. and Murawski H., 1981, Thin-skinned tectonics in the northern Rhenish Massif, Germany: Nature 290:399–401.

Meneley R.A., 1986, Oil and gas fields in the East Coast and Arctic Basins of Canada, *in* M.T. Halbouty (ed.), Future petroleum provinces of the world: Am. Assoc. Petrol. Geol. Mem. 40:143–176.

Meneley R.A., Henao D. and Merritt R.K., 1975, The northwest margin of the Sverdrup Basin, *in* C.J. Yorath, E.R. Parker and D.J. Glass (eds.), Canada's continental margins and offshore petroleum exploration: Can. Soc. Petrol. Geol. Mem. 4:531–544.

Menzies A.W., 1982, Crustal history and basin development of Baffin Bay, *in* P.R. Dawes and J.W. Kerr (eds.), Nares Strait and the drift of Greenland: A conflict in plate tectonics: Meddel. Grønland, Geoscience 8:295–312.

Metz P.A., Egan A. and Johansen O., 1982, Landsat linear features and incipient rift system model for the origin of base metal and petroleum resources of northern Alaska, *in* A.F. Embry and H.R. Balkwill (Eds.), Arctic geology and geophysics: Can. Soc. Petrol. Geol. Mem. 8: 101–112.

Miall A.D., 1975, Post-Paleozoic geology of Banks, Prince Patrik and Eglington Islands, Arctic Canada, *in* C.J. Yorath, R.N. Parker and D.J. Glass (eds.), Canada's continental margins and offshore petroleum exploration: Can. Soc. Petrol. Geol. Mem. 4:557–587.

Miall A.D., 1981, Late Cretaceous and Paleogene sedimentation and tectonics in the Canadian Arctic Island, *in* A.D. Miall (ed.), Sedimentation and tectonics in alluvial basins: Geol. Assoc. Can. Spec. Paper 23:221–272.

Miall A.D., 1983, The Nares Strait problems: A re-evaluation of the geological evidence in terms of a diffuse oblique-slip plate boundary between Greenland and the Canadian Arctic Basin: Tectonophysics 100:227–239.

Miall A.D., 1984a, Sedimentation and tectonics of a diffuse, oblique-slip plate boundary, the Canadian Arctic Islands from 80 Ma B.P. to the present: 27th Internat. Geol. Congress, Moscow, Arctic Geology, Coll. 04, reports vol. 4, Publ. office "Nauka", Moscow, p. 109–124.

Miall A.D., 1984b, Sedimentation and tectonics of a diffuse plate boundary: The Canadian Arctic Islands from 80 Ma B.P., to the present: Tectonophysics 107:261–277.

Miall A.D., 1986, The Eureka Sound Group (Upper Cretaceous-Oligocene), Canadian Arctic Islands: Bull. Can. Soc. Petrol. Geol. 34(2):240–270.

Miall A.D., Balkwill H.R. and Hopkins W.S. Jr., 1980, The Cretaceous–Tertiary sediments of Eclipse Trough, Bylot Island, Arctic Canada, and their regional setting: Geol. Surv. Can. Paper 79–23.

Michard A., 1976, Elements de Géologie Marocaine: Notes et memoires du Service Géologique No. 252, Editions du Serv. Geol. Maroc, 408 p.

Michard A., Whitechurch H., Ricou L.E., Montigny R., and Yazgan E., 1984, Tauric subduction (Malatya–Ealzig provinces) and its bearing on the tectonics of the Tethyan realm in Turkey, *in* J.E. Dixon and A.H.F. Robertson (eds.), The geological evolution of the eastern Mediterranean: Geol. Soc. Publ. 17: 361–373.

Milanovsky E.E., Khain V.E., Vyalov O.S., Asianian A.T., Tvalchrelidze G.A. and Shikhalibeili E.S., 1984, Structure and geological history of the Mediterranean fold belt of the USSR: 27th Int. Geol. Congr., Moscow, Coll. 01, Geology of the USSR, "Nauka" Publ. Office, Moscow, p. 99–119.

Milnes A.G. and Pfiffner O.A., 1980, Tectonic evolution of the Central Alps in the cross section St. Galle--Como: Ecl. Geol. Helv. 73(2):619–633.

Mirouse R., 1980, Introducion a la geologia del Pirineo: Bol. Geol. Minero. XCL–I:91–106.

Mitchell A.H.G., 1981, The Grampian Orogeny in Scotland and Ireland: Almost an ancient Taiwan: Proc. Geol. Soc. China 24:113–129.

Mitchell R.H. and Platt R.G., 1984, The Freemans Cove volcanic suite; Field relations, petrochemistry and tectonic setting of nephelin—basanite volcanism associated with rifting in the Canadian Archipelages: Can. J. Earth Sci. 21:428–436.

Moorbath S. and Welke H., 1968, Lead isotope studies on igneous rocks form the Isle of Skye, northwest Scotland: Earth Planet. Sci. Lett. 5:217–230.

Moore T.E. and Nilsen T.H., 1984, Regional variations in the fluvial Upper Devonian and Lower Mississippian Kanayut conglomerate, Brooks Range, Alaska, *in* T.H. Nislen (eds.), Fluvial sedimentation and related tectonic framework, western North America: Sed. Geol. 38:465–497.

Morel P. and Irving E., 1978, Tentative palaeocontinental maps for the early Phanerozoic and Proterozoic: J. Geol. 86(5):535–561.

Morelli C., 1985, Geophysical contribution to knowledge of the Mediterranean crust, *in* D.J. Stanley and F.-C. Wezel (eds.), Geological evolution of the Mediterranean Basin: New York/Berlin/Heidelberg/Tokyo, Springer-Verlag, p. 65–82.

Moretti I. and Pinet B., 1987, Discrepancy between lower and upper crustal thinning, *in* C. Beaumont and T. Tankard (eds.), Sedimentary basins and basin-forming mechanisms: Can. Soc. Petrol. Geol. Mem 12, Atl. Geosci. Soc. Spec. Publ. 5: 233–239.

Morgan P. and Baker B.H., 1983, Introduction: processes of continental rifting: Tectonophysics 94:1–10.

Mørk A. and Bjorøy M., 1984, Mesozoic source rocks on Svalbard, *in* A.M. Spencer et al. (eds.), Petroleum geology of the north European margin: Norw. Petrol. Soc., London, Graham and Trotman, p. 371–382.

Mørk A., Knaurud R. and Worsley D., 1982, Depositional and diagenetic environments of the Triassic and Lower Jurassic succession of Svalbard, *in* A.F. Embry and H.R. Balkwill (eds.), Arctic geology and geophysics: Can. Soc. Petrol. Geol. Mem. 8: 371–389.

Mörner N.A., 1977, Eustasy and instability of the geoid configuration: Geologiska Föreningens, Stockholm Forhandlingar. 99:369–376.

Mörner N.A., 1981, Revolution in Cretaceous sea-level analysis: Geology 9:344–346.

Morris W.A., 1976, Transcurrent motion determined palaeomagnetically in the northern Appalachians and Calidonides and the Acadian Orogen: Can. J. Earth Sci. 13:1236–1243.

Morton A.C., 1982, Lower Tertiary sand development in the Viking Graben, North Sea: Bull. Am. Assoc. Petrol. Geol. 66(10):1542–1559.

Mosher S. and Rast N., 1984, The deformation and metamorphism of Carboniferous rocks in maritime Canada and New England, D.H.W. Hutton and D.J. Sanderson (eds.), Variscan tectonics of the North Atlantic region: Geol. Soc. Lond. Spec. Publ. 14:233–243.

Mostardini F. and Merlini S., 1986, Appennino Centro Meridionale, Sezioni geologiche e proposta di modello strutturale: 73° Congresso Societa' Geologica Italiana, Romo 1986, AGIP Publication, 59 p.

Mougenot D., 1981, Une phase de compression au Crétacé terminal à l'ouest du Portugal: Quelques arguments: Bol. Soc. Geol. Portugal 21:233–239.

Mountrakis D., 1986, The Pelagonian zone in Greece: a Polyphase-deformed fragment of the Cimmerian continent and its role in the geotectonic evolution of the Eastern Mediterranean: J. Geol. 94:335–347.

Mulder C.J., 1973, Tectonic framework and distribution of Miocene evaporites in the Mediterranean, *in* W.C. Drooger (ed.), Messinian events in the Mediterranean: Geodynamics Scientific Report No. 1, on colloquium held in Utrecht, 2-4 March 1973, Amsterdam/London, North-Holland Publ. Co., p. 44–60.

Mulder C.J. and Parry G.R., 1977, Late Tertiary evolution of the Alboran Sea at the eastern entrance of the Straits of Gibraltar, *in* B. Bijou-Duval and L. Montadert (eds.), International Symposium of the Structural History of the Mediterranean Basin: Split, Paris, Edit. Technip, p. 401–410.

Mulder C.J., Lehner P. and Allen D.C.K., 1975, Structural evolution of the Neogene salt basins on the eastern Mediterranean and Red Sea: Geol. Mijnbouw 54(3–4):208–221.

Müller S., 1982, Deep structure and recent dynamics in the Alps, *in* K.J. Hsü (ed.), Mountain building processes: London/New York, Academic Press, p. 181–199.

Murray J.W. and Wright C.A., 1974, Paleogene foraminifera and palaeoecology- Hempshire and Paris Basin and the English Channel: Palaeont. Assoc. London Spec. Papers Pal. 14:175 p.

Mutter J., Talwani M. and Stoffa P.L., 1982, Origin of seaward dipping reflectors in oceanic crust off the Norwegian margin by "subaerial sea floor spreading": Geology 10:353–357.

Myhre A.M., Eldholm O. and Sundvor E., 1982, The margin between Senja and Spitsbergen fracture zones: Implications from plate tectonics: Tectonophysics 89:33–55.

Nachtmann W. and Wagner L., 1987, Mesozoic and Early Tertiary evolution of the Alpine foreland in western Austria: Tectonophysics 137: 61–76.

Nalivkin V.D., 1982, La fosse bordière de Pré-Oural, *in* Tectonics of Europe and adjacent areas, Variscides, Epi-Paleozoic Platforms, Alpides. Explanatory note to the International Tectonic map of Europe and adjacent areas. Scale 1:2500000: Moscow, "Nauka" Publ. Office, p. 206–213.

Naylor D. and Shannon P.H., 1982, The geology of offshore Ireland and western Britain: London, Graham and Trottman, 161 p.

Neev D., Greenfield L. and Hall J.K., 1985, Slice tectonics in the eastern Mediterranean, *in* D.J. Stanley and F.-C. Wezel (eds.), Geological evolution of the Mediterranean Basin: New York/Berlin/Heidelberg/Tokyo, Springer-Verlag, p. 249–269.

Nesterov I.I.N., Podsosova L.C., Rudkevich M.Y. and Trofimuk A.A.T., 1984, Geology of West Siberian Platform: Proc. 27 Internat. Geol. Congr., Coll. 01, Reports Vol. 1, "Nauka" Publ. Office, Moscow, p. 52–61.

Neugebauer H.J., 1983, Mechanical aspects of continental rifting: Tectonophysics 94:91–108.

Neugebauer H.J. and Gao X, 1985, Dynamics of convergent plate boundaries and the stress field of East Asia: Ter. Cogn. 5(2-3):311–312 (abstract).

Neumann E.-R., 1985, Rift-related magmatism in the Oslo Rift, southeast Norway, *in* International Symposium on Deep Internal Processes and Continental Rifting (abstracts), Sept. 9-13, Chengdu, China, Beijing, China Academic Publishers, p. 117–118.

Newman P.H., 1982, Marine geophysical study of the Nares Strait, *in* P.R. Dawes and J.W. Kerr (eds.) Nares Strait and the drift of Greenland, a conflict in plate tectonics: Meddel. Grønland, Geoscience 8:255–260.

Nilsen T.H., 1973, Devonian (Old Red) sedimentation and tectonics of Norway, *in* M.G. Pitcher (ed.), Arctic geology: Am. Assoc. Petrol. Geol. Mem. 19:471–481.

Nilsen T.H., 1983, Influence of the Greenland-Scotland ridge on the geological history of the North Atlantic and Norwegian-Greenland Sea areas, *in* H.P. Bott, S. Saxov, M. Talwani and J. Thiede (eds.), Structure and development of the Greenland-Scotland Ridge—new methods and concepts: New York/London, Plenum Press, p. 457–478.

Noe-Nygaard A., 1976, Tertiary igneous rocks between Shannon and Scoresby Sund, East Greenland, *in* A. Escher and W.S. Watt (eds.), Geology of Greenland: Geol. Surv. Greenland, p. 387–402.

Norling E. and Bergström J., 1987, Mesozoic and Cenozoic evolution of Scania, Southern Sweden: Tectonophysics 137: 7–19.

Norris D.K. and Yorath C.J., 1981, The North American Plate from the Arctic Archipelago to the Romanzof Mountains, *in* A.E.N. Nairn, M. Churkin Jr. and F.G. Stehli (eds.), The oceans basins and margins. Vol. 5. The Arctic Ocean, New York/London, Plenum Press, p. 37–103.

Norton M.G., 1986, Late Caledonide extension in western Norway: Tectonics 5(2):195–204.

Nunns A.G., 1982, The structure and evolution of the Jan Mayen Ridge and surrounding regions, *in* J.S. Watkins and C.L. Drake (eds.), Studies in continental margin geology: Am. Assoc. Petrol. Geol. Mem. 34:193–208.

Nunns A.G., 1983, Plate tectonic evolution of the Greenland–Scotland Ridge, *in* M.H.P. Bott, S. Saxov, M. Talwani and J. Thiede (eds.), Structure and development of the Greenland–Scotland Ridge—new methods and concepts: new York/London, Plenum Press, p. 11–30.

Nunns A.G., Talwani M., Lorentzen G.R., Vogt P.R., Sigurgeirsson T., Kristjansson L., Larsen H.C. and Voppel D., 1983, Magnetic anomalies over Iceland and surrounding areas, *in* M.H.P. Bott, S. Saxov, M. Talwani and J. Thiede (eds.), Structure and development of the Greenland–Scotland Ridge—new methods and concepts: New York/London, Plenum Press, p. 661–678.

Nysaether E., 1976, Investigations on the Carboniferous and Permian stratigraphy of the Torell Land area, Spitsbergen: Norsk Polarinstitutt Arbok 1976:21–42.

Oberli F., Sommerauer J. and Steiger R.H., 1981, U-(Th)-P systematics and mineralogy of single crystals and concentrates of accessory minerals from the Cacciola granite, Central Gotthard Massif, Switzerland: Schweiz. Mineral. Petrogr. Mitt. 61:373–348.

O'Brian S.J., Wardle R.J. and King A.F., 1983, The Avalon Zone: A pan-African terrane in the Appalachian Orogen of Canada: Geol. J. 18:195–223.

Oftedahl C., 1968, Magmen-Entstehung nach Lava-Stratigraphie im südlichen Oslo-Gebiet: Geol. Rundsch. 57:203–218.

Ogniben L. and Vezzani L., 1975, Nappe structure in Sicily and Lucania, Italy, *in* C.A. Squyres (ed.), Geology of Italy: Tripoli, The Earth Sciences, Society of the Libyan Arab Republic 2:83–104.

Okay A.I., 1984, Distribution and characteristics of the northwest Turkish blueshists, *in* J.E. Dixon and A.H.F. Robertson (eds.), The geological evolution of the eastern Mediterranean: Geol. Soc. London Spec. Publ. 17:455–466.

Olade M.A., 1975, Evolution of Nigeria's Benue Trough (Aulacogen): A tectonic model: Geol. Mag. 112:575–983.

Oldow J.S., Avé Lallemand H.G., Julian F.E. and Seidensticker C.M., 1987, Ellesmerian (?) and Brookian deformation in the Franklin Mountains, northern Brooks Range, Alaska and its bearing on the origin of the Canada Basin: Geology 15:37–41.

Oliveira J.T., 1982, The Devonian–Carboniferous stratigraphy and geodynamics of southern Portugal: Some comments: N. Jb. Geol. Palaeont. 163:(2):276–284.

Olivet J.-L., Bonnin J., Beuzart P. and Auzende J.-M., 1982, Cinematique des plaques et paleogéographie: Une revue: Bull. Soc. Géol. France (7)XXIV(5):857–892.

Olivet J.-L., Bonnin J., Beuzart P. and Auzende J.-M., 1984, Cinématique de l'Atlantique Nord et Central: Publ. Cent. Nat. Expl. Oceans, Rap. Sci. Tech. 54:108 p.

Olsen K.H., 1983, The role of seismic refraction data for the studies of the origin an devolution of continental rifts: Tectonophysics 94:349–370.

Osadetz K., 1982, Eurekan structures of the Ekblaw Lake Area, Ellesmere Island, Canada, *in* A.F. Embry and H.R. Balkwill (eds.), Arctic geology and geophysics: Can. Soc. Petrol. Geol. Mem. 8:219–232.

Osberg p.H., 1983, Timing of orogenic events in the US Appalachians, *in* P.E. Schenk (eds.) Regional trends in the geology of the Appalachians-Caledonian-Hercynian-Mauretanid Orogen: Dordrecht, D. Reidel Publ. Co., p. 315–337.

Owen H.G., 1973, Ammonite faunal provinces in the middle and upper Albian and their palaeogeographic significance, *in* R. Casey and P.F. Rawson (eds.), The Boreal Lower Cretaceous: Geol. J. Spec. Iss. 5:145–154.

Oxburgh E.R., 1974, Eastern Alps, *in* A.M. Spencer (ed.), Mesozoic–Cenozoic orogenic belts, data for orogenic studies: Geol. Soc. London Spec. Publ. 4:109–126.

Pakulska Z. and Kuna H. (eds.), 1981, International symposium Central European Permian proceedings: Wydawnictura Geologiczne, Warszawa, 656 p.

Pamic J.J., 9184, Triassic magmatism of the Dinarides in Yugoslavia: Tectonophysics 109:273–307.

Papa A., 1970, Conceptions nouvelles sur la structure des Albanides (présentation de la carte tectonique de l'Albanie au 500.000): Bull. Soc. Géol. France (7)XII(6):1096–1109.

Parker J.R., 1975, Lower Tertiary sand development in the central North Sea, *in* A.W. Woodland (ed.), Petroleum and the continental shelf of NW Europe. Vol. I. Geology: Barking, England, Applied Science Publishers, p. 447–452.

Pattinson J., Smith D.B. and Warrington G., 1973, A review of Late Permian and Early Triassic biostratigraphy in the British Isles: Can. Soc. Petrol. Geol. Mem. 2:220–260.

Pedersen K.R., 1976, Fossil floras of Greenland, *in* A. Fischer and W.S. Watt (eds.), Geology of Greenland: Geol. Surv. Greenland, p. 519–535.

Pedersen S.A.S., 1986, A transverse, thin-skinned, thrust-fault belt in the Paleozoic North Greenland fold belt: Geol. Soc. Am. Bull. 97:1442–1455.

Pedersen S.A.S. and Holm P.M., 1983, The significance of a Middle Devonian K/Ar age of an intrusive rock in the southern part of the North Greenland Belt: Bull. Geol. Soc. Denmark 31:121–127.

Pegrum R.M., 1984, The extension of the Tornquist Zone in the Norwegian North Sea: Norsk Geol. Tidss. 64:39–64.

Pegrum R.M. and Ljones T.E., 1984, 15/9 Gamma gas field offshore Norway, new trap type for the North Sea Basin with regional structural implications: Bull. Am. Assoc. Petrol. Geol. 68:874–902.

Peltier W.R., 1980, Models of glacial isostasy and relative sea level, *in* A.W. Bally, P.L. Bender, T.R. McGetchin and R.I. Walcott (eds.), Dynamics of plate interiors: Am. Geophys. Union, Geol. Soc. Am. Geodynam. Ser. 1:111–128.

Pe-Piper G. and Piper D.J.W., 1984, Tectonic setting of the Mesozoic Pindos Basin of the Peleponnese, Greece, *in* J.E. Dixon and A.H.F. Robertson (eds.), The geological evolution of the eastern mediterranean: Geol. Soc. London, Spec. Publ. 17:563–568.

Pe-Piper G., Panagos A.G., Piper D.J.W. and Kotopouli C.N., 1982, The (?) mid Triassic volcanic rocks of Lakonia, Greece: Geol. Mag 119(1):77–85.

Perch-Nielsen K., Bromley R., Asgaard and Aellen M., 1972, Field observations in Palaeozoic and Mesozoic sediments of Scoresby Land and northern Jameson Land: Grønlands Geol. Unders. Rapp. 48:39–59.

Perrier G. and Ruegg J.C., 1973, Structure profonde du Massif Central Francais: Annls. Géophys. 29:435–502.

Perroud H. and Bonhommet N., 1981, Palaeomagnetism of the Ibero-Armorican Arc and the Hercynian Orogeny in Western Europe: Nature, London, 292:445–448.

Perroud H. and Voo R. van der, 1983, Palaeozoic evolution of the Armorican plate on the basis of palaeomagnetic data: Tectonophysics 91:271–283.

Perroud H., Voo R. van der and Bonhommet N., 1984, Palaeozoic evolution of the Armorican plate on the basis of palaeomagnetic data: Geology 12:579–582.

Peryt T.M. and Peryt D., 1977, Zechstein foraminifera from the Fore-Sudetic monocline area (West Poland) and their palaeoecology: Annl. Soc. Géol. Pol. XLVII:301–326.

Pfeiffer H., 1971, Die variszische Hauptbewegung (sogenannte Sudetische Phase) im Umkreis der äusseren Kristallinzone des variszischen Bogens: Geologie 20:945–958.

Philip H., Andrieux J., Dolala H., Chihi L. and Ben Ayed N., 1986, Evolution tectonique mio-plio-quaternaire du fossé de Kasserine (Tunésie Centrale): Implications sur l'évolution géodynamique recente de Tunésie: Bull. Soc. Géol. France (8)II(4):559–568.

Phillips W.E.A., Stillmann C.J. and Murphy T., 1976, A Caledonian plate tectonic model: J. Geol. Soc. London 132(6):579–609.

Pierce J.W., 1982, The evolution of the Nares Strait lineament and its relation to the Eurekan Orogeny, *in* P.R. Dawes nad J.W. Kerr (eds.), Nares Strait and the drift of Greenland: Conflict in plate tectonics: Meddel. Grønland, Geoscience 8:237–252.

Pieri M., 1975, An outline of Italian geology, *in* C.H. Squires (ed.), Geology of Italy: Tripoli, The Earth Sciences Society of the Libyian Arab Republic, p. 75–143.

Pieri M., 1983, Seismic profiles through the Po Valley, *in* A.W. Bally (ed.), Seismic expression of structural styles, a picture and work atlas: Am. Assoc. Petrol. Geol. Stud. Geol. Ser. 15, Vol. 3:3.4.1.8–3.4.1.2.6.

Pieri M. and Groppi G., 1981, Subsurface geological structure of the Po Plain, Italy: Publication No. 414, del Progetto Finalizzato Geodinamica, p. 11.

Pieri M. and Mattavelli L., 1986, Geological framework of Italian petroleum resources: Bull. Am. Assoc. Petrol Geol. 70(2):103–130.

Pinet B., Montadert L., Mascle A., Cazes M. and Bois C., 1987, New insight on the structure and the formation of sedimentary basins from deep seismic profiling in Western Europe, *in* J. Brooks and K. Glennie (eds.), Petroleum geology of northwest Europe: London, Graham and Trotman, p. 11–31.

Piqué A., 1981, Un segment de chaîne intracontinentale: La Meseta marocaine nord-occidentale, influence des fractures du socle précambrien sur la sédimentation et la déformation de la couverture Paléozoique: Bull. Soc. Géol. France (7)XXIII(1):3–10.

Piqué A. and Kharbouche F., 1983, Distension intracontinentale et volcanisme associé, le Meseta Marocaine nord-occidentale au Devonien-Dinantien: Bull. Cent. Rech. Explor.-Prod. Elf-Aquitaine 7(1):377–387.

Pitman W.C., III, 1978, Relationship between eustasy and stratigraphic sequences on passive margins: Geol. Soc. Am. Bull. 89:1389–1403.

Pitman W.C., III, and Golovchenko X., 1983, The effect of sea level changes on the shelf edge and slope of passive margins; Soc. Econ. Paleont. Mineral. Spec. Publ. 33:41–51.

Plaziat J.C., 1975, Signification paléogéographique des "Calcaires conglomérés," des brèches et des niveaux a Rhodeophycées dans la sédimentation carbonatée du bassin Basco-Béarnais à la base du Tertiaire (Espagne-France): Rev. Géogr. Phys. Géol. Dynam. XVII(3):239–258.

Plaziat J.C., 1981, Late Cretaceous to late Eocene palaeogeographic evolution of southwest Europe: Palaeogeogr., Palaeoclim. Palaeoecol. 36:263–320.

Plein E., 1978, Rotliegend Ablagerungen im Norddeeutschen Becken: Zeitschr. Deutsch. Geol. Ges. 129:71–97.

Pogrebitsky Y.E., 1982, Le système plissé du Taimyr, *in* Tectonics of Europe and adjacent areas, Varicides, Epi-Paleozoic platforms, Alpides. Explanatory note to the International Tectonic Map of Europe and adjacent areas, Scale 1:2500.000, Moscow, "Nauka" Publ. Office, p. 229–230.

Poisson A., 1984, The extension of the Ionian Trough into southwest Turkey, *in* J.E. Dixon and A.H.F. Robertson (eds.), The geological evolution of the eastern Mediterranean: Geol. Soc. Spec. Publ. 17:241–249.

Poka T., 1982, Chemical evolution of the Inner Carpathian Neogene and Quaternary magmatism and the structural formation of the Carapthian Basin, *in* F. Horvath (ed.), Evolution of extensional basins within regions of compression, with emphasis on the Intra-Carpathians: Eötvös University, Budapest Publ., p. 46–48.

Pommerole C., 1978, Evolution paléogéographique et structurale du Bassin de Paris du Précambrien à l'actuel, en relation avec les régions avoisinantes: Geol. Mijnbouw 57:533–543.

Poole W.H., 1977, Evolution of the Appalachian belt in Canada, *in* La Chaîne varisque d'Europe moyenne et occidentale. Colloque Internat. C.R.N.S. Rennes 243:587–603.

Poole W.H., Sanford B.V., Williams A. and Kelley D.G., 1970, Geology of southeastern Canada, *in* Geology and economic minerals of Canada: Economic Geology Report No. 1, 5th edition Dept. of Energy, Mines and Resources, Ottawa, Canada, p. 227–304.

Pozaryska K., 1977, On the upper Eocene in Poland: Kwart. Geol. 21:59–68.

Pozaryska K., 1978, Differences between the late Eocene foraminiferal faunas in western and eastern Europe: Paläont. Z. 52:47–56.

Pozaryski W. and Brochwicz-Lewinski W., 1978, On the Polish Trough: Geol. Mijnbouw 57:545–558.

Pozaryski W. and Dembowski Z. (eds.), 1984, Geological map of Poland and adjoining countries without Cenozoic, Mesozoic, and Permian formations: Publ. House Wydawnictwa Geologicene, Warsaw.

Pozaryski W. and Zytko K., 1979, Aulakogen srodkowopolski a geoscynklina Karpacka: Przeglad Geol. XXVII–6(314):305–311.

Pozaryski W., Tomczyk H. and Brochwicz-Lewinski W., 1982, Tectonics and palaeotectonic evolution of the pre-Permian Paleozoic between Koszalin and Tarun (Pomerania): Przeglad Geol. XXX (12):658–665 (in Polish).

Preston J., 1981, Tertiary igneous activity, in C.H. Holland (ed.), A geology of Ireland: Edinburgh Scotish Academic Press, p. 213–223.

Prestvik T., 1977, Cenozoic Plateau lavas of Spitsbergen: A geochemical study: Norsk Polar Inst. Arbok. 1977:129–142.

Price I. and Rattey R.P., 1984, Cretaceous tectonics off Mid-Norway: Implications for the Rockall and Faeroe-Shetland troughs: J. Geol. Soc. London 141(6):985–992.

Price P.D. and Shade B.D., 1982, Reflection seismic interpretation and seafloor spreading history of Baffin Bay, in A.F. Embry and H.R. Balkwill (ed.), Arctic geology and geophysics: Can. Soc. Petrol. Geol. Mem. 8:245–265.

Priem H.N.A. and den Tex E., 1984, Tracing crustal evolution in the NW Iberian Peninsula through the Rb-Sr nd U-Pb systematics of Palaeozoic granitoids: A review: Phys. Earth Planet. Inter. 35:121–130.

Prinzlau I. and Larsen O., 1972, K/Ar age determinations on alkaline olivine basalts, from Skåne, South Sweden: Geol. För. Stockholm Förh. 94:259–269

Puffer J.H., Hurtubise D.O., Geiger F.J. and Lechler P., 1981, Chemical composition and stratigraphic correlation of Mesozoic basalt units of the Newark Basin, New Jersey, and the Hartford Basin, Connecticut: Summary: Geol. Soc. Am. Bull. 92(1):155–159.

Pugdefabregas C. and Souquet P., 1986, Tectono-sedimentary cycles and depositonal sequences of the Mesozoic and Tertiary from the Pyrenees: Tectonophysics 129:173–203.

Quennell A.M., 1984, The western Arabian rift system, in J.E. Dixon and A.H.F. Robertson (eds.), The geological evolution of the eastern Mediterranean: Geol. Soc. London Spec. Publ. 17:775–788.

Quinlan G.M. and Beaumont C., 1984, Appalachian thrusting, lithospheric flexure and the Paleozoic stratigraphy of the eastern interior of North America: Can. J. Earth Sci. 21:973–996.

Raczynska A., 1979, The stratigraphy and lithofacies development of the younger Lower Cretaceous in the Polish Lowlands: Pr. Inst. Geol. Warszawa LXXXIX:78 p.

Radulescu D. and Sandulescu M., 1980, Correlation des phases de déformation, de métamorphisme et de magmatisme dans les Carpathes, in J. Aubouin, J. Debelmas and M. Latreille (eds.), Geology of the Alpine chains born of the Tethys: Mem.

B.R.G.M. 115:301–302.

Räheim A., 1974, A post-Caledonian syenite porphyry dyke in the western Gneiss region, Tustna, Central Norway: Norsk Geol. Tids. 54:130–147.

Ramberg I.B., 1976, Gravity interpretation of the Oslo Graben and associated igneous rocks: Norg. Geol. Unders. 325:1–194.

Raoult J.-F., 1986, Le front Varisque du Nord de la France d'après les profils sismiques, la géologie de surface et les sondages: Rev. Géol. Dynam. Geogr. Phys. 27(3–4):247–268.

Rast N., 1983, The northern Appalachian traverse in maritime Canada, in N. Rast and F.M. Delany (eds.), Profiles of orogenic belts: Am. Geophy. Union, Geol. Soc. Am., Geodynam. Series 10: 243–274.

Rast N., 1984, The Alleghenian orogeny in eastern North America, in D.H.W. Hutton and D.J. Sanderson (eds.), Variscan tectonics of the North Atlantic region: Geol. Soc. Lond. Spec. Publ. 14:197–218.

Rast N. and Skehan J.W., 1983, The evolution of the Avalon plate: Tectonophysics 100:257–286.

Rat P., 1974, Le systèm Bourgogne–Morvan–Bresse (articulation entre le bassin parisien et le domaine péri-alpin), in J. Debelmas (ed.), Géolgie de la France, Vol. II: Paris, Doin Editeur, p. 480–500.

Rat P., 1978, Les phases tectoniques du Tertiaire dans le nord du fossé bressan et ses marges bourguignonnes en regard des systèmes d'érosion et sédimentation: Cent. Rech. Somm. Soc. Géol. Fr. 5:231–234.

Rawson P.F., 1973, Lower Cretaceous (Ryazanian-Barremian) marine connections and cephalopode migrations between Tethyan and Boreal realms, in R. Casey and P.F. Rawson (eds.), The Boreal Lower Cretaceous: Geol. J. Spec. Iss. 5:131–144.

Rawson P.F. and Riley L.A., 1982, Latest Jurassic–Early Cretaceous events and the "Late Cimmerian unconformity" in the North Sea area: Bull. Am. Assoc. Petrol. Geol. 60(2):2628–2648.

Rawson P.F., Currey D., Dilley F.C., Hancock J.M., Kennedy W.J., Neal J.W., Wood C.J. and Worssam B.C., 1978, A correlation of Cretaceous rocks in the British Isles: Geol. Soc. London Spec. Rep. 9:70 p.

Rehault J.P., Boillot G. and Mauffret A., 1984a, The Western Mediterranean Basin, geological evolution: Mar. Geol. 55(3–4):447–477.

Rehault J.P., Mascle J. and Boillot G., 1984b, Evolution géodynamique de la Méditerranée depuis l'Oligocène: Mem. Soc. Geol. It. 27:85–96.

Rehault J.P., Boillot G. and Mauffret A., 1985, The Western Mediterranean Basin, in D.J. Stanley and F.-C. Wezel (eds.), Geological evolution of the Mediterranean Basin: New York/Berlin/Tokyo/Heidelberg, Springer-Verlag, p. 101–129.

Reidiger C.L., Bustin R.M. and Rouse G.E., 1984, New evidence for the chronology of the Eurekan orogeny for south-central Ellesmere Island: Can. J. Earth Sci. 21:1286–1295.

Reutter, K.-J., 1981, A trench-forearc model for the Northern Apennines, in F.-C. Wezel (ed.), Sedimentary basins of Mediterranean margins: C.N.R. Italian Project of Oceanography, Bologna, Tecnoprint, p. 433–443.

Rex D.C., Geldhill A.R., Brooks C.K. and Steenfelt, 1978, Radiometric ages of Tertiary sialic instrusions near Kong Oscars Fjord, East Greenland: Grønlands Geol. Unders. Rapp., 95:106–109.

Reynolds P.H., Zentilli M. and Mücke G.K., 1981, K-Ar and Ar $^{40}$/Ar$^{39}$ geochronology of granitoid rocks from southern Nova Scotia: Its bearing on the evolution of the Meguma Zone of the Appalachians: Can. J. Earth Sci. 18:386–394.

Ribeiro A., Iglesias M., Ribeiro M.L. and Pereira E., 1983, Modèle géodynamique des Hercynides Ibériques: Comun. Serv. Geol. Portugal 69(2):291–293.

Ricci-Lucchi F., 1975, Miocene palaeogeography and basin analysis in the Periadritic Apennines, in C.H. Squires (ed.) Geology of Italy: Tripoli, The Earth Science Society of the Libyan Arab Republic, p 129–237.

Ricci-Lucchi F., 1978, Turbidite dispersal in a Miocene deep-sea plain: The Marnoso arenacea of the northern Apennines: Geol. Mijnbouw 57(4):559–576.

Rice P.D. and Shade B.D., 1982, Reflection seismic interpretation and seafloor spreading history of Baffin Bay, in A.F. Embry and H.R. Balkwill (eds.), Arctic geology and geophysics: Can. Soc. Petrol. Geol. Mem. 8:245–265.

Richter D., 1978, Die geodynamische Entwicklung der Helleniden in Spiegel ihrer Flysch und Molasse Bildung: Z. Geol. Wiss. Berlin 6(12):1439–1459.

Richter F. and McKenzie D., 1978, Simple plate models of mantle convection: J. Geophys. 44:441–478.

Ricou L.E. and Siddans A.W.B., 1986, Collision tectonics in the Western Alps, in M.P. Coward and A.C. Ries (eds.), Collision tectonics: Geol. Soc. Spec. Publ. 19:229–244.

Ricou L.E., Marcoux J. and Whitechurch H., 1984, The Mesozoic organization of the Taurides: One or several ocean basins, in J.E. Dixon and A.H.F. Robertson (eds.), the geological evolution of the Mediterranean: Geol. Soc. London Spec. Publ. 17:349–359.

Ricou L.E., Dercourt J., Geyssant J., Grandjacquet C. and Leprier C., 1986, Geological constraints on the Alpine evolution of the Mediterranean Tethys: Tectonophysics 123:83–122.

Ridd M.F., 1981, Petroleum geology west of the Shetlands, in L.V. Illings and D.G. Hobson (eds.), Petroleum geology of the continental shelf of north-west Europe: London, Institute of Petroleum, p. 414–425.

Ridd M.F., 1983, Aspects of the Tertiary geology of the Faeroe-Shetland Channel, in M.H.P. Bott, S. Saxov, M. Talwaini and J. Thiede (eds.), Structure and development of the Greenland–Scotland ridge—new methods and concepts: New York/London, Plenum Press, p. 91–108.

Riddihough R.P. and Max M.D., 1976, A geological framework for the continental margin to the west of Ireland: Geol. J. 11(2):109–120.

Rizun P.B. and Senkovskiy, 1973, Position of the southwestern boundary of the East European Platform in the Ukraine: Geotectonics 1973(4):211–214.

Robardet M., 1981, Late Ordovician tillites in the Iberian Peninsula, in M.J. Hambrey and W.B. Harland (eds.), Earth's pre-Pleistocene glacial record: Cambridge, Cambridge Univ. Press., p. 585–589.

Roberts D., 1983, Devonian tectonic deformation in the Norwegian Caledonides and its regional perspective: Norg. Geol. Unders. 380:85–96.

Roberts D. and Gale E.H., 1978, The Caledonian–Appalachian Iapetus Ocean, in D.H. Tarling (ed.), Evolution of the Earth's crust: London, Academic Press, p. 255–342.

Roberts D.G., 1975, Tectonic and stratigraphic evolution of the Rockall Plateau and Trough, in A.W. Woodland (ed.), Petroleum and the continental shelf of north-west Europe, vol. I,

Geology: Barking, England, Applied Science Publ., p. 77–92.

Roberts D.G. and Ginzburg A., 1984, Deep crustal structure of SW Rockall Plateau: Nature London, 308:435–439.

Roberts D.G., Masson D.G. and Miles P.R., 1981a, Age and structure of the Southern Rockall Trough: New evidence: Earth Planet. Sci. Lett. 52:115–128.

Roberts D.G., Masson D.G. and Montadert C., 1981b, Continental margin from the Porcupine Seabight to the Armorican Marginal Basin, in L.V. Illing and G.D. Hobson (eds.), Petroleum geology of the continental shelf of north-west Europe. Vol. 1. Geology: London, Institute of Petroleum, p. 455–473.

Roberts D.G., Bott M.H.P. and Uruski C., 1983, Structure and origin of the Wyville-Thomson Ridge, in M.H.P. Bott, S. Saxov, M. Talwani and J. Thiede (eds.), Structure and development of the Greenland–Scotland Ridge—new methods and concepts: New York/London, Plenum Press, p. 133–158.

Roberts D.G., Backman J., Morton A.C., Murray J.W. and Keene J.B., 1984, Evolution of volcanic rifted margins: Synthesis of Leg 81 results on the western margin of the Rockall Plateau, in D.G. Roberts, D. Schnitker et al. (eds.), Initial Reports of Deep Sea Drilling Project, 81, Washington, DC, U.S. Gov. Printing Office, p. 883–911.

Robillard D., 1979, Tectonique synsédimentaire du Moyen-Atlas septentrional au sud de Tarza (Maroc): Bull. Soc. Géol. France (7)XXI(4):441–447.

Robinson K.W., Shannon P.M. and Young D.G.G., 1981, The Fastnet Basin, an integrated analysis, in L.V. Illings and G.D. Hobson (eds.), Petroleum geology of the continental shelf of north-west Europe: London, Heyden and Son Ltd., p. 444–454.

Rochow K.A., 1981, Seismic stratigraphy of the North Sea "Palaeocene" deposits, in L.V. Illings and G.D. Hobson (eds.), Petroleum geology of the continental shelf of north-west Europe, London, Heyden and Son Ltd., p. 255–266.

Roddick J.C., Cameron W.E. and Smith A.G., 1979, Permo-Triassic and Jurassic 40Ar–39Ar ages from Greek ophiolites and associated rocks: Nature, London 279:788–790.

Roeder D., 1978, Three Central Mediterranean orogens, a geodynamic synthesis, in H. Closs, D. Roeder and K. Schmidt (eds.), Alps, Apennines, Hellenides: Stuttgart, Schweizerbartsche Verlagsbuchhandlung, p. 589–620.

Roeder D., 1980, Geodynamics of the Alpine-Mediterranean system—a synthesis: Ecl. Geol. Helv. 73:353–377.

Rögel F. and Steininger F.F., 1983, Von Zerfall der Tethys zu Mediterran und Paratethys. Die neogene Palaeogeographie und Palinspastik des zirkum-mediterranean Raumes: Ann. Natur. Hist. Mus. Wien 85A:135–163.

Rolet J., 1983, La "phase Bretonne" en Bretagne: État des connaissances: Bull. Soc. Géol. Minéral. Bretagne 1982(C)14(2):63–71.

Rolet J., Le Gall B., Darboux J.-R., Thonon P. and Gravelle M., 1986, L'évolution géodynamique dévono-carbonifère de l'extrémité occidentale de la chaîne hercynienne d'Europe sur le transect Armorique-Cornwall: Bull. Soc. géol. France (8)II(1):43–54.

Rolle F., 1985, Late Cretaceous-Tertiary sediments offshore central West Greenland: Lithostratigraphy, sedimentary evolution, and petroleum potential: Can. J. Earth Sci. 22:1001–1019.

Rondeel H.E. and Simon O.J., 1974, Betic cordilleras, in A.M. Spencer (ed.), Mesozoic-Cenozoic orogenic belts, data for orogenic studies: Geol. Soc. London Spec. Publ. 4:23–35.

Rønnevik H.C. and Beskow B., 1983, Structural and stratigraphic evolution of the Barents Sea: Norwegian Petroleum Directorate, Contribution No. 1, 29 p.

Rønnevik H. and Jacobsen H.P., 1984, Structural highs and basins in the western Barents Sea, in A.M. Spencer et al. (eds.), Petroleum geology of the north European margin: Norw. Petrol. Soc., London, Graham and Trotman, p. 19–32.

Ronov A., Khain V. and Seslavinsky K., 1984, Atlas of lithological-palaeogeographical maps of the world. Late Precambrian and Paleozoic of continents: Leningrad, USSR Academy of Science, 70 p.

Ross C.A. and Ross J.R.P., 1985, Carboniferous and Early Permian biogeography: Geology 13:27–30.

Roussel J., Lécorché J.P., Ponsard J.F., Sougy J. and Villeneuve M., 1984, Panafrican to Hercynian deformations in the Mauretanides and tectonic significance of gravity anomalies; Tectonophysics 109:41–59.

Rowley D.B. and Sahagian D., 1986, Depth-dependent stretching: A different approach: Geology 14:32–35.

Royden L.H., 1985, The Vienna Basin: A thin skinned pull-apart basin, in K.T. Biddle and N. Christie-Blick (eds.), strike-slip deformation, basin formation and sedimentation: Soc. Econ. Paleont. Mineral. Spec. Publ. 37:319–338.

Royden L. and Keen C.E., 1980, Rifting process and thermal evolution of the continental margin of eastern Canada determined from subsidence curves: Earth Planet. Sci. Letts. 51:343–361.

Royden L., Sclater J.G. and Herzen R.P., 1980, Continental margin subsidence and heat flow: Importance parameters in formation of petroleum hydrocarbons: Bull. Am. Assoc. Petrol. Geol. 64(2):173–187.

Royden L.H., Horváth F. and Burchfiel B.L., 1982, Transform faulting, extension, and subduction in the Carpathian Pannonian region: Geol. Soc. Am. Bull. 93:717–725.

Rudkewich M.Y., 1976, The history and dynamics of the development of the West Siberian platform: Tectonophysics 36(1–3):275–287.

Ruellan E. and Auzende J.M., 1985, Structure et évolution du plateau sous-marin de El Jadida (Mazagan, ouest Maroc): Bull. Soc. Géol. France (8)I(1):103–114.

Ruzencev S.V. and Samygin S.G., 1979, Die tektonische Entwicklung des Südurals im unteren und mittleren Paläozoikum: Z. Geol. Wiss. Berlin 7(10):1123–1186.

Salomon J., 1983, Les phases "fossé" dans l'histoire du bassin de Soria (Espagne du nord) au Jurassique supérieur–Crétacé inférieur: Bull. Cent. Rech. Expl.-Prod. Elf-Aquitaine 7(1):399–407.

Salveson J.O., 1981, Rift basins—a tectonic model, in Papers presented to the Conference on the Processes of Planetary Rifting, Napa Valley, California, 3-5 December 1981, Lunar and Planetary Institute, Contribution No. 457, p. 39–42.

Sancho A., Duée G., Hervouet Y. and Telliez H., 1987, Evolution de la sédimentation dans une zone de décrochement complexe: Le Crétacé supérieur sur le rebord nord-ibérique entre le pic d'Orhy et Sainte-Jean-Pied-de-Port: Bull. Soc. Géol. France (8)III(2):235–243.

Sandulescu M., 1975, Essai de synthèse structurale des Carpathes: Bull. Soc. Géol. France 7(XVII)3:299–358.

Sandulescu M., 1978, The Moesian Platform and the north Dobrugean Orogen, in M. Lemoine (ed.), Geological areas of Alpine Europe and adjoining areas: Amsterdam/Oxford/New York, Elsevier Sci. Publ. Co., p. 427–442.

Sandulescu M., 1982, Les Carpathes, in Tectonics of Europe and adjacent areas. Variscides, Epi-Paleozoic platforms, Alpides. Explanatory note to the International Tectonic Map of Europe and adjacent areas, scale 1:2.500.000, Moscow, "Nauka" Publishing Office, p. 405–457.

Sandulescu M., 1984, Geotectonica României: Bucaresti, Ed. Technica, 334 p.

Sannemann D., Zimdars J. and Plein E., 1978, Der basale Zechstein (A2-T1) zwischen Weser und Ems: Z. Dt. Geol. Ges. 129:33–69.

Savostin L.A., Sibuet J.C., Zonnenshain L.P., Le Pichon X. and Roulet M.J., 1986, Kinematic evolution of the Tethys Belt from the Atlantic Ocean to the Pamirs since the Triassic: Tectonophysics 123:1–35.

Sawyer D.S., Toksöz M.N., Sclater J.G. and Swift B.A., 1983, Thermal evolution of the Baltimore Canyon Trough and Georges Bank Basin, in J.S. Watkins and C.L. Drake (eds.), Studies in continental margin geology: Am. Assoc. Petrol. Mem. 34:743–762.

Scandone P., 1975a, The pre-orogenic history of the Lagonegro Basin (Southern Apennines), in C.H. Squyres (ed.), Geology of Italy: Tripoli, The Earth Science Society of the Libyan Arab Republic 2:305–316.

Scandone P., 1975b, Triassic seaways and the Jurassic Tethys Ocean in the central Mediterranean area: Nature, London 256:117–119.

Schenk P.E., 1978, Synthesis of the Canadian Appalachians, in I.G.C.P. project 27 Caledonian-Appalachian Orogen of the North Atlantic region: Geol. Surv. Can. Paper 78–13: 111–136.

Schenk P.E., 1981, The Meguma Zone of Nova Scotia—a remnant of Western Europe, South America or West Africa, in J.W. Kerr, A.J. Ferguson and L.C. Machan (eds.), Geology of the North Atlantic borderlands: Can. Soc. Petrol. Geol. Mem. 7:119–148.

Schenk P.E. and Lane T.E., 1981, Early Palaeozoic tillite of Nova Scotia, Canada, in M.J. Hambrey and W.B. Harland (eds.), Earth's pre-Pleistocene glacial record: Cambridge, Cambridge University Press, p. 707–710.

Schermerhorn L.J.C., Priem H.N.A., Boelrijk N.A.I.M., Hebeda E.H., Verdurmen E.A.T. and Verschuren R.H., 1978, Age and origin of the Messejana Dolerite fault-dyke system (Portugal, Spain) in the light of the opening of the North Atlantic Ocean: J. Geol. 86:299–309.

Schlüter H.-U. and Hinz K., 1978, The continental margin of West Spitsbergen: Polarforschung 48(1/2):151–169.

Schmidt K. and Franke D., 1975, Stand und Probleme der Karbonforschung in der DDR: Z. Geol. Wiss. Berlin 3:819–849.

Schminke H.U., 1982, Volcanic and chemical evolution of the Canary Islands, in U. von Rad, K. Hinz, M. Sarntheim and E. Seibold (eds.), Geology of the northwest African margin: Berlin/Heidelberg/New York, Springer-Verlag, p. 273–306.

Schönlaub H.P., 1979, Das Paläozoikum in Osterreich: Abh. Geol. Bundes. Wien 33:124 p.

Schopf T.J.M., 1974, Permo-Triassic extinctions: Relation to sea floor spreading: J. Geol. 82:129–143.

Schott J.J., Montigny R. and Thuizat R., 1981, Palaeomagnetism and potassium-argon age of the Messejana Dyke (Portugal and Spain): Angular limitation to the rotation of the Iberian Peninsula since the Middle Jurassic: Earth Planet. Sci. Lett. 53:457–470.

Schröder B., 1987, Inversion tectonics along the western margin of the Bohemian Massif: Tectonophysics 137:93–100.

Schwab F.L., 1981, Evolution of the western continental margin, French-Italian Alps: Sandstone mineralogy as an index of plate tectonic setting: J. Geol. 89:349–368.

Schwan W., 1980, Geodynamic peaks in Alpinotype orogenies and changes in ocean-floor spreading during Late Jurassic-Late Tertiary time: Bull. Am. Assoc. Petrol. Geol. 64:359–373.

Sclater J.G. and Christie P.A.F., 1980, Continental stretching: An explanation of the post-Mid-Cretaceous subsidence of the Central North Sea Basin: J. Geoph. Res., 85(137):3711–3739.

Sclater J.G. and Tapscott C., 1979, The history of the Atlantic: Sci. Am. 240:120–133.

Sclater J.G., Royden L., Horvath F., Burchfiel B.L., Semken S. and Stegena L., 1980, The formation of the Itnra-Carpathian Basin as determined from subsidence data: Earth Planet. Sci. Lett. 51:139–162.

Sclater J.G., Hellinger M. and Shore M., 1986, An analysis of the importance of extension in accounting for post-Carboniferous subsidence of the North Sea Basin: University of Tulsa, Institute for Geophysics, Technical Report No. 44, 38 p.

Scotese C.R., 1984, An introduction to the volume: Paleozoic paleomagnetism and the assembly of Pangea, in R. van der Voo, C.R. Scotese and N. Bonhommet (eds.), Plate reconstruction from Paleozoic paleomagnetism: Am. Geophys. Union, Geol. Soc. Am. Geodynam. Ser. 12:1–10.

Scotese C.R., Bambach R.K., Barton C., Voo R. van der and Ziegler A.M., 1979, Palaeozoic base maps: J. Geol. 87(3):217–277.

Scotese C.R., Snelson S., Rose W.C. and Dodge L.A., 1980, A computer animation of continental drift: J. Geomag. Geoelectr. 32 (suppl. III): SIII61–SIII70.

Scotese C.R., Voo R. van der, Johnson R.E. and Giles P.S., 1984, Paleomagnetic results from the Carboniferous of Nova Scotia, in R. van der Voo, C.R. Scotese and N. Bonhommet (eds.), Plate reconstruction from Paleozoic paleomagnetism: Am. Geophys. Union, Geol. Soc. Am. Geodynam. Ser. 12:63–81.

Scotese C.R., Voo R. van der and Barrett S.F., 1985, Silurian and Devonian base maps: Phil. Trans R. Soc. London B309:57–77.

Scrutton R.A., 1986, The geology, crustal structure and evolution of Rockall Trough and the Faeroe-Shetland Channel: Proc. Roy. Soc. Edinburgh 88b:7–26.

Secor D.T. Jr., Snoke A.W. and Dallmeyer R.D., 1986, Character of the Alleghenian orogeny in the southern Appalachians. Part III. Regional tectonic relations: Geol. Soc. Am. Bull. 97:1345–1353.

Seemann U., 1984, Tertiary intrusives on the Atlantic continental margin of southwest Ireland: Ir. J. Earth Sci. 6:229–236.

Séguin M.K., 1983, Palaeomagnetism of some lithological units from the lower Palaeozoic of the Vendée, France: Tectonophysics 96:357–279.

Seguret M. and Daignières M., 1985, Coupes balancées d'échelle crustale des Pyrenees: C.R. Acad. Sci. Paris 301, Ser II(5):341–346.

Senes J. and Marinescu F.C., 1974, Cartes paleogeographiques du Néogène de la Paratéthys centrale: Mem. B.R.G.M. 78:785–792.

Sengör A.M.C., 1977, Mid-Mesozoic closure of Permo-Triassic Tethys and its implications: Nature, London 279:590–593.

Sengör A.M.C., 1984, The Cimmeride Orogenic System and the Tectonics of Eurasia: Geol. Soc. Am. Spec. Paper 195:82 p.

Sengör A.M.C., 1985, The story of the Tethys: How many wives did Okeanos have? Episodes 8(1):3–12.

Sengör A.M.C. and Canitez N., 1982, The North Anatolian Fault, in H. Berkhemer and K. Hsü (eds.), Alpine-Mediterranean geodynamics: Am. Geophys. Union, Geol. Soc. Am., Geodynam. Ser. 7: 205–210.

Sengör A.M.C. and Kidd W.S.F., 1979, Post-collisional tectonics of the Turkish–Iranian Plateau and comparison with Tibet: Tectonophysics 55:361–376.

Sengör A.M.C. and Yilmaz Y., 1981, Tethyan evolution of Turkey: A plate tectonic approach: Tectonophysics 75:181–241.

Sengör A.M.C., Yilmaz Y. and Sungurlu O., 1984, Tectonics of the Mediterranean Cimmerides: Nature and evolution of the western termination of Palaeo-Tethys, in J.E. Dixon and A.H.F. Robertson (eds.), The geological evolution of the eastern Mediterranean: Geol. Soc. Lond. Spec. Publ. 17:77–112.

Sestini G., 1974, Northern Appenines, in A.M. Spencer (ed.), Mesozoic-Cenozoic orogenic belts, data for orogenic studies: Geol. Soc. Lond. Spec. Publ. 4:61–84.

Sibuet J.-C., Mathis B., Pastouret L., Auzende J.-M., Foucher J.-P., Hunter P.M., Guennoc P., de Graciansky P.-C., Montadert L. and Masson D.G., 1985, Morphology and basement structure of the Goban Spur continental margin (northeast Atlantic) and the role of the Pyrenean orogeny, in P.C. de Graciansky, C.W. Poag, et al., Initial Reports of Deep Sea Drilling Project, 80, Washington D.C., U.S. Govt. Printing Office, p. 1153–1165.

Sider H. and Ohnenstetter M., 1986, Field and petrological evidence for the development of an ensialic marginal basin related to the Hercynian orogeny in the Massif Central, France: Geol. Rundsch. 75(2):421–443.

Siedlicka A. and Sielicki S., 1972, A contribution to the geology of the Downtonian sedimentary rocks of Hitra: Norg. Geol. Unders. 275:1–28.

Simon O.J. and Kozur H., 1977, New data on the (Permo) Triassic of the Betic Zone (southern Spain): Cuad. Geol. Iber. 4:307–322.

Sineriz B.G., Querol R., Castillo F. and Ramon J., 1980, A new hydrocarbon province in the western Mediterranean: Proc. 10th World Petrol. Congr. 1979, vol. II, p. 191–197.

Sittler C., 1969a, The sedimentary trough of the Rhine Graben: Tectonophysics 8:543–560.

Sittler C., 1969b, La fossé Rhénan en Alsace, aspect structural et histoire géologique: Rev. Geogr. Phys. Geol. Dyn. (2)6(5):465–494.

Skehan J.W., 1983, Geological profiles through the Avalonian Terrain of south eastern Massachussetts, Rhode Island and eastern Connecticut, USA, in N. Rast and F.M. Delany (eds.), Profiles of orogenic belts: Am. Geophys. Union, Geol. Soc. Am., Geodynam. Ser. 10:275–300.

Skehan J.W. and Rast N., 1983, Relationship between Precambrian and lower Paleozoic rocks of southeastern New England and other North Atlantic Avalonian Terrains, in P.E. Schenk (ed.), Regional trends in the geology fo the Appalachian-Caledonian-Hercynian-Mauretanide Orogen: Dordrecht, D. Reidel Publ. Co., p. 131–162.

Skogseid J. and Eldholm O., 1987, Early Cenozoic crust at the Norwegian continental margin and the conjugate Jan Mayen Ridge: J. Geophys. Res., in press.

Slaczka A., 1976, Atlas of palaeotransport of detrital sediments in the Carpathian–Balkan Mountain System. Part 1. Tithonian–Lower Cretaceous: Geological Association Carpathian–Balkan Sedimentological commission, Geological Institute, Warszawa.

Sleep N.H., 1973, Crustal thinning on Atlantic coastal margins:

Evidence from old margins, *in* D.H. Tarling and S.K. Runcorn (eds.), Implications of continental drift to earth sciences, Vol. 2, Part 6: London, Academic Press, p. 685–692.

Sleep N.H., 1976, Platform subsidence mechanisms and "eustatic" sea-level changes: Tectonophysics 36:45–56.

Slezinger A.E. and Jansin A.L., 1979, Die strukturelle Position der jungpaläozoischen Depressionsfazies im südlichen Vorural: Z. Geol. Wiss. Berlin 7(10):1187–1195.

Smith A.G. and Briden J.C., 1977, Mesozoic and Cenozoic paleocontinental maps: Cambridge Earth Science Series, Cambridge University Press, 63 p.

Smith A.G. and Spray J.G., 1984, A half-ridge transform model for the Hellenic-Dinaric ophiolites, *in* J.E. Dixon and A.H.F. Robertson (eds.) The geological evolution of the eastern Mediterranean: Geol. Soc. Lon. Spec. Publ. 17:629–644.

Smith D.B., 1981, The evolution of the English Zechstein Basin, *in* Z. Pakulska and M. Kuna (eds.), International Symposium Central European Permian, Proceedings, Geologiczni, Warszawa, Wydawnictwa Geologiczni, p. 7–47.

Smith D.G., Harland W.B., Hughes N.F. and Pickerton C.A.G., 1977, The Geology of Kong Karls Land, Svalbard: Geol. Mag. 113(3):193–304.

Smith G.P. and Stearn C.W., 1982, The Devonian-Carbonate-Clastic sequences on Southwest Ellesmere Island, Arctic Canada, *in* A.E. Embry and H.R. Balkwill (eds.), Arctic geology and geophysics: Can. Soc. Petrol. Geol. Mem. 8:147–154.

Smythe D.K., 1983, Faeroe-Shetland escarpment and continental margin north of the Faeroes, *in* M.H.P. Bott, S. Saxov, M. Talwian and J. Thiede (eds.), Structure and development of Greenland–Shetland Ridge—new methods and concepts: New York/London, Plenum Press, p. 109–119.

Smythe D.K., Skuce A.G. and Donato J.A., 1980, Geological objections to an extensional origin of the Buchan and Witchground Graben in the North Sea: Nature, London 287:467–468.

Sobczak K.W., Mayer U. and Sweeney J.F., 1986, Crustal section across the polar continent-ocean transition in Canada: Can. J. Earth Sci. 23:608–621.

Sobolev I.D., 1982, Chaîne plissée de l'Oural, *in* Tectonics of Europe and adjacent areas, Variscides, Epi-Paleozoic platforms, Apides. Explanatory note to the International Tectonic map of Europe and adjacent areas, scale 1:2500000, Moscow, "Nauka" Publ. Office, p. 185–203.

Solli M., 1976, En Seismisk Skorepeundersøkelse Norges-Shetland: Thesis, University of Bergen.

Sonnenfeld P., 1985, Models of upper Miocene evaporite genesis in the Mediterranean region, *in* D.J. Stanley and F.-C. Wezel (eds.), Geological evolution of the Mediterranean Basin: New York/Berlin/Heidelberg/Tokyo, Springer-Verlag, p. 323–346.

Sonnenfeld P. and Finetti I., 1985, Messinian evaporites in the Mediterranean: A model of continuous inflow and outflow, *in* D.J. Stanley and F.-C. Wezel (eds.), Geological evolution of the Mediterranean Basin: New York/Berlin/Heidelberg/Tokyo, Springer-Verlag, p. 347–353.

Soper N.J. and Hutton D.H.W., 1984, Late Caledonian sinistral displacements in Britain: Implications for a three-plate collision model: Tectoncis 3(1):781–794.

Soper N.J., Higgins A.C., Downie C., Matthews D.W. and Brown P.E., 1976, Late Cretaceous-Early Tertiary stratigraphy of the Kangerdlugssuaq area, east Greenland, and the age of opening of the north-east Atlantic: J. Geol. Soc. London 132:85–

104.

Sørensen K., 1985, Danish basin subsidence by Triassic rifting on a lithosphere cooling background: Nature, London 319(6055):660–663.

Sørensen S., Jones M., Hardman R.F.P., Leutz W.K. and Schwarz P.H., 1986, Reservoir characteristics of high- and low-productivity chalks from the Central North Sea, *in* A.M. Spencer et al. (eds.), Habitat of hydrocarbons on the Norwegian continental shelf: London, Graham and Trotman, p. 91–110.

Spakman W., 1986, Subduction beneath Eurasia in connection with the Mesozoic Tethys: Geol. Mijnbouw 65:145–153.

Spariosu D.J. and Kent D.V., 1983, Paleomagnetism of the Lower Devonian Traveler Felsite and the Acadian orogeny in the New England Appalachians: Geol. Soc. Am. Bull. 94:1319–1328.

Spariosu D.J., Kent D.V. and Keppie J.D., 1984, Late Paleozoic motions of the Meguma Terrane, Nova Scotia: New paleomagnetic evidence, *in* R. van der Voo, C.R. Scotese and N. Bonhommet (eds.), Plate reconstruction from Paleozoic paleomagnetism: Am. Geophys. Union, Geol. Soc. Am., Geodynam. Ser. 12:82–97.

Spencer A.M., Home P.C. and Berglund L.T., 1984, Tertiary structural development of the Western Barents Shelf: Troms to Svalbard, *in* A.M. Spencer et al. (eds.), Petroleum geology of the north European margin: Norw. Petrol. Soc., London, Graham and Trottman, p. 199–209.

Spjeldnaes N., 1981, Lower Palaeozic palaeoclimatology, *in* C.H. Holland (ed.), Lower Palaeozoic of the Middle East, eastern and South Africa and Antarctica: New York, John Wiley and Sons Ltd., p. 199–256.

Spohn T. and Schubert G., 1983, Convective thinning of the lithosphere: A mechanism for rifting and mid-plate volcanism on Earth, Venus and Mars: Tectonophysics 94:67–90.

Spray J.G., Bébien J., Rex D.C. and Roddick J.C., 1984, Age constraints on the igneous and metamorphic evolution of the Hellenic-Dinaric ophiolites, *in* J.E. Dixon and A.H.F. Robertson (eds.), The geological evolution of the eastern Mediterranean: Geol. Soc. London Spec. Publ. 17:619–628.

Srivastava S.P., 1978, Evolution of the Labrador Sea and its bearing of the early evolution of the North Atlantic: Geophys. J.R. Astr. Soc. 52:313–357.

Srivastava S.P., 1983, Davis Strait: Structure origin and evolution, *in* M.H.P. Bott, S. Saxov, M. Talwani and J. Thiede (eds.), Structure and Development of the Greenland–Scotland Ridge—new methods and concepts: New York/London, Plenum Press, p. 159–189.

Srivastava S.P., 1985, Evolution of the Eurasian Basin and its implications to the motion of Greenland along Nares Strait: Tectonophysics 114:29–53.

Srivastava S.P. and Falconer R.K.H., 1982, Nares Strait: A conflict between plate tectonics and geological interpretation, *in* P.R. Dawes and J.W. Kerr (eds.), Nares Strait and drift of Greenland: A conflict in plate tectonics: Meddel. Grønland, Geoscience 8:339–352.

Srivastava S.P., Falconer R.K.H. and MacLean B., 1981, Labrador Sea, Davies Strait, Baffin Bay; Geology and geophysics—a review, *in* J.W. Kerr, A.J. Fergusson and L.C. Machan (eds.), Geology of the North Atlantic borderlands: Can. Soc. Petrol. Geol. Mem. 7:333–398.

Srivastava S.P., MacLean B., Macnab R.F. and Jackson H.B., 1982, Davies Strait: Structure and evolution as obtained from a systematic geophysical survey, *in* A.F. Embry and

H.R. Balkwill (eds.), Arctic geology and geophysics: Can. Soc. Petrol. Geol. Mem. 8:267–295.

Stadler G. and Teichmüller R., 1971, Zusammenfassendes Uberblick über die Entwicklung des Bramscher Massivs und des Niedersächsischen Tektogens: Fortsch. Geol. Rheinld Westf. 18:547–564.

Stancu-Kristoff G. and Stehn O., 1984, Ein grossregionaler Schnitt durch das Nordwestdeutsche Oberkarbon Becken vom Ruhrgebiet bis in die Nordsee: Fortschr. Geol. Rheinland u. Westf. 32(1):35–38.

Steckler M.S., 1985, Uplift and extension at the Gulf of Suez—indications of induced mantle convection: Nature, London 317:135–139.

Steckler M.S. and Watts A.B., 1982, Subsidence history and tectonic evolution of Atlantic-type continental margins, *in* R.A. Scrutton (ed.), Dynamics of passive margins: Am. Geophys. Union, Geol. Soc. Am. Geodynam. Ser. 6:184–196.

Steel R.J., 1976, Devonian basins of West Norway: Sedimentary response to tectonism and varying tectonic context: Tectonophysics 36:207–224.

Steel R. and Gloppen T.G., 1980, Late Caledonian (Devonian) basin formation, western Norway: Signs of strike-slip tectonics during infilling: Spec. Publ. Int. Ass. Sediment. 4:79–103.

Steel. R.J. and Worsley D., 1984, Svalbard's post-Caledonian strata—an atlas of sedimentational patterns and palaeogeographic evolution, *in* A.M. Spencer et al. (eds.), Petroleum geology of the north European margin: Norw. Petrol. Soc., London, Graham and Trotman Ltd., p. 109–136.

Steel R.J., Dalland A., Kalgraft K. and Larsen V., 1981, The Central Tertiary Basin of Spitsbergen: Sedimentary development of a sheared-margin basin, *in* J.W. Kerr, A.J. Fergusson and L.C. Machan (eds.), Geology of the North Atlantic borderlands: Can. Soc. Petrol. Geol. Mem. 7:647–664.

Steel R., Gielberg J., Helland-Hansen W., Kleinspehn K., Nø ttvedt A. and Rye-Larsen M., 1985, The Tertiary strike-slip basins and orogenic belt of Spitsbergen, *in* K.T. Biddle and N. Christie-Blick (eds.), strike-slip deformation, basin formation and sedimentation: Soc. Econ. Paleont. Mineral. Spec. Publ. 37:339–359.

Stegena L. and Horváth F., 1982, Review of the Pannonian Basin, *in* F. Horváth (ed.), Evolution of extensional basins within regions of compression, with emphasis on the Intra-Carpathians; Eötvös University, Budapest Publ., p. 19–25.

Steiner J. and Falk F., 1981, The Ordovician Lederschiefer of Thuringia, *in* M.J. Hambrey and W.B. Harland (eds.), Earth's pre-Pleistocene glacial record: Cambridge, Cambridge University Press, p. 579–581.

Steininger F.F. and Rögel F., 1984, Paleogeography and palinspastic reconstruction of the Neogene of the Mediterranean and Paratethys, *in* J.E. Dixon and A.H.F. Robertson (eds.), The geological evolution of the eastern Mediterranean: Geol. Soc. London Spec. Publ. 17:659–668.

Stemmerik L. and Sørensen M., 1980, Upper Permian dykes in southern Scoresby Land, East Greenland: Grønland Geol. Unders. Rapp. 100:108.

Stets J. and Wurster P., 1981, Zur Strukturgeschichte des Hohen Atlas in Marokko: Geol. Rundsch. 70(3):801–841.

Stets J. and Wurster P., 1982, Atlas and Atlantic—structural relations, *in* V. von Rad, K. Hinz, M. Sarnthein and E. Seibold (eds.). Geolgoy of the north-west African continental margin: Berlin, Springer-Verlag, p. 69–85.

Stévaux J. and Winnock E., 1974, Les bassins du Trias et du Lias inférieur d'Aquitaine et leurs épisodes évaporitiques: Bull. Soc. Géol. France (7)XVI(6):679–695.

Stevens G.R., 1973a, Jurassic belemnites, *in* A. Hallam (ed.), Atlas of palaeobiogeography: Amsterdam, Elsevier Sci. Publ. Co., p. 258–274.

Stevens G.R., 1973b, Cretaceous belemnites, *in* A. Hallam (ed.), Atlas of palaeobiogeography: Amsterdam, Elsevier Sci. Publ. Co., p. 385–401.

Steward F.H., 1965, Tertiary igneous activity, *in* G.Y. Craig (ed.), The geology of Scotland: Edinburgh/London, Oliver and Boyd, p. 417–465.

Stewart A.D., 1978, Limits to palaeogravity since the Precambrian: Nature, London 271:153–155.

Storedvedt K.M., 1987, Major late Caledonian and Hercynian sinistral dextral movements on the Great Glen Fault: Tectonophysics, 143(4): 253–267.

Storedvedt K.M. and Tørsvik T.H., 1983, Palaeomagnetic re-examination of the basal Caithness Old Red Sandstone; aspects of local and regional tectonics: Tectonophysics 98:151–164.

Strong D.F. and Harris A., 1974, The petrology and Mesozoic alkaline intrusives of central Newfoundland: Can. J. Earth Sci. 11(9):1208–1219.

Sturt B.A., Pringle I.R. and Ramsey D.M., 1978, The Finnmarkian phase of the Caledonian Orogeny: J. Geol. Soc. London 135:597–610.

Sturt B.A., Dalland A. and Mitchell J.L., 1979, The age of the sub-Mid Jurassic tropical weathering profiles of Andoya, northern Norway, and the implication for the late Palaeozoic palaeogeography in the North Atlantic region: Geol. Rundsch. 68(2): 523–542.

Sullivan K.D., 1983, The Newfoundland Basin: Ocean-continental boundary and Mesozoic sea floor spreading history: Earth Planet. Sci. Lett. 62:321–339.

Surlyk F., 1977a, Stratigraphy, tectonics and palaeogeography of the Jurassic sediments of the areas north of Kong Oscar Fjord, East Greenland: Grønl. Geol. Unders. 123:53 p.

Surlyk F., 1977b, Mesozoic faulting in East Greenland: Geol. Mijnbouw 56(4):311–327.

Surlyk F., 1978, Jurassic basin evolution of East Greenland: Nature, London 274(5667):130–133.

Surlyk F., 1984, Fan-delta to submarine fan conglomerates of the Volgian-Valanginian Wollaston Foreland Group, East Greenland, *in* E.H. Koster and R.J. Stell (eds.), Sedimentation of gravels and conglomerates: Can. Soc. Petrol. Geol. Mem. 10:359–382.

Surlyk F. and Clemmensen L.B., 1983, Rift propagation and eustacy as controlling factors during Jurassic inshore and shelf sedimentation in northern East Greenland: Sed. Geol. 34:119–143.

Surlyk F. and Hurst J.M., 1984, The evolution of the early Paleozoic deep water basin of North Greenland: Geol. Soc. Am. Bull. 95:131–154.

Surlyk F., Clemmensen L.B. and Larsen H.C., 1981, Post-Palaeozoic evolution of the East Greenland continental margin, *in* J.W. Kerr and A.J. Fergusson (eds.), Geology of the North Atlantic borderlands: Can. Soc. Petrol. Geol. Mem. 7:611–645.

Surlyk F., Piasecki S., Rolle F., Stemmerik C., Thomsen E. and Wrang P., 1984, The Permian basin of East Greenland, *in* A.M. Spencer (ed.), Petroleum geology of the north European margin: London, Graham and Trotman, p. 303–315.

Surlyk F., Hurst J.M., Piasecki S., Rolle F., Scholle P.A., Stemmerik L. and Thomsen E., 1986, The Permian of the western margin of the Greenland Sea—a future exploration target, *in* M. T. Halbouty (ed.), Future petroleum provinces of the world: AAPG Mem. 40: 630–659.

Svoboda J., 1966, The Barrandian Basin, *in* J. Svoboda (ed.), Regional geology of Czechoslovakia. Part I. The Bohemian Massif: Geol. Surv. Cech. Publ., p. 281–341.

Sweeney J.F., 1977, Subsidence of the Sverdrup Basin, Canadian Arctic: Geol. Soc. Am. Bull. 88:41–48.

Sweeney J.F., 1985, Comments on the age of the Canadian Basin: Tectonophysics 114:1–10.

Sweeney J.F., Weber J.R. and Blasco S.M., 1982, Continental ridges in the Arctic Ocean: Lorex constraints: Tectonophysics 89:217–237.

Sweeney J.F., Balkwill H., Franklin R., Mayr U., McGrath P., Snow E., Sobczak L.W. and Wetmiller R.J., 1986, North American Continent-Ocean Transect Program, Corridor G., Somerset Island to Canada Basin: Geol. Surv. Can. Open File 1093.

Swift S.A., Ebinger C.J. and Tucholke B.E., 1986, Seismic stratigraphic correlation across the New England seamounts, western North Atlantic: Geology 14:346–349.

Talwani M. and Eldholm O., 1977, Evolution of the Norwegian-Greenland Sea: Geol. Soc. Am. Bull. 88:969–999.

Talwani M. and Udintsev G., 1976, Tectonic synthesis: Initial Reports of Deep Sea Drilling Project, 37, Washignton, DC, U.S. Govt. Printing Office, p. 1213–1242.

Tamain A.L.G., 1978, L'évolution Calédono-Varisque des Hespérides, *in* IGCP Project 87, Caledonian-Appalachian Orogen of the North Atlantic Region: Geol. Surv. Canada Paper 78-13: 183–492.

Tapponnier P., 1977, Evolution tectonique du system alpin en Mediterranée: Poinconnement et écrasement rigide-plastique: Bull. Soc. Géol. France (7)XIX(3):437–460.

Tarakovsky A.N., Fishman M.V., Shkola I.V. and Andreichev V.L., 1983, Vozrast trappov Zemli Frantsa-Josifa, *in* G.I. Kavardin (ed.), Prognozirovaniye i otsenka niklenosnosti novykh rudnykh rayonov na severe Sibirskoy Platformy, Sbornik nauchnylch statey, L. P.G.O. "Sevmogeo," p. 100–107.

Tarling D.H. and Gale N.H., 1968, Isotopic dating and palaeomagnetic polarity in the Faroe Islands: Nature, London 218:1043–1044.

Taylor J.C.M., 1984, Late Permian-Zechstein, *in* K.W. Glennie (ed.), Introduction to the petroleum geology of the North Sea: Oxford, Blackwell Sci. Publ., p. 61–83.

Taylor P.N., Parson L.M., Morton A.C., Hertogen J. and Gibson I.L., 1986, Petrogenesis of the Vøring Plateau volcanic sequence drilled on Leg 104: Interaction of mantle and crust derived melts during formation of a constructive plate margin: Geol. Soc. Newsl. 15(6):38 (abstract).

Taylor P.T., Kovacs L.C. and Vogt P.R., 1981, Detailed aeromagnetic investigation of the Arctic Basin: J. Geophys. Res. 86(B7):6323–6333.

Teichmüller M., Teichmüller R. and Barenstein H., 1984, Inkohlung und Erdgas—eine neue Inkohlungs—Karte der Karbon Oberfläche in Nordwest Deutschland: Fortschr. Geol. Rheinld. Westf. 32(1):4–34.

Thélin P. and Aryton S., 1983, Cadre évolutif des evènements magmatico-métamorphiques du socle anté-triasique dans le domaine penninique (Valais): Schweiz. Mineral.-Petrogr. Mitt. 63(2/3):393–402.

Thiede J., 1979, Paleogeography and paleobathymetry of the Mesozoic and Cenozoic North Atlantic Ocean: Geo. J. 3(3):263–272.

Thiede J. and Eldholm O., 1983, Speculation about the palaeodepths of the Greenland-Shetland Ridge during late Mesozoic and Cenozoic times, *in* H.P. Bott, S. Saxov, M. Talwani and J. Thiede (eds.), Structure and development of the Greenland-Scotland Ridge—new methods and concepts: New York/London, Plenum Press, p. 445–456.

Thiele O., 1977, Zur Tektonik des Waldviertels in Niederösterreich (südliche Böhmische Masse): Nov. Act. Leopold. N.F. 244:67–82.

Thierry J., 1982, Thethys, Mésogée et Atlantique au Jurassique: Quelques réflexions basées sur les faunes d'Ammonites: Bull. Soc. Géol. France (7)XXIV(5–6):1053–1067.

Thomas B. and Gennesseaux M., 1986, A two stage rifting in the basins of the Corsica-Sardinia Straits: Mar. Geol. 72:255–239.

Thompson R.N., 1982, Magmatism of the British Tertiary volcanic province: Scott. J. Geol. 18:49–107.

Tollmann A., 1978, Plattentektonische Fragen in den Ostalpen und der plattentektonische Mechanismus des Mediterranen Orogen: Mitt. österr. Geol. Ges. 69:291–351.

Tollmann A., 1980, Grosstektonische Ergebnisse aus den Ostalpen im Sinne der Plattentektonik: Mitt.östen. Geol. Ges. 71/72:37–44.

Tollmann A., 1984, Entstehung und früher Werdegang der Tethys mit besonderer Berücksichtigung des Mediterranen Raums: Mitt. Osterr. Geol. Ges. 77:93–113.

Tollmann E.K. and Tollmann A., 1982, Die Entwicklung der Tethystrias und Herkunft ihrer Fauna: Geol. Rundsch. 71(3):987–1019.

Torsvik T.H., Løvlie R. and Storedvedt K.M., 1983, Multicomponent magnetisation in the Helmsdale Granite, North Scotland; geotectonic implication: Tectonophysics 98:111–129.

Trettin H.P., 1973, Early Palaeozoic evolution of the northern parts of the Canadian Archipelago, *in* M.G. Pitcher (ed.), Arctic geology, Am. Assoc. Petrol. Geol. Mem. 19:57–75.

Trettin H.P., 1987, Pearya: A composite terrane with Caledonian affinities in northern Ellesmere Island: Can. J. Earth Sci. 24:224–245.

Trettin H.P. and Balkwill H.R., 1979, Contributions to the tectonic history of the Innuitian Province, Arctic Canada: Can. J. Earth Sci. 17(3):748–769.

Trettin H.P. and Parrish R., 1987, Late Cretaceous bimodal magmatism, northern Ellesmere Island: Isotope age and origin: Can. J. Earth Sci. 24:257–265.

Trettin H.P., Parrish R. and Loveridge W.D., 1987, U-Pb age determinations on Proterozoic to Devonian rocks from northern Ellesmere Island, Arctic Canada: Can. J. Earth Sci. 24:246–256.

Tröger K.-A., 1978, Probleme der Paläontologie, Biostratigraphie und Paläogeographie Oberkretazischer Faunen (Cenoman-Turon) Westeuropas und der Russichen Tafel Z. Geol. Wiss. Berlin 6:557–570.

Trümpy R., 1980, Geology of Switzerland—a guide book. Part A. Outline of the geology of Switzerland: Basel/New York, Wepf. & Co. Publ., 102 p.

Trümpy R., 1982, Alpine paleogeography: A re-appraisal, *in* K.J. Hsü (ed.), Mountain building processes: London, Academic Press, p. 149–156.

Trunko L., 1969, Geologie von Ungarn: Beiträge zur regionalen Geologie, Vol. 8, Berlin/Stuttgart, Bornträger, 257 p.

Tszyn Z.I., 1967, Devonian of the Timan-Pechora region, *in* D.H. Oswald (ed.), International Symposium on the Devonian System, Calgary 1976, Alberta Soc. Petrol. Geol. 1:397–412.

Tucholke B.E. and Fry V.A., 1985, Basement structure and sediment distribution in northwest Atlantic Ocean Bull. Am. Assoc. Petrol. Geol. 69(12):2077–2097.

Tucker R.M. and Arter G., 1987, The tectonic evolution of the North Celtic Sea and Cardigan Bay basins with special reference to basin inversion: Tectonophysics 137:291–307.

Turcotte D.L., 1981, Rifts—tensional failures of the lithosphere, *in* papers presented to the Conference of Processes of Planetary Rifting, Napa Valley, California, 3-5 December, 1981, Lunar and Planet. Inst. Contrib. 451:5–8.

Turcotte D.L. and Emerman S.H., 1983, Mechanisms of active and passive rifting: Tectonophysics 94:39–50.

Udias A., 1982, Seismicity and seismotectonic stress field in the Alpine-Mediterranean region and their implications to tectonic processes, *in* H. Berkhemer and K. Hsü (eds.), Alpine-Mediterranean geodynamics: Am. Geophys. Union, Geol. Soc. Am. Geodynam. Ser. 7:75–82.

Udias A., 1985, Seismicity of the Mediterranean Basin, *in* D.J. Stanley and F.-C. Wezel (eds.), Geological evolution of the Mediterranean Basin: New York/Berlin/Heidelberg/Tokyo, Springer-Verlag, p. 54–63.

Ulmishek G., 1982, Petroleum geology and resource assessment of the Timan-Pechora Basin, USSR, and the adjacent Barents-Northern Kara Shelf: Argonne National Laboratory, U.S. Department of Commerce, National Technical Information Service DE83-004421, 197 p.

Ulmishek G., 1984, The geology and petroleum resources of basins in the Asian Arctic and offshore East Greenland: Argonne National Laboratory Publ.ANL/EES-TM-247, p. 104.

Umpleby D.C., 1979, Geology of the Labrador Shelf: Geol. Sur. Can. Paper 79-13:34 p.

Ussami N., Karner D. and Bott M.H.P., 1986, Crustal detachment during South Atlantic rifting and formation of Tucano-Gabon basin system: Nature, London 322:629–632.

Ustritsky V.I., 1973, Permian climate, *in* A. Logan and L.V. Hills (eds.), The Permian and Triassic systems and their mutual boundary: Can. Soc. Petrol. Geol. Mem 2: 733–744.

Uyeda S., 1981, Subduction zones and back-arc basins—a review: Geol. Rundsch. 70(2):552–269.

Uyeda S., 1982, Subduction zones: An introduction to comparative subductology: Tectonophysics 81:133–159.

Vai G.B., 1975, Hercynian basin evolution of the southern Alps, *in* C.H. Squyres (ed.), Geology of Italy: Tripoli, The Earth Science Society of the Libyan Arab Republic, 1:293–298.

Vai G.B., 1979, Tracing the Hercynian structural zones across "Neo-Europa," an introduction: Mem. Geol. Soc. Italy 20(1979):39–45.

Vai G.B., 1980, Pré-Palaéozoique et Paléozoique pré-Varisque, *in* Introduction à la géologie générale d'Italie, 26th Congr. Géol. Int., Paris, G-13, p. 53–60.

Vai G.B. and Cocozza T., 1986, Tentative schematic zonation of the Hercynian chain in Italy: Bull. Soc. Géol. France (8)II(1):95–114.

Vai G.B. and Spalletta C., 1982, Devonian Palaeo-Tethyan carbonate platform-basin system of the southern Alps: Evolutionary trend and comparative analysis: Ter. Cogn. 2:109–115.

Vail P.R. and Todd R.G., 1981, Northern North Sea Jurassic unconformities, chronostratigraphy and sea level changes from seismic stratigraphy, *in* L.V. Illings and G.D. Hobson

(eds.), Petroleum geology of the continental shelf of northwest Europe: London, Institute of Petroleum, p. 216–235.

Vail P.R., Mitchum R.M, Jr., Todd R.G., Widmier J.M., Thompson S., Sangree J.B., Bubb J.N. and Hatlelid W.G., 1977, Seismic stratigraphy and global changes of sea level, *in* C.E. Payton (ed.), Seismic stratigraphy application to hydrocarbon exploration: Am. Assoc. Petrol. Mem. 26:49–212.

Vaillard P., 1985a, Hypothèse sur la polarité des déformations alpines aux marges "pyrénéennes" de la plaque Europe et Ibérie: C.R. Acad. Sci. Paris (300)II(2):1019–1024.

Vaillard P., 1985b, Ibérides et Ibérie; un exemple de relations entre tectogenèse intracontinentale et tectonique des plaques: C.R. Acad. Sci. Paris (300)II(6):217–222.

Vann I.R., 1978, The siting of Tertiary vulcanicity, *in* D.R. Bowes and B.E. Leake (eds.), Crustal evolution in N.W. Britain and adjacent regions: Geol. J. Spec. Iss. 10:393–414.

Vegas R. and Banda E., 1983, Tectonic framework and Alpine evolution of the Iberian Peninsula: Earth Evol. Sci. 2(4):320–343.

Vielzeuf D. and Kornprobst J., 1984, Crustal splitting and the emplacement of Pyrenean iherzolites and granulites: Earth Planet. Sci. Lett. 67:87–96.

Villemin T. and Bergerat F., 1987, L'évolution structurale du fossé rhénan au cours du Cénozoique: Un bilan de la déformation et des effects thérmiques de l'extension: Bull. Soc. Géol. France (8)III(2):245–255.

Vinogradov A.P. (ed.), 1969, Atlas of the lithological-palaeogeographical maps of the USSR, Vol. 2, Devonian, Carboniferous and Permian, Moscow, Akad. Sci. USSR.

Vinsjakov I.V., Glusko V.V., Pomjanovkaja G.H. and Chiznjakov A.V., 1984, Grundzüge der geologischen Entwicklung des SW-Randes der Osteuropäischen Tafel im Zeitraum Oberproterozoikum-Palaeozoikum auf dem Territorium der Ukraine, Zeitschr. Angew. Geol. 30(1):34–39.

Vischer A., 1943, Die postdevonische Tektonik von Ostgrönland zwischen 74° und 75° n Br. Kuhn Ø, Wollaston Forland, Clavering Ø und angrenzender Gebiete: Meddr. Grønland 133:1–195.

Voigt W.A., 1962, Über Schollenränder und ihre Bedeutung im Gebiet der Mitteleuropäischen Senke und angrenzender Gebiete: Z. Dt. Geol. Ges. 114:378–418.

Vogt P.R., 1973, Early events in the opening of the North Atlantic, *in* D.H. Tarling and S.K. Runcorn (ed.), Implications of continental drift to earth sciences, Vol. 2: London, Academic Press, p. 693–712.

Vogt P.R., 1983, The Iceland Mantle Plume: Status of the hypothesis after a decade of new work, *in* M.H.P. Bott, S. Saxov, M. Talwani and J. Thiede (eds.), Structure and development of the Greenland-Scotland Ridge—new methods and concepts: New York/London, Plenum Press, p. 191–213.

Vogt P.R., Perry P.K., Feden R.H., Fleming H.S. and Cherkis N.Z., 1981, The Greenland-Norwegian Sea and Iceland environment: Geology and geophysics, *in* A.E.M. Nairn, M. Churkin Jr., and F.G. Stehli (eds.), The ocean basins and margins. Vol. 5. The Arctic Ocean: New York/London, Plenum Press, p. 493–598.

Vogt P.R., Taylor P.T., Kovacs L.C. and Johnson G.L., 1982, The Canadian Basin: Aeromagnetic constraints on structure and evolution: Tectonophysics 89:295–336.

Vogt P.R., Kovacs L.C., Perry R.K. and Taylor P.T., 1984, Amerasian Basin, Arctic Ocean: Magnetic anomalies and their decipherment: 27th Internat. Geol. Congr. Moscow, "Nauka,"

Publ. Office Moscow, Arctic Geology, Coll. 04, Reports Vol. 4, p. 152–161.

Volker F. and Altherr R., 1987, Lower Carboniferous calcalkaline volcanics in the Northern Vosges: Evidence for a distructive continental margin: Terr. Cogn. 7(2–3):174–175 (abstract).

Voo R. van der, 1983, Paleomagnetic constraints on the assembly of the Old Red Continent: Tectonophysics 91:271–283.

Voo R. van der and Peinado J., 1984, A paleomagnetic reevaluation of Pangera reconstructions, in R. van der Voo, C.R. Scotese and N. Bonhommet (eds.), Plate reconstructions from Palaeozoic paleomagnetism: Am. Geophys. Union, Geol. Soc. Am., p. 11–26.

Voo R. van der and Scotese C.H., 1981, Palaeomagnetic evidence for a large (c. 2000 km) sinistral offset along the Great Glen fault during the Carboniferous: Geology 9:583–589.

Voo R. van der, Briden J.C. and Duff A., 1980, Late Precambrian and Palaeozoic palaeomagnetism of the Atlantic bordering continents, in J. Cogné and M. Stansky (eds.), Géologie de l'Europe: B.R.G.M. Mem. 108:203–212.

Wade J.A., 1981, Geology of the Canadian Atlantic Margin from Georges Bank to the Grand Banks, in J. W. Kerr, A.J. Fergusson and L.C. Machan (eds.), Geology of the North Atlantic borderlands: Can. Soc. Petrol. Geol. Mem. 7:447–460.

Walker G.P.K., 1975, A new concept in the evolution of the British Tertiary intrusive centres: J. Geol. Soc. London 131:121–141.

Walliser O.H. and Alberti H., 1983, Flysch, olistromes and nappes in the Harz Mountains, in H. Martin and F.W. Eder (eds.), Intracontinental fold belts: Berlin/Heidelberg, Springer-Verlag, p. 144–169.

Wanless R.K., Stevens R.D., Lachance G.R. and Delabio R.N.D., 1974, Age determinations and geological studies K-Ar isotopic ages, Report 12: Geol. Surv. Can. Paper 74–2.

Waterlot G., 1974, Le Paléozoique du Nord de la France et de la Belgique (Ardennes et Boulonnais), in J. Debelmas (ed.), Géologie de la France. Vol. 1. Vieux massifs et grandes bassin sédimentaires: Paris, Doin Editeurs, p. 42–62.

Watson H.J., 1982, Casablanca field offshore Spain, a paleogeomorphic trap, in M.T. Halbouty (ed.), The deliberate search for the subtle trap: Am. Assoc. Petrol. Geol. Mem. 32:237–250.

Watson J., 1985, Northern Scotland as an Atlantic-North Sea divide: J. Geol. Soc. London 142(2):221–243.

Watt W.S., 1969, Coast parallel dike-swarm of southwest Greenland in relation to the opening of the Labrador Sea: Can. J. Earth Sci. 6:1320–1321.

Watts A.B. and Steckler M.S., 1979, Subsidence and eustasy at the continental margin of eastern North America: Maurice Ewing Symposium, Series 3, Am. Geophys. Union, p. 218–234.

Watts A.B. and Steckler M.S., 1981, Subsidence and tectonics of Atlantic type continental margins: Proc. 26th Internat. Geol. Congr. Geology of Continental Margins Symp., Oceanologica Acta. Supp. Vol. 4:143–154.

Watts A.B. and Thorne J., 1984, Tectonics, global changes in sea level and their relationship to stratigraphic sequences at the U.S. Atlantic continental margin: Mar. Petrol. Geol. 1(4):319–339.

Watts A.B., Karner G.D. and Steckler M.S., 1982, Lithospheric flexure and the evolution of sedimentary basins, in Sir Peter Kent, M.H.P. Bott, D.P. McKenzie and C.A. Williams (eds.), The evolution of sedimentary basins: Phil. Trans. R. Soc. London A305: 249–281.

Watts N.L., Lapré F.S., Schijndel-Goester F.S. van and Ford A., 1980, Upper Cretaceous and Lower Tertiary chalks of the Albuskjell area, North Sea: Deposition in a slope and base of slope environment: Geology 8:217–221.

Watznauer A., Tröger K.A. and Möbus G., 1976, Gleichheiten und Underschiede im Bau der Saxothuringischen Zone westlich und östlich des Elbelineaments, in A. Watznauer (ed.), Frankzkossmat Symposium: Nov. Act. Leopold. N.F. 224:93–110.

Weber J.R. and Sweeney J.F., 1985, Reinterpretation of morphology and crustal structure in the Central Arctic Ocean Basin: J. Geophys. Res. 90(B1):663–677.

Weber K., 1984, Variscan events: Early Palaeozoic continental rift metamorphism and late Palaeozoic crustal shortening, in D.H.W. Hutton and D.J. Sanderson (eds.), Variscan tectonics of the North Atlantic region: Oxford, Blackwell Sci. Publ. p. 3–22.

Wedepohl K.H., Meyer K. and Mücke C.K., 1983, Chemical composition and genetic relations of meta-volcanic rocks from the Rhenohercynian belt of northwest Germany, in H. Martin and F.W. Eder (eds.), Intracontinental fold belts, case studies in the Variscan Belt of Europe and the Damara Belt in Namibia: Berlin, Springer-Verlag, p. 231–256.

Weissert H.J. and Bernouilli D., 1985, A transform margin in the Mesozoic Tethys: Evidence from the Swiss Alps: Geol. Rundsch. 74(3):665–679.

Wendlandt R.F., 1981, Experimental petrology as a probe of rifting processes, in papers presented to the Conference on Processes of Planetary Rifting, Napa Valley, California, 3-5 December 1981, Lunar Planet. Inst. Contrib. 457:126–133.

Wendlandt R.F. and Morgan P., 1982, Lithospheric thinning associated with rifting in East Africa: Nature, London 298:734–736.

Wendt J., 1985, Disintegration of the continental margin of northwestern Gondwana: Late Devonian of the eastern Anti-Atlas (Morocco): Geology 13:815–818.

Wernicke B., 1981, Low-angle normal faults in the Basin and Range province: Nappe tectoncis in an extending orogen: Nature, London 291:645–647.

Wernicke B., 1985, Uniform-sense normal simple shear of the continental lithosphere: Can. J. Earth Sci. 22:108–125.

Wernicke B. and Burchfiel B.C., 1982, Modes of extensional tectonics: J. Struct. Geol. 4:105–115.

Wessely G., 1987, Mesozoic and Tertiary evolution of the Alpine-Carpathian Foreland in eastern Austria: Tectonophysics 137:45–59.

Westphal M., Bazhenov M.L., Laner J.P., Pechersky D.M. and Sibuet J.C., 1986, Paleomagnetic implications on the evolution of the Tethys Belt from the Atlantic Ocean to Pamir since Trias: Tectonophysics 123:37–82.

Wever T. and Meissner R., 1986, About the nature of reflections from the Lower Crust: Ter. Cogn. 6(3):346 (abstract).

Wezel F.-C., 1982, The structure of the Calabro-Sicilian Arc: Result of a post-orogenic intra-plate deformation, in J.K. Legget (ed.), Trench- forearc geology: Sedimentology and tectonics on modern and ancient active plate margins: Geol. Soc. London Spec. Publ. 10:345–354.

Wezel F.-C., 1985, Structural features and basin tectonics of the Tyrrhenian Sea, in D.J. Stanley and F.-C. Wezel (eds.), Geological evolution of the Mediterranean Basin: New York/Berlin/Heidelberg/Tokyo, Springer-Verlag, p. 153–194.

Whitechurch H., Juteau T. and Montigny R., 1984, Role of the eastern Mediterranean ophiolites (Turkey, Syria, Cyprus) in the history of the Neo-Tethys, *in* J.E. Dixon and A.H.F. Robertson (eds.), The geological evolution of the eastern Mediterranean: Spec. Publ. Geol. Soc. London 17:301–317.

Wiedmann J., 1979, Prä-Driftzusammenhänge und Faunenprovinzen in der Kreide: Neues Jb. Geol. Paläont. Abh. 57:213–218.

Wijhe D.H. van, 1987, Structural evolution of inverted basins in the Dutch offshore: Tectonophysics, 137: 171–220.

Wildi W., 1983, La Chaîne tello-rifaine (Algérie, Maroc, Tunisie): Structure, stratigraphic of evolution du Trias au Miocène: Rev. Geol. Dynam. Geogr. Phys. 24(3):201–297.

Williams H. and Hatcher R.D. Jr., 1983, Appalachian suspect terranes: Geol. Soc. Am. Mem. 158:33–53.

Wilson J.T., 1966, Did the Atlantic close and then reopen? Nature, London 211:676–681.

Wilson L.M., 1981, Circum-North Atlantic tectono-stratigraphic reconstruction, *in* J.W. Kerr, A.J. Fergusson and L.C. Machan (eds.), Geology of the North Atlantic borderlands: Can. Soc. Petrol. Geol. Mem. 7:167–184.

Winkler W. and Bernoulli D., 1986, Detrital high-pressure/low-temperature minerals in a late Turonian flysch of the eastern Alps (western Austria): Implications for early Alpine tectonics: Geology 14:598–601.

Winnock E., 1981, Structure du bloc pélagien, *in* F.-C. Wezel (ed.), Sedimentary basins of Mediterranean margins: C.N.R. Italian Project of Oceanogrpahy, Bologna, Tecnoprint, p. 445–464.

Winterer E.L. and Bosellini A., 1981, Subsidence and sedimentation on a Jurassic passive continental margin (Southern Alps, Italy): Bull. Am. Assoc. Petrol. Geol. 65:394–421.

Winterer E.L. and Hinz K., 1984, The evolution of the Mazagan continental margin: A synthesis of geophysical and geological data with results of drilling during Deep Sea Drilling Project Leg 79, *in* K. Hinz, E.L. Winterer et al., Initial Reports of Deep Sea Drilling Project, 79, Washington, DC U.S. Govt. Printing Office, p. 893–919.

Wintsch R.P. and Sutter J.F., 1986, A tectonic model for the late Paleozoic of southeastern New England: J. Geol. 94:459–472.

Wjalow O.S. and Medwedew A.P., 1977, Die präalpidische Struktur der westlichen Ukraine und Südpolens und ihre Wechselbeziehungen zwischen Tafel-und Geosynklinalgebieten: Zeitschr. Angew. Geol. 23(10):517–521.

Wood A.W., 1981, Extensional tectonics and the birth of the Lagonegro Basin (southern Italian Apennines): N. Jb. Geol. Paläont. Abh. 161(1):93–131.

Wood R. and Barton P., 1983, Crustal thinning and subsidence in the North Sea: Nature, London 302:134–136.

Worsley D. and Edwards M.B., 1976, The upper Palaeozoic succession of Bjørnøya: Norsk Polar Arbok. 1974:17–34.

Worsley D. and Gjelberg J., 1980, Excursion guide to Bjørnøya, Svalbard: Contrib. Paleont. Museum, Oslo, Norway, No. 258, 33 p.

Wortel M.J.R., 1986, Dynamical aspects of active continental margins: Geol. Mijnbouw 65:119–132.

Wurster P. and Stets J., 1982, Sedimentation in the Atlas Gulf. II: Mid-Cretaceous events, *in* V. Rad, K. Hinz, M. Sarnthein and E. Seibold (eds.), Geology of the northwest African continental margin: Berlin/Heidelberg/New York, Springer-Verlag, p. 69–85.

Wynne P.J., Irving E. and Osadete K., 1983, Paleomagnetism of the Esayoo Formation (Permian) of northern Ellesmere Island: Possible clue to the solution of the Nares Strait dilemma: Tectonophysics 100:241–256.

Ziegler A.M., Scotese C.R., McKerrow W.S., Johnson M.E. and Bambach R.K., 1979, Palaeozoic palaeogeography: Ann. Rev. Earth Planet. Sci. 7:473–502.

Ziegler P.A., 1969, The development of sedimentary basins in western and Arctic Canada: Alberta Soc. Petrol. Geol., 89 p.

Ziegler P.A., 1980, Northwestern Europe: Geology and hydrocarbon provinces: Can. Soc. Petrol. Geol. Mem. 6:653–706.

Ziegler P.A., 1982a, Geological atlas of western and central Europe: Amsterdam, Elsevier Sci. Publ. Co., 130 p. and 40 plates.

Ziegler P.A., 1982b, Triassic rifts and facies patterns in western and central Europe: Geol. Rundsch. 71(3):747–772.

Ziegler P.A., 1983a, Crustal thinning and subsidence in the North Sea; matters arising: Nature, London 304:561.

Ziegler P.A., 1983b, Inverted basins in the Alpine foreland, *in* A.W. Bally (ed.), Seismic expression of structural styles—a picture and work atlas: Am. Assoc. Petrol. Geol. Stud. Geol. Ser. 15, Vol. 3:3.3.3.–3.3.12.

Ziegler P.A., 1984, Caledonian and Hercynian crustal consolidation of western and central Europe—a working hypothesis: Geol. Mijnbouw 63(1):93–108.

Ziegler P.A., 1986, Geodynamic model for Palaeozoic crustal consolidation of western and central Europe: Tectonophysics 126:303–328.

Ziegler P.A., 1987a, Celtic Sea-Western Approaches area—an overview: Tectonophysics 137:285–289.

Ziegler P.A., 1987b, Evolution of the Western Approaches Trough: Tectonophysics 137:341–346.

Ziegler P.A., 1987 c, Late Cretaceous and Cenozoic intra-plate compressional deformations in the Alpine foreland—a geodynamic model: Tectonophysics 137:389–420.

Ziegler P.A., 1987d, Manx-Furness Basin: Tectonophysics 137:335–340.

Ziegler P.A. (ed.), 1987e, Compressional intra-plate deformations in the Alpine foreland: Tectonophysics 137(1–4):420 p.

Ziegler P.A. and Louwerens C.J., 1979, Tectonics of the North Sea, *in* E. Oele, R.T.E. Schüttenhelm and A.J. Wiggers (eds.), The Quaternary history of the North Sea: Acta Univ. Ups. Symp. Univ. Ups. Annum Quingentesimum Celebrantis: 2, Uppsala, p. 7–22.

Ziegler W.H., Doery R. and Scott J., 1986, Tectonic habitat of Norwegian oil and gas, *in* A.M. Spencer et al. (eds.), Habitat of hydrocarbons on the Norwegian continental shelf: London, Graham and Trotman, p. 3–19.

Znosko J. and Pajchlowa M., 1968, Geological cross sections, *in* J. Znosko (ed.), Geological atlas of Poland, 1:200.000, Geological Institute, Warsaw.

Zonenshain L.P. and Le Pichon X., 1986, Deep basins of the Black Sea and Caspian Sea as remnants of Mesozoic back-arc basins: Tectonophysics 123:181–211.

Zonenshain L.P. and Savostin L.A., 1981, Movements of lithospheric plates relative to subduction zones; formation of marginal seas and active continental margins: Tectonophysics 74:57–87.

Zonenshain L.P., Korinevsky V.G., Kazmin V.G. and Pechersky D.M., 1984, Plate tectonic model of the south Urals development: Tectonophysics 109:95–135.

Zwart H.J. and Dornsiepen V.F., 1978, The tectonic framework of central and western Europe: Geol. Mijnbouw. 57:627–564.

# Index

A reference is indexed according to its important, or "key" words.

Four columns are to the left of a keyword entry. The first column, a letter entry, represents the AAPG book series from which the reference originated. In this case, ME stands for AAPG Memoir Series. Every five years, AAPG will merge all its indexes together, and the letters ME will differentiate this reference from those of the Studies in Geology Series (ST) or from the AAPG Bulletin (B).

The following number is the series number. In this case, 43 represents a reference from AAPG Memoir 43. The third column lists the page number of this volume on which the reference can be found. The fourth column represents the type of entry: K = keyword, A = author, and T = title.

Index entries without page numbers represent the title or author of this volume.